IRELAND

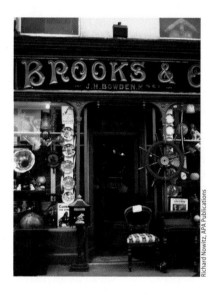

Editorial Director   Cynthia Clayton Ochterbeck

THE GREEN GUIDE IRELAND

Editors   Jonathan P. Gilbert, Rachel Mills
Principal Writer   Paul Murphy
Production Manager   Natasha G. George
Cartography   Alain Baldet, Michelle Cana, Peter Wrenn
Photo Editors   Lydia Strong, Yoshimi Kanazawa
Proofreader   Alison Coupe
Layout & Design   John Higginbottom, Natasha G. George
Cover Design   Ute Weber, Laurent Muller

Contact Us: The Green Guide
                            Michelin Maps and Guides
                            One Parkway South
                            Greenville, SC 29615
                            USA
                            www.michelintravel.com
                            michelin.guides@us.michelin.com

                            Michelin Maps and Guides
                            Hannay House
                            39 Clarendon Road
                            Watford, Herts WD17 1JA
                            UK
                            ☎ (01923) 205 240
                            www.ViaMichelin.com
                            travelpubsales@uk.michelin.com

Special Sales: For information regarding bulk sales,
                            customized editions and premium sales,
                            please contact our Customer Service
                            Departments:
                            USA   1-800-432-6277
                            UK   (01923) 205 240
                            Canada 1-800-361-8236

With thanks to Tourism Ireland and Fáilte Ireland, in particular: John Lahiffe,
Charlene Boyle, Belfast Visitor & Convention Bureau and Fáilte Ireland SW.

Note to the Reader

One Team…
A Commitment to Quality

There's just one reason our team is dedicated to producing quality travel publications—you, our reader.

Throughout our guides we offer **practical information**, **touring tips** and **suggestions** for finding the best places for a break.

Michelin driving tours help you hit the highlights and quickly absorb the best of the region. Our descriptive **walking tours** make you your own guide, armed with directions, maps and expert information.

We scout out the attractions, classify them with **star ratings**, and describe in detail what you will find when you visit them.

Michelin maps featured throughout the guide offer vibrant, detailed and easy-to-follow outlines of everything from close-up museum plans to international maps.

Places to stay and eat are always a big part of travel, so we research **hotels and restaurants** that we think convey the essence of the destination and arrange them by geographic area and price. We walk you through the best shopping districts and point you towards the host of entertainment and recreation possibilities available.

We **test**, **retest**, **check and recheck** to make sure that our guidebooks are truly just that: a personalized guide to help you make the most of your visit. And if you still want a speaking guide, we list local tour guides who will lead you on all the boat, bus, guided, historical, culinary, and other tours you shouldn't miss.

In short, we remove the guesswork involved with travel. After all, we want you to enjoy exploring with Michelin as much as we do.

The Michelin Green Guide Team

PLANNING YOUR TRIP

INTRODUCTION TO IRELAND

H. Champollion/MICHELIN

CONTENTS

DISCOVERING IRELAND

HOW TO USE THIS GUIDE

PLANNING YOUR TRIP

The blue-tabbed PLANNING YOUR TRIP section at the front of the guide gives you **ideas for your trip** and **practical information** to help you organize it. You'll find tours, a host of breaks in the great outdoors, a calendar of events, information on shopping, sightseeing, kids' activities and more.

INTRODUCTION

The orange-tabbed INTRODUCTION section explores **Nature** from the river Shannon to the Wicklow Mountains. The **History** section spans from Celtic Ireland to 20C partition and independence. The **Art and Culture** section covers architecture, art, literature, traditions and folklore, while the **Country Today** delves into modern Ireland.

DISCOVERING

The green-tabbed DISCOVERING section features Ireland's Principal Sights,

arranged alphabetically, featuring the most interesting local **Sights**, **Walking Tours**, nearby **Excursions**, and detailed **DrivingTours**.

⚏ Contact information, ⚏ admission charges, 🕐 hours of operation, and a host of other **visitor information** is given wherever possible. Admission prices shown are normally for a single adult.

STAR RATINGS★★★

Michelin has given star ratings for more than 100 years. If you're pressed for time, we recommend you visit the ★★★, or ★★ sights first:

★★★	Highly recommended
★★	Recommended
★	Interesting

Address Books - Where to Stay, Eat and more...

WHERE TO STAY

We've made a selection of hotels and arranged them by price category to fit all budgets (⏺ *see the Legend on the cover flap for an explanation of the price categories*). For the most part, we've selected accommodations based on their unique regional quality, their regional feel, as it were.

⏺ *See the back of the guide for an index to where to stay.*

⏺ *See the red-cover Michelin Guide Great Britain and Ireland for more addresses.*

WHERE TO EAT

We thought you'd like to know the popular eating spots in Ireland. So, we selected restaurants that capture the regional experience. We're not rating the quality of the food per se; as we did with the hotels, we selected restaurants for many towns and villages, categorized by price to appeal to all wallets.

⏺ *See the back of the guide for an index to where to eat.*

⏺ *See the red-cover Michelin Guide Great Britain and Ireland for more addresses.*

MAPS

- **Principal Sights map** and **Driving Tours Map** on the cover.
- Detailed maps for **major cities** and **villages**, including **driving tour maps** and larger-scale maps for **walking tours**.

All maps in this guide are oriented north, unless otherwise indicated by a directional arrow. The term "Local Map" refers to a map within the chapter or Tourism Region. A complete list of the maps found in the guide appears at the back of this book, along with a comprehensive index.

A Bit of Advice

Green advice boxes found in this guide contain practical tips and handy information relevant to the sight in the DISCOVERING section.

See the map Legend at the back of the guide for an explanation of map symbols.

ORIENT PANELS

Vital statistics are given for each principal sight in the DISCOVERING section:

- **Information:** Tourist Office/Sight contact details.
- **Orient Yourself:** Geographic location of the sight with reference to surrounding boroughs, towns and roads.
- **Parking:** Where to park.
- **Don't Miss:** Unmissable things to do.
- **Organising Your Time:** Tips on organising your stay; what to see first, how long to spend there, crowd avoidance, market days and more.
- **Especially for Kids:** Sights of particular interest to children.
- **Also See:** Nearby PRINCIPAL SIGHTS featured elsewhere in the guide.

SYMBOLS

- **Spa Facilities**
- **Interesting for Children**
- **Also See**
- **Tourist Information**
- **Hours of Operation**
- **Periods of Closure**
- **Closed to the Public**
- **Entry Fees**
- **Credit Cards not Accepted**
- **Wheelchair Accessible**
- **Tours**
- **On-site Parking**
- **Directions**
- **On-site eating Facilities**
- **Camping Facilities**
- **Beaches**
- **Breakfast Included**
- **A Bit of Advice**
- **Warning**

Contact – Addresses, phone numbers, opening hours and prices published in this guide are accurate at the time of press. We welcome corrections and suggestions that may assist us in preparing the next edition. Please send your comments to:

UK
Michelin Maps and Guides
Hannay House
39 Clarendon Road
Watford, Herts WD17 1JA
travelpubsales@uk.michelin.com
www.michelin.co.uk

USA
Michelin Maps and Guides
Editorial Department
P.O. Box 19001
Greenville, SC 29602-9001
michelin.guides@us.michelin.com
www.michelintravel.com

Signpost near Kilkenny
P. Hurlin/MICHELIN

MHIC TREOIN
W ROSS 27

MHIC ANNDÁIN
OMASTOWN 11

JERPOINT ABBEY
VISITOR CENTRE

km

19

NORE VALLEY
PARK

MICHELIN DRIVING TOURS

Ireland By Car

See the Driving Tours map.

These tours were devised to help you plan visits to the main cities of Dublin, Belfast, Cork and Sligo, and important attractions nearby. A grand tour including all the major sights is also provided (tour 8) although you may find you want to linger longer in some places to enjoy the scenery, the warmth of the people and the craic! Itineraries all start and end at a convenient port of entry by air or sea.

1 DUBLIN AND ENVIRONS – ONE WEEK

Dublin demands at least two days for its many attractions and vibrant atmosphere, after which, it is good to foray into the countryside to see some of the country's major sights – the prehistoric monuments of the Boyne Valley, great houses and gardens, early-Christian Glendalough in its remote valley, busy country towns and charming seaside harbours.
From **Dublin**, head north to picturesque Howth, the aristocratic demesne (former estate lands) of Malahide and bustling **Drogheda**, the nearby prehistoric grave sites of Newgrange and Knowth, and the tranquil setting for the decisive Battle of the Boyne.
West of the capital, follow the road to the vast Anglo-Norman castle at Trim, the splendid Palladian mansion of Castletown, and Curragh: the heartland of Irish horse-breeding and racing near **Kildare**. Proceed to the Great House at Russborough, and climb up into the Wicklow Mountains, to the highly evocative monastic remains at Glendalough. After a night in the seaside town of **Wicklow**, return to **Dublin** via the magnificent gardens of Powerscourt and the capital's attractive southern suburbs.

2 ASPECTS OF ULSTER – ONE WEEK

Northern Ireland comprises only six of Ulster's nine counties: to get a view of the whole province, consider a longer itinerary (*see Route 7*). Route 2 takes in the major towns, wonderful natural landscapes and an array of man-made attractions, including a number of world-class museums. Head east out of **Belfast**, pausing at the fascinating Ulster Folk and Transport Museum, to the coastal resort of **Bangor**. On the way to St Patrick's town of Downpatrick, visit the great houses and gardens of Mountstewart and Castle Ward before driving on to **Newcastle**. Continue through the spectular Mourne Mountains before arriving at Ireland's holy city of **Armagh**. The less grand but equally interesting country houses of Ardress and The Argory are worth a detour on the way to Lough Neagh, Ireland's largest lake. From here, consider calling in at the Peatlands Park to learn about local wildlife and turf-cutting, before going to Ardboe to see the High Cross, and the archetypal plantation towns of Cookstown and Draperstown. Visit the Ulster-American Folk Park on the way to the last walled city to be laid out in Europe, **Londonderry**. Follow the coastal road east through Portrush and Portstewart to the spectacular Giant's Causeway and the pretty seaside resort of **Ballycastle**. Return to **Belfast** via the imposing landscapes of the Antrim Glens and the corniche of the Antrim Coast Road.

3 SIGHTS OF THE SOUTHEAST – ONE WEEK

Follow in the footsteps of the Anglo-Normans as they spread across Ireland, building great castles, churches and abbeys, and relish one of the great sights of ancient Ireland: the holy hill of Cashel. The Republic's second city,

Cork, has its own distinctive character, while the southeastern coast is renowned for its beauty.

From the ferry port of Rosslare, and the Viking city of **Wexford**, make your way to Johnstown Castle and the Irish Agricultural Museum. Drive through the National Heritage Park to the old towns of Enniscorthy and New Ross, past the lovely abbey ruins at Jerpoint to medieval **Kilkenny** (2 nights), one of Ireland's most compelling towns. The **Rock of Cashel** is magical. From here, head south through Caher with its castle, and Fermoy with its splendid river, crossing to the Republic's second city, **Cork** (2 nights)

From Cork take the road east along the coast to Cobh, overlooking the broad waters of Cork Harbour, and on via delightful old Youghal to the southeast's other Viking city of **Waterford**, renowned for its opera festival and lively cultural life.

A ferry crosses Waterford Harbour to the abbeys, gardens, castles and beaches of the Hook Peninsula. The return is then direct to Rosslare.

④ THE SOUTHWEST: COUNTIES CORK, KERRY AND LIMERICK – TEN DAYS

The Southwest corner—with its rocky peninsulas stretching far into the Atlantic, the country's highest mountains and lush inland landscapes—is perhaps the most alluring region for visitors to Ireland.

From Shannon Airport, follow the road to 15C Bunratty Castle and its Folk Park to the Republic's third largest city, historic **Limerick**. Explore the country towns of Kilmallock and Mallow on the way to bustling **Cork** (2 nights). The coastal road west of Cork takes you through attractive fishing villages and little maritime towns like **Kinsale**. More coastal delights include Skibbereen, Skull and **Bantry** on its great sea-inlet and Bantry Bay, famous for its fish. The splendidly scenic coastal road, the Ring of Beara, runs around the Beara Peninsula, to pretty **Kenmare**. The panoramic Ring of Kerry offers wonderful views of the glorious Iver-

agh Peninsula to the distant drowned mountain top of Great Skellig Island, once an austere monastic retreat, before reaching the world-famous lake and mountain setting of **Killarney** (2 nights). From here, continue to the Gaelic harbour town of Dingle and the tip of the Dingle Peninsula with its beehive huts and panoramic views of the wave-battered Blasket Islands, before turning inland via Tralee, Ardfert Cathedral and Glin Castle. Return to **Limerick** and Shannon.

⑤ GLORIES OF GALWAY, CONNEMARA AND SLIGO – ONE WEEK

Connemara sometimes appears to consist more of sky, sea, bog and lake than terra firma, despite its mountains, including the splendidly rounded Twelve Bens - very different from the bleak arid limestone landscapes of the Burren and lively city of Galway.

From Knock airport, head north to the cheerful regional capital of **Sligo** with its many associations with W B Yeats. From here, head west to north Mayo through vast stretches of bog, to Stone Age vestiges at Ceide Fields and the high cliffs of **Achill Island**.

On the way to the elegant town of **Westport**, featuring Westport House, one of the finest Great Houses in the West, detour to Castlebar and its state-of-the-art National Museum of Country Life at Turlough. From the road south-west, you will see St Patrick's holy mountain, Croagh

Travel by horse and cart in the Burren

Patrick. Continue south through the Sheffry Hills, round the end of the fjord-like Killary Harbour and past the opulent 19C country house of Kylemore Abbey to charming little **Clifden**. Archetypal Connemara landscapes can be enjoyed on the way to Inverin. From here there are flights to Inishmore, the largest of the **Aran Islands**, where Gaelic is spoken and life is steeped in traditional ways.

Back on the mainland, it is tempting to linger at the vibrant city of **Galway**. The south of Co Galway includes the strange moonscapes of **The Burren** and the lofty Cliffs of Moher, some of the tallest in Europe.

The tour returns to Knock via Ennis, (the miniature capital of Co Clare), the Heritage Town of Athenry and the little cathedral city of Tuam.

6 THE HEART OF IRELAND, THE UNKNOWN MIDLANDS – ONE WEEK

As well as outstanding monuments like the great monastic complex of Clonmacnoise and the enigmatic earthworks around Tulsk, this itinerary introduces the inquisitive visitor to a few hidden treasures: castles and country houses, bustling small towns off the tourist trail, unexpected uplands, the banks of the Shannon, and one of the country's most extensive and well-preserved boglands.

Head northwest out of **Dublin** to Trim with its great Anglo-Norman castle, to the prehistoric burial mounds of Loughcrew and the ancient seat of the Pakenham family at Tullynally, before arriving at the midland market town of **Mullingar** for the night.

Co Longford has some intriguing features, notably the delightful estate village of Ardagh. Co Roscommon boasts Strokestown House, which has its own estate village and an authoritative Famine Museum; the small town of **Boyle** is graced by handsome abbey ruins. From here, head south to Tulsk, where the Cruachan Aí visitor centre provides an insight into the mysteries of the Celtic past, then continue to Ballinasloe and **Athlone**

at the southern end of Lough Ree on the River Shannon.

The monastic precinct of Clonmacnoise is one of the great ecclesiastical sights of Ireland, as is the extraordinary little Romanesque cathedral of Clonfert. This itinerary now leaves the Shannon for the little Georgian town of **Birr**, the anteroom to the great house and grounds of the Birr Castle Demesne. To the East of Birr rise the green summits of the relatively little visited Slieve Bloom Mountains, while to the northeast, close to little Tullamore, lies the vast, strange, and potentially perilous expanse of Clara Bog. From here, it is a straight run back to **Dublin**.

7 ULSTER ODYSSEY – TWO WEEKS

This near-comprehensive tour of the old province of Ulster, including the six counties of Northern Ireland and three over the border in the Republic, takes in the quiet countryside of Cavan and Monaghan, and the wild scenery of Donegal's coast and mountains.

From **Belfast** take the road to the old coastal resort of **Bangor**. Visit the great houses and demesnes at Mountstewart and Castle Ward before taking the ferry across the mouth of Strangford Lough to St Patrick's city of Downpatrick, and heading for the seaside town of **Newcastle**.

Snake your way through the Mourne Mountains to **Armagh**, another holy city, the seat of both Archbishops of Ireland. The following day, head south-west into the Republic through Monaghan and Cavan, before turning northwest to the Fermanagh Lakeland and its capital, **Enniskillen**.

After Belleek, with its famous pottery, cross into Co Donegal. West of Donegal Town rise the dramatic cliffs of Slieve League where the village of Glencolumbkille is perched, still breathing the spirit of its founder St Columba. From here, the route heads inland to the tweed town of Ardara and north via Glenveagh National Park to the quiet little resort of **Dunfanaghy** in the lee of Horn Head.

Spectacular scenery in Northern Ireland

Take the N56 back past the ancient fortress of Grianan of Aileach to the renowned walled city of **London-derry** in Northern Ireland. Divert to the **Sperrin Mountains** for the Ulster-American Folk Park. East of the mountains there is the typical plantation settlement of Cookstown, a famous High Cross at Ardboe on the shores of Lough Neagh, the country's greatest lake, and the 17C planter's house of Springhill. Drive north to Drapers-town, another plantation settlement and continue to the favourite seaside resorts of **Portrush** and Portstewart. The Giant's Causeway and the Causeway Coast demand a day of anyone's time, and a choice of accommodation is available at **Ballycastle**.

The return to **Belfast** is along the Antrim Coast Road through the superlative landscapes of the Glens of Antrim, with a final stop at the great Anglo-Norman castle at Carrickfergus.

8 IRISH HIGHLIGHTS, GRAND TOUR – TWO WEEKS

This route highlights the very best that Ireland has to offer to the first-time visitor. From **Dublin**, drive out to one of the country's finest mansions, Russ-borough, and on through the Wicklow Mountains to the monastic ruins of Glendalough in their deep wooded valley, before arriving at the historic city of **Kilkenny** (2 nights). Spend a day absorbing the atmosphere of Ireland's Acropolis, the Rock of **Cashel** before heading for the Republic's second city, **Cork**, and then west on to **Killarney** (2 nights) in its incomparable setting of lakes and mountains. The classic drive around the Iveragh Peninsula, the Ring of Kerry, is a great experience, as is the Dingle Peninsula, with its ancient stone huts and enclosures, and views of the rocky Blasket Islands.

Old **Limerick** is an up-and-coming town, while Co Clare offers its little capital, Ennis, the mighty Cliffs of Moher and the weird limestone landscapes of the Burren.

North of The Burren is one of the Ireland's most attractive towns, **Galway**. From here, make your way to **Clifden** through what many regard as the most Irish of landscapes: the bogs, shining lakes, and rounded mountains of Connemara. Pass close to St Patrick's mountain, Croagh Patrick, to **Westport**. After Castlebar and the excellent Museum of Country Life at Turlough, follow signs to the busiest town in the northwest, **Sligo**. Northern Ireland is entered at **Enniskillen**, in the heart of the glorious Fermanagh Lakeland. An essential stop on the way to the walled city of **Londonderry** is the Ulster-American Folk Park. Don't miss the country's greatest natural attraction, the Giant's Causeway, before driving on to the province's capital, **Belfast**. Return to **Dublin** along the **Boyne Valley** with its battle site and magnificent prehistoric monuments.

WHEN AND WHERE TO GO

When To Go

CLIMATE

Extreme temperatures are rare in Ireland but unfortunately there is the probability of rain throughout the year. The southeast enjoys the most sun and the east coast is drier than the west.

The best time to visit Ireland is the summer, with the sunniest months of the year in May–June and the warmest in July–August. However, whatever time of year you go, rain gear and umbrellas are a must!

Information about the weather in both the Republic and Northern Ireland is available at www.discoverireland.com/weather, or www.meto.gov.uk.

Themed Tours

HISTORIC ROUTES

Sarsfield's Ride
This historical route (70mi/113km signed) makes a wide loop around Limerick along byroads through small villages and unspoilt countryside, following the route taken by General Patrick Sarsfield when he set out to intercept an English siege train. In August 1690 King William III of England was encamped at Caherconlish

Touring the traditional way; by horse-drawn caravan

Bord Fáilte, Dublin

(8 miles east of Limerick) awaiting the arrival of heavy siege guns from Dublin, while his army besieged Limerick. Acting on information from a deserter, Sarsfield slipped out of King John's Castle in Limerick with 600 cavalry and headed northeast along the right bank of the Shannon via Bridgetown, fording the river upstream of Killaloe Bridge, which was held by the Williamites. At about this point he was joined by local guides who showed him a route by Kiloscully and Ballyhourigan Wood, pausing to rest before climbing over the Silvermine and the Slievefelim Mountains via Toor and Rear Cross. From Doon they continued south on the county boundary to Monard, and turned west. In Cullen they discovered the password for the Williamite camp was Sarsfield; so after midnight they travelled the last two miles to Ballyneety and destroyed the siege train.

Siege of Kinsale
The sites of the various camps and engagements of the opposing forces are marked by a dozen signs erected by the roadsides around Kinsale.

SCENIC ROUTES

Several Scenic Routes, designated by the local Tourist Boards, are marked by signs (Slí) – **Inis Eoghain Scenic Drive** in Donegal, **Arigna Scenic Drive** around Lough Key near Boyle, **Slea Head Drive** on the Dingle Peninsula, the **Ring of Kerry** round the Iveragh Peninsual west of Killarney and the **Ring of Beara** round the Beara Peninsula west of Glengarriff.

LITERARY ROUTES

Explore the places where Oliver Goldsmith spent his childhood (*see ATHLONE*), visit the towns where Anthony Trollope lived during his residence in Ireland, or follow the trail of sights associated with Patrick Kavanagh.

Dublin Literary Pub Crawl (www.dublin pubcrawl.com) is highly recommended.

Ideas for your Visit

Always allow plenty of time when touring Ireland: part of the enjoyment is stopping for an idle chat, a pint of Guinness or a spectacular view.

2-DAY BREAKS

Dublin City

Begin with a visit to Trinity College and that masterpiece of Irish art, the Book of Kells, before going up Grafton Street and its side streets, enjoying the buskers and Dublin's elegant shopping area. Wander around the gardens of St Stephen's Green before returning to the streets off the north side to find a place for lunch. In the afternoon visit the National Museum or the National Gallery, walk through Merrion Square and admire the Georgian houses, notably Number Twenty Nine. Spend the evening exploring Temple Bar.
On the second day explore the old town and the art in the Chester Beatty Library, then refresh yourself with a tour around the Guinness Storehouse. Alternatively, book a guided tour of Dublin Castle or look into Christ Church Cathedral or St Patrick's Cathedral. After lunch take the bus to Kilmainham Gaol for a lesson in recent Irish history and pop in to admire displays in the Irish Museum of Modern Art installed in the Royal Kilmainham Hospital.

Kilkenny

Visit Kilkenny Castle and the Kilkenny Design Centre. After lunch plunge into Dunmore Cave. Head south down the Nore Valley to the magnificent ruins of Jerpoint Abbey, calling in on Inistioge, and on over Brandon Hill to Graiguenamanagh on the River Barrow.

Sligo

Visit the Niland Gallery (reopen after redevelopment Spring 2009), featuring paintings by Jack B Yeats, and stroll through the Abbey ruins. After lunch, take a boat trip on Lough Gill, visiting the lake isle of Innisfree and Parke's Castle.
Drive through Yeats' Country to the tomb of W B Yeats at Drumcliff in the shadow of Benbulben, and Lissadell, home of Countess Markievicz, before turning inland to Glencar Waterfall.

3-DAY BREAKS

Cork City

Highlights include the English Market, Grand Parade and St Patrick's Street. Admire the exuberant architecture of William Burges at St Fin Barre's Cathedral. After lunch cross the river to try your hand at ringing Shandon Bells and see how criminals were treated in Cork City Gaol.
On the second day take a trip to Blarney Castle to kiss the Blarney stone and make a round trip to Mallow and Fermoy on the Blackwater River.
On the third day drive out to Fota House and the Wildlife Park, make a lunchtime visit to Cobh and end the day sampling whiskey at the Old Midleton Distillery.

Westport and District

Stroll round the charming little town, and the Quayside, a good spot for lunch, then visit Westport House.
Drive west to explore the Murrisk Peninsula, which presents some of the most beautiful landscapes in the west of Ireland – Croagh Patrick and Killary Harbour.
Take the road north to the Marian Shrine at Knock and the Museum of Country Life at Turlough near Castlebar.

Enniskillen

Stroll through the town and visit Enniskillen Castle and its museums. In the afternoon tour the stately rooms of Castle Coole.
Drive southwest to Florence Court, another less austere country house with flamboyant plasterwork, and the Marble Arch Caves, part of which is visited by boat.

Cruising on the River Shannon

Make a tour round the shores of Lower Lough Erne taking in Devenish Island, Castle Archdale and White Island, the Janus Figure, Belleek Pottery, the Cliffs of Magho viewpoint and Tully Castle.

Londonderry

Walk round the walls and visit the Tower Museum, the Cathedral and Long Tower Church.

Make a tour in the Sperrins Mountains – Roe Valley Country Park, Glenshane Pass, Dungiven Priory, Wellbrook Beetling Mill, Beaghmore Stone Circles, Ulster Plantation Centre in Draperstown, Springhill, Ulster History Park, Sperrin Heritage Centre, Ulster American Folk Park, Gray's Printery in Strabane.

Tour north round the Inishowen (Inis Eoghain) Peninsula – visiting the many prehistoric and early Christian relics – Grianán of Aileach, Carrowmore High Crosses, Clonca Church and Cross. Visit Malin Head, famous from the shipping forecasts, and Fort Ree Military Museum.

4-DAY BREAKS

Dublin and District

For your first two days, explore Dublin City as described under 2-day breaks.
Drive south into the Wicklow Mountains to Russborough or Powerscourt and further on to the monastic ruins at Glendalough.

Take the motorway north via Slane to Newgrange in the Boyne Valley and return via Trim and Tara or Malahide and Newbridge House.

Killarney and District

Wander around the town centre and explore the National Park on foot – Knockreer Demesne and Ross Castle – or by car – Muckross House, Muckross Friary and the Muckross Peninsula, and Torc Waterfall and Ladies View.

Take a guided tour through the Gap of Dunloe if it is a fine day, or drive round the Ring of Kerry, enjoying the fine views of the landscape.

Go north to the Dingle Peninsula, part of the Gaeltacht, which has many relics dating from a former way of life.

Limerick and District

Visit the treasures in the Hunt Museum and walk up to the Castle and St Mary's Cathedral.

Drive northwest into Co Clare to visit Bunratty Folk Museum and Castle, Quin Friary, Knappogue Castle and Cragganunowen Centre.

Make a round trip south of Limerick visiting the prehistoric remains at Lough Gur Interpretive Centre, the walled town of Kilmallock and the childhood haunts of Eamon de Valera in Bruree, before returning down the Maigue Valley via Croom, Monasteranenagh Abbey and charming Adare with its thatched cottages.

Drive north via Ennis and Ennistimon to the barren landscape of the Burren – the Cliffs of Moher, Lisdoonvarna, Corkscrew Hill and Aillwee Cave.

Belfast and District

Visit the city centre and the waterfront. Ride the Belfast Wheel and lunch in the Crown Liquor Saloon. In the afternoon visit the Ulster Museum (closed until 2009 for redevelopment) and take a stroll in the Botanic Gardens with its two glass houses. Alternatively take a tour of the city's famous political Murals.

On day two, drive east to the Ulster Folk and Transport Museum at Cultra; after lunch explore the splendours of Mount Stewart on the east shore of Strangford Lough.

Head south up the Lagan Valley to learn about the traditional Irish linen industry in the Lisburn Museum. Visit charming Hillsborough and the plants and shrubs at Rowallane.

Take a full day out to drive north via Ballymena and Ballymoney to marvel at the volcanic columns of the Giant's Causeway. In the afternoon drive south along the coast and glens of Antrim, not missing the Carrick-a-rede Ropebridge.

5-DAY BREAK

Galway and District

Stroll round the medieval city centre and in the afternoon take the road to Aughnanure Castle and the charming fishing village of Oughterard on Lough Corrib.

Take the road up the east shore of Lough Corrib via Annaghdown and Ross Errily Abbey to Cong.

Take the road west through Connemara to Clifden, returning by the coast.

In Kiltartan country south of Galway visit Athenry heritage town, Thoor Bal-lylee, once the home of William Butler Yeats, and Coole Park.

Book a day-trip to Aranmore, the larg-est of the Aran Islands, where tourism has softened the once harsh island way of life.

LONGER BREAKS

For trips of a week or more, see Driving Tours.

ACTIVITY HOLIDAYS

See WHAT TO SEE AND DO.

Discover Ireland (the Irish tourist board) provides information on all kinds of holidays and summer schools.

Horse-Drawn Caravan

The caravan provides accommodation as well as a leisurely way of exploring the Irish country roads:

Slattery's Horse-drawn Caravans, 1 Russell Street, Tralee, Co Kerry. ☎066 26277.

Mayo Horsedrawn Caravan Holidays Ltd, Belcarra, Castlebar. ☎094 903 2054. www.horsedrawn caravan.com.

Boating and Cruising

Ireland is blessed with many lakes and waterways, and is surrounded by sea. Good waterways for cruising include the River Shannon, Shannon–Erne Waterway and Lough Erne; canal barges are recommended on the River Barrow, the Grand Canal and the River Shannon. Details of local operators are given in the relevant chapters.

Visit **www.waterwaysireland.org** for general information. Try to hire from a boat operator that is a member of the Irish Boat Rental Association: **www.boatholidaysireland.com**.

Walking, Cycling and Horse Riding

Holidays – even chauffeur-driven – can be organised around a variety of activities, which include tracing ances-tors, gardens and golf.

Tailormade-Ireland. ☎059 916 1473. www.tailormade-Ireland.com.

Irish Language and Culture

Several course are on offer in the Irish speaking districts (the Gaeltacht), either specialising in language or combining language with culture. Workshops include tin-whistle playing, Bodhrán playing, set-danc-ing, sean-nós singing, hill-walking, lectures on Irish folklore, poetry reading, traditional music concerts, cultural activity courses on archaeol-ogy, marine painting, Celtic pottery and much more.

Oideas Gael, Gleann Cholm Cille, Co Donegal. ☎074 973 0248. www.oideas-gael.com.

Bord Fáilte, Dublin

Irish soda bread

Cooking

Various country hotels have set up cookery schools. **Berry Lodge** (Annagh, Miltown Malbray, Co Clare; ☎065 708 7022; www.berrylodge. com) for example, offers 'A Taste of Irish Cooking'.

OTHER WAYS OF EXPLORING

In addition to the ideas listed below, you may like to check out rail and bus trips from the major towns organised by Irish Rail Service (Iarnród Éireann), Northern Ireland Railways, Bus Eireann and Ulster Bus (*see GETTING THERE*).

By Tourist Train

There are a few tourist railways in Ireland that occasionally operate steam trains on the national network. Advance booking is essential.

Railway Preservation Society of Ireland (RPSA), PO Box 171, Larne, Co Antrim BT40 1UU. ☎028 260 803 or (Dublin) 01 280 9147; www.rpsi-online.org.

Irish Steam Preservation Society Ltd, Steam Museum, Stradbally, Co Laois. ☎086 389 0184. www.irishsteam.ie.

By Bicycle

Ireland is an ideal place to cycle because much of the country is gently undulating. Bicycles can be taken on planes, trains and buses so travelling around is generally straightforward. There are also various tour operators offering well-organised group itineraries and independent holidays (*see WHAT TO SEE AND DO; Cycling*).

Irish Tourism.com Ltd, River House, Killarney Road, Newcastle West, Limerick. ☎069 77686; www.irishtourism.com

Irish Cycling Safaris www.cycling safaris.com ☎01 260 0749

The Táin Trail

This trail (365mi/585km) retraces as closely as possible the route through the Midlands from Rathcroghan to the Cooley Peninsula and back taken by Maeve's armies in pursuit of the Brown Bull of Cooley, a tale told in the *Cattle Raid of Cooley (Táin bó Buailgne)*, one of the great Irish legends.

The circular route can be joined at any point as it passes through historic places of interest – on the northern leg, starting from Rathcroghan, the trail goes through Strokestown, Longford, Fore, Kells, Louth, Dundalk and Omeath to Carlingford; on the southern leg, starting in Carlingford, it runs through Monasterboice, Slane, Kells, bypasses Mullingar, and continues through Kilbeggan, Clara, Athlone and Roscommon to Rathcroghan.

On Foot

Ireland has over 30 waymarked routes *(yellow arrow and walking figure)*

Cycling on a remote country road

Bord Fáilte, Dublin

A welcome sign of fair weather

following disused roads, lanes and forest trails across the country.

As the weather can change quickly it is important to let someone know where you are going and when you are expected to return, to be properly equipped with suitable clothing, compass, maps and guidebook.

In addition to the trails described below, you will find others listed in the appropriate chapter– Beara Way (&see KENMARE), Burren Way (&see The BURREN), Mourne Trail (&see MOURNE MOUNTAINS), Wicklow Way (&see WICKLOW MOUNTAINS).

The Bangor Trail

This is an old drovers' trail (approx. 20mi/32km) in the west of Ireland from Newport on the shores of Clew Bay northwards through the Nephin Beg Mountains to Bangor Erris. This area of northwest Connacht consists of hills encircled by a vast area of trackless bog, without trees or houses, nothing between the heather and the sky but the occasional shepherd or farmer.

The Cavan Way

In north-west Co Cavan between Blacklion and Dowra (16mi/25km) over the hills to Shannon Pot, the source of the River Shannon, and then mainly by road to Dowra where it links up with the Leitrim Way (&see below).

The Dingle Way

A circular walk (104mi/168km) to and from Trale,e which takes in the beautiful scenery of the Dingle Peninsula.

The East Munster Way

This walk (44mi/70km) starts from Carrick-on-Suir, passes through Clonmel and finishes in Clogheen in Co Waterford; it includes forest tracks, open moorland and a river towpath.

The Kerry Way *(Slí íbh Ráthach)*

This is the longest waymarkedwalk (133mi/214km) and can be done clockwise or anti-clockwise, starting and finishing in Killarney. It winds through the Macgillycuddy Reeks before reaching the coast at Glenbeigh and running south and east through Caherciveen, Waterville, Derrynane, Sneem and Kenmare.

The Leitrim Way *(Slí Liatroma)*

Consists of old and new tracks (30mi/48km) from Drumshanbo, along the east shore of Lough Allen at the foot of Slieve Anierin, through Dowra the first town on the River Shannon, up the Owennayle Valley, over a moorland plateau, past Doo Lough (panoramic views), through lowland and forest, over the Tullykeherny Plateau and down a country road into Manorhamilton.

KNOW BEFORE YOU GO

Useful Websites

www.discoverireland.com
The official tourist board website for all of Ireland.

www.discover northernireland.com
The official regional tourist board website for Northern Ireland.

www.irlgov.ie
Republic of Ireland government.

www.ireland.com
Irish Times, daily newspaper.

www.12travel.com
The website of My Guide Ireland, customized Ireland holiday specialists.

www.emigrant.ie
News for the global Irish community.

www.irishgenealogy.ie
The Irish Genealogical Project, answering questions about Irish ancestry.

Tourist Offices

For information, brochures, maps and assistance in planning a trip, contact:

IRISH TOURIST BOARD (BORD FÁILTE)

Australia
Level 5, 36 Carrington Street, Sydney, NSW 2000. ☎029 299 6177.

Canada
2 Bloor Street West, Suite 3403, Toronto ON M4W. ☎1 416 925 6368

Denmark
Nyhavn 16, 3rd Floor, DK 1051 København K. ☎33 15 80 45.

France
33 rue de Miromesnil, Paris, 75008. ☎01 53 43 12 35

Italy
Piazza Cantore 4, Milan 20123. ☎02 58 17 73 11

United Kingdom
103 Wigmore Street, **London** ☎020 7518 0800. James Millar House, 7th Floor, 98 West George Street, **Glasgow**. ☎0141 572 4030.

United States
345 Park Avenue, 17th Floor, New York, NY 10154. ☎212 418 0800/212 371 9052.

NORTHERN IRELAND TOURIST BOARD *(NITB)* OFFICES

United Kingdom
Britain Visitor Centre, 1 Regent Street, London SW1Y 4XT (appointment only). www.visitbritain.com.

Republic of Ireland
www.discovernorthernireland.com St Anne Court, 59 North Street, Belfast BT1 1NB. ☎028 9023 1221 16 Nassau Street, Dublin 2. ☎01 679 1977.

TOURISM ORGANISATIONS

Armagh
40 English Street, Armagh. ☎028 3752 1800. www.visitarmagh.com.

Belfast Visitor and Convention Bureau
47 Donegall Place, Belfast. ☎028 9024 6609. www.gotobelfast.com

The Causeway Coast and Glens
11 Lodge Road, Coleraine. ☎028 7032 7720. www.causewaycoastandglens.com.

Derry Visitor and Convention Bureau
44 Foyle Street, Londonderry. ☎028 7126 7284. www.derryvisitor.com.

Dublin Tourism
Dublin Tourism Centre, Suffolk Street.
☎01 605 7700. www.visitdublin.com.

Fermanagh Lakeland Tourism
Wellington Road, Enniskillen.
☎028 6632 3110.
www.fermanaghlakelands.com.

Cork & Kerry Tourism
Grand Parade, Cork.
☎021 425 5100. www.corkkerry.ie.

Ireland West Tourism
Aras Failte, Forster Street, Galway.
☎091 537 700. www.irelandwest.ie.

East Coast and Midlands Tourism
Dublin Road, Mullingar,
Co Westmeath. ☎0444 8761.
www.ecoast-midlands.travel.ie.

South East Tourism
41 The Quay, Waterford.
☎051 875 823.
www.southeastireland.com.

North West Tourism
Aras Reddan, Temple Street, Sligo.
☎071 916 1201.
www.irelandnorthwest.ie.

Shannon Development
Shannon Town Centre, Co Clare.
☎061 361 555.
www.shannonregiontourism.ie

The Kingdoms of Down
40 West Street, Newtownards,
Co Down. ☎028 9182 2881.
www.kingdomsofdown.com.

LOCAL TOURIST OFFICES

*In this guide the contact details for
Tourist Information Centres are identified by the* 🖪 *symbol.*

Some local tourist offices are only
open during the summer months.
The centres can supply town plans,
timetables and information on
sightseeing, local entertainment and
sports facilities. Many have bureau de
change facilities and a hotel reservation service.

International Visitors

IRISH EMBASSIES

Australia
20 Arkana Street, Yarralumla,
Canberra. ☎06273 3022.
Consulate General –
Level 26, 1 Market Street.
Sydney NSW 2000, ☎612 9264 9635.

Canada
Suite 1105, 130 Albert Street, Ottawa,
Ontario KIP 5G4. ☎613 233 6281.

Denmark
Østbanegade 21, DK-2100
Copenhagen. ☎035 423 233.

Japan
Ireland House 5F, 2-10-7 Kojimachi,
Chiyoda-Ku, Tokyo 102-0083.
☎03 3263 0695.

New Zealand
Level 7, Citibank Building, 23 Customs
Street East, Auckland. Postal address
PO Box 279, Auckland 1001.
☎09 977 2252.

Norway
Haakon VIIs gate 1, 0244 Oslo.
☎047 2201 7200.

South Africa
1st Floor, Southern Life Plaza, 1059
Schoeman Street, Arcadia 0083, Pretoria 0001. Postal address PO Box 4174
Pretoria 0001. ☎(27) 12 342 5062.

Sweden
Ostermalmsgatan 97, PO Box 10326,
100 55, Stockholm. ☎08 66 18 005.

United Kingdom
17 Grosvenor Place, London
SW1X 7HR. ☎020 7235 2171.

United States
2234 Massachusetts Avenue NW,
Washington DC 20008-2849.
☎202 462 3939.
www.embassyofireland.org.

FOREIGN EMBASSIES AND CONSULATES IN IRELAND

Australia
Fitzwilton House (7th floor), Wilton Terrace, Dublin 2. ☎01 664 5300.

Canada
Canada House, 65 St Stephen's Green, Dublin 2. ☎01 417 4100.

Denmark
7th Floor, Block E, Iveagh Court, Harcourt Road. Dublin 2. ☎01 475 6404.

Japan
Nutley Building, Merrion Centre, Nutley Lane, Dublin 4. ☎01 202 8300.

South Africa
Alexandra House, Earlsfort Centre, Earlsfort Terrace, Dublin 2. ☎01 661 5553.

Sweden
13-17 Dawson Street, Dublin 2. ☎01 474 4400.

United Kingdom
29 Merrion Road, Ballsbridge, Dublin 4. ☎01 205 3700.

USA
42 Elgin Road, Ballsbridge, Dublin 4. ☎01 668 8777.

ENTRY REQUIREMENTS

Visitors entering Ireland must be in possession of a **valid national passport** (except British nationals). In case of loss or theft report to the appropriate embassy and the local police. Visitors who require an **entry visa** for the Republic of Ireland or Northern Ireland should apply at least three weeks in advance to the Irish Embassy or the United Kingdom Embassy. Useful information for US nationals on visa requirements, customs regulations, medical care etc. for international travel can be found by visiting www.travel.state.gov. Visitors from outside the EU should have comprehensive travel insurance. Visitors from EU countries should carry a **European Health Insurance Card (EHIC)**, and have adequate travel insurance for the duration of their stay. In case of the loss or theft of any document, report it to the local police.

CUSTOMS REGULATIONS

Tax-free allowances for various commodities are governed by EU legislation. Details of these allowances are available at most ports of entry to the Republic of Ireland / United Kingdom, and from customs authorities. It is against the law to bring into the Republic of Ireland firearms, explosives, illicit drugs, meat and meat

Torc Waterfall, Killarney National Park

©Dickon Whitehead/Fotolia.com

products, plant and plant products (including seeds). It is against the law to bring into the United Kingdom drugs, firearms and ammunition, obscene material featuring children, counterfeit merchandise, unlicensed livestock (birds or animals), anything related to endangered species (furs, ivory, horn, leather) and certain plants (potatoes, bulbs, seeds, trees).

Customs and Excise, Passenger Terminal, Dublin Airport, Co Dublin. ☎01 844 5538. www.revenue.ie.

Customs and Excise, Custom House, Belfast BT1 3ET. ☎028 9056 2600 or 028 9023 4466. www.hmrc.gov.uk.

HM Customs and Excise, ☎0845 010 9000 (National Advice Helpline). www.hmrc.gov.uk.

For US nationals returning to the US after travelling abroad there is useful information in the leaflet *Know Before You Go* available as a downloadable pdf from www.cbp.gov.

DOMESTIC ANIMALS

No animals, pets or other, may be brought into the Republic of Ireland, except from the United Kingdom. Domestic animals (dogs, cats) with vaccination documents are allowed into the United Kingdom (Great Britain and Northern Ireland).

Department of Agriculture, Food and Rural Development, Agriculture House, Kildare Street, Dublin 2. ☎01 607 2000

HEALTH

For emergencies, dial ☎999.

In Ireland hospital treatment is available in emergencies, but is not free of charge except to Irish nationals. Emergency help can be obtained from the Casualty Department of a hospital or from a pharmacy/chemist. Nationals of non-EU countries should take out comprehensive insurance.

National of EU countries should apply to their own National Social Security Offices for a **European Health Insurance Card (EHIC)**, (not obligatory for UK nationals; proof of identity only necessary), which entitles them to medical treatment under an EU Reciprocal Medical Treatment arrangement, provided treatment is sought from a doctor in Ireland whose name is on the Health Board Panel of Doctors (list available from the local health board).

Accessibility

Where sights described in this guide are accessible, or mostly accessible to disabled visitors, they are indicated by the ⚐ symbol. Absence of a symbol does *not* indicate that there are no facilities for disabled visitors at the site or attraction in question, just that there are certain difficulties to overcome. As ever, call ahead to plan your visit.

The red-cover **Michelin Guide Great Britain and Ireland** indicates hotels with facilities suitable for disabled travellers. The following organisations provide further information:

- **Everybody's Hotel Directory** www.everybody.co.uk. www.allgoher.com. Useful information about accommodation.
- **Direct Enquiries** www.directenquiries.com. Information about holidays and travel in the UK and Northern Ireland (though not the Republic of Ireland).
- **Tourism for All**. www.tourismforall.org.uk. ☎0845 124 9971. National UK charity dedicated to making tourism welcoming to all
- **Fáilte Ireland** has developed a scheme for the validation and provision of information on registered and approved accommodation that provides for those needs of various grades of disability. www.discoverireland.ie.

GETTING THERE AND GETTING AROUND

By Air

Many international airlines operate flights to the international airports in Ireland – Dublin, Shannon, Knock and Belfast. All airports are linked by bus to the neighbouring towns.
Regional airports offering scheduled flights to Dublin, the UK and Europe are Kerry Airport (Farrannfore), Galway Airport, Knock International Airport, Sligo, Donegal and Derry (London-derry) Airports.
Several airlines offer non-stop trans-Atlantic flights to Dublin and Shannon. Others fly to Belfast and to Knock. Information, brochures and timetables are available from the airlines and from travel agents. Fly-Drive schemes are operated by most airlines.

 Aer Arran
www.aerarann.com

 Aer Lingus
www.aerlingus.com

 Air France
www.airfrance.co.uk

 Air Southwest
www.airsouthwest.com

 British Airways
www.britishairways.com

 British European
www.flybe.com

 bmi/bmi baby
www.flybmi.com
www.flybmibaby.com

 Easyjet
www.easyjet.com

 Euromank Airways
www.euromanx.com

 flybe
www.flybe.com

 Jet2.com
www.jet2.com

Luxair
www.luxair.lu

Manx2
www.manx2.com

 Ryanair
www.ryanair.com

XL.com
www.xl.com

By Sea

Details of passenger ferry and car ferry services to Ireland from the United Kingdom and France can be obtained from travel agencies or from the main carriers. Information about ferries to the offshore islands is given in the *Discovering* section of the guide.

Brittany Ferries
www.brittany-ferries.com.
General enquiries ☎021 4277 801 (Ireland); 0870 9076 103 (UK).
Roscoff (France)-Cork

Irish Ferries
www.irishferries.com.
General enquiries ☎01 855 2222.
Holyhead (Wales) -Dublin; Pem-broke Wales)-Rosslare. Cherbourg and Roscoff (France)-Rosslare.

Norfolkline
www.norfolkline.com.
☎0844 499 0007.
Liverpool-Belfast and Dublin.

Stena Line
www.stenaline.com
☎08705 204 204 (Northern Ireland) 01 204 7777 (Dublin). Fishguard-Rosslare; Holyhead to Dublin and Dun Laoghaire; Fleetwood (Lancs, England)-Larne; Stranraer (Scotland)-Belfast.

P&O Irish Sea
www.poirishsea.com.
UK ☎0871 66 44 999. Dublin ☎01 407 34 34. Larne-Troon or Cairnryan (Scotland); Dublin-Liverpool

Swansea Cork Ferries
www.directferries.co.uk.
☎0871 222 3312.

Steam Packet Company
www.steam-packet.com
Isle of Man-Belfast and Dublin.
☎0871 222 1333.

By Coach / Bus

Regular coach services operate between the major Irish towns and the major cities in Great Britain and the Continent via the car ferry ports at Rosslare, Dublin Ferryport and Larne. As an example of journey times it takes around 11 hours to get from London to Dublin.

National Express
www.nationalexpress.comeurolines

Bus Éireann
www.buseireann.ie.

Dublin Bus (Bus Atha Cliath)
www.dublinbus.ie. ☎01 873 4222.

Ulsterbus
www.translink.co.uk.
(♿ *See By Rail*).

By Car

Nationals of EU countries wishing to drive in Ireland require a **valid national driving** licence; nationals of

Ferry crossing the Irish Sea

R Holzbachova, Ph Benet/MICHELIN

non-EU countries require an **International Driving Permit (IDP)**. This is obtainable in the US from the National Auto Club, 1151 E Hillsdale Boulevard, Foster City CA 94404; www.thenac. com or from a local branch of the American Automobile Association. ☎1 800 622 2136. Nationals of other non-European countries should check before leaving their home country. If you plan to bring your own car to Ireland you will need your vehicle's **registration papers** ("log-book") and an approved **nationality plate**. Vehicle **insurance cover** is compulsory. Although no longer a legal requirement, the International Insurance Certificate (Green Card) is the most effective proof of insurance cover and is internationally recognised by the police and other authorities. In the case of loss or theft of any document, report it to the local police.

CAR HIRE / RENTAL

There are car rental agencies at airports, railway stations and in all large towns throughout Ireland. European cars usually have manual transmission; automatic cars need to be specified at the time of booking.
Before crossing the border between the Republic and Northern Ireland it is important to check that the insurance cover extends to the other country. It is invariably cheaper to return a hire car to its pick-up point than to leave it elsewhere.

On the Sky Road, Connemara

DRIVING IN IRELAND

The road network consists of a limited network of motorways, some high standard major roads, some older ones with an inside lane for farm vehicles, and plenty of narrow country roads. In the peatlands where the road surface may be undulating it is a good idea to slow down.

HIGHWAY CODE

- The **minimum driving age** is 16 in the Republic of Ireland and 17 in Northern Ireland.
- Traffic drives on the **left**.
- Traffic on main roads and on roundabouts has priority.
- Give way to traffic coming from the right at roundabouts.
- The driver and front-seat passenger must wear **seat belts**. Rear-seat belts must be worn where they are fitted; children under 12 must travel in the rear seats.

Speed limits Republic of Ireland:
30mph/48kph: in built-up areas
60mph/96kph: on country roads
70mph/112kph: on motorways
Northern Ireland:
30mph/48kph: in built-up areas
60mph/96kph: on country roads
70mph/112kph: on dual carriageways and motorways

- Full or dipped **headlights** should be switched on in poor visibility and at night; use **sidelights** only when the vehicle is stationary in an area without street lighting.
- It is obligatory to carry a red warning triangle or to have hazard warning lights to use in the case of a **breakdown** or **accident**.

PARKING

There are multi-storey car parks in towns, disc systems, parking meters and paying parking zones; in the last two cases, small change is necessary and in the last case tickets must be obtained from the ticket machines and displayed inside the windscreen. In Northern Ireland city centre parking may be restricted and the usual regulations are as follows:

- **Double red line** – no stopping at any time (freeway)
- **Double yellow line** – no parking at any time
- **Single yellow line** – no parking for set periods as indicated on panel
- **Dotted yellow line** – parking limited to certain times only

PENALTIES

In the Republic
Parking offences may attract an on-the-spot fine. Drivers suspected of **speeding** are liable for an on-the-spot fine. Drivers suspected of **driving while under the influence of alcohol** are liable to be checked with a breathalyser and to prosecution.

In Northern Ireland
Failure to display a parking ticket may result in a fine. Illegal parking will lead to a Penalty Charge Notice and, in some cases, to the vehicle being clamped or towed away.
Drivers suspected of **driving while under the influence of alcohol** are liable to be checked with a breathalyser and to be prosecuted.

Drivers suspected of **speeding** are liable to be prosecuted; there are speed camera warning signs beside the road before you enter a speed check area. Speed cameras are yellow.

ROAD SIGNS

The colour code for different types of road signs is as follows:

- **blue** for motorways
- **green** for major roads
- **black** on white for local
- **brown** for tourist signs

ROAD TOLLS

Tolls are levied on the East Link Bridge (Dublin), which spans the Liffey estuary; the West-Link Bridge (Dublin), which runs north–south on the western edge of the city; on the M1 Drogheda By-pass; and the M4 Kinnegad-Enfield-Kilcock road.

PETROL/GAS

Most service stations have dual-pumps; **unleaded pumps** are identified by a green stripe or green pump handles. Prices tend to be cheaper in the Republic than in Northern Ireland.

MOTORING ORGANISATIONS

In Ireland and the UK accident insurance and breakdown service schemes are available through motoring organisations. Members of the American Automobile Club should obtain the brochure.

Automobile Association (AA)
Ireland: ☎01 617 9999.
www.aaireland.ie
UK: ☎0800 085 2721 (sales).
☎0870 600 0371 (general enquiries).
www.theaa.com.

Royal Automobile Club (RAC)
Ireland: 01800 805 498
(Customer Services). www.rac.ie
UK: ☎020 8917 2500. 08705 722 722
www.rac.co.uk.

MAPS AND PLANS

For Route Planning use the maps in this guide, **Michelin Map 712 Ireland** and the **Michelin Atlas Great Britain and Ireland**. The atlas and map 712 show the major roads (N or A) and many of the minor roads (R/L or B).

By Rail

Irish Rail Service, (Northern Ireland Railways and the various British railway companies operate train services between the major cities in Ireland and the United Kingdom.

Iarnród Éireann / Irish Rail
Online timetables and ticket reservation; ☎1850 366 222; www.irishrail.ie. Talking timetable; ☎1890 77 88 99
Iarnròd Eireann Travel Centre, 35 Lower Abbey Street, Dublin 1.
☎01 703 4070.

Railtours Ireland – (using train and coach). www.railtoursireland.com
Dublin Tourism Centre, Suffolk Street, Dublin 2 or opposite Connolly Station; ☎01 856 0045.

CIE – national coach/rail/Dublin Bus operator. International and national routes, timetables, fares on www.cie.ie

Northern Ireland Rail
Online timetables and journey planner for public transport by rail and road; www.translink.co.uk
Central Station, Belfast BT1 3PB.
☎028 9066 6630 (enquiries) international services and short breaks. ☎028 9024 2420

WHERE TO STAY AND EAT

Where to Stay

A variety of different types of accommodation are available in Ireland. Hotels and restaurants are described in the Address Books within the *Discovering* section.

In town centres **parking** can be a problem but many hotels have a car park on site or a short walk away.

In a small town the only hotel often doubles as the **local disco** and it may be very noisy until the early hours on a Saturday night, especially if there is a wedding party.

At **breakfast** most establishments offer a light Continental-style breakfast of coffee and bread and jam, as well as the traditional cooked breakfast. The latter is often a feature of bed and breakfast accommodation and comes in very generous portions.

ACCOMMODATION TYPES

Hotels

Traditionally hotels tend to be medium to large establishments, where the bedrooms have en-suite facilities and a full-range of services. The terms hotel and guesthouse are

| 1 FINGAL | 2 SOUTH DUBLIN | 3 DÚN LAOGHAIRE-RATHDOWN | ○ County Towns |

used fairly loosely, usually at the whim of the proprietors, and apply to a broad range of accommodation.
In the last few years the general standard of Irish hotels has come on in leaps and bounds. Throughout Ireland you can now find some of the finest 5-star, de-luxe, state-of-the-art design and boutique hotels in the British Isles. Country Houses and even castles have also seized upon the resort trend and many now offer luxurious spas, golf courses and a complete outdoor sports and leisure pursuits package within their estates.

A welcome sign in Kenmare

Bord Fáilte, Dublin

Guesthouses
The term guesthouse describes a smaller operation than a hotel, with fewer facilities, which generally appeals more to visitors on holiday than to those on business.
The properties vary from modern purpose-built premises to Georgian and Victorian houses.

Inns/Pubs with Rooms
In the smaller towns and villages the local inn often has rooms to let.

Bed & Breakfast
The distinction between Bed-and-Breakfast places and guesthouses is often blurred but the traditional Bed-and-Breakfast is a family-run affair, offering one or two bedrooms at a moderate price. This simple form of accommodation is found all over Ireland in properties ranging from a simple bungalow to a Great House.

Farm Holidays
Being a predominantly agricultural country, Ireland has a great range of farms, many of which welcome visitors in the summer season.

Self Catering
In many parts of the country, particularly the tourist districts, there are purpose-built holiday villages consisting of a cluster of well-appointed cottages.
See Budget Accommodation.

University Residences
Accommodation in universities (single rooms and self-catering apartments) is available during school vacations, particularly in Dublin, Cork, and Galway.
See Budget Accommodation.

Hostels
There are around 50 **youth hostels** in the Republic and six in Northern Ireland.
See Budget Accommodation.

Camp Sites
Ireland has many officially graded caravan and camping parks with modern facilities and a variety of sports facilities.

USEFUL WEBSITES

www.goireland.com
The accommodation booking service developed for the Irish Tourist Board (Bord Fáilte) and the Northern Irish Tourist Board (NITB), and their networks of regional tourist boards. Information on flights, ferries, special interest holidays. ☎00800 369 87412 in Ireland; ☎0800 783 8359 in the UK; ☎1 888 827 3028 in the US.

www.discoverireland.com
Has thousands of offers on accommodation, travel, holiday packages, attractions and activities and more.

Places to stay

Overnight stop
Sightseeing centre
Resort
Seaside resort
Spa
Marina
Beach
Surf
Nature reserve
Garden
Golf
Racecourse
Greyhound track
Waymarked footpath
Wildlife/Safari park, Zoo
Country park
Forest, Forest park, National park
Airfield
Airport
Tourist or steam railway
Fishing

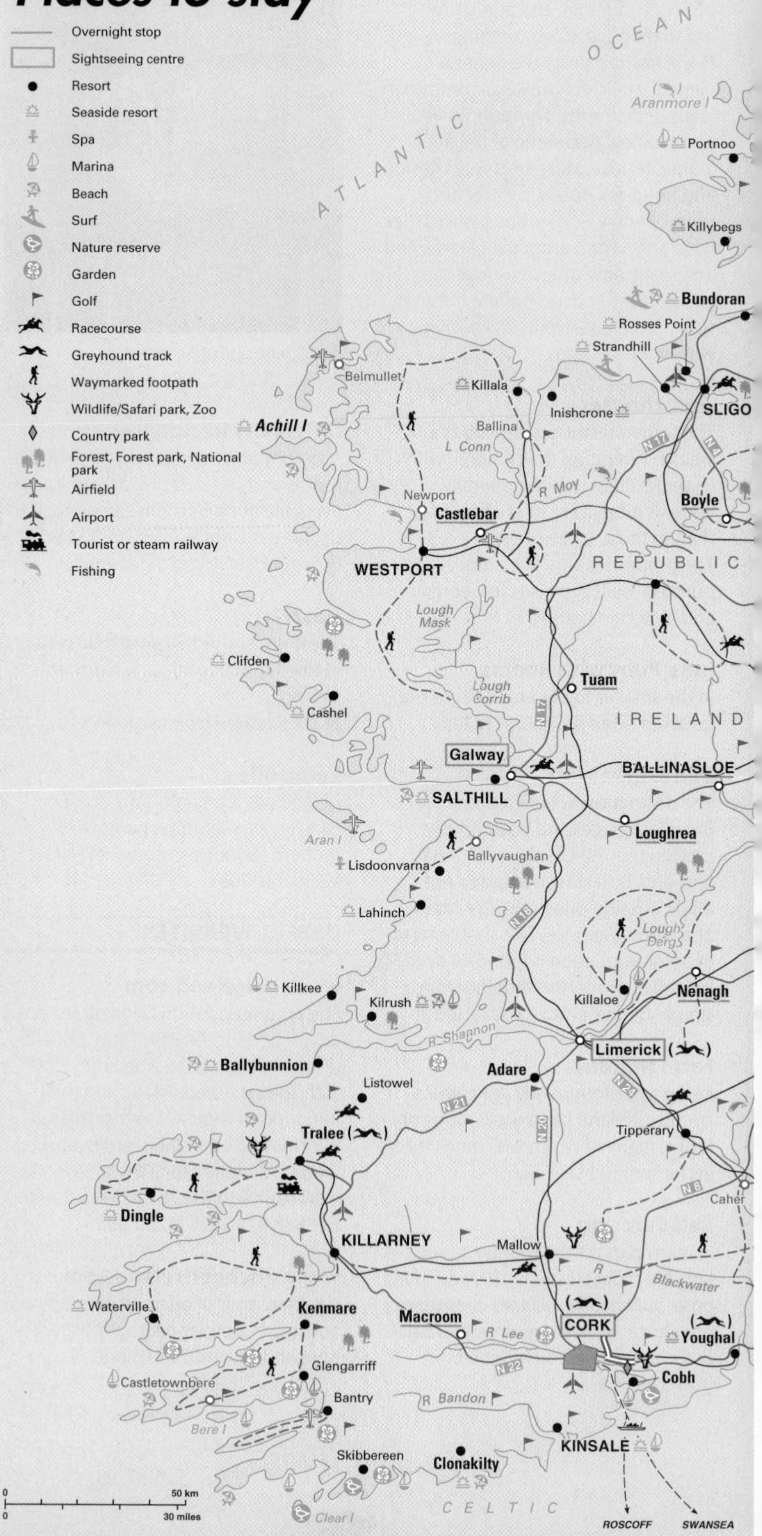

ATLANTIC OCEAN

Aranmore I
Portnoo
Killybegs
Bundoran
Rosses Point
Strandhill
SLIGO
Belmullet
Killala
Inishcrone
Achill I
Ballina
L Conn
R Moy
Boyle
Newport
Castlebar
REPUBLIC
WESTPORT
Lough Mask
Clifden
Lough Corrib
Tuam
IRELAND
Cashel
Galway
BALLINASLOE
SALTHILL
Loughrea
Aran I
Ballyvaughan
Lisdoonvarna
Lahinch
Lough Derg
Killee
Kilrush
Killaloe
Nenagh
R Shannon
Limerick
Ballybunnion
Listowel
Adare
Tipperary
Tralee
N 21
Caher
N 8
Dingle
KILLARNEY
Mallow
Blackwater
Waterville
Kenmare
Macroom
R Lee
CORK
Youghal
Glengarriff
Cobh
Castletownbere
Bantry
R Bandon
Bere I
Skibbereen
Clonakilty
KINSALE
Clear I
CELTIC

0   50 km
0   30 miles

ROSCOFF   SWANSEA

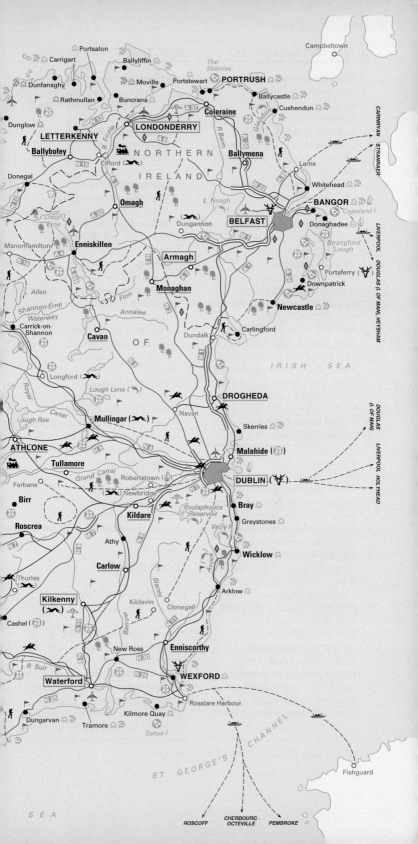

HOTELS AND GUESHOUSES

- **The Irish Hotels Federation**
  ☎01 497 6459
  www.irelandhotels.com
- **Manor House Hotels
  and Irish Country Hotels**
  ☎01 808 281 281 from within the
  Republic of Ireland; ☎+353 1295
  8900 from elsewhere;
  www.manorhousehotels.com.
- **The Hidden Ireland**
  Accommodation in historic Irish
  houses in town and country.
  ☎01 662 7166 or 098 66650;
  www.hidden-ireland.com
- **Ireland's Blue Book**
  Irish country houses and
  restaurants affiliated to the
  Historic Hotels of Europe/America.
  ☎01 676 9914; toll free
  from the USA ☎1 800 323 5463.
  www.irelands-blue-book.ie.
- **Irish Farmhouse Holidays**
  B&B and self-catering options on
  farms across the land. ☎061 309
  955. www.irishfarmholidays.com.

BED AND BREAKFAST ACCOMMODATION

- **Town and Country
  Homes Association**
  Over 1 100 B&B's in town, city
  and countryside locations across
  Ireland. They also publish *Bed and
  Breakfast Ireland*. ☎071 982 2222.
  www.townandcoutry.ie.
- **Elegant Ireland**
  Exclusive rented castles, country
  houses and cottages. ☎01 473
  2505. www.elegant.ie.
- **Premier Collection of Ireland**
  Over 40 guesthouses.
  ☎01 205 2826.
  www.premierguesthouses.com.
- **Irish Cottages and
  Holiday Homes Association**
  Over 5 000 holiday cottages and
  houses to rent. ☎01 205 2777.
  www.irishcottageholidays.com.

BUDGET ACCOMMODATION

Simple accommodation is available
in hostels (single, twin and 4/6-
bedded rooms) through the following
organisations:

- **Independent Holiday
  Hostels Ireland**
  ☎01 836 4700.
  www.hostels-ireland.com.
- **Northern Ireland
  Hostelling International**
  Modern smart hostels in Armagh,
  Belfast, Bushmills, Enniskillen,
  Newcastle, and Whitepark Bay.
  ☎028 9032 4733.www.hini.org.uk.
- **An Oige**
  Youth Hostel Association.
  26 youth hostels in the Republic.
  ☎01 830 4555. www.irelandyha.org.
- **Usit**
  Student travel specialists
  and information centre.
  Hostel/ hotel booking service.
  ☎01 602 1906. www.usit.ie
- **Ireland in Summer**
  Modern apartment accommoda-
  tion at 10 separate locations,
  serving all of ireland's universities:
  Belfast, Londonderry, Dublin (4),
  Cork, Limerick, Coleraine,
  Maynooth.
  www.irelandinsummer.com.
- **Irish Caravan &
  Camping Council**
  Over 100 camping and caravan
  parks; www.camping-ireland.ie.

Where to Eat

*For more on eating and drinking
see the INTRODUCTION.*

Ireland offers a huge range of places
to eat from top-class restaurants offering the highest quality produce and
the latest in the culinary art; wine bars,
bistros and brasseries; and fast food
outlets such as pizzerias, cafés and
fish and chips shops. Many historical
sights, like National Trust properties in
Northern Ireland, also provide lunch
and tea.

St. Patricks Day dinner with corned beef and a pint of Guinness

For a selection of the eating choices available, try the Restaurants Association of Ireland, whose website (www.rai.ie) lets you search for your nearest affiliated restaurant.

See Other Publications.

EATING OUT

Restaurants are usually open at lunchtime from noon to 2.15pm depending on their location, and in the evening from 6.30pm to 10pm. Many close one day a week and they may close early (between 7pm and 8pm on Sundays and Mondays in Northern Ireland). It is always advisable to book in the evening, particularly at the weekend. Portions are usually generous.

SPECIALITIES

Being an agricultural country, Ireland produces very good home-reared meat, particularly beef and lamb, and excellent dairy products – local cheeses, butter and cream. Near the coast there should be a good choice of fish; salmon is usually available everywhere. In the less-expensive restaurants the menu may not offer much in the way of fresh fruit and vegetables but the potatoes are usually very good. Look out for soda bread, for potato cakes (even at breakfast), for oysters and Guinness, for black pudding – a speciality in Co Cork – and for *carrageen*, a form of seaweed that is used in savoury and sweet dishes.

TIPPING

Tipping is optional but it is common to leave 10 per cent if the service has been good. You are generally not obliged and in some cases even expected to tip. Often a discretionary service charge (often 12.5 per cent) is included in the bill, which you may choose not to pay if the service has been poor. Some unscrupulous restaurants may make a service charge *and* leave the total open on a credit card slip, encouraging customers to unwittingly tip twice. To ensure that the staff get your tip, leave cash.

Other Publications

Consult the red-cover **Michelin Guide Great Britain and Ireland** or the **Michelin Eating Out in Pubs in Britain and Ireland**, for even more places to stay and eat throughout Ireland. The red guide provides comprehensive coverage of hotels, guesthouses and restaurants, while the pub guide covers all of the best spots for a good pint and pub lunch.

WHAT TO SEE AND DO

Activities for Children Kids

Sights of interest to children are indicated in this guide with a Kids symbol.

At first glimpse Ireland may not seem the ideal place for children. The classic Irish holiday itinerary of scenic tours, a game of golf, long walks and enjoying the craic in the pub listening to traditional music, is hardly likely to appeal to children. Neither are there any theme parks, or the kind of major family attractions to be found on the British mainland. However with a bit of planning, creativity and perseverance there is no reason why all the family can't have a great time.

Animal Magic

Dublin Zoo, Fota Wildlife Park and Belfast Zoo present a variety of animals to view. Connemara ponies roam wild in the Connemara National Park and there are herds of deer in several parks – Glenveagh National Park in Co Donegal, Doneraile Wildlife Park near Mallow and Parkanaur Forest Park near Dungannon. There are many riding schools offering the chance of a pony or horse ride or you can take a trip in one of the jaunting cars in Killarney.

Railway Children

A number of the old railways are being brought back into service. The longest is the Tralee-Blennerville Railway; there are shorter rides on the Fintown Railway in Co Donegal; the Foyle Valley Railway Centre in Londonderry, Downpatrick; and on two former peat bog trains—the Clonmacnoise and West Offaly Railway near Birr and the narrow gauge railway at Peatlands Park between Dungannon and Lough Neagh. There are model railways at the West Cork Model Railway Village near Clonakilty and the Fry Model Railway at Malahide.

The Good Old Days

Most children enjoy watching demonstrations of old crafts at the open-air museums – try Muckross Farms near Killarney, Ulster Folk and Transport Museum near Bangor and the Ulster-American Folk Park north of Omagh in the Sperrin Mountains.
Children are also likely to enjoy seeing how Irish ancestors lived in earlier centuries at the Craggaunowen Centre near Ennis, where the Brendan is on view, at the Lough Gur Interpretive Centre south of Limerick, at the Irish National Heritage Park near Wexford and the Ulster History Park north of Omagh in the Sperrin Mountains.
A great selection of vintage vehicles is on view at the Museum of Transport in Clonmel, the National Transport Museum in Howth Castle north of Dublin, the Museum of Irish Transport in Killarney and the Ulster Folk and Transport Museum near Bangor. Other delights for the mechanically minded are the Great Telescope at Birr Castle, which has been restored to working order.

Going Underground

The action of water on the landmass has produced several caves that can be safely explored – Aillwee Cave in the Burren, Mitchelstown Cave near Caher, Dunmore Cave near Kilkenny, Crag Cave near Tralee and Marble Arch Caves near Enniskillen.

Entertainment

TRADITIONAL MUSIC

The most typically Irish, and also generally the most popular form of evening entertainment, is the traditional music and singing performed in the bars up and down the country, in cities, towns and in rural areas.
The instruments played are commonly the violin – called the fiddle by traditional musicians – the flute,

the goatskin drum (*bodhrán*) and the free-reed instruments such as the accordion, melodeon and concertina; more recently the guitar and banjo have joined in. That other very genteel and quintessentially Irish instrument, the Irish harp, is now rarely played in public though there are two harp festivals (𝒸 *see CALENDAR OF EVENTS*). Ask at the tourist Information centre for bars with traditional music.

A feature of Irish traditional music is **dancing**, including individual old-style (*sean-nós*) dancing and particularly **set dancing**, an adaptation of military dances to existing tunes such as jigs, reels, hornpipes and polkas.

Set dancing has enjoyed a huge revival in popularity largely thanks to the efforts of the ebullient, American-born **Michael Flatley**, whose lavish stage production of *Riverdance* (followed by *Lord of the Dance and Feet of Flames*) became an international phenomenon in the mid-1990s.

CULTURAL FESTIVALS

Ireland hosts a number of literature and music festivals in honour of individual artists, or groups of artists. Many are accompanied by bands, parades, horse races and regattas.

IRISH BANQUETS

For a truly Irish evening's entertainment, try a medieval banquet accompanied by music and poetry – they take place at Knappogue Castle; Bunratty Castle; Dunguaire Castle; Killarney Manor; and Brú Ború in Cashel.

THEATRES

Ireland has a lively theatrical scene with theatres in many provincial towns, as well as Dublin and Belfast. In Dublin, modern and classic plays are performed at the **Abbey Theatre** and the **Gate Theatre**.

The traditional seasonal festivals and rural way of life are evoked in music, song, dance and mime in the performances of the **National Folk Theatre of Ireland** in Tralee, which

Fishing at Maam Cross in Connemara

R Holzbachova, Ph Benet/MICHELIN

draw on the local Gaelic tradition. Productions in the Irish language are put on by the Irish Theatre **(Taibhearc na Gaillimhe)** in Galway, which is a state-sponsored body.

CLASSICAL MUSIC

In Dublin, the **National Concert Hall** (Earlsfort Terrace) has a regular programme of classical and modern orchestral music. Over in Belfast, the **Waterfront Hall** offers a varied programme of events.

Concerts of **chamber music** are given by Irish and international musicians in some of the great Irish houses in the summer; details are available from the National Concert Hall in Dublin.

Opera is performed in Dublin and Belfast and also at various **opera festivals**, notably in Wexford.

Heritage

Historic Properties

- **Dúchas** – The Irish Heritage Service is the State body responsible for the protection and conservation of natural and built heritage. The **Heritage Card** provides unlimited admission to all sites managed by The Office of Public Works, available at most properties or from Dublin Tourism. ☎01 661 3111. www.heritageireland.ie.

- **Heritage Towns** – Some 25 towns have been designated Heritage

Towns for their architecture, history, or character, which is illustrated in the local heritage centre. www.heritagetowns.com

- **Historic Monuments** In Northern Ireland are the responsibility of the Department of the Environment. www.ehsni.gov.uk.
- **National Trust** – The Trust owns over 200 historic house and gardens and 49 industrial monuments and mills in the United Kingdom. Members may use their membership cards to visit NT properties in Northern Ireland. Annual membership offering free admission to all NT sites is available at most sites. **Head Office in Northern Ireland**. ☎028 9751 0721. www.nationaltrust.org.uk.
- In August, during **National Heritage Week/ European Heritage Open Days**, there are walks, lectures, exhibitions, music recitals, pageants and demonstrations at several historic properties, some exclusively at this time. www.heritageweek.ie.

Nature Reserves and National Parks

Ireland has four **national parks**: Glenveagh, Connemara, Wicklow Mountains and Killarney. Many **forest parks** and **country parks** are managed for public use and recreation, There are numerous **nature reserves** (wildfowl sanctuaries, peat bogs and sand dunes) both sides of the border :

- **National Parks and Wildlife Service** – www.npws.ie.
- **Birdwatch Ireland (BWI)** – www.birdwatchireland.ie.
- **Irish Peatland Conservation Council** – www.ipcc.ie.
- **Royal Society for Protection of Birds (RSPB)** – www.rspb.org.uk/nireland.

Outdoor Fun

Ireland is naturally well-endowed with a variety of different physical environments for outdoor **sports and leisure activities**. The long, indented coastline provides facilities for bathing, scuba-diving, wind-surfing, sailing, sea-angling and deep-sea fishing. The many inland lakes and waterways are good for cruising, canoeing and water-skiing and attractive to anglers. For golfers there are both inland and links courses. The magnificent mountain ranges that fringe the Atlantic coast from north to south provide exhilarating locations for walking, rambling, orienteering and mountaineering. Hunting and horse racing are concentrated in the flatter, agricultural counties of the south and midlands; pony trekking is available countrywide. Information on all activities is available from tourist boards.

ADVENTURE SPORTS

Climbing and Mountaineering

Information on mountaineering, rock climbing and orienteering:

- **Mountaineering Council of Ireland** – www.climbing.ie.
- **Tollymore Mountain Centre** – Mountaineering and canoeing courses. Bryansford, Newcastle. ☎028 4372 2158. www.tollymoremc.com.

Multi-sport centres

- **Killary Tours** – Sailing, kayaking, surfing, bungee jumping, high ropes, cycle tours, clay pigeon etc. Leenane, Connemara, Co Galway. ☎095 43411. www.killary.com

AIRBORNE SPORTS

Gliding
Irish Hang-Gliding and Paragliding Association – www.ihpa.ie or www.uhpc.f9.co.uk (for Northern Ireland).

Parachuting
Irish Parachute Club – www.skydive.ie.

HORSE RIDING

Association of Irish Riding Establishments (AIRE) – www.aire.ie.
Equestrian Holidays Ireland – www.ehi.ie.

LAND SPORTS

Cycling

Cycling is becoming increasingly popular in Ireland. As a result, bicycle hire is available almost everywhere.

◆ **Walking Cycling Ireland** – Walking and Cycling Tour Holiday operators in Ireland. www.irelandwalkingcycling.com.

Tour operators:

◆ **Irish Cycling Safaris** – University College Dublin, Dublin 4. ☎01 260 0749. www.cyclingsafaris.com.
◆ **Irish Cycle Hire** – Unit 6 Ardee Enterprise Centre, Co Louth. ☎041 685 3772; www.irishcyclehire.com. Guided and self-guided holidays.
◆ **Cyclewest Ireland** – 12 Dun Na Mara, Renmore, Co Galway. ☎091 861 001. www.cyclewest.com.

Golf

Ireland Let's Golf is a complete online resource, including details of over 400 courses and specialist tour operators: www.golf.ireland.ie.

Rambling

The Irish Tourist Board publishes brochures on **national waymarked ways** in the Republic of Ireland. Detailed information sheets for individual long-distance walks are also available. Waymarked ways are reserved for walkers and are unsuitable for horses or mountain bikes. For details on all kind of walks, from short city and rural strolls to serious waymarked treks, visit www.discoverireland.com/walking, or www.discovernorthernireland.com/walking

◆ **East–West Mapping** are specialists in recreational and tourism mapping ☎053 937 7835. http://eastwestmapping.ie.

Hunting, Shooting, Fishing

The main website for field and country sports is www.irishfieldsports.com For hunting with hounds contact:

◆ **Hunting Association of Ireland** – www.hai.ie.

In the Republic of Ireland **shooting permits** are available from the Department of the Environment and Local Government. In Northern Ireland permits are available on application to the Forestry Service – www.forest service.ni.gov.uk

◆ **National Parks and Wildlife Service** – 7 Ely Place, Dublin 2. ☎01 888 2000; Www.npws.ie/PermitsLicences.
◆ **District Forest Office** – The Grange, Castlewellan Forest Park, Castlewellan BT31 9BU. ☎028 4377 2257.
◆ **District Forest Office** – Inishkeen House, Killyhevlin, Enniskillen BT74 4EJ. ☎028 6634 3123.

The Irish tourist Board lists details on game **angling**, sea angling and coarse angling, river trout angling, pike angling, River Moy angling, a Lough Derg fishing guide and more. For extensive details on fishing in both the north and south of the country, just search the tourist board websites. Fishing permits are available in Northern Ireland from tackle shops and fishery authorities:

◆ **Central Fisheries Board**, Swords Business Campus, Swords, Co Dublin. ☎01 884 2600. www.cfb.ie .
◆ **Shannon Fishery Board** www.shannon-fishery-board.ie.
◆ **Angling News**. www.anglingnews.net.

RACING

Horse Racing

There are racecourses dotted across much of Ireland. Those in the Dublin area include The Curragh, Punchestown, Leopardstown and Fairyhouse. The most popular festivals are **Fairyhouse** *(Easter)*, **Killarney** *(May)*, **Curragh** *(June)*, **Killarney** *(July)*, **Galway**, **Tramore** and **Tralee** *(August)*, **Galway** and **Listowel** *(September)* and **Leopardstown** and **Limerick** *(December)*. **Irish Horseracing Authority**, Thoroughbred County House, Kill, Co Kildare. ☎045 842 800. www.hri.ie.

The Sport of Kings

The Irish are passionate about racing and their horses, which have a worldwide reputation for excellence. Some people believe that the country's legendary emerald pastures are so rich in calcium and other nutrients that they produce horses with strong, light bones. The Ballydoyle Stables in County Tipperary are world famous, producing some of the finest horses ever raced including Ninjinsky, Sir Ivor, Alleged and The Minstrel.

Although horseracing in Ireland is popular with every class of folk, it is known as "the sport of kings". This may go back to Celtic times, when Brehon law dictated that it should be limited to princes and noblemen.

Horse riding in Galway

Greyhound Racing

There are 18 race tracks for this popular evening entertainment: Ballyskeagh, Cork, Dublin, Dundalk, Dungannon, Enniscorthy, Galway, Kilkenny, Lifford, Limerick, Londonderry, Longford, Mullingar, Newbridge, Thurles, Tralee, Waterford and Youghal.

Bord na gCon – Irish Greyhound Board, Limerick. www.igb.ie.

WATER SPORTS

Canoeing and Kayaking

The many lakes and rivers provide good sport, as does the sea
- **Irish Canoe Union** – www.irishcanoeunion.com.

Traditional Sailing Boats, Betraboy Bay

- **Irish Sea Kayaking Association (ISKA)** – www.irishseakayaking association.org.
- **National Mountain and White-water Centre** – www.tiglin.com.

Sailing / Cruising

Ireland Waterways co-ordinates the management and promotion of inland navigable waterways: www.waterwaysireland.org.

There are sailing marinas all round the coast of Ireland and on the inland lakes. All yacht clubs are linked to the Irish Sailing Association which lists racing, training and cruising activities on its Web site.
- **Irish Sailing Association** – www.sailing.ie.
- **Saii Ireland Charters** – yacht charters from Kinsale and Dingle. www.sailireland.com.
- **Waveline Cruisers Ltd** – Cruising on the Shannon and Erne waterways. ☎090 648 5711. www.waveline.ie.
- **Celtic Canal Cruisers Ltd** – Tullamore, Co Offaly. ☎0506 21861; www.sailingireland.com/celtic.htm.
- **Sail Northern Ireland** – Luxury Yacht Charter Cruises and High Speed Ribs (rigid inflatable boat).

☎07809 155 856.
www.sailnorthernireland.com.

Scuba Diving

Ireland has a beautiful underwater coastline, particularly on the west coast where the Gulf Stream brings an abundant marine life into the clear Atlantic waters.

- **Irish Underwater Council** – ☎01 284 4601. www.cft.ie.
- **Activity Ireland Dive Centre** – Based on the Dingle Peninsula, Waterworld is Ireland's largest diving and leisure centre - ☎066 713 9292. www.waterworld.ie.

Swimming (and Bathing)

There are swimming pools in the Leisure Centres of most of the larger towns and seawater baths in many seaside resorts.

Water Skiing and Wakeboarding

Top spots include Macroom, Cork; Craigavon Lakes in County Armagh; Upper and Lower Lough Erne; The Lower Bann; Farran Forest Park, Parknasilla, Ring of Kerry; Blessington Lakes, Co Wicklow; Ballymore Eustace, County Kildare; and Lough Muckno in County Monaghan.

Irish Water Ski Federation (IWSF) – www.iwsf.ie

Surfing

The best conditions are to be found on the northwest and the mid-west coasts; good conditions prevail on the north, southwest and south coast. Surfing on the east coast is practicable only during a storm or strong southerly winds. Surfboards are available for hire.

- **Irish Surf Association** ☎096 49428. www.isasurf.ie.
- **Irish Sailing Association** – See Sailing.

Windsurfing

The elite of the windsurfing community regard Ireland as one of the best windsurfing locations in the world; top venues include Brandon Bay, Clew Bay and Portstewart. Inland, hundreds of lakes offer excellent opportunities, Some of the most popular places for windsurfing (also known as sailboarding or boardsailing) are in northwest Ireland on the coast of Co Mayo at **Easky**, where international championships have been held, and on the coast of Co Donegal at **Bundoran**, where the European championships draw large crowds.

- **Oysterhaven Centre** – One of Ireland's leading centres for sailing and windsurfing, 6mi/10km from Kinsale, Co Cork. ☎021 4770 738. www.oysterhaven.com.

Shopping

Ireland produces a number of articles that have an international reputation, such as **Waterford Crystal**, **Aran sweaters** and **Donegal tweed**. The **Kilkenny Design Centre**, set up in the early 1960s, infused new life into domestic and industrial design in Ireland and markets a good range of craftwork (see KILKENNY and DUBLIN). Throughout the country there are many less well-known enterprises and individual craftsmen and women producing top quality hand-made articles.

Manufacturers of textiles, glass and porcelain usually offer a tour of the factory and have showrooms and shops on the premises; their goods are often available in department stores, specialist shops in the major towns and tourist shops in the popular country districts.

Some craft workers are grouped in certain regions, such as weavers in Donegal. Others congregate in the special **craft villages**, set up by the Government in Dingle, Donegal town, Blennerville near Tralee or Roundstone in Connemara.

Folk museums and folk villages usually organise crafts demonstrations.

GLASS

The most famous and oldest glass factory in Ireland is in **Waterford**

41

Aran Sweaters keep out the wind and rain

(&see WATERFORD), but since its revival in 1951 several smaller enterprises have started to produce hand-blown lead crystal, which is cut, engraved or undecorated – Cavan Crystal, Galway Crystal, Grange Crystal, Sligo Crystal, Tipperary Crystal, Tyrone Crystal. Most have factory shops where first- and second-quality pieces can be bought. Many offer a guided tour of their workshops.

KNITWEAR

The thick cream-coloured (undyed) knitwear associated with the Aran Islands is the best known of Irish knitwear and is on sale throughout the country. Ireland produces a great variety of other knitted garments in a variety of textures and colours, particularly thick sweaters to keep out the wind and rain, using the traditional stitches – basket, blackberry, blanket, cable, diamond, moss, plait, trellis and zigzag.

Irish Souvenirs

LACE

In the 19C there were many lace-making centres in Ireland, but few have survived. In most cases the skill was fostered by nuns; the traditional lacemakers of Clones and Carrickmacross have now formed themselves into cooperatives. Kenmare needlepoint lace is the most difficult to make; Clones is a crochet lace, but the other centres produce "mixed lace" on a base of machine-made cotton net.

LINEN

The demand for bed linen, table linen and tea towels keeps some 20 Irish linen houses in business. The popularity of linen as an apparel fabric has revived in recent years, since blending with synthetic or other natural fibres has reduced its tendency to crease. It is now used by top fashion designers all over the world who appreciate its sheen and interesting texture, its durability and versatility – it is cool in summer and a good insulator in winter; it dyes well in bright clear colours. Some tour guides offer a *Linen Homelands Tour* which visits the **Irish Linen Centre** (&see LISBURN), as well as various linen manufacturers in and around Lisburn.

METALWORK

Throughout the country, and especially in the craft villages, artists are employing traditional techniques in gold, silver, bronze, pewter and enamel to produce flatware and jewelry; the traditional Claddagh rings (&see GALWAY) worked in gold show a heart with two clasped hands (&see MULLINGAR, TIMLOIN).

PORCELAIN AND POTTERY

The largest and most famous porcelain factory in Ireland is at **Belleek** (&see ENNISKILLEN), which produces fine translucent Parian ware and specialises in woven basket pieces and naturalistic flower decoration. Similar wares are produced by Donegal Irish

Parian china. The Irish Dresden factory preserves and develops the tradition of delicate ornamental porcelain figures, which originated in Germany. There are many studio potteries in Ireland producing hand-turned articles, such as those in Connemara and the Stephen Pearce Pottery in Shanagarry.

TWEED

The term *tweed* was first recognised late in the 19C to describe the hand-woven woollen cloth produced in Co Donegal. Donegal tweed is still the most well-known and is now mainly produced on power looms by four firms in Ardara, Donegal Town, Downies and Kilcar. Three of these companies also employ out-workers using hand-looms; most have also diversified into the production of knitwear and ready-made garments or into weaving with other natural fibres – linen, cotton and silk. The original tweeds were made from natural undyed wool – grey, brown or cream. As coloured wool was produced only in small quantities from natural dyes derived from plants, lichens, turf, soot and minerals, it was introduced as speckles when the wool was carded. Avoca Weavers were founded in 1723, the Kerry Woollen Mills later in the 18C. Foxford and Blarney were started in the 19C.

WOODWORK

There are a number of craftsmen producing hand-turned articles such as bowls, lamp stands and ornaments; the unique pieces are the graceful and delightful carvings produced by artists from skeletal pieces of **bogwood**. Some wood-turners produce musical instruments, such as pipes and drums (bodhráns) (&see Roundstone in CONNEMARA).

FOOD AND DRINK

Take home a bottle of Irish whiskey, an Irish liqueur or, if you are not travelling far, Irish cheeses, smoked salmon and other smoked fish or meat.

Spas

Spas in this guide are highlighted with the Spa *symbol, and rated with the fountain symbol (⚜), instead of stars.*

The only active spa resort in Ireland is **Lisdoonvarna** in The Burren, which has been popular since the 18C. The waters contain magnesia, iodine and iron and are reputed to have restorative and therapeutic powers. The Victorian Spa Complex and Health Centre features sulphur baths, massage, wax treatments and saunas. The Victorian Pump House is open daily.

THALASSOTHERAPY

The abundant supplies of seaweed on the Irish coast are used not only as food but also in hot seaweed baths at Enniscrone west of Sligo and for therapeutic purposes at the outdoor baths in Ballybunnion north of Tralee and at Waterworld in Bundoran in Co Donegal, where you can enjoy various health treatments using heated sea water, local seaweed and sea water drench showers.

RETREATS

Ireland's beautiful natural landscapes provide perfect settings for retreats, yoga centres and health farms. Go to www.discoverisland.com or www.discovernorthernisland.com and use their Search facility for these terms.

Seaweed Baths

Seaweed baths, once again popular in Ireland, date from Edwardian times, when they were much more widespread than they are now with baths in most large seaside towns. Seaweed baths are individual baths filled with hot seawater and seaweed – generally wracks such as Fucus serratus. The wrack is usually steam-treated prior to use so that it releases minerals, trace elements, and polysaccharides such as alginates. Ask at the tourist office for your nearest baths.

Another good alternative lifestyle website is www.sustainable.ie

Books

ART

Ireland's Traditional Houses
by Kevin Dunaher, Bord Failte
Irish Art and Architecture by Peter Harbison, Homan Potterton, Jeanne Sheehy (Thames & Hudson 1978)
A Guide to Irish Country Houses
by Mark Bence-Jones (1988)
The Painters of Ireland
by Anne Crookshank and the Knight of Glin (1978/9)
Exploring the Book of Kells
by George Otto Simms (1988)

AUTOBIOGRAPHY

Twenty Years A-Growing
by Maurice O'Sullivan (1953, 1992)
Wheels within Wheels
by Dervla Murphy (1981)
Angela's Ashes by Frank McCourt (1997)

FICTION

Castle Rackrent
by Maria Edgeworth (1800)
The Macdermots of Ballycloran, The Kellys and the O'Kellys, Castle Richmond and *The Landleaguers* by Anthony Trollope (1847, 1848, 1860, 1883)
Experiences of an Irish RM
by E Somerville and M Ross (1899)
The Playboy of the Western World
by JM Synge (1907)
A Portrait of the Artist as a Young Man
by James Joyce (1916, 1960)
Ulysses by James Joyce (1922)
The Last September
by Elizabeth Bowen (1929)
Troubles by JG Farrell (Fontana 1970)
Good Behaviour
by Molly Keane (1981, 1988)
Hungry Hill by Daphne du Maurier (1983)

GEOGRAPHY

The Book of the Irish Countryside
edited by Frank Mitchell (Blackstaff Press 1987)

Reading the Irish Landscape
by Frank Mitchell and Michael Ryan (TownHouse 2001)
Atlas of the Irish Rural Landscape
edited by F H A Aalen, Kevin Whelan and Matthew Stout (Cork University Press 1997)
The Personality of Ireland- Habitat, Heritage and History
by E Estyn Evans (Lilliput 1992)

HISTORY

Brendan the Navigator by George Otto Simms (O'Brien Press)
The Celts edited by Joseph Raftery (The Mercier Press, Dublin 1988)
An Introduction to Celtic Christianity
by James P Mackey (T & T Clark, Ltd, Edinburgh 1989)
Ancient Ireland by Jacqueline O'Brien and Peter Harbison

Films

⚅ *For more on Irish Cinema see the INTRODUCTION*

The Quiet Man (1952)
A slice of stereotypical pre-industrial Irishness directed by John Ford (of Irish descent himsef), starring John Wayne in a memorable role as a homecoming brawling boxer.

Darby O'Gill and the Little People (1959)
Delightful Disney film that leaves no quaint Irish image or myth unturned.

Ryan's Daughter (1970)
A young married Irishwoman falls for an officer of the British garrison amid the magnificent wild and very wet landscapes and seascapes of the west.

MyLeft Foot, 1989
Poignant oscar-winning performance from Daniel Day-Lewis as a cerebral palsy victim.

The Committments (1991)
The "World's Hardest Working

Band," not only brought sweet soul music to the people of Dublin, but also a great film, and even spawned a spin-off touring band.

The Crying Game (1992)
Neil Jordan's gripping account of the relationship between an IRA gunman and a black British bisexual soldier.

In the Name of the Father (1993)
The failure of justice following the IRA's bombing of a Guildford pub.

Michael Collins (1996)
Neil Jordan's blockbusting biopic of the life and times of the charismatic, doomed Republican leader.

The Wind that Shakes the Barley (2006)
Ken Loach's bloody epic tells of the struggle for freedom from occupation: as the Irish Republican Army fights against British rule.

CALENDAR OF EVENTS

Annual Events

FEBRUARY

All Ireland Irish Dancing Championships – Open to competitors from Ireland and abroad. **Different town every year**. www.clrg.ie/english.

MARCH

17 March: St Patrick's Day Parade – 4-day spectacle of fireworks, carnival, marching bands and theatre. **Dublin and all major towns**. www.stpatricksday.ie.

Feis Ceoil – 10-day classical music festival for aspiring instrumentalists and singers. **Dublin**. http://feisceoil.ie.

APRIL

All Ireland and International Dancing Championships – Competition involving over 4000 dancers from everywhere in the world (6 days at Easter). **Different town every year**. www.irishdancingorg.com.

Pan Celtic International Festival – Inter-Celtic poetry, dancing, musical and arts extravaganza.

Letterkenny, Donegal. www.panceltic.ie.

MAY

Bantry Mussel Fair – Seafood festival promoting the mussel industry; free street entertainment.

Bantry Fleadh Nua – Folk festival of musicians, singers, dancers and more. **Ennis**.

Irish Open Golf Championship – Different venue each year.

MAY / JUNE

Castle Ward Opera – Three weeks of opera performed at an elegant Georgian country house on the shores of **Strangford Lough**. www.castlewardopera.com.

Raft Race Weekend – Bands, street theatre, parachute displays and the Raft Race, raising funds for the RNLI. **Portrush**

Writers' Week – Ireland's oldest literary festival with workshops, exhibitions and a book fair. **Listowel**. www.writersweek.ie.

National Country Fair – Ireland's premier country sports event

Stepdance

and country fair for all the family. **Moira Demesne**, **Co Down**. www.irishfieldsports.com.

JUNE

Fleadh Amhrán agus Rince – Traditional festival of song, music and dance. **Ballycastle**.

16 June: Bloomsday – Annual celebration of James Joyce's great novel *Ulysses* – readings, re-enactments, music, theatre, street theatre. **Dublin**. www.jamesjoyce.ie.

Galway Hookers' Regatta – *(Crinniú na mBád)* – Traditional boat gathering and regatta on Strangford Lough. **Portaferry**.

Irish Country Lifestyle Festival – Game fair, carriage-driving, clay

St Patrick's Festival, a week-long celebration of Ireland's national day

pigeon shooting, dog shows; Irish Medieval Festival **Shanes Castle**, **Co Antrim**. www.countrysports andcountrylife.com.

Loughcrew Garden Opera – In the round production in Loughcrew Gardens. **Loughcrew**. www.loughcrew.com/opera.html.

JUNE–JULY

County Wexford Strawberry Festival – Strawberries and cream, arts and crafts exhibitions, Irish dancing and mumming, horse and greyhound racing, band recitals… **Enniscorthy**. http://enniscorthystrawberryfestival.com.

JULY

Willie Clancy Summer School – Major festival of traditional Irish music (particularly *uilleann* pipes) and dance. **Milltown Malbay**, **Co Clare**. www.setdancingnews.net/wcss

James Joyce Summer School – Lectures, seminars and social events in Newman House, St Stephen's Green, where Joyce himself studied *(2 weeks)*. **Dublin**. www.jamesjoyce.ie.

Twelfth of July Parades – Bands, banners and brethren of the Orange Order celebrating the anniversary of the Battle of the Boyne. **Belfast**.

International Rose Week – International rose Trials. **Belfast**, **Dixon Park**.

Galway Arts Festival – Theatre, dance, music and street entertainment, Ireland's premier multidisciplinary arts festival *(13 days)*. **Galway**. www.galwayartsfestival.com.

Dublin Circus Festival – Four days of clowning around plus spectacular outdoor performances from Irish and international circus acts, including musical comedy, daring acrobatics and a lot more. **Temple Bar**, **Dublin**. www.temple-bar.ie.

JULY–AUGUST

Yeats Festival – Literature, music and drama. **Sligo**. www.yeats-sligo.com.

All-Ireland Intermediate Road Bowls Finals – Ancient game, played only in Co Armagh and Co Cork, in which competitors used to throw cannonballs. **Armagh**.

AUGUST

O'Carolan Harp and Traditional Music Festival – Performance of his works, international harp competition, Irish music, ceilidhs, concerts, song and set dancing, many open-air events. August Bank Holiday. **Keadew**. www.ocarolanharpfestival.ie.

Steam Engine Rally – Stradbally Steam Museum annual steam and vintage show. August Bank Holiday. **Stradbally**. www.irishsteam.ie.

Failte Ireland Dublin Horse Show – International team jumping competitions held at the Royal Dublin Society ground in Ballsbridge; a grand equestrian and social event. **Dublin**. www.dublinhorseshow.com.

Kilkenny Arts Festival – Ten days of music, visual art, theatre, literature, children's arts and outdoor events. **Kilkenny**. www.kilkennyarts.ie.

10-12 August: Puck Fair – One of the oldest street festivals in Ireland, centred on a billy goat enthroned in a chair, with a traditional horse fair, busking, open air concerts, parades and fireworks. **Killorglin**. www.puckfair.ie.

MICHELIN

Lambeg Drums, an impressive sight in the marching season in Northern Ireland

Gathering of the Boats – *(Crinniú na mBád)* Galway hookers' regatta. **Kinvara**. www.kinvara.com/cnb.html.

Clifden Connemara Pony Show – Grand showing of Ireland's only native pony. **Clifden**. www.cpbs.ie.

Fleadh Cheoil na hEireann – The biggest traditional Irish music festival *(7 days)*. The largest showcase of traditional Irish musicians, singers and dancers, with over 10,000 performers taking part (♦ *see 'Fleadh Season' Box*) .

Fleadh Season

Festivals are an essential part of the Irish experience; there are so many in summer that you would have to go out of your way to avoid them. A term you may well come across is the gaelic *Fleadh* (pronounced *flaa*) which simply means festival and is now synonymous with typical Irish entertainment. The biggest Fleadh of them all is simply entitled "Fleadh (plus the year)", each August, with over 200,000 people gathering from all over the world for a week long cultural celebration at Tullamore, Co Offally. The world record for the largest Irish traditional music session was set at Fleadh 2007 when 2,700 musicians performed together in O'Connor Square, Tullamore.

Ould Lammas Fair, a traditional horse fair held in Ballycastle in the Antrim Glens

Tullamore, County Offaly.
www.fleadh2008.com.

Rose of Tralee Festival – Bands, parades, a famous beauty parade, dancing, horse racing and many other activities, celebrating the art of being Irish. **Tralee**. http://roseoftralee.ie.

Ould Lammas Fair – Oldest traditional Irish fair with horse trading, street entertainment, competitions and market stalls. **Ballycastle**. www.lammasfair.com.

AUGUST / SEPTEMBER

Lisdoonvarna Matchmaking Festival – Europe's biggest singles event with music and dance and horse racing *(late August to early October)*. **Lisdoonvarna**. www.matchmakerireland.com.

Appalachian & Bluegrass Music Festival – Europe's premier bluegrass music festival attracts thousands of visitors to watch International stars and award-winning Irish artists.
Ulster American Folk Park, **Omagh**. www.folkpark.com, www.bluegrassomagh.com.

All Ireland Hurling Finals – Annual national hurling championships at Croke Park. **Dublin**. www.hurlingchampionship.gaa.ie.

Clarinbridge Oyster Festival – Food and stout, music, dance. **Clarinbridge**. www.clarenbridge.com

Laytown Strand Races – Unique horse race held annually in East Meath at low tide. **Laytown**.

All Ireland Football Finals – Annual Gaelic Football championship finals at Croke Park. **Dublin**. www.footballchampionship.gaa.ie.

Galway International Oyster Festival – World Oyster-opening Championships, held in the pubs, oyster tasting, music, song and dance. **Galway**. www.galwayoysterfest.com.

SEPTEMBER / OCTOBER

Waterford International Festival of Light Opera – Competitive musical festival for amateur musical societies held at the Theatre Royal, **Waterford**. www.waterfordfestival.com

Dublin Theatre Festival – Best of world theatre and new productions from all the major Irish companies. **Dublin**. www.dublintheatrefestival.com

OCTOBER

Cork International Film Festival – Ireland's oldest film event presents the best of international and new Irish cinema. **Cork City and region**. www.corkfilmfest.org.

O'Carolan Harp Cultural and Heritage Festival – Harp and instrumental workshops and competitions, traditional Irish music concerts, step and set dancing, traditional festival Mass in Irish, seminars and lectures. **Nobber**.

Kinsale International Gourmet Festival – The best of fine food and wines in a convivial party atmosphere with music, dance and wine tasting. **Kinsale**. www.kinsalerestaurants.com.

Great October Fair – One of the three great country fairs of Ireland for buying and selling horses, also featuring traditional music, tug-of-war competitions, bareback riding, show jumping, a carnival and street traders. **Ballinasloe, Co Galway**. www.ballinasloe octoberfair.com.

Cork Guinness Jazz Festival – Great jazz and an imperative rendez-vous for the greatest names in this genre. **Cork**. www.corkjazzfestival.com.

Baboro - International Arts Festival for Children– Workshops, story-telling, theatre. (6 days). **Galway**. www.baboro.ie.

OCTOBER / NOVEMBER

Wexford Festival Opera – Production of rare operas and other cultural activities (10 days). **Wexford**. http://wexfordopera.com.

Belfast Festival at Queen's – Largest arts festival in Ireland: music from classical to folk and jazz, drama, ballet and cinema. **Belfast**. www.belfastfestival.com.

USEFUL WORDS & PHRASES

Alt	- cliff	**Dearg**	- red
Ard	- high, height, hillock	**Díseart**	- desert, hermitage
Áth	- ford	**Droichead**	- bridge
Bád	- boat	**Dubh**	- black
Baile	- town, townland, homestead	**Dún**	- fort
Beag	- little	**Eaglais**	- church
Beal	- opening, entrance, river mouth	**Eas**	- waterfall
Bealtaine	- 1 May, month of May	**Fear**	- man
Boireann	- large rock, rocky district	**Fir**	- men
Bóthar	- road	**Gall**	- foreigner
Buí	- yellow	**Gorm**	- blue
Bun	- end, bottom	**Gort**	- field
Cabhán	- hollow	**Inis**	- island
Caiseal	- castle, circular stone fort	**Lár**	- centre
Caisleán	- castle	**Leithinis**	- peninsula
Caladh	- harbour, landing place	**Mór**	- large
Capall	- horse	**Óg**	- young
Carraig	- rock	**Oileán**	- island
Cath	- battle	**Poll**	- hole, cave
Cathair	- circular stone fort, city	**Sagart**	- priest
Cealtrach	- old burial ground	**Sean**	- old
Céide	- hillock	**Slí**	- route, way
Cill	- church	**Sliabh**	- mountain
Cloch	- stone	**Teach**	- house
Cluain	- meadow	**Trá**	- beach, strand
Cno	- hill	**Túr**	- tower
		Uachtar	- top, upper part

BASIC INFORMATION

Abbreviations

Dúchas – Heritage of Ireland, Gaeltacht and the Islands;
HM – Historic Monuments Branch of the Department of the Environment in Northern Ireland; **NT** – National Trust.

Communications

TELEPHONES

The telephone service in the Republic of Ireland is Eircom (www.eircom.ie). Pre-paid callcards for national and international calls from public phones are available from post offices and some shops (newsagents, tobacconists). Card phones are cheaper than pay phones.

It is usually more expensive (+ 30 per cent) to make a long-distance telephone call from a hotel than from a pay phone.

To make an **international call** dial 00 followed by the country code, followed by the area code (without the initial 0). The codes for direct dialling to other countries are printed at the front of telephone directories.

When dialling from the Republic to Northern Ireland, remove the 028 and substitute the 028 prefix with 048 followed by the number.

Discounts

If you are intending to apply for a reduced price pass, take some passport-size photos with you, and all relevant documentation to qualify for your entitlement as a senior citizen or student.

SEASON TICKETS AND PASSES

For a one-off payment **The Dublin Pass** includes transport from the airport to the city, entrance to 30 of Dublin's top attractions and special offers in over 24 of Dublin's top shops, restaurants, tours and entertainment venues: www.dublinpass.ie/dublin pass. Belfast has not yet implemented such a scheme, thought the *Belfast regional* voucher booklet, available from tourist offices, contains many useful discount offers.

The annual **Heritage Card** provides free admission to all Heritage sites, available from most fee-paying sites, or online from www.heritageireland. ie/en/HeritageCard/

DISCOUNT RAIL / BUS FARES

Irish Rover, **Irish Explorer** and **Emerald Card** tickets are available, which enable passengers to travel throughout all of Ireland, by rail only or by rail and bus. The latter is a better option due to the relatively limited rail coverage throughout the country. Ask for details at any major station or tourist office, or visit www.irishrail.ie (for the Republic) and www.translink.co.uk (for the North). If you intend to travel only within the North, there is the option of the **Freedom of Northern Ireland** Pass. Non-European residents should visit the **Eurail** site www.railpass.com.

DISCOUNTS FOR U.S. NATIONALS

Eurorail Pass, **Flexipass** and **Saver Pass** are options available in the US for travel in Europe and must be purchased in the US, ☎212 308 3103; ☎1-800-4 EURAIL, 1-888-BRITRAIL and 1-888-EUROSTAR (automated lines for callers within the US only); www.raileurope.com/us.

DISCOUNTS FOR STUDENTS

Students with an **International Student Card** can apply for **Student Travelsave** to obtain reductions on Irish Rail and Bus Éireann.
USIT – Dublin ☎01 602 1904; Belfast ☎028 90 327 111; www.usit.ie.

Electricity

The electric current is 230 volts AC (50 hertz); 3-pin flat or 2-pin round wall sockets are standard.

Emergencies

☎*999* – Ask for Fire, Police, Ambulance, Coastguard and Sea Rescue, Mountain Rescue or Cave Rescue.

Mail

Irish postage stamps must be used in the Republic, British stamps in Northern Ireland; they are available from Post Offices and some shops (newsagents and tobacconists).

OPENING HOURS

In the Republic post offices are open Mon–Sat, 8am–5pm or 5.30pm; they are closed on Sun and public holidays and for 1hr 15min at lunchtime; sub-post offices usually close at 1pm one day a week.
In Northern Ireland post offices are open Mon–Fri, 9am–5.30pm, and Sat, 9am–12.30pm; sub-post offices close at 1pm on Wednesdays.

Media

In the **Republic of Ireland** the national newspapers on sale are *The Irish Times*, *The Independent* and *The Examiner*. The last broadcasts in the Irish language appear on 4 television channels: RTE1, RTE2, TV3 and TG4.
In **Northern Ireland** the national newspapers are *The Times*, *The Independent*, *The Daily Telegraph* and *The Guardian*. There are 5 terrestrial television channels – BBC1, BBC2, ITV, Channel 4 and Channel 5.

Money

In the Republic of Ireland the currency is the euro (€1 = 100 cent); in Northern Ireland it is Pounds Sterling (£). There is no limit on the amount of currency visitors can import into the Republic of Ireland.

BANKS

Money can be withdrawn from banks using a credit card and a PIN. There is no commission charge for EU travellers on cash drawn from Cash Point /ATM machines in the Republic of Ireland.

TRAVELLERS' CHEQUES

Some form of identification is necessary when cashing travellers' cheques in banks. Commission charges vary; hotels and shops usually charge more than banks.

CREDIT CARDS

All major credit cards are widely accepted in shops, hotels, restaurants and most petrol stations in towns. If you are travelling to more remote rural areas however cash is always preferred and in some cases all that is accepted.

American Express Travel Services – www.americanexpress.com/uk.

Public Holidays

On public holidays, shops, museums and other monuments may be closed or may vary their times of admission. In the Republic of Ireland, national museums and art galleries are usually closed on Mondays.
In addition to the usual school holidays at Christmas and in the spring and summer, there are mid-term breaks at Hallowe'en (31 October) and around St Patrick's Day (17 March).

- ◆ 1 January – New Year's Day.
- ◆ 17 March – St Patrick's Day (Republic only).
- ◆ Monday nearest 17 March (Northern Ireland only).
- ◆ Good Friday (Republic only).
- ◆ Easter Monday.
- ◆ Monday nearest 1 May – May Day Holiday (Northern Ireland only).

Conviviality Irish style in a Doolin pub

- ◆ Last Monday in May – Spring Bank Holiday (Northern Ireland only).
- ◆ First Monday in June – June Holiday (Republic only).
- ◆ 12 July – Orangeman's Day (Northern Ireland only).
- ◆ First Monday in August – August Bank Holiday (Republic only).
- ◆ Last Monday in August – August Bank Holiday (Northern Ireland only).
- ◆ Last Monday in October – October Holiday (Republic only).
- ◆ 25 December- Christmas Day.
- ◆ 26 December (St Stephen's Day/Boxing Day).

Sightseeing

⏱ ADMISSION TIMES

Ticket offices usually shut 30min before closing time; only exceptions are mentioned. Admission times and charges vary, the information printed in this guide is for guidance only.

Dialling codes
00 61: Australia
00 1: Canada
00 353: Republic of Ireland
00 64: New Zealand
00 44: United Kingdom (including Northern Ireland)
00 1: United States of America

🔗 CHARGES

Charges in this guide, given in the local currency, are for a single adult. Reductions are nearly always made for families, children, students, senior citizens (old-age pensioners) and the unemployed. Note too that for some of the most popular attractions that it is sometimes cheaper to book tickets online, and by doing so you can also, usually, avoid having to wait in line. Groups should apply in advance, as many places offer special rates for group bookings and some have special days for group visits.

⛪ CHURCHES

Many Church of Ireland (Anglican) and Presbyterian churches are locked when not in use for services.

Smoking

A smoking ban was introduced in 2004, prohibiting smoking in enclosed public places - including pubs and bars, restaurants and places of entertainment.

Time

In winter, standard time throughout Ireland is Greenwich Mean Time (GMT). In summer (mid March to October) clocks are advanced by one hour for British Summer Time (BST), which is the same as Central European Time. Time may be expressed according to the 24-hour clock or the 12-hour clock.

VAT

The Value-Added Tax (VAT) refund is available to non EU residents. Stores participating in the Tax Back Service must be members of the Retail Export Scheme. Details are available in major department stores.

CONVERSION TABLES

Weights and Measures

	(US)	(UK)	
1 kilogram (kg) 6.35 kilograms 0.45 kilograms	**2.2 pounds (lb)** 14 pounds 16 ounces (oz)	**2.2 pounds** 1 stone (st) 16 ounces	*To convert kilograms to pounds, multiply by 2.2*
1 metric ton (tn)	**1.1 tons**	**1.1 tons**	
1 litre (l) 3.79 litres 4.55 litres	**2.11 pints (pt)** 1 gallon (gal) 1.20 gallon	**1.76 pints** 0.83 gallon 1 gallon	*To convert litres to gallons, multiply by 0.26 (US) or 0.22 (UK)*
1 hectare (ha) **1 sq. kilometre (km²)**	**2.47 acres** 0.38 sq. miles (sq.mi.)	**2.47 acres** 0.38 sq. miles	*To convert hectares to acres, multiply by 2.4*
1 centimetre (cm) **1 metre (m)**	**0.39 inches (in)** 3.28 feet (ft) or 39.37 inches or 1.09 yards (yd)	**0.39 inches**	*To convert metres to feet, multiply by 3.28; for kilometres to miles, multiply by 0.6*
1 kilometre (km)	**0.62 miles (mi)**	**0.62 miles**	

Clothing

Women				Men			
	35	4	2½		40	7½	7
	36	5	3½		41	8½	8
	37	6	4½		42	9½	9
Shoes	38	7	5½	Shoes	43	10½	10
	39	8	6½		44	11½	11
	40	9	7½		45	12½	12
	41	10	8½		46	13½	13
	36	6	8		46	36	36
	38	8	10		48	38	38
Dresses	40	10	12	Suits	50	40	40
& suits	42	12	14		52	42	42
	44	14	16		54	44	44
	46	16	18		56	46	48
	36	06	30		37	14½	14½
	38	08	32		38	15	15
Blouses &	40	10	34	Shirts	39	15½	15½
sweaters	42	12	36		40	15¾	15¾
	44	14	38		41	16	16
	46	16	40		42	16½	16½

Sizes often vary depending on the designer. These equivalents are given for guidance only.

Speed

KPH	10	30	50	70	80	90	100	110	120	130
MPH	6	19	31	43	50	56	62	68	75	81

Temperature

Celsius (°C)	0°	5°	10°	15°	20°	25°	30°	40°	60°	80°	100°
Fahrenheit (°F)	32°	41°	50°	59°	68°	77°	86°	104°	140°	176°	212°

To convert Celsius into Fahrenheit, multiply °C by 9, divide by 5, and add 32.
To convert Fahrenheit into Celsius, subtract 32 from °F, multiply by 5, and divide by 9.
NB: Conversion factors on this page are approximate.

Derryclare Lough, Connemara
H. Champollion/MICHELIN

NATURE

Visitors come to Ireland for many reasons: to meet the friendly and convivial people and explore their Celtic heritage; for the folk music and the Guinness; or to visit the western-most edge of the European continent; but, the country's greatest draw is the wonderful scenery. The "Emerald Isle" is wondrously green, variegated by its bare mountains and strange rock formations, stark cliffs and sandy strands, flower-rich boglands and tree canopied desmesnes.

Lay of the Land

Unlike the archetypal island, which is supposed to rise from coastal lowlands to a mountain core, Ireland's heartland is mostly low-lying country, enclosed by highland ramparts. Only from Dublin northwards is there an extensive opening of the land to the sea, a fifty-mile doorway of fertile land, through which successive waves of invaders have entered the country. Overlooking Dublin from the south, the Wicklow Mountains rise to a peak of 3 035ft/925m at Lugnaquilla, but the country's highest point and the most dramatic mountain scenery are to be found in the far southwest, where Carantuohill (3414ft/1038m) and Macgillycuddy's Reeks preside over the glories of the Killarney lakelands and the Iveragh Peninsula. This peninsula is one of several and part of a much wider set of parallel mountain folds running roughly east–west, which were violently folded in Hercynian times, and which include the granites of Brittany and the Harz massif in Germany. In Ireland they also include a whole series of ranges dividing the Midlands from the island's southern coastline. Their equivalents in the north are the northeast–southwest pointing ranges, folded in the Caledonian period and crossing the Atlantic edge in Donegal and Connaught and the narrow strait separating Ulster from Scotland.

Bounded by these ancient mountain systems, the central regions of the country are largely underlaid by a much-eroded foundation of carboniferous limestone: the basis of the rich pasturelands for which Ireland is famous, it is far from monotonous, producing such dramatic features as the great escarpment of Benbulben, glowering over Sligo, and the eerie moonscapes of The Burren in Co Clare.

Invermore River, Connemara

B Pérousse/MICHELIN

Much of the Midlands landscape is profoundly marked by the impact of the Ice Ages. The retreating glaciers left unconsolidated deposits of clay, sand and gravel, great tracts of which remain badly drained today, though the worm-like, winding ridges of sandy gravel called *eskers* – deposited by streams running beneath the glaciers – have always provided dry areas in an otherwise almost impenetrable land. The ice sheets also moulded great swarms of **drumlins**, low egg-shaped mounds, most clearly visible when partially submerged as in Clew Bay and Strangford Lough. In the north, a broad band of drumlins extends right across the island, the waterlogged land around them forming a barrier to communication which may well have helped establish Ulster's distinctive identity in ancient times.

Saving the turf, Inishowen

PEAT BOGS

One of the most intriguing features of the Irish landscape is its peat bogs, the most extensive in Europe, occupying something like a sixth of the land surface, and playing an important role in the country's history, economy, and collective memory.

There are two types of bogs in Ireland although the peat in both is formed in water-logged conditions by the accumulation of dead and incompletely decomposed plant material. **Blanket bog** occurs in areas of high rainfall and humidity, mostly in the mountains of the western seaboard, and comprises dead grass and sedge. It is usually shallower (6ft/2m to 20ft/6m) than **raised bog**, which is more of a lowland phenomenon, occurring where there is less rainfall, growing above the ground-water level, and formed by dome-shaped bog moss (sphagnum). This type of peat-bog, up to 19ft/12m deep, is scattered over much of the Midlands, where it forms a distinctive, open and natural-seeming landscape in contrast to the farmland beyond. Raised bogs have developed over time without appreciable human interference, whereas the blanket bog has been fashioned by burning and the clearance of scrub and woodland for grazing. The history of the land is preserved by the peat layers, revealing the nature of forests and of Neolithic fields beneath the blanket bogs of the west.

In more recent times, the Irish bogs have provided places of refuge for rebels and outlaws, while their inaccessibility and unfamiliarity have made it difficult for invaders to extend their control over the whole country.

The early disappearance of tree cover and scarcity of coal deposits meant that peat – known locally as turf – became the most important source of fuel. The turfs are traditionally cut with a *slane*, a narrow spade with a side blade set at a right angle, and laid out to dry. When thoroughly dry, they are stacked into clamps near the house. In a fine summer, a family can harvest enough fuel for several years. The cuts sliced deep into the bog and the stacks of drying peat make distinctive patterns in the landscape that appear quite alien to visitors from abroad, while the sight, sound and smell of the turf fire glowing in the corner of living room or pub evokes strong emotions in every Irish heart.

Since the mid-20C peat has been harvested on an industrial scale to provide the country with electric power as well as yielding moss peat for horticultural purposes. The mechanical harvesters of the Bord na Móna (Peat Development Authority) are an impressive sight as they scrape huge quantities of sun-dried milled peat from a bog that has been drained for a period of five to seven years. The harvested peat is made into briquettes for domestic use or burned in one of five electricity generating stations.

CLIMATE

Confronting the Atlantic as it does, Ireland has an oceanic climate, tempered by the influence of the warm waters of the Gulf Stream flowing northwards along its western shores. Successive weather systems blow in from the southwest, bringing abundant precipitation and ever-changing cloudscapes. The temperature range is limited; it is rarely very hot nor very cold. In the coolest months of January and February temperatures vary between 4° and 7° Celsius, in the warmest months of July and August between 14° and 16°. Snowfalls are uncommon except on the highest mountains, where the total annual precipitation can exceed 2.4m. The southwest is the wettest part of the country and the east the driest, but it is not so much the amount of rainfall, rather its persistence that is characteristic. However, although there may not be many days without rain or a touch of drizzle, it should always be remembered that its occurrence is in no small part responsible for the freshness of the atmosphere and the luminous look of the landscape.

COAST

The country's rock foundation is most dramatically exposed at the interface of land and ocean, particularly in the west, where mountainous peninsulas frequently end in bold headlands, while sea inlets and fjords penetrate far inland. The northern shore of Co Antrim boasts what is surely Ireland's most famous natural wonder, the countless clustered columns of the Giant's Causeway, formed 60 million years ago by violent volcanic disturbances. Few natural ramparts are as spectacular as the bands of shale and sandstone making up the 5mi/8km stretch of the

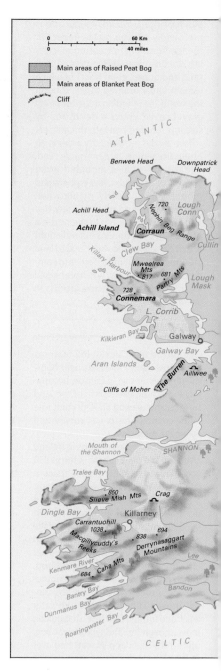

Cliffs of Moher, rising 200m over the Atlantic breakers on the edge of the Burren in Co Clare. The limestones of The Burren leap seaward to form the Aran Islands, where the abrupt cliffs of Inishmore, though less high, are equally

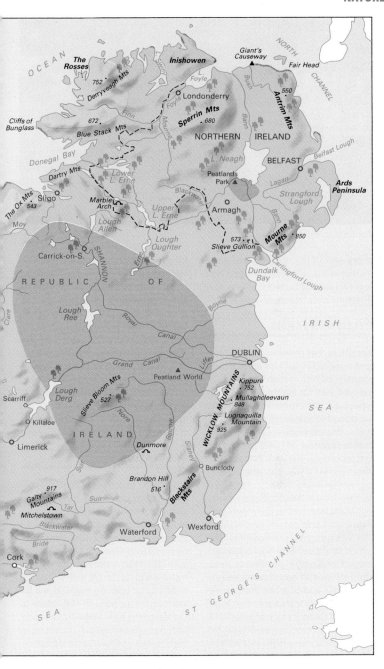

awe-inspiring. The discontinuous archipelago along the western coast offers other equally extraordinary sights, none more so than the drowned mountaintop of Skellig Michael, a rocky refuge for a hardy monastic community in the days of Early Christianity. The tallest cliffs are those of the Slieve League peninsula, where a great bastion of quartzite stands some 1 972ft/601m above the waves.

New Ross, Co Wicklow

In the east of the country, coasts are characterised by splendid natural harbours formed by drowned valleys, low limestone cliffs and glorious beach.

FIELDS AND FARMS

Despite recent economic trends, Ireland is still very much an **agricultural country**, with more than 80 per cent of the land used for farming. Most of this is **pasture**; it is estimated that Ireland has around 95 per cent of the best grassland in the whole European Union, but **arable farming** prospers in the drier east, notably in the Ards Peninsular in Ulster and in Co Wexford, where barley is grown on a large scale.

As elsewhere in Atlantic Europe, farmland is **enclosed** rather than open, with a variety of field patterns reflecting a complex historical development. The typical field boundary is a hedgebank topped with native shrubs and trees, often allowed to grow spontaneously rather than laid to make them stockproof. It is these leafy banks that make up for the country's lack of woodland, transforming the rolling landscape into picturesque scenery. In the rocky peninsulas of the west and elsewhere, stone is used to form boundary walls: most notably in the Aran Islands, where tiny enclosures are bounded by drystone walls built to be permeable to strong local winds. In areas of poor soil and high rainfall, '**lazy beds**' were made. These were cultivation ridges, created by laying a strip of manure and inverting sods over it from both sides. The raised bed drained easily into the trenches on either side and its soil was warmed by the sun from the side as well as the top, highly advantageous characteristics in a cool, wet country. Lazy beds came into their own with the widespread cultivation of the potato in the pre-Famine years, and whole landscapes are marked by the wrinkled pattern of the subsequently abandoned ridges, sometimes at an elevation where cultivation of any crop would seem doomed to failure.

VEGETATION

Most of the country was originally covered in trees, particularly forests of sessile oak. Clearance for agriculture began in Neolithic times and continued until virtually no natural or even semi-natural woodlands were left. One of the last assaults on the native forest was made by the British in the 17C and 18C, on the one hand for building materials and for smelting, on the other to deny refuge to the rebellious Irish. Remnants of natural forest can be found in the southern Wicklow Mountains and around Killarney, where there are also marvellous specimens of the arbutus or strawberry tree. In the 18C considerable replanting efforts were made by many owners of demesnes eager to landscape their estates in the English manner. Exotic trees like Scots pine, beech, sweet chestnut, monkey puzzle and cedar of Lebandon were introduced to supplement the native species. As some six per cent of the land surface was held in demesnes, the landscape impact was considerable, though it was much reduced subsequently through the break-up and parcelling-out of many estates. The fate of the Anglo-Irish so-called Big House is well known; less familiar is the felling of its heritage of trees and ornamental woodland and their conversion into ordinary farmland or conifer plantations. Nevertheless a number of demesnes have survived, some in the form of **Forest Parks** in public ownership, others in the hands of the National Trust in Northern Ireland.

Generations of gardeners have exploited the country's favourable, frost-free environment to create gardens famous for their broad spectrum of plants, notably in areas sheltered from the wind. Several sub-tropical paradise gardens such as Garinish Island in Glengarriff Harbour, manage to have flowers in bloom all year round. Conditions favoured by rhododendrons and fuchsias account for why these shrubs grow in woodlands and hedgerows. Botanically speaking, Ireland's most fascinating landscape is perhaps The Burren, where a profusion of acid and lime-loving plants grow in harmonious co-existence.

RIVERS AND LAKES

Not surprisingly, water is ever-present in the Irish landscape. The country's rivers have a total length of 16,530mi/26,000km and lakes/loughs cover an area of 560sq mi/1,450sq km. Ireland's low population density and the relative lack of polluting industries means that most of this water is unpolluted and well-stocked with fish and other wildlife.

The watercourses rising on the seaward side of mountains tend to be short and steep, draining straight into the sea. Those that rise inland form slow-moving lowland streams, lined by water-meadows and often widening out into lakes. The **Shannon**, the country's longest river (230mi/370km) behaves in this way, winding sluggishly through the Midlands countryside and forming the great expanses of Lough Ree and Lough Derg, before discharging into its immensely long estuary below Limerick. In Ulster, **Lough Neagh** is far more impressive than the River Bann, which flows through it – though shallow, it is Ireland's largest body of water, covering an area of 153sq m/400sq km, and teeming with eels. The country's loveliest lakeland is that which has developed along the course of the Erne, comprising countless lesser lakes as well as island-studded **Upper** and **Lower Lough Erne** themselves.

In the south, rivers rising far inland have cut their way through upland chains to reach the sea; the valleys thus formed by the Blackwater, Nore, Suir, Barrow and Slaney are often of great beauty.

Youghal Harbour, Co Cork

HISTORY

Ireland continues to carry the scars of its troubled history more than most European countries. However, the Republic of Ireland has enjoyed booming prosperity since joining the European Union, and since the political breakthroughs of the last couple of years, Northern Ireland, and Belfast in particular, has also begun to harvest the fruits of peace, reconciliation and reconstruction.

Timeline

CELTIC IRELAND

6000-1750 BC—Stone Age; c 3000 BC hunter-gatherer people begin farming. Construction of passage graves.

1750–500 BC—Bronze Age.

500 BC–AD 450—Iron Age; Celtic invasion from Europe; inter-tribal strife for supremacy and the title of High King (Ard Rí).

55 BC–early 5C AD—Roman occupation of Britain (not Ireland): trade links proved by coins and jewellery found.

4C–5C— Irish Celts (known as Scots) colonise the west of England and Scotland.

432–61—**St Patrick's mission** to convert Ireland to Christianity.

6C–11C—Monastic age; Irish missionaries travel to the continent.

795— **Viking Invasions**—Vikings from Norway and Denmark raid the monasteries near the coasts and waterways; in 841 they begin to settle.

1014— **Battle of Clontarf – Brian Ború**, king of Munster, defeats the Danish Vikings and the king of Leinster's allied forces.

1156— Death of Turlough O'Connor, last powerful native ruler.

1159— Henry II (1154–89), receives the title "Lord of Ireland" from Pope Adrian IV and is permitted to invade Ireland.

ANGLO-NORMAN IRELAND

1169— Invited by Dermot, King of Leinster, to oust his opponents, Strongbow (Richard de Clare) lands with his Anglo-Norman army and in 1171, Strongbow declares himself King of Leinster to the discomfiture of Henry II. England's involvement in Irish affairs is now constant, though the interests of the two frequently diverge.

1177— **Anglo-Norman** invasion of Ulster by John de Courcy.

1185— **Prince John**, "Lord of Ireland", visited the country, to which he returned in 1210.

1297— First **Irish Parliament** convened.

1315–18—**Bruce Invasion** – Edward Bruce, brother to King Robert of Scotland, lands at Carrickfergus with 6 000 Scottish mercenaries (gallowglasses); he is crowned king in 1316; but dies at the Battle of Faughart near Dundalk in 1318.

1348–50—**The Black Death** kills one-third of the population.

1366— **The Statutes of Kilkenny** promulgated to maintain the distinction between Anglo-Normans and native Irish. Prohibition of fosterage, bareback riding, hurling, the Irish language and Irish dress and patronage of Irish story tellers and poets largely fails in their purpose.

1394 & 1399—**Richard II** landed in Ireland with an army to re-establish control.

1446— First mention of **The Pale** to describe the area of English influence; by the 15C it was only a narrow coastal strip from Dundalk to south of Dublin.

1471—	The Earl of Kildare appointed **Lord Deputy**, marking the rise to power of the Geraldines.
1487—	The pretender Lambert Simnel crowned Edward V of England in Dublin by the Earl of Kildare.
1491—	Perkin Warbeck, pretender to the English throne, landed in Cork without the opposition of the Earl of Kildare.
1494—	Sir Edward Poynings appointed Lord Deputy: under **Poynings' Law** the Irish parliament could not meet or propose legislation without royal consent.
1534–40—	Failure of the **Kildare (Geraldine) Revolt** and the end of Kildare ascendancy.

REFORMATION AND PLANTATION

1539—	**Reformation** and **Dissolution of the Monasteries**.
1541—	Henry VIII declared **King of Ireland** by the Irish Parliament.
1556—	Colonisation of Co Laois (Queen's County) and Offaly (King's County) by English settlers.
1579—	**Desmond (Munster) Rebellion** severely crushed by Elizabeth I; confiscation and colonisation.

1585—	Ireland mapped and divided into counties; 27 sent members to Parliament.
1588—	**Spanish Armada** – After its defeat in the English Channel, the Spanish Armada, driven by the wind, sailed up the east coast of Great Britain and round the north coast of Scotland. Off the Irish coast stormy weather further depleted its ranks.
1598—	**Hugh O'Neill, Earl of Tyrone**, leads rebellion and defeats English army at the **Battle of Yellow Ford** (see DUNGANNON).
1601—	**Siege of Kinsale** – 4 000 Spanish troops land in Kinsale to assist Hugh O'Neill but withdraw when besieged.
1603—	Submission of Hugh O'Neill (Earl of Tyrone) and Rory O'Donnell (Earl of Tyrconnell) at Mellifont to **Lord Mountjoy**, Queen Elizabeth's Deputy. In 1607 they sail from Rathmullan (see DONEGAL) into exile on the continent. This **Flight of the Earls**, marks the end of Gaelic Ireland's political power.
1607–41—	**Plantation of Ulster** under James I: Protestants from the Scottish lowlands settle in the northern part of Ireland.
1641—	**Confederate Rebellion** provoked by policies of the King's

The Wrecks of the Spanish Armada

In 1588 some 30 ships of the Spanish Armada were wrecked off the Irish coast between Antrim and Kerry, with an estimated loss of 8 000 sailors and gunners, 2 100 rowers, 19 000 soldiers and 2 431 pieces of ordnance.

The *Gerona*, a galleass (oar-propelled galley), went down at Port na Spaniagh on the Giant's Causeway; all perished; treasures recovered by divers in 1968, are displayed in the Ulster Museum. The *Juliana*, *La Levia* and *La Santa Maria de Vision* all foundered at Streedagh Point, north of Sligo; over 1 300 are thought to have died. *La Duquesa St Anna* and *La Trinidad Valencia* was wrecked on the Inishowen Peninsula at Kinnagoe Bay. A map on the clifftop *(at the road junction)* plots the sites of the many ships that were lost during those fateful storms.

One survivor who came ashore at Streedagh, Captain Francisco de Cuellar, wrote an account of his escape from Sligo through Leitrim, Donegal and Derry to Antrim; from where he sailed to Scotland, then on to Antwerp and Spain.

Dublin Volunteers on College Green by Francis Wheatley

National Gallery of Ireland, Dublin

Deputy and the desire of the dispossessed to recover their land: widespread slaughter of Protestant settlers.

1642— **Confederation of Kilkenny** is an alliance between the Irish and Old English Catholics to defend their religion, land and political rights.

1649— **Oliver Cromwell** "pacifies" Ireland with great brutality, storming Drogheda and Wexford and sending thousands of Irish to the West Indies.

1653— Under the **Cromwellian Settlement** most Roman Catholic landowners judged unsympathetic to the Commonwealth were dispossessed and ordered to retreat west of the Shannon.

1660— **Restoration** of Charles II and restitution of some land to Roman Catholic owners.

1678— The **Oates Conspiracy** was a pretext for the arrest, imprisonment and even death of various Roman Catholics, among them Oliver Plunkett, Archbishop of Armagh (♻ *see DROGHEDA*).

1685— Revocation of the Edict of Nantes in France forces many **Huguenots** (Protestants) to flee to England and Ireland.

1688— **Glorious Revolution:** James II is deposed; William of Orange accedes to the English throne. 13 Londonderry Apprentice Boys shut the city gates in the face of King James's troops; the following year the city endures a three-month siege by a Jacobite army.

1690— **Battle of the Boyne** – King William III of England and his allies representing the Protestant interest defeat King James II who flees to France.

1691— **Siege of Limerick** – Following the battles of Athlone and Aughrim (♻ *see ATHENRY*), the Irish army retreats to Limerick, after a siege it surrenders 'with honour' as per the military terms of the **Treaty of Limerick**; known as the **Wild Geese**, these soldiers are granted leave to sail to France; many join the French army.

ANGLO-IRISH ASCENDANCY

1695— The provisions of the Treaty of Limerick guaranteeing Roman Catholic rights are soon ignored; **Penal Laws** (♻ *see Religion*) impose severe restrictions on their rights to property, freedom of worship and education.

1711— **Linen Board** established to control quality of linen for export; other improvements to canals, roads, and urban planning contribute to growing prosperity.

1778— **Volunteers** rally to defend Ireland against the French; support a call for an independent Irish parliament.

1782— **Repeal of Poynings' Law** and the establishment of an independent Irish Parliament, known as Grattan's Parliament after Henry Grattan a leading campaigner for independence.

1791— Formation in Belfast of the mostly Presbyterian **United Irishmen**, to promote the idea of a republican country with no religious distinctions.

1791–93—**Catholic Relief Acts**.

1795— Rural violence between Protestant Peep O'Day Boys and Catholic Defenders and the foundation of the **Orange Order** (see AR-MAGH).

1796— Abortive French invasion in Bantry Bay (see BANTRY).

1798— **Rebellion of the United Irishmen** launched by Wolfe Tone; main engagements in Antrim, Wexford and Mayo; the rising was brutally suppressed and 30 000 rebels killed. Tone is captured and commits suicide in prison.

IRELAND IN THE UNITED KINGDOM

1800— **Act of Union** and suppression of the Irish Parliament: members take up 100 seats in the House of Commons and 32 in the Upper House in London.

1803— The abortive **Emmet Rebellion** led by Robert Emmet (1778–1803) ends with his hanging but provides inspiration to future nationalists.

1823— **Daniel O'Connell** (1775–1847), a Roman Catholic lawyer, is elected MP for Clare after campaigning for the rights of Catholics and the repeal of the Act of Union. The **Roman Catholic Emancipation Act**, passed in 1829, enables Roman Catholics to enter Parliament.

1845 –49—A blight destroys potato crops, leading to the **Irish Potato Famine** and the deaths of an estimated 800 000 people. Even more emigrate to Great Britain and the USA.

1848— Abortive **Young Ireland Uprising** led by William Smith O'Brien (1803–64).

1858— Founding of the rebel **Irish Republican Brotherhood (IRB)** known as Fenians.

1867— **Manchester Martyrs**: three Fenians are executed for the death of a policeman during an attack to release two Fenian prisoners. The convic-

The Great Famine (1845–49)

When potato blight *(phytophthora infestans)* destroyed the potato crop on which much of the population depended, around 800 000 people died of hunger, typhus and cholera. Thousands of starving people overwhelmed the workhouses and the depot towns distributing the Indian corn imported by the government; the workhouse capacity was 100 000 but five times that number qualified for relief. The Quakers did most to provide relief: soup kitchens were set up by compassionate landlords and by Protestant groups seeking converts; public works were instituted to provide employment relief. Other landlords evicted penniless tenants (in 1847 16 landlords were murdered) or arranged for their emigration, though so many people died en-route or in quarantine that the vessels became known as coffin ships. Over one million emigrated to England, Scotland, Canada and the USA.

Marriage of Strong Bow and Eva (1854) by Daniel Mac Lise

tion on doubtful evidence undermines Irish confidence in British justice.

1869— Disestablishment of Anglican **Church of Ireland**.

1870–1933—17 Land Acts transfer ownership of large estates from landlords to tenants.

1874— 59 Home Rulers elected to Parliament. In 1875 Protestant landowner **Charles Stewart Parnell** (1846-91)

takes his seat, lobbying for home rule and landowner rights.

1879–82—Land League formed by Michael Davitt to campaign for the reform of the tenancy laws and land purchase.

1886— First **Home Rule Bill** granting Ireland autonomy to decide certain domestic matters is rejected by Parliament.

1891–1923—Congested Districts' Board use funds from the disestablished Church of Ireland to build harbours, promote fishing, fish curing and modern farming methods in poor areas.

1893— Second **Home Rule** Bill rejected by Parliament.

1905–08—Sinn Féin (Ourselves) founded to promote the idea of a dual monarchy.

1912— Third **Home Rule** Bill introduced by Asquith: fierce opposition in Ulster where 75 percent of the adult population represented by **Sir Edward Carson** sign a convenant to veto it. Rival militias are armed with smuggled weaponry to form the Ulster Volunteer Force *(north)* and Nationalist Irish Volunteers *(south)*.

1914— **First World War:** postponement of Home Rule and

The Easter Rising 1916

While **John Redmond**, leader of the moderate Nationalists, hoped that Irish contribution to the British war effort would be rewarded by Home Rule, the Military Council of the Irish Republican Brotherhood secretly organised a national uprising. Despite the capture of Sir Roger Casement and a cargo of arms from Germany, the plan went ahead. On Easter Monday columns of Volunteers marched into Dublin and seized various key sites. Outside the General Post Office, Patrick Pearse announced the establishment of a republic, but the insurgents were hopelessly outnumbered and outgunned; on Saturday they surrendered. Initially the insurrection was not especially popular, but attitudes changed when the ringleaders were court marshalled and executed.

civil strife. Irishmen volunteer for the British army.

1917— **Sinn Féin** reorganised under Eamon de Valera to campaign for an independent Ireland.

1918— **General Election:** Redmond's Home Rulers defeated; Sinn Féin win 73 seats.

1919— **Declaration of Independence** in the Irish Assembly (*Dáil Éireann*).

1919–20—War of Independence – Irish Republican Army (IRA) aims to block the British administration; martial law proclaimed; the Royal Irish Constabulary reinforced by British ex-servicemen (Black and Tans) notorious for their brutal tactics.

1920— **Government of Ireland Act** provides for partition: six Ulster counties remain part of the UK as per the will of the majority, to be ruled by a separate parliament; dominion status granted to the remaining 26 counties, which form the Free State.

PARTITION AND INDEPENDENCE

1921— **Anglo-Irish Treaty**

1922–23—Civil War: Michael Collins and the Free State Army clash with the Republicans against even the temporary partition of the country. Casualty numbers surpass those of the War of Independence. Collins is assassinated, the Republicans are defeated.

1922— **Irish Free State**; the two-tier legislature comprises the Senate and *Dáil Éireann*.

1937— Change of name to **Éire**.

1938— Three British naval bases (Cork Harbour, Bere Island and Lough Swilly) granted under the Anglo-Irish Treaty are returned to Ireland.

1939–45—Second World War (referred to as the Emergency): Éire is neutral but gives covert aid to the Allies.

1949— Éire renamed the **Republic of Ireland**; withdrawal from the Commonwealth.

1952— Ireland joins the United Nations.

1965— Anglo-Irish Free Trade Area Agreement.

1973— The Republic of Ireland and United Kingdom of Great Britain and Northern Ireland join the European Union (EU). EEC funds stimulate development in the Republic.

1998— The Northern Ireland Assembly is established as a result of the Belfast Agreement of 10 April 1998. David Trimble and John Hume awarded the Nobel Peace Prize.

2002— **Euro currency** goes into circulation in the Republic. Northern Ireland Assembly suspended following the arrest of three Sinn Fein party members on spying charges.

2004— Sinn Fein fail to provide Unionists (DUM and UUP) evidence that the IRA has been decommissioned. Hope for achieving a devolved Parliament is suspended.

2005— The Provisional IRA orders all its units to disarm and to cease all activity not related to peaceful political programs.

2006— Official census reveals that Republic population has risen to its highest level since 1861 (4 234 925).

2007— Following an historic meeting between Dr Ian Paisley (the leader of the DUP) and Gerry Adams (the leader of Sinn Fein) at Stormont, both parties made a commitment to set up an **Executive Committee** in a Northern Ireland Assembly to which devolved powers were restored on 8 May 2007.

2008— **Irish Referendum** on the new EU consitution dismays EU leaders after the proposal is narrowly rejected.

ART AND CULTURE

Architecture

Architecture in Ireland has been strongly influenced by stylistic developments originating in Britain or continental Europe, but Irish building has many distinctive features. For example, the medieval round towers with their conical caps have become an emblem of Irishness. The array of prehistoric monuments and medieval fortified structures is extraordinary, while the town and country buildings of the Georgian era are particularly fine.

PREHISTORIC ERA

Although the first traces of human habitation in Ireland date from c 7,000 BC, the first people to leave structural evidence of their presence were Neolithic farmers who lived in Ireland from their arrival c 4,000 BC, until 2,000 BC. Traces of their huts have been found at Lough Gur (&see Limerick).

Megalithic Tombs

The most visible and enduring monuments of these people are their elaborate **burial mounds**.

The most impressive are the **passage tombs** at Newgrange, Knowth and Dowth in the Boyne Valley, on Bricklieve Mountain, at Loughcrew, at Fourknocks and Knockmany. Each grave consisted of a passage leading to a chamber roofed with a flat stone or a corbelled structure, sometimes with smaller chambers off the other three sides and sometimes containing stone basins. It was covered by a circular mound of earth or stones, retained by a ring of upright stones. Passage graves date from 3000–2500 BC.

The earliest Megalithic structures, **court tombs**, consisted of a long chamber divided into compartments and covered by a long mound of stones retained by a kerb of upright stones. Before the entrance was a semicircular open court flanked by standing stones as at Creevykeel (&see SLIGO) and Ossian's Grave (&see ANTRIM GLENS).

A third style of Megalithic tomb is known as the **portal tomb**; like Proleek (&see DUNDALK), they are found mostly near the east coast of Ireland. The tomb consisted of two standing stones in front with others behind supporting a massive capstone, which was hauled into place up an earth ramp long since removed. They date from c 2,000 BC.

Bronze Age Structures

Stone circles, which date from the Bronze Age (1750–500 BC), are mostly found in the southwest of the country

Glendalough

J Malburet/MICHELIN

(*see DONEGAL GLENS, KENMARE, DOWNPATRICK, SPERRIN MOUNTAINS*). The circle at Dromberg (*see Kinsale*) seems to have been used to determine the shortest day of the year.

Single standing stones probably marked boundaries or grave sites. Some were made into Christian monuments with a cross or an Ogham inscription (*see Gaelige*).

Of similar antiquity is the cooking pit *(fulacht fiadh)*, which was filled with water; hot stones were placed in the water to bring it to boiling-point.

Iron Age Dwellings

By the Iron Age, men were living in **homesteads**, approached by a causeway. A ringfort was enclosed by an earth bank *(ráth or dún)* or by a stone wall *(caiseal)* and was surrounded by a ditch. An artificial island *(crannóg)* was formed by heaping up stones in a marsh or lake. Many such dwellings were in use from the Iron Age until the 17C. There is a replica at Craggaunowen (*see ENNIS*). Stone forts *(cashels)* like Dún Aonghasa (*see ARAN ISLANDS*) and Grianán of Aileach (*see BUNCRANA*), although restored at various periods, illustrate the type, built on a hill with massive walls and mural chambers.

Within the homestead individual huts were built of wattle and daub or of stone with a thatched roof. In the west, beehive huts *(clocháin)* were built entirely of stone using the same technique of **corbelling** inwards to form a roof that was used in the passage graves. Similar stone huts are also found in the monastery on Great Skellig and at Clochan na Carraige on the Aran Islands. They demonstrate the use of drystone construction in a treeless land.

At the centre of the homestead there was often an underground stone passage, called a souterrain, used for storage or refuge.

IRISH MONASTIC SETTLEMENTS

Little remains of most early Christian settlements, as the buildings were made of perishable material – wood or wattle and daub. The records describe beautiful wooden churches made of smooth planks constructed with great craft and skill. Unfortunately none has survived. Early monasteries consisted of an area enclosed by a circular wall or bank and divided into concentric rings, as at Nendrum (*see STRANGFORD LOUGH*), or into sectors assigned to different uses. The most important sector was the graveyard, since it was seen as the gateway to heaven.

Round Towers

The sites of early monasteries are marked by slender tapering round towers, just as much a symbol of Ireland as the high crosses. Almost unique to Ireland, they were built between about AD 950 and 12C as bell-towers where hand bells, the only kind available, were rung from the top floor to announce the services. The towers were also used to store treasures and possibly as places of refuge; in almost every case the entrance was several feet (10ft/3m) above ground level. Intact towers vary in height (from 50ft/17m to over 100ft/30m). All were surmounted by a conical cap, sometimes replaced by later battlements. About 65 survive in varying condition, with 12 intact. Most were constructed without foundations and all are tapered.

Tomb Shrines

Some saints' graves are marked by a stone **mortuary house**, which resembles a miniature church. These structures, such as St Ciaran's at Clonmacnoise, are among the earliest identifiable stone buildings in Ireland.

Churches

Most early **stone churches** consisted of a single chamber with a west door and an east window; churches with a nave and chancel date from the 12C. None of the surviving churches are very large, but there are often several churches on one site. The very large stones employed accentuate the smallness of the churches. The roofs would have been made of thatch or shingles.

The rare **stone-roofed** churches, an Irish peculiarity, employ the corbelling technique. The simplest is Gallarus Oratory; St Doulagh's near Malahide is a

Jerpoint Abbey Cloisters

H Champollion/MICHELIN

13C church still roofed with stone slabs; St Columba's House, St Mochta's House, St Flannan's Oratory and Cormac's Chapel have a small room between the vaulted ceiling and the roof. The earliest examples are devoid of ornament; an exception to this rule is found on White Island in Co Fermanagh, where seven figurative slabs are attached to the walls —these may be later insertions.

MIDDLE AGES

Norman / Romanesque

The first church in the Romanesque style introduced from the Continent in the 12C, was Cormac's Chapel of 1139 at Cashel. In Ireland Romanesque churches are always small; their typical features, to which carved decoration is limited, are round-headed doorways, windows and arches. Ornament includes fantastic animals, human masks and geometric designs such as bosses, zigzags and "teeth". Cormac's Chapel has fine carvings, several series of blind arcading, painted rib vaults and the earliest extant frescoes.

Profusely ornamented west doorways are perhaps unique to Ireland, exemplified by Clonfert (after 1167), Ardfert and St Cronan's in Roscrea.

Norman Castles

The first castles built by Normans were of the **motte and bailey** type. The motte was a natural or artificial mound of earth surrounded by a ditch and usually surmounted by a wooden tower as at Clough in Co Down; the bailey was an area attached to the motte and enclosed by a paling fence. From the start of the 13C, the Normans built more solid stone donjons (keeps), which were square with corner buttresses, as at Trim, Carrickfergus and Greencastle, polygonal as at Dundrum and Athlone or round as at Nenagh. During the 13C entrance towers became more important and barbicans were added for additional defence. In the latter half of the 13C a new symmetrical design was developed consisting of an inner ward with four round corner towers and a combined gatehouse/donjon in the middle of one wall, as at Roscommon.

Gothic Churches

Gothic architecture, introduced to Ireland in the late 12C, is on a much smaller scale than elsewhere and few examples have survived. Most cathedrals show English and Welsh influences, whereas monasteries, founded by Continental monastic orders, are built according to their usual plan of a quadrangle enclosed by cloisters bordered by the church on the north side, the sacristy and chapter-house on the east, the refectory and kitchens on the south and the store on the west, with dormitories above the east and south ranges.

Early in the 13C many cathedrals were remodelled; the two Anglican cathedrals in Dublin underwent building works in this period, although they have been much altered since. St Patrick's Cathedral in Dublin, completed in 1254, to which a tower was added in 1372, is very English in its form and decoration.

A second period of building occurred in the 15C and coincided with the construction of many Franciscan houses in the west. Most existing churches were altered to conform to the new fashion. Broad traceried windows were inserted, which let in more light and provided the stonemasons with opportunities for decoration. There is a distinctive Irish character to the capitals and high relief carving in the cloisters at Jerpoint (15C).

Tower Houses

After the Black Death (1348–50) building resumed on a more modest scale. In 1429 a £10 subsidy was offered by Edward VI for the construction of a castle or tower. Over 70 per cent of tower houses, which were erected by native and settler alike, are south of the Dublin–Galway axis.

The most distinctive feature is their verticality, one room on each of four to five storeys, sometimes with a hidden room between two floors.

Defences consisted of corner loop holes, battering at the base, double-stepped merlons, known as **Irish crenellations**, and external machicolations over the corners and the entrance. Most such towers, which were built between 1450 and 1650, were surrounded by a **bawn**, an area enclosed by a defensive wall. Only in the later and larger castles is decoration evident.

PLANTATION PERIOD

Plantation Castles

As the country came more firmly under English control in the late 16C, more luxurious rectangular houses were built with square corner towers, as at Kanturk (c 1603), Portumna (c 1618), Glinsk (c 1620) and Ballygally (1625). Often an existing tower house was extended by the addition of a more modern house, as at Leamaneh, Donegal and Carrick-on-Suir. These buildings show a Renaissance influence in plain and regular fenestration with large mullioned windows.

Planter's Gothic

This style was introduced in the early 17C by settlers from England and Scotland who built many parish churches throughout Ireland, a few of which survive unaltered; one of the best examples is St Columb's Cathedral in Londonderry.

Coastal Fortifications

In the Restoration period several important towns were provided with star forts; the most complete surviving fortifica-

tion is Charles Fort in Kinsale (from 1671). Signal towers were built on the coast after the French invasion of Bantry Bay in 1796 and Killala in 1798. The building of Martello towers began in 1804; about 50 of these squat structures with very thick walls punctuate the coast from Drogheda to Cork and along the Shannon estuary. The so-called Joyce Tower in Sandycove, built of ashlar granite, is typical.

18C–19C CLASSICAL

Country Houses

Between the Battle of the Boyne (1690) and the Rebellion (1798) there was a period of relative peace and prosperity during which most of the important country houses were built. While Dutch gables and red brick are attributed to the influence of William of Orange, in general English and French inspiration predominated in the late 17C. In the 18C the influence was mainly Italian sources, often distilled through England and latterly Greek-inspired architects, while in the 19C the English Gothic and Tudor revivalists were influential. Most country houses were built of local stone.

The most popular style in the 18C was the **Palladian villa**, which consisted of a central residence – two or three storeys high – flanked by curved or straight colonnades ending in pavilions (usually one storey lower) which housed the kitchens or stables and farm buildings.

The major architect of the first half of the 18C was **Richard Castle** (originally Cassels) (1690–1751), of Huguenot origin. Castle's many houses – Powerscourt, Westport, Russborough, Newbridge – tend to be very solid. He took over the practice of **Sir Edward Lovett Pearce**, who had the major role in designing Castletown (&see MAYNOOOTH) and who built the Houses of Parliament (from 1729), now the Bank of Ireland in Dublin.

The influence of **Robert Adam** (1728–92) arrived in Ireland in 1770, the date of the mausoleum he designed at Templepatrick. Sir William Chambers' work in Ireland is exemplified by The Casino, Marino (1769–80), an expensive neo-Classical gentleman's retreat cum folly.

R Holzbachova, Ph Benet/MICHELIN

Dublin Castle in 1792 by James Malton

James Gandon (1742–1823) was brought to Ireland in 1781 to design Emo Court. His Classical style is well illustrated by the Customs House and the Four Courts in Dublin.

The chief work of **James Wyatt** (1746–1813) was at Castle Coole but he also contributed to Slane Castle.

One of the best known Irish architects was **Francis Johnston** (1761–1829), an exponent of both the Classical and the Gothic styles, the former exemplified by Dublin's General Post Office, the latter by Dublin Castle's Chapel Royal.

Interior Decoration

Many interiors were decorated with exuberant stuccowork executed by the Swiss-Italian **Lafranchini** brothers, one of whom executed the stairwell plasterwork at Castletown. Contemporary work of similar quality was carried out by Robert West and at Powerscourt House in Dublin by Michael **Stapleton**, the principal exponent of Adam decor.

Churches

Classical details began to be used in the 17C. St Michan's in Dublin (c 1685) and Lismore (1680) by William Robinson retain some details of 17C work. The early Georgian St Anne's in Shandon, Cork, has an imposing west tower with an eastern flavour.

The neo-Classical rectangular building with a pillared portico, inspired by the Greek temple, was popular with all the major denominations: St Werburgh's (1754–59), St George's (1812), St Stephen's (1825) and the Pro-Cathedral (finished after 1840) in Dublin, St John the Evangelist (1781–85) at Coolbanagher by Gandon and St George's (1816) in Belfast.

REVIVAL STYLES

The Gothic Revival style first appeared in Ireland in the 1760s at Castle Ward and at Malahide Castle where two tall Gothic towers were added to the medieval core. At first Gothic features and intricate stuccowork vaulted ceilings were added to buildings that were basically Classical and symmetrical, such as Castle Ward. In addition to crenellations, machicolations and pointed arches, one of the key features of the Gothic style was asymmetry. Existing medieval castles or tower houses or Classical mansions, such as Kilkenny Castle (c 1826) by William Robertson, and Dromoland Castle (1826) by George and James Pain, were enlarged and reworked in Gothic or Tudor style. Johnstown Castle and Ashford Castle are later examples of such Gothicising, which was romantic in flavour but distinctly Victorian in convenience.

Some new houses were built entirely in an antiquated style; Gosford Castle is neo-Norman; Glenveagh was designed in the Irish Baronial style; for Belfast Castle, Lanyon and Lynn chose the Scottish Baronial style, which was also used for Blarney Castle House.

Gothic Revival Churches

Many early 19C Gothic churches, such as the Church of the Most Holy Trinity (formerly the Chapel Royal) in Dublin Castle, are filled with ornament, with decorative galleries, plaster vaulting and rich oak carvings. Later the influence of Augustus Welby Pugin, who practised widely in Ireland, and JJ McCarthy, promoted antiquarian correctness, as at St Fin Barre's in Cork (1862) by William Burges. McCarthy's greatest achievement was probably the completion in Decorated Gothic style of the great new cathedral at Armagh (after 1853). This was only one example, albeit an outstanding one, in the spate of building that followed the Emancipation Act when many Roman Catholic cathedrals and parish churches were constructed in eclectic Gothic variations.

19C-20C

The Gothic style was often used in the second half of the 19C for civic buildings as well as detached houses and mansions; Trinity College Museum (completed 1857) by Deane and Woodward is a classic of the Venetian Gothic revival. The Arts and Crafts movement did not find much architectural expression in Ireland; Cavan Town Hall (1908) by William Scott is a notable exception with expressive use of planes and textures. University College Dublin in Earlsfort Terrace (1912) by RM Butler and the College of Sciences in Upper Merrion Street in Dublin (1904–13) by Sir Aston Webb exemplify the Classical revival. Perhaps the most grandiose structure of this period is the huge City Hall (1906) in Belfast, a "great wedding cake of a building" (J Sheehy) with a dome and corner towers. The young Free State restored with admirable promptness the bombed General Post Office, the Four Courts and the Custom House, but the record of new design is relatively poor.

Modernism

Architectural Modernism was slow to come to Ireland but an early and very striking example was the Church of Christ the King (1927) at Turner's Cross in Cork by Barry Byrne of Chicago. The changes in practice introduced by Vatican II favouring worship in the round, have inspired many exciting church designs, some of which reflect local physical features – St Conal's Church, Glenties, Co Donegal; St Michael's Church, Creeslough, Co Donegal; Dominican Church, Athy; Prince of Peace Church, Fossa, near Killarney; Holy Trinity, Bunclody. Modern civic architecture arrived in Ireland with the construction of the Ardnacrusha hydroelectric plant in 1929 and the Dublin Airport terminal building of 1940.

IRISH DISTINCTION

Towns and Cities

Early Irish villages (clachans) were formed of clusters of wattle-and-daub cottages arranged in a haphazard manner. The first towns were founded by the Vikings, invariably on estuaries; among them were Drogheda, Dublin, Waterford and Wexford. Most such places had a Tholsel (toll stall), often an arch or gateway several storeys high, where payment for rights of privilege or passage was made. Norman settlements were mostly confined to the south and east of the country. Towns were often enclosed within town walls, parts of which have survived at Athenry, Kilmallock, Youghal, Fethard and Londonderry.

The first widespread foundation of towns occurred in the late 16C and 17C during the plantations of Ulster, Munster and some parts of Leinster; they consisted of timber-framed houses, which have not survived, set out round a green or lining a street. The green was often known as "The Diamond" although rarely a true diamond shape; many such "Diamonds" survive in Ulster. In many Irish towns one of the most elegant buildings is the market and the courthouse, sometimes combined in one structure.

Town Planning

In the 18C and 19C many country landlords indulged in town planning, setting out wide streets as in Strokestown and Moy, tree-lined malls as in Westport,

Birr and Castlebar, unusual formal street plans, such as the X-shape in Kenmare, rows of cottages built of local stone as at Glassan, northeast of Athlone, and Shillelagh in Co Wicklow or the picturesque thatched houses of Adare.

In the major towns elegant terraces of houses of Classically inspired design were built of local stone or red brick, some of which was imported from Somerset via Bristol. In 19C Dublin the materials used were grey brick from local clays, local limestone and grey Wicklow granite. Although most terraces were erected piecemeal and lack a unified aesthetic, the influence of the **Wide Streets Commissioners** (in Dublin from 1758) led to distinctly Irish Georgian doorways – usually flanked by columns – and ordered fenestration. The tallest windows are on the principal floor, decreasing in size towards the roofline parapet. Some later terraces by the Wide Streets Commissioners and others were more standardised – Fitzwilliam Street and Square (south side) in Dublin, and Pery Square in Limerick. Internal decoration was often of a very high standard, with Classical motifs common in chimneypieces, plasterwork and timberwork.

20C town planning in Ireland has had few notable successes. Grandiose plans for the reconstruction of Dublin following the devastation of 1916 were drawn up but never implemented. Many of the close-packed terraced streets of late 19C Belfast have been replaced by planned housing schemes of various kinds, the least succesful of which consisted of Brutalist blocks of flats. The attempt to create the "New Town" of Craigavon on the British model, based on the existing urban areas of Lurgan and Portadown, has only been partially realised. In the South, rural prosperity and lax planning controls have led to the abandonment of the picturesque but sub-standard cabin with a scatter of comfortable but visually inappropriate houses and bungalows.

Vernacular Houses

The Irish countryside is full of buildings and other structures of traditional vernacular architecture – not only dwellings and outhouses but also structures such as sweathouses and forges.

The small stone sweathouse, was used to treat pleurisy and other ailments and also as a type of sauna. A fire was lit inside and, when the interior was hot, the ashes were raked out and a layer of rushes placed on the floor to protect the feet from the heat.

The 1841 Census identified four grades of housing, of which the most modest was a windowless one-room mud cabin with a thatched roof *(bothán)*, a type of dwelling that predominated west of a line from Londonderry to Cork. Such houses contained little or no furniture; more windows or rooms meant higher rents. The half door, which is to be found all over Ireland, allowed in light while keeping out animals.

The middle grades of house, single- and two-storey farmhouses, have survived in greater numbers, with glazed windows, hearths and a hierarchy of rooms for distinct social uses.

The Irish **long house**, in which all the rooms were interconnecting with the stairs at one end, was a style that lasted from the Middle Ages to the 18C; the one at Cratloe (*see Limerick*) is a rare survivor.

The box-style Georgian house with symmetrical elevation, some Classical detailing such as Venetian or Wyatt windows and a fanlit and columnated doorcase, was very popular with people of more substantial means.

Simple dwellings were often destroyed during evictions or fell into decay. Some have been discovered under layers of modernisation; others, threatened with demolition, have been reconstructed or

Merrion Square North

B.Juge/MICHELIN

recreated in Bunratty Folk Park, Glencolmcille Folk Village, the Ulster-American Folk Park and the Ulster Folk Park near Bangor.

Stained Glass

No medieval stained glass has survived in-situ in Ireland but there was a revival of interest in this craft in the 1770s with the enamelling work of Thomas Jervais and Richard Hand, much of which was secular. The fashion for the neo-Gothic style of architecture in the 19C for both churches and houses created a great demand for stained glass; good examples from this period are St Patrick's Roman Catholic Church in Dundalk, which has glass by Early of Dublin, Hardman of Birmingham and Meyer of Munich, the east window of St Patrick's Anglican Church in Monaghan by the German FS Barff, and the altar window of the Cathedral of the Assumption in Tuam by Michael O'Connor (1801–67).

The outstanding contribution made by 20C Irish artists in this field was nurtured by the foundation of **An Túr Gloine** (the Tower of Glass) (1903–63) at the instigation of Edward Martyn and Sarah Purser.

The portrait painter Sarah Purser did designs for several windows including Cormac of Cashel in St Patrick's Cathedral, and another founder member was Michael Healy (d 1941) whose work can be seen in Loughrea Cathedral.

Wilhelmina Margaret Geddes worked for An Túr Gloine from 1912 to 1925 and works by her can be seen in the Municipal Gallery of Modern Art in Dublin – *Episodes from the Life of St Colman* (strong black line used) and in the Ulster Museum – *The Fate of the Children of Lir* (1930).

Evie Hone joined An Túr Gloine in 1934. Her work, which was often inspired by Irish medieval sculpture, includes *The Ascension* (1948) for the Roman Catholic church in Kingscourt, Co Cavan, and *The Beatitudes* (1946) for a chapel in the Jesuit Retreat House at Tullabeg near Tullamore.

Harry Clarke (1889–1931) developed a distinctive personal style as early as 1915, drawing from iconography and legends in a symbolist manner. His first public commission, 12 windows for the Honan Chapel in University College Cork, is one of his greatest works. His "Geneva Window" (1928) is in the Municipal Gallery of Modern Art in Dublin. Just before his death he executed his most important ecclesiastical commission *The Last Judgement with the Blessed Virgin Mary and St Paul* for St Patrick's Church in Newport.

A current revival is headed by James Scanlon and Maud Cotter, both based in Cork.

St Wilfrid and St John Berchmans (1927) by Harry Clark

ABC of Architecture

Ecclesiastical Buildings

Romanesque (Norman)

CLONFERT CATHEDRAL, Co Galway – West door – 12C
The inner arch immediately surrounding the door is 300 years later than rest of the doorway, which consists of five rows of columns and five rows of round-headed arches framing the door, surmounted by a hood moulding containing a triangular pediment, the whole capped by a finial.

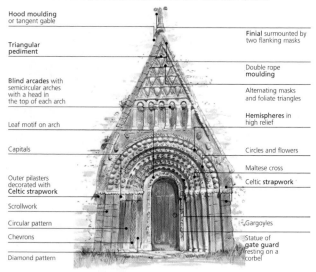

Hood moulding or tangent gable

Triangular pediment

Blind arcades with semicircular arches with a head in the top of each arch

Leaf motif on arch

Capitals

Outer pilasters decorated with Celtic strapwork

Scrollwork

Circular pattern

Chevrons

Diamond pattern

Finial surmounted by two flanking masks

Double rope moulding

Alternating masks and foliate triangles

Hemispheres in high relief

Circles and flowers

Maltese cross

Celtic strapwork

Gargoyles

Statue of gate guard resting on a corbel

Medieval

JERPOINT ABBEY, Co Kilkenny – 12C with 15C tower

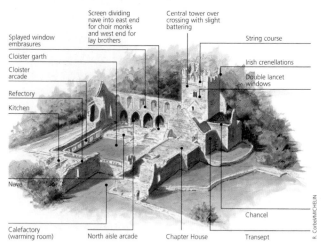

Splayed window embrasures

Cloister garth

Cloister arcade

Refectory

Kitchen

Nave

Calefactory (warming room)

North aisle arcade

Screen dividing nave into east end for choir monks and west end for lay brothers

Central tower over crossing with slight battering

String course

Irish crenellations

Double lancet windows

Chapter House

Chancel

Transept

R. Corbel/MICHELIN

Gothic

ST PATRICK'S CATHEDRAL, Dublin – 13C
Construction begun in the Early English style but extensively restored in the 19C.

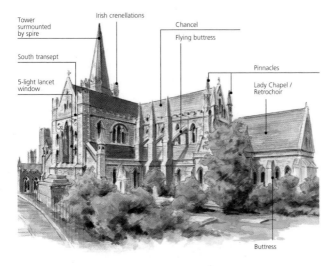

Tower surmounted by spire

Irish crenellations

Chancel

Flying buttress

South transept

5-light lancet window

Pinnacles

Lady Chapel / Retrochoir

Buttress

Neo-Classical

CHRIST CHURCH CATHEDRAL, Waterford – 18C

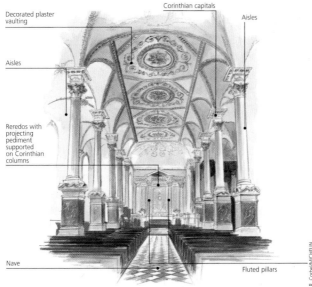

Decorated plaster vaulting

Corinthian capitals

Aisles

Aisles

Reredos with projecting pediment supported on Corinthian columns

Nave

Fluted pillars

R. Corbel/MICHELIN

77

Neo-Gothic

CHURCH OF THE MOST HOLY TRINITY (formerly Chapel Royal), Dublin Castle – 19C

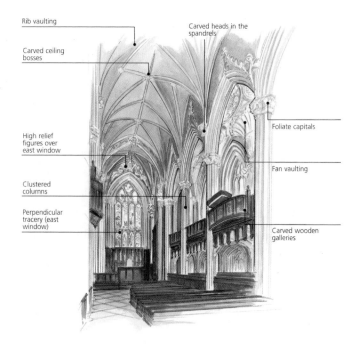

Rib vaulting

Carved ceiling bosses

High relief figures over east window

Clustered columns

Perpendicular tracery (east window)

Carved heads in the spandrels

Foliate capitals

Fan vaulting

Carved wooden galleries

Military Structures

Norman

Motte and bailey

In the immediate post-invasion years, the Normans built timber castles, surmounting a natural or artificial earthern mound (motte). A outer stockaded enclosure (bailey) contained stables, storehouses etc. Later castles were built of stone.

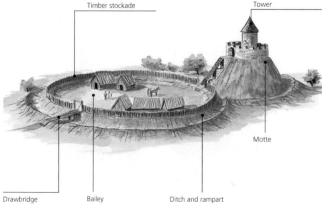

Timber stockade

Tower

Motte

Drawbridge

Bailey

Ditch and rampart

R. Corbel/MICHELIN

15C-17C

DUNGUAIRE CASTLE, Co Galway – 1520 restored in the 19C

Fortified dwelling, consisting of a **tower house** surrounded by a courtyard, known as a **bawn**, enclosed by defensive wall; the main living accommodation with windows was on the upper floors.

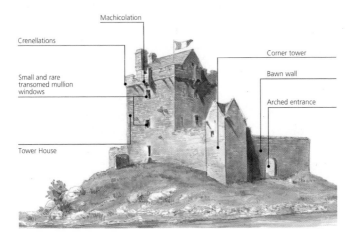

Machicolation

Crenellations

Small and rare transomed mullion windows

Tower House

Corner tower

Bawn wall

Arched entrance

17C

CHARLES FORT, Co Cork – c 1670

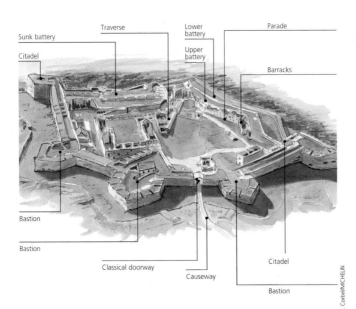

Traverse

Sunk battery

Citadel

Lower battery

Upper battery

Parade

Barracks

Bastion

Bastion

Classical doorway

Causeway

Citadel

Bastion

R. Corbel/MICHELIN

Secular Buildings

16C

PORTUMNA CASTLE, Co Galway – 1518
Semi-fortified house, with symmetrical fenestration, approached through formal walled gardens.

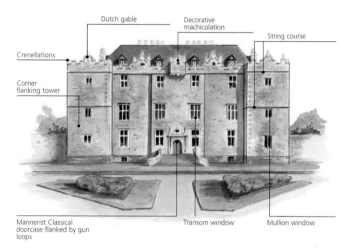

Dutch gable

Decorative machicolation

String course

Crenellations

Corner flanking tower

Mannerist Classical doorcase flanked by gun loops

Transom window

Mullion window

17C

SPRINGHILL, Co Tyrone – c 1680 with 18C additions
Unfortified house with symmetrical facade and large and regular fenestration.

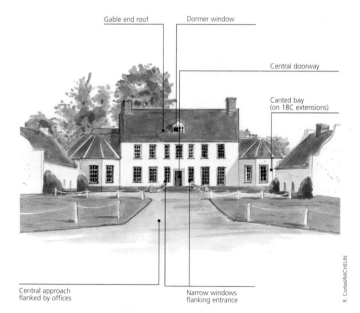

Gable end roof

Dormer window

Central doorway

Canted bay (on 18C extensions)

Central approach flanked by offices

Narrow windows flanking entrance

R. Corbel/MICHELIN

18C

GEORGIAN URBAN HOUSING

Urban terrace houses built of red brick, with 4 storeys over basement, three bays wide, with regular fenestration, composed of sash windows with wooden glazing bars. The tall windows emphasized the importance of the first floor reception rooms.

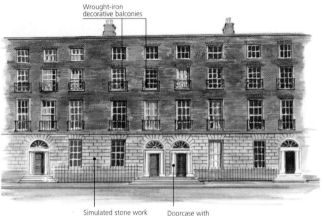

Wrought-iron decorative balconies

Simulated stone work

Doorcase with pillars and fanlight

Doorcases and fanlights (1740s)

Door case capped by a lantern fan light and flanked by pillars with Ionic capitals

Door case capped by a decorated fan light and flanked by pillars with Ionic capitals

Door case capped by a decorative fan light and flanked by pillars with Ionic capitals and by side lights and door scrapers

Door case capped by a decorated fan light and flanked by pillars with Ionic capitals

18C

RUSSBOROUGH, Co Wicklow – 1743-56

House in the **Palladian style** consisting of a main **residential block** linked by curved or straight colonnades to two **flanking service blocks** containing the kitchens and stables.

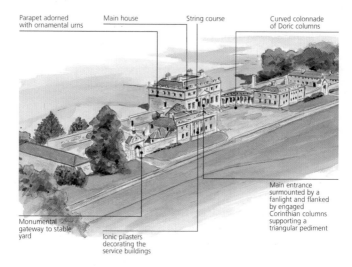

Parapet adorned with ornamental urns

Main house

String course

Curved colonnade of Doric columns

Main entrance surmounted by a fanlight and flanked by engaged Corinthian columns supporting a triangular pediment

Monumental gateway to stable yard

Ionic pilasters decorating the service buildings

18C plasterwork

FLORENCE COURT, Co Fermanagh – 1740s

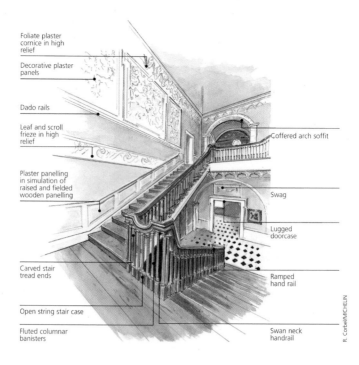

Foliate plaster cornice in high relief

Decorative plaster panels

Dado rails

Leaf and scroll frieze in high relief

Plaster panelling in simulation of raised and fielded wooden panelling

Carved stair tread ends

Open string stair case

Fluted columnar banisters

Coffered arch soffit

Swag

Lugged doorcase

Ramped hand rail

Swan neck handrail

R. Corbel/MICHELIN

MONAGHAN MARKET HOUSE, Co Monaghan – 1791

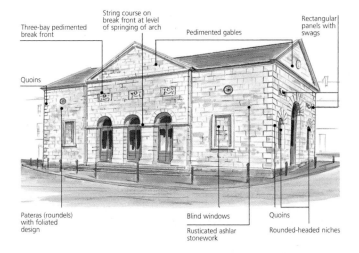

Three-bay pedimented break front

String course on break front at level of springing of arch

Pedimented gables

Rectangular panels with swags

Quoins

Pateras (roundels) with foliated design

Blind windows

Rusticated ashlar stonework

Quoins

Rounded-headed niches

Revival styles

Medieval styles such as Gothic and Norman were revived featuring asymmetric façades and fenestration and varied rooflines.

LISMORE CASTLE, Co Waterford – 19C Neo-Gothic

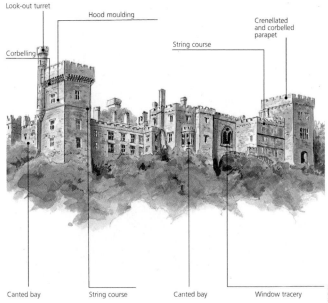

Look-out turret

Hood moulding

Crenellated and corbelled parapet

Corbelling

String course

Canted bay

String course

Canted bay

Window tracery

R. Corbel/MICHELIN

Irish Art

Constantly receptive to influences from Britain and the rest of Europe and often giving them a specifically local flavour, Irish art was unsurpassed in its originality and creativity in the Early Christian era, when sculptors, jewellers, illuminators and other artists found inspiration in the country's glorious heritage of Celtic arts and crafts. A fainter echo of Celtic achievement came in the paintings and graphic arts associated with the Gaelic revival of the late 19C and early 20C, but before this, Ireland, quite as much as England, had become a stronghold of the arts and crafts of the Georgian era; the brilliant and sometimes eccentric life of the Anglo-Irish Ascendancy is reflected in the painting of the time as much as in architecture and the decorative arts.

CELTIC ART

Circles are an integral part of Celtic art; the outline of the design was marked out on the piece to be decorated with an iron compass. Other decorative motifs were S-and C-shaped curves, spirals

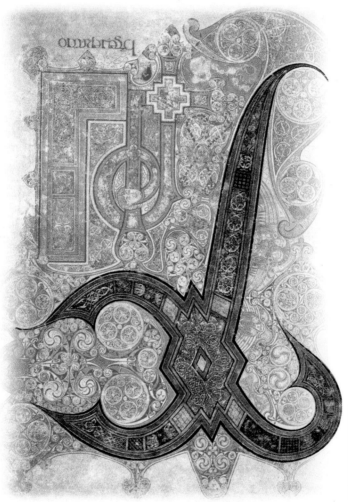

Book of Kells

R Holzbachova, Ph Benet/MICHELIN

and swirls and zig-zags, with intricate, interlaced patterns in the interstices. Similar designs, identified by archaeologists as **La Tène** (after the continental Celtic centre found at La Tène which flourished during the last five centuries BC), are found on two granite monuments – at Turoe (*see ATHENRY*) and Castlestrange (*see STROKESTOWN*) – which date from the 3C BC. They are the only two such monuments to have survived in Ireland and were probably used in religious ceremonies. They resemble the Greek *omphalos* at Delphi, a site raided by the Celts in 290 BC.

Ardagh Chalice (8C)

The finest Celtic pieces are designed in gold. In making a torc (a neckband), the goldsmith stretched the metal into long narrow strips and then twisted them around each other to make a golden rope which was then shaped to fit around the warrior's neck. The Celts made personal ornaments – brooches, horse harnesses and sword sheaths – which they often decorated with enamel favouring the colour red but also using blue, yellow and green. A regular motif in Celtic design is the triskele, a figure with three arms or legs, symbolising earth, fire and water.

Some early sculptures display a nude (and often very lewd) female figure with open legs, known as *Sheila-na-gig*, which owes much to pagan traditions but is usually found in or about churches. Many interpretations have been given to these often grotesque carvings which were probably linked to a fertility cult.

A Golden Age

The first important example of an illuminated manuscript is a copy of the Psalms dating from around AD600 and traditionally attributed to St Columba. Compared with later achievements, it is relatively simple, its principal feature being a large decorated initial at the beginning of paragraphs. Its ornamentation of Celtic spirals and stylised animals is further developed in the course of the 7C in the **Book of Durrow**, where a variety of coloured inks is used as well as the black of Columba's manuscript. Whole "carpet pages" are given over to decoration rather than text, and the charac-

teristic motif of interlaced bands makes its appearance. Over the next century and a half, the scribes' increasing skill resulted in ever greater intricacy and exuberance, culminating in the sublime achievement of the **Book of Kells** dating from around 800. Of equal virtuosity are a number of products of the metalworker's and jeweller's art. The almost monumental **Ardagh Chalice** (c 700) is a masterpiece of colourful decoration; its extraordinarily elaborate base, with three friezes in gold around a central rock crystal, would have been visible only briefly when raised during Mass. In a similar way, the splendid ornamentation of the underside of the renowned **Tara Brooch** (also c 700) would have only been seen by its owner.

Tara Brooch (8C)

PAINTING

When Gaelic culture waned in the 17C the chief influences on art in Ireland were English and European. A guild of painters was founded in Dublin in 1670, but there was little development until the Dublin Society's Schools were set up in 1746 to promote design in art and manufacture. The first master, Robert West (d 1770), and his assistant, James Mannin (d 1779), had trained in France. The School's most outstanding pupil was probably **Hugh Douglas Hamilton** (1739–1808), who excelled at pastel portraits; in 1778 he visited Italy and while in Rome developed as a painter in oils.

Susanna Drury (1733–70), whose paintings of the Giant's Causeway are in the Ulster Museum, was a member of the Irish school of landscape painting, which emerged in the 18C. **George Barret** (c 1732–84), who moved to England in 1763, introduced the Romantic element into his landscapes. Several Irish artists travelled to Italy. Thomas Roberts (1748–78), a pupil of the Dublin Society's Schools and a brilliant landscape artist, was familiar with Dutch and French painting and exhibited several works in the style of Claude Vernet. The dominant figure of the 18C is **James Barry** (1741–1806), who produced large-scale works in the neo-Classical tradition. He travelled widely, including in Italy, studying painting and sculpture. Joseph

Ardboe High Cross

Peacock (c 1783–1837) from Dublin was famous for his outdoor fair scenes.

Among the visitors to 18C Dublin were Vincent Valdré (1742–1814), who painted three ceiling panels for Dublin Castle, and Angelica Kauffmann (1741–1807), who was the guest of the Viceroy, Lord Townshend for several months in 1771. In 1823 the **Royal Hibernian Academy** was incorporated by charter to encourage Irish artists by offering them an annual opportunity to show work.

After the Act of Union in 1800 many Irish artists moved to London: Martin Archer Shee (1769–1850), who became President of the Royal Academy in 1830, and Daniel Mac Lise (1806–70), a popular historical painter. Nathaniel Hone (1831–1917) spent 17 years in France painting outside like the painters of the Barbizon school. Roderic O'Conor (1860–1940) studied in Antwerp and in France where he met Gauguin, whose influence, together with that of Van Gogh, is obvious in his work. **Sir John Lavery** (1856–1948), who also studied in Paris, is known for his portraits, although he also painted scenes from the French countryside. Another artist who studied abroad is **Sarah Purser** (1848–1943), a prolific portrait painter and a founder of *An Túr Gloine*.

The 20C has produced several artists of note. **Jack B Yeats** (1871–1957), brother of the poet, painted his views of Irish life with bold brushstrokes in brilliant colours. **Paul Henry** (1876–1958) is known for his ability to represent the luminous quality of the light in the west of Ireland. **William Orpen** (1878–1931), who trained at the Metropolitan School of Art in Dublin and the Slade in London, became a fashionable portrait painter and an official war artist; among his Irish pupils were **Seán Keating** (1889–1977) and **Patrick Tuohy** (1894–1930). Cubism was introduced to Ireland by **Mainie Jellett** (1897–1944) and **Evie Hone** (1894–1955), who is better known for her work in stained glass.

In 1991 the National Gallery and the Hugh Lane Gallery were joined by the Irish Museum of Modern Art at Kilmainham, all in Dublin.

SCULPTURE

Cross-slabs and pillar-stones

Among the earliest stone monuments are the slabs laid flat over an individual grave between the 8C and the 12C. The largest collection is at the monastic site at Clonmacnoise. Of somewhat earlier date are cross-decorate pillar-stones, some set up as grave markers. A number of them may be recycled prehistoric standing stones.

High Crosses

One of the great symbols of Ireland, the free-standing highly-decorated crosses are most numerous in the east of Ireland but they are also found in western and northern Britain. The best groups are at Monasterboice, Clonmacnoise, Kells and Ahenny. It is thought that high crosses are the successors to small painted or bronze-covered wooden crosses used as a focus for kneeling congregations. Most stand on a pyramidal base; the head of the cross is usually ringed and surmounted by a finial often in the shape of a small shrine.

The early carving on late 8C crosses is mostly decorative consisting of spirals and interlacing. In the 9C and 10C, panels of figures appear illustrating stories at first from the New and then from the Old Testament; interestingly, such biblical figures or scenes are rare in early Christian art. Animal scenes are often executed on the base.

The 12C crosses are not a direct continuation and often lack a ring. By this date the figure of a bishop or abbot in the Continental style predominates.

Middle Ages to the Renaissance

A distinctive feature of the medieval period is the box tomb found in the chancel of many churches. These often have lids bearing a carved effigy of the deceased and sometimes that of his wife; while the sides are decorated with figures of the Apostles and saints. In the 15C and 16C, figures and scenes from the crucifixion were carved in high relief (see KILDARE and KILKENNY Cathedrals). Although predominantly religious, 17C sculpture, such as the Jacobean Segrave or Cosgrave stucco

Statue of Justice, Dublin Castle

© Marek Slusarczyk/Bigstockphoto.com

tableaux in St Audeon's Church in Dublin, widened in scope to include stone and timber carved chimneypieces; there are two fine examples of the former in the castles in Donegal and Carrick-on-Suir. Renaissance-inspired 17C tombs are to be found in St Mary's Cathedral in Limerick, St Nicholas' Church in Carrickfergus and in Youghal Parish Church. Carvings from the Restoration period – fine wood relief and stone – survive, especially at the Kilmainham Hospital.

18C to the Present

A spate of building in the 18C provided much work for sculptors. The figures of **Justice** and **Mars** above the gates of Dublin Castle are the work of **Van Nost** as is a statue of George III, now in the Mansion House. **Edward Smyth** (1749–1812), who was a pupil of the Dublin Society's Schools, created the riverine heads on the keystones of the arches and the arms of Ireland on the Custom House and also worked on the Four Courts under James Gandon and on the Bank of Ireland; he had been apprenticed to Simon Vierpyl (c 1725–1810), who worked on the Marino Casino. Vierpyl's work at the Casino includes the urns flanking the external steps; the lions adjacent are the work of the English sculptor Joseph Wilton.

The 19C saw the dominance of a taste in Greek Revival detailing; in St Patrick's

Church in Monaghan there is a good collection of monuments, notably the one to Lady Rossmore (c 1807) by Thomas Kirk (1781–1845). John Hogan (1800–58) is acknowledged as a most distinguished sculptor – see his fine plaster *The Drunken Faun* in the Crawford Art Galley in Cork. Among his contemporaries, two stand out: Patrick MacDowell (1799–1870) who carved the group of Europe on the base of the Albert Memorial in London, and John Henry Foley (1818–74) who sculpted the bronze figure of Prince Albert; Foley's best work in Dublin is the O'Connell Monument and the statues of Burke, Goldsmith and Grattan on College Green. The best work of Thomas Farrell (1827–1900) is the Cullen Memorial (1881) in the Pro-Cathedral in Dublin.

The Wellington Testimonial (c 1817) in Phoenix Park in Dublin by English architect Sir Robert Smirke, has bronze reliefs on the base by the sculptors Joseph Robinson Kirk, Farrell and Hogan. The work of Oliver Sheppard (1864–1941) is strongly influenced by the Art Nouveau style. The Parnell Monument in O'Connell Street in Dublin was designed by Augustus St Gaudens in 1911. The portrait sculptor **Albert Power** (1883–1945), a resident of Dublin, was elected Associate of RHA in 1911; there are examples of his work in Cavan Cathedral, Mullingar Cathedral and in Eyre Square in Galway. The Belfast sculptor FE McWilliam (1909–92) is represented by a series of bronze figurative sculptures in the Ulster Museum.

More recent work of note includes the *Children of Lir* by Oisin Kelly (1916–81) in the Garden of Remembrance in Dublin. A pleasing aspect of contemporary urban renewal is the placing of sculpture in places where it is readily encountered by the public, who have often responded with affection and amusement.

Literature

Irish men and women of letters have made a significant contribution to English literature through poetry, novels and drama. Poetry was an art form practised by the Celtic bard and medieval monk, but theatrical performances were unknown to Gaelic society. The Irish brought a talent for fantasy, wit, satire and Gaelic speech patterns to the English language. Four Irish writers have been awarded the Nobel Prize for Literature: William Butler Yeats (1923), George Bernard Shaw (1925), Samuel Beckett (1969) and Seamus Heaney (1995).

CELTIC INFLUENCE

The Celts may not have left a written record but their oral tradition has bequeathed a rich legacy of myth and history to inspire later generations.

The work of the monks in the scriptorium of a Celtic Church was to copy biblical and other religious texts and to write their own commentaries. They decorated their work, particularly the first capital letter of a chapter, with highly ornate Celtic patterns. Several of these **illuminated manuscripts**, of which the most famous is the Book of Kells, are displayed in the Old Library of Trinity College in Dublin.

One account from this early period is *Navigatio*, written in medieval Latin, an account of the voyage from Ireland to America made by St Brendan in the 6C (see *ENNIS*).

ANGLO-IRISH LITERATURE

The first flowering of Anglo-Irish literature came in the late 17C and 18C when George Farquhar (1678–1707) wrote his stage works, Oliver Goldsmith (1728–74) composed poetry, novels and plays and Richard Brinsley Sheridan (1751–1816) published his satirical comedies – *School for Scandal*.

The major figure of this period was **Jonathan Swift** (1667-1745) who was born in Ireland, studied at Trinity College, Dublin, and spent many years in England before being appointed Dean of St Patrick's Cathedral in Dublin where he stayed until his death. *Gulliver's Travels* is the most famous of his satirical writings on 18C Irish society. His friend and fellow student, **William Congreve** (1670–1729), meanwhile, wrote witty costume dramas, such as *The Way of the World*, which inspired Wilde and Shaw.

After spending his early childhood among his mother's relatives in Ireland, **Laurence Sterne** (1713-68), made his name in England as an innovator among novelists with *Tristram Shandy* and *A Sentimental Journey*; he is also seen as a forerunner of the stream of consciousness technique practised by James Joyce.

Many Irish writers who achieved success and fame moved to London, where they made a significant contribution to English literature and theatre. The name of the novel *Dracula* is better known than its author **Bram Stoker** (1947-1912), who worked for several years as an Irish civil servant, writing drama reviews, before moving to London as Henry Irving's manager; only his first novel, *A Snake's Pass*, is set in Ireland. George Moore (1852–1933) described high society in Dublin *(Drama in Muslin)* and introduced the realism of Zola into the novel *(Esther Waters)*. **Oscar Wilde** (1854–1900) achieved huge success in the London theatre with his poetry, comic plays *(Lady Windermere's Fan, The Importance of Being Earnest)* and in society with his distinctive dress and style, his disgrace and prison term in Reading Gaol. **George Bernard Shaw** (1856–1950) commented on the Anglo-Irish dilemma in his journalism and his play *John Bull's Other Island* and explored the contradictions of English society *(Pygmalion)*.

IRISH THEMES

Several successful authors chose Irish themes for their work. Maria Edgeworth (1767–1849) achieved international fame and the admiration of Sir Walter Scott with her novels *Castle Rackrent* and *The Absentee*; William Carleton (1794–1869) wrote about rural life in County Tyrone. The theme of the novel *The Collegians* by Gerald Griffin (1803–40) was reworked by Dion Boucicault for the stage as *The Colleen Bawn* and by Benedict as an opera, *The Lily of Killarney*. **Anthony Trollope** (1815–82), who began his literary career while working for the Post Office in Ireland, wrote several novels on Irish themes. Canon Sheehan (1852–1913) was admired in Russia by Tolstoy

and in the USA for his novels about rural life. Somerville and Ross, a literary partnership composed of **Edith Somerville** (1858–1949) and her cousin Violet Florence Martin (1862–1915), whose pen-name was **Martin Ross**, produced novels about Anglo-Irish society, *The Real Charlotte* and the highly humorous *Experiences of an Irish RM*, adapted for TV in the 1980s.

IRISH LITERARY RENAISSANCE

At this time, as part of the **Gaelic Revival** (👆 *see ART AND CULTURE, Gaelige*), a literary renaissance deeply rooted in folklore was taking place in Ireland. One of its early influential figures was George Russell (1867–1935), known as AE, mystic, poet and painter, economist and journalist. The leader of this literary movement and the dominant writer of traditional Irish myths and legends, was **William Butler Yeats** (1856–1939), who established his name as a poet and playwright and was a founder member of the Abbey Theatre. He lived for a number of years in County Sligo and came to recognise the power of the native imagination in Irish oral tradition, especially in the heroic tales and in mythological material, which greatly influenced his writing. His own understanding of the occult influenced his involvement in and interpretations of Irish lore. His *Fairy and Folk Tales of the Irish Peasantry*, first published in 1888, was followed by

William Butler Yeats (1856-1939)

National Gallery of Ireland, Dublin

Irish Fairy Tales in 1892. Here he made the distinction among folktale, legend and myth; he was among the first writers to interpret Irish folklore. He admired Douglas Hyde because of Hyde's honest commitment to the Irish language and to native Irish lore. Yeats was part of a group of people who associated Anglo-Irish writing as part of a revival of a culture that was in danger of disappearing, to a large extent owing to social development. Another leading light in this movement was **Isabella Augusta**, **Lady Gregory** (1852-1932), who lived in County Galway and became friendly with Yeats. They were much influenced by one another and collected folklore together. Among her best-known works is *Visions and Beliefs in the West of Ireland* (1920), which is based on 20 years of work in this area with Yeats.

The *Kiltartan History Book* (1909) contained, for the first time, accounts and descriptions of many aspects of historical lore, unchanged from the oral narration of local people. She was one of the first to publish unedited folklore material faithfully reproducing what she had collected. In common with Yeats, she recognised the richness of folklore among the "farmers and potato-diggers and old men" in her own district, the unbroken chain of tradition and the wealth of ballads, tales and lore that played such an important part in the everyday life of the ordinary people around her in County Galway.

Some of the greatest successes written for the **Abbey Theatre** were the plays of **John Millington Synge** (1871–1909). These included *Riders to the Sea* and *Playboy of the Western World*, inspired by the Aran Islands, and *The Shadow of the Glen*, inspired by the Wicklow Mountains, where language dominates in the bleak landscape; and the pacifist plays of **Sean O'Casey** (1880–1964), *The Shadow of a Gunman*, *Juno and the Paycock* and *The Plough and the Stars*, written in the aftermath of the First World War.

LITERARY EXILES

The narrow-mindedness of Irish society is expressed in the drama and fiction of George Moore (1852-1933), who spent part of his early life in Paris, and even more so in the work of **James Joyce** (1882-1941), often considered to be the greatest and certainly the most innovative of 20C writers in English. The appearance of his short story collection, *Dubliners*, was long delayed because of the publisher's attempts to impose cuts. Joyce's anti-clerical and anti-nationalist views led him to leave Dublin in 1904 for exile, first in Trieste, then in Zürich and Paris. His most influential work, the vast novel *Ulysses*, recounts a day in the life of Jewish Dubliner Leopold Bloom as he moves around the city in a strange reprise of the wanderings of Homer's hero. The novel revels in the English language and pushes it to its limits, exploiting the devices of interior monologue and stream of consciousness to extraordinary effect. Dwelling on the most intimate details of everyday life, it was banned not just in Ireland but in Britain and America as well. The even more monumental *Finnegan's Wake* takes these developments even further, exploiting not just the potential of English but of scores of other languages and delighting in word-play and paradox of the utmost complexity.

Much influenced by Joyce, and an associate of his during the older writer's sojourn in Paris, **Samuel Beckett** (1906-89) is remembered mainly as one of founders of the Theatre of the

James Joyce (1882-1941)

© White Images/Scala 2008

Absurd. Like Joyce, Beckett found life in Ireland unbearably constricting and spent most of his life in France, being decorated for his work in the Resistance in the Second World War. Unlike Joyce, Beckett honed his language to the bare minimum required to convey his grim vision of human life as an "intolerable existence not worthwhile terminating". His best-known work is the play *En Attendant Godot/Waiting for Godot*, written in French and then translated by the author himself. First produced in 1953 and provoking acclaim and bafflement in equal measure, it is the austere and apparently inconsequential tale of two tramps waiting in vain for a mysterious being who never makes an appearance.

MODERN WRITING IN IRELAND

The early 20C produced the bleak realistic poetry of **Patrick Kavanagh** from Monaghan (1904–67 *Ploughman and Other Poems*) – whose influence can be seen in the work of John Montague (b 1929 *Poisoned Lands* and *Rough Field*) and Northern poet **Seamus Heaney** (b 1939 *The Death of a Naturalist*) – and of Louis MacNeice (1907–63), who was a member of Auden's circle and an early influence on the poet / playwright Derek Mahon (b 1941 *The Hudson Letter*). Novelists included Flann O'Brien (1911–66, real name Brian O'Nolan), who wrote a famous newspaper column as Myles na Gopaleen.

The theme of the Big House survives in the work of Elizabeth Bowen (1899–1973 *The Last September*), **Molly Keane** (1897-1974) writing as MJ Farrell (1905–97 *The Last Puppetstown*), Aidan Higgins (b 1927 *Langrishe, Go Down*), Jennifer Johnston (b 1930 *The Illusionist*) and *Woodbrook* (1974) by David Thompson.

Influential writers include **John B Keane** (1928-2002), whose work is firmly set in Co Kerry – his first play *Sive* won the all-Ireland drama festival; *The Field* was made into a film in 1990 and his best novel is *The Bodhran Makers*; also **Edna O'Brien** (b 1932 *The Country Girls*), whose frank accounts of female sexuality in the 1950s were banned in Ireland on first publication and publicly burned in her home village in Co Clare, and the highly acclaimed short-story writer **John MacGahern** (1934-2006 *Amongst Women*) who grew up in Co Leitrim. *Troubles* by **JG Farrell** (1935-79) brings rare humour to the grim reality of the War of Independence. **Maeve Binchy** (b 1940) writes in lighter vane about episodes in Irish family life. **Brendan Behan** (1923-64), who was involved in IRA activity at an early age and imprisoned in both Britain and Ireland, made use of these experiences in the vivid and humorous writing of the plays *The Quare Fellow* and *The Hostage* (the latter originally written in Irish) and in his autobiography *Borstal Boy*.

Northern Irish writers Brian Moore (b 1921 *The Lonely Passion of Judith Hearne)*, Patrick McCabe (b 1955 *Butcher Boy)* and Eoin MacNamee (b 1960 *Resurrection Man)* have all seen their work quickly turned into films, as have many writers from the south, including **Roddy Doyle** (b 1958 *The Commitments* and *Paddy Clarke Ha Ha Ha*, which won the Booker prize) and Colin Bateman (b 1962 *Cycle of Violence, Belfast Confidential*), or from outside Ireland such as **Frank McCourt**, who won the Pulitzer Prize in 1997 with *Angela's Ashes*, about his childhood in Limerick.

Among the established pillars of Irish drama are **Brian Friel** (b 1929 *Dancing at Lughnasa*, adapted as a film in 1998), Thomas Kilroy (b 1934 *The Secret Fall of Constance Wilde*), Thomas Murphy (b 1935 *A Whistle in the Dark, Baileangaire*) and Frank McGuinness (b 1956 *Observe the Sons of Ulster Marching towards the Somme*). Alongside them a new wave of young Irish writers is making an international impact. Encouraged by the Abbey and the Gate Theatres in Dublin, the Royal Court in London and independent theatre companies, such as Rough Magic in Dublin, the Druid Theatre Company in Galway and Red Kettle in Waterford, this new wave includes Martin McDonagh (*The Leenane Trilogy*), Conor McPherson (b 1971 *The Weir*), Marina Carr (b 1964 *The Mai*) and Enda Walsh (*Disco Pigs*).

The Gaelic Revival at the end of the 19C was responsible for the rescue of writing in Irish, which, at the start of that century had fallen to a very low point indeed. An important figure was Peter O'Leary (tAthair Peadar) (1839-1920); his folk-tale *Séadna* of 1910 eschewed archaic literary convention in favour of the vigour of the contemporary spoken language, as did the short stories of Pádraig O'Conaire (1882-1928).

Among the best-known authors is the Connemara-born Máirtín O Cadhain (1906-70), former professor of Irish at Trinity College, whose novel *Cré na Cille (The Clay of the Graveyard* – 1949*)* is the best-known prose writing in recent times. Those who lived and worked on the Great Blasket Island, off the coast of Co Kerry, have produced several works describing island life before the people left in the early 1950s. Modern Irish poetry, composed by Seán O Ríordéin, Máirtín O Direáin and Nuala ní Dhomhnaill among others, has appeared in a number of languages.

Music

Ireland is unusual in having a musical instrument – the harp – as its national emblem. Music plays a very important role in Irish life. Traditional music, song and dance are among the most vibrant aspects of Irish culture. Performances take place frequently and spontaneously in all parts of the country, and it is this very unpredictability which is responsible for much of its attraction. New songs and tunes are constantly being composed.

The harp dominated the musical scene from the Middle Ages until it was proscribed by the English because of its nationalist allure. It was used to accompany the singing or recitation of poetry. Irish harpists, who trained for many years, were admired for their rapid fingerwork and their quick and lively technique; they enjoyed high social status. **Turlough O'Carolan** (Carolan) (1670–1738) started too late in life to reach the highest standard of skill but he was an outstanding composer, much in demand; he left over 200 tunes, which show remarkable melodic invention and are still played today.

The first documented mention of mouth-blown pipes in Ireland occurs in an 11C text and the earliest depiction dates from the 15C; these pipes appear to have been primarily for entertainment purposes. The particularly Irish form of pipes, the **uilleann (elbow) pipes**, which have regulators and drones operated by the fingers, emerged in the 18C. These pipes are renowned for the unique sound produced by highly skilled musicians and are closely identified with Irish traditional music, which in recent years has become an important industry.

The workshop of a violin maker

NITB, Belfast

TRADITIONAL MUSIC TODAY

During the 20C traditional Irish music, which formerly had been played as the accompaniment to dancing, came to be valued in its own right, and is no longer confined to isolated regions. Nowadays, traditional musicians come together in pubs throughout the country for sessions that may be formal, commercial and structured, while others are informal and free of charge. Apart from the pipes, the most popular instruments tend to be the fiddle, flute, tin whistle, accordeon, concertina, melodeon, banjo, guitar, bodhrán, keyboard and the spoons.

Schools and festivals are held throughout the year with people coming from far and wide to learn an instrument or study some other aspect of Irish music. Several schools celebrate the name of a local musician, the best known being the **Willie Clancy Summer School**, which runs in early July in Milltown Malbay in County Clare. Specialist classes in regional styles of instrumental playing are also held at many schools, such as the fiddle classes in Glenties, Co Donegal, each October.

TRADITIONAL TO POP

Traditional music was popularised through the recordings made by the Irish in America and the formation of *Ceoltóirí Chualann* by Seán O'Riada in the early 1960s. This group of the highest calibre of traditional musicians created a more formalised style and generated an appreciation of Irish music. Out of this group the **Chieftains** were formed and brought Irish traditional music to a worldwide audience. In the same decade in the United States the Clancy Brothers and Tommy Makem achieved the popularisation of the Irish ballad tradition. In subsequent years many traditional music groups emerged including the **Dubliners**, the **Bothy Band**, **De Dannan**, **Planxty** and **Altan**. Members of the Brennan family of the Irish-speaking region of Donegal penetrated the realm of popular music singing in both Irish and English as the group **Clannad**, while another member of the family, **Enya**,

J Malburet/MICHELIN

forged a highly successful international career as a solo artist.

During the 1950s and 1960s showbands entertained in ballrooms throughout Ireland. Musicians such as **Rory Gallagher** and **Van Morrison** began their careers in showbands before pursuing solo careers. Today showband members such as Joe Dolan still have a considerable Irish following among the over 50s age group. Country/Irish music has a large fan base in Ireland. One of the most popular singers is Daniel O'Donnell who has been recording since the mid-1980s.

Traditional Irish music has influenced the bands of recent decades, so much so that Irish rock has often been described as "Celtic Rock". **Thin Lizzy** and **Rory Gallagher** were among the first to gain international celebrity. **Van Morrison** and **U2** still continue to maintain their positions on the international stage, entertaining new generations with their brand of Irish music. More recent international celebrities **The Pogues**, **The Cranberries**, **Sinéad O'Connor** and **The Corrs** have created a worldwide interest in "Celtic" music. **Bono** of U2 and **Bob Geldof**, originally of the Boomtown Rats, have used their pop fame to espouse worthier causes and have become world famous for their statesmen-like approach to the issue of world poverty.

By contrast with the raw energy of Bono and Geldof, the rather bland **Boyzone**, **B*witched** and more recently **Westlife** have had huge commercial success. Boyzone members have embarked on solo careers; Ronan Keating has the largest following to date.

Bands who came to the fore in the 1990s making the charts in both Ireland and the UK are Northern Ireland's Divine Comedy and Ash. At the forefront of the Club Scene is David Holmes, a DJ turned Pop Star, who has gained a considerable reputation for his remixing and soundtrack work.

Many bands that have not yet entered the charts, nor ever will, still have many loyal fans who flock to their gigs – this underground music scene was brilliantly captured in Roddy Doyle's book and subsequent film *The Commitments*.

DANCE

Set dancing originated in Ireland in the 18C; it consists of figure dances, developed by travelling dancing masters, who adapted the original French dance movements to suit Irish music. Set-dancing is very popular and can be seen at many public venues; classes are held on a regular basis at hundreds of venues. Although it could not really be described as "traditional", the phenomenon of **Riverdance**, created in 1994

and seen on five continents, has done for Irish dance what the Chieftains did for Irish music. Although Michael Flatly, the virtuoso American dancer and brilliant mind behind *Lord of the Dance* quit the show that he had devised and starred in after a contractual dispute, he has followed his original huge success in no small measure with *Lord of the Dance* and *Feet of Flames*.

SONG

Singing forms part of many of the music festivals held in Ireland, and at least one festival is devoted solely to this art and is held each June in Ennistymon, Co Clare. Traditional singing is usually called old style *(sean-nós)* singing, and is especially closely identified with singing in Irish; songs are also sung in English in this style. Traditional songs in Irish date for the most part from the last two or three hundred years, although some are older and the style is a good deal older still. Songs in English include recently composed songs and also many songs from the medieval ballad traditions. The style is individual, unaccompanied, free and ornate, with many regional variations. The Irish-speaking area of Rath Cairn, Co Meath, hosts the Irish-language singing festival *Eigse Dharach Uí Chatháin* in October each year.

Religion

Christianity was probably introduced to Ireland from Roman Britain or Gaul in the 4C. Palladius, the first bishop, was appointed in 431 by Pope Celestine I but his mission met with little success and it is Patrick, the country's much-revered patron saint, who is held responsible for the country's definitive conversion.

The majority (75 percent) of the population of Ireland is Roman Catholic but most of the country's Catholic churches are of recent date; the traditional religious sites are usually occupied by Anglican churches, a reminder that for many years the Protestant Church of Ireland was the country's established church. Many Catholic churches stand in new centres of population though

St Patrick, Bangor Abbey

MICHELIN

others were built close to a ruined monastery where the faithful heard Mass in the Penal Days and where they continue to be buried.

NATIONAL SAINTS

St Patrick

The patron saint of Ireland was born on the west coast of Roman Britain where he was captured as a young man by Irish raiders. After six years of slavery near Sliabh Mis (Slemish in Co Down), he escaped to France and then returned to his birthplace. Inspired by a vision that the people of Ireland were calling him, he went to France to study, possibly at the monasteries of Lérins, Tours and Auxerre. In 432 in middle age he returned to Ireland to convert the people to Christianity. He is thought to have founded his first church at Saul and then travelled to Slane where he challenged the power of the High King and his druids.

In 444, after a visit to Rome, he founded the cathedral church of Armagh, still the ecclesiastical capital of Ireland, as well as many other churches. When he died, probably at Saul in 461, the country was organised into dioceses based on the petty Irish kingdoms.

Patrick is the subject of numerous tales and legends, according to which he banished monsters and drove the snakes out of Ireland.

On St Patrick's day (17 March) people wear a sprig of **shamrock** *(seamróg)*, a comparatively recent custom, being first documented in the later part of the 17C; it is claimed that the saint used this trefoil plant to illustrate the doctrine of the Holy Trinity.

St Bridget

Brigit was a Celtic goddess, whose name means "the exalted person"; it is significant that the same name is given to the most popular female saint in Irish tradition and second only to St Patrick among all the saints. This Leinster saint ("Bríd"), who died c AD 524, established a convent in Kildare (*Cill Dara* meaning "the church of the oak tree") and this may have been a sacred spot in pre-Christian times. Bridget is perceived to be the protectress of animals and crops, with which she is closely associated.

The most popular legend of St Bridget is associated with Kildare, where she wished to build a convent. The local king refused to grant her more land than could be covered by her cloak, but when she spread her garment it expanded to cover a vast area.

On St Bridget's day (1 February) it is customary to honour the saint by making straw or rush crosses *(Cros Bhríde)*, which have numerous regional variations in design and form.

CELTIC CHURCH

As continental Europe was overrun by barbarians, the church in Ireland developed a distinctive form of organisation

---

Irish Missionary Monks

Monks from Ireland played a leading role in re-Christianising Europe, particularly in the conversion of the powerful Frankish kingdom. In the late 6C, **Columbanus** founded monasteries in Luxeuil, Annegray and Fontaines in France and Bobbio in Italy ; his disciple **Gall** gave his name to Switzerland's most renowned monastery, which has preserved a fine collection of Irish manuscripts. **Columba (Colmcille** in Irish) left his native country to found the monastery on Iona ; monks from there moved on to Lindisfarne in the north of England and to the court of Charlemagne. **Fursey** founded a monastery at Lagny near Paris, while **Johannes Eriugena** achieved renown as a philosopher at Laon. Several Irish monks went to Germany and beyond, **Kilian** to Würzburg, **Virgil** in the 8C to Salzburg, **Marianus Scottus** in the 11C to Cologne, Fulda and Mainz, and a namesake, a member of an important Donegal family, to Regensburg. The most-travelled monk, however, was probably **Brendan** (*see ENNIS*), who may have reached America.

based on monasticism. In the mid 6C and 7C a great many monasteries were founded and by the 8C the administration of the church had been taken over by the abbots. Although bishops continued to perform the sacramental duties and new bishops were consecrated, they were not appointed to particular sees.

Some **monasteries** grew up round a hermit's retreat but many were founded by the head of a clan; members of the family entered the religious life and filled the various offices, as abbot, bishop, priest, teacher or ascetic. The manual work was done either by the monks or by the original tenants of the land, married men with families, whose elder sons usually received a clerical education in the monastery school. Most monasteries were self-sufficient communities providing their own food, clothing, books, tools and horses. Some monasteries seem to have been founded on sites which had pagan religious associations; others were set up by the main highways, often on the boundaries of a kingdom.

The monastic **libraries** contained copies of the Scriptures, the early Fathers, some classical authors and some history; much early Christian scholarship was preserved in Ireland after the fall of the Roman Empire. In the scriptorium the monks made copies of existing texts or wrote their own learned works, using meticulous techniques which are well described and illustrated at the Colmcille Heritage Centre (see DONEGAL GLENS).

Irish monks developed a strong tradition of **asceticism** with a threefold classification of martyrdom. Ascetics seeking to contemplate the presence of God would form small monastic communities in remote places, particularly on islands like the harsh and remote rock of Great Skellig.

ROMANISATION

Following four synods held in the first half of the 12C the Irish church lost its distinctive character and was gradually reorganised on the Roman pattern. Four provinces and 33 new dioceses were created, each with a bishop. Some monastic churches became cathedrals, others were used as parish churches.

Monastic orders from the continent were introduced. The Augustinians took over earlier monastic centres to be near the people. The Cistercians chose new and remote sites in accordance with their ascetic rule, which attracted many Irish monks; by 1272 there were 38 Cistercian houses in Ireland. The Franciscans settled in the towns in the 13C; in the 15C the Observants spread to the west and north.

The Irish church was further diminished by the Normans with the encouragement of King Henry II and Popes Adrian IV and Alexander III so as "to extend the bounds of the Roman Church". Under the Statute of Kilkenny (1366) Irishmen were forbidden to enter English-run monasteries, and English-speaking clergy were to be appointed to English-speaking parishes.

REFORMATION

In the 16C the churches in England and Ireland were declared independent of Rome; the monasteries were suppressed. Trinity College in Dublin was founded in 1591 to provide Irish priests for the established church; although Roman Catholics were admitted to degrees in 1793, membership was confined to Anglicans until 1873. The 16C reforms were only intermittently enforced in Ireland; the majority of the people remained faithful to the Roman church and many monasteries continued until suppressed by Cromwell. Early in the 17C the Plantation of Ulster with lowland Scots introduced fervent Presbyterianism.

PENAL LAWS

Under the repressive measures introduced after the Battle of the Boyne (1690), Roman Catholics were barred from the armed forces, law, commerce, from civic office or office under the crown, from land purchase; Roman Catholic estates could pass *in toto* to an eldest son if he converted to the established church but otherwise had to be divided among all the sons. No Roman

Catholic could attend school, keep a school or go abroad to school. Education was conducted in **hedge schools**, which taught Latin, Greek, arithmetic, Irish, English, history and geography; the masters, who were paid in money or kind, were respected members of the Irish community; several were poets. All Roman Catholic bishops and regular clergy were banished from Ireland, and Roman Catholic worship was forbidden. Roman Catholic priests travelled the country in disguise and said mass out of doors in remote places or in ruined monastery churches; they used sacramental vessels which could be dismantled to avoid detection.

DISSENTERS

Roman Catholics were not alone in suffering repression. The Scottish Presbyterians who had migrated to Ulster were frequently regarded with disfavour, though the Protestant Ascendancy could not afford to alienate them completely. The Toleration Act of 1719 granted them freedom of worship, but they continued to endure various disabilities and particularly resented the obligation to pay tithes to the established Church of Ireland; in the 18C many of them emigrated to America, though the majority remained. Their dissatisfaction with the existing order found expression in widespread support for the rebellion of 1798, when a large proportion of the membership of the United Irishmen was composed of Presbyterians. The English Quakers who came to Ireland during the Civil War period also faced discrimination of various kinds, though by the beginning of the 18C this had diminished. Like their counterparts elsewhere, and despite their generally humble beginnings, many Quakers later achieved prominence in commerce and industry.

DENOMINATIONAL FREEDOM

The Catholic Relief Acts of 1791 and 1793 finally allowed freedom of worship and education. In 1795 **Maynooth Seminary** was established for training Roman Catholic clergy. In 1820 Edmund Rice (1762–1844), a former pupil of a hedge school, obtained papal recognition of the **Christian Brothers** (*see KILKENNY*), an order that established many boys' schools in Ireland. In 1831 the 18C hedge schools were replaced by the National Schools. In 1869 the Church of Ireland, a member of the Anglican Communion, was disestablished. Apart from Trinity College and two short-lived 16C colleges at Maynooth and Galway, Ireland had no medieval universities. In 1845 charters were issued to incorporate three colleges in Belfast, Cork and Galway but, owing to Roman Catholic opposition, only Queen's College in Belfast thrived. The Catholic University, founded in Dublin in 1854 with Cardinal Newman as Rector, was incorporated as University College when the National University of Ireland was founded in 1908; two years later Maynooth was also recognised as a college of the National University.

PILGRIMAGES AND PATTERNS

Since the 8C, by which time Ireland was an almost entirely Christian country, the lives of the **saints** have played a major role in popular devotion and also stimulated an entire body of related legends and lore. Saints were seen to be powerful in many spheres of life on earth and in the afterlife; in many instances, they were seen as popular heroes and heroines. Some were said to have had a miraculous birth; others wielded

Pilgrims climbing Croagh Patrick

SLIDE FILE, Dublin

supernatural powers and could triumph against the enemy. Saints had healing powers and even their posessions or relics could effect a cure.

Oral tradition has been profoundly influenced by biographies of saints; the lore of saints is widespread throughout Ireland. Thousands of **holy wells**, many associated with local saints, are scattered throughout the countryside; they are said to have curative powers – of a general type or more specific – and are visited frequently, particularly on saints' days.

People still observe the feast days of local saints and the **pattern** (modern Irish *pátrún*; the word is a corruption of patron) when they make a communal visit to a holy well or other religious site under the protection of the local patron saint. In many places holy wells are associated with **rag trees**, named after the hundreds of coloured pieces of cloth attached to their branches, and used to invoke divine assistance, often of a curative kind.

Many traditional religious sites are still visited by pilgrims: Glencolumbkille on St Columba's Day (9 June); Clonmacnoise on St Kieran's Day (9 September); Croagh Patrick in July, when people climb barefoot to the summit. The most rigorous pilgrimage takes place at St Patrick's Purgatory, an island in Lough Derg (southeast of Donegal) where St Patrick spent 40 days in prayer and fasting; during the season (1 June to 15 August) pilgrims spend three days barefoot, take part in an all-night vigil and exist on one meal a day of bread and hot black tea or coffee.

Castlestrange Stone

SLIDE FILDE, Dublin

Myths and Lore

Some of the best sources for understanding the Celtic mind and imagination are the Irish myths and tales populated with colourful descriptions of gods and goddesses, and the fabulous exploits of mortal heroes and heroines. Although most of the earlier stories originated in Ireland, they were written down by Christian monks.

RELIGION

The Celts seem to have acknowledged many divinities – gods of war and hunting, goddesses of fertility, harvest and healing. Among those worshipped in Ireland were Brigit, Daghdha and Cernunnos – god of animals, plants and forests, whose emblem was a set of antlers. Different tribes each venerated its own tribal god or goddess who might reside in a special sacred well and hold the power to cure and protect people who regarded not only wells, but trees and certain springs and rivers – particularly the River Boyne – as sacred, indeed, they carved images of their gods on tree-trunks. Assemblies, at which games and races took place, were held at ancient royal or assembly sites, such as Tara and Tullaghoge. The Celts buried their dead, sometimes cremated, with offerings of food and ornaments; they believed that after death they went to join their ancestors, the gods of the Otherworld, who were thought to live in sacred mounds, now known to be prehistoric burial mounds such as at Newgrange, Tara and Rathcrogan.

FAIRYLORE

The belief in the **Otherworld** is still an important factor in Irish tradition. This "Otherworld" may exist in a fort or in a mountain, under a lake or beneath the sea. Hundreds of tales and legends associated with the fairies and their world survive, as the landscape and its placenames bear witness. In Irish the fairies are called *sí* or *na daoine maithe* – the good people, or *na daoine beaga* – the little people. The fairies are said variously to be fallen angels, the ancient gods – the Tuatha Dé

The giddy little creature depicted here is Ireland's national fairy, the leprechaun. About two feet high – when upright! – and usually of rather wizened appearance, the leprechaun is a cobbler by trade, though he is better known as the crafty guardian of a hidden crock of gold. A mischievous player of tricks on the human race, he steals into their houses at night to create havoc in kitchen and cellar.

S Allegret/MICHELIN

Danann or sometimes the community of the dead. These supernatural beings are invisible to mortals, inhabiting the earth, the air and water. The earthen tumuli – known as *rath* and *lios* – are often said to be fairy forts and sometimes fairy music can be heard to emanate from them. Many legends are told describing how the fairies "borrowed" or "stole" a mortal to assist them in some task of their own, such as nursing a fairy child or playing music at a fairy wedding. On occasions, fairies have been said to remove a mortal child, leaving one of their own in its place; when the unsuspecting parents returned from their chores, they would be shocked to discover a sick or dying child in the cradle, referred to as a "**changeling**".

BANSHEE

The Banshee *(Bean Sí)* is a solitary female spirit whose eerie cry is said to portend death. Superstition associated with

the banshee is still very strong and an excuse for the retelling of many legends, often depicting her combing her long hair. One story describes how a man found her comb and brought it home; the following night he heard wailing and knocking at his window: so, catching the comb in a pair of tongs he passed it out of the window; the comb was removed by the banshee and the tongs broken as a warning that had the man put out his hand, it would have met the same fate.

The banshee is associated with lamenting, keening and death. The keen *(caoineadh)* was performed by women at funerals and at wakes as part of the lament for the dead. Certain, usually older, women in the community came to the house where the corpse was laid out and took it in turns to perform the keen which was usually composed *ex tempore* and sung to music with a regular refrain during the days of the wake and later at the graveyard. During the wake people also told stories, smoked clay pipes, drank whiskey and played games. The clergy disapproved of many of the wake customs and of the keen.

THE MYTHOLOGICAL AND HISTORICAL CYCLES

The stories from the four great ancient Irish cycles are arguably among the finest expressions of Irish imagination and are still a source of artistic inspiration.

The **Mythological Cycle** tells of the heroes or gods who inhabited Ireland before the arrival of the Celts and contains the story of the Battle of Moytura, the Children of Lir and the Wooing of Etain.

The **Ulster Cycle** *(Rúraíocht)* recounts the deeds of the Red Branch Knights of Navan Fort; it includes the **Cattle Raid of Cooley** *(Táin Bó Cuailgne)*, an epic poem that describes how Queen Maeve of Connaught set out to capture the famous brown bull of Cooley and how Ferdia, the Connaught champion, was defeated by the Ulster champion, Cúchulain, which translates as the hound of Culann.

The **Ossianic Cycle**, also known as the **Fenian Cycle** *(Fiannaíocht)*, is set in the time of Cormac mac Airt, who is said to have reigned at Tara in the 3C, and tells about Fionn mac Cumhaill and the Fianna, whose capital was on the Hill of Allen. The Fenian tales and lore tell of the great deeds of the Fianna or Fenian warriors.

Hundreds of neolithic tombs are called Diarmuid and Gráinne's bed *(Leaba Dhiarmuid agus Ghráinne)* in the belief that these lovers from the Fenian tales slept here during their travels in Ireland.

The **Historical Cycle**, which is also known as the **Cycle of the Kings**, is probably a mixture of history and fiction. Many place-names and sites identify with characters and episodes from mythological tales.

A vast number of tales and episodes from these cycles were central to the living storytelling tradition in Ireland until very recently. In addition to their preservation in written literature, the stories were kept alive in oral form, both in Irish and in English, and formed an important part of the repertoire of the storyteller *(seanchaí)*, a person of great social importance.

Gaelige

Gaelige, Irish or Gaelic – whichever name is used – is a subtle and extremely expressive language. Although rarely used, it has had a profound influence on the way the Irish use English, which has largely replaced it. Irish is an Indo-European language, one of the Celtic group – Scots Gaelic, the extinct Manx, Welsh, Cornish and Breton – and is closest to Scots Gaelic and Manx. Its stylish alphabet, abandoned in the 1960s, can still be seen in old road signs and where its decorative qualities are exploited.

Once the natural language of the whole island, Irish has been remorselessly displaced by English, and today is spoken as a first language by only a small minority, some 60 000 in all. Nevertheless it enjoys official status as the first official language of the Republic, remains an

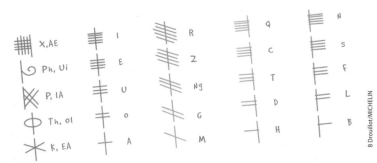

Ogham Script

B Drouillot/MICHELIN

important badge of Irish identity and has been consistently promoted by government and cultural organisations since independence; over 40 per cent of adults claim to be able to speak Irish. It has a complex grammar and a pronunciation that most outsiders find difficult to grasp; consonants may remain mute or change their sound according to their position. Even monoglot English speakers have become familiar with the use of the Irish language in official expressions; the prime minister is always referred to as the Taoiseach, the Parliament as Dáil Eireann, the Tourist Board as Bord Fáilte, the national railway as Iarnród Éireann, and all buses heading for the city centre in Dublin bear the direction An Lár.

OGHAM SCRIPT

The earliest known form of writing in the Irish language is in **Ogham script**, which survives in inscriptions on memorials to the dead dating from the 4C to 7C. The script is based on the Latin alphabet and was probably adapted by poets and wise men before the Latin alphabet became more generally familiar in Christian Ireland. The script consists of 20 characters written as groups of a maximum of five straight lines on either side of, or horizontally or diagonally through, a central line which was usually cut into the vertical edge of a standing stone – many of which are to be found in the southern districts of Ireland.

TRANSITION TO ENGLISH

The decline in the use of Irish was caused by the gradual imposition of English law and administration in the 16C and the repressive clauses of the Penal Laws (*see HISTORY*) in the 17C. Many Irish people turned to English to achieve a position in society. This trend was accelerated by the teaching of English in the National Schools, which were set up in 1831. During and after the famine (1845–49) many Irish speakers died or emigrated. In 1835 half the population was estimated to speak Irish; in 1851 one-quarter of the population was recorded as Irish-speaking; by 1911 the number had fallen to one-eighth.

GAELIC REVIVAL

The 19C saw a revival of interest in Ireland's Gaelic heritage, largely because of its close association with nationalist politics, precipitating various societies set up to promote Irish language and culture.

The **Irish Literary Society** was founded in 1892; early members included William Butler Yeats, Edward Martyn and Lady Gregory; in 1899 the society became the **Irish Literary Theatre** (later the Irish National Theatre at the Abbey Theatre) and George Moore returned to Dublin especially to take part in the new movement.

In 1893 the **Gaelic League** (*Conradh na Gaeilge*) was founded by Douglas Hyde (*see STROKESTOWN*) dedicated to the "de-Anglicisation of Ireland" through the revival of Gaelic as a spoken language and a return to Irish cultural roots. It instituted an annual festival of native culture and campaigned sucessfully for St Patrick's Day (17 March) to be a national holiday.

In 1922 the Constitution stated that Gaelic was an official language and its study was made compulsory in primary schools. The following year it became an obligatory qualification for entry into the Civil Service of the Irish Free State and the Constitution of 1937 named it as the first official language.

In 1925, in order to foster the use of Irish, the new government set up a Commission to investigate conditions in the Gaelic-speaking districts. As a result of its report two organisations – **Gaeltarra Éireann** (1935) and **Údarás na Gaeltachta** (1980) – were established to develop the resources of these areas, collectively known as the **Gaeltacht**. With a total population of over 80,000 (not all of whom are Irish speaking), these are mostly sparsely populated, remote and beautiful western parts of the country – Donegal, Mayo, Galway and Kerry – though there are pockets in the south – near Cork, in Co Waterford and Co Meath. Today, the government's Department of Arts, Heritage, Gaeltacht and the Islands is charged with their social and economic welfare and with the promotion of the Irish language. The radio station *Raidío na Gaeltachta* has broadcast in Irish since 1972, and since 1996 there has been a national television service, *Telefís na Gaeilge*. The summer schools started during the 19C Gaelic revival have become a permanent feature of the Gaeltacht, inspiring and entertaining each new generation.

Cinema

Cinema first appeared in Ireland on 20 April 1896 with a projection of a film by the Lumière brothers in Dublin and by 1909 the Volta in Dublin had been opened by James Joyce himself. Very soon the movies were playing a major role in Irish life. They continue to do so, and in recent years, government support has encouraged cinematic activity; many foreign films have been shot in Ireland and the local industry has produced some memorable works.

In 1904 JT Jameson, a newsreel cameraman, founded the Irish Animated Company (IAC); together with the American cinema, which was anxious to please the many Irish immigrants in the States, it made cinema acceptable in Ireland and launched the local industry. In 1916 and 1917 two more companies were set up – Film Company of Ireland (FCOI) and General Film Supply (GFS). It was not, however, until the founding of the Free State in 1922 that Irish cinema truly flourished in Ireland. Political events supplied the first themes such as the Easter Rising of 1916 in *Irish Destiny* (1926) by Isaac Eppel; incidents in the War of Independence feature in *Guest of the Nation* (1935) by Denis Johnston and *The Dawn* (1936) by Tom Cooper.

Perhaps the internationally best known film made in Ireland in the 1930s was the documentary *Man of Aran*. The work of an American of Irish descent, Robert O'Flaherty, it presents a compelling and beautiful picture of the harsh traditional life of the people of the Aran Islands, but is more a romantic evocation of humanity's epic struggle against the elements than an accurate record of a particular place, period, or people.

One of the earliest non-Irish films to make extensive use of Ireland as a location was Laurence Olivier's *Henry V*. Shot in 1944 as a deliberate wartime morale booster, it used the Powerscourt estate in neutral Ireland as a setting for the large-scale re-creation of the battle of Agincourt. Hundreds of local farmers hired as extras proved themselves more than adequate as stalwart cavalrymen. Plenty of other films have exploited Ireland as a background to films set elsewhere, among them Mel Gibson's *Braveheart* (1996), in which the town of Trim, its great castle and its surroundings stand in for the Scotland of rebel William Wallace. Earlier, in 1956, the little port of Youghal was transformed into New Bedford, Massachusetts, becoming the harbour town from which Captain Ahab sets out in search of the great whale in *Moby Dick*. More often, however, the cinematic role of Ireland has been as itself, or at least as a version of itself. In what is probably the most celebrated of all films with an Irish setting, *The Quiet Man* (1952), in which the country appears as a kind of mysterious, pre-industrial rural paradise, inhabited by quaint, stereotypical Irishmen and Irishwomen. The work of the great John Ford, himself of Irish descent, it revolves around the return to his native land of a boxer, memorably played by John Wayne, and features one of cinema's longest fight scenes, in which Wayne and his rival brawl their way through the village from farmyard to pub. Conflict of another kind was portrayed by David Lean in *Ryan's Daughter* (1970), in which a young married Irishwoman falls for an officer of the British garrison. Its evocation of the wild landscapes and seascapes of the west has never been excelled.

In more recent years, film-makers from home and abroad have moved beyond this backward-looking vision of the country, taking their themes from contemporary politics and social questions as well as from history and from literature. Neil Jordan's blockbusting biopic *Michael Collins* (1996), an account of the life and times of the charismatic but doomed Republican leader, was second only to *Titanic* in its success with Irish audiences, not least thanks to the performance of Liam Neeson in the title role. Neeson was only one of several Irish stars like Gabriel Byrne, Stephen Rea and Pierce Brosnan, to emerge in this period with international reputations. Jordan's earlier *The Crying Game* (1992) dealt with the relationship of an IRA gunman and a black British soldier, while his *The Butcher Boy* (1997), in which a young boy from a dysfunctional family descends into madness and murder, has been seen as a metaphor for a country still coming to terms with its troubled history. Jim Sheridan's *The Field* (1991) was equally sombre in its treatment of a farmer's refusal to let his land pass into alien hands. Previously, in 1989, Sheridan had filmed the poignant story of the cerebral palsy victim Christy Brown in *My Left Foot*, in which Daniel Day-Lewis won an Oscar for his extraordinarily moving performance. Day-Lewis also appeared in *In the Name of the Father* (1993), Sheridan's account of the failure of justice following the IRA's bombing of a Guildford pub.

The Oscar-winning *Crying Game* was based on the classic short story by Frank O'Connor, and numerous other works of literature have been translated with varying degrees of success to the screen. Among them are James Joyce's *Dubliners* (1987) by John Huston and, perhaps surprisingly, his *Ulysses* (1967) by Joseph Strick. *Angela's Ashes* (1999), was a not altogether convincing adaptation by Alan Parker of Frank McCourt's best-selling autobiographical memoir of his rain-soaked and wretched Limerick childhood. A similarly grim social story is retold in *The Magdalene Sisters* (2003), set in a women's asylum run by Roman Catholic nuns.

Roddy Doyle's sensitive and sometimes hilarious novels of contemporary Dublin's low life have inspired *The Commitments* (1991) by Alan Parker and *The Van* (1996) by Stephen Frears.

Mention should also be made of the work of the expatrite director **Ken Loach** – *Hidden Agenda* (1990), *Land and Freedom* (1995), *Carla's Song* (1997) and *Sweet Sixteen* (2002). In 2006 his film *The Wind that Shakes the Barley* was awarded the prestigious Palme d'Or at Cannes for his portrayal of the struggle for freedom from occupation: in this instance the Irish Republican Army fights against the yoke of British rule, whose escalating loss of control was epitomised in the 1920s by the Black and Tans and intense scenes of violence on both sides.

Three Irish TV series have earned great popularity in the UK – *Father Ted*, *The Ambassador* starring Pauline Collins and partly filmed in Ely Place in Dublin, and *Ballykissangel,* filmed in Avoca in the Wicklow Mountains.

THE COUNTRY TODAY

Ireland's prosperous economy owes much to forceful government intervention and enthusiastic membership of the European Union in the last decades of the 20C. The effects of new-found affluence, from a high level of car ownership to individual house-building, can be seen everywhere. Social change has been profound, but at the same time many of the characteristics of the Irish way of life, which so endear the country to its visitors, remain as pronounced as ever, and Irish identity is far from being eroded by the country's whole-hearted entry into the mainstream of contemporary international life.

Economy

CELTIC TIGER

In the 19C, Union with Britain failed for the most part to bring Ireland the benefits or indeed the problems of the Industrial Revolution. The great exception was Belfast, where the linen and food processing industries stimulated the growth of general engineering. The city joined the ranks of British industrial centres, its role confirmed in the first half of the 20C, when Harland and Wolff built liners like the *Titanic* and Short built famous flying boats. Between 1939–45, the North's economy was further stimulated by the needs of war production and by the presence of British and American military bases.

By contrast, in the years following independence, the Republic concentrated on being self-sufficient rather than on modernising its economy, which remained over-reliant on farming and on the export of agricultural products

Financial Centre, Dublin

to Britain. Some stimulation came from government initiatives like the Shannon hydro-electric scheme, but the high level of emigration of people of working age was a fundamental weakness. The world depression of the 1930s and a trade war with Britain further hindered progress. Ireland's neutral stance during 1939–45 may have made political sense, but brought none of the benefits of intensified production nor of the American aid that helped restore the postwar economies of other European countries. However from the 1950s onwards, a series of measures were taken to open up the economy and stimulate growth; tax concessions and incentives encouraged export-based, modern industries and attracted foreign investment. A further boost was given when the country joined the European Economic Community in 1972. Despite intermittent setbacks, the highly qualified and largely un-unionised workforce, together with investment in research and development, brought about astonishing economic expansion; by the 1990s, the country's growth rate was twice the European Union's average, and modern industries like chemicals, pharmaceuticals, electronics, biotechnology, and information technology constituted 75 per cent of the total industrial output. The strength of the "Celtic Tiger's" economy meant that Ireland was able to join the single European currency project as one of the few countries complying with the criteria set by the Maastricht Treaty of 1992. The outward migration which had been such a negative feature of Irish life for centuries came to an end and net immigration began, many of the migrants being

Skibbereen, Co Cork

young professionals bringing with them expertise acquired abroad.

Northern Ireland, once in advance of the South in terms of industry and employment, has suffered like the rest of the United Kingdom from the decline in traditional heavy industries. Government sponsored initiatives have not always ended in success and the halting progress of the peace process has inhibited the inflow of investment. A mitigating factor is the exceptionally high level of employment in the public sector.

Tourism has become the Republic's second largest indigenous industry. Six million overseas visitors come here every year, drawn by unspoilt landscapes, clean rivers and lakes, peace and quiet, the Celtic heritage, and the friendly welcome extended by local people. Fishing and golf remain major attractions. The once rudimentary visitor facilities are being replaced by state of the art interpretative centres while the previous somewhat carefree attitude to conservation has given way to the meticulous work of Dúchas, the government body charged with preservation of national heritage.

Modern tourism began with the spread of the railway network in the 19C. The mountain, lake and coastal scenery of the west particularly appealed to Victorian sensibilities. Today, more than half the Republic's visitors still come from Britain, about a million from North America, and many from the over-crowded conurbations of western Europe.

People

ORIGINS

The Irish are commonly thought of as being a Celtic people, but this is more of a cultural than ethnic definition. Around 8,000BC, long before the arrival of the Celts, the coastal areas and river valleys were settled by Mesolithic hunter-gatherers who had moved across the land-bridge that still connected Ireland with Scotland. The dominant Celts seem to have come in several waves during the second half of the last millennium BC, pushed to the western fringe of the continent by the expansion of the Roman Empire and pressure from Germanic tribes in Central Europe. By the time of the coming of Christianity in the 5C, the population may have amounted to a quarter of a million. Viking attacks began towards the end of the 8C but, although the Norsemen's original objective was pillage, they later settled, founding coastal towns and eventually becoming absorbed into the local population. Subsequent immigration mostly originated from Britain, the Anglo-Norman invaders and their followers being succeeded in the 16C and 17C by a planned influx of settlers and colonists. By the beginning of the 18C, perhaps a quarter of the population of just over two million was of English, Welsh and Scottish origin. Other groups, though far less numerous, added their distinctive flavour; Huguenots in the late 17C, Jews mostly in the late 19C and early 20C. Before the last decades of the 20C, the backwardness of the economy meant that immigration from non-European countries remained statistically insignificant.

DISTRIBUTION AND STRUCTURE

The country has a population of around 5.7 million, of whom 1.7 million or so live in Northern Ireland and 4 million in the Republic. This represents a substantial increase over the low point of the early 20C of about 4.5 million, the result of a falling birthrate and continuing emigration. The size of the current population is largely due to net inward migration, but it is still well short of the total of over 8 million in the period immediately preceding the Famine.

Population density compared with other western European countries is low – 52 people per sq km – and a large proportion of the population still lives in small towns or the countryside. Villages are relatively few and the isolated family farm is the most typical form of rural settlement; many places that elsewhere in Europe would be classified as villages with a total population of perhaps a few hundred, have a full range of urban functions such as a market, shops, pubs, and professional offices.

Recent rural building has confirmed the scattered nature of settlement, with new farmhouses and homes standing proudly in the middle of fields and a ribbon development of bungalows along the roads.

The larger towns are all on the coast. Greater Dublin has a disproportionate number of inhabitants, with 1,122,600 in total; Greater Belfast has some 277,391. No other regional centre in the Republic approaches the capital in population size; Cork has around 180 000 inhabitants, while the other leading cities have

under 100 000. In the Republic, birth rates have fallen recently, but the population is relatively young, with more than 40 per cent under the age of 25, and 24 per cent under the age of 15.

RELIGIOUS AFFILIATION AND MINORITIES

In recent years, the power and authority of the Roman Catholic Church may have been sapped by recurrent scandals, but the Republic of Ireland is still a demonstrably Catholic country, with 91 per cent of the population declaring their adherence to the Roman Catholic Church. Attendance at Mass is high, though no longer universal, and much lower in inner city districts of Dublin than in rural areas. The Church's teachings on matters such as abortion continue to command widespread respect; attempts to liberalise restrictions on termination of pregnancy have been defeated when put to referendum. Protestants, who once formed a quarter of the total population, and almost 50 per cent of the inhabitants of Dublin, have declined in number, either through emigration or intermarriage. Today they number around 3 per cent of the Republic's population, most of them members of the Church of Ireland.

The strength of religious observance is paralleled in Northern Ireland, whose majority Protestant population is split between Presbyterians, Methodists, members of the Church of Ireland and of various minor denominations. Roman Catholics form about one third of the Northern population, a proportion that is steadily increasing.

Ethnically indistinguishable from their fellow-citizens, Travellers are perhaps the most visible minority in southern Ireland. Previously known by the now demeaning name of "tinkers", they move their lorries and caravans from one roadside site to another and earn a living mostly from scrap-metal dealing. There are small numbers of Chinese and other Asians in both North and South. The Republic, especially its remoter western areas, has long attracted individuals from other European countries, particularly Germany.

Leisure

MUSIC

Music plays a major role in Irish life; not only through the sessions of traditional music played in the bars in the evenings all over the country but also the dancing for which many of the tunes were written (ℓ see WHAT TO SEE AND DO).

SPORTS

Most forms of sport are played enthusiastically in Ireland, none more so than those that are uniquely Irish; **hurling** *(iománaíocht)* and **Gaelic football** *(peil),* These, together with **handball** *(liathróid láimhe)* and rounders, are administered by the **Gaelic Athletic Association** *(Cumann Lúthchleas Gael),* a largely rural movement, founded in 1884 in Thurles. The national 80,000 spectator GAA stadium – Croke Park, Dublin – is named after the Association's first patron, Archbishop Croke (1824–1902). The high point of the Gaelic sporting year comes in September, when both the hurling and football national finals are held at Croke Park. The history of the Association and the exploits of the hurling and football champions are excellently illustrated in the GAA Museums at Croke Park and in Thurles.

Hurling is a fast-moving and high-scoring game of great antiquity, played by two teams of fifteen using long curved hurley *(camán)* sticks to hit the cork and leather ball into or over the rugby-style goal. Allowing the ball to be handled under certain circumstances increases the excitement of the game, which can seem violent and chaotic to the non-initiated. *Camogie* is a version of hurling adapted for women participants, with a shorter playing time, teams of 12, and a smaller pitch.

Gaelic football is played with a spherical ball, uses the same pitch as hurling and has similar rules; neither game is played outside Ireland to any extent, but Australian Rules football owes much to its Gaelic ancestor.

Hurling

SLIDE FILE, Dublin

HORSE RACING

The horse plays a special role in Irish life and the great Horse Fairs still figure in the Irish calendar. Breeding and racing horses have deep roots in Irish culture; the earliest horse races were part of pre-Christian festivals. Swimming races, which ceased only recently, also had Celtic origins, in the ritual of immersion. The focal point of Ireland's breeding, racing and training is at the Curragh in Co Kildare.

There are about 28 race courses in Ireland. At Laytown Strand, south of Drogheda, the times of races are dictated by the tide and horses are often exercised on the seashore. The first recorded prize is a plate donated in 1640 by the Trustees of the Duke of Leinster. In 1684 King James II presented the King's Plate at Down Royal "to encourage the sport of horse racing". The first steeplechase, a race over obstacles invented by Lord Doneraile, took place in 1752 from Buttevant Church to St Leger Church near Doneraile (4.5mi/7km). In the past, men challenged one another to pounding matches, in which the participants, accompanied by their grooms, had to follow the leader over any selected obstacle or admit defeat.

BARS AND PUBS

More varied and more interesting than its derivatives, which have been such a marketing success world-wide, the Irish pub or bar remains the centre of much social life, particularly in the countryside and in small towns, where some still double as general stores. Big-city pubs in both Belfast and Dublin can be places of almost Baroque splendour, redolent with literary or political associations. Drinking and conversation remain the patrons' principal preoccupations, but more and more pubs serve good food and very few remain an exclusively male preserve. Strangers seeking company are unlikely to remain lonely for long, and the pub is the best place to enjoy fun and good talk, the famous *craic*, as well as music, traditional or contemporary.

Irish Diaspora

Forty million people of Irish descent live in the USA, 5 million in Canada, 5 million in Australia and innumerable millions in Great Britain. Estimates suggest that over 60 million people in the world are of Irish origin. The influence of Irish people worldwide is immeasurable in comparison to the country's size.

The imposition of the Anglican Reformation in the reign of Elizabeth I caused many to leave Munster for Spain and Portugal. The conquest of 1603 caused more departures to Spain and Brittany. Cromwell transported whole regiments, possibly 34 000 men, to Spain and Portugal, while many civilians were shipped to the West Indies, where they could be sold as slaves. The Treaty of Limerick in 1691 was followed by the flight of the so-called *Wild Geese*, military men who, together with their wives and children, emigrated to France, where they served in the French army until 1697; some of them moved on to Spain, where three Irish regiments were formed. The most famous name among the merchants who settled on the western coast of Europe is that of Richard Hennessy, from Cork, who started the Cognac company.

The first transatlantic emigrants were mostly Presbyterians, the Ulster-Scots (known in the USA as Scots-Irish or Scotch-Irish), descendants of lowland Scots who had settled in Ulster in the 17C. Whole families emigrated early in the 18C owing to religious strictures and rising rents. The Roman Catholic Irish tended to emigrate as single young adults, both men and women.

The Scotch-Irish have enjoyed great influence in America despite their limited numbers, particularly in the War of Independence and in education. The heartland of Ulster settlement was in the Appalachian back country; the name hillbilly derives from King William III. Many of the settlers were involved in pushing the frontier westwards and building the American railways. Over a quarter of the Presidents of the USA are descended from Scotch-Irish settlers. This Irish-American connection is traced in detail at the Ulster-American Folk Park (&see SPERRIN MOUNTAINS) and Andrew Jackson Centre (&see CARRICKFERGUS), as well as several other family homesteads. Allied military leaders in the Second World War who were of Ulster stock include Alanbrooke, Alexander, Auchinleck, Dill and Montgomery.

Following the Napoleonic Wars emigration recommenced and during the next 25 years over a million Irish men and women emigrated to Great Britain and the USA. Emigration reached its peak during the Great Famine when Ireland lost 4 million people through death and emigration. During the worst years about 1 million fled and another 2.5 million emigrated in the following decade. The great wave of 19C emigrants was largely composed of Roman Catholics from Donegal, Connaught, Munster and Leinster; counties that until then had not seen much emigration. Many landed first in Canada then later crossed the frontier into the USA to escape from British rule. Their descendants include John Fitzgerald Kennedy, Ronald Reagan and William Jefferson Clinton.

Ulster-Scots – Scotch-Irish

Theodore Roosevelt's mother, speaking of her family who came from Co Antrim, described them as:

"A grim, stern people, strong and simple, powerful for good and evil, swayed by gusts of stormy passion, the love of freedom rooted in their very hearts' core… relentless, revengeful, suspicious, knowing neither ruth nor pity; they were also upright, resolute and fearless, loyal to their friends and devoted to their country".

Emigrant Ship by E Hayes

R. Holzbachova, Ph. Benet/MICHELIN – National Gallery of Ireland, Dublin

The numbers who emigrated to Australia and New Zealand were smaller and included some who were transported to the penal colonies.

The flow of immigrants into Great Britain has waxed and waned since the Irish established colonies in Wales and Scotland in the 5C. Many, particularly those who left Ireland during the Famine in the hope of reaching America but were too weak or penniless to continue, settled in Liverpool and Glasgow. London has a flourishing Irish community, particularly north of the river. Margaret Thatcher, ex-Prime Minister of the UK (1978–91), is descended from Catherine Sullivan, who emigrated in 1811 from Kenmare and became a washerwoman in England.

Many Irishmen who went to work in Britain on the canals or in agriculture and the building trade In the 18C and 19C, returned home for the winter. Those who went to America or Australasia seldom returned to the mother country. Despite their rural origins, most Irish emigrants settled in the big cities rather than on the land of their adopted countries.

Irish emigrants in the late 20C and early 21C are highly qualified young men and women seeking employment not only in English-speaking countries like the UK and the USA, but also throughout the European Union. In recent years emigration has declined and immigration has increased. In 1997 there was a net inflow of 15 000 people, the highest such figure since the 1970s. Many of these people are former emigrants, returning to a higher standard of living and a culturally revitalised society.

TRACING ANCESTORS

Many visitors, particularly from Australia, New Zealand and the USA, hope to trace their ancestors who left Ireland and settled abroad. This task is more difficult than it might have been, due to the destruction during the Civil War of the national archives, whose records went back to 1174. In the latter years of the 20C a great project was set in motion to collect all the information available from parish records, tombstones and other sources throughout Ireland. Access to these computer records and assistance in tracing ancestors can be obtained through the many regional Genealogical Centres that are listed in the Address Books of the appropriate chapters in the *Discovering Ireland* sections. If you have no idea where in Ireland your ancestors came from, it is best to consult one of the national organisations in Dublin (*see Planning Your Trip*). A good way of exchanging news or meeting long-lost relatives, is to attend one of the annual clan gatherings, held on ancestral sites by some of the 243 Irish clans.

Food and Drink

There are two Irish culinary traditions: the elaborate meals served in town and country mansions, and the simple dishes of earlier centuries.

IRISH CUISINE

The **gourmet festival** of Kinsale celebrates Irish cuisine, based on first-class local produce, from the renowned Dublin Bay prawn and succulent Galway oyster to the humble potato.

Breakfast

The traditional **Irish Fry**, known in the north as an "Ulster Fry", consists of fried egg, sausage, bacon, black pudding, potato farls, mushrooms, tomatoes and sometimes soda bread. The Irish, English, Scottish and Welsh each have their own version of the 'fry-up', though the Scottish and Welsh fry ups are the most unique, with the addition of unusual specialities, such as haggis or laverbread (fried seaweed and oatmeal patties).

Fish and Meat

The king of the freshwater fish is the **salmon**, wild or farmed; as a main dish it is usually poached or grilled. Irish smoked salmon is traditionally cured with oak wood. The other most frequently served freshwater fish is **trout**, farmed or wild. **Shellfish**, such as crab, lobster, scallops, mussels and Dublin Bay prawns (also known as langoustines or scampi) are usually available near the coast, particularly in the southwest.

The Irish fishing grounds produce Dover sole (known locally as Black sole), lemon sole, plaice, monkfish, turbot, brill, John Dory, cod, hake, haddock, mackerel and herring.

Prime **beef** is raised on the lush pastures in the east and south of Ireland; lamb comes from the uplands. **Pork** is presented in many ways: as joints and chops; as ham or bacon; as pigs' trotters (*crúibíní*), known in English as crubeens; in white puddings; in black puddings (*drisheen*) flavoured with tansy and eaten for breakfast. The most popular game is rabbit but hare and pheasant are also served.

Traditional Dishes

There is no official recipe for **Irish stew**, which consists of neck of mutton layered in a pot with potatoes, onions and herbs. **Colcannon** is a Harvest or Hallowe'en dish of mashed potatoes, onions, parsnips and white cabbage, mixed with butter and cream. **Champ** is a simpler dish of potatoes mashed with butter, to which are added chopped chives or other green vegetables such as parsley, spring onions (scallions), chopped shallots, nettles, peas, cabbage or even carrots (cooked in milk that is added to the purée). Nettles are also made into soup. To make **coddle**, a forehock of bacon, pork sausages, potatoes and onions are stewed in layers. Collar and cabbage is composed of a collar of bacon, which has

SLIDE FILE, Dublin

Table laid for a Farmhouse Tea

Whiskey or Whisky

The origins of Irish whiskey (usually but not always spelled with an "e") are lost in the mists of time, but it was being distilled and drunk throughout Ireland by the 16C and Elizabeth I seems to have had a taste for it. Illicit whiskey *(poteen)* appeared in the 17C when the government introduced a tax on distilling (1661) and set up a department of Excisemen (Gaugers) to police the distilleries. By the end of the 17C, the substance was being exported all over the British Empire. Exports to the USA dwindled with prohibition in the 1920s and the British Empire market was closed off by the War of Independence. In 1966 the few surviving distilleries joined to form the Irish Distillers Company and founded a new distillery in Midleton; in the early 1970s they took over Bushmills but were taken over by Pernod-Ricard in 1989.

Despite the popularity of blended whisky from Scotland, Irish distillers have preferred to maintain the lightness and fuller flavour of their traditional product, achieved by **Triple Distillation.** The grain, including the husks, is milled to produce "grist" which is mixed with hot water in a large vessel (mash tun) to release the sugars; the liquid is then drawn off. This process is repeated twice and the liquid from the first and second mashing (wort) is pumped into vessels called washbacks; yeast is added, which reacts with the sugars to produce a light brown liquid. When fermentation is complete the liquid is distilled three times. The spirit is matured in old sherry or Bourbon casks and then blended (vatted) for two or three days.

been boiled, coated in breadcrumbs and brown sugar, baked, then served with cabbage cooked in the bacon stock. Various sorts of **seaweed**, a highly nutritious source of vitamins and minerals, were traditionally used to thicken soups and stews. **Carrageen** is still used to make a dessert with a delicate flavour. **Dulse** is made into a sweet.

Dairy Products

Irish cookery makes liberal use of butter and cream. Ice-cream is particularly popular as a dessert. In recent years many hand-made **cheeses** have appeared on the market, such as: **Cashel Blue** (a soft, creamy, blue-veined cheese made from cow's milk in Tipperary; milder than Stilton), **Cooleeny** (a Camembert-type cheese from Thurles in Co Tipperary), **Milleens** (a distinctive spicy cheese from West Cork) and **Gubbeen** (a soft surface-ripening cheese from Skull in Co Cork).

Bread

A wide variety of breads and cakes is baked for breakfast and tea. The best-known is **soda bread**, made of white or brown flour and buttermilk. **Barm**

Brack is a rich fruit cake made with yeast (*báirín breac* – speckled cake).

BEVERAGES

Stout made by **Guinness** or Murphys is the traditional thirst-quencher in Ireland, but the drinking of ales (bitter) and lagers is not uncommon. Black Velvet is a mixture of stout and champagne.

Although there are now only three **whiskey** distilleries in Ireland – Bushmills in Co Antrim, which produces the only malt, and Midleton in Co Cork, both owned by the same company, and Cooley in Dundalk – there are many different brands of whiskey. Their distinctive flavours arise from subtle variations in the production process.

The Flag is a patriotic drink that mixes crème de menthe, tequila and Southern Comfort—the green, white and orange of the Republican tricolor.

Irish Coffee, a delicious creation, consists of a measure of whiskey, brown sugar and very hot black coffee mixed in a heated glass and topped with a layer of fresh cream.

Custom House, Dublin
SLIDE FILE, Dublin

ABBEYLEIX

POPULATION 1 299

At the height of the Anglo-Irish Ascendancy in the mid-18C, Viscount de Vesci followed the contemporary trend for demolishing tenant cottages, re-housing the residents in a carefully planned new settlement at the gates of his great mansion. Scarcely changed since those days, Abbeyleix (Mainistir Laoise) is one of the best examples of this type of aristocratic estate development, preserved by its designation as a Heritage Town. However, its origins are much older, since it occupies the site of a late 12C Cistercian abbey built on an earlier monastery.

- **Information:** Portlaoise. ☎ 057 86 64132.
- ▶ **Orient Yourself:** Abbeyleix lies on N8, 61mi/98km SW of Dublin towards Cork.
- **Don't Miss:** an excursion to Emo Court.
- **Also See:** ATHY, CASHEL, KILDARE, KILKENNY, ROSCREA, TULLAMORE.

Visit

Abbeyleix Heritage House

♿⚘*Open Mar–Sept, Mon–Fri, 9am–5pm, (May–Sept, Sat–Sun, 1pm–5pm).* €3. ☒ 🅿 ☎057 873 1653. www.heritagehouse museum.com.

The exhibition in the old school traces the history of Abbeyleix, its industries and role in the evolution of the region. In the walled garden of the former convent, the **Abbey Sense Garden** has been designed and planted to appeal to touch, taste, smell, sound and sight.

Excursions

Emo Court★★

15mi/24km NNE of Abbeyleix by N 8, M 7 and R 422. (Dúchas) Gardens: ⚘*Open daylight hours. House: Easter–Oct, 10am–6pm; last tour at 5pm.* ⚘*Closed 25–26 Dec. House* €2.90. ☒ *(Easter–Oct).* 🅿. ☎057 862 6573. www.heritage ireland.ie/en.

This splendid domed Classical mansion surrounded by extensive gardens, was designed by **James Gandon** in 1792. After many years of use as a Jesuit seminary, the rotunda and superb stucco work has been restored and re-furnished including a collection of Wedgwood pottery.

A magnificent avenue of Wellingtonias, the first in Ireland, links the house to the Dublin Road; azaleas, rhododendrons and Japanese maples feature in the Clucker Garden; statues of the Seasons and a ring garden adorn the lawns; a Grapery planted with trees and shrubs descends to the lakeside walk.

Rock of Dunamase★

15mi/24km NE of Abbeyleix by R 245, R 247 and N 80 NW.

The rock rising straight from the plain is crowned by the extensive ruins of the O'More clan fortress, destroyed by Cromwell's army in the mid 17C. It offers excellent **views**★ from the summit (200ft/60m high).

Stradbally

13mi/21km NE of Abbeyleix by R 245, R 247 and N 80 SE.

In the Stradbally Market Place stands an unusual pagoda-like structure with a red roof. It commemorates Dr William Perceval, a local man who died in 1899 after 54 years of local practice.

Address Book

ADDRESS BOOK

Morrissey's Bar – Many travellers make a point of stopping off at Morrissey's Bar, a wonderful combination of grocer's shop and pub, which, like the town itself, seems little altered since it was built.

Grantstown Lake – *8mi/13km W by R 433* – Woodland walks beside a lake (fishing).

Stradbally Steam Engine Rally

The **Steam Museum**★ (⌖⏰*call museum for opening hours,* ⊜€5, *railway Bank Holiday Sun–Mon, 2.30pm–5pm; steam rally August Bank Holiday weekend;* ☎057 86 41878/086 38 90184; www.irishsteam. ie) *displays 1930s steam-powered farm machinery. Some are brought out for the annual rally at Stradbally Hall. A narrow-gauge steam railway (1mi/1.6km) runs through the woods.*

Timahoe

9mi/15km NE of Abbeyleix by R 430 east and a minor road N.
The fine **Round Tower**★ (96ft/29m high) leaning 2ft/0.6m from the verti-cal, was probably built in the 12C; it has a lovely Romanesque double doorway.
Richard Nixon, President of the USA (1969–74), whose ancestors came from the village, visited Timahoe in 1970.

Heywood Gardens, Ballinakill

(Dúchas) 3.5mi/6km SE of Abbeyleix by R 432. ⌖⏰*Open 8.30am–dusk.* ☎056 7721450. www.heritageireland.ie/en.
The gardens were completed in 1912, by **Edwin Lutyens** (1869–1944) and **Gertrude Jekyll** (1843–1932), with ter-races, clipped yew hedges, an Italianate sunken garden, ponds, and walks with fine prospects of distant towers.

ADARE★

POPULATION 1 042

This tiny town in fertile wooded countryside at the tidal limit of the River Maigue is often described as the prettiest village in Ireland, with its unusual rows of pretty, colour-washed cottages with overhanging thatched roofs built in the mid-19C by the local landowner, the Earl of Dunraven, who succeeded in making his corner of west Limerick resemble something from the English shires. Adare *(Átha Dara)* is a designated Heritage Town.

- **Information:** Adare Heritage Centre. ☎061 396 255.
- **Organising Your Time:** Allow a day to see the town and environs.
- ▶ **Orient Yourself:** Adare is 10mi/17km SW of Limerick on the N 21 Tralee road.
- **Also See:** LIMERICK, TRALEE.

Town

There is more to Adare than picturesque thatched cottages: the **heritage centre** provides a historical survey of Norman invaders, medieval abbeys and the influential Dunraven family. The square tower and the south wall of the present RC **Church of the Most Holy Trinity** on Main Street were part of a monastery, the only house in Ireland of the **Trinitarian Order**, constructed about 1230 by Maurice Fitzgerald, 2nd Baron of Offaly. The 50 monks were put to death in 1539 at the Dissolution of the Monasteries. The ruins were restored by the 1st Earl of Dunraven and enlarged in 1852. The **dovecot** at the rear (restored) dates from the 14C.

Adare's Anglican **Parish Church**★ is fashioned from the nave and part of the choir of an Augustinian priory founded in 1315. The cloisters were converted into a mausoleum for the family of Quin, the Earls of Dunraven. The exuberantly neo-Gothic **Adare Manor** (1832) by the River Maigue, now a hotel, was designed in part by James Pain and **Augustus Welby Pugin**.

Adare Friary★
Access via Adare Golf Course; ask at the Club House.
The evocative riverside ruins marked by **Kilmallock Gate** are those of the Franciscan friary founded by the Earl of Kildare in 1464, and extended in 15–16C.

Desmond Castle (Co Limerick)
Visit by guided tour, Jun–mid-Sept by appointment. ☎061 396 6666.
The strategic importance of **Desmond Castle** (also known as Adare Castle) had already dwindled by the time much of it was demolished by Cromwell's forces. A large square tower stands in the inner ward of the early 14C stronghold surrounded by a moat. The upper storey of the building in the southwest corner of the outer ward was the **great hall**. Nearby are the ruins of **St Nicholas Church** (11C) and the **Desmond Chapel** (14C).

Address Book

⌖For coin ranges, see the Legend on the cover flap.

WHERE TO STAY

⌂**Berkeley Lodge** – Station Road. 6rm. ☎061 396 857. www.adare.org. Simple, clean accommodation competitively priced and centrally located. True 'home from home' feeling. Bedrooms at the rear of the house are quieter.

⌂–⌂**Carrabawn Guesthouse** – Killarney Road, 0.5mi SW on N 21. 8rm. ☎061 396 067. www.carrabawnhouse adare.com. A welcoming and immaculately kept guesthouse, ten minutes walk from the town centre.

⌂⌂⌂⌂**Adare Manor** – Adare. 113rm, 35 suites, 23 townhouses. ☎061 396 566. www.adaremanor.com ✗. Imposing and impressive Gothic manor sympathetically extended with 800 acres/323ha park: fishing, golf (host to the Irish Open in 2008), luxury spa and leisure facilities. Classic menu; bedrooms in the main house have the most character.

SHOPPING
Irish Dresden – Dromcollogher. 20mi/32km SW of Adare by R 515 via Ballingarry and Kilmeedy. Delicate porcelain figures representing musicians and dancers, ladies in flounced skirts, angels and figures for the Christmas crib, birds and animals. The range is cast from original master moulds from Mueller Volkestedt in Germany brought to Ireland after the original factory was bombed in WWII, with the addition of new ones of Irish inspiration. *Showroom: open Mon–Fri, 9am–1pm and 2pm–5pm. Factory: Visit by guided tour only (20min), by appointment.* ☎063 83236

TRACING ANCESTORS
The **Irish Palatine Heritage Centre** at Rathkeale provides a **genealogical service**.

R Holzbachova, Ph Benet/MICHELIN

Thatched Cottages, Adare

Excursions

Rathkeale

7.5mi/13km W of Adare by N 21.
The Norman tower of **Castle Matrix**★ was built in 1440 by the 7th Earl of Desmond. The Great Hall houses a fine **library** and objets d'art. The castle also houses an **international arts centre** and the **Heraldry Society of Ireland**. It was at Castle Matrix that the poet Edmund Spenser, and Walter Raleigh met for the first time in 1580 and began a lifelong friendship. &⊙*Open by appointment.* ☎*069 64284.*
The **Irish Palatine Heritage Centre**★ (& ⊙ *open mid-May–mid-Sept, Tue –Sat 2pm–5pm (Sun and Bank Hol Mon, Jul–mid-Sept);* ☞€5; *Genealogy service;* 🖵 🅿; ☎*069 63511; www.irishpalatines. org*) presents photographs, documents, articles and artefacts relating to the German Protestant settlers, their innovative farming methods, their impact on Methodism and their dispersion throughout the English-speaking world.

Newcastle West★

16mi/26km W of Adare by N 21.
This thriving market town, known for its spring water, takes its name from the **castle** that belonged to the **Knights Templar** before passing to the **Earls of Desmond**. The banqueting hall, now known as **Desmond Hall**, with an oak minstrel's gallery (restored) and a hooded fireplace (reconstruction),

stands over a 13C vaulted stone chamber, lit by ecclesiastical lancet windows. The remains of the **castle** *(Halla Mór; Dúchas;* & ⊙ *open mid-Jun–mid-Sept, 10am–6pm (5.15pm last tour);* ☎*069 77408; www.heritageireland.ie/en)* include the adjoining Great Hall.

Askeaton

13mi/20km NW of Adare by N 21 and R 518.
On a small island in the River Deel stand the ruins of **Askeaton Castle**, probably founded by William de Burgo c 1199, with tower and walls (15C) largely intact; the banqueting hall (1440–59) erected by the 7th Earl of Desmond, was one of the largest of its kind in Ireland. North of the town by the river, are the ruins of **Askeaton Franciscan Friary**, a 15C foundation; note the depiction of **St Francis** in the northeast corner of the cloisters.

Foynes

21mi/34km W of Adare by N 21, R 518 and N 69.
Before and during the Second World War the small seaport in the Shannon Estuary was the operational base for the flying boats which pioneered transatlantic air travel. The old terminal building now houses the **Flying Boat Museum** (& ⊙ *open Mar–Sept, 10am–6pm; Oct– Dec, 10am–4pm; Last admission one hour before closing;* ☞€8; 🖵 🅿; ☎*069 65416; www.flyingboatmuseum.com)* dis-

Irish Palatines

In 1709, following two invasions, a bitter winter and religious oppression, many German Protestants left the Rhineland area known as the Palatinate, and travelled to England where the government promised to subsidise their ongoing journey to Carolina, USA. However, funds ran out and many were stranded in London. The Dublin government offered to take the 821 families, and landlords were offered subsidies to accept them. The majority settled on the estate of Lord Southwell in Rathkeale, where their names – Bovenizer, Corneille, Delmege, Miller, Rynard, Piper, Sparling, Stark, Switzer, Teskey – sounded a foreign note. These industrious people introduced new farming practices, and being pious people, mostly **Lutherans** or **Calvinists**, they responded enthusiastically to the preaching of **John Wesley**, who visited them on several occasions from 1756 onwards.

playing models, photographs, log books and technical equipment relating to the precursor of Shannon Airport.

Glin Castle Hotel★

29mi/47km W of Adare by N 21, R 518 and N 69. ☎*068 34173. www.glincastle.com.* The Knights of Glin have lived close to the village of **Glin** for 700 years. Their original stronghold was destroyed by Queen Elizabeth's forces in 1600, so a replacement was built (1780–85) and gothicized around 1820. The **interior** is outstanding, with superb stuccowork, excellent examples of Georgian mahogany furniture, family portraits and other paintings, and a very unusual flying **staircase** with a Venetian window overlooking the formal gardens.

ARAN ISLANDS★

POPULATION 2 000

Keeping watch over the mouth of Galway Bay are the islands of Inishmore, Inishmaan and Inisheer, great slabs of limestone linked geologically to the Burren on the mainland. People have inhabited these lonely isles since ancient times, using the limestone to build great prehistoric forts like Dún Aonghasa and Dún Conor as well as the close-knit network of drystone walls bounding tiny, flower-rich fields. Tellingly evoked in the writings of J M Synge and Robert Flaherty's classic semi-documentary film *Man of Aran*, the islanders' traditional, extremely harsh way of life lasted until relatively recently. The islands remain a stronghold of the Gaelic language.

- **Information:** Kilronan, Inishmore. ☎099 61263.
- **Orient Yourself:** The three Aran Islands extend in an oblique line across the mouth of Galway Bay. The smallest, Inisheer is the closest (5mi/8km) to the mainland; the middle island is the slightly larger Inishmaan (6sq mi/7.77sq km; the largest, Inishmore, lies about7mi/11.3km from the coast of Connemara.
- **Don't Miss:** An excursion to see the stone cliff-top fort Dún Aonghasa.
- **Also See:** THE BURREN, CONNEMARA, GALWAY.

A Bit of History

The Aran Islands rise in natural terraces from a flat sandy shore facing Galway Bay to high cliffs (300ft/91m) confronting the Atlantic. They get less rainfall than the mainland, and are never touched by frost. Despite the lack of soil, wild flowers thrive but trees are rare: the traditional crops of rye and potatoes were grown on artificial soil created laboriously over the years by layering sand and seaweed on the bare rock. Traditionally, the white-washed cottages were thatched with straw tied down against the wind. Fishing and farming were the main activities; cows would graze the summer pastures in Connemara and winter on Aran, unlike the ponies which wintered in Connemara and worked on Aran in summer months. Illicit whiskey and peat were imported by boat from Connemara in exchange for potatoes and limestone.

The Aran Islands have been inhabited for centuries: the ruins of great stone forts date from prehistoric times, while in the early and medieval Christian period (5C–16C), the Aran monasteries prospered as centres of culture. Today, tourism is the dominant industry, ensuring the survival of traditional crafts, notably the distinctive cream-coloured **Aran knitwear** designed using patterns of stitches that evoke elements in nature and an ancient way of life that include the women spinning the wool and men knitting using goose quill needles.

Inishmore (Arainn)

The largest island (9mi/14.5km x 2.5mi/4km) is served by one road running north from the airstrip along the shore of Killeany Bay *(Cuan Chill Éinne)*, to **Kilronan** *(Cill Rónáin)* and then west to the remote hamlet of Bun Gabhla overlooking **Brannock Island** *(Oileán Dá Bhranóg)* and the lighthouse. The old tracks and walls (7 000mi/11 265km) run from northeast to southwest following natural rifts and man-made ruts created by the carting of seaweed from the shore to field. At the roadside stand square pillars topped with crosses erected in memory of islanders who died abroad or at sea. The Atlantic waves constantly batter the grim, southwestern cliffs and send spectacular spurts of spray through the "puffing-holes" at the island's eastern extremity. On the northwestern shore by Port Chorrúch, lives a colony of seals.

Address Book

GETTING THERE

There are flights to all three islands from Connemara Regional Airport at Inverin *(20mi/32km W of Galway by R 336)*; they can also be reached by ferry from Rossaveal *(23mi/37km west of Galway*, and from Doolin in the Burren (Inisheer only).

Aran Islands Air Service – *Operates regular flights: up to 8 per day in summer; 3 in winter (9min). €45 Return.* ☎*091 593 034 (Aer Arann). www.aerarannislands.ie*

Rossaveal – Aran Islands Ferry – *Operates 2–5 sailings per day. €25 Return. Online booking service; bus service from Galway City Centre (Return €6).* ☎*091 568 903. www.aranisland ferries.com*

Rossaveal – Aran Direct – *Operates (35min) from Rossaveal 2 to 3 sailings per day. Return €25. Bus from Galway City Centre departs 1hr 15min before ferry sailing.* ☎*091 566 535, (Aran Direct). www.aran direct.com*

Doolin (Co Clare) – Aran Islands Ferry – *Operates (weather permitting) Apr–Oct: to Inishmore (45min), 3 times daily; to Inisheer (20min), up to 5 times daily. See website for details. Return €40.* ☎*065 707 4455, 707 4189 (Doolin Ferry Co). www.doolinferries.com*

GETTING AROUND

The best way to explore **Inishmore** is on foot or by hired bicycle. Regular but infrequent bus service operate along the island's main road, and minibus operators meet planes and ferries, offering tours of the principal sights. As well as the Tourist Information Centre by the harbour in Kilronan, the Aran Heritage Centre and the visitor centre below Dún Aonghasa are useful sources of information. Buy the meticulously crafted *Map of the Aran Islands*, by Tim Robinson, to get to know the landscape in detail.

SHOPPING

Aran Sweater Market, *Kilronan* – Wide range of the famous sweaters with their distinctive family stitches and patterns. ☎*064 39756. www.clanarans.com*

Bord Fáilte, Dublin

Dún Aonghasa

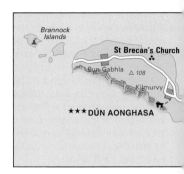

Kilronan

The Aran Heritage Centre, **Ionad Arann** (🕐*open Apr, May, Sept, Oct 11am–5pm; Jun–Aug 10am–7pm; ☎099 61355; www. visitarandislands.com)*, introduces the landscape, monuments, traditions and culture of the islands. Note the currach, the seemingly frail craft of hide or canvas stretched over a frame of laths and powered by blade-less oars.

Dún Aonghasa★★★

4.5mi/7.2km W of Kilronan; 10min on foot from Kilmurvy (Cill Mhuirbhigh) Visitor Centre (Dúchas). 🕐*Open Mar–Oct 10am–6pm, Nov–Feb 10am–4pm.* 🎟€2.10 *(no charge after hours).* 💬☎099 61008. www.heritageireland.ie/en.

This great drystone fort in a spectacular setting is one of the finest prehistoric monuments in Europe, with three lines of defence. Between the outer and the middle wall, stone stakes spike the ground, set at an angle to impede attack. A square tunnel in the thickness of the wall leads into the inner compound. The inner wall, which has steps up to wall walks, follows a semicircle, beginning and ending on the cliff edge.

St Kieran's Church (Teampall Chiaráin)

1mi/1.7km NW of Kilronan.

Half way down the slope to the shore stands a small ruined church dedicated to **St Kieran of Clonmacnoise**, home to four cross-inscribed stones and St Kieran's Well.

Monastic Sites

5.5mi/8.8km NW of Kilronan.

Tucked away in a hollow on the north coast overlooking a small bay is an ancient monastic site, also known as Na Seacht d'Teampall, the Seven Churches. In fact, only two ruins are churches: the larger, **St Brecan's Church (Teampall Bhreacáin)**, marks the grave of St Brecan *(opposite west door)*. The other structures are thought to be outbuildings or pilgrim hostels. In the southeast corner of the graveyard is a stone inscribed to seven Roman saints.

Dún Dúchatair★

2mi/3km SW of Kilronan.

The Black Fort is a splendid example of a promontory fort, with a massive curving

---

Words and Images

The Gaelic-speaking islanders are talented music-makers and story-tellers, skills encouraged by the austere life on Aran as portrayed by Liam O'Flaherty (1896–1984) in *Thy Neighbour's Wife* (1924). Local stories feature in JM Synge's play *Riders to the Sea* set on Inishmaan, and in *The Playboy of the Western World*. WB Yeats urged Synge to study the islands and 'express a life that has never found expression;' the result was *The Aran Islands* (1907), made into a film in 1924. *Stones of Aran: Pilgrimage* by Tim Robinson (1935–) is more factual.

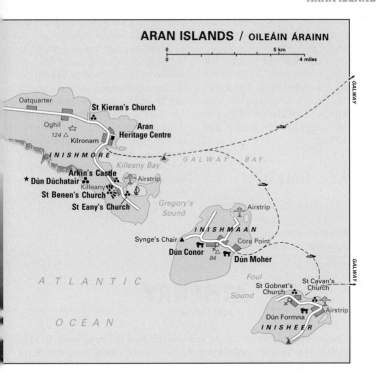

ARAN ISLANDS / OILEÁIN ÁRAINN

wall 20ft/6m high and almost as thick, guarding the headland.

Arkin's Castle (Caisleán Aircín)
1 mi/1.6km S of Kilronan in Killeany.
On the south shore of Killeany Bay stand the ruins of this castle, a tower house probably built by John Rawson to whom the islands were granted by Elizabeth iin 1588. It was fortified by Lord Clanrickard, using stone from St Enda's Church and the nearby friary to strengthen its defences against the Cromwellians.

St Eany's Church
(Teaghlach Éinne)
1.5mi/2.4km S of Kilronan.
On the coast south of the airstrip, stand the early ruins of **St Eany's Church (Teaghlach Éinne)** set among countless tombstones. **St Enda** is said to be buried here on the site of a monastery he founded (c 490) from which his reputation as a teacher spread far and wide, attracting St Kieran of Clonmacnoise, St Finnian of Moville on Inishowen, St Jarlath of Tuam, St Colman of Kilmacduagh south of Galway among scores of others. As some 227 saints are buried across the island, it has been known as Aran of the Saints.

Short Walk
1mi/1.6km S of Kilronan; in Killeany bear right; 10min there and back on foot.
A path climbs the hill past St Eany's oratory (6C-7C) with a narrow north door and a slim east window. From **St Benen's Church (Teampall Bheanáin)**, there is a good **view** of Killeany Bay and of the mainland.

Inishmaan (Inis Meáin)

Inishmaan (3mi/5km x 1mi/2km) is the most remote of the three islands.
A bleak and bare rocky plateau slopes northeast to a sandy shore, providing little shelter to the isolated houses.
Inishmaan exercised a particular fascination for J M Synge, who is said to have loved one particular spot called Synge's Chair *(Cathaoir Synge)* on the western cliffs overlooking Gregory's Sound *(Sunda Ghrióra)*.

The island's main monument is the huge prehistoric fort **Dún Conor (Dún Chonchúir)** perched on high ground keeping watch over the narrow valley: its main enclosure (227ft/69m x 115ft/35m) is contained by a thick wall (17.5ft/5.65m. A second stone fort, **Dún Moher or Dún Fearbhaigh** (103ft/31m x 90ft/27m) overlooks the landing pier at Cora Point.

Inisheer (Inis Oírr)

The smallest Aran island is mainly populated along its north coast. The gentle landscape of the interior is transformed in springtime by countless daffodils. The ruins by the airstrip are those of **St Cavan's Church** (*Teampall Chaomháin*): its east window dates from the early 10C; the chancel arch and south door are medieval. The grave of **St Cavan**, the brother of St Kevin of Glendalough, lies nearby *(NE)*. Among the central settlements stands **Dún Formna**, a stone fort (170ftx123ft/52mx37m) containing the ruins of a tower house, probably built by the O'Briens in the 14C and destroyed by the Cromwellians in 1652. Northwest of the houses are the ruins of **St Gobnet's Church** (*Kilgobnet*): a small medieval oratory.

ATHENRY

POPULATION 1 612

Now a peaceful little market centre and a designated Heritage Town, in 1316 Athenry (Baile Átha an Rí) was the scene of one of Ireland's most savage medieval battles, when an Anglo-Norman force massacred a huge army of native Irish. The bloody encounter is commemorated in the town's 14C seal, which features the severed heads of the Irish chieftains displayed on spikes above a gateway. This was probably the North Gate, still the main feature of the defensive walls built in the early 13C by the town's founder, the Anglo-Norman nobleman, Meiler de Bermingham.

- **Information:** Athenry Arts & Heritage Centre, St Mary's, The Square. ☎091 844661. www.athenryheritagetown.com.
- **Organising Your Time:** Allow a day to see the town and environs.
- **Orient Yourself:** Athenry is in South Galway just north of the main road (N 6) between Galway and Loughrea.
- **Parking:** Park by the Castle.
- **Also See:** BIRR, CLONMACNOISE, GALWAY, PORTUMNA, STROKESTOWN.

Visit

Athenry Heritage Centre

Open Apr–Sept 10am–6pm. ☎091 844 661. www.athenryheritagetown.com. This lively interpretive centre within a 19C church, itself built within the 13C ruins of the medieval Parish Church. traces the history of the town.

Athenry Castle

(Dúchas) *Open Easter–Sept, 10am –6pm, Oct 10am –5pm.* €2.90. ☎091 844 797. www.heritageireland.ie/en.

Built by Meiler de Bermingham c 1250, the castle was destroyed in 1597. Among the ruins there is a central keep with a vaulted undercroft, The main entrance at first-floor level, is enclosed within massive walls and towers.

Dominican Friary

(Dúchas) Key available from Mrs Sheehan in Church Street.
Down by the river on the east side of town are the ruins of a friary founded in 1241 by Meiler de Bermingham. In 1574 the friary was confiscated and burned

War of the Two Kings - Battle of Aughrim

Aughrim was the last great battle in the War of the Two Kings *(Cogadh an Dá Rí)* between King James II of England, aided by Louis XIV of France, and King William III of England and his allies. Having retreated west after the **Battle of Athlone**, the Jacobites, led by the French general St Ruth, faced the Williamites commanded by the Dutchman General Ginkel at Aughrim on 12 July 1691: 20 000 Irish, French, Germans and Walloons fought against 25 000 Irish, English, Dutch, Germans and Danish; 9 000 perished. St Ruth fell in mid-battle; in the ensuing confusion, the Williamites seized victory from the Jacobites. It is said that the Williamites were buried at Clontuskert Priory, while the Jacobites bodies were stripped and left to rot.

by the Burkes; in 1627 it reverted to the friars. After restoration, the complex was made into a university (1644), then in 1652, the friars were expelled by the Cromwellians.

Excursions

East of Athenry

Loughrea
11mi/18km S by R 348 and R 349.
The town on the north shore of Lough Rea facing the **Slieve Aughty Mountains** was built around a Norman stronghold c. 1300 constructed by Richard de Burgo. The local **Carmelite Priory**, now in ruins, is where General St Ruth, killed at the Battle of Aughrim (*see 'Battle of Aughrim' box*), is said to be buried. Part of one of the medieval **town gates** can be seen on the edge of the cathedral precinct. The neo-Gothic **St Brendan's Cathedral**★, head church of the Roman Catholic diocese of Clonfert was designed by William Byrne in 1897. Beyond a rather dull exterior is a richly decorated interior and Celtic Revival arts and crafts furnishings. The **Clonfert Diocesan Museum** (&⊘open *Mon–Thu 2pm–4pm (call to confirm);* ☎*091 841 212; if the museum is locked, enquire at the Cathedral Presbytery;* 🅿 ☎*091 841 212)* displays vestments, missals and church plate.

Turoe Stone★
10mi/1.6km S of Athenry by R 348 and a minor road S from Kiltullagh to Bullaun.
The granite boulder (3ft/1m high) in the field *(right)* is presumed to be a Celtic ritual stone. Its domed cap is carved

with the finest early Celtic decoration in Ireland.

Kilconnell Franciscan Friary
15mi/18km E of Athenry by R 348.
Extensive ruins of a monastery founded in 1353 occupy the site of an earlier complex begun in the 6C by St Conall. Note the tomb niche with the figures of six saints.

St Joseph by M Healy in Loughrea Cathedral

B Lynch/Bord Fáilte, Dublin

Address Book

For coin ranges, see the Legend on the cover flap.

WHERE TO EAT

Morans Oyster Cottage – *The Weir, Kilgogan* ☎*091 796113. www.moransoystercottage.com. Oysters and seafood are the house specialities in this sixth generation family restaurant.
Paddy Burke's Oyster Inn – *Clarenbridge* ☎*091 796226. www.paddy* *burkesgalway.com.* Pub established in 1650, home of the famous Clarenbridge Oyster Festival, held in mid September.
Raftery's – *Craughwell.* ☎*091 846 004.* Well-kept, family-run pub; seafood specials.

EVENTS AND FESTIVALS

Athenry Annual Medieval Festival *(weekend nearest 15 August)* – Open air theatre and concerts, and fireworks.

Battle of Aughrim Interpretative Centre

Ballinasloe. 5mi/8km S of Kilconnell by minor road. ○*Open Tue–Sat 10am–6pm, Jun–Aug Sun 2pm–4pm (Call to confirm).* ∞*€4.* ☞ ℗ ☎*0905 73939.*

Various relics make up a re-creation of the bloody battle of Aughrim as described by Captain Walter Dalton, one of the combatants. Fought on 12 July 1691 between the forces of William of Orange and James II, it was the bloodiest battle in Irish history. Some 9000 men died in total, the vast majority being from the Jacobites, whose forces in Ireland would never recover.

Clontuskert Augustinian Priory

10mi/16km SE of Aughrim by N 6 to Garbally and S by R 355; 5min on foot from roadside ℗ *(left).*

The first monastery here was founded by **St Baedán** (d c 809). By the end of the 13C the **Augustinians** had established one of the richest monasteries in the diocese. Most of the present ruins are from the 15C.

Kiltartan Country

Thoor Ballylee★

23mi/37km S of Athenry by R 348, R 349, N 6 and N 66 (sign). ℗○*Open Jun–Sept, 10am–6pm.* ∞*€6.* ℗ ☎*091 631 436.*

The 16C **tower house** served as **William Butler Yeats'** summer house for 11 years, and often featured in his poetry. In the year he married Georgie Hyde-Lees, he sought a property near Coole Park, where his friend Lady Gregory resided. The local Kiltartan Society has restored the four-storey building, miller's cottage and mill wheel: the tower now houses rare editions of Yeats' works.

Kiltartan Gregory Museum

3.5mi/5km W of Thoor Ballylee by minor road and N 18 S. ○*Open Jun–Aug, 10am–6pm; Sept–May, Sun 1pm–5pm.* ☎*091 632346. www.gortonline.com/gregory museum.*

The old schoolhouse, built by the Gregory family, displays mementos of Augusta, Lady Gregory (1852–1932), co-founder with WB Yeats, of the Abbey Theatre in Dublin.

Coole Park

Gort. 2mi/3km S from Kiltartan by N 18. ℗○*Visitor Centre open Apr–Sept, 10am–5pm (6pm Jun–Aug); last admission 1hr before closing.* ∞*€2.90.* ☞ ℗. ☎*091 631 804. www.coolepark.ie.*

In the walled garden stands a great copper beech, the **autograph tree**★, on which many Irish Literary greats – William Butler Yeats, George Bernard Shaw, G Russell (AE), John Millington Synge and Sean O'Casey – cut their initials while guests at Lady Gregory's house (demolished). The **visitor centre** provides information on the national park. A forest walk *(0.5mi/0.8km)* leads to the lake, where petrified trees protrude from the water.

Kilmacduagh Churches and Round Tower★

3.5mi/50km SW of Gort by R 460.

The main landmark of the former monastic site set against the strange Burren landscape, is the well-preserved leaning **round tower**. Founded in the 7C by **St Colman**, son of Duagh, the monastery suffered many Viking attacks in the 9C–10C; after the Reformation it was acquired by Richard, 2nd Earl of Clanrickard. The 13C **Glebe House** was probably used by the abbot. Beside the round tower stands the **cathedral** with folk art Crucifixions *(north transept)*. **St Mary's Church**, across the road, was built c 1200. **O'Heyne's Church** *(NW)* contains early-13C carvings.

Dunguaire Castle★
Kinvara. 20mi/32km NW of Kilmacduagh by minor road to Tirneevin, Killinny and Kinvara. Open May–Sept, 9.30am–5pm (4.30pm last admission). Medieval banquets nightly, 5.30pm, 8.45pm (reservation required). Castle €5.50; banquet €53.50. 061 711 200. www.shannonheritage.com.

Facing **Kinvara**, a charming little port, the castle is a four-storey **tower house** built in 1520.

ATHLONE
POPULATION 7 691

The county town of Westmeath occupies a strategic position straddling the Shannon south of Lough Ree, in the very heart of Ireland. From early on the river crossing was defended by a fortress built by the Kings of Connacht. The present stronghold dates from the Anglo-Norman era. In the early days of the Free State, Athlone *(Baile Átha Luain)* was considered to be a suitable site for the capital. Though the town escaped this distinction, it is a bustling place served by good rail and road links, within easy reach of major attractions like Clonmacnoise and Lough Ree.

- **Information:** Athlone Castle. 090 6494630. www.eastcoastmidlands.ie. www.athlone.ie.
- **Organising Your Time:** Allow a full day, to include a river cruise.
- **Orient Yourself:** Athlone is located on N 6, the Dublin to Galway road, at the junction with N 55 and N 61.
- **Also See:** ATHENRY, BIRR, CLONMACNOISE,LONGFORD, MULLINGAR, STROKESTOWN, TULLAMORE.

A Bit of History

Siege of Athlone
Athlone has been repeatedly fought over but the town's worst moment came in the course of the Williamite War, when it suffered the most devastating bombardment in Irish history. Following the Battle of the Boyne the Jacobite forces retreated to Athlone.

In June 1691 the Williamite army under Ginkel made a determined assault on the bridge; Sergeant Custume, who died heroically, is commemorated in the name of the local barracks. After 10 days of sustained attack the town and castle fell; Ginkel was made Earl of Athlone; the Jacobites withdrew southwest to Aughrim.

Irish Tenor
The greatest lyric tenor of his day, **John McCormack** (1884–1945), born in Athlone, first sang in the Palestrina Choir of the Pro-Cathedral in Dublin. At 23 he made his debut at Covent Garden, and went on to perform there annually until 1914. His voice and charisma made him one of the most widely honoured and decorated singers in the world, the only Irish tenor to reach such an international standard. He was made a Count of the Papal Court for his charity work.

Address Book

🪙 *For coin ranges, see the Legend on the cover flap.*

SIGHTSEEING

Athlone Cruises – *90min excursion on Lough Ree or private charter.* ☎090 6472892. www.iol.ie/wmeathtc/acl.

Viking Tours – *excursions in a replica Viking longship on the Shannon and Lough Ree.* ☎0902 73383 – www.iol. ie/wmeathtc/viking.

Shannon Safari – *Powerboat trips on the Shannon and around Clonmacnoise.* €20/hr. ☎086 2849108. www. shannonsafari.ie.

WHERE TO STAY

🍽 **Glasson Stone Lodge** – *Glasson, 5mi NE of Athlone on N 55. 5rm.* ☎090 6485004. www.glassonstonelodge.com. Tea and cakes on arrival and generous breakfasts; bright bedrooms, all with power showers.

🍽 **Riverview House B&B** – *Summerhill, Galway Road, 2.5mi W of Athlone on N 6.* ☎0906 494532. www.riverviewhouse-bandb.com. 4rm. Purpose-built house with a neat garden on a small tributary of the Shannon, bedrooms all ensuite. Good base for fishing.

🍽 **Shelmalier House** – *Retreat Road, Cartrontroy , 1.5mi E of Athlone by Dublin Road (N 6). 7rm.* ☎090 6472245. www.shelmalierhouse.com. Purpose-built accommodation with sauna/outdoor tub. Bedrooms decorated to a high standard.

WHERE TO EAT

🍽🍽 **The Olive Grove** – *Custume Place, Athlone.* ☎0902 76946. www.theolive grove.ie. Modern Irish cooking in bright buzzy surroundings

🍽🍽🍽 **Wineport Lodge** – *Glassan, 5mi NE of Athlone on N 55 and 1mi SW of Glassan.* ☎0906 439010. www.wineport.ie. Modern Irish cooking in a spectacular waterside location

EVENTS AND FESTIVALS

John McCormack Golden Voice of Athlone *(late Jun)* is a competition for young classical singers
Lough Ree Yaght Club Regatta *(Aug)*

TRACING ANCESTORS

Dún na Sí (Fairy Fort) – Knockdomney, Co Westmeath. *Genealogy service.* ☎090 64 81183. www.irish-roots.net.

Town

Market Square

Early in the 13C John de Grey, Justiciar of Ireland, built **Athlone Castle**. The curtain wall and its three fortified towers date from the late 13C. The oldest part, however, is the central polygonal **keep;** early in the 19C the upper part was altered to accommodate heavy artillery, supplemented by new defences, known as the Batteries, west of the town. A video in the exhibition centre details the Siege of Athlone and the life story of **John McCormack**. The **Castle Museum** *(in the keep;* 🕐 *open Easter/ May–early-Oct, 10am–4.30pm (last admission);* 🎫€6; 🅿 ; ☎090 6492912) covers local history and folk life.

The monumental **Church of St Peter and St Paul** was designed by **Ralph Byrne** (1937). Much of the striking stained glass comes from the **Harry Clarke** studios, while the window in the priest's sacristy is by the portrait painter **Sarah Purser**.

From the bridge, the main street curves east through town towards the site of the Dublin Gate. In a side turning *(left)* stand the remains of Court Devenish *(private)*, a Jacobean house (1620). The Bawn, a narrow street *(left)*, contains the birthplace of **John McCormack** (🪙 *see 'Irish Tenor' box)*. The **Franciscan Church** (1931) was built in the Hiberno-Romanesque style inspired by old Irish designs. The **Strand** along the river bank to Burgess Park provides a fine view of the weir, the eel fisheries and the old port on the west bank.

ATHY

POPULATION 5 306

Clustered round a fortified crossing of the river, Athy (Baile Àtha was once the largest town in Co Kildare. Today little more than a large village, it is a bustling centre for an extensive rural area and attracts streams of visitors looking to cruise, sail and fish the River Barrow, the Barrow Line, and the Grand Canal.

- **Information:** Town Hall, Emily Square. ☎059 863 3075. www.athyheritagecentre-museum.ie.
- **Organising Your Time:**. Allow half a day.
- **Orient Yourself:** Athy stands on N 78, and the county boundary between Kildare and Carlow.
- **Also See:** ABBEYLEIX, KILDARE, KILKENNY, TULLAMORE.

Town Centre

The present bridge, known as Crom-a-Boo Bridge (from the bizarre war cry of the local Geraldine family) dates from 1796; White's Castle (*private*) alongside is 16C.

Facing onto the main square is the **Courthouse**, the former Corn Exchange (1856), and the mid-18C **Town Hall** (*Open Mon–Fri, 10am–5pm; ⊜€3; ☎059 863 3075*), which as well as the information centre, also houses a gene-alogy and heritage centre. It celebrates the arctic explorer SIr Ernest Shackelton, born locally.

The striking, fan-shaped **Dominican Church** is furnished with stained-glass windows and Stations of the Cross by the artist **George Campbell** (1917–79).

Driving Tour

East of Barrow Valley

20mi/32km.

- *From Athy take N 67 E and a minor road (right) via Burtown.*

Ballitore

The great Irish statesman and political theorist Edmund Burke (1729–97) was at school here. The **House of Mary Lead-better** now accommodates a library and **Quaker Museum** (*open Tue–Sat, noon –5pm; Jun–Sept, Sun 2pm–6pm; ⌂; ☎059 862 3344; http://kildare.ie/library/ballitore-library.asp*) describing the 18C Yorkshire Quakers' sober and industrious way of life.

- *Take N 9 S to Timolin.*

Irish Pewter Mill, Museum and Crafts Centre, Timolin

Open Mon–Fri, 9.30am–4.30pm. Closed Easter weekend, 25 Dec. ☎059 862 4164. www.kildare.ie.

Ireland's oldest pewter mill continues to cast, spin and polish the alloy into objects of all kinds. A museum displays moulds, tools and dies used since the Middle Ages.

- *Continue S by N 9.*

Moone High Cross★

The scant ruins of a 6C monastery founded by **St Columba** enclose an unusual, early 9C high cross (17.5ft/5.3m high).

The slender shaft and tapering base carry a wealth of crude but very expres-sive carved panels of biblical scenes: one shows the Feeding of the Five Thousand with five loaves, two highly stylised eels, and a pair of smiling fish.

- *Continue S by N 9 to Castledermot; continue 9.5mi/16km SE by R 418.*

Castledermot High Crosses★

The site of a monastery founded by **St Dermot** is marked by two gran-ite **high crosses** carved with biblical scenes, and a 10C **round tower** top-ped by medieval battlements. Ruined chancel walls recall the Franciscan friary founded in 1302.

▶ *From Castledermot take minor road E; in Graney turn left to Baltinglass.*

Baltinglass

The main square of the tiny town is dominated by a memorial to Michael Dwyer, who escaped British soldiers in 1798 when his comrade Sam MacAllister selflessly drew their fire onto himself. Beside the 19C Anglican church are the ruins of **Baltinglass Abbey**, founded by **Dermot MacMurrough**, King of Leinster, in 1148 and suppressed in 1536: six Gothic nave arches, the 19C tower and parts of the original cloisters (restored) still stand.

BANTRY ★

POPULATION 2 777

The market and fishing town of Bantry (Beanntraí) stands near the head of the deep-water inlet known as Bantry Bay. Long familiar to mariners as a safe anchorage, the bay was the scene in 1796 of a dramatic episode in British and Irish history, when an attempted French invasion was frustrated by foul weather.

- 🄸 **Information:** Old Court House, Bantry. ☎027 50229. www.corkkerry.ie.
- 🕓 **Organising Your Time:.** Allow at least a day.
- ▶ **Orient Yourself:** Bantry lies between Cork and Killarney (N 71) on the south shore of Bantry Bay (30mi/48km long) between Skibbereen and Glengarriff.
- 🄳 **Also See:** KENMARE, KILLARNEY, SKIBBEREEN.

Sights

Bantry House ★

🄳🕓*Open mid Mar–Oct, daily 10am–6pm. ⊜House and garden €10; Gardens and Armada Centre €5. ⊡☎027 50047. www.bantryhouse.ie.*

This splendid symmetrical Georgian mansion of 1740 and its **terraced**

Italianate gardens stand in contrast to the vast scale and wild nature of Bantry Bay. The house is full of tastefully chosen treasures: some are intimately connected with the events of **1796**, for which the owner Richard White (1767–1851) was given a peerage in recognition of his role as commander of the local militia (🄳*see 'The Invasion*

Ch Legrand/MICHELIN

Dining Room, Bantry House

The Invasion That Never Was, 1796

An expeditionary force of 15,000 French troops, commanded by General Hoche, accompanied by the Irish rebel Wolfe Tone, set sail from Brest intent on invading Ireland and expelling the British. Fog and adverse winds prevented most of the fleet from entering Bantry Bay. Then a storm blew up, impeding any attempts at landing so the ships retreated. Had the soldiers managed to come ashore, things might well have been very different, as only a scratch force of militiamen commanded by Richard White, owner of Bantry House, could be mustered.

Ten French warships were lost; the frigate *La Surveillante* was scuttled on 2 January 1797. The 17cwt/863kg French anchor, recovered by a trawler in 1964, sits by the N17 south of Bantry; a captured French longboat is now in Dún Laoghaire.

That Never Was' box) Others are linked to Viscount Berehaven (1800–68) who travelled widely in Europe, accumulating extraordinary curiosities from Pompeii, Savonnerie carpets, Aubusson tapestries once owned by Marie-Antoinette, a Russian travelling shrine with 15C and 16C icons, and Spanish leather with which to clad the sides of the staircase. There are family portraits throughout the house, while the spectacular **dining room** is hung with those of King George III and Queen Charlotte, presented by the king at the time of White's ennoblement. The East Stables now house an exhibition on the **1796 Bantry French Armada**.

Whiddy Island

The island has had a varied history, as its monuments tesify: Kilmore church and graveyard; Reenavanig Castle – the first residence of the White family; and fortifications, including three gun batteries, erected as part of the British naval defences in 1801. An American sea plane base operated from here at the end of the First World War.

Excursions

Gougane Barra Forest Park★

23mi/38km – half a day. From Ballylickey take R 584 E inland.
The approach road climbs inland between the vertical rock walls of the **Pass of Keimaneigh** (2mi/3.2km). West of the lake, the source of the **River Lee**, a **forest drive** (3mi/4.8km) makes a loop through the extensive park (walks and nature trails) which rises up the steep mountain slopes beside the tumbling mountain stream. St Finbar, the 6C founder of Cork, had a hermitage on the island in the lake. A small causeway leads to the modern island chapel built in the Irish Romanesque style.

Kilnaruane Inscribed Stone

2mi/3km S of Bantry by N 71; turn left at the Westlodge Hotel (sign).
On the hilltop stands a 9C stone pillar, possibly the shaft of a high cross. Carved panels depict a boat – possibly a curragh – with four oarsmen navigating through a sea of crosses, a figure at prayer, St Paul and St Anthony of the Desert.

BIRR

POPULATION 3 355

With elegant 18C houses lining its shady streets, Birr (Biorra) is a fine example of a planned Georgian town laid out at the gates of a great house, and now a Heritage Town. The local landowners, the Parsons family, later ennobled as the Earls of Rosse, were also responsible for creating one of the richest collections of exotic trees and shrubs anywhere: one of many bequests left by a line of eminent men, innovators and inventors – another being what for many years was the world's most powerful telescope.

- **Information:** Brendon Street. ☎050 920110. www.midirelandtourism.ie.
- **Organising Your Time:** Allow 2 days to include driving tour.
- **Orient Yourself:** Birr is situated on N 52 between Tullamore and Nenagh on the country boundary SW of Tullamore in the O'Carroll country.
- **Don't Miss:** Birr Castle and the Great Telescope.
- **Also See:** ABBEYLEIX, ATHLONE, CLONMACNOISE, PORTUMNA, ROSCREA, TULLAMORE.

A Bit of History

Birr figures in the early records as the site of an important monastery, which produced the Macregol's Gospels and where the Law of Adamnan was accepted by abbots and chieftains at the Synod of Birr in 697. Owing to its central position in Ireland, Birr was referred to in the Down Survey as *Umbilicus Hiberniae*. Until the establishment of the Free State, Birr was known as Parsonstown in King's County (the old name of Co Offaly). In 1620 the village was granted to **Sir Lawrence Parsons**. He started weekly markets, set up a glass factory and built most of the castle. In 1642 much of Birr was destroyed by fire during a siege by local clans; in 1690 it was garrisoned by the Williamites and besieged by the Duke of Berwick. During the more peaceful 18C and 19C, the town, castle and demesne were much extended.

American Connection

One of the signatories of the American Declaration of Independence in 1776, **Charles Carroll** of Carrollton, was the grandson of Charles Carroll, who emigrated in 1688 from Letterluna in the Slieve Bloom mountains to the USA, where he was granted land in Maryland.

Sir William Parsons, a patron of Handel, enabled the composer to stage the first performance of *Messiah* in Dublin in 1742. His grandson, another Sir William, the 4th baronet, devoted much time to the late-18C Volunteers. **Sir Lawrence**, the 5th baronet, was more nationalist in political sentiment and a friend of **Wolfe Tone** but he retired from politics after the Act of Union in 1800. In the 19C the family genius was invested in **scientific discoveries** and in the 20C was directed towards the collection and propagation of the **rare botanical species** for the magnificent gardens.

Walking Tour

Birr Town★

The principal axis is **Oxentown Mall** which runs between the castle gates and the Anglican church between rows of elegant houses and mature trees. The town centre is formed by **Emmet Square**; among the best Georgian houses is Dooley's Hotel (1740). **John's Mall** is graced by a statue of the 3rd Earl of Rosse, and beside the delightful little Greek temple (1833) is the **Birr Stone**, a large limestone rock, which may once have marked the supposed meeting place of the mythical Fianna warriors near Seffin. In 1828 it was removed to a mansion in Co Clare for secret celebrations of the Mass; it was returned in 1974.

Town

Birr Castle Demesne★★

♿ ◷ *Open daily 9am–6pm.* ☕€9. *Check website for times of telescope demonstration and summer evening concerts.* ☕ 🅿 ☎ *057 9120336. www.birrcastle.com.*

Gardens

Each of the many walks through these pleasure grounds (100 acres/40ha), either by the water or among thousands of species of trees and shrubs, is a delight. Highlights include tall box hedges and the flora from China and the Himalayas. Extensive herbaceous displays adorn the terraces below the crenellated 17C **castle** *(private).*

Great Telescope★★

In the 1840s, the 3rd Earl of Rosse built a telescope named the **Leviathan of Parsonstown**, providing a more extensive view of space than was hitherto possible. Its mirror (72in/183cm) was cast in a furnace built at the bottom of the castle moat, and fired with turf from nearby bogs. Astronomers came from far and wide to use the telescope, considered to be the most powerful in the world for 60 years, until 1908.

Ireland's Historic Science Centre

Part of the stable yard is given over to an account of the brilliant family achievements – the building of the first-known example of a wrought-iron suspension bridge by the 2nd Earl; the construction of the great telescope and the discovery of distant galaxies by the 3rd Earl; the invention of the steam turbine engine by Charles Parsons in the 1890s; the pioneering work in photography by Mary Countess of Rosse in the 1850s; the world-wide plant-collecting expeditions conducted by the 5th and 6th Earls.

Driving Tours

Slieve Bloom Mountains★

Round tour of 46mi/73km.

▷   *From Birr take R 440 E.*

After the monotonous landscapes of the Midlands, the plantations of pine and spruce, and mountains rising from the bog to 1728ft/527m (Arderin) are a refreshing change. A good way to enjoy the scenery is to walk sections of the 44mi/70km **Slieve Bloom Way**. Otherwise take the drive east from the village of Kinnitty, past Forelacka Glen to Drimmo, then north through The Cut to Clonaslee.

Kinnitty

The village, set among idyllic scenery has considerable charm. The **Kinnitty Pyramid** in the churchyard south of the village (on the Roscrea road), is an extraordinary mausoleum modelled on

Great Telescope, Birr

Address Book

For coin ranges, see the cover flap.

SIGHTSEEING

Silverline Cruisers – *Banagher Marina.* ☎057 9151112. www.silverlinecruisers. com. Cruisers for hire on the Shannon.

WHERE TO STAY

Ring Farmhouse – *Ballinree. 2km from Birr off N62. 13rm.* ☎057 9120976. www.irishfarmhouseholiday.com. Friendly farmhouse B&B built on the site of a medieval Loretto Castle cirled by hedges. Good location for walking in the Slieve Bloom mountains.

Maltings Guesthouse – *Castle Street. 13rm.* ☎0509 21345. themaltings birr@eircom.net. Built in 1810 as a maltstore for Guinness, this establishment also houses a craft centre. It offers spacious accommodation and a simple restaurant overlooking the river.

Ardmore House B&B – *The Walk Kinnitty. 5rm.* ☎057 9137009. www. kinnitty.com. This charming Victorian period house makes an ideal base for walks in the Slieve Bloom mountains.

WHERE TO EAT

The Thatch – *Crinkill. 1.5mi S off N 52.* ☎0509 20682. www.thethatchcrinkill .com. Thatched pub kept by fifth generation of landlords. Open for bar lunches and dinner in the restaurant.

SPORTS AND LEISURE

Walking: Birr Castle Demesne, along the River Camcor, beside the Grand Canal, and in the Slieve Bloom mountains.
Boating: on the Shannon, Grand Canal.
Fishing: Shannon and Brosna rivers for salmon, pike, trout and most coarse species; River Suck and Grand Canal for pike, bream and perch.

EVENTS AND FESTIVALS

Birr Vintage Week *(late Aug)* : events include a Sunday parade, a Georgian Cricket Match played in period costume according to the 1744 rules and the Irish Independent Carriage Driving Championships, held in the Castle demesne, including music, theatre, fireworks.

---

the pyramid of Cheops in Egypt, honouring the Bernards of Kinnitty Castle.
For details on walking trails and the flora and fauna of the area, contact the **Slieve Bloom Centre** (*open Apr–Sept, Tue–Fri lunchtimes;* ☎086 2789147; www. slievebloom.ie).

Shannon Valley
Drive of 20mi/32km.

▶ *From Birr take R 439 N.*

Banagher (Beannchar)

The town on the **Shannon** was an important crossing point, defended on the Connacht bank by Cromwell's Castle. A tower house with bastions was added c. 1650. The Revd Arthur Nicholls came from Banagher, and when he married **Charlotte Brontë**, the couple spent their honeymoon nearby. Another literary resident was **Anthony Trollope** (*see 'Anthony Trollope in Ireland' box*).

▶ *From Banagher take R 356 E ; turn left to Shannon Harbour.*

Shannon Harbour

The junction of the **Grand Canal** and the Shannon is now a popular mooring for river cruisers. In its commercial heyday, a dry dock, warehousing, a customs post and hotel (now in ruins) served the lock and canal basin; the local population numbering 1 000, saw the trans-shipment of some 300 000 tons of produce and over 250 000 people on the barges, many of them emigrants on their way via Limerick and Cobh to Australia, Canada and America.
The area provides excellent coarse fishing and birdwatching when rare birds, including the corncrake, visit the Shannon Callows wet grasslands.

▶ *Beyond Shannon Harbour in Clonony; left into R 357 to Shannonbridge.*

Anthony Trollope in Ireland

Having been in the employ of the Post Office since 1834, Anthony Trollope was appointed a Surveyor's Clerk in1841 and went to Ireland. His first appointment, to which he travelled from Dublin by canal boat, was in **Banagher**, where he took up hunting, and visited Sir William Gregory of Coole Park, a contemporary at Harrow School. In 1843 during a visit to Drumsna he was inspired to begin his first novel, *The Macdermots of Ballycloran*, published in 1847.

On 11 June 1844 he married Rose Heseltine. Later that year they moved to **Clonmel**, renting rooms on the first floor of a house in O'Connell Street (then High Street) where two sons were born – Henry Merivale (March 1846) and Frederic James (September 1847). In 1845 Anthony began his second novel *The Kellys and the O'Kellys*, which was published in 1848. The family then moved to **Mallow** (1848–51) and Anthony was able to indulge his passion for hunting with various great hunts including the Duhallow, the oldest in Ireland. While on secondment in the Channel Islands in 1853, Trollope implemented the idea of the first **post boxes**, which were painted sage green. In 1854, after a year in Belfast as Acting Surveyor, he was appointed Surveyor of the Northern District of Ireland but obtained permission to reside in Dublin, where he lived at 5 Seaview Terrace, Donnybrook. As his work involved a good deal of travelling, he created a portable desk so that he could write on the train.

He began his third Irish novel, *Castle Richmond*, which takes place during the Great Famine, in 1859, the year in which he transferred permanently to England. At the end of his life he began a fourth Irish novel, *The Landleaguers*, about agrarian reform, but died in December 1882 before it was finished.

Clonmacnoise and West Offaly Railway
&. *Apr–Sept on the hour; mid Oct–Mar Mon–Fri by request* ⊗ €6.50. ☎ 090 9674450. www.bnm.ie.
This narrow-gauge railway takes passengers on a guided tour (45min, 5.5mi/8km) of the **Blackwater Bog**, part of the Bog of Allen (20 000 acres/8 090ha) which is one of the largest unbroken raised bogs in Ireland. The tour includes a view of the various stages in the process of harvesting the peat to fuel the electricity power station at Shannonbridge, including a half-way halt to see the bog.

BOYLE

POPULATION 1 695

On the River Boyle at the foot of the Curlew Mountains (867ft/264m), this pleasant little town (Mainistir Na Búille) has one of the loveliest set of abbey ruins in Ireland and fascinating reminders of one of the most ruthless and ambitious Anglo-Irish landowning dynasties, the King family. The river and the nearby loughs give excellent fishing.

- 🛈 **Information:** King House, Boyle. ☎071 9662145.
- 🕐 **Organising Your Time:** Allow a day to include excursions, longer if taking the driving tour.
- **Especially for Kids:** Lough Key Forest Park.
- ▸ **Orient Yourself:** Boyle lies on N 4, the Dublin to Sligo road, south of the Curlew Mountains between Lough Key and Lough Gara.
- 👌 **Also See:** CARRICK-ON-SHANNON, KILLALA, KNOCK, SLIGO, STROKESTOWN.

Address Book

EVENTS AND FESTIVALS

O'Carolan Harp Festival – Performance of O'Carolan's works (🕮 *see Turlough O'Carolan' box*), music, song and dancing, many open-air events. *Late-Jul or early-Aug.* ☎*071 9647247. www.ocarolanharpfestival.ie.*
Boyle Arts – *King House.* Summer (*Late-Jul–early-Aug*) festival of contemporary art, comedy, storytelling, drama, jazz classical music and more. *www.boylearts.com.*

Sights

Boyle Abbey★

2mi/3.2km E of Boyle by N 4. (Dúchas) 🚹🕐*Open Easter–Oct, daily 10am–6pm (5.15pm last admission).* 🎫*€2.10.* ☎*071 966 2604. www.heritageireland.ie.*

A **Cistercian** house was founded here n 1161 by monks from Mellifont. The church, built over several decades, shows the transition from the Romanesque to the Gothic style. Normally frowning on exuberance of any kind, here at Boyle the austere Cistercians gave free rein to their masons, who endowed the capitals with carvings of men, beasts and foliage. The abbey buildings were occupied by the Cromwellians who showed them their usual disrespect; thereafter they served as barracks until the 18C. Information on the monastic life is provided in the **gatehouse**.

Dining Room in King House, Boyle

King House★

🕐*Open Apr–Sept, 10am–6pm; last admission 5pm.* 🎫*€7.* 🍴 🅿 ☎*071 966 3242. www.kinghouse.ie.*

The Palladian mansion of the King family stands at the east end of the main street. It was built around 1730. The first King was Sir John, a Staffordshire gentleman sent here a century earlier, charged with subjugating the native Irish and rewarded with the lands confiscated from the local ruling clan, the MacDermots. The Kings became increasingly powerful, acquiring the title of Earls of Kingston, and moving to a more splendid residence in the vast Rockingham estate.

King House has been carefully restored to accommodate descriptions of the old rulers – O'Connors, Kings of Connaught and MacDermots of Moylurg – and the exploits of the King family who displaced them. The **Boyle Civic Art Collection** is considered to be among the finest collections of contemporary Irish painting and sculpture anywhere.

Excursion

Lough Key Forest Park★ [Kids]

2mi/3.2km E of Boyle by N 4. 🚹🕐*Open Mar–Oct, daily 10am–6pm (Jul–Aug, Fri–Sun 9pm). Nov–Feb, Fri–Sun noon–4pm. Last admission 1–2hrs before closing.* 🎫*€7.50 Lough Key Experience; €16 Boda Borg. €19.50 adult day pass. €5 child day pass Adventure Play Kingdom.* 🍴🅿 *(€4).* ☎*071 967 3122. www.loughkey.ie.*

With its woodlands, bog garden, ornamental trees and estate buildings, this vast forest park (865 acres/350ha) looks out over Lough Key and its islands. Until 1959 it formed part of the Rockingham estate, the demesne of the Earls of Kingston, who built themselves a great house here on the site of a MacDermot castle. In the early 19C, the house was remodelled by John Nash and the estate was landscaped by Humphry Repton. In 1959 the house was destroyed by fire.

The **Lough Key Experience** takes visitors on an audio trail through 19C underground tunnels to the top of the 5-storey **Moylurg Tower** (132 steps) and along a 300m steel-and-timber **Tree Canopy Walk** rising 9m above the forest floor, offering panoramic views over the woods, lakes and hills. Younger visitors enjoy the **Adventure Play Kingdom** play area while **Boda Borg** is a more cerebral area of puzzles and tasks.

Driving Tour

Mountains and Lakes of Moylurg★

Round-trip of 50mi/80km.

▸ *From Boyle take N 4 N.*

As it climbs over the **Curlew Mountains** (867ft/264m) the road provides splendid **views**★ of the lakes *(east)*.

Ballinafad

The Castle of the Curlews, now in ruins, was built in 1590 to protect the Curlew Mountain pass. It had four round corner towers with square interiors.

▸ *Continue N on N 4. In Castlebaldwin turn left signed to Carrowkeel Cemetery; at the fork bear left. Park at the gate if locked; 1hr on foot there and back.*

Carrowkeel Megalithic Cemetery

The bleak hilltop in the **Bricklieve Mountains** (1 057ft/321m), provides a fine **view**★★ of the surrounding country. The stone mounds contain passage graves dating from around 2500 to 2000 BC. On a lower ridge (east) are about 50 round huts, probably dwellings.

▸ *From Castlebaldwin take the road along the shore of Lough Arrow. At the end of the lake turn left. In Ballyfarnan turn left into a steep minor road to Altgowlan.*

Arigna Scenic Drive (Slí)★

From the **viewpoint**, you see Lough Skean and Lough Meelagh. As the road crosses the watershed, more fine views extend over the steep Arigna Valley.

Turlough O'Carolan (1670–1738)

The blind harpist who wrote poetry and music, including the melody of *The Star-Spangled Banner,* was born in **Nobber** in Co Meath. In 1684 his family moved to Carrick-on-Shannon, where Mrs MacDermot Roe became his patron and provided for his education and musical studies. She even gave him a horse so that he could perform his compositions at the big houses. After his marriage in 1720 he lived several years in Mohill. His death in **Keadew** (Keadue) was marked by a 4 day wake. Annual harp festivals are held in his honour in Keadew and Nobber.

▸ *At the T-junction turn right; after 2.5mi/4km turn left into Arigna. In Arigna cross the river and turn left uphill; after 1.5mi/2.4km turn right (sign) onto a very steep and narrow road. At the next junction turn right.*

As the road descends from the bare and rugged heights there is an extensive **view**★ of **Lough Allen**, the most northerly of the great Shannon lakes. Nearby, the river rises in a bog at Shannon Pot *(9mi/14.5km north)*, running past Slieve Anierin (1 927ft/586m), the highest point in the Iron Mountains.

▸ *At the bottom of the hill turn right onto R 280 to Drumshanbo.*

Drumshanbo (Droim Seanbho)

An angler's haven on Lough Allen.

Woodbrook

The name of the house, situated between Lough Key and the main road, which was once the home of the Kirkwood family, is also the name of a charming book by David Thomson, an 18 year old Oxford student who took a summer job as tutor to Phoebe Kirkwood in 1932 and wrote about the experience.

▶ *From Drumshanbo return N on R 280; turn left onto R 285 and drive through Keadew (Keadue).*

O'Carolan's Grave

The tombstones mark the site of **Kilronan Abbey**, founded in the 6C: the doorway is 12C–13C; in the transept is the tombstone of **Turlough O'Carolan**.

▶ *Return to the last junction; turn right. In Knockvicar turn right to Corrigeen-roe; in Corrigeenroe turn left to return to Boyle, past Lough Key.*

BOYNE VALLEY★★

Upstream from Drogheda, the River Boyne winds through a fertile and well-wooded landscape with an extraordinary concentration of ancient and prehistoric sites. Huge grave mounds, laboriously constructed and enigmatically decorated, testify to the skill and sophistication of the people who thrived here long before work started on the pyramids of Egypt. Much later, in the pre-Christian era, the High Kings of Ireland held court at the Hill of Tara. Christianity was brought to the region by St Patrick himself; the early monastic site at Monasterboice evokes the Irish church before its 12C Romanisation, in contrast to the later, European style of monastery at Mellifont. The clash of arms on the banks of the river in 1690 was an event of European as well as local importance, and the outcome of the Battle of the Boyne is still a factor in contemporary Irish politics.

- 🔲 **Information**: Bru na Boinne Visitor Centre, Donore. ☎041 988 0300. www.heritageireland.ie.
- ▶ **Orient Yourself:** The Boyne Valley runs inland from Drogheda; the sights can be reached from N 51 on the north bank of the River Boyne, from M 1 which passes just west of Drogheda or from N 2 which passes through Slane.
- 🕐 **Organising Your Time:** Allow at least a day.
- 😊 **Don't Miss:** Newgrange – a UNESCO World Heritage Site, and Monasterboice.
- 🚶 **Walking Paths:** River Boyne towpath, Oldbridge Estate, Townley Hall grounds (nature trail).
- 🚲 **Also See:** DROGHEDA, FINGAL, KELLS, TRIM.

Prehistoric Sites

The prehistoric burial sites at Knowth, Dowth and Newgrange are the oldest in the British Isles. They were built by a farming and stock-raising community in the Neolithic era (3,500–2,700 BC), overlooking the Boyne, then a main through route.

Present knowledge suggests that Dowth was built first to align with the setting sun. It was followed by Newgrange where the rising sun penetrates the inner chamber at the winter solstice. Knowth was built later facing east–west to align with the rising sun in March and the setting sun in September.

Altogether, there are some 40 graves, consisting of three major graves and many satellites: only the major graves have been systematically excavated.

Brú na Bóinne Visitor Centre

(Dúchas) 🚶🚗 *Visit by guided tour only May–Sept, daily, 9am–6.30pm (7pm Jun–mid-Sept); Mar–Apr and Oct–Feb, daily, 9.30am–5.30pm (5pm Nov–Feb). 🕐Closed 24–27 Dec. 😊 Arrive early in high season as tours sell out quickly. 🚌Visitor Centre only 🎟€2.90; Centre and Newgrange (2hr) €5.80; Centre and Knowth (Easter to Oct), 2hr, €4.50. All three sites €10.30. Ticktet includes shuttle-bus service 🚌 🅿. ☎041 988 0300. www.heritageireland.ie.*

Informative displays with replicas of the monuments provide an excellent introduction to the archaeological sites: details of the people, their clothing, food and

Neolithic dwellings are integrated into descriptions of their expertise and ability to move stones on rollers: 500 years before the pyramids of Egypt.

Newgrange★★★

Newgrange is one of the best examples of a passage grave in western Europe, its dimensions imposing, the enigmatic stone carving a marvel of imagination. The **mound** (1.25 acres/0.5ha, between 260ft/79m and 280ft/85m in diameter, and 37ft/11m high) consists of a cairn of medium-sized stones enclosed within a circle of 97 kerbstones, some of which are decorated, set on their long edges, ends touching, surmounted by a facing of round granite boulders. Excavations in 1963 made it possible to reconstruct the original south front **revetment** of white quartz stones, except where the entrance has been enlarged to accommodate visitors. Above the entrance, which was originally closed by an upright slab *(right)*, is the **roof box**, a unique structure with a finely decorated lintel, through which the rays of the rising sun penetrate to the inner chamber for 17 minutes at the winter solstice (21 December).

The passage, which is lined with large standing stones, some decorated and all dressed, leads into a corbelled **chamber** a third of the way into the mound. The three decorated recesses contain stone **basins**, which held the bones of the

Newgrange

dead together with funeral offerings of stone and bone beads and pendants, bone pins and small stone balls resembling marbles. The corbelled vaulted roof, completed by a central capstone (4 tonnes), is quite waterproof as the outer faces of the stones are grooved to drain off water.

The mound was surrounded at a distance (39x49ft/12x15m) by a **great circle** of standing stones. The four opposite the entrance are among the largest.

South of the mound are traces of a late-Neolithic to early-Bronze Age **pit circle**.

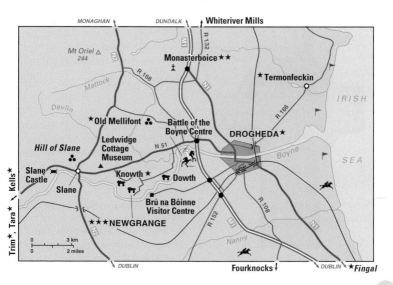

Battle of the Boyne

The battle fought on 12 July 1690 was the decisive engagement in the War of the Two Kings *(Cogadh an Dá Rí)* and ended the Stuart cause. The army of **King James II** of England, supported by Louis XIV of France, numbered some 25,000. King William III of England (**William of Orange**) and his allies (British, Danish, Dutch, Finnish, French, German, Irish, Polish, Prussian and Swiss) counted 36,000.

While the French Jacobites were under orders to delay William, the latter was keen for a speedy victory. As he surveyed his troops on the morning of the battle, a bullet tore his coat and grazed his shoulder. The king despatched troops upstream to the French left flank, they forded the Boyne at Oldbridge and attacked the Jacobite army on the south bank; five crossings were made between 10am–2pm.

William lost 500 men; James double that. On hearing William had crossed the river, James left for Dublin, rode on to Duncannon and sailed to Kinsale and France. In the hope of reversing the Cromwellian land settlement, the Irish fought on until the following year when they suffered defeats at Athlone, Aughrim and Limerick.

Knowth★

The mound (40ft/12m high, 220ft/67m in diameter) probably dates from 2500 to 2000 BC. It contains two decorated passage graves discovered in 1967 and 1968; one is simply an enlargement of the passageway but the other is circular and corbelled with side chambers. It is aligned east–west and is surrounded by smaller tombs facing the large central mound. In the early centuries AD the central mound was surrounded by deep defensive ditches. In about 8C AD the settlement expanded and several souterrains and rectangular houses were built. From the 12C to 14C the site was occupied by the Normans who constructed a rectangular stone structure on the top of the mound.

Excavations conducted since 1962 have made it possible to reconstruct the smaller tombs which had collapsed owing to the passage of time and conversion of the material to other uses.

Dowth

The mound (☛ *closed for excavation*), which was raised by man in 3000 BC (1 acre/0.4ha, 280ft/85m in diameter, 50ft/15.24m high), contains two tombs and a souterrain connecting with the north tomb. The base of the mound was enclosed by about 100 kerb stones, many ornamented, although most are covered by landslip.

Other Sites

Tara★

5mi/8km S of Navan by N 3. (Dúchas)
& ⏱ *Site: Open all year. Visitor Centre and guided tour: mid-May–mid-Sept, 10am–6pm (5.15pm last tour).* ☞€2.10. ☕ P ☎ 046 9025903. www.heritage ireland.ie.

The name of Tara conjures up the spirit of Irish Celtic greatness; the Hill of Tara, also known as Tara of the Kings, played a significant part in Irish legends. Its origin as a religious site is lost in prehistory; it

High Cross, Monasterboice

B Kaufmann/MICHELIN

achieved its greatest prestige under the pagan High Kings of Ireland, and even after the introduction of Christianity it retained its significance as the nominal seat of the High King until it was abandoned in 1022.

During the 1798 rebellion a skirmish took place on the hill. In the 19C O'Connell chose it as the site of one of his huge rallies (monster meetings) in the cause of Roman Catholic emancipation; 250 000 people came to hear him speak.

The **bare hill** pockmarked with earthworks does not readily suggest a royal palace. An effort of the imagination is required to envisage the many small buildings, of wood or wattle and daub, where the king held his court.

The history of Tara is recounted in an audio-visual presentation in the early-19C **St Patrick's Church**, which incorporates a medieval window.

In the churchyard stands a red sandstone pillar stone, known as **St Adamnán's Cross**, which bears a carved figure which may be the ancient Celtic god **Cernunnos**.

West of the graveyard is the **Rath of the Synods**, a ringfort with three banks. Farther south is an Iron-Age ringfort, enclosed by a bank and a ditch, known as the **Royal Enclosure**. Within it is the **Mound of the Hostages**, a small passage grave which dates from about 1800 BC. In the centre of the enclosure are two ringforts, known as the **Royal Seat** and **Cormac's House;** beside the statue of St Patrick, is a standing stone known as the **Lia Fáil**, which was moved from its original position near the Mound of the Hostages to be a memorial to those who died in 1798.

South of the Royal Enclosure is part of another earthwork known as **King Laoghaire's Rath**. To the north of the churchyard is a hollow flanked by two long parallel banks, which may have been the grand entrance but which is known as the Banqueting Hall. On the west side are three circular earthworks; the first is known as Gráinne's Fort, the other two as the Sloping Trenches.

South of the hill *(0.5mi/0.8km – visible from the road)* is part of another ringfort, known as **Rath Maeve**, surrounded by a bank and ditch.

Fourknocks

11mi/18km S of Drogheda by R 108; after 10mi/16km turn right.

The **passage grave** (*key available from Mr White;* ☎*041 980 9950*), which dates from c 1500 BC, is unusually large compared with the size of the mound. The interior contains stones decorated with zigzags and other prehistoric designs and a human face. It contained over 60 burials.

Battle Site

Battle of the Boyne Visitor Centre

&⃞ ⏰*Open Mar–Apr daily, 9.30am–5.30pm. May–Sept, daily 10am–6pm. Oct–Feb, daily 9am–5pm. Last admission 1 hr before closing. Living History weekends, May–Sept.* ⬮€3.70. ⛶ ☎*041 980 9950. www.battleoftheboyne.ie.*

The battlefield site, now part of the Oldbridge estate, granted to the Williamite commander Coddington, contains a museum and interpretive centre including an audio-visual presentation. There are walks on the estate and beside the river from the Obelisk Bridge.

Monastic Sites

Monasterboice★★

8mi/13km N of Drogheda by N 1.

Overlooked by a half-ruined **round tower**, three **high crosses** of outstanding beauty and interest mark the site of the famous 6C monastery founded by **St Buithe** (**Boethius**), an important centre of learning closely connected with Armagh.

The **South Cross** was erected by Muiredach in the 9C. The west face shows the Crucifixion, Christ with Peter and Paul, the raised Christ flanked by Apostles and the Mocking of Jesus; on the east face are the Last Judgement, the Adoration of the Magi, Moses striking the Rock, David and Goliath, the Fall of Man, and Cain slaying Abel.

The **West Cross** (*between the two ruined churches*) is unusually tall (23ft/7m) and the subjects of the carvings are unusual: the Crucifixion, the Arrest of Christ,

Christ surrounded by Apostles, the Resurrection of the Dead, the Soldiers at the Tomb; Christ Militans, Christ walking on the water, Simon Magus and the Fiery Furnace, Goliath, Samuel anointing David, the Golden Calf, the Sacrifice of Isaac, David killing a lion.

The **North Cross** *(NE corner of the graveyard)* also shows the Crucifixion. The original shaft is contained in the same enclosure as well as a monastic sundial indicating the hours of the Divine Office.

Behind the north church lies an early **grave slab** bearing the name Ruarcan. The **tower** and its treasures were burned in 1097.

Mellifont Old Abbey★

6mi/10km W of Drogheda by N 51, R 168 and a minor road west of Tullyallen. (Dúchas) &⊙*Visitor Centre: open May–Sept, 10am–6pm (5.15pm last admission).* ⊛€2.10. ▣ ☎041 982 6459. www.heritage ireland.ie/en.*

The first Cistercian house in Ireland was founded here, on the banks of the **River Mattock** by St Malachy in 1142 with four Irish and nine French monks. It no doubt owed its name ("Honey fountain" in Latin) to the beauty of its surroundings.

Still standing are the ruined **gatehouse**, the vaulted **Chapter House** (14C) and four faces of the two-storey **octagonal lavabo** (12C). The 12C church, which was consecrated in 1157, was designed by one of the Frenchmen; it had a crypt at the west end and three transept chapels. In 1225 the chancel and transepts were extended. In 1556 the abbey became a private house which was abandoned in 1727.

Hill of Slane

This hilltop with its wide-ranging views is one of the key sites in the story of Irish Christianity. In 433 St Patrick travelled from Saul (in Co Down) by sea and on foot to Slane, where he lit a fire on the hilltop on Easter Eve to challenge the druids who were holding a festival at Tara. As anyone who kindled a fire within sight of Tara did so on pain of death, Patrick was brought before Laoghaire, the High King, to whom he preached the Gospel. Although the king remained a pagan, he allowed his subjects freedom of conscience. One of them, Erc, converted and founded a monastery at Slane; he is said to be buried in the ruined mortuary house in the graveyard.

The church, which was in use until 1723, was part of **Slane Friary**, a Franciscan house, founded in 1512 by Sir Christopher Flemyng, whose arms are on the west wall of the courtyard. The friary, which housed four priests, four lay-brothers and four choristers, was suppressed in 1540, occupied by Capuchins in 1631 and abandoned under Cromwell. On the west face of the hill is a motte raised by Richard le Flemyng of Flanders, who arrived in Ireland in 1175.

Termonfeckin★

6mi/10km N of Drogheda by R 167 E or R 166 and a minor road E. (Dúchas) Key available from the cottage opposite.

In the graveyard of St Fechin's Church stands a 10C **high cross** depicting the Crucifixion and Christ in Glory; it marks the site of a monastery founded by St Fechin of Fore. Close to the shore stands a 15C or 16C three-storey **tower house** which has an unusual corbelled roof *(45 steps)*: **view** of the coast from Drogheda *(S)* to Clogher Head *(N)*.

Slane

The "square" at the centre of the village was laid out by Viscount Conyngham in the late 18C; it is lit by oil lamps and bordered by four nearly identical Georgian houses, each flanked by two smaller houses. The Gothic Gate *(S of the crossroads)* was designed by **Francis Johnston** c 1795 as an entrance to Slane Castle. From the bridge over the Boyne there is a **view** of Slane Castle, Slane Mill (1766), the weir and the canal; the towpath goes upstream to Navan and downstream to Drogheda.

Slane Castle

0.25mi/0.5km W of Slane by N 51. ⌁⌁*Guided tour May–early-Aug, Sun–Thu noon–5pm.* ⊛€7. ☎041 988400. www.slanecastle.ie.*

The impressive raised **site** overlooking the **River Boyne** is surmounted by an elegant assembly of turrets, crenellations and machicolations. The present house was built between 1785 and 1821 on the site of a confiscated **Fleming** fortress purchased by the Conynghams in 1641. Only the best architects were employed, among them James Gandon, James Wyatt, Francis Johnston and Thomas Hopper, while Capability Brown designed the stables and landscaped the grounds.

Ledwidge Cottage Museum

0.5mi/0.8km E of Slane by N 51.
&🕒*Open daily, 10am–1pm, 2pm–5.30pm.* ∞*€3.* ☎*041 982 4544.*
www.francisledwidge.com.
The four-roomed semi-detached cottage built under the Labourers' Dwellings Act (1886) was the childhood home of the poet, **Francis Ledwidge** (1887–1917), who wrote about his love of the Meath countryside. Today, it displays some of his manuscripts.

BUNCRANA

POPULATION 3 112

With its long sandy beach facing west across Lough Swilly to the mountains of Donegal, Buncrana (Bun Cranncha) is a busy seaside resort and the largest town on the Inishowen Peninsula, crowded in summer with holidaymakers from Londonderry, a mere dozen miles away on the far side of the border. Approached by a six-arched bridge spanning the Crana River, O'Docherty's Keep is all that remains of the castle built by the Anglo-Normans and later held by the local lords, the "O'Dochertys tall from dark Donegal" (Benedict Kiely).

- **Information:** Buncrana; ☎074 9362600.
  The Diamond, Inishowen; ☎074 9374933. www.visitinishowen.com.
- **Orient Yourself:** Buncrana is set on the east shore of Lough Swilly, NW of Londonderry. It is a good place to start a tour of the Inishowen Peninsula.
- **Don't Miss:** Malin Head and Grianán of Aileach.
- **Organising Your Time:** allow at least 1 day for the driving tour.
- **Also See:** DONEGAL, DONEGAL COAST, DONEGAL GLENS, LONDONDERRY, SPERRIN MOUNTAINS.

Driving Tour

Inishowen (Inis Eoghain) Scenic Drive★★

100mi/160km.

This drive follows the coast of the Inishowen Peninsula to Malin Head, the most northerly point in Ireland. The landscape is composed of rugged mountains covered in blanket bog, fringed by steep cliffs or broad sweeps of sand. The peninsula is named after Eoghain, a 5C ruler who was a contemporary of St Patrick. By the 15C the powerful clan of the O'Dochertys held sway, but when their chief was killed in 1608, the land passed into the possession of the Eliza-

bethan adventurer Sir Arthur Chichester, whose family eventually became the largest landowners in Ireland.

- *Take coast road N to Dunree Head.*

Fort Dunree Military Museum★

🕒*Open May–Sept,10.30am (1pm Sun) –6pm; Oct–May, Mon–Fri 10.30am–4.30pm, Sat–Sun 1pm–6pm.* ∞*€5.* ⌣.
☎*074 9361817 – www.dunree.pro.ie.*
A drawbridge spans the narrow defile which separates this late 18C fort from the desolate headland of Dunree Head. The fort itself has been converted into a **military museum** containing the original guns; modern interactive technology and a video explain their role in a coastal defence battery and describe

the evolution of the fort from a fortified earthen embankment, built in 1798 under the threat of French invasion, to an important element in a chain of forts on the shores of Lough Swilly defending a Royal Navy base at Buncrana. In 1914 the entire British Grand Fleet sheltered behind a boom in the Lough. Knockalla Fort is visible across the narrow channel on the opposite shore.

▶ *Return to the junction and turn left; at the crossroads turn left.*

Gap of Mamore★

The road climbs past rocky outcrops to the **viewpoint** and sights of Dunaff Head.

▶ *Turn left past Lenan Strand to Lenan Head, through Dunaff to Clonmany and continue N on R 238.*

Ballyliffin (Baile Lifín)

Beyond Lenon Head where a gun battery (1895) used to command the entrance to Lough Swilly, lies this attractive holiday village, slightly set back from Pollan Bay and Pollan Strand.

▶ *Continue E on R 238.*

Carndonagh High Cross★

At the top of the hill next to the Anglican church stands an 8C **high cross**, decorated with an interlaced cross and a Crucifixion and flanked by two **pillars**: one shows David with his harp. In the graveyard stands a **cross pillar**, known as the Marigold Stone.

▶ *Continue N on R 238 and R 242.*

Malin

The 17C Plantation village retains its original layout, including its triangular green.

Lag Sand Dunes★

Massive sand dunes line the north shore of Trawbreaga Bay, the estuary of the Donagh River.

Malin Head★★

The tiny fishing village shelters in the lee of the great headland. On the cliffs stands a tower, originally built in 1805 by the British Admiralty to monitor shipping and later used as a signal tower by Lloyds. North across the sound *(1.5mi/2.4km)* lies Inishtrahull Island, once the site of a hermitage but now deserted. The road circles the headland providing dramatic **views**★★ *(southwest)* to Pollan Strand and Dunaff Head.

▶ *Take the coast road S via Portaleen to Culdaff. Take R 238 S; turn left into minor road.*

Bocan Stone Circle

In a field *(left)* are the traces of a stone circle which may have comprised 30 standing stones.

▶ *Return to last junction; turn right into R 238 ; drive towards Culdaff; turn left into minor road.*

Clonca Church and Cross

In the 6C St Buodán founded a monastery at Clonca. The ruined church dates

Dunagree Point

H Champollion/MICHELIN

from the 17C/18C but the carved lintel is earlier. Inside is the 16C tombstone of Magnus MacOrristin, who probably came from the Hebrides, showing a sword and a hurley stick and bearing a rare Irish inscription. In the field opposite the church door is **St Buodán's high cross** depicting the miracle of the loaves and fishes.

▷ *Continue to the next junction, turn left and then right.*

Carrowmore High Crosses

The monastery founded by Chionais, St Patrick's brother-in-law, is now marked by two **high crosses**, a decorated slab and a boulder inscribed with a cross.

▷ *Return to the last junction; turn right; in Gleneely take R 238 S; after 3.5mi/4km turn left to Leckemy and take the minor road NE to Kinnagoe Bay.*

Kinnagoe Bay

The sandy beach is sheltered by steep headlands. A map *(at the road junction)* plots the sites of the Spanish Armada ships wrecked off the Irish coast; many military relics have been recovered from *La Duquesa St Anna* and *La Trinidad Valencia*, which foundered in the bay. *Clifftop footpath to Inishowen Head.*

▷ *Take the minor road S to Greencastle, turn left to Inishowen Head.*

Inishowen Head★

The headland (295ft/90m) above the tiny harbour next to the lighthouse on **Dunagree Point** commands a fine view east along the Antrim coast to the Giant's Causeway. *Clifftop footpath to Kinnagoe Bay.*

▷ *Take the coast road S past the golf course.*

Greencastle

The beach makes this a popular resort. North of the town, on the cliffs opposite Magilligan Point, commanding the narrow entrance to Lough Foyle, stand the overgrown ruins of a castle built in 1305 by Richard de Burgo, the Red Earl of Ulster, so-called because of his florid complexion. It was captured by Edward Bruce in 1316, fell into the possession of the O'Donnells in the 14C and was granted to Sir Arthur Chichester in 1608; the adjoining fort (1812) was used in the defence of Lough Foyle until the end of the 19C.

▷ *From Greencastle take R 241 S.*

Moville (Bun an Phobail)

Moville (pronounced with the accent on the second syllable), once a bustling port where emigrant ships set sail for the United States, is now a seaside resort. The granite mass of **St Pius' Roman Catholic Church** (1953) masks its handsome mahogany interior. The cliffs and beaches overlooking Lough Foyle have been incorporated into a landscaped coastal walk, **Moville Green**.

▷ *From Moville take R 241 S; after 2mi/3.2km turn right.*

In **Cooley** at the graveyard gate stands a **high cross** (10ft/3m) with a hole in its head through which people clasped hands to seal an undertaking. The graveyard contains a **mortuary house**, or tomb shrine, known as the Skull House.

The Warrior Coirrgend

This fierce fighter had committed the terrible crime of murdering the son of the king. As punishment, he was ordered to carry the body and a burial stone to **Grianán Mountain**. The burden killed him and he died crying "Á, leac!" ("Alas, stone!") – the origin of the name of the site.

▷ *Continue S on R 241. In Muff turn right to Burnfoot; take the minor road to Speenoge.*

Grianán of Aileach★★

This pre-Christian circular stone fort crowning the exposed hilltop (☞*see 'The Warrior Coirrgend' box*) is among the most spectacular of its kind in the country, though its present form is a late 19C reconstruction. It served as the seat of the O'Neill clan from the 5C-11C but even before then was included in Ptolemy's map of the world as a "royal residence". It was destroyed in 1101 by the King of Munster, Murtogh O'Brien, in retaliation for the destruction of his own royal seat at Kincora. A tunnel pierces the stone wall (13ft/4m thick) which contains small chambers and steps to the ramparts and encloses a circle (77ft/23m in diameter). From the ramparts is an extensive **view**★★ *(east)* of Derry and the Sperrin Mountains, *(northeast)* of Lough Foyle, *(north)* of the Inishowen Peninsula, and *(west)* of Inch Island, Lough Swilly and Knockalla Mountain. At the foot of the hill is **St Aengus Church**, a magnificent modern building designed by Liam McCormick.

▷ *Return downhill to Burnfoot. Take R 238 N to Fahan.*

Fahan Cross-Slab

On the south side of the village in the old graveyard beside the Anglican church stands a 7C **cross-slab**, decorated with a cross formed of interlaced bands, one flanked by two figures. It marks the site of a monastery which was founded by St Mura in the 7C and survived until at least 1098.

▷ *Take R 238 N to Buncrana.*

THE BURREN★★

Covering much of County Clare, the austere limestone plateau of the Burren (*Boireann – Place of Rock*) is one of Ireland's strangest but most compelling landscapes. Six thousand years of human occupation have largely denuded the Burren of its trees, but in spring and early summer, the bleak scenery is coloured by extraordinary carpets of diverse flowers, with Mediterranean and Alpine species flourishing side by side.

- ⊞ **Information:** Cliffs of Moher, Liscannor, Co Clare.
  ☎065 708 1171. www.shannonheritage.com.
- ⊙ **Organising Your Time:** It could take several days to explore The Burren!
- ▷ **Orient Yourself:** The Burren covers the northern part of Co Clare extending south from Ballyvaughan to Ennistimon and Corofin.
- ☺ **Don't Miss:** The Cliffs of Moher.
- ☝ **Also See:** ARAN ISLANDS, ATHENRY, CONNEMARA, ENNIS, GALWAY.

A Bit of History

The Burren gently inclines south, its outer limits generally marked by steep escarpments. The classic karstic features of limestone pavements and underground drainage systems are accompanied by sink holes, which, when filled by a rise in the water table, become temporary lakes known as *turlach*. Fissures (grykes) between the slabs (clints) forming the limestone pavements contain enough soil to support a remarkably rich flora. The human impact has been considerable; drystone walls define field patterns and enclosures of immense variety, some dating back to neolithic times, and there are a multitude of tombs, forts and traces of ancient settlements.

The old Celtic practice of booleying – moving cattle and sheep to summer pastures on higher ground or moorland – is practised in reverse: in winter, the cattle are kept on the higher ground, where it remains relatively dry partly due to the Gulf Stream, partly because the limestone absorbs heat and releases it later; then , in summer, when the uplands may suffer from drought, the animals are kept near the homesteads, where they can be tended and watered.

Driving Tour
Round trip of 80mi/128km.

Ennistimon (Inis Díomáin)
The **waterfalls** on the River Cullenagh are visible from the seven-arch bridge, the river bank *(through arched entry in the Main Street)* and from the grounds of the Falls Hotel. The town itself is noted for its traditional shop fronts with Irish writing.

▷ *Take N 67 and R 481 N.*

Address Book

For coin ranges, see the Legend on the cover flap.

SIGHTSEEING
Aran Islands – From Doolin there is a ferry to the Aran Islands. ☎065 7074455. www.doolinferries.com.

WHERE TO EAT
Linnane's Lobster Bar – *Opposite The Burren Centre.* ☎065 7088157. Perched on the rocks, above Galway Bay. Pews and pine tables and a menu that makes the most of local seafood; from chowder to mussels, crab cakes and fresh lobster.
Vaughan's – *Kilfenora.* ☎065 708 8004. Live music most nights and set dancing (Thu, Sun); menu ranges from sandwiches to beef and Guinness casserole.

ENTERTAINMENT/NIGHT-LIFE
Irish Traditional Music – **Doolin** has an international reputation both for the audience and for the quality of the musicianship. Other places for sessions in summer are Ballyvaughan, Kilfenora, Lisdoonvarna and Ennistimon.

SHOPPING
The **Burren Smokehouse** in Lisdoonvarna sells fish, cheese and other gourmet items. *Visitor Centre open* 9am/10am–5pm (6pm May–Sept; 4pm Jan–Feb). ☎065 7074432; mail order service www.burrensmokehouse.ie.
National Knitting Centre and Crana Knits – *St Orans Road, Buncrana. Traditional and contemporary hand-knits to suit all.* ☎074 936 2355.
Burren Perfumery (*see Driving Tour*).

SPORTS AND LEISURE
Seaside Resorts – To the south at **Liscannor**, **Lahinch** (long sand beach with lifeguard) and **Milltown Malbay**; also to the north at **Fanore** (*S of Black Head*) and at **Finavarra** (*NE of Ballyvaughan*).
Burren Way – Walking trails between Ballyvaughan and Liscannor (*26mi/42km*) in the Caher Valley, mostly on Green Roads, through Doolin and along the Cliffs of Moher before turning inland to Liscannor. Good walk from Lisdoonvarna south across the bog at Cnoc na Madre.

FESTIVALS
The **Willie Clancy Summer School** (*July*) Milltown Malbay: major festival for all music, song and dance, particularly of the elbow (*uilleann*) pipes.
An annual summer school is held in **Ennistimon** to celebrate the work of Brian Merriman (b. 1749 in Ennistimon), whose poem *The Midnight Court* is unique in Irish Literature.

Kilfenora

Kilfenora was once an important episcopal see. Its cathedral, now in partial ruin, has superb carved capitals, crude effigies, and an elegant east window. Outside stand three 12C **high crosses**★. The famous Doorty's Cross, despite its eroded condition, is carved with figures of Christ, a bishop, and Celtic decoration. A fourth cross *(100yd/90m W in a field)* shows the Crucifixion.

The Burren Centre★

&♿⏱*Open Jun–Sept, 9.30am–6pm; Mar–May and Oct, 10am–5pm.* ✆€6. ✗🅿 ☎*065 708 8030. www.theburrencentre.ie.*

Excellent displays provide a clear insight into the unique natural history of the Burren, and the human impact on it.

▶ *Take R 476 NW.*

Lisdoonvarna
(Lios Dúin Bhearna)

Ireland's only operating spa developed in the 19C round three mineral springs; naturally sulphurous water is served by the glass or the bottle at the Spa Wells; the health centre provides sulphur baths and other treatments.

▶ *Take N 67 N.*

Corkscrew Hill

There is a fine **view** of the terraced limestone landscape from Corkscrew Hill on the road between Ballyvaughan and Lisdoonvarna *(N 67)*.

Newtown Castle and Trail

🕐*Open May–Sept, Mon–Fri, 10am–5.30pm.* ☎*065 707 7200. www.burren lawschool.org.*

The spiral stone staircase of this fine 16C defensive tower house leads to a series of exhibits illustrating the importance of the region in medieval times as a centre for the study of law.

A trail on the hillside behind the tower leads to a variety of natural and historic

Brides for Bachelors

Lisdoonvarna is the scene in September of a famous – or notorious – Match-making Festival, whose original function was to provide partners for lonely lads living on isolated farms deep in the countryside. For several days the little spa town is filled with hordes of merrymakers, less intent nowadays on the serious business of finding a bride than of having a raucously good time. The Match-making Festival takes place from late August to early October with dancing, singsongs, evening pub sessions and walks.

Cliffs of Moher

Botanising

The best months to view the 1000 or so species of flowering plants and ferns in the Burren are May or June but there is something to enjoy in every season. The rarer plants favour the more extreme habitats – the sunniest, shadiest, driest or wettest – look for cracks *(grikes)* shallow enough to admit light but deep enough to give shelter. Keep to naked limestone or grassy hill slopes, avoiding the cultivated farmland.

man-made features including an early lime kiln and a Victorian gazebo.

▷ *Take R 480 SE.*

Aillwee Cave★

♿🚶Visit by guided tour (35min) only, Jan–Nov daily 10am–6pm. ✆€12. ☕ ☎065 707 7036. www.aillweecave.ie.
Fluctuating water levels make the underground Burren perilous. This cavern has a single tunnel (0.75mi/1km) with stalactites, stalagmites and a **waterfall**★ which is impressively floodlit from below. At the back of the Highway, the largest chamber, there is a vertical drop. The **visitor centre** explains the formation of the cave and its discovery in 1940 by a local herdsman, Jack McCann.

Poulnabrone Portal Tomb★

In a magnificent stony setting on the road between Aillwee and Leamaneh Castle *(R 480)* stands this **dolmen**, the most famous and much photographed megalithic tomb in the Burren.

Leamaneh Castle

Only the shell remains of a four-storey Elizabethan-style fortified house with mullioned windows which was built in the 17C by Conor O'Brien, killed in 1651 during the Cromwellian wars.

▷ *Return N on R 480 SE ; bear right into a minor road to Carran.*

Burren Perfumery

🕐Open daily 9am–6pm/7pm (5pm Oct–Apr). ☕ (Easter–Sept). ☎ 065 708 9102. www.burrenperfumery.com.
The astonishing diversity of Mediterranean and Alpine flowers in this seemingly inhospitable landscape are the inspiration for a range of perfumes and soaps made here by traditional methods of distilling and blending.

▷ *Turn right into N 67.*

Corcomroe Abbey★

The ruins of this Cistercian abbey founded around 1180 blend harmoniously with the limestone of the surrounding Burren. The monks dedicated their abbey to St Mary of the Fertile Rock, perhaps in response to abundance of flowers in the stony countryside. There

are carved capitals and fine vaulting in the choir and transept chapels. It was here that William Butler Yeats set his verse play *The Dreaming of the Bones*. On Turlough Hill (925ft/282m) are the ruins of three 12C churches.

▷ *Take N 67 W to Ballyvaughan.*
Turn R 477 W.

Scenic Route★★

The coast road south of Black Head provides a fine view of the huge boulders, deposited at the end of the Ice Age, resting on the bare limestone pavement; in fine weather the Aran Islands, of similar geological formation, are clearly visible offshore.

▷ *W of Lisdoonvarna take*
N 67 and R 478 S.

Cliffs of Moher★★★

♿🕐 *Site: Open daily. Visitor Centre: open daily. Mar, Apr, Oct, 9am–6pm. May–Sept, 8.30am–7pm (Jun–Aug 8.30pm). Nov–Feb 9am–5pm.* 🍴 ☎ *065 708 6141. www.cliffsofmoher.ie.*

These great dark sandstone cliffs (600ft/182m high – nearly 5mi/8km long) are among the country's most stunning natural sights. Rising sheer from the Atlantic, the Cliffs of Moher are home to one of the major colonies of cliff nesting seabirds in Ireland. The best view is from **O'Brien's Tower**, built in 1853 by Cornelius O'Brien. The **New Visitor Experience** centre provides information on the flora and fauna of the area.

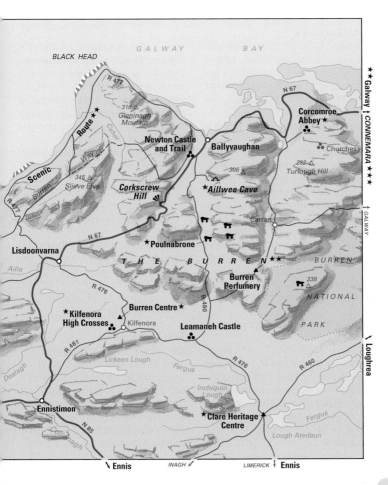

CAHIR

POPULATION 2 236

In a fine location on the River Suir at the foot of the Galty Mountains, Cahir (An Cathair) – also known as Caher and pronounced *care* – is a busy little cross-roads town. This designated Heritage Town now benefits from a bypass carrying the main Dublin–Cork highway. Its formidable castle, built on a rocky islet in the river, was the site of Brian Ború, the High King of Ireland's residence, in the 10/11C. The present stronghold was begun in the 13C, then greatly modified and extended by one of the greatest of Ireland's Anglo-Norman dynasties, the Butlers, who retained possession until it passed to the State in 1961.

- **Information:** Castle Street, Cahir. ☎052 41453. www.cahirtourism.ie.
- **Organising Your Time:** Half a day for the town. longer for excursions.
- **Orient Yourself:** Cahir marks the junction of N 8 and N 24, S of Cashel and NW of Clonmel.
- **Don't Miss:** the guided tour of the Castle.
- **Also See:** CASHEL, CLONMEL, LISMORE.

Walking Tour

Cahir Castle★★

(Dúchas) ♿🕐*Open daily. Mid-Mar–mid-Jun, mid-Sept–mid-Oct 9.30am–5.30pm. Mid-Jun–mid-Sept 9.30am–7pm. Rest of year, closes 4.30pm* 🕐*Closed Dec 24–30.* ✑*€2.90.* ☎*052 41011. www.heritageireland.ie/en.*

Though much restored, Cahir castle is one of the largest and finest examples of a late medieval stronghold in Ireland, with high outer wall, outer, middle and inner wards, a barbican, sturdy towers and a splendid keep. It expresses the power and pride of the Anglo-Norman Butlers, Earls of Ormond, who held sway over much of southeastern Ireland, even though its defences failed to save it from falling to an assault by troops led by Queen Elizabeth I's favourite, the Earl of Essex. The guided tour explores its passageways, spiral staircases, sentry walks and great hall.

- *Walk along Castle Street to the Square.*

The **Cahir House Hotel**, the former family seat of the Butlers after the castle had fallen into disrepair, and the Market House (now the library) are part of the 18C transformation of the town centre by the Butlers; the mills also date from this period.

- *Walk along Old Church Street (N 24 to Clonmel).*

The ruined church, last used in the 1820s, had a curtain wall, which allowed Roman Catholics and Protestants to worship simultaneously; in the 19C, when Cahir was an important garrison town, part of the adjoining cemetery was reserved for military burials. Many Cahir men fell in the First World War and are commemorated by the Great War Memorial, a rarity in an Irish town.

- *Return to the Square and turn right into Church Street (N 8 north towards Cashel).*

The Anglican **St Paul's Church** was designed in 1820 by John Nash, the famous Regency architect.

Excursions

Swiss Cottage★

1mi/2km S of Caher by R 670 or on foot along the riverbank. (Dúchas) 📷*Visit by guided tour (40min) only, mid-Apr–mid-Oct, 10am–6pm. Mid-Mar–mid-Apr and mid-Oct–mid-Nov Tue–Sun and Bank Hols 10am–1pm, 2pm–6pm (4.30pm Oct–Nov).* ✑*€2.90.* ☎*052 41144. www. heritageireland.ie/en.*

Office of Public Works

Swiss Cottage, Caher

While in Cahir, John Nash also turned his hand to the design of this elaborate thatched cottage, built in 1812–14 as a fishing and hunting lodge for Lord Caher. In one of the two ground-floor rooms, the hand-painted French wallpaper shows views of the Bosporus.

Mitchelstown Cave

9mi/14.5km W by N 8; in Boolakennedy turn left. ⊙*Open daily 10am–6pm (Nov–Jan 11am–5pm).* ⊛€5. ☎*052 67246.*

A flight of 88 steep steps leads into three massive caverns (1mi/2km) containing dripstone formations – stalactites and stalagmites, curtains and pipes: the most impressive being the Tower of Babel, a huge calcite column, measuring 250ft/76m long.

CARRICK-ON-SHANNON ★

POPULATION 1 868

On the main road and railway between Dublin and Sligo, the county to of Co Leitrim (Cora Droma Rúisc) is a major crossing point on the River Sh In recent years its status as a busy centre for boating and cruising h boosted by the reopening of the Ballyconnell-Ballinamore Canal, c the Shannon-Erne Waterway.

- **Information:** The Old Barrel Store, The Marina. ☎071 9620170. www.leitrimtourism.com.
- **Organising Your Time:** You'll want to spend a day here, p exploring the river.
- ▶ **Orient Yourself:** Carrick-on-Shannon lies on N 4, the D on the east bank of the River Shannon, close to Lough
- **Especially for Kids:** a ride on the Cavan and Leitrir
- **Also See:** BOYLE, CAVAN, KNOCK, LONGFORD, STP

Town

The **Costello Chapel** (⊙*open Mar–Oct, daily (or ask at tourist office);* ☎*078 20251)* on Bridge Street is a mortuary chapel

built h
to h'
m

T
16
str
Jan

The
which
was bi
to scho
now live
a master
and exam
interest in
neighbours

152

Shannon–Erne Waterway

This canal was built (1847–58) as the **Ballinamore–Ballyconnell Navigation** by the engineer John McMahon to join the River Shannon with Lough Erne: the final link in a waterway system devised to enable barges to travel between Dublin, Belfast, Limerick and Waterford. Competition from the railway and a lack of industry meant that the scheme failed and the canal was abandoned in 1869. By 1880 it was derelict. The course (40mi/65km) includes 16 locks and 34 stone bridges as it runs through Lough Scur, St John's Lough, Garadice Lough, and along Woodford River. It joins the River Shannon in **Leitrim** *(4mi/8km north of Carrick by R 280).*

Address Book

SIGHTSEEING

Moon River, *Main St, Carrickon Shannon – Cruises on the Shannon. Saturday night party cruises all year, 11.30pm boarding.* €12. ☎071 962 1777. www.moon-river.net.

Cavan and Leitrim Railway – *Dromond. Open Sat–Mon (acccording to demand), 10am (1pm Sun) to 5.30pm.* €8. Train ride (20min). ☎071 9638599. www.irish-railway.com. Narrow gauge steam railway and tour.

Leitrim Way – *The Leitrim Way Map Guide,* available from tourist offices, details a number of walks.

At the east end of **St George's Terrace** stands the Town Clock (1905). The **Market House** and yard *(south side)* were built in 1839 and elegant **Hatley Manor** *(north side)*, also built in the 1830s. Next to it stands the Courthouse of 1821, once linked by underground passage to the neighbouring County Gaol, the site of which is now occupied by the **marina**.

Driving Tour

Shannon Valley

25mi/40km.

▶ *Take N 4 southeast.*

Jamestown

The fortified settlement established in 1622 to guard the river crossing downstream from Carrick is named after James I.

John McGahern

...author of *Amongst Women,* ...won the Booker prize in 1991, ...ought up in Cootehall, went ...l in Carrick-on-Shannon and ...near Mohill. McGahern is ...at describing provincial life ...ning the effect of people's ...or indifference to their ...lives.

Drumsna

Anthony Trollope was inspired by the ruins of the Jones family mansion and the story of their downfall to write his first novel, *The Macdermots of Ballycloran* (1847)

▶ *South of Drumsna turn left onto R 201 to Mohill.*

In **Mohill** is a statue of long-time resident **Turlough O'Carolan (Carolan)** *(see BOYLE)* seated at his harp.

▶ *Leave Mohill by R 201 which bears right at the end of the main street; at the fork bear right onto L 112; at next fork bear right; after 0.75mi/1.2km turn left onto a narrow road (sign).*

Lough Rynn Castle Hotel★

☎071 9632710. www.loughrynn.ie. This extensive domain was acquired by the **Clements** family in 1750 but it dates mostly from Victorian times. Its walled gardens and an exotic arboretum are open to non-residents.

▶ *Exit right. At the T-junction turn right; after two side turnings and two crossroads bear right to Dromod.*

Dromod and **Roosky** are attractive Shannonside villages popular for cruising.

▶ *From Roosky continue south on N 4; after 3mi/4.8km turn left (sign) to Cloonmorris Abbey (1mi/1.6km).*

Beside the graveyard entrance of the ruined 12C **Cloonmorris church** stands an **Ogham stone** inscribed Qenuven.

▶ *Return to N 4 and continue south; in Newtown Forbes bear right onto a minor road (direction Killashee); turn right onto N 4 and then bear left to Cloondara. Rejoin N 5 west of the village and continue to Termonbarry.*

Bord Fáilte, Dublin

Cruising on the River Shannon

CASHEL★★★

POPULATION 2 346

Rising like a mirage over the vastness of the Tipperary plain, the Rock of Cashel (Caiseal) is Ireland's Acropolis; its ruined buildings are wonderfully evocative of the spirit of Celtic Christianity and Irish kingship. From the limestone outcrop (200ft/60m) rises a cluster of structures – castle and fortress, chapel, cathedral and round tower – forming the country's greatest landmark. At close quarters, the Rock reveals a wealth of pattern and texture, the primordial geometry of triangular gable, high-pitched roof, cubes, cones and cylindrical tower set off by battlements, blind arcades, slender window openings, and ornate carving.

▪ **Information:** Heritage Centre, Main Street, Cashel. ☎062 61333 or 62511. www.casheltouristoffice.com.
🕐 **Organising Your Time:** Come early morning before the coach parties descend upon the town. Allow at least half a day.
▶ **Orient Yourself:** Cashel stands on the N 8 between Cork and Portlaoise.
🅿 **Parking:** Public car park beside the Rock.
👁 **Don't Miss:** Cormac's Chapel, and an excursion to Holy Cross Abbey.
🕐 **Also See:** ABBEYLEIX, CAHER, CLONMEL, KILKENNY, ROSCREA.

A Bit of History

Royal Seat
Between c. AD370–1101, the rock was the seat of the kings of Munster, and therefore the provincial capital, comparable in regal stature to Tara, home of the High Kings of Ireland. St Patrick visited Cashel in 450 when he baptised King Aengus; there is a legend that during the ceremony, St Patrick accidentally pierced the king's foot with the point of his staff but the king, believing it to be part of the ritual, remained composed. Cashel was a place of great importance during the 10C when it was the strong-

hold of the holy Cormac MacCullinan, king and bishop.

Ecclesiastical Site
The first cathedral was founded in 1169 and in 1172 the country's clergy assembled to honour the claim of Henry II to rule all Ireland.

In 1494 it was burned down by Gerald Mor, the Great Earl of Kildare. In 1647, when Lord Inchiquin, seeking the presidency of Munster under the Cromwellian regime, attacked the town of Cashel; hundreds fled to the rock, so Lord Inchiquin ordered turf to be piled against the walls of the cathedral; in the subsequent fire, many were roasted to death. By the end of that terrible day, most of the population of 3 000 had perished.

In 1749 the Anglican Archbishop of Cashel, tiring of the climb from his palace to the cathedral, decided to move the cathedral into town. The great storm of 1847 did much damage to the abandoned building.

Rock of Cashel★★★

(Dúchas) ♿⏰*Open daily, 9am–5.30pm (early Jun–mid-Sept 7pm; mid Oct–mid-Mar 4.30pm). Last admission 45min before closing.* ⏰*Closed 25–26 Dec.* ⊙ €5.30. ☎062 61437. www.heritageireland.ie/en.*

Cormac's Chapel★★

Cashel's greatest treasure is the chapel started by Cormac MacCarthy in 1127. It is a highly ornate Romanesque building with twin towers, decorated with some of the earliest frescoes in Ireland and array of carvings, the most elaborate of their date. The human heads and animals are Celtic in style, while the interlace carving on a sarcophagus is of Viking inspiration.

Round Tower★

In perfect condition, the tower, standing 92ft/28m high, is built from irregularly coursed sandstone).

Cathedral

Most of the ruin dates from the 13C, the central tower from the 14C. In the south wall of the choir is the tomb (1) of Archbishop Miler MacGrath, the Scoundrel of Cashel, who changed his religious beliefs several times and served as both Anglican and Roman Catholic bishop of Cashel during the reign of Elizabeth I; he died in 1621 at the age of 100. The west tower (91ft/28m), also called the **castle**, was built as a fortified residence by Archbishop O'Hedigan in 1450.

Museum★

The museum, in the undercroft of the 15C Hall of the Vicars Choral, displays articles associated with the Rock: the stone cross of St Patrick (12C); an evil eye stone; and replicas of the 9C Cashel bell and brooch.

Hall of the Vicars Choral

Extensively renovated in the 1970s) this was the clergy residence. The main hall *(upstairs)* contains a huge 17C stone fireplace and fine items of medieval-style furniture made by modern craftsmen.

Rock of Cashel

H Champollion/MICHELIN

Address Book

ENTERTAINMENT / NIGHT-LIFE

Brú Ború Theatre – For a **traditional Irish evening** followed by a banquet (⌂ see Rock of Cashel).

SHOPPING

Farney Castle Visitor Centre, *Holycross, Co Tipperary* – the home, design studio and retail outlet of Irish International Designer, Cyril Cullen, Farney Castle, built in 1495 and augmented in 1800, is the only round tower in Ireland occupied as a family home. Cullen's rare Jacob sheep wool sweaters and Fine Parian porcelain figurines are on sale. *Open Mon–Sat 10am–6pm. €4.* ⌂ ☎0504 43281. www.tipp.ie/placesof interest/farney.htm

SPORTS AND LEISURE

Walking in the Galty Mountains.
Greyhound Racing in Thurles.

TRACING ANCESTORS

Brú Ború – (⌂ see Rock of Cashel).
Tipperary Family History Research – *Tipperary Exel. Open Mon–Fri, 9.30am– 5.30pm. ☎062 80555. www.tfhr.org.*

The kitchen has been restored to its original state. A video presentation in the Dormitory sets Cashel in the context of Irish history.

Brú Ború

&. ☉*Open May–Sept, 9am– 5pm. Genealogy service. Folk Theatre (music, song, dance): mid-Jun–mid-Sept, Tue–Sat at 9pm. ☜Multimedia show €5, Theatre show €18 (inc dinner €48).* ☲ ⚹. *☎062 61122. www.comhaltas.com/locations.*
A modern village green is a fitting focal point for this cultural centre, which presents performances of native Irish music, song and dance, story-telling and folk theatre. The principal attraction by day is the multimedia show.

Walking Tour

▸ *From the Rock take Bishop's Walk down through Cashel Palace Hotel Gardens into Main St.*

Cashel Palace Hotel Gardens★

☎062 62707. www.cashel-palace.ie.
This Palladian mansion, now a luxury hotel, was built in 1730 as the archbishop's palace. The gardens contain a 1702 mulberry tree and hop plants, descendants of those used in 1759 to brew the first ever Guinness, invented by Richard Guinis, agent to the Archbishop of Cashel, and brewed in Dublin by his better known son, Arthur.

Cashel Heritage Centre

☉*Open Mar–Oct, 9.30am–5.30pm (Mon–Fri, Nov–Feb). ☎062 61333 or 62511. www. casheltouristoffice.com.*
Displays traces the history of Cashel, its royal heirlooms and charters, and relics of the house of McCarthy Mor.

▸ *From Main St walk up John St.*

Cathedral and Library

The austere Anglican cathedral dedicated jointly to St John and to St Patrick of the Rock (1749- 84), has a fine panelled ceiling and stalls for Dean and Chapte. In the graveyard a number of

Cormac's Chapel

H Champollion/MICHELIN

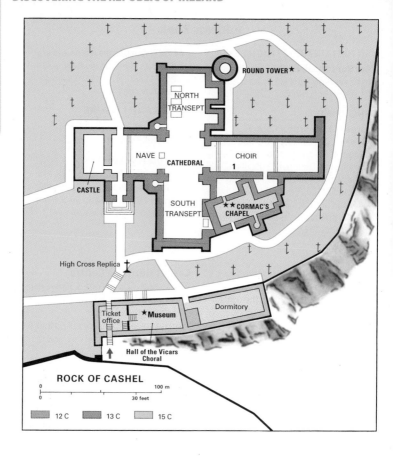

ROUND TOWER ★

NORTH TRANSEPT

NAVE ☐

CATHEDRAL

CHOIR
1

CASTLE

SOUTH TRANSEPT

★★ **CORMAC'S CHAPEL**

High Cross Replica ✝

Ticket office

★ **Museum**

Dormitory

⬆ **Hall of the Vicars Choral**

ROCK OF CASHEL

0   100 m

0   30 feet

12 C   13 C   15 C

13C carved stone coffin lids have been placed against the walls, which are part of 14C town defences.

Bolton Library★ (⊙ *open May–Sept, usually Mon–Wed, 9.30am–5.30pm (call to confirm);* 🅿 ; ☎ *062 61232; www. cashel.anglican.org/cashel.shtm),* built in 1836, contains some 12 000 books. Among its treasures is a monk's encyclopedia (1168), two leaves from Chaucer's *The Book of Fame* printed by William Caxton at Westminster in London in 1483, a note signed by Jonathan Swift and a collection of ecclesiastical silver.

▸ *Walk through to Friar St.*

Parish Church

The Roman Catholic church of St John the Baptist, the oldest RC church in use in Ireland, was opened in 1795, screened by a row of cottages. The mosaics on the façade were added to commemorate the Eucharistic Congress in Ireland (1932). The interior is unusual in that two galleries run the full length of the building and the ceiling resembles the upturned hull of a ship.

▸ *Walk down to the end of Friar St; turn left into Main St and right into Dominic St.*

Folk Village

♿ ⊙ *Open Easter to mid-Oct, 10am–6pm.* ⬅ €3.50. 🅿 . ☎ *062 62525.*
A small reconstruction of 18C Irish rural life including various traditional thatched village shops, a forge, other businesses and a penal Chapel.

Dominican Friary

The friary was founded by Archbishop David MacKelly (*Dáibhí Mac Ceallaigh*), a Cork Dominican, in 1243 and suppressed in 1540. The church, which was rebuilt after a fire in 1480, has a long narrow nave and choir.

Excursions

Holy Cross Abbey★★

9mi/16km north of Cashel by R 660. ◷*Open 10am–6pm.* ⛟*Guided tour: Jun–Sept.* ☎*0504 43241 or 43124. www. holycrossabbey.ie.*

Holy Cross is one of the finest examples of 15C church architecture in the country and today serves as a flourishing parish church. It was originally founded for the Benedictines by Donal O'Brien, King of Munster (1168) and became a major place of pilgrimage, as it was reputed to contain a relic of the True Cross. After the Dissolution it passed to the Earls of Ormond, though the monks (by, now Cistercians) continued in residence into the 17C. The popularity of the abbey as a centre of pilgrimage made it rich, allowing the 15C rebuilding to be completed to the highest standard. There are windows with stained glass, fine original stonework, and a rare **wall-painting**, showing hunters about to kill a stag beneath an oak tree. The **grounds** contain a replica of the Vatican gardens, including the Stations of the Cross.

The eight-arch **bridge** spanning the River Suir, a copy of the original, was constructed in 1626.

Lár na Páirce

14mi/23km north of Cashel by R 660 to Thurles; Slievenamon Road. ◷*Open Apr–Sept, Mon–Fri, 10am–5pm.* ⛉€3. ☎*0504 22702.*

This elegant 19C building houses a display on the history of the Gaelic Games.

Hore Abbey

0.5mi/0.8km west of Cashel by N 74.

The last Cistercian house to be founded in medieval Ireland, established by monks from Mellifont in 1272. Most of the present extensive ruins date from the late 13C.

Athassel Priory★

5mi/8km west of Cashel by N 74 and minor road S from Golden; across two fields.

This was once one of the most extensive and prosperous establishments of its kind in Ireland, surrounded by a town. The priory was destroyed in 1447 but parts of the main church survive.

Tipperary

10m/16km west of Cashel by N 74. Mitchell Street, 062 80520 www.tipperary-excel.com/ Tourism.php.

This pleasant small county town, with enough old buildings and 19C shop-fronts to merit Heritage Town status, was a centre of Land League agitation and later the headquarters of the 3rd Tipperary Brigade of the IRA which fought many battles in the War of Independence. It owes much of its fame, however, to the First World War marching song:

It's a long way to Tipperary,
it's a long way to go
It's a long way to Tipperary,
to the sweetest girl I know.
Goodbye Piccadilly,
Goodbye Leicester Square,
It's a long, long way to Tipperary
but my heart lies there.

Glen of Aherlow★

2m/3.2km S of Tipperary by R 664.

This lovely vale runs for 16m/26km between the forests of the Slievenamuck ridge and the Galty Mountains, Ireland's highest inland range. The glen, once woodland, is now lush farmland. Head for the panoramic **viewpoint**★★ above Newtown. A gleaming white statue of Christ the King looks to the Galtees, their splendid swooping ridgeline reaching its highest point (3018ft/919m) at the summit of Galtymore.

CAVAN

POPULATION 3 509

The little capital of Co Cavan – (An Cabhán) lies in drumlin country – a tranquil, undulating, well-wooded landscape, scattered with countless small lakes. Nearby is Lough Oughter, the largest lake in Co Cavan, fed by the River Erne.

🗓 **Information:** Johnston Central Library, Farnham Street, Cavan.
☎049 43 77 200. www.cavan.tourism.com.

▶ **Orient Yourself:** Cavan is set at the junction of the N 3 Dublin-Donegal road 70mi/112km north west of Dublin.

⟲ **Also See:** CARRICK-ON-SHANNON, ENNISKILLEN, LONGFORD, MONAGHAN.

Town

There is little to deter visitors in Cavan itself, its places of interest lie outside town. The Roman Catholic **Cathedral** (1942) designed by **Ralph Byrnes** and sculptures by **Albert Power** (1883–1945), is variously described as "sham Renaissance" or "the last flamboyant fling of historicism" and the crenellated **Anglican Church** with west tower and steeple by John Bowden, who also designed the Classical **Courthouse**.

Excursions

Ballyjamesduff

10mi/16km S of Cavan by N 3, N 55 and a minor road via Cross Keys.
This small town, named after Sir James Duff, the commander of British troops in the 1798 uprising, clusters around the Market House (1813). It is home to the **Cavan County Museum** (⟲⟳open Tue–Sat 10am–5pm; Jun–Oct, also Sun 2pm–6pm; ⟳€3; ⟳. ☎049 85 44070, www.cavanmuseum.ie). This fine collec-

tion includes archaeological artefacts tracing the heritage of County Cavan, including a rare three-faced pre-Christian Corleck Head and Stone Age dugout. Other galleries trace 1950s rural life, art, famine, costume, The Nun's Story, Percy French (⟲see 'Cavan's Literary Cavalcade' box) and GAA sports.

Carraig Craft Visitor Centre

Mount Nugent ,15mi/24km S of Cavan via the N 3, N 55 and R 154.
⟳*Open Apr–Oct, Mon–Fri, 10am–6pm; Sun 2pm–6pm; Nov–Mar by appointment.* ⟳€3.50. ⟳. ☎049 8540179.
The art of basket-making, old and new, is celebrated in this museum shop with donkey creels, pigeon panniers; bee skeps; straw, reed and willow containers for eggs, turf, potatoes, fish, poultry, flowers and more.

Kilmore Cathedral

3mi/5km W of Cavan on the R 198.
⟳*By appointment or during services.* www.cornafean.com/kilmore.htm.
The neo-Gothic Anglican cathedral known as the **Bedell Memorial Church**

Cavan's Literary Cavalcade

Several famous writers are connected with County Cavan: the playwright **Richard Brinsley Sheridan** was the grandson of Dr Thomas Sheridan, the headmaster of Cavan Royal School and a good friend of Jonathan Swift, who lived at Quilcagh House near Mullagh. An ancestor of **Edgar Allan Poe** (1809–49) emigrated to America from Killeshandra in the mid 18C. William James, a Presbyterian from Baillieborough who settled in America, was the grandfather of **Henry James** (1843–1916). The song-writer and painter **Percy French** (1854–1920), born at Cloonyquin (west of Strokestown), worked in Cavan for 7 years as an inspector of loans to tenants. He began penning lyrics while studying at Trinity College, Dublin.

Address Book

For coin ranges, see the Legend on the cover flap.

WHERE TO STAY

Rockwood House – *Cloverhill, Belturbet.* 047 55351. www.bedand-breakfastireland.net/cavan_rockwood. htm. 4rm. Lovely good value B&B set among woods with a bright conservatory, attractive garden. Bedrooms simply, yet pleasantly, furnished. Hospitable owners.

Eonish Lodge Farm Guesthouse – *Killeshandra, 5mi SW of Cavan on N 55 and 2.5mi W of Bellinagh by N 55 off Arva road.* 049 433 4487. www.eonishlodge. com. Peaceful location, convenient for boating, lake fishing, horse riding, and exploring Killykeen Forest Park.

WHERE TO EAT

The Olde Post Inn – *Cloverhill.* 047 55555. www.theoldepostinn. com. Guesthouse and award winning restaurant for use of locally-sourced ingredients; vegetarian menu.

SHOPPING

Cavan Crystal – *Dublin Rd.* 049 433 1800. www.cavancrystal.com. The second-oldest lead-crystal glass factory in Ireland, recently transformed into the Cavan Crystal Hotel, including an extensive contemporary glass gift shop.

Bear Essentials – *Tiernawannagh, Bawnboy.* 049 952 3461 www.bear essentials.ie. Collectible handcrafted mohair teddy bears.

SPORTS AND LEISURE

Lough Oughter, a collection of many small lakes interlinked by short slow moving rivers, is the perfect place **boating** and **canoeing**.
Coarse fishing takes place on the lake and along stretches of the Annalee, a tributary of the Erne, for roach, bream, hybrids, pike, perch; **trout fishing** on Lough Annagh; **game angling** for salmon and trout.
Watersport facilities include windsurfing and waterskiing.

EVENTS AND FESTIVALS

Belturbet Festival of the Erne. www.ernefestival.com. Live music, a talent competition, marching bands, fireworks a very popular fancy dress party and the Lady of The Erne pageant *(late Jul–early Aug)*.

TRACING ANCESTORS

Cavan Genealogy Research Centre – *Cana House, Farnham St. Open Mon–Fri 9.30am–4.30pm.* 049 436 1094.

---

is dedicated to **St Felim** *(Fethlimidh)*, who brought Christianity to the region in the 6C. The fine 12C Romanesque north doorway may have belonged to an earlier church or to the abbey on Trinity Island in Lough Oughter.

Killykeen Forest Park★

5mi/8km W of Cavan on the R 198. www.cornafean.com/Attractions.htm. This 600-acre (243-ha) Forest Park replicates the patchwork of land and water so characteristic of the River Erne in counties Cavan and Fermanagh. Marked nature trails thread through the park, and there is a wildfowl sanctuary by the Sally Lake. Other facilities include a tennis court, children's play area, bicycle and boat hire.

On Trinity Island at the southern end of **Lough Oughter** stands the ruin of a Premonstratensian Priory, established in 1250 by monks from Lough Key

William Bedell (1571–1642)

William Bedell was born in Sussex, studied at Cambridge and travelled widely in Europe, before being appointed Provost of Trinity College in Dublin in 1627. In 1629 he became Bishop of Kilmore and tried to introduce reforms. During the 1641 Rebellion he was imprisoned for two years by the Confederates in Clogh Oughter Castle.

CLONMACNOISE★★★

POPULATION 1 695

Founded in 545 by St Kieran (Ciarán), Clonmacnoise (Cluain Mhic Nóis) was once a pre-eminent monastic site, second only to Armagh, where the Kings of Connaught and Tara are interred. With its churches, cathedral, high crosses, ancient grave slabs and round towers, it draws thousands of visitors, tourists and pilgrims, most notably on 9 September (St Kieran's Day).

- **Information:** Shannonbridge, Athlone. ☎090 96 74134.
- ▶ **Orient Yourself:** Clonmacnoise is situated on the east bank of the River Shannon 13mi/21km south of Athlone on the N 6 and N 62 or 13mi/20km from Ballinasloe along the R357.
- 🕐 **Organising Your Time:** Allow 1–2 hours for your visit but beware that t this is a very busy site and you may experience delays during the summer months.
- ♿ **Also See:** ATHENRY, ATHLONE, BIRR, PORTUMNA, TULLAMORE.

A Bit of History

The monastery's position beside the Shannon now seems remote but in earlier centuries transport was easier by water than over land. The old Pilgrims' Road approached from the north along the esker (or ridge). As its reputation grew the settlement expanded from an original wooden oratory to a cluster of stone churches, numerous monks' dwellings and a round tower within an earth or stone enclosure. None of the surviving ruins predate the 9C, having been successively plundered by the Irish, Vikings and Anglo-Normans, until it was finally reduced to ruin in 1552 by the English garrison from Athlone.

A castle built by the Normans in 1212 on the river was slighted in the Cromwellian period.

Walking Tour

Visitor Centre

(Dúchas)♿🕐*Open daily: mid-May–mid-Sept 9am–7pm; rest of year 10am–6pm (5.30pm Nov–mid-Mar); last admission 45min before closing.* 🕐*Closed 25 Dec.* 🎫*€5.30.* 🍴*.* ☎*090 96 74195. www.heritage ireland.ie.*

The **Visitor Centre** displays the original **high crosses** and a collection of **grave slabs**★ (those on site are replicas), confirming Cloncmanoise's status as an

Clonmacnoise

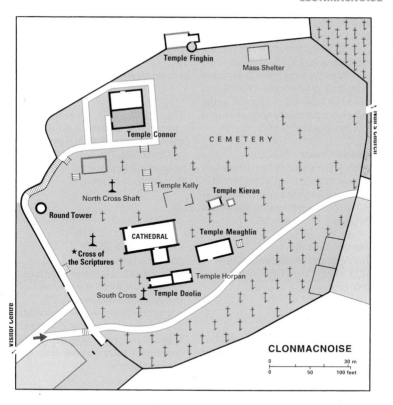

Temple Finghin

Mass Shelter

Temple Connor

CEMETERY

Main S Church

Temple Kelly

North Cross Shaft

Temple Kieran

Round Tower

CATHEDRAL

Temple Meaghlin

★ Cross of
the Scriptures

Temple Horpan

South Cross

Temple Doolin

Visitor Centre

CLONMACNOISE

| 0 | | 30 m |
| 0 | 50 | 100 feet |

important stone-carving centre from the 8C to 12C.

Monuments

The most important monuments include the early 9C **South Cross** (12ft/3.6m) with a carving of the Crucifixion, decorative spirals and interlacing recall designs on crosses at Kells, on Iona and Kildalton in Scotland. **Temple Doolin** is the pre-12C church named after Edward Dowling when he restored it (1689) as a mausoleum; **Temple Meaghlin or Temple Rí** has special windows that echo those at Clonfert and O'Heyne's Church at Kilmacduagh. **Temple Kieran** is the tiny church said to contain the grave of St Kieran. The **North Cross Shaft** (c 800) is decorated with lions biting their tail and a cross-legged figure thought by some to be the Celtic god Cernunnos. The sandstone **Cross of the Scriptures**★, related to the crosses at Monasterboice, was erected in the 10C possibly by King Flann (d 916); unusually, its arms protrude upwards from the circle – note scenes of the Crucifixion, the Last Judgement, the Passion (soldiers resting on their spears), and one showing Abbot Colman and King Flann founding the monastery.

Cathedral

The simple rectangular building has been modified many times. The oldest parts may date from the 10C when the

St Kieran

St Kieran was born at Roscommon, trained by St Finnian at Clonard before going to Inishmore, among the Aran Islands. His vision of a great tree growing in the heart of Ireland was interpreted by his tutor St Enda as a church growing on the banks of the Shannon. After a stay on Hare Island in Lough Ree, St Kieran and seven companions settled at Clonmacnoise, the field of the sons of Nos. He died months later of the plague, aged 33.

original wooden church was replaced with a stone structure. The Romanesque west doorway dates from the 12C; the sacristy may be 13C. The elaborate north doorway with three plaques depicting St Dominic, St Patrick and St Francis, was added by Dean Odo in the 15C at the same time that the chancel was divided into three vaulted chapels.

Round Tower

This is a typical round tower despite having lost its conical cap, possibly built in the 10C by Fergal O'Rourke and repaired in 1120 by Abbot O'Malone. The arched doorway is most likely 12C.

Temple Connor

The Anglican church may date from 1010 when it was endowed by Cathal O'Connor.

Temple Finghin and Nun's Church

The 12C church, modified in the 17C, comprises a nave and chancel. Unusual features include the south door and mini round tower incorporated into the chancel.

▶ *From the centre of the enclosure follow the old path E across the extended graveyard and along the road.*

The ruined Nun's Church with nave and chancel was completed according to the Annals of the Four Masters in 1167 by Dervorgilla. The west doorway and chancel arch have striking Irish Romanesque style decoration.

Excursion

Clonfinlough Stone

2mi/3km E by the minor road and 0.5mi/0.8km S by the minor road; park by the church; 10min there and back on foot up the path and over the stile.
A large boulder bearing symbols similar to the Bronze Age rock art of Galicia in Spain are suggestive of human figures. To the south there is a **view** of the Brosna and Shannon.

CLONMEL ★

POPULATION 15 215

The principal town of Co Tipperary (Cluain Meala) stands in a lovely fertile valley. To the south rise the Comeragh Mountains in Co Waterford: a fine backdrop to the many historic buildings of the town, which recall its great period of prosperity in the 18C and 19C.

- **Information:** Old St Mary's Church. ☎052 22960. www.clonmel.ie.
- ▶ **Orient Yourself:** Clonmel is 30 mi/50km west of Waterford on the N 24 on the boundary between Co Tipperary and Co Waterford.
- **Don't Miss:** The scenic drive through the Nier Valley.
- **Especially for Kids:** Fethard Folk Farm and Museum.
- **Also See:** CAHER, CASHEL, KILKENNY, YOUGHAL.

A Bit of History

The town is said to pre-date the Vikings. and its name comes from the Irish words for "a meadow of honey" – an Early Christian reference to the great fertility of the Suir valley. Viking longships sailed up the River Suir from Waterford and, according to tradition, fought at Clonmel in 916 or 917 against the local O'Neill clan.

Edward I granted the town a charter and the **walls** were built in the early 14C. Later, it became an important stronghold of the Butler family, the Earls of Ormond. In the 17C, the garrison is said to have put up more resistance to Cromwell than any other Irish town.
Four English novelists had close links with Clonmel: **Anthony Trollope** wrote his first two novels here (1844–48);

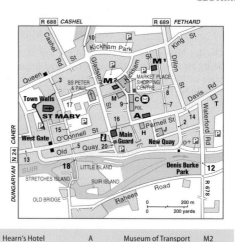

CLONMEL

George Borrow who attended a local school refers to Clonmel in *Lavengro*; **Marguerite Power**, the Countess of Blessington, a noted early-19C literary figure, was born at Suir Island in 1789; **Laurence Sterne** (1713–68), author of *Tristram Shandy*, was born in Mary Street and his family lived at Suir Island.

Town

Landmarks

The Anglican **Old St Mary's Church**★, with its unusual octagonal tower, was built in the 19C incorporating parts of earlier 14C buildings: it now accommodates an information centre.

The town's mock-Tudor gateway (1831) was built on the site of the medieval **Westgate** separating the Anglo-Norman borough from its suburb, Irishtown. Cromwell's troops destroyed Clonmel's original courthouse during the 1650 siege. Its 1674 three-storeyed replacement, **Main Guard**, adorned with the town's coat of arms, is one of Ireland's earliest public classical buildings, inspired by the architecture of Sir Christopher Wren.

Riverside

The 17C **Old Bridge** links Little Island, Suir Island and Stretches Island (named after 16C Italian immigrants called Stroccio).The north bank between the Old Bridge and the 18C **Gashouse Bridge** forms the town **quay**, where ships used to unload their cargoes. Note the memorial to the Manchester Martyrs and the elegant **Georgian** terraces of houses and tall warehouses.

Museums

The **Tipperary County Museum**★ (◷ *open Tue–Sat 10am–5pm;* ☎ *052 34550; www.southtippcoco.ie/museum*) displays artefacts from the Stone Age to the 20C: rare early coins confirm links with the Roman Empire; fascinating documents relating to a famous trial of rebels (1848) and to the Royal Irish Regiment, based here until its demise in 1922 after the signing of the Anglo-Irish Treaty. There is also a good selection of paintings by Irish artists.

Moving the Masses

Charles Bianconi (1786–1875) was the son of an Italian immigrant from Lombardy. He arrived in Dublin in 1801 with no English language skills and sold pictures on the street. Eventually making his way to Clonmel he set up business in 1809 (at No 1 Gladstone Street), as a "carver and gilder of the first class". However, his breakthrough was to come in the area of cheap public transport. Noting from his own hard experience, selling "on the road", how little transport there was in early 19C Ireland, he cleverly bought up cheap ex-army horses, surplus after the defeat of Napoleon, and developed carriages, which became known as "Bians" (after Bianconi). These ran to Wexford, Waterford, Cork and Kilkenny. As demand grew elsewhere, a network of communications, with Clonmel at the hub, spread over the whole of Ireland. At its peak the service employed 1 400 horses and 100 vehicles painted crimson and yellow, creating a nationwide revolution in the carrying of mail, freight and passengers that was only superseded by the advent of railways in the late 19C. Bianconi was voted Mayor of Clonmel twice.

One of the old mail cars ran between Clonmel and Dungarvan well into the 1920s, long after Bianconi retired in 1865. A mail coach horn and the clock (now handless) by which the departures were timed are preserved in the foyer of Hearn's Hotel.

Driving Tour

Nier Valley Scenic Route★★

Round tour of 40mi/64km.
From Clonmel take the R 678 south.
After 5mi/8km turn right; after 4mi/6km make a detour left to a viewpoint. In Ballymacarbry turn right onto the R 671 to return to Clonmel.
The road goes through the dark green forests, moorland and imposing escarpments of the **Comeragh Mountains** which culminate in Knockanaffrin at 2478ft/753m.

Carrick-on-Suir

13mi/21km east on the N 24.
This bustling little town enjoys a prime location on the tidal Suir between Slievenamon and the Comeragh foothills). The 15C Old Bridge is the lowest river crossing before the estuary, built when the wool trade was at its height. You can trace this history at the **Heritage Centre** (&♿⏰*open daily May–Aug 10am–5pm; Sept–Apr Mon–Fri 10am–5pm;*☎*051 640 200),* located in a 13C church off Main Street, which also serves as a tourist information office.
Ormond Castle★ *(Dúchas ✎admission by guided tour only (45min) mid-Jun–early Sept, daily 10am–6pm;*☎*051 640 787; www.heritageireland.ie),* is the best example of an Elizabethan manor house in Ireland. It was built around 1568 by the 10th **Earl of Ormond** to receive his cousin, Queen Elizabeth, who disappointingly never visited Ireland at all. Highlights include fine **ornamental plasterwork**, a long gallery hung with Elizabethan portraits, and a fascinating collection of charters tracing the rise in status of the Ormond family.

Kilkeeran High Crosses

17mi/27km east via the N 24 and R 697.
Three crosses, probably from the 9C, mark the site of an early monastery. The **West Cross** has eight horsemen and an unusual cap, like the plainer, possibly unfinished, East Cross. The Long Shaft Cross is the only one of its type in Ireland.

Ahenny High Crosses★

19mi/31km east via the N 24 and R 697.
The decorative interlacing and spirals so characteristic of the Book of Kells are repeated here in stone, which may mean that the two crosses (note their unusual caps) may date from as early as the 8C. The figures on the base represent seven clergymen carrying croziers, led by a cross-bearer.

Office of Public Works

Ormond Castle, Carrick-on-Suir

Fethard★

8mi/13km N by R 689.

Fethard, an Anglo-Norman town of some importance, has retained its late-14C **town walls** and a 15C **Castle** in one of three keeps. Its **church** features a late-15C crenellated tower, and boasts a huge roof-span; the east window is copied from Kilcooley Abbey. Among the ruins of a 12C Augustinian **priory** lie tombs dating from the 16C and 17C.

The **Fethard Folk Farm and Museum** (Kids ⏱ ⏰ *open Sun and Bank Hol Mon 11.30am–5pm; ⚬€5; ☐; ☏052 31516, www.fethard.com/attra/Museum.html)* is dedicated to the rural and domestic life of earlier centuries, including bicycles, washing machines and hearses. One of Ireland's biggest car boot sales takes place here every Sunday afternoon with dealers coming from all over Ireland.

COBH★

POPULATION 6 468

Facing the sheltered water of Cork Harbour, Cobh (An Cóbh) – pronounced cove – has been an important naval base for generations.

🛈 **Information:** Old Yacht Club, Cobh. ☏021 4813 301. www.visitcobh.com.

▶ **Orient Yourself:** Cobh lies on the south side of Great Island, linked by road and rail to Fota Island and the mainland, 12 mi/19km south east of Cork.

◉ **Don't Miss:** An excursion to Fota Island.

Kids **Especially for Kids:** Fota Wildlife Park.

⏱ **Also See:** CORK, KINSALE, MIDLETON, YOUGHAL.

A Bit of History

Cobh developed in the late 18C when Royal Navy ships assembled here for operations in the American War of Independence and later against France.

The Royal Navy continued to operate from here well after Independence until Cobh was handed back to the Free State with the other "Treaty Ports" (1938). Until the 1960s, large transatlantic cruise liners like the *Queen Mary* and the *Queen Elizabeth* would stop here: an era recorded in period photographs and paintings hanging in the bar of the Commodore Hotel.

On a much sadder note Cobh also witnessed the departure of around

2.5 million of the six million Irish people who emigrated to North America between 1848 and 1950. They are commemorated in the statue of Annie Moore, the very first emigrant to pass through the Ellis Island immigration reception centre in New York.

A period as a health resort in the 19C left a fine legacy of Italianate buildings and neo-Gothic villas, which merit the classification of Heritage Town. Cobh was also once known as Queenstown after Queen Victoria disembarked here in 1849 on her first visit to Ireland.

Sights

St Colman's Cathedral★

The neo-Gothic Catholic cathedral designed by Pugin and Ashlin (1868–1915) was clearly modelled on the French medieval cathedrals of Amiens, Chartre and Laon; the sculpture echoes Rheims. The tall **spire** houses a carillon of 47 bells. The interior is typically Victorian in style.

Lusitania Memorial★

The 1 500 lives lost when the *Lusitania* was torpedoed in 1915 are commemorated by an elaborate sculpture in Casement Square, designed by Jerome Connor (1876–1943) who was born in Cork; it was completed posthumously by Seamus Murphy.

Nearby in Pierce Square, a more modest memorial recalls the demise of the *Titanic* which docked at Cobh on 11 April 1912 before sailing on her fateful maiden voyage.

Museums

At the **Cobh Heritage Centre** (&⊙*open year-round daily 9.30am–6pm; Jan–Apr & Nov–Dec 5pm; Last admissions 1hr before closing;* ⊙*closed 23 Dec–2 Jan;* ✗*;* ⊜*€7.10;* ☎*021 481 3591, www.cobh heritage.com)*, **The Queenstown Story** explains how convicts were expelled to Australia and how thousands more emigrated to America from here; a separate display is dedicated to the *Titanic.*

House in the former Scots Presbyterian Church on the High Road above the Heritage Centre, the **Cobh Museum** (⊙*open Mar–Oct Mon–Sat 11am–1pm and 2pm–5.30pm; Sun 2.30pm–5pm;* ⊜*€1.50;* ☎*021 481 4240, www.cobh museum.com)* displays historical material relating to Cobh and the Great Island.

Excursion

Fota Island★★

4mi/6km N by R 624.

Until 1975, this 780 acre/316ha island in Cork Harbour belonged to the descendants of its 12C Anglo-Norman Lord Philip de Barri. In the early 19C the family's

---

Address Book

&*For coin ranges, see the cover flap.*

GETTING AROUND

Cork Harbour Car Ferry across the River Lee between Carrigaloe *(east bank)* and Glenbrook *(west bank)* – Operates daily, 7am–12.15am. Car €6 (return), €4 single; pedestrian €1. ☎021 481 1223.

Cork Harbour Cruises – Operate from Kennedy Pier (1hr: harbour forts, Spike Island, Naval base and major harbour industries) May–Sept daily noon, 2pm, 3pm, 4pm. €5.50. ℗(5–10min walk). ☎021 427 7085.

Rail Service – Operates between Cobh and Cork via Fota Island, daily. ☎021 481 1655 (Cobh Railway Station); www.irishrail.ie

WHERE TO STAY / EAT

⊖⊖ **Robin Hill House** – Rushbrooke 0.1mi NE on the R 624. ☎021 481 1395; www.irelandwide.com/acom/robinhill. This converted 19C rectory is set in mature gardens overlooking Cork Harbour. It has contemporary fittings and decor including work by local artists. The cuisine (⊖⊖) is locally sourced Modern Irish and there is an extensive wine list.

P Thebault/MICHELIN

Cobh harbour and the cathedral

hunting lodge was converted by John Smith Barry into a fine neo-Classical gentleman's residence to plans by the leading architects Richard and William Vitruvius Morrison; other additions included sea defences, walls, lodges, workers' cottages and outbuildings, a landscaped parkland and a famous arboretum. Much of the island is now given over to one of the country's finest wildlife parks, and the house has been saved from near-dereliction.

Fota House and Gardens★★

&🕓Open Apr–Sept Mon–Sat 10am–5pm and 11am–5pm Sun and Bank Hols. Oct–Mar daily 11am–4pm. 🕓Closed at Christmas. ⊚€5.50. 🖵.☏021 481 5543. www.fotahouse.com.

This Regency mansion is notable for its series of exquisite interiors set off by fine furniture. The Morrisons' masterly manipulation of space is particularly evident in the entrance hall, while below stairs, the servery, kitchen and scullery are models of their kind.

A short distance from the house is a delightful little **orangery**, and a walled garden.

The great **arboretum**★ was laid out by John Barry Smith, a prominent plant collector, and sustained by his successors into the 20C. Its warm brown earth soils and mild climate favour species from North America, Chile, Australasia, Japan and China, and this is one of the finest collections of rare and tender trees and

shrubs grown outdoors in Ireland and Britain.

Fota Wildlife Park★   Kids

&🕓Open daily 10am (11am Sun) to 5pm. Last admission 3.30pm. ⊚€13.50, child €8.50. ✕.🅿€3. ☏021 481 2678. www.fotawildlife.ie.

This spacious park, comprising 70 acres/28ha, was established by the Zoological Society of Ireland in 1983 to breed endangered species like cheetah, Oryx, Macaque. Zebra, antelope and kangaroo roam freely while giraffe, monkeys, flamingoes, pelicans, penguins and other waterfowl thrive in designated areas. A special attraction is the Cheetah Run feeding time, every day at 3pm. Their food is suspended on a wire that travels 10ft/3m off the ground, at approximately 40mph/65kph which encourages them to act naturally by sprinting after it.

A land train ferries visitors around the grounds.

Water Club

The world's first yachting fraternity, the Water Club, was founded in Cobh in 1720. Its successor, the Royal Cork Yacht Club, is now based at Crosshaven (&see CORK), but its old headquarters still stands, an elegant waterfront pavilion designed in 1854 by the architect Anthony Salvin.

CONG
POPULATION 197

Once the seat of the kings of Connaught, the attractive little settlement of Cong (Conga) sits close to the ruins of a famous abbey, on the narrow neck of land (conga in Irish) separating Lough Corrib and Lough Mask, on the Mayo-Galway border. It is a popular base for exploring the lakes, the mountains of Connemara and Joyce Country to the west. The Wilde family had a holiday house on the shore of Lough Corrib; in 1867 Oscar's father, Sir William Wilde ,wrote an antiquarian guidebook *Lough Corrib, its Shores and Islands*, still in print today. Cong was put back on the map in 1952 when the *The Quiet Man*, starring John Wayne, was made here.

- ⓘ **Information:** Cong Tourist office, opposite the Abbey.
  ☎094 954 6542. www.discoverireland.ie/west.
- 🕐 **Organising Your Time:** Allow half a day in Cong.
- ▶ **Orient Yourself:** Cong is 27 mi/43km north of Galway via the N 84 and R 334.
- ⌚ **Also See:** ATHENRY, CONNEMARA, GALWAY, KNOCK, WESTPORT.

Walking Tour

Cong Abbey

The Augustinian abbey beautifully set by the river was founded in the 12C, probably by Turlough O'Conor, King of Connaught and High King of Ireland, on the site of an earlier monastic foundation (6C/7C). It features some very fine examples of stone carving, a lovely Romanesque doorway, **cloisters** (c 1200), a sculpted **chapter house**, and the Guest Refectory with a twisted chimney stack remain. The **Cross of Cong**, the famous gold cross which is believed to have once contained a relic of the True Cross of Christ, is now in the National Museum in Dublin. West of the abbey grounds on an island in the river is the **monks' fishing house** (12C) with a hole in the floor through which a net could be lowered, and when a fish was caught, a bell rang in the kitchen.

Quiet Man Heritage Cottage Museum

🕐*Open Easter to mid-Oct 10am–5pm.*
✎€5. ☎094 954 6089. www.museums ofmayo.com.
The interior, a typical Irish cottage of the 1920s is furnished as a replica of the house used in the film.

Ross Errily Abbey

H Champollion/MICHELIN

Captain Boycott

From Lough Mask House (on the eastern shore of the lake) **Captain Charles Boycott** administered the estates of Lord Erne with a severity that made him extremely unpopular with his tenants. In 1880, after evicting a number for non-payment of rent, Parnell's Land League made him the first victim of the process that subsequently bore his name.

The wretched man and his family were shunned and ostracised, and the land could only be worked by Ulstermen protected by troops. Boycott fled to England, securing lexicographical immortality.

Address Book

For coin ranges, see the cover flap.

SIGHTSEEING

Lough Corrib Cruises – *Operate daily. Daytime/evening sailings* ☎092 46029. www.corribcruises.com. Excursions to Inchagoil Island's 5C / 12C ruins, or Asford Castle for dinner.

WHERE TO EAT

John J Burke & Sons – *Clonbur* ☎094 9546175. www.burkes-clonbur. com. *Mon–Sat 1pm–5pm; Apr–Sept 6pm–9pm daily*. Try the Irish stew.

Ashord Castle – ☎094 9546003 (*see Walking Tour*). Luxurious dining in sumptuous context.

Upstairs is a local collection of historic artefacts dating back to 7000 BC.

Ashford Castle

Pedestrian entrance south of the Abbey; vehicle entrance on R 346 east of Cong. *Grounds and gardens open to non-guests daily 9am–6pm.* €5. ☎094 95 4600. www.ashford.ie.

The Guinness family transformed the 13C castle, built by the de Burgos into a huge baronial residence of great sumptuousness in the 19C. It is now a luxury hotel with formal gardens, a golf course, and equestrian, falconry and fishing facilities. You can also take a cruise to Inchagoill Island (*see Address Book*) to see St Patrick's Church, reputedly built by the saint in 450 AD, Europe's second oldest Christian inscription (dating from 470 AD), and an ornate Augustinian church built by the monks of Cong in 1178.

Excursion

Ross Errilly Abbey★

10mi/16km SE of Cong by R 346 and R 344.

Although in ruins, Ross Abbey, on the banks of the Black River, is one of the best-preserved Franciscan friaries in Ireland, founded around 1351 and extended in 1496 at a time when the Franciscans felt the need to take control of an idle and corrupt official church. In 1596 the complex was requisitioned by the English for use as barracks, in 1656 it was looted by the Cromwellians, in 1753 the last monks moved away.

Among its fascinating features, note the **cloister buildings**, a second courtyard with a postern gate for entry after dark, the **kitchen** with its big round **fish tank** and huge fireplace backing onto a large circular oven in the adjoining **bakery**. The **central tower** (70ft/21.5m), probably added in 1498, provides good **views**★.

Cong's dry canal

Lough Mask and Lough Corrib are linked by the River Cong, which runs mainly through caves and underground channels in the limestone. The idea of creating a navigable waterway between the two great lakes seemed about to come to fruition, when men doing relief work during the famine laboured for six years to dig a canal (4mi/7km) with three locks. In March 1854 work was suspended; costs had risen, new railways threatened competition and attempts to fill the canal came to nothing when the water drained away into the porous limestone rock. No vessel has ever floated on Cong's dry canal.

CONNEMARA★★★

The largest Gaeltacht (irish-language area) in Ireland, with many road-signs in Gaelic only, Connemara is a wild and beautiful region of mountains, lakes, tumbling streams, undulating bog, sea-girt promontories, unspoilt beaches and panoramic views. Its beauty and remoteness, together with its traces of a traditional way of life, have attracted a large crafts community who are happy to introduce visitors to their handweaving, knitting, screen printing and carving, marble inlay, jewellery and pottery.

🛈 **Information:** Galway Road, Clifden. ☏095 21163. www.discoverireland. ie/west. http://www.experienceconnemara.com. www.goconnemara.com.

🕐 **Organising Your Time:** Allow at least three days, longer if you wish to explore Connemara's many walking trails.

▸ **Orient Yourself:** Connemara comprises all of County Galway, to the west of Galway City and occupies the broad peninsula between Killary Harbour and Kilkieran Bay. The unofficial capital of Connemara is Clifden.

👁 **Don't Miss:** The scenery along the cliffs north of Clifden Bay and around Lough Corrib.

👶 **Also See:** ARAN ISLANDS, CONG, GALWAY, WESTPORT.

A Bit of History

The mountains at the heart of Connemara are the **Twelve Bens** or **Pins**, that culminate with Benbaun (2 388ft/728m). The sharp grey peaks of quartzite rock resistant to weathering rise sharply out of the blanket-bog. The Bens are drained by mountain streams and ringed by a chain of lakes where trout are plentiful. Between the foot of the Twelve Pins and the southern coastline extends the level **Connemara Bog** dotted with innumerable tiny lakes. On a bright day the stretches of water act like mirrors reflecting the sun; in the rain, it all turns to water.

In this remote region with unyielding soils and harsh climate, the people of

Connemara lived in settlements dotted along the coast, resisting invaders and colonisation. For centuries the ferocious O'Flaherty clan held sway until dislodged by Cromwell, whose ruthless troop stayed on in their stronghold on Inishbofin. The population was decimated by the Famine but its Irish-speaking, peasant culture survived, exercising great fascination on Gaelic revivalists and on nationalists like Patrick Pearse. Throughout Connemara's history, enterprising individuals have doggedly tried to implement improvements: **John D'Arcy**, a member of a long-established Galway family which had originally settled in Ireland in the reign of Elizabeth I, moved to the estate he inherited in 1815 and set about developing the new harbour town of Clifden, constantly importuning the authorities for funds to build roads to link his new settlement to Galway and Westport. The Galway road was completed in the 1820s, running through miles of uninhabited countryside between the Twelve Bens and the Connemara bog, built by labourers who had to be supplied with tents and cooking utensils. Although a railway line to the area was eventually opened in 1895, it closed in 1935. Another reformer nurtured in this wild land was **Richard Martin**, also known as "Humanity Dick",

Connemara Pony

R Holzbachova, Ph Benet/MICHELIN

Address Book

For coin ranges, see the Legend on the cover flap.

GETTING AROUND

Ferries and various cruises from Cleggan to Inishbofin. ☎095 45819 or 45894. *http://inishbofinislanddiscovery.com.*

SIGHTSEEING

Maritime Wildlife cruises and sea angling cruises from Letterfrack.

WHERE TO STAY

Letterfrack Lodge – *Letterfrack.* ☎095 41222. www.letterfracklodge. com. *11rm.* Self-catering B&B hostel in dorms or en-suite rooms in a beautiful rural setting. Lively infrmative hosts. Excellent value.

Dolphin Beach Country House – *Lower Sky Rd, Clifden.* ☎095 21204. www.dolphinbeachhouse. com. *9rm.* Comfortable modernised farmhouse in a secluded location overlooking the bay and sandy beach. The welcoming hosts produce excellent home-cooked dinners () and award-winning breakfasts featuring local produce.

The Quay House – *Beach Rd, Clifden.* ☎095 21369. www.thequay house.com. *14rm.* The elegant harbour master's house, the oldest building in Clifden has been converted into a stylish townhouse hotel; national winner of Guesthouse of the Year and Irish Breakfast Awards (both 2006).

Ballynahinch Castle Hotel – *Ballynahinch.* ☎095 31006. www. ballynahinch-castle.com. *37rm/3 suites.* The castle lies in a vast estate of 450 acres/183ha featuring scenic walks, salmon and trout fishing, sailing, shooting, horse-riding and golf. Log fires, quiet reading rooms, fine dining in the outstanding Owenmore Restaurant ().

WHERE TO EAT

O'Dowds – *Roundstone.* ☎095 35923. www.odowdsbar.com. This lively pub is famous for its locally-sourced seafood, and is especially busy at weekends with family lunches.

SHOPPING

For crafts try the IDA craft village at **Roundstone** (*see South Connemara driving tour*) the craft shop at **Kylemore Abbey** (*see North Connemara driving tour*) and, for woollen goods, the **Leenane Cultural Centre** (*see North Connemara driving tour*).

SPORTS AND LEISURE

BEACHES

There is a long sandy beach on the north shore of Clifden Bay west of the harbour.

Scubadive West, Renvyle. ☎095 439 22. www.scubadivewest.com. Ireland's leading PADI dive centre.

SEA ANGLING

In Clifden, at Letterfrack and at the **Roundstone Sea Angling Centre**. ☎095 359 52.

FRESHWATER FISHING

In Lough Corrib, Lough Mask, Lough Nafooey, in the Joyce River, at Maam Cross and Recess.

RAMBLING

Visitors intending to walk in the hills should be properly equipped (map and compass, stout waterproof footwear, warm clothes and food) and should notify someone, preferably at the **National Park Visitor Centre** (*see North Connemara driving tour*), of their route and expected time of return. The National Park Visitor Centre offer guided walks (2–3 hrs) during July and August.

EVENTS AND FESTIVALS

Connemara Pony Show – Clifden *(August).* Over 400 ponies from all over Ireland are on show at the Clifden Showground. www.cpbs.ie.

Galway International Oyster Festival – *September.* www.galwayoysterfest. com. Four days and nights of music, partying and oysters in Galway City.

who founded the Society for the Prevention of Cruelty to Animals; his family home, **Ballynahinch Castle** on the south shore of Ballynahinch Lake, is now a hotel.

Driving Tours

North Connemara
Round trip of 60mi/96km – 1 day.

Clifden
Sited at the head of a long sea-inlet and still consisting mainly of John d'Arcy's original triangle of broad streets, Clifden is the heart of Connemara. In August, people flock to the Clifden Connemara Pony Show, a major event in the local calendar. Ireland's native pony breed is celebrated at the **Station House Museum** (♿ ⏰*open May–Oct Mon–Sat 10am–5pm, Sun noon–6pm; ≋€2; ☎ 095 21494, www.connemarapony. ch/museum1.htm*), together with local history and two events that (briefly) put Connemara "in the forefront of communications technology": the opening of the Marconi radio station in 1905 at nearby Derryginlagh and the first transatlantic flight, which concluded with Alcock and Brown's crash-landing in Derryginlagh bog (*see South Connemara Driving Tour*).

▶ *From Clifden take the cliff road W.*

Sky Road★★
A steep and narrow road climbs along the cliffs on the north side of Clifden Bay past the site of Clifden Castle, John D'Arcy's house. Looking south across Clifden Bay you can see the round hump of Errisbeg (987ft/300m). As the road bears north-west over the ridge, a magnificent **view**★★ stretches north west along the coastline and offshore islands. The road descends in a curve to the head of Kingstown Bay and then continues inland along the south shore of Streamstown Bay.

▶ *At the T-junction turn left onto the N 59. To visit Inishbofin go west to Cleggan (4mi/6.5km).*

Inishbofin
Ferry from Cleggan (⏰see Address Book). The Island of the White Cow, where St Colman of Lindisfarne founded a monastery in the 7C, is nowadays inhabited by farmers and fishermen. The fort was used by Grace O'Malley, whose ancestors seized the island from the O'Flahertys in the 14C, then by Cromwell, who expelled the monks and interned Catholic priests there.

Connemara National Park (Páirc Náisiúnta Chonamara)★
(*Dúchas*). ♿ ⏰*Visitor Centre open daily: Mar–May and Sept–Oct 10am–5.30pm Jun–Aug 9.30am–6.30pm.☎095 41054 or 41006. www.heritageireland.ie/en/ West.*

The park (4 942 acres/2 000ha) preserves some of the finest scenery in the Twelve Bens range of mountains with areas of heath, blanket bog, grassland and natural oak and birch woodland. The flora includes Mediterranean, alpine and arctic species. The **red deer** and the **Connemara pony**, Ireland's only native pony, roam the park. From Diamond Hill (1 460ft/445m) there is a good view of the Polladirk River.

The visitor centre in Letterfrack village offers a good introduction to the park including a 15min audio-visual presentation and information on walking trails and guided walks during July and August.

▶ *Continue north on the N 59. In Letterfrack make a detour left to Rinvyle.*

Rinvyle Peninsula
From **Rinvyle (Currath) Castle**, a ruined tower house belonging to the O'Flaherty clan with a spiral stair and huge fireplace, there is a good view of the Mweelrea (Muilrea) Mountains (*northeast*) and offshore islands – Inishbofin (*west*), Inishturk and Clare Island (*north*). Rinvyle House, nearby, was once home to the Dublin wit and socialite, Oliver St John Gogarty, who loved his "long, long house in the ultimate land of the undiscovered West".

▶ *Return to the N 59 and continue east.*

B Perousse/MICHELIN

Kylemore Abbey

Kylemore Abbey★

♿🕐*Visitor Centre, Abbey & Church open daily 9am–5pm. Walled garden mid-Mar–Oct 10am–4.30pm.* 🕐*Closed Good Fri and Christmas week.* ⊗*€12.* ✕. ☎*095 41146. www.kylemoreabbey.com.*

The Irish name *Coill Mhór* refers to the "big wood" on the north shore of Lough Pollacappul at the foot of Doughrough Mountain. The turreted and crenellated neo-Gothic castle, built (1860–67) of Dalkey granite, now houses a community of Irish Benedictine nuns and a convent school. The lavish mansion was built for the Manchester financier, MP and socialite, Mitchell Henry (1826–1901). The history of the castle and convent is retold with photographs and a 12min film. The **Gothic church** dating from 1878 *(5min walk)* is a replica of Norwich Cathedral.

The magnificent 6acre/2.5ha **Victorian walled garden**★ *(shuttle bus)* is restored to its late 19C state when it was one of the most admired in Ireland. A stream and belt of trees divide the flower garden and geometrical parterres from the vegetable garden with in exemplary lazy-beds. The buildings comprise a castellated bothy, a head gardener's house and spectacular glasshouses.

The Abbey's extensive **Craft and Retail** complex is famous for its homemade jam and its Pottery Studio.

▶ *Continue east on the N 59.*

Killary

Killary harbour★ has a fine view of the deep fjord and Erriff River estuary.

At the **Leenane Cultural Centre** (🕐*open Apr–Oct, 9.30am–7pm (9am, Aug–Jul)* ; ⊗ *€3;* 🍴; ☎*095 42323)* you can learn how fleece is transformed into woollen cloth.

▶ *Take the R 336 south; after 4.5mi/8km turn left onto a steep, narrow mountain road.*

Joyce Country★

This beautiful area takes its name from a Welsh family which settled in the mountains between Lough Mask and Lough Corrib after the Anglo-Norman invasion in the 12C. **Lough Nafooey**★ lies at the foot of Maumtrasna (2 207ft/671m), while **Lough Mask** stretches towards the Parry Mountains *(west)*.

▶ *At the T-junction turn left; in Clonbur turn right onto the R 345.*

Lough Corrib★★

The second largest lake in Ireland, almost 30mi/48km long, is dotted with islands. On one stands the ruin of **Hen's Castle**, an O'Flaherty stronghold that was twice defended by Grace O'Malley.

Alexander Nimmo (1783–1832)

Alexander Nimmo was a Scot who came to Ireland in 1809 to assist in surveys into the economic potential of Connemara's bogland. Fortunately for the natural beauty of the area, his scheme for converting the bogs into farmland was never implemented. However his legacy to the area is the village of Roundstone plus Connemara's highway network and a number of piers and harbours.

▶ *At the T-junction turn left onto the R 336. In Maam Cross turn right onto the N 59.*

Galway–Clifden Road

Maam Cross (An Teach Dóite) and **Recess** (Sraith Salach) are two popular angling villages; beyond lie the many islands of **Derryclare Lough**. In the glaciated valley between the Maumturk Mountains *(east)* and two of the Twelve Pins, Bencorr and Derryclare *(west)*, lies **Lough Inagh**.

Lettershear

The **Connemara Heritage and History Centre** (✆*open Apr–Oct daily 10am–6pm; ✆€7.50; ⌗; ✆095 21808; www. connemaraheritage.com)* introduces visitors to the history and landscapes of the region; the **Dan O'Hara homestead** re-creates a farmholding typical of a Connemara family with seven children before the potato famine.

South Connemara

Round trip of 75mi/121km – 1 day.

On the way to Roundstone

South of Clifden, the Owenglin River tumbles down a great waterfall towards Ardbear Harbour. After 2mi/3,2km, you see the **Alcock and Brown Monument** up on the hill commemorating the first non-stop transatlantic flight by Alcock and Brown who crash-landed in Derryginlagh Bog on 15 June 1919. At **Errisbeg**, outcrops of dense gabbro

rock (987ft/300m) shelter two lovely sand beaches.

Roundstone (Cloch na Rón)★

The delightful harbour village created by **Alexander Nimmo** (✆*see 'Alexander Nimmo' box)* was originally populated with fisherfolk from Scotland. On the south side of the town is the **IDA Craft Village**, where Malachy Kearns' workshop makes the traditional *bodhrán* (goatskin drum).

▶ *Right In Toombeola onto the R 342.*

Cashel★

At the foot of a hill overlooking Bertraghboy Bay sits the village of Cashel, known for its angling.

▶ *Turn right onto the R 340.*

Carna Peninsula

Offshore *(south)* lies **St MacDara's Island** where the 6C saint founded a monastery. The little church (c 10C, restored) built of huge stone blocks, has distinctive projections on the gable ends known as *antae* bend inwards that meet at the roof ridge, possibly aping timber cruck construction. The island can be reached by boat from **Carna**, a lobster fishing village, which holds celebrations on the saint's feast day (16 July), sailing over to St MacDara's island for Mass, followed by a series of regattas.

Patrick Pearse's Cottage

7mi/11.3km north of Kilkieran. Dúchas. ♿✆*Open late May–Sept daily 10am–6pm.* ✆€1.60. ✆091 574292. www.heritage ireland.ie/en/West.
On the west shore of Lough Aroolagh is the tiny thatched holiday cottage built by Patrick Pearse (1879–1916) one of the leaders of the 1916 Rising (✆*see DUBLIN)* where he studied the Irish language.

▶ *Return to the R 340 and continue east. At the T-junction EITHER turn left onto the R 386 and left again in Maam Cross onto N 59 to return to Clifden OR turn right onto the R 386 to take the coast road to Galway.*

CORK ★★

POPULATION 127 187

The Republic of Ireland's second city, Cork (Corcaigh), is a major port and commercial centre, with a university, a distinct historical and cultural identity, and a vibrant and welcoming atmosphere. The city centre is built on reclaimed marshland between two arms of the River Lee, whose estuary, Cork Harbour, forms the largest natural harbour in Europe. Until the 19C many of the streets were open waterways where ships moored – likened in 1780, by Arthur Young, to the towns of the Netherlands. North of the river the land rises steeply, this is now covered by **Montenotte**, the city's most exclusive residential district.

- **Information:** Grand Parade; ☎021 425 5100; www.corkkerry.ie. Blarney, Castle Gates, The Square, Macroom; ☎021 438 1624.
- ▸ **Orient Yourself:** Cork sits at a major cross-roads: 75mi/120km south west of Waterford on the N 25, 65mi/104km south of Limerick on the N 20, and 55mi/88km south east of Killarney on the N 22.
- **Parking:** Disc parking in the street; parking discs available at the Tourist Office and other outlets in Cork.
- **Don't Miss:** The Anglican Cathedral, the Shandon Bells carillon, and an excursion to Blarney Castle.
- **Organising Your Time:** Allow at least a day in Cork City plus an extra day or two for excursions.
- **Especially for Kids:** Cork City Gaol.
- **Also See:** COBH, KINSALE, MALLOW, MIDLETON, YOUGHAL.

A Bit of History

"A Marshy Place" – Cork derives its name from the Irish for a "marshy place", where St Finbar founded a church in 650 on the banks of the River Lee near the present site of University College. Its early development was disrupted in 860 by Viking raids, and in 1172 by the invasion of the Anglo-Normans who eventually broke the Danish hold on the city.

"Rebel Cork" – Cork's political independence is rooted in its long-standing commercial success. In 1492 **Perkin Warbeck**, the pretender to the English throne, arrived and soon won the support of the mayor and other leading citizens who accompanied him to England, where he proclaimed himself Richard IV, King of England and Lord of Ireland. They were all later hanged at Tyburn. In the 1640s Cork supported the royal cause; when Cromwell entered the city

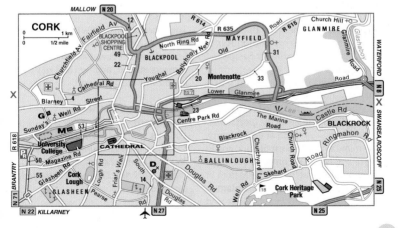

Artistic Cork

Among those sons of Cork who made their mark in the world are **John Hogan** (1800–58), a sculptor whose work is found not only in Cork but elsewhere in Ireland, **Frank O'Connor**, who penned short stories, and **Frank Browne**, a Jesuit and photographer extraordinaire of life in Ireland at the beginning of the 20C but especially of the first stages of the fatal maiden voyage of the *Titanic*.

in 1649, he inflicted great damage on it; then, in 1690 the city endured a five-day siege, until the army of William III breached the walls and destroyed the fortifications.

In the early 18C Cork accommodated many Huguenots fleeing from religious persecution in France – hence the name of French Church Street.

In the 19C, the city lived up to its rebellious reputation becoming a stronghold of Fenian (🌣*see HISTORY*) agitation.

The War of Independence and the subsequent Civil War were bitterly fought in and around Cork. In 1920 the Black and Tans (🌣*see HISTORY*) set fire to a substantial portion of the city centre. The political unrest was aggravated by the deaths of two Lord Mayors of Cork: Terence McSwiney died on hunger strike in Brixton Prison; while Tomás McCurtain was shot in his bed by Crown Forces in the presence of his wife and children.

Commercial and Industrial Centre – Cork began trading in the 12C exporting hides and cloth, and importing wine from Bordeaux. By the 18C the city had become a major producer of butter, shipping it to Britain, Europe and America.

In 1852 Cork staged Ireland's first national Industrial Exhibition, modelled on the GreaT Exhibition in London.

Henry Ford, founder of the great American car firm, was born at Ballinascarty, 28 mi/44km south west of Cork, and in 1917 the Ford car company set up its first overseas factory at the Marina in Cork. Dunlop started its Cork plant in the 1930s. Both Ford and Dunlop ceased

operations in 1980 and shipbuilding died shortly afterwards. The principal commercial activity is now related to computer manufacturing.

Historic Landmarks

St Patrick's Street★ and Grand Parade★

St Patrick's Street, Cork's main thoroughfare is lined with shops and leads to the Merchant's Quay Shopping Centre. The covered **English Market**★ (1610), the main aisle of which remained a waterway until the early 19C to allow merchandise to be brought in by boat, is renowned for its food.

Grand Parade has been the principal commercial street since the 18C when its handsome bow-fronted buildings, hung with grey slates, were built with steps down to an open water channel draining into the River Lee, where merchants would have tethered their boats. Merchants responsible for running the Butter Exchange lived at the east end of **South Mall**★, in the Commercial Rooms (now part of the Imperial Hotel).

The **South Chapel** (1766) contains a sculpture of the Dead Christ beneath the high altar, produced by local artist John Hogan (1800–58). A short distance away, stands a square tower, the last vestige of Cork's oldest building, **Red Abbey**, an Augustinian friary founded in 1300.

The **Elizabethan Fort**★ was originally built in the 1590s for "overawing the citizens of Cork". The existing building dates from c1624 and was used as a prison from 1835. In 1922 the Anti-Treaty forces set light to it.

The **Beamish and Crawford Brewery** (🖙*tours available; www.beamish.ie*) in South Main Street was acquired by the brewers in 1791, and by 1809 was the largest brewery in Ireland.

St Fin Barre's Cathedral (Anglican)★★

🕘*Open summer Mon–Sat 9.30am–5.30pm Sun 12.30pm–5pm; winter Mon–Sat 10am–12.45pm, Sun 2pm–5pm.* ✎*€3.* ☎*021 496 3387. www.cathedral. cork.anglican.org.*

South Mall, Cork

Cork's most exuberant church (1865) was designed by William Burges in an early pointed French Gothic style on the site used since medieval times. The tallest of three spires rises to 240ft/73m; the apse is lit by18 stained glass windows. A brass floor plate marks the resting place of Elizabeth Aldworth who is said to have hidden in a clock-case during a Masonic lodge meeting in her husband's house in 1712 and, when discovered, was made a Mason to secure her silence.

Church of Christ the King★

Evergreen Road, Turner's Cross, 1mi/1.6km south of city centre. ☎021 431 2465. www.turnerscross.com/church.
A magnificent **panorama** of the city can be enjoyed from the bell tower of this strikingly modern Catholic church completed in 1937.

North of the River

Shandon Bells (St Anne's Church)★★

⏰Open Mon–Sat 9.30am–5.30pm (Nov–Easter 10am–3pm). ✆€5. 🅿. ☎021 450 5906. www.shandonbells.org.
St Anne's Anglican Church dates from 1722 and the eight bells producing the famous carillon were hung in the Shandon steeple in 1752. Unusually, two of

the tower facings are limestone, two sandstone; its clock has been affectionately called the 4-faced liar on account of the fact that the time is rare synchronised. There is a fine view from the top of the tower, reached by 133 steps. The circular building at the back of the church is the old **butter market**, which opened in 1770 and traded for 150 years bringing much prosperity to Cork. The butter was brought to market in wooden caskets called 'firkins'. Today it is home to an arts and performance centre.

Cork City Gaol (& Radio Museum Experience) Kids

⏰Open year-round daily 9.30am–6pm (Nov–Feb, 10am–5pm). Last admission 1hr before closing. ✆€6. ☎021 430 5022. www.corkcitygaol.com.
The fortress-like prison in Convent Avenue, designed by Sir Thomas Deane, was in use from 1825 to 1923. Descriptions

Road Bowls

The ancient Irish sport of road bowling is still played on Sundays in Co Cork and Co Armagh. A heavy iron ball (28oz/794g; 7in/18cm) is hurled underarm along a stretch of quiet winding country road in as few throws as possible. Betting, as usual in Ireland on any sport, is heavy!

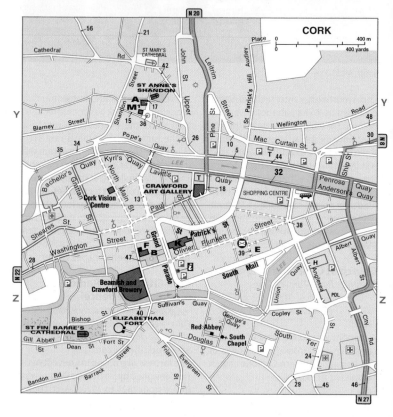

of the felonies committed by prisoners, their diet (porridge) and regime (oakum picking, treadmill, solitary confinement) are provided, and the role of the school (1856–79), the hospital and 20C graffiti are explained. The **Radio Museum** explains how Marconi made early transmissions from Ireland, and how Cork Radio was first broadcast from the prison governor's house in 1927.

South of the river

Crawford Art Gallery★
Emmet Place.
Open Mon–Sat, 10am–5pm. Closed 24–27 Dec, 1–2 Jan. ✕. 021 49 07855. www.crawfordartgallery.com.
Named after its founding benefactor, WH Crawford, the gallery is housed in the Custom House of 1724 (later extended) and has a representative collection of 19C and 20C works by Irish artists such as William Conor, John Keating, Sir William Orpen and Seán O'Sullivan,and by John Hogan and Daniel Maclise from Cork. There are frequent touring exhibitions of contemporary art.

Cork Public Museum★
Open year-round Mon–Sat 11am–1pm and 2.15pm–5pm (Sat 4pm); Sun (Apr–Sept only) 3pm–5pm. Closed Bank Hols. P. 021 42 70679. www.corkcity.ie/ourservices.
A Georgian house in Fitzgerald Park houses historical artefacts relating to Cork from prehistoric to modern times including Civic Regalia and displays relating to 19C–20C crafts and trade. There are notable collections of 18C Cork silver, Cork glass, needlepoint lace from Youghal and temporary exhibitions on local social history.

Cork Vision Centre
North Main Street. Open Tue–Sat 10am –5pm. 021 427 9925. www.corkvisioncentre.com.
St Peter's Church is the venue for temporary visual arts exhibitions. Its centrepiece is a detailed 1:500 scale model of Cork City.

Lewis Glucksman Gallery (University College)
Open year-round Tue–Sat 10am– 5pm (8pm Thu), Sun noon–5pm. ✕. 021 4901844. www.glucksman.org.
University College Cork (UCC), now part of the National University, was founded by charter in 1845 as one of three Queens Colleges alongside Galway and Belfast. The original buildings were designed by Benjamin Woodward (1816–61). The striking **Lewis Glucksman Gallery** exhibits contemporary

Kissing the Blarney Stone

art and offers daily programs of lectures and activities.

Excursions

Blarney Castle★★
5mi/8km north west via the N 20.
Castle open year-round Mon–Sat 9am–6.30pm (7pm Jun–Aug; dusk, Oct–Apr). Sun 9.30am–5.30pm or dusk. Gardens and Lakeland Walk open Apr–Aug Mon–Sat 10am–4pm. Blarney House (open by guided tour only) Apr–mid-Jun Mon–Sat 10am–2pm. Closed 24–25 Dec. €10. P. 021 4385 252. www.blarneycastle.ie.
The central feature of the castle is the massive keep, a fine example of a tower house. In addition there are halls and dungeons, but the main reason why the castle attracts so many visitors is the **Blarney Stone**, said to bestow the gift of eloquent speech on all those who kiss it. This is harder than it sounds since the famous piece of rock is set inside the parapet at the top of the castle and can be reached only by lying upside-down with a guide holding one's legs.
There are a number of legends on the stone's origins: some say it is the pillow of Jacob or St Columba, or the Stone of Ezel brought back to Ireland during the Crusades, or the "Stone of Destiny" (a magical part of the king's throne), or even the rock struck by Moses to call the waters of the Nile to crush the pursuing Egyptian army.

In the 16C Queen Elizabeth I commanded the Earl of Leicester to take the castle from the head of the McCarthy clan.

The Earl was frustrated in his mission but he sent back numerous progress reports which so irritated the Queen that she referred to them as "all Blarney".

Blarney House★ built in 1874 in the Scottish baronial style with fine corner turrets and conical-roofed bartizans, has recently been opened to the public for the first time. It is one of the most elegant and gracious of Ireland's stately homes, beautifully situated overlooking Blarney Lake. Inside is a fine collection of early furniture, family portraits, tapestries and works of art.

On a druidic site beside the Blarney River is the romantically landscaped dell known as **Rock Close**. Laid out in the 19C, the gardens contain wishing steps – ideally negotiated up and down with eyes closed. Two dolmens are sited in the close, which has a Fairy Glade with a sacrificial rock, also said to have druidic connotations.

Blarney Woollen Mills

&⏰*Open year-round daily, 9.30am–6pm (10am Sun).* ⓧ*Closed 25–26 Dec, 1 Jan.* ✗. ☎*021 451 6111.*

Established in the 19C, this is the enormous flagship store of the famous Irish chain and the successor to the 13 mills developed around the castle as an industrial enterprise in the 18C.

It is housed in one of Ireland's oldest and most authentic Irish woollen mills and is almost as popular as the Blarney Stone.

Address Book

⚪*For coin ranges, see the Legend on the cover flap.*

ARRIVING

Cork International Airport – 5mi/8km south of Cork city. ☎*021 431 3131.* www.corkairport.com.

SIGHTSEEING

Day Coach Tours to Kinsale, Killarney, Kerry, Kenmare. ☎*021 454 5328.* www.easytourscork.com

Cork Historic Walking Tours – 80min tours of central Cork. *Apr–Sept, Mon–Fri 10am, 2pm, 4pm from Cork Tourist Office in Grand Parade.* €*7.* ☎*0851 007 300.* www.walkcork.ie.

WHERE TO STAY

⚪**Acorn House** – *14 St Patrick's Hill.* 9rm. ☎*021 450 2474.* www.acornhouse-cork.com. Georgian house 5-minute walk from the centre of town, decorated with sympathetic period charm; the high ceilinged bedrooms have modern touches and facilities.

⚪⚪**Achill House** – *Western Road.* 6rm. ☎*021 427 9447.* www.achillhouse.com. Comfortable elegant period guest-house five-minutes walk from the city centre.

⚪⚪**Crawford House** – *Western Road.* 13rm. ☎*021 427 9000.* www.crawford guesthouse.com. Rooms are spacious with king-size beds and designed in a contemporary fashion. Quality features including oakwood and marble furniture. 10min walk from city centre.

⚪⚪**Garnish House** – *Western Road* 14rm. ☎*021 427 5111.* www.garnish.ie. Victorian-style guest house five-minutes walk from the city centre; generous breakfasts; some rooms with jacuzzi.

WHERE TO EAT

⚪⚪**Jacobs on the Mall** – *30A South Mall. Closed Sun. Booking essential.* ☎*021 425 1530.* www.jacobsonthemall.com. Former 19C Turkish baths converted into one of the city's most stylish restaurants, showcasing modern Irish art. Attentive service, modern cooking using the best local ingredients and some original combinations.

⚪⚪**Jacques** – *Phoenix St. Lunch, Mon–Fri; dinner Mon–Sat. Booking essential.* ☎*021 427 7387.* Well-established restaurant located in a colourful little side street in the city centre. Always busy with locals yet retaining an intimate atmosphere. Modern menu with the emphasis on locally sourced ingredients from small producers.

No 5 Fenn's Quay – *Sheares Street. Closed Sun.* ☎*021 427 9527. www.fennsquay.ie.* Converted mews house, bright and informally run. Open all day for snacks, light lunches, more substantial dinner all freshly prepared.

Blair's Inn – *Cloghroe, 5 mins from Blarney on the R 579.* ☎*021 4381 470. www.blairsinn.ie.* Friendly pub in a charming and secluded wooded setting by the Owennageara river. Traditional bar menu, more elaborate Modern restaurant menu. Live music Monday nights May–Sept.

Cafe Paradiso – *16 Lancaster Quay, Western Road. Closed Sun. Booking essential.* ☎*021 427 7939. www.cafeparadiso.ie.* Scrubbed pine tables, vivid colours, pleasant and efficient service, very inventive (albeit pricey) vegetarian dishes from a multi-award winning chef. Contemporary townhouse-style accommodation (☺☺☺) available.

ENTERTAINMENT

Everyman Palace Theatre – *15 MacCurtain Street.* ☎*021 450 1673. www.everymanpalace.com.* Cork's principal theatre, producing a wide range of entertainment.

Kino Cinema – *Washington Street.* ☎*021 427 1571. www.kinocinema.net.* The only independent arthouse cinema in Ireland.

Opera House – *Emmet Place.* ☎*021 427 0022. www.corkoperahouse.ie.* Opera, dance, drama, musicals, concerts and family entertainment.

The Half Moon Theatre – *Emmet Place, at the back of the Opera House* ☎*021 427 0022. www.halfmoontheatre.ie.* Experimental range of interdisciplinary projects mixing drama with music and comedy.

UCC Granary Theatre – *Mardyke.* ☎*021 490 4275. www.granary.ie.* New, experimental and often controversial work by artists across the disciplines.

Triskel Arts Centre –*Tobin Street.* ☎*021 427 2022. www.triskelart.com.* A popular arts centre, with mainstream and avant garde performers. Also open throughout the day (*Tue–Sat 10am–5pm*).

Busker in Cork City

SHOPPING

The main shopping street is **Patrick Street**. **North Main Street** is one of the oldest shopping areas. The picturesque **English Market** (*just off Patrick Street; open Mon–Sat 9am–5.30pm*) offers a wide range of high quality fresh produce from both local and international producers.

The **Huguenot Quarter** is a bohemian district dotted with cafés, boutiques, antique shops; the **Shandon Crafts Centre**, housed in the old **Butter Exchange** (1750), is fun for crystal, jewellery and textiles (*open Mon–Sat, 9am–5pm;* ☎*021 427 3251*).

For woollen goods visit the **Blarney Woollen Mills** (🍀*see Excursions*).

Merchant's Quay Shopping Centre – *1 Patrick Street. Open Mon–Sat 9am–6pm (Fri 9pm), Sun 2pm–6pm. www.merchantsquaycork.com* is the city's best shopping mall.

EVENTS AND FESTIVALS

Cork International Choral and Folk Dance Festival (late July) – *www.corkfolkdancefest.com.*

Beamish Cork Folk Festival (late Aug–early Sept) – *www.beamish.ie/festivals-folk.asp.*

Guinness Cork Jazz Festival (October) – *www.corkjazzfestival.com*

Corona Cork Film Festival (October) – *www.corkfilmfest.org*

TRACING ANCESTORS

Cork City and County Archives – *Great William O'Brien Street, Blackpool. Open by appointment Tue–Fri, 10am–1pm and 2.30pm–5pm.* ☎*021 4505886. www.corkcity.ie/ourservices/rac/archives.*

DINGLE PENINSULA★★

The Dingle Peninsula is extreme western Ireland at its most spectacular and atmospheric; a Gaelic-speaking area with sheer cliffs, harsh mountain-sides, an intricate network of tiny stone-walled fields, and an extraordinary concentration of ancient stone monuments – ring-forts, beehive huts, and inscribed stones. Brandon Mountain (3 121ft/951m) on the north coast, the second-highest in Ireland, is clothed in blanket bog and takes its name from St Brendan of Clonfert, a 6C monk, who is reputed to have set out on a transatlantic voyage from **Brandon Creek**, the narrow sea-inlet at the west foot of the mountain.

- **Information:** Strand Street. ☎066 9151188. www.dingle-peninsula.ie.
- ▶ **Orient Yourself:** Dingle is the main town on the Dingle Peninsula, 40 mi/65km west of Killarney via the N 70.
- **Don't Miss:** Slea Head, Gallarus Oratory, the view from Connor Pass before walking along Stadbally Strand.
- ◷ **Organising Your Time:** Allow at least a day in Dingle and a day of touring.
- **Especially for Kids:** Dingle Oceanworld Aquarium. Fungie the dolphin. Stradbally Strand - Ireland's longest beach.
- **Also See:** KILLARNEY, TRALEE.

A Bit of History

Extensive Bronze Age monuments have been recorded on the northern side of the Conor Pass near Cochlane. Later, the possibilities of the great natural harbour of Dingle were quickly realised by the Anglo-Normans; in 1257 Henry III of England imposed customs duties on exports. The peak of its commercial importance was reached in the 16C when Dingle had particularly strong trading links with Spain; in 1583 the town received permission to build a wall of enclosure.

In the same year a long period of local rule by the house of Desmond came to an end when Gearóid, the rebel Earl, was killed.

Three years earlier 600 Spanish and Italian troops sent to aid the Desmond Rebellion had been massacred by government forces at Dún an Óir on the west side of Smerwick Harbour. Following the rebellion of 1641 and the Cromwellian wars, Dingle declined significantly as a port for nearly a century, although during the late 18C it had a substantial linen industry.

Driving Tour

Dingle (An Daingean)★

Dingle, the principal centre of population, is the home port of one of Ireland's largest fishing fleets; when the catch is unloaded, the pier (0.25mi/0.4km long) is a scene of frantic activity. The town has developed as a popular tourist resort, with brightly painted houses and numerous pubs, restaurants, and places to stay.

Dingle

Address Book

For coin ranges, see the Legend on the cover flap.

GETTING AROUND

Blasket Islands Ferry – Dún Chaoin Ferry Co. Ltd. operate daily (weather permitting) *Easter–Oct 9.55am–4.55pm hourly from Dunquin Pier. ☎066 915 4864 or 87 2316131; www.blasketislands.ie.*

WHERE TO STAY

Captains House – *The Mall, Dingle* ☎*066 915 1531. http://homepage.eircom. net/~captigh. 9rm.* A warm welcome is guaranteed at this B&B with a distinctive homely feel; well-tended garden.

Greenmount House – *Upper John Street, Gortonora.* ☎*066 915 1414. www. greenmount-house.com. 12rm.* Request one of the superior rooms at the top of the B&B overlooking the town. A highlight is the sumptuous breakfast served in the conservatory.

Heatons – *The Wood.* ☎*066 915 2288. www.heatonsdingle.com. 16rm.* Excellent position by the water a 5-minute walk from town; elegant bedrooms decorated to a high standard. Extensive breakfast menu.

Pax House – *Upper John Street.* ☎*066 915 1518. www.pax-house.com. 12rm.* Fabulous views of Dingle Bay from an elevated position a short walk from the town centre. Clean and roomy accommodation.

Milltown House – *0.75mi west on the R 559 (Slea Head Drive).* ☎*066 915 1372 www.milltownhousedingle.com. 10rm.* Robert Mitchum lived here for a year while filming Ryan's Daughter! Wonderful view of the harbour; light menu offered from midday to 7pm. Hearty Irish breakfast.

Emlagh House – *Off N 86.* ☎*066 915 2345. www.emlaghhouse.com.*

10rm. Luxury country house with spacious and individually themed bedrooms with antique furniture; wonderful bay views; some rooms with private patio.

WHERE TO EAT

Doyle's Seafood Restaurant – *4 John St* – ☎*066 915 1174. www. doylesofdingle.com. Closed Sun.* Choose your lobster, the house speciality, from the tank in the bar, then pick one of the kitchen tables. Stone floors and an old kitchen range add to the rustic feel of this renowned seafood bar. Accommodation ( )available in the adjacent town house.

SHOPPING

John Weldon – *Green Street.* ☎*066 915 2522. www.johnweldonjewellers.com.* Gold and silver jewellery featuring the finest Celtic knotwork.

The Weavers Shop/Siopana bhFiodoiri – ☎*066 915 1688. www.lisbeth mulcahy.com.* Weavings, hangings and tapestries by the Danish-born Lisbeth Mulcahy.

Louis Mulcahy Pottery Workshop – *Clogher, Ballyferriter. Studio open Easter–Sept daily 10am–5pm. Open Oct–Easter Mon–Fri 10am–5pm.* ☎*066 915 6229. www.louismulcahy.com.* One of the last workshops making every piece by hand at their studio on the Dingle peninsula.

SPORTS AND LEISURE

Beaches – At Ventry Harbour, Smerwick Harbour, Stradbally Strand.
Rambling – Make the pilgrimage up the **Saint's Road** *(7mi/12km)* from Kilmalkedar (*see Driving Tour*) up the southwest face of Mount Brandon to the oratory and shrine dedicated to St Brendon on the summit.

Oceanworld Aquarium 〔Kids〕

Open year-round daily 10am–5pm. €12, child €7. ☎*066 91 52111. www.dingle-oceanworld.ie.*
The region's largest aquarium features an Amazonian display including piranhas and poison-dart frogs, a shark tank, a touch pool and a walk-through perspex tunnel bisecting the largest tank.

Diseart

Open Mon–Sat 9am–5.30pm. €2, €3.50 included guided tour. ☎*066 915 2476. www.diseart.ie.*
This institute of Education and Celtic Culture promotes language courses, traditional festivals, art, poetry, music and storytelling. You can visit the garden and a famine kitchen, specially built to feed

Failure and Fame for Ryan's Daughter

Despite the fact that it was a critical and box office failure when released in 1970, for many viewers this is one of the most atmospheric and powerful films to have been made in Ireland. *Ryan's Daughter* was directed by David Lean and starred Sarah Miles, Robert Mitchum, Trevor Howard and, most memorably, John Mills in his role as Michael, the mute village idiot. He won an Oscar for Best Supporting Actor and created history at the awards ceremony for the shortest ever acceptance speech, merely nodding in the character of Michael and picking up his award without saying a word!

Filming on the **Dingle Peninsula** was very difficult and expensive and it is said that the local economy gained the then princely sum of around £3 million. Stormy weather is prominent in the film and tragedy nearly struck for real when Robert Mitchum almost drowned.

as many poor souls as possible during the Irish Potato Famine (see HISTORY) and a secret tunnel leading between the convent and the church. There is also a small exhibition on the making of the film 'Ryan's Daughter' (see "Failure and Fame for Ryan's daughter' box).

Diseart's pride and glory however lies in the attached former Convent of the Presentation Sisters, designed by the architect J J McCarthy. Its chapel contains twelve outstanding **stained glass windows**★ created in 1922 by Harry Clarke, one of the greatest artists of the last century in this genre (see ART AND CULTURE).

J J McCarthy, often called "the Irish Pugin", also designed the adjacent **St Mary's Church**★ (1862); although the steel girders and copper sheet roof is modern.

Dingle Library (open Mon–Sat, 10am–5pm; 8pm Thu; ☎066 91 51499, www.kerrycountylibrary.com) displays material relating to local hero **Thomas Ashe** (1885–1917), who took a leading role in the 1916 Easter Rising.

▶ *From Dingle take the R 559 west (signed Ceann Sléibhe).*

Celtic and Prehistoric Museum

Kilvicadownig, 6 miles west of Dingle, 3 miles west of Ventry. Open Mar–mid-Nov Mon–Sat 10am–5.30pm. €4. ☎066 915 9191. www.celticmuseum.com.

A large archeological collection with over 500 artefacts from the Stone, Bronze, and Celtic Iron Ages as well as Viking, Saxon and Roman objects. It claims the world's largest fossil Woolly Mammoth skull and tusks, a fossil dinosaur egg nest, and a complete fossil baby dinosaur skeleton.

Slea Head (Ceann Sléibhe)★★

On the steep south-facing slopes of Mount Eagle (1 696ft/516m), both east and west of the ford at Glenfahan, the agricultural landscape of Early Christian – possibly even prehistoric – times has been largely preserved in all its multi-layered complexity. Though some have been unthinkingly cleared, drystone walls define a filligree pattern of tiny fields, among which are more than 400 **clocháin** or **beehive huts**★ *(privately owned)*, some set within ringforts like **Cathair na gConchúireach** *(admission charge may be requested)*, where their superb workmanship can be admired.

Dunbeg Promontory Fort (An Dún Beag)

Fahan, 2mi/3.2km east of Slea Head. Visitor Centre open year-round daily 9am–7pm (6pm Nov–Mar). €3. ☎066 915 9755. www.dunbegfort.com.

This "fort" occupies a dramatic site at the base of Mount Eagle and projects right into Dingle Bay. Inside is a circular clocháin (see Slea Head) with a square interior. It seems to have been in use from c. 800 through Celtic times and up to the 10C. Despite its current name however its purpose – defensive, ritual, or merely domestic dwelling – remains a mystery. A 10-min audio-visual presentation offers some clues.

H Champollion/MICHELIN

Gallarus Oratory

Blasket Islands★

Accessible by boat from Dunquin.

These islands have been uninhabited since 1953 when the last 22 residents abandoned a harsh and demanding life. The largest island, **Great Blasket** (4mix0.75mi/6kmx1.2km), is now a national historic park with buildings restored as holiday accommodation. In Blasket Sound, two Spanish Armada ships, *San Juan* and *Santa Maria de la Rosa*, founded in 1586.

Dunquin

It was here that David Lean filmed the beach scenes in *Ryan's Daughter* (&see 'Ryan's Daughter' box) although the main (fictional) village of Kirrary was actually built in the mountains above Carhoo.

The starkly modern **Great Blasket Centre**, *(Dúchas; &* *open Easter–Oct daily 10am–6pm (7pm Jul–Aug); last admission 45min before closing; in winter by appointment; €3.70; ; 066 915 6444 ,www.heritageireland.ie)* also known as the The Blascaod Centre (Ionad and Bhlascaoid Mhóir) - celebrates the unique heritage and fine Gaelic literary tradition of the Blasket Islands, their folktales and traditional way of life until 1953.

▶ *Take the R 550 north to Ballyferriter.*

Ballyferriter

The **Corca Dhuibhne Regional Museum**★ *(* *open Apr–Oct 10am–6pm and by request; €2.50; 066 91 56333, www.corca-dhuibhne.com/museum. html, in Gaelic only)* describes life on the Dingle peninsula with displays of ancient monuments, Blasket Island literature, and an extensive folk collection.

Gallarus Oratory★★

Ireland has several examples of Early Christian oratories built like beehive huts with dry stone walls corbelled inwards but none is so complete as this

---

Blasket Island Authors

The early 20C Blasket islanders were literate in both Irish and English, and were encouraged by their visitors to develop their literary talents and evoke their elemental way of life before it vanished. Among the better-known works are three novels translated from Irish: *Twenty Years A-Growing* by Maurice O'Sullivan, *Peig* by Peig Sayers, and *The Islandman* by Tomás Ó'Criomhthain, described by E M Forster as "an account of Neolithic life from the inside." Another fine account, albeit from the point of view of an outsider, is *Western Island* by the Englishman Robin Flower.

Dingle's Famous Flipper

Dingle's most unusual resident is a male bottlenose dolphin, named **Fungie** by the locals. He weighs in at around 250 kg and measures around 13ft/4m long. Fungie was first spotted in 1984, escorting the town's fishing boats to and from the port. Since then he has been studied regularly by many cetacea experts and enthusiasts and has developed into a playful, even mischievous, companion to humans. A small cave under the cliffs at Burnham is thought to be his home.

Fungie still accompanies the fishing vessels that regularly cross his chosen territory and he has been seen to clear the water to the height of a vessel's bridge. Usually though a roll in the bow wave is his signature. It is by no means unique to find these usually social, open creatures living alone in such a small "restricted" zone or befriending humans. But it is still relatively rare and Fungie is Ireland's first recorded occurrence. From observation of body scarring it seems that Fungie does still frequently encounter other cetaceans but his habit of returning to the bay may indicate that he finds it a welcoming and safe environment.

During the summer months Fungie is often seen taking garfish in the harbour mouth, another oddity as this has never before been recorded as part of a dolphin's diet. During the winter months he has to travel further afield for his food. Dingle Boatmen's Association (Kids ☎066 915 2626 or 915 1967, www.dingledolphin.com |€16, child €7) organise **boat trips** throughout the day year-round (weather permitting) to see Fungie. These depart from The Pier and last approximately 1hr; there is a "no-show money back guarantee" which apparently has never had to be paid out!

---

one, built with exceptional care in the 9C in the shape of an inverted boat. Unlike other beehive huts it is rectangular rather then circular in plan, a feature which in every other example has led to collapse, since the resulting walls are inherently unstable.

A **visitor centre** (◷open daily 10am–7pm (9am Jun–Aug); ⦿€3; ⌧; ☎066 91 55333) shows a video about the oratory and the local natural history.

Kilmalkedar★

This ruined Romanesque church, probably built in the 12C as part of a medieval religious complex, echoes the famous Cormac Chapel at Cashel (⦿see CASHEL): inside there is an alphabet stone and fine stone carving and an Ogham stone. The chancellor's house *(400yd/370m south)* would have served the chancellor of the diocese of Ardfert. From here an old track, the **Saint's Road** runs for 7mi/12km up the southwest face of Brandon Mountain to an oratory and shrine dedicated to St Brendan.

▶ *Return to Dingle and take the minor road NE (signed) to the Connor Pass.*

Connor Pass★★

Enjoy great **views** from the highest pass in Ireland (1 496ft/456m)of Dingle Harbour, Brandon Mountain, Brandon Bay, the Castlegregory Peninsula and Tralee Bay.

Stradbally Strand★★   Kids

Nestling in the beautiful horseshoe-shaped **Brandon Bay** is Ireland's longest sandy beach (12mi/19km); at the north end sit the **Magharee Islands** or The Seven Hogs. At low tide, Illauntannig, the largest island (early-Christian monastery) is linked to Reennafardarrig Island.

▶ *Continue E to Camp; turn right onto the N 86 towards Dingle; turn left.*

Minard Castle

The great square fortress built by the Knight of Kerry in the 15C and largely destroyed by Cromwellian forces in the 17C occupies an excellent vantage point overlooking Dingle Bay.

DONEGAL

POPULATION 2 296

Donegal (Dún na nGall) **is an attractive small town at the mouth of the River Eske, a perfect spot from which to explore the glens and mountains north, the dramatic coastal scenery west and the seaside resorts on Donegal Bay to the south.**

- **Information:** Quay Street, Donegal; ☎972 1148; www.discoverireland.ie/northwest.aspx. www.donegaldirect.com. Main Street, Bundoran; ☎072 41350.
- **Orient Yourself:** Donegal is situated on the south side of the Blue Stack Mountains, overlooking Donegal Bay on N 15 which links Sligo with Strabane on the border with Northern Ireland.
- **Don't Miss:** A stroll along Rossnowlagh Strand.
- **Especially for Kids:** A trip to Waterworld, Bundoran (*see Address Book*)
- **Also See:** BUNCRANA, DONEGAL COAST, DONEGAL GLENS, ENNISKILLEN, LONDONDERRY.

A Bit of History

Dún na nGall (the fort of the foreigners) was established by the Vikings; for 400 years the O'Donnell clan ruled the area until the flight of the Earl of Tyrconnell in 1607. In 1610 it was granted by the English crown to Sir Basil Brooke who rebuilt the castle and laid out the new Plantation town round the triangular Diamond 'square'.

The Irish mounted an unsuccessful attack during the 1641 rebellion; during the Williamite war the town was burned by the Jacobite Duke of Berwick, but the castle held firm. In 1798 two French ships, carrying reinforcements for General Humbert's army, anchored in Donegal Bay but cut their cables on learning of his defeat. The anchor abandoned by the *Romaine* is now displayed on the quay.

Visit

Donegal Castle★

(*Dúchas*) ♿ ◷*Open mid–Mar–Oct daily 10am–6pm, Nov–mid–Mar Thu–Mon 9.30am–4.30pm. Last admission 45 mins before closing.* ◷ *Closed 25–26 Dec.* ⊛€3.70. 🅿. ☎073 22405. www.heritage ireland.ie.

Perched on a bluff in the centre of town on the south bank of the River Eske, the original O'Donnell stronghold was largely destroyed by Hugh Roe O'Donnell in 1604 to prevent it falling into English hands. The remains were incorporated into a splendid five-gabled Jacobean mansion with a great hall, furnished in the style of the 1650s.

Donegal Railway Heritage Centre

◷*Open year-round Mon–Fri 10am–5pm also Sat–Sun in Summer.* ⊛€4. ☎074 97 22655. www.cdrrl.com.

The old station museum is dedicated to the narrow gauge County Donegal Railway, run between 1900 and 1959.

Donegal Friary (Abbey)

On the south bank of the estuary overlooking Donegal Bay are the ruins of a

Donegal Castle

SLIDE FILE, Dublin

Franciscan house, once a famous centre for learning founded by Red Hugh O'Donnell and his wife Nuala (1474). Substantial damage was caused by an explosion during the English occupation in 1601.

Driving Tour

South of Donegal
22mi/36km – allow half a day.

▷ *From Donegal take the N 15 south. After 4mi/6.4km in Ballintra turn right onto the R 231 to Rossnowlagh.*

Rossnowlagh Strand★★
A small village with a large hotel overlook a wonderful beach some 2.5mi/4km long – perfect for swimming, surfing, horse riding. Across Donegal Bay rise the cliffs of the Slieve League (◔*see DONEGAL COAST*).

▷ *Continue south on the R 231.*

Abbey Assaroe
In the late 12C **Cistercian monks** from Boyle Abbey settled by the Erne estuary. The history of their monastery is told in the restored **Mill** (◔*open Jun–Sept 11am–7pm; Oct–May, Sun, 2.30pm–7pm.* ▱*).*

Address Book

◔*For coin ranges, see the Legend on the cover flap.*

GETTING AROUND
Donegal Airport – ☏074 954 8284. www.donegalairport.ie.

SIGHTSEEING
The Waterbus offers 80min tours of Donegal Bay. ☏*074 972 3666. www.donegalbaywaterbus.com.*

WHERE TO STAY
⌒**Ardeevin** – *Lough Eske, Barnesmore. 5.5mi north east of Donegal.* ☏*074 9721790. http://members.tripod. com/~ardeevin. 6rm.* Peaceful location with stunning views of Lough Eske. Cosy traditional rooms.
⌒**Island View House** – *Ballyshannon Road, 0.75mi from town.* ☏*074 972 2411. dowdsb@indigo.ie. 4rm.* This purpose-built guest house enjoys views of the surrounding countryside and lough. Simply decorated with the emphasis on value for money.

SHOPPING
The famous woollen **Donegal tweed** is made and sold locally.
Magee of Donegal. *The Diamond.* ☏*074 9722660. www.mageeclothing.com*
The **Craft Village** on the southern outskirts of the town, specialises in contemporary craftsmanship in wood, handweaving, jewellery, glass and

stone. *Ballyshannon Road.* ☏*074 9722 225. www.donegalcraftvillage.com.*

SPORTS AND LEISURE
Drumcliffe Walk – A pleasant wooded walk from the river bridge in Donegal downstream along the north bank of the River Eske overlooking the estuary.
Rossnowlagh Strand is ideal for bathing, surfing and horse riding.
Bundoran town beach can be dangerous but there are sandy beaches for bathing up and down the coast.
Indoor facilities at **Waterworld** Kids *(Bundoran; open daily Jun–Aug 10am–7pm, Apr–May and Sept, Sat–Sun, also Easter week; €9.50 (including sauna/steam rooms);* ☏*071 9841172; www.waterworldbundoran.com)* – tidal wave, aqua volcano, tornado slide, water rapids, sea-based treatments; seaweed baths and health suite.
Also at Bundoran is **Donegal Adventure Centre** *(*☏*071 98 42418 www. donegaladventurecentre.net)*, one of Ireland's best surf school and outdoor activity centres.

EVENTS AND FESTIVALS
Ballyshannon Folk and Traditional Music Festival – Irish music in marquees, open air concerts, busking competitions and workshops *(late Jul–early August. www.ballyshannonfolkfestival.com)*

Ballyshannon

Ballyshannon guards an important crossing point on the **River Erne**. In 1597 the English under Sir Conyers Clifford were defeated here by Red Hugh O'Donnell. Today, it is best known for its popular Folk and Traditional Music Festival (🎵*see Address Book*).

▶ *From Ballyshannon take the N 15 south.*

Bundoran (Bun Dobhráin)

Bundoran is a major seaside resort with fine views across Donegal Bay to Slieve League cliffs (🎵*see DONEGAL COAST*), and the great square mass of Benbulben rock, north of Sligo.

Four Masters

Michael O'Cleary (b 1580), a Franciscan from **Donegal Abbey**, and three lay Gaelic scholars, compiled the *Annals of the Kingdom of Ireland*, an account of Irish history known as the Annals of the Four Masters in the 17C while the authors were in refuge at a Franciscan house by the River Drowes south of **Bundoran** (🎵*see Driving Tour*). They are commemorated by the obelisk (1967) in the Diamond, and in the dedication of the Roman Catholic church built in 1935 of local red granite in the Irish Romanesque style.

DONEGAL COAST★★

Facing the full force of Atlantic gales in winter, this remote and rugged coastline of deep sea-inlets, jagged cliffs and sandy beaches is backed by spectacular mountains and blanket bog. Its pristine landscapes are largely unaffected by modern development; on the north coast the land is divided into fields by walls of huge round stones and dotted with tiny white houses with thatched roofs roped down against the furious winter weather.

- 🛈 **Information:** The Quay, Dungloe. ☎074 952 1297. www.ireland-northwest.travel.ie.
- 😊 **Don't Miss:** Cliffs of Bunglass, Glencolmcille Folk Village and the views from Glengesh Pass.
- 😮 **Warning:** The coastal roads are narrow and winding with spectacular views. Watch the road and only pull over when it is safe to do so.
- 🕐 **Organising Your Time:** Allow a full day for each of the three tours below.
- 🕑 **Also See:** BUNCRANA, DONEGAL, DONEGAL GLENS, LONDONDERRY.

Driving Tours

Donegal to Naran
70mi/113km – allow 1 day.

▶ *From Donegal take the N 56 west of Dunkineely, turn to St John's Point, then left again.*

Killaghtee Cross
In the graveyard of the ivy-covered 12C Killaghtee Church stands a 7C **cross-slab**.

▶ *Return to the N 56 and continue west. After 3mi/4.8km turn left.*

Killybegs
This bustling little town, set on the River Strager, and with a natural deepwater harbour is one of the country's foremost fishing ports and is said to be the most productive port in Ireland. With the decline in fishing stocks the boats are moving further out but at any one time you may still be able to count over 50 boats.

In the mid 19C it became a centre for hand-tufted carpets, celebrated in the local Heritage Centre. Within the gates of St Catherine's Church, which was designed by JB Papworth c1840, *(turn right uphill)* stands the **tomb slab** *(left)* of Niall Mor MacSweeney; allies of the O'Neills, the MacSweeneys originally came to Ireland as gallowglasses (mercenaries) and the slab shows several of these hardy Scottish warriors.

▶ *Continue west on the R 263; after 3mi/4.8km turn left onto the Coast Road.*

Kilcar (Cill Cárthaigh)

This is a major centre for tweed (◐see *Address Book*), set at the confluence of two rivers. Several sandy beaches nearby are ideal for swimming.

▶ *Continue west. In Carrick turn left to Teelin (Teileann); take the second right to Bunglass.*

Cliffs of Bunglass★★

The road leads to one of the most spectacular sights in the whole of Ireland, an awe-inspiring prospect of ocean, mountain and enormous cliffs. After climbing steeply (over 1 000ft/305m) and skirting Lough O'Mulligan, stop at the top to contemplate the view of the Cliffs of Bunglass rising 300m from the sea, and the sheer south flank of Slieve League sea cliffs (1 972ft/601m).

▶ *Return to Carrick and turn left onto the R 263. After 2mi/3.2km bear left to Malin Beg (Málainn Bhig).*

Glenmalin Court Cairn

In marshy ground beside a small stream are the substantial remains of a court tomb, known locally as Cloghanmore, meaning Big Stone.

▶ *Continue to the crossroads; turn left along the coast.*

Trabane Strand★

The sheltered sandy bay faces south across Donegal Bay to Benbulben (◐see *SLIGO*).

▶ *Return to the crossroads and go straight ahead to Glencolumbkille.*

Glencolmcille Folk Village★★

♿⏰*Open Easter Sat–Sept daily 10am–6pm (noon Sun).* 🎫€3.50. 💬. ☎074 974 300 17. www.glenfolkvillage.com.

The folk village was one of the many initiatives undertaken by **Father James McDyer** (1910–87) who resolved to put a stop to the traumatic exodus of emigrants from this poor and remote area. He helped build a community centre, had electricity connected and roads improved. In 1967 he initiated the idea of preserving traditional practises by building a folk village with a cottage for each century, furnished with artefacts donated by his parishioners. The school, craftshop and shebeen (the illicit bar, now selling seaweed wine and country wines, quite legally!) were added later. The actual village of **Glencolumbkille** *(Gleann Cholm Cille)* lies inland from its sandy beaches guarded by a Martello tower on Glen Head (745ft/227m). In this remote and rugged valley St Columba *(Colmcille)* built himself a house of retreat for quiet prayer. On his feast day (9 June), pilgrims make a penitential tour (3mi/5km) of the glen between midnight and 3am, stopping at Stations of the Cross marked by cairns, boulders, pagan standing stones and early-Christian cross-slabs.

The **Ulster Cultural Institute** *(Foras Cutúir Uladh)*, a centre for Gaelic studies, offers a variety of activities and language courses (☎074 97 30248. www.oideas-gael.com).

▶ *Take the road to Ardara. After 10mi/16km there is a viewing point on the left.*

Glengesh Pass★★

Stop at the head of the pass to view the glaciated, green valley, enclosed by steep and rugged mountains. Hairpin bends carry the road down to join the river.

Ardara (Ard an Rátha)

Ardara (pronounced with the accent on the last syllable) is an attractive market town on the Owentocker River at the head of a deep sea-inlet, famous for its production of Donegal Tweed. The **Ardara Heritage Centre** (⏰*open Easter–*

Glengesh Pass

Sept daily 10am (2pm Sun) to 6pm; ; *074 95 541473)* celebrates the local tweed industry; weaving demonstrations and Aran knitting tradition.

▶ *Take the N 56 east.*

Glenties (na Gleannta)

Glenties is the home town of **Patrick MacGill** (1890–1963), the "Navvy Poet" known for his uncompromising depictions of the hard life led by migrant labourers (*see 'The Irish Navvy' box*). At the age of 12 MacGill was sold to a farmer to be used as a labourer by his parents, Two year later he had moved to Scotland where he became a navvy working on the railway.

Despite his lack of formal education he taught himself reading and writing and at the age of 19 years self-published 8,000 copies of a small book (56pp) printed by *The Derry Journal* which he called "Gleanings from a Navvy's Scrapbook". By the following year (1911) Patrick was working as a journalist for the *Daily Express* in London. He is honoured in a festival each summer (*July/August*).

St Connall's Church (Roman Catholic), one of Liam McCormick's masterpieces of modern architecture echoes the landscape between Big Glen and Wee Glen, with marvellous use of natural light and collection of rainwater for the water gardens.

Opposite the church is the excellent **St Connell's Museum & Heritage Centre** (*open year-round Mon–Sat 10am–1pm & 2pm–4.30pm; €2.50; 075 51277),* which includes the prison cells of the late 19C courthouse and has many artefacts pertaining to the famine in South West Donegal.

▶ *Take the N 56 west. In Maas take the R 261 west; after 3mi/5km turn right.*

The twin resorts of **Naran** and **Portnoo**, which face Inishkeel in Gweebarra Bay, have broad sandy beaches. These are excellent places for cliff walks, surfing, sailing, fishing and golf.

The Irish Navvy

The term navvy is abbreviated slang (often perjorative) for navigator and has been stereotypically applied to Irish labourers for centuries. The term comes from the late 18C when numerous canals ("navigations") were being built in Britain and a navvy came to mean anyone who was manually working on canals, roads and railways. In fact, Irish seasonal and migrant workers were a highly mobile and flexible workforce, vital to Britain's booming 19C economy and economic revival after the Second World War. Many of these men came from Donegal.

Naran to Dunfanaghy
70mi/113km – allow 1 day excluding island visits.

▶ *East of Naran take the R 261 east. In Maas take the N 56 north.*

The Rosses★
After the beautiful **Gweebarra Estuary**★ comes **Dunglow** *(An Clochán Liath)* an attractive small town regarded as the capital of The Rosses – a bleak flat rocky Gaelic-speaking region (100sq mi/259km²) dotted with tiny lakes.

▶ *Take the R 259 north west.*

Burtonport (Ailt an Chorráin)
The tiny harbour provides regular ferry services *(2mi/3.2km)* to Arranmore Island *(see Address Book).*

Arranmore Island
Around 800 people live on this unspoiled rock. The scenic attractions are rugged cliffs on the northern and western shores, and several lakes. There are seven pubs which hold regular traditional music sessions.

▶ *Continue north on the R 259. In Crolly turn left onto the N 56. After 1mi/1.6km turn left onto the R 258; turn left to Bunbeg.*

Bunbeg (An Bun Beag)
Beyond the signal tower on the narrow winding Clady estuary is this lovely little harbour, well protected from the Atlantic storms. Boats sail from here to Tory Island.

▶ *Take the R 257 north.*

Bloody Foreland Head
The headland owes its name to the reddish colour of the rocks, exaggerated in the evening sun. Offshore Inishbofin and its islands point north towards Tory Island.

Tory Island (Toraigh)
Access by boat from Meenlaragh (Magheroarty) and Gortahork (see Address Book); from Gortahork follow the signs to Bloody Foreshore; right down to the pier.

Although it is only 7mi/11km from the mainland, bad weather means that Tory Island is frequently cut off; most notably in 1974 when it was inaccessible for 8 weeks due to storms and full-scale evacuation plans had been drawn up.

This bleak and windswept rock, measuring 2.5mi/4km by around 1mi/1.6km ,is largely inhabited by Gaelic-speaking fishermen and ruled since time immemorial by their "king". The population is around 150.

Little is left of the monastery founded in the 6C by St Columba (Colmcille) other than a round tower, Tau cross and two ruined churches. At the Tory School of Primitive Art, islanders produce striking paintings in a naive folk style; examples are on show at Glebe House.

▶ *Turn left onto the N 56.*

Ballyness Bay
The sheltered sea-inlet is overlooked by two Gaelic-speaking villages, **Gortahork** *(Gort an Choirce)* and **Falcarragh** *(An Fál Carrach).*

Dunfanaghy
In the lee of Horn Head, this picturesque former fishing port was transformed into a resort when the harbour silted up. The **Dunfanaghy Workhouse Heritage Centre** (*open Apr–Sept Mon–Sat 10am–5pm; €4. 50. ; 074 9136540, www.dunfanaghyworkhouse.ie)* is one of many such built across Ireland in the 1840s, in response to the Great Potato Famine, and, at its peak, the Workhouse supported over 600 people. It explains how the Famine devastated the area, highlighting the plight of one Hannah Harraty, who survived hunger, a wicked stepmother, a life of beggary, and still reached the age of 90. There is also an art gallery and craft shop here.

Horn Head Scenic Route★
30min drive.
This headland, a breeding colony for seabirds, rises to high cliffs (over 600ft/183m) on the north coast; the blow-hole to the south west is known as McSwyne's Gun. There are magnificent 360-degree **views**.

Address Book

For coin ranges, see the Legend on the cover flap.

GETTING AROUND

Arranmore Ferry – *Passenger/car ferry operates from Burtonport to Leadgarrow: 30min crossing, up to 8 sailings per day in summer. ☎074 952 0532. www.arranmoreferry.com.*

Tory Island Ferry – *Operates (weather permitting) Bunbeg to Tory Island (1hr 30min). Magheroarty to Tory Island (45min) up to 3 times/day. ☎074 9531 1320. www.toryislandferry.com.*

Donegal Coastal Cruises. *Coastal Cruises from Bunbeg/Magheroarty (Meenlaragh) ☎074 953 1320 – www.toryislandferry.com*

WHERE TO STAY

Atlantic House – *Main Street, Dunglow. ☎074 952 1061. www.atlantichousedungloe.com. 10rm.* Simple accommodation in central location.

Ostan Gweedore – *Bunbeg. ☎074 9531177.* Very well-equipped modern hotel with comprehensive leisure, health and spa facilities; comfortable, luxurious bedrooms and great views over Gweedore. Seafood restaurant and Wine & Tapas bar.

WHERE TO EAT

The Mill Restaurant – *Dunfanaghy, 0.5mi south west on the N 56. ☎074 36985. www.themillrestaurant.com.* A converted flax mill in a super location on New Lake, with terrific views of Mount Muckish. Pleasant bedrooms and a pretty restaurant with Modern Irish cooking. *6rm.* Delightful rooms with ensuite facilities.

SHOPPING

The famous **Donegal tweed** is on sale in several centres – Donegal, Kilcar, Ardara and Downies.

Studio Donegal, The Glebe Mill, Kilcar (☎74 973 8194, www.studiodonegal.ie), makes and sells hand-woven tweed: throws, clothing, hats.

Also in Kilcar the **Doogan Donegal Factory Shop** (☎74 973 8256) sells knitted woolllens.

SPORTS AND LEISURE

Beaches at Naran and Portnoo. Angling in Glenties at the confluence of the Owenea and Stracashel Rivers.

Walking: 4 long-distance waymarked coastal paths – Bealach na Gaeltachta, Dun na nGall – details from North West Tourism Office, Letterkenny (☎074 9121160). (*see DONEGAL Address Book*)

EVENTS AND FESTIVALS

International Mary from Dungloe Festival – *Dungloe. One week late-Jul–early-Aug (www.maryfromdungloe.com).* Music and dancing and outsdoor events

TRACING ANCESTORS

Donegal Ancestry Centre – *The Quay, Rathmelton. Open Mon–Fri 9.30am–4.30pm (3.30pm Fri). ☎074 915 1266. www.donegalancestry.com*

Dunfanaghy to Letterkenny

80mi/130km – allow 1 day.

▶ *N56 E from Dunfanaghy.*

Portnablagh

This fishermen's hamlet was transformed by the Portnablagh Hotel (1923).

Ards Forest Park

The park (1 188 acres/481ha), once part of an extensive estate owned by the prominent Stewart family of Scottish descent, includes the north shore of the Ards Peninsula, the Binnagorm headland, Sheep Haven Bay (bathing beaches). It includes a broad variety of woodland, fenland, sand dunes, salt-marsh, a dolmen, ringforts and a lough.

▶ *Continue south on the N 56.*

Creeslough

Muckish Mountain (2 197ft/670m) stands guard over the village of Creeslough, lending its profile to **St Michael's**

H Champollion/MICHELIN

Rathmelton Bridge

Church (Roman Catholic), another of Liam McCormick's outstanding modern churches (1971). Frequent past visitors include artists and writers such as W B Yeats, AE Russell, Percy French and G K Chesterton.

The ruins of **Doe Castle**★ stand in a strategic position on a promontory in Sheep Haven Bay protected by the sea, a rock-cut moat and drawbridge. Built in the 1500s by Scottish mercenaries, the MacSweenys, the stronghold played an important role in local history until after the Battle of the Boyne (1690). A **tomb slab** (*Dúchas; closed for restoration; ☎074 9138445*) carved with an elaborate cross may have belonged to one of the Scottish McSweeneys, sometime lords of the castle, moved here from the ruins of the neighbouring Franciscan monastery.

▶ *On leaving the castle turn left over a hump-backed bridge; turn left onto the R 245. At Carrigart (Carraig Airt), follow the R 248 north west.*

Rosguill Peninsula
Atlantic Drive★
9mi/14.5km drive.
This scenic route follows the great curve of sand dunes alongside the Rosapenna golf links, before climbing up to **Downies** *(Na Dúnaibh)*, renowned for its tweed. From here it stretches past the deep inlet of Sheep Haven Bay, backed by Horn Head, providing glorious views of the sheltered beach of Tranarossan Bay, Melmore Head and the sandy coves and islands of Mulroy Bay.

▶ *In Carrigart take the R 245 east to Mulroy Bay and Millford.*
Turn left onto the R 246. 2mi/3.2km north of Carrowkeel, fork left onto the coast road.

Fanad Peninsula
A string of hamlets lines the east shore of Mulroy Bay and Broad Water. North of Kindrum, grass-covered dunes, dotted with white cottages and small lakes, extend to the sandy shore. The lighthouse on Fanad Head marks the entrance to Lough Swilly. Dunaff Head, the Urris Hills and Dunree Head come into view on the opposite shore. **Portsalon** is a small resort at the north end of Warden Beach.

▶ *From Portsalon take the R 246; after 1mi/1.6km turn left onto the coast road.*

Knockalla Viewpoint★
The north end of Knockalla Mountain (1 194ft/364m) provides panoramic **views**.

▷ *At the junction bear left onto the R 247.*

Rathmullan (Ráth Maoláin)

This pretty little place facing Lough Swilly is famous for being the departure point in 1607 of the Irish clan leaders including the earls, Aodh Uî Neill (Hugh O'Neill) and Rudhraighe Ó Domhnaill (Rory O'Donnell), who were leaving Ireland to secure military help from Spain. This episode, which came to be known as The Flight of the Earls, is cited as the end of the old Gaelic order in Ireland. The story is told in the **Rathmullen Heritage Centre** (⊙*open Easter–Sept Mon–Sat 10am–1pm & 2pm–5pm, Sun noon–5pm; ⊸€5; ☎074 58229)* housed in an old Napoleonic battery beside the pier.

▷ *Continue SW on R 247.*

Rathmelton (Ráth Mealtain)★

This typical Plantation town stands on a salmon river flowing into Lough Swilly. Among the 18C warehouses along the quay is the old Steamboat Store housing the **Donegal Ancestry Centre** and **Rathmelton Story** exhibition (⊙*open Jun–Sept Mon–Sat 9.30am–5pm. ☎ 074 9151266. www.donegal ancestry.com)*.

▷ *Take the R 245 south to Letterkenny.*

DONEGAL GLENS

The centre of County Donegal is mountainous country interrupted by long and sometimes serpentine glens: the Barnesmore Gap running south of the Blue Stack Mountains (2 205ft/672m) to Donegal, the Barnes Gap north of Kilmacrenan to the east of Muckish Mountain (2 197ft/670m), and Muckish Gap at the foot of the south face. The most spectacular of the high peaks is Errigal (2 466ft/752m), a cone of white quartzite, towering over Dunlewy.

- ▯ **Information:** Neil T Blaney Road, Letterkenny.
  ☎074 9121160. www.donegaldirect.com.
- ▷ **Orient Yourself:** Most of the roads follow the course of the rivers through the glens. The N 15 runs between Donegal and Letterkenny, which is linked by N 13 to Londonderry over the border. Letterkenney is the best touring base.
- ☺ **Don't Miss:** Glenveagh National Park.
- Kids **Especially for Kids:** The Old Courthouse Lifford, Fintown Railway, Dunlewy Centre.
- ♿ **Also See:** BUNCRANA, DONEGAL, DONEGAL COAST, LONDONDERRY.

Glens

Sites listed in rough clockwise order from Letterkenny.

Letterkenny

Large by local standards, and with a good range of facilities, this undistinguished town on the River Swilly has the longest main street in Ireland and is the seat of the diocese of Raphoe.

The vast Gothic Revival **Cathedral** has an interior with an uneasy mixture of neo-Celtic carving and Italianate decor.

The **Donegal County Museum** (♿ ⊙ *open Mon–Fri 10am–4.30pm, Sat 1pm–4.30pm; ☎074 912 4613, www.dun-na-ngall.com/museum.html)* housed in the old 19C workhouse, traces the folklore and traditions of Donegal, its history, archaeology and geology.

Newmills Corn and Flax Mills

(Dúchas). ⊙*Open late May–late Sept daily 10am–6.30pm (last admission 5.45pm).* ☎074 25155. www.heritageireland.ie.
A tour of the water-powered corn and flax mill, boasting one of the oldest and largest waterwheels in working order in

St Columba

St Columba, or St Colmcille, (521–597), was a native of Donegal and active in the transition from pagan to Christian Ireland. He was born an O'Neill in Gartan of a noble family, and as a boy was fostered at Kilmacrenan, which was then the custom.

Over a period of 15 years he founded monasteries at Tory, Drumcliffe, Kilmore, Swords, Moon and Durrow). In c 560 he embraced the "white martyrdom" by giving up all he loved and leaving Ireland for Iona off the coast of Scotland, where he established a famous monastic community. He died in 597, the year in which Augustine landed in Kent.

Ireland, explains how the corn was dried and milled, and how the flax was treated by retting, rolling, scutching and buffering, to produce linen thread.

Lake Finn
4mi/6km N via the R 624. 19mi/31km west of Letterkenny via the R 250 to Fintown.
Fintown's attractions include paddle boats for hire from the pier, and the restored narrow-gauge **Fintown Railway** Kids (*An Mhuc Dhubh;* ⚙ 🕐 *services operate Jun Thu–Sun and Jul–Sept daily*

Mon–Fri 11am–4pm, Sun 1pm–5pm; ⚙ *€8, child €5;* ☎ *074 954 6280, www. antraen.com).*

Colmcille
St Columba (⚙ *see 'St Columba' box*), born by Gartan Lough, is commemorated in the **Colmcille Heritage Centre** (♿ 🕐 *open Easter and May–early Oct 10.30am–6.30pm (1pm Sun);* ⚙ *€3;* ☎ *074 9137306).*

The Regency **Glebe House and Gallery** ★ houses the **Derek Hill Collection** of some 300 paintings by 20C artists (Braque, Corot, Degas, Picasso, Renoir, Graham Sutherland), notable Irish artists (J B Yeats) and by the inhabitants of Tory Island (⚙ *see DONEGAL COAST*) who paint in a primitive style producing striking "folk" works.

Glebe House (*Dúchas;* 🕐 *open Easter daily 10am–6.30pm, Jun–Sept Sat–Thu 11am–6.30pm;* 🖼 *house open by guided tour only, last tour 5.30pm;* ⚙ *gallery free, house €2.90.* ☎ *in summer;* ☎ *074 9137071, www.heritageireland.ie)* is richly furnished with Oriental prints, William Morris fabrics, William de Morgan tiles and Wemyss ware pottery; artworks by John Sherlock, Victor Pasmore, Basil Blackshaw, Augustus John, Evie and Nathaniel Hone, Sir William Orpen, Oskar Kokoshka, Cecil Beaton and John Bratby.

On the hillside, facing southeast over Lough Akibbon, are the scanty remains of **St Colmcille's Oratory**, a monastery associated with St Colmcille: a holy well, two crosses and the ruins of a church in a graveyard.

Glenveagh National Park★★

(Dúchas) ◷ *Open year-round daily 10am–6pm.* ◄ *Castle open by guided tour only. (5pm last admission).* ◄ *Castle €3, Minibus between Visitor Centre and Castle €2.* ✕ ⌂. ☎ *074 91 37090. www. heritageireland.ie. www.glenveagh nationalpark.ie.*

The National Park (23 887 acres/9 667ha) consists of Lough Beagh and the surrounding wild landscape of bogs, moorland, and rugged mountain clad in natural woodlands of oak and birch. By contrast the romantic granite castle sits on a promontory beside the lake surrounded by luxuriant **gardens**★★ The estate was created by John George Adair through the amalgamation of several smaller holdings from which he evicted all the tenants in 1861.

The **Visitor Centre** provides information about the park and there is a video about the conservation of the flora and fauna, including the largest herd of **red deer** in Ireland.

The beautiful gardens are designed to provide colour and interest through the seasons. Stone statuary provides a formal note to the **Terrace** (1966) and in the **Italian Garden** (1958). From the long lawn at the centre of the **Pleasure Grounds**, paths lead up to the **Belgian Walk**, which was constructed during the First World War by convalescing Belgian soldiers billeted at the house. Within the **walled garden** is an Orangery (1958) designed by Philippe Jullian. From the south end of the gardens there is a long **view** up Lough Beagh to the head of the glen below the peak of Slieve Snaght (2 441ft/683m).

The castellated façade of the **castle** conceals a large Victorian house, designed in 1870 by John Adair's cousin, John Townsend Trench. It was lit by oil lamps until 1957.

Dunlewy Centre (Ionad Cois Locha) [Kids]

◷*Open daily 17 Mar–early Nov 10.30am–6pm (Sun 11am).* ◄€*5.50 (homestead); €5.50 (boat trip).* ✕. ☎*074 9531 699. www.dunlewycentre.com.*

On the shore of the lake stands an old weaver's homestead which is the focal point of a family-oriented visitor centre providing tweed weaving demonstrations, pony treks, boat trips, adventure play area, farmyard animals to feed and lakeside walks.

Glenveagh Castle

B Perousse/MICHELIN

The road from Dunlewy east to Letterkenny (R 251) offers wonderful **views** of the lake and its valley, known as the **Poisoned Glen**. The most likely explanation for the name is that it was once called Glen of Heaven. As the Irish for 'of heaven' - neimhe - and 'of poison' - nimhe - are similar in spelling (if not pronunciation) it is thought an English cartographer confused the two, and over the centuries the name has stuck.

Doon Well and Rock

The rags on the bush show that people still believe in the curative properties long attributed to the well. Until the 16C the **Doon Rock** was the place of inauguration of the O'Donnells, the chiefs of Tirconail. Its flattened top (*5min there and back on foot*) provides a fine **view** of the surrounding country.

Kilmacrenan

St Columba built the first church here, on a site between the road to Millford and the Leannan River now marked by the ruins of a 17C church and the remains of Kilmacrenan Friary.

Raphoe

The village of Raphoe is grouped around its Diamond, an attractive triangular green. In the south corner stands **Raphoe Cathedral**, a Gothic building with 18C tower and transepts, incorporating several carved fragments dating from the 10C to the 17C. The gaunt ruin south of the church was the Bishop's Palace, built in 1636 destroyed by fire in 1839.

South of Raphoe stands the Bronze Age **Beltany Stone Circle** (*west up a track – sign Stone Circle, 10min return on foot*) commanding fine views. The circle which is about 4ft/1m high, comprises 64 stones although there were originally many more.

The Old Courthouse, Lifford [Kids]

&. ○Open year-round Mon–Fri 10am–5pm, Sun noon–5pm. Last tour 4pm. ○Closed bank holidays. ◉€6, child €3. ✕ (Sun). ☏074 9141733. www.liffordold courthouse.com.

The county town's **courthouse** (1746) has been converted into an historical attraction where visitors experience a taste of 18C prison life. This includes arrest "by our vicious Gaoler", solitary confinement in the dark dungeons deep in the heart of the Old Courthouse. Children will be disciplined by the school master, taken to the lunatic asylum, charged, fingerprinted and face public humiliation in the stocks!

Cavanacor House

Ballindrait, 2mi/3km west of Lifford on the N 14. &. ○Open Easter week and summer Tue–Sat noon–6pm, Sun 2pm–6pm. ▱. ☏074 9141143. www.dun-na-ngall.com/cav.html. www.cavanacorgallery.ie.

This is one of the oldest inhabited 17C houses in the province. James II once dinied in the garden and it was home to descendants of the 11th US President James Knox Polk. Now furnished with Jacobean and Georgian furniture, It is home to a contemporary art gallery.

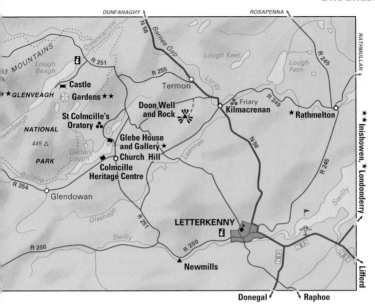

DROGHEDA ★

POPULATION 24 460

Straddling the River Boyne close to its mouth, Drogheda (Droichead Átha) was one of the most important towns of medieval Ireland, with a long and eventful history. It is still a place of some consequence, located on the main Dublin-Belfast road and railway, with varied industries and a harbour. There is an attractive coastline to the north and inland lies the **Boyne Valley.**

🅸 **Information:** Bus Eireann Bus Depot. ☎041 983 7070. Millmount. ☎041 984 5684. www.drogheda-tourism.com. www.louthholidays.com.
▸ **Orient Yourself:** Much of the town centre is set on the steep north bank of the river with narrow lanes and flights of steps linking the different levels.
🕓 **Organising Your Time:** Allow a full day.
🖒 **Also See:** BOYNE VALLEY, DUNDALK, FINGAL, KELLS, TRIM.

A Bit of History

The town was founded in 911 by Norsemen. In the late 12C, Hugh de Lacy, Lord of Meath, made it an important Norman stronghold with two separate parishes, Armagh and Meath. Little remains of the many monasteries which flourished in Drogheda in the Middle Ages and only the **Butter Gate** on Millmount and St Laurence Gate remain of the town walls built in 1234.

Parliament often met in Drogheda and in 1494 it was here declared that the Irish Parliament was to be placed under the authority of the English Parliament. During the Confederate Rebellion Drogheda was twice besieged, most infamously in 1649 when it was attacked by **Oliver Cromwell.** During the siege, many people took refuge in St Peter's Church and perished when the wooden steeple was set alight by Cromwell's troops. Eventually the city wall was breached on the southeast side of Millmount near St Mary's Church and, according to Cromwell's own estimate, 2 000 died

Cadaver tombstone

SLIDE FILE, Dublin

> *Turn right along West Street, turn left into Old Abbey Lane.*

The roofless nave and crossing tower of **St Mary's Abbey** stand on the oldest monastic site in Drogheda, where, according to tradition, a monastery was founded after St Patrick's visit in 452. In 1206 a Norman settler, Ursus de Swemele and his wife, founded a hospital which was later administered by the Augustinian Friars until the Dissolution in 1543.

by the sword; most of the survivors were transported to Barbados.

> *From West Street turn right uphill into Fair Street.*

The **Courthouse**, with its distinctive weather vane on the corner of Fair Street and Bolton Street, was completed in 1790.

Town Centre Tour

> *Walk east along Fair Street and turn left into Magdalene Street.*

St Peter's Roman Catholic Cathedral

(♿ ⏰ *open year-round 8.30am–6pm;* ☎ *041 983 8537; www.armagharch diocese.org*) a neo-Gothic building (1881) on West Street contains the shrine of **Oliver Plunkett** (1625–81), the Roman Catholic Archbishop of Armagh.

St Peter's Anglican Church

⏰ *Open for services and concerts.* ☎*041 982 7345. www.drogheda.armagh. anglican.org.*
A new church was built in 1753 to replace the medieval church burnt by Cromwell.

Address Book

💰*For coin ranges, see the Legend on the cover flap.*

WHERE TO STAY

🍽**Boyne Haven House** – *Dublin Road 2.5mi SE of Drogheda on N 1.* ☎*041 983 6700. taramcd@ireland.com. 4rm.* A bungalow surrounded by a mature garden Welcoming fire, impressive Irish breakfast, attractively bedrooms.
🍽**Windsor Lodge B&B** – ☎*041 984 1966. www.barwindsorlodge.com* Comfortable modern guesthouse 5min walk from town.

WHERE TO EAT

🍽**The Boiled Onion** – *32 Shop Street.* ☎*041 987 5566. www.theboiledonion. com. Dinner only.* Bright modern eaterie serving international bistro-style cooking.

🍽**The Black Bull Inn** – *Dublin Rd.* ☎*041 983 7139.* Local pub serving traditional Irish and Modern Irish cooking.
🍽🍽**Buttergate Restaurant** – *Millmount Square. Booking advisable.* ☎*041 9834759.* Good French cuisine, a wide range of dishes including vegetarian options and spectacular views of the River Boyne and old Drogheda.

SHOPPING

Millmount Craft Centre *by Martello Tower. Open Tue–Sat, 10am–5pm.* ☎*041 984 1960. www.millmount.net.* Designers and craftsmen working from their studios: jewellery, hand-painted silks, ceramics and knitwear.

SPORTS AND LEISURE

Extensive beaches at Bettystown (south).

The Last Catholic Martyr to Die in England

Oliver Plunkett (1629–81) was a member of a notable Anglo-Irish family from Loughcrew in Co Meath. Educated in Rome, Plunkett was appointed Archbishop of Armagh and Primate of Ireland in 1670. Using family connections with the establishment, he used his authority to reverse years of neglect following the Cromwellian era and the Penal Laws, travelling extensively in the north of Ireland. In his wake, a school for pupils of all ages was set up, priests were ordained and bishops annointed.

Repression following the marriage of Charles II's bother, James Duke of York, to the Roman Catholic Mary of Modena, prompted Plunkett to go into hiding. Anti-monarchists in London accused him of complicity in the "Popish Plot" fabricated by Titus Oates and implicated in the organisation of an invasion of 40 000 men in Carlingford. He was arrested in 1679 and brought to trial in Dundalk but no one would give evidence against him. Convicted of treason in London, he was condemned to be hanged, drawn and quartered at Tyburn. He was canonised in 1975.

It suffered a serious arson attack in 1999 and has subsequently been much rebuilt with the provision of a new space for concerts and other performances.

The three rows of Georgian houses (c 1730) beyond the graveyard, with its **cadaver tombstone**, (at the east gate) were built for clergy widows.

▶ *Continue up Magdalene Street. turn right into Upper Magdalene Street.*

Magdalene Tower (14C) marks the site of a Dominican monastery founded in 1224 by Lucas de Netterville, Archbishop of Armagh, where in 1395 four Irish princes submitted to Richard II.

▶ *Continue along Upper Magdalene Street, turn right into King Street; continue into Palace Street, turn left.*

St Laurence Gate★: this well-preserved three-storey barbican, an integral part of the 13C gate, is unique in Ireland. It was built by the Normans using stone from the walls erected by the Vikings. A section of the town wall still stands on the south side.

▶ *Walk west along Laurence Street to Shop Street.*

The **Tholsel** stands at the crossroads in the town centre; a clock tower and a lantern surmount the limestone building (1770) where Corporation meetings and law courts were held until 1889.

Millmount

South Bank.

Generations of rulers left their mark on the hill dominating the south bank of the Boyne; it was possibly the site of a passage grave and subsequently crowned by an Anglo-Norman motte, then by 18C fortifications. From the **Martello Tower** of **Millmount Fort** there is a fine **view** of the town centre and **railway viaduct** built in 1855 across the Boyne estuary.

Drogheda Millmount Museum★

🕐*Open Mon–Sat 9.30am–5.30pm, Sun 2pm–5pm.* 📷*Last tour 1 hr before closing.* 💶*€4.50.* 🅿️ *.*☎*041 983 3097. www. millmount.net.*

Located in the old Officers' quarters (1820) this museum is dedicated to its military use, local industries, a folk kitchen, geology and archaeology. The Martello Tower (fort) offers fine views over Drogheda.

Excursion

Whiteriver Mills

4mi/6km N by R 624. Dunleer; 9mi/14.5km north of Drogheda by N 1 and R 132. 🕐*Open Apr–Sept daily 10am (2pm Sun)-6pm.* 💶*€4.* ☎*041 985 1141.*

A restored three-storey 18C working flour mill.

DUBLIN★★★

Ireland's famous capital – the fair city – bestrides the River Liffey and looks seawards to its port and the broad waters of Dublin Bay. The distinctive outline of the Wicklow Mountains forms a magnificent backdrop to the south, while suburbs stretch far inland as well as north to the Ben of Howth and south to Dalkey Headland. Something like a third of the country's population lives in the greater Dublin area, and a disproportionate amount of the country's business is carried out here. Georgian architectural elegance and the increasingly cosmopolitan life of street, cafe, restaurant and bar make the city an irresistible destination, not just for a weekend, but for longer periods of exploration.

- **Information:** Dublin Tourism Centres: Suffolk Street; 14 Upper O'Connell Street; Arrivals Hall, Airport; Dun Laoghaire Ferry Terminal. ☎01 605 7700; ☎0800 0397000 (from UK). www.visitdublin.ie. Temple Bar Cultural Information Centre, 12 East Essex St; ☎01 677 2255; www.templebar.ie.

- **Orient Yourself:** Dublin is set on the east coast, on the estuary of the River Liffey and the shores of Dublin Bay. It forms the hub of the road and rail network and has direct connections with all the major provincial towns. It is served by an international airport (north of the city centre) and by shipping lines from Liverpool, Holyhead and the Isle of Man.

- **Parking:** There are carparks throughout the city (*see Address Book*).

- **Don't Miss:** Trinity College, Dublin Castle and KilmainhamGaol are special.

- **Organising Your Time:** Allow at least three days for the highlights.

- **Especially for Kids:** Dublinia, Dublin Zoo.

- **Also See:** BOYNE VALLEY, FINGAL, KILDARE, MAYNOOTH, TRIM, WICKLOW MOUNTAINS.

A Bit of History

Viking Settlement – The name Dublin (Baile Átha Cliath) is derived from *Dubh Linn*, the Dark Pool at the confluence of the Poddle and the Liffey; the Irish name, *Baile Átha Cliath*, means the city by the hurdle ford. The first permanent settlement beside the Liffey was established at Wood Quay in the 9C by the Vikings, who then spread north of the river where their settlement was known as Oxmantown; at the Battle of Clontarf on the north shore of Dublin Bay in 1014 their power was curbed by Brian Ború.

Anglo-Norman Stronghold – After the Anglo-Norman invasion late in the 12C Dublin was granted to the port of Bristol as a trading post by Henry II in 1172. Under constant harassment by the Irish tribes and an unsuccessful attack in 1316 by Edward Bruce of Scotland, the extent of the Anglo-Normans' influence waxed and waned but they never lost control of Dublin, which gradually became the seat of Parliament and the centre of government. Early Lord Deputies operated from their own power bases in the Pale – Trim, Maynooth and Kilkenny – but in the 16C Sir Henry Sidney, who was four times Lord Deputy, took up residence in the castle and put it in good repair. Gradually the medieval fortress evolved into an administrative centre and viceregal court.

Kildare Revolt – The most serious incident occurred in 1534 when Thomas Fitzgerald, known as "Silken Thomas" because of the silk embroidery on his men's apparel, was acting as Vice Deputy during his father's absence in London. On hearing a false report that his father had been beheaded, he renounced his allegiance to Henry VIII in St Mary's Abbey and launched a rebellion which became known as the Kildare or Geraldine Revolt. He laid siege to the Castle into which the Constable

SLIDE FILE, Dublin

Grand Canal

and his retinue had barricaded themselves, but the citizenry turned against Thomas; the besieged proclaimed the arrival of the king's army and made a sortie, whereupon the besiegers took fright and scattered. Fitzgerald himself escaped but he was forced to surrender some months later and was executed in London together with his five uncles.

Georgian Dublin – In the relative peace of the 18C, restrictions eased and trade flourished. Buildings were constructed to house public bodies; terraces of fine houses were erected first north and then south of the river; men of property, drawn to the capital on parliamentary and other business, commissioned fine mansions.

Under the activities of the Wide Streets Commissioners, established in 1758, Dublin developed into an elegant city, embraced by the Royal and Grand Canals and bisected by the Liffey, now embanked between quays and spanned by several bridges. With the Act of Union (1800) political affairs removed to London and, although known as the "second city of the Empire", Dublin stagnated. Despite many grievous losses, Dublin can still claim to be the finest Georgian city in the British Isles.

Capital of the Republic – There was much destruction during the Easter Rising and the Civil War but key buildings like the Four Courts, the GPO and the Custom House were eventually restored to something like their former glory. The refurbishment projects carried out in the last decades of the 20C meant that Dublin well deserved the title European City of Culture in 1991. Temple Bar has been transformed from a dilapidated district into a network of pedestrian streets, vibrant with pubs, cafés, restaurants, hotels, nightspots, crafts and clothes shops. The district of Smithfield, west of O'Connell Street, has recently been regenerated under the Harp Project.

Walking Tours

The three walks covering the city centre start and finish at O'Connell Bridge or Ha'penny Bridge.

South Bank

This is the city's youngest quarter, vulnerable as it was to Irish raiding parties swooping down from the Wicklow Mountains. Until the construction of the Old Parliament in 1728 there was little building east of the old town except for Trinity College.

The district began to develop into a fashionable suburb in the 1750s when the Duke of Leinster erected the first nobleman's house south of the river; his prediction that fashionable society would follow soon proved true. Some of the most elegant Georgian terraces

B Perousse/MICHELIN

Trinity College

are to be found east and south of his mansion. In 1815 the Leinster property was bought by the Royal Dublin Society, and the National Museum, the National Library and the National Gallery were built in the grounds. After 1922 the mansion was converted to serve as the Parliament of the newly established Free State.

▶ *From O'Connell Bridge walk south along Westmoreland Street passing (right) the Bank of Ireland.*

College Green

This triangular open space, formerly known as Hoggen Green, was an old Viking burial ground *(haugen)* and meeting place *(thengmote)*. At the centre stands a statue of **Henry Grattan** by John Foley (1879) and a modern iron sculpture designed by Edward Delaney in memory of **Thomas Davis** (1814–45), poet, leader of the Young Ireland movement and founder of *The Nation*.

Trinity College★★

Trinity College, Dublin, sometimes known as TCD, was founded in 1592 by Elizabeth I on the site of All Hallows, an Augustinian monastery suppressed at the Dissolution.

It developed according to the tradition of the Oxford and Cambridge colleges and long remained an Anglican preserve. Roman Catholics were excluded until 1873, while the Roman Catholic Church for its part strongly disapproved of the faithful studying here well into the 1960s. Women were first admitted in 1903. The College stands in its own grounds, **College Park**: an open space set aside for sport – cricket, rugby, running and hurling – although this has been encroached upon by the science and medical faculties. The film *Educating Rita*, starring Michael Caine and Julie Walters, was filmed here.

Beside the entrance gates stands an elegant Georgian house built for the Provost in 1758. Statues by Foley of

Dublin Waterways

The urban landscape of Dublin is greatly enhanced by the five waterways which traverse the city – **River Liffey**, personified as Anna Livia Pluribella, which flows through the city centre before entering the sea in Dublin Bay; two tributaries, the **River Dodder** on the south bank and the **River Tolka** on the north bank; and two canals, the **Grand Canal** (1757–1803), which passes through the southern suburbs to join the Shannon at Shannon Harbour, north of Birr, and the **Royal Canal** (1790–1817), which passes through the Northside to join the Shannon west of Longford.

Address Book

GETTING ABOUT

Dublin International Airport – ☎01 814 1111. www.dublinairport.com. **AirLink** is a bus service operated by Dublin Bus (🚌 see below) between Dublin Airport and central Dublin; pick-up points – O'Connell Street, Central Bus Station (Store Street); Connolly Railway Station; Heuston Rail Station. An alternative service is provided by Aircoach which runs to Grafton Street. www.aircoach.ie.

Dublin city is served by a bus network and a railway line along the coast. The **DART** (Dublin Area Rapid Transport) is a **rail service** along the coast (25mi/40km) from Howth in the north to Greystones in the south. It serves three stations in central Dublin – Connolly, Tara Street and Pearse. The service operates daily between around 6.30am (9am Sunday) and 11.45pm with trains running every 5–10min during peak times and every 15min off-peak. All-day tickets available at any station – rail only within the short hop zone €7.20; rail and bus €8.80. *Further details from 35 Lower Abbey Street;* ☎*01 836 6222 (Passenger information).* www.dublin.ie/transport/dart.htm

The **Dublin LUAS System** is a **light rail transit** system with several routes radiating from the city centre – Abbey Street southwest via Drimnagh to Tallaght; St Stephen's Green south via Ranelagh and Dundrum to Sandyford. Trams run Mon–Sat 5.30am (6.30am Sat)–12.30am; Sun 7am–11.30pm, every 5 to 10min (every 15min, 10.30pm onward). Ticket prices from €1.50 (single), €2.70 (return). ☎1800 300 604. www.luas.ie.

Dublin Bus (CIE) operates the **bus network** which covers the whole city from the Central Bus Station (Busáras) in Store Street (behind the Custom House); any bus bearing the direction *An Lár* is going to the city centre. The price of a single ticket varies according to the number of stages from €1 to €2 (over €4 for outer suburbs). All-day tickets: bus only, €6; bus and rail, €8.80; bus and LUAS, €6.50. All-day tours are available north along the coast to Howth and Malahide; south along the coast to Bray and Greystones returning inland via Enniskerry. *Further details from Dublin Bus, 59 Upper O'Connell Street, Dublin 1,* ☎*01 873 4222.* www.dublinbus.ie.

Nitelink buses run from the City Centre to the suburbs, every Fri–Sat on the half hour 12.30am–4am.

In the city centre there are **paying car parks**, **parking meters**, **pay and display machines** and **disc parking areas**; an electronic panel, advertising parking spaces, is visible from the west side of St Stephen's Green.

There is **no parking** on double yellow lines at any time; no parking on **single yellow lines** during the hours indicated on the time plate; no parking in **clearways and bus lanes** during the hours indicated on the time plate.

Parking bays for the **disabled** may be used only if a disabled parking permit is displayed. Cars parked illegally may be **clamped**; declamping costs at least €80.

A system of numbered car parks linked to numbered road junctions on the outskirts of Dublin makes it much easier to find the right route into the city centre. The major **toll roads** are the Dublin East-Link (€1.50) which spans the Liffey estuary, and the Dublin West-Link (€2), which runs north south on the western edge of the city. The M1 Drogheda bypass (€1.60) and M4 motorway, just west of Lucan to west of Kinnegad also collect a toll (€2.75, at Enfield).

SIGHTSEEING

The **Dublin Pass** can be purchased on the Web (at a discount) or at any of the five Dublin tourist information offices. Pass includes free admission to 30 visitor attractions, 26 special offers and an airport transfer with AirCoach from the airport into the city. Passes start at €31 and may be purchased for 1, 2, 3, or 6 days. ☎01 605 7756. www.dublinpass.ie. Several companies organise **circular bus tours** of the city centre including a comprehensive open-top bus tour (2hr 45min) of all the famous sights and a running commentary given by an approved guide; **hop-on-hop-off bus**

tours giving unlimited travel throughout the day.

Dublin Bus City Tour – *Operates daily, 9.30am –5pm, every 10 –15min; 5pm–6.30pm, every 30min. Hop-on-hop-off circular tour (20 stops; minimum 1hr 15min) starting from 59 Upper O'Connell Street. €14. ☎01 703 3028. www.dublinbus.ie.*

City-Sightseeing Dublin – *Hop-on-hop-off circular bus tours operate every 6–15min. €16. ☎01 708 866 000. www.guidefriday.com*

Viking Splash Tours – Sightseeing tour of Dublin by land and water in an amphibious military vehicle starting from Bull Alley Street beside St Patrick's Cathedral and entering the water at the Grand Canal Basin in Ringsend. *Operate early Feb–Nov daily 10am–5pm every 30 mins. €20. ☎01 707 6000. www.vikingsplash.ie.*

More active sightseers may consider a **bicycle tour** (bicycles provided) of Dublin, accompanied by a guide, who will point out the cultural and historical sights and avoid the busier roads.

Full-day and half-day tours to attractions in the Dublin area are organised by various bus companies including **Gray Line Tours Ireland** – *Excursions to the Wicklow Mountains, valleys and lakes (including Glendalough); Dublin Bay and Malahide Castle. €24–38. ☎01 458 0054. www.grayline.com.*

For **steam train excursions** visit *www.rpsi-online.org.*

To see the famous Dublin landmarks while learning about key events in Irish history, join a specialised **walking tour**. **Heritage trails**, walking tours with historical themes, are organised by Dublin Tourism. *www.visitdublin.com.* There are aslo several excellent privately run themed tours:

Historical Walking Tours of Dublin – *Operates May–Sept, daily 11am, 3pm; Apr and Oct, daily 11am; Nov–Mar, Fri–Sun 11am. €12. ☎87 688 9412. www.historicalinsights.ie.*

1916 Rebellion Walking Tour – *Operates Mar–Oct, Mon–Sat 11.30pm; Sun, 1pm. €12. ☎86 858 3847. www.1916rising.com*

Dublin Literary Pub Crawl – Conducted by two actors who introduce the city's most famous writers and act out scenes from their works this very amusing tour is highly recommended. *Operates Apr–Nov daily, Dec–Mar Thu–Sun 7.30pm and Sun noon. €12. ☎01 670 5602. www.dublinpubcrawl.com.*

Traditional Irish Musical Pub Crawl Pub tour led by two professional musicians who perform tunes and songs while telling the story of Irish music. Highly recommended. *€12. Operates nightly 7.30pm (Nov–Apr Thu–Sat only). ☎01 475 3313. www.visitdublin.com.*

For coin ranges, see the Legend on the cover flap

WHERE TO STAY

Pembroke Townhouse – *90 Pembroke Road. ☎01 660 0277. www.pembroketownhouse.ie. Closed 21 Dec–2 Jan. 48rm.* A quiet location in a smart suburb avoids the bustle of the city centre. Thoughtfully furnished and faithful to its Georgian origins yet with all mod cons.

Trinity Lodge – *12 South Frederick Street. ☎01 679 5044. www.trinity-lodge.com. Closed 22–27 Dec. 16rm.* This modernised Georgian townhouse with clean, comfortable and well-furnished bedroom is in one of the quieter streets in the city centre.

Brownes Townhouse – *22 St Stephen's Green. ☎01 638 3939. www.brownesdublin.com. Closed 25–27 Dec. 12rm. Restaurant .* It would be hard to beat the location of this sympathetically recently restored Georgian house which overlooks St Stephen's Green in the heart of the city. The original staircase and numerous four-poster beds add to the period atmosphere.

The Clarence – *6–8 Wellington Quay. – ☎01 407 0800; www.theclarence.ie. 43rm, 5 suites. Restaurant .* Its stylish interior, merging the contemporary with the traditional, has made The Clarence, owned by Bono and The Edge of rock group U2, highly popular with the cognoscenti. Staff are alert to guests' every needs.

Harrington Hall – *70 Harcourt Street. ☎01 475 3497. www.harringtonhall.com. 28rm.* Standing in an elegant terrace of classic Georgian properties, Harrington Hall offers sophisticated levels of comfort and service. All the bedrooms are of a generous size, especially the three junior suites which have ornate ceilings and huge windows.

The Mercer – *Lower Mercer Street. ☎01 478 2179. www.mercerhotel. ie. Closed 23–29 Dec. 41rm. Restaurant*. Keen shoppers will like this location, next to Grafton Street in the middle of the city. The hotel offers pleasantly furnished and air-conditioned bedrooms, decorated with a certain amount of individuality.

The Merrion – *Upper Merrion Street. ☎01 603 0600. www.merrion hotel.com. 122rm. 20 suites. Restaurant*. If you are looking for sumptuous surroundings and pampered service you will be more than satisfied at this elegant hotel, consisting of a row of carefully restored, ornately decorated Georgian townhouses arranged around a private garden.

WHERE TO EAT

The Bad Ass Café – *Crown Alley. ☎01 671 2596. www.badasscafe.com.* It's loud and it's brash but it ain't half bad, and it offers an undemanding menu of assorted grilled dishes and pizza that pleases its many regulars.

Bleu – *Joshua House, Dawson Street. ☎01 676 701. www.bleu.ie.* This bistro moderne epitomises the new sleek cosmopolitan Dublin and offers Modern European cooking.

Bang Café – *11 Merrion Row. ☎01 676 089. www.bangrestaurant. com. Closed 1 week Christmas, Sun and Bank Holiday Mon – Booking essential.* Captures the zeitgeist, with a suitably un-stuffy atmosphere that matches the bustle of the surrounding streets. Service is chatty and the open plan kitchen produces a mix of the classical and the more creative.

Bistro One – *3 Brighton Road. ☎01 289 7711. bistroone@eircom.ie. Closed 25–27 and 31 Dec, 1 Jan, Sun and Mon. Booking essential.* Gingham tablecloths and a blackboard menu contribute to the relaxed, informal feel. Somewhat hidden in a residential area to the south of the city. Modern cooking with the occasional added Asian influence.

Brownes Brasserie – *22 St Stephen's Green (at Brownes Townhouse). ☎01 638 3939. www. brownesdublin.com. Closed 24 Dec– 4 Jan and Sat lunch. Booking essential.* Distinctive continental atmosphere and 'belle époque' feel. The strength of the European-influenced menu lies in its seafood.

Bruno's – *30 East Sussex Street. ☎01 670 6767. www.brunos.ie. Closed 25 Dec–2 Jan, Sat lunch and Sun. Booking essential.* Its Temple Bar location, wood flooring, mirrors and moody lighting make this another example of the city's new wave of contemporary, informal dining establishments. The menu features some original touches and the wine list is reasonably priced.

Cafe Mao – *2–3 Chatham Row. ☎01 670 4899. www.cafemao.com.* If you're looking for a culinary change of pace you should head for this drop-dead trendy South East Asian restaurant The original in this highly popular small chain is spread over two floors in a clean, minimalist style with vivid, ersatz Warhol prints. Helpful and attentive service assured.

The Cellar Restaurant – *Upper Merrion St (at The Merrion Hotel) – ☎01 603 0631. www.merrionhotel.com.* It's best to book for the very popular lunch at this restored Georgian cellar with its vaulted ceiling and exposed brick walls, and a menu that features classic Irish dishes. There is a popular bar attached. **Chapter One** – *18–19 basement of The Dublin Writers Museum, Parnell Square. ☎01 873 2266. www.chapteronerestaurant.com. Closed 24 Dec–9 Jan, Sun, Mon, Sat lunch and Bank Hols.* Cavernous room beneath the Dublin Writers's Museum. Contemporary art hangs on the thick granite walls. The cooking is innovative and the service careful. Splendid choice of wines.

Dobbin's – *15 Stephen's Lane, off Lower Mount Street. ☎01 676 4679. www. dobbins.ie. Closed 1 week Christmas– New Year, Sun, Mon dinner, Sat lunch and Bank Hols. Booking essential.* Set in the middle of the financial district and recently refurbished Dobbins' lively and convivial atmosphere bears testament to its reputation as one of the city's institutions.

La Cave – *28 South Anne Street.*
☎01 679 4409. www.lacavewinebar.com.
Just off Grafton Street is Dublin's oldest
French wine bar serving light French
food or full classic Irish meals.

La Stampa – *35 Dawson Street
(at La Stampa Hotel). ☎01 677 8611.
www.lastampa.ie. Booking essential.*
Look no further if you're after a true
flavour of Dublin's buzzing restaurant
scene. The atmosphere reverberates
around this converted 19C ballroom
with its large mirrors, original artwork
and ornate mosaic ceiling. Appropriately modern cuisine.

Nancy Hands Pub & Restaurant
– *30–32 Parkgate Street. ☎01 677 0149,
www.nancyhands.ie.* Famed for its
vast collection of Irish whiskeys and its
mildly schizophrenic décor which lends
it a certain Victorian charm, including
a collection of Guinness antiques and
advertising. Superior pub fare and
generously portioned.

Roly's Bistro – *7 Ballsbridge
Terrace. ☎01 668 2611. www.rolysbistro.
ie Closed 25–27 Dec. Booking essential.*
A veritable institution and one of the
city's most celebrated restaurants.
The tables are set close together so you
virtually rub shoulders with your neighbour but that's all part of its charm.
Modern menu; particularly
good value lunch.

Jacob's Ladder – *4–5 Nassau
Street. ☎01 670 3865. www.jacobsladder.
ie. Closed 17 March, Good Fri, first week of
August, 25 Dec–Jan 7. Booking essential.*
A particularly good value lunch is
offered at this first-floor restaurant
overlooking Trinity College park. The
chef owner provides modern Irish cooking in appropriately modern surroundings, complemented by a well-chosen
wine list.

Mermaid Café – *69–70 Dame
Street. ☎01 670 8236. www.mermaid.ie.
Closed Good Fri , 24–26 and 31 Dec, 1 Jan.
Booking essential.* Draws in the young,
well-heeled and fashionable with its
effervescent atmosphere. The food
here has an eclectic Mid-Atlantic hue,
drawing influences from all over the
world and also offers daily-changing
blackboard specials.

The Tea Room – *6–8 Wellington
Quay (at The Clarence Hotel). ☎01 670*
*7766. www.theclarence.ie. Closed lunch
Sat. Booking essential.* Double height
windows ensure that this fashionable
restaurant is flooded with light during
the day. Cool, pastel shades add to the
understated, airy feel and the menu
offers modern Irish cooking using top
quality ingredients.

Patrick Guilbaud –
*21 Upper Merrion Street. ☎01 676 4192.
www.restaurantpatrickguilbaud.ie.
Closed Good Fri, first week Jan, 25 Dec,
Sun and Mon.* The city's most renowned
restaurant occupies a Georgian townhouse adjacent to the Merrion hotel.
The superlative cooking – modern Irish
cooking using fresh Irish produce in
season – combined with cosmopolitan
surroundings and courteous service all
help to make this one of the ultimate
dining experiences.

TAKING A BREAK

Abbey Tavern – *Howth. ☎01 832 20 06;
www.abbeytavern.ie. Open daily from
10.30am.* This charming 1879 pub north
of the city exudes a genuine sense of
authenticity and a very convivial atmosphere. Known for its long-established
traditional Irish concerts every evening
in the adjacent barn, from 8.30pm,
with the 'Abbey Tavern Singers and
Musicians'.

Brazen Head – *20 Lower Bridge Street.
☎01 679 5186. www.brazenhead.com
Open Mon–Sat from 10.30am, Sun
noon–midnight.* Claims to be the oldest
pub in the city, being on the site of a
12C tavern. Although popular with tourists this doesn't seem to detract from
the atmosphere. Worth getting there
early to get a seat for the nightly music.
Has a pleasant terrace.

Butlers Chocolate Café – *24 Wicklow
Street. ☎01 671 0599; www.butlerschoco
lates.com. Open daily 8am–7pm.* One
of a chain of several Butlers Chocolate
Cafés throughout the city , this is not
only the best place for sipping a cup
of hot chocolate but also a very good
place to buy chocolates for presents/
souvenirs. For the taste of Ireland try
the Jameson Truffle, filled with Irish
Whiskey. They also do a wide range of
teas and coffees.

Bewley's Cafe – *Grafton St ☎635 5470;
www.bewleyscafe.com. Daily 7.30am*

(coffee only until 8am) to 11.30am. An Irish instiution which every Dublin visitor should sample at least once, Bewley's *is* the essence of Irish café society. Come here for a coffee and cake or their famous full breakfast, or pizzas, pastas and salads in the Bar Deli section. Particularly worth seeing is the recently refurbished Harry Clarke room renowned for its stained glass windows, and do try to get tickets for the Café Theatre. This is Dublin's foremost stage for lunchtime drama *(Mon–Sat 1.10pm)* and one of the city's best venues for evening cabaret, jazz and comedy.

Café-en-Seine – *40 Dawson Street. ☎01 677 4567. www.capitalbars.com. Mon–Sat 9am–2.30pm (12.30pm Mon).* With its fin-de-siecle Parisian decor, this café represents the new wave of establishments which combine the café, bar and brasserie. Despite being open for several years now it's still a magnet for the young and hip with its fashionably long bar.

Davy Byrne's – *21 Duke Street. ☎01 677 5217. www.davybyrnes.com. Open daily 10.30am (11.30am Sun)–11pm (1am Thu–Fri).* This is the most famous of Dublin's many literary pubs and is closely associated with James Joyce. Despite the changes made over the years, Davy Byrne's is still a very pleasant bar with a few remaining Art Deco touches and 1940s murals. It is also renowned for its food, particularly fresh salmon, smoked salmon, crab and oysters.

Doheny & Nesbitt – *5 Lower Baggot St reet. ☎01 676 2945. Open daily from 10.30am.* A classic pub, recently renovated but still full of character and popular with government workers from the neighbourhood, especially civil servants from the Ministry of Finance. Hence the reason why Dubliners like to refer to the pub as the Doheny & Nesbitt School of Economics.

Johnnie Fox Pub – *Glencullen. ☎01 295 5647; www.jfp.ie. Open Mon–Sat 10.30am–1.30am. Sun, noon–11.30pm.* It may look as if it were built for a film set but Johnnie Fox's has been in business since 1798. Situated in Glencullen on top of the Dublin mountains, this is not only one of Ireland's oldest and most famous pubs, it is also the highest pub in the country. Traditional

music here every evening; worth the half-hour drive from the city centre.

Knightsbridge Bar/Arlington Hotel – *23–25 Bachelor Walk, O'Connell Bridge. ☎01 804 9100. www.arlington.ie. Open daily from 11am.* In the evenings this vast bar in the heart of the city really comes alive. There's entertainment every night of the week, be it song or dance, and it's all free. Although it's blatantly touristy, it's still an enjoyable-experience.

Messrs Maguire – *1–2 Burgh Quay. Open daily from 10.30am. www.messrs-maguire.ie.* This 19C building facing the Liffey is a good example of the fusion of the old and the new worlds, combined as all things to all drinkers. It has cosy little nooks and crannies, a library bar, micro-brewery, cafe and brasserie/restaurant serving a fusion of Irish, continental and world cuisine. From Wednesday to Sunday a DJ pounds out the music from 9pm and drinkers take to its dance floor.

Mulligan's – *8 Poolbeg Street. ☎01 677 5582. www.mulligans.ie. Mon–Sat 10.30am–11.30pm (12.30am Fri–Sat); Sun, 12.30pm–11pm.* This celebrated old pub is the genuine article. James Joyce and John F Kennedy are just two of the famous luminaries who have enjoyed a pint here. The Victorian interior with its mahogany and screens is ideal for those looking for more intimacy and is regularly frequented by journalists and those who take their drinking seriously.

Oliver St John Gogarty – *58–9 Temple Bar. ☎01 671 1822. www.gogartys.ie. Open daily from 10.30am.* Located in the heart of Temple Bar, this is always a very popular bar with visitors to the city. There's a first floor restaurant, live music every night until 2am and it acts as the starting point for the 'Musical Pub Crawl'.

O'Donoghue's – *14 Merrion Row. ☎01 660 7194. www.odonoghues.ie. Open daily from 10.30am.* Although it is a bit touristy, this pub has excellent traditional Irish music nightly and all day Sunday. The famous group the Dubliners came roaring on the music scene here in 1962. Often very crowded, especially weekends.

Temple Bar – *48 Temple Bar. ☎01 671 2324. www.thetemplebarpub.com.*

Open daily from 10.30am. The most photographed pub in Dublin (if not Ireland!) this is nonetheless a very agreeable and popular choice for a good night out. The musical programme is varied, the acoustics are good and on a summer's day it all moves into the garden. There's a shop attached selling all manner of Temple Bar merchandise.

The Auld Dubliner – *Fleet Street.* ☎*01 677 0527. Open daily from 10.30am.* Despite its name, this is a relatively recent arrival on the Temple Bar pub scene, and has a good reputation for its daily traditional music sessions.

The Long Hall – *51 South Great George Street.* ☎*01 475 1590. Open Sun–Wed 4pm–11.30pm, Thu–Sat 1pm–12.30am.* This wonderful Victorian bar has remained largely unchanged since 1880 and is noted for its extraordinarily long counter. It's a welcoming and sociable place, attracting visitors from all parts of the globe.

The Porter House – *16 Parliament Street.* ☎*01 679 884. www.porterhouse brewco.com. Open daily from 11.30am (noon Sat, 12.30pm Sun).* The city's first micro-brewery has rapidly become a fashionable hangout. It offers a large range of modern beers and thus makes an ideal stop for those wanting a break from the 'black stuff'. Traditional music at weekends, modern during the week.

ENTERTAINMENT

Abbey Theatre – *26 Lower Abbey Street.* ☎*01 878 7222. www.abbeytheatre.ie. Despite the unprepossessing exterior* the Abbey is a proud symbol of Irish culture. Works by Ireland's best-known authors are performed here regularly (Shaw, Synge, Yeats, O'Casey) as are pieces by less famous dramatists.
The Peacock Theatre, in the same building, specialises in contemporary and experimental work.

Gaiety Theatre – ☎*01 677 1717. www. gaietytheatre.ie. Mon–Sat 10am–8pm.* Opera and musicals are the main fare here, but the Gaiety Theatre Late Night Club also boasts four bars with DJs and top quality live bands at the weekend.

Gate Theatre – *1 Cavendish Row.* ☎*01 874 4045. www.gate-theatre.ie.* A proud Dublin institution, founded in the 1920s, this theatre includes Irish and non-Irish works in its repertoire.

Irish Film Institute – *6 Eustace Street, Temple Bar.* ☎*01 677 8788. www. irishfilm.ie.* Film buffs are catered for all year round here. The programme ensures that Irish films as well as the well-known classics are always being shown.

Jurys Irish Cabaret – *Jury's Ballsbridge Hotel.* ☎*01 614 2649 (tickets).www. jurysdoyle.com/cabaret. Open early May–early Oct, Wed–Sun.* It began in 1960 and today they put on 2000 shows a year. These 2hr 30min spectaculars incorporate music, singing and dancing in both modern and traditional styles. You can just have a drink with the show (*€45.50, inc two drinks*) or a 4-course meal (*€59, inc show*).

National Concert Hall – *Earlsfort Terrace.* ☎*01 417 0000. www.nch.ie.* Dublin's premier performing arts venue hosts everything from the Irish Youth Orchestra to Japanese drummers and informal ceilidhs.

Olympia Theatre – *72 Dame Street.* ☎*01 679 3323. www.mcd.ie/olympia. Mon–Sat from 10.30am.* An eclectic mix of shows from Derren Brown to Bob the Builder plus big names in pop (often from yesteryear) and a good slice of comedy.

The Burlington Cabaret – *The Burlington Hotel, Upper Leeson Street.* ☎*01 64 3186, www.jurysdoyle.com/cabaret. Open May–Sep, Mon, Wed–Sat.* Top class comedy, music, song and dance even though it is squarely aimed at large tourist groups. You can just have a drink with the show (*€45.50, inc two drinks*) or a 4-course meal (*€59 inc show*).

NIGHTLIFE

Rí-Rá – *11 Dame Court.* ☎*01 671 1220; www.rira.ie. Open Mon–Sat 11.30pm– 2.30am.* Spread over two floors, this night-club is loud, funky and popular with the 'in crowd' despite, or because of, being slightly more expensive than others in the city. Next door The Globe Bar and Cafe is a good place to warm up and meet up.

Zanzibar – *Lower Ormond Quay.* ☎*01 878 7212. Open daily 4pm–3am.* A classic example of the Dublin theme pub with its eccentric Arabic decoration as imagined by Walt Disney. Geared unashamedly to groups out for the night and frequented mostly by 20-

somethings. Queues begin to form later in the evening when it turns into a night-club.

SHOPPING

The **central shopping** area extends from Grafton Street *(south bank)* to O'Connell Street *(north bank)*. Nassau Street *(parallel with the south side of Trinity College)* contains several good shops selling a range of **Irish goods** from high fashion to modest souvenirs – clothing, craftwork, pottery, Irish music and instruments, family crests. Bookshops congregate at the north end of Dawson Street. The renovated **Smithfield Village** is worth a look for crafts and jewellery. The **Temple Bar** area offers an eclectic mix of individual little shops and outdoor stalls. For **antiques** go to Francis Street.

Street market-goers should visit :
Moore Street market *(Mon–Sat)*, where barrow boys sell fresh fruit and vegetables; **Dublin Corporation Fruit and Vegetable Market** under a cast-iron roof *(Mary's Lane; Sat am)*; **Temple Bar Market** *(Meeting House Square; Sat am)* selling local food produce (cheeses, sauces, bread, chocolates, vegetable drinks, pizzas, pies and sausages).

Avoca Mills, *Suffolk Street* – ☎01 677 4215. www.avoca.ie. A 7-level mini-department store filled with quirky gifts and fashionable design items.

Blarney Woollen Mills – *21–23 Nassau Street* ☎01 671 0068. www.blarneywoollenmills.com. Mon–Sat from 9am. There's a huge choice of knitted items and classic Aran sweaters as well as knitwear with more imaginative patterns and designs. They also offer for sale a large choice of crystal, from Waterford, Galway and Tipperary.

Brown Thomas – *88–95 Grafton Street* ☎01 605 6666. www.brownthomas.com. Dublin's smartest department store deals in designer brands from fashions and accessories to cosmetics and homewares.

Celtic Note – *14 Nassau Street.* ☎01 670 4157. www.celticnote.com. No trip to Ireland is complete without hearing some traditional Celtic music and this is the number one shop if you want to take home a musical reminder. There's a vast selection of recorded music, as well as traditional instruments.

Claddagh Records – *Dame House, Dame Street.* ☎01 677 8943. www.claddaghrecords.com. Specialist in folk, traditional and ethnic music.

Dublin Woollen Mills – *41 Lr Ormond Quay.* ☎01 677 5014. www.woollenmills.com; call for opening times. This family firm can lay claim to having once employed James Joyce as an agent during his sojourn in Trieste. A wide selection of authentic knitwear is available, as well as accessories such as scarves, caps and ties.

House of Ireland – *Nassau Street.* ☎01 671 1111. www.houseofireland.com. If it's made in Ireland then it is probably available in this well known shop. Although perhaps a little expensive the range is vast; from woollens to crystal, porcelain to jewellery.

Kevin & Howlin – *31 Nassau Street.* ☎01 677 0257. www.kevinandhowlin.com. The definitive temple of Donegal tweed in all its forms. The range available at this family firm includes jackets, suits, waistcoats and ties. Alternatively, fabric can be bought by the metre and fashioned into garments by your own tailor.

Kilkenny Shop – *6 Nassau Street.* ☎01 677 7066. www.kilkennyshop.com. Tweeds, Aran sweaters, lace and Celtic jewellery are just some of the products for sale iat what is claimed to be the largest emporium of traditional Irish products. Wilting shoppers can refuel in the cafe or award-winning restaurant.

Mitchell & Son – *21 Kildare Street.* ☎01 676 0766. www.mitchellandson.com. This wine merchants was founded in 1805 and the sixth generation of the family is now at the helm. Celebrated for its famous 'Green Spot' whiskey, aged in sherry casks, they also offer a vast range of wines, rare malts, spirits and cigars.

Market Arcades – *South Great George Street.* This covered passage is home to over twenty shops, some offering second-hand clothing. There are some real bargains to be found, especially in tweed jackets.

Mother Redcap's Market – *Back Lane, Fri–Sun 10am–5.30pm.* This emporium has a little bit of everything: old records and second-hand clothes, Aran Island

sweaters, lucky charms, dishes, knick-knacks, incense and patchouli.
National Museum Shop – *Kildare Street and Benburb Street*. Top quality reproductions of items based on exhibits in the country's national museums.
The **Powerscourt Centre** – *South William Street*. ☎*01 671 7000. www.powerscourtcentre.com*. An 18C town house converted into an attractive shopping centre with 43 individual shops.
Rory's (Fishing Tackle) – *17A Fleet Street*. ☎*01 677 2351, www.rorys.ie.* A Dublin institution and a must for fishermen. All the equipment you could ever need is here, including a huge range of flies made at the shop. They are more than willing to help with advice on what to buy and where to fish.

SPORTS AND LEISURE

Croke Park – *Drumcondra*. ☎*01 819 2300. www.crokepark.ie*. The stadium where the national finals of home of Gaelic games – hurling and football – are held. It will also be home to international football and rugby matches until Lansdowne Road is completed around 2010. Stadium tours and home to the GAA Museum.

Horse Racing is held at **Leopardstown** (south) and **Fairy House** (north). **Punchestown**, the home of Irish National Hunt racing, is 26 mi/42km away.
Greyhound Racing takes place at Shelbourne Park and Harold's Cross.

EVENTS AND FESTIVALS

Bloomsday (16 June) – Annual celebration) of James Joyce's great novel *Ulysses* – including readings, re-enactments, music, theatre, street theatre.
St Patrick's Festival (mid March) – This five-day extravaganza of music, street theatre, carnival, dance, pageantry, comedy and more, is one of the world's biggest street parties, climaxing on St Patrick's Day ('Paddy's Day'), 17 March.
Temple Bar Trad Festival of Irish Music & Culture (late Jan) – Dublin's premier celebration of traditional Irish music and culture.
Six Nations Rugby Internationals (Feb–Mar) – Any rugby international featuring Ireland playing at home in Dublin turns the city into a raucous but good-natured place to be.
Heineken Green Energy Festival (1 Apr–31 May) – rock music festival.

Oliver Goldsmith and Edmund Burke flank the main gate.
The buildings in **Front Court** date from the mid 18C; the wings terminate in the **Theatre** (*south*) and the **Chapel** (*north*), both designed by Sir William Chambers with stuccowork by Michael Stapleton. The chapel is mainly lit by high semi-circular windows. The theatre (1777–91) is used for degree ceremonies, Senate meetings, musical and theatrical events; it is hung with portraits of Elizabeth I, Edmund Burke, George Berkeley, Jonathan Swift.
Library Court is dominated by the **Campanile** (1853) designed by Charles Lanyon. Among the trees in the centre is *Reclining Connected Forms* (1969), a sculpture by Henry Moore. The area behind the north range is called **Botany Bay**, after the Australian penal colony (possibly because of unruly student

antics). The red-brick range on the east side, known as Rubrics, is the oldest building in the college: the south side is closed by the Old Library and Treasury. The **Museum** (1850) (*south side of New Square*) was designed by Sir Thomas Deane and Benjamin Woodward in the Venetian style promoted by Ruskin; the delightful stone carving of flowers, leaves and animals is by the O'Shea brothers from Cork.

▷ *Turn left into Nassau St.*

On the corner with Kildare Street stands the former home of the **Kildare Street Club**, the oldest and most staunchly Unionist of Dublin's gentleman's clubs.

▷ *Continue along Nassau St and Clare St to Merrion Sq.*

Merrion Square★

The jewel of Georgian Dublin was laid out in 1762 by John Ensor for the 6th Viscount Fitzwilliam under the policy of the Wide Streets Commissioners. Delicate fanlights surmount the elegant doorways of the perfectly proportioned red-brick houses; commemorative plaques mark the homes of famous people – Oscar Wilde's father, Sir William Wilde, at no 1, William Butler Yeats at no 82. The west side is graced by the gardens of Leinster House, flanked by the Natural History Museum and the National Gallery. The southeast vista is closed by **St Stephen's Church**, designed in 1821 by John Bowden and completed by Joseph Welland: its domed tower, known as the "Pepper Canister", was inspired by three Athenian buildings – the Erechtheum, the Tower of the Winds and the Monument of Lysicrates. ☎01 2880663 (vicarage)

▸ *Walk south up Merrion St past the Natural History Museum and Government Buildings (see Inner Dublin).*

Among the many handsome Georgian houses are the town house of the Wellesley family, where the Duke of Wellington spent some of his childhood, and the Merrion Street Hotel, with its splendidly restored interior.

▸ *Turn right into the north side of St Stephen's Green.*

The **Shelbourne Hotel** (1867), still a centre of Dublin's social life, was built by Martin Burke on the site of Kerry House, residence of the Earl of Shelburne, in 1824.

▸ *Turn right into Kildare St.*

Half way down, set back from the street, is the front of **Leinster House** – now seat of the *Dáil*, the Irish Parliament (see Inner Dublin) – flanked by the **National Museum** (right) and the **National Library** (left).

▸ *Turn left into Molesworth St and left into Dawson St.*

St Ann's Church

🕒*Open 10am–4pm.* ☎*01 676 7727. www.stannschurch.ie.*
St Ann's was one of the earliest Georgian churches in Dublin, an elegant and fashionable place of worship designed by Isaac Wills and not really improved by the addition of a Victorian neo-Romanesque west front and stained glass. The bread shelf in the chancel was established in 1723 by a charitable bequest to provide 120 loaves of bread each week for the poor. The church is highly regarded for the quality of its regular concerts.

Mansion House

Mansion House was built in 1705 by Joshua Dawson and bought by the City of Dublin in 1715 as the residence of the Lord Mayor. The spacious Round Room was added for the visit of George IV in 1821; it was here that the first Irish parliament met in 1919 to adopt the Declaration of Independence.

▸ *At the top of Dawson St cross the road into the gardens of St Stephen's Green.*

St Stephen's Green

(Dúchas) 🕒*Open daily 7.30am (9.30am Sun and Bank Hols)– dusk.* ☎*01 475 7816 www.heritageireland.ie/en.*
Formerly common land first enclosed in 1663, the beautifully landscaped and well-maintained **gardens** (22 acres/9ha) are a wonderful asset in this densely built-up part of the city. They were laid out in 1880 by Lord Ardilaun, a mem-

St Stephen's Green

ber of the Guinness family, who is honoured with a statue on the west side. The bronze sculpture by Henry Moore was erected in memory of **William Butler Yeats** in 1967. The **Fusiliers' Arch** (*northwest entrance*) commemorates those who died in the Boer War and the **German Monument** (*southeast entrance*) expresses the gratitude of the people of the Federal Republic of Germany for help it received after the Second World War.

The **Royal College of Surgeons** (*west side*), designed by Edward Parke in 1806, was captured during the Easter Rising in 1916 by a party of insurgents led by Constance Markievicz.

On the south side are **Newman House**, **Iveagh House** (designed by Richard Castle and now the Department of Foreign Affairs) and the **University Church** (1854), designed at the behest of Cardinal Newman by John Pollen in the highly ornate Byzantine and Italian early-Christian style advocated by John Ruskin.

▷ *From the SE corner of the square turn left into Harcourt St then left into Clonmel St.*

Iveagh Gardens
Entrances in Clonmel St and Earlsfort Terrace. (Dúchas) ○*Open 8am (10am Sun and Bank Hols)–dusk (5pm Feb and*

Nov; 6pm Mar–Oct; 4pm Dec–Jan). www.heritageireland.ie/en.

Lawns and tree-lined walks, enhanced by statuesque fountains, a rosarium and a maze, provide respite from the city bustle. The main axis is terminated by a massive rock-work cascade based on the Bains d'Apollon at Versailles.

▷ *Return to St Stephen's Green; walk south and into Grafton St.*

Grafton Street★
Dublin's finest shopping street is now a bustling pedestrian precinct and a favourite haunt of street musicians; in the 19C it was paved with pine blocks to deaden the sound of carriage wheels. **Bewley's Oriental Café** with its distinctive mosaic façade and stained-glass windows by Harry Clarke started in the 1840s but was re-opened in 1927; the previous building there was Whytes School, attended by Robert Emmet, Thomas Moore, Richard Sheridan and the Duke of Wellington.

▷ *Turn left into Johnson Ct.*

Powerscourt Centre★
○*Open Mon–Fri 10am–6pm (8pm Thu), Sat 9am–6pm, Sun noon–6pm.* ☎*01 671 7000. www.powerscourtcentre.com.*
This 18C town house with fine stucco ceilings was designed in 1771 by Robert

Mack for Viscount Powerscourt; it is now a shopping centre.

▶ *Return to Grafton St and continue north to College Green and O'Connell Bridge.*

Old Dublin

The heart of old Dublin occupies the ridge between the Liffey and its southern tributary, the Poddle River, which now flows underground. Excavations (1974–81) at **Wood Quay**, where the modern Civic Offices of Dublin Corporation now stand, revealed the remains of 150 Viking buildings at 13 different levels (AD 920–1100). The town expanded eastwards along Dame Street to meet the development taking place around Leinster House, and also westwards along the **High Street** into the **Cornmarket**, where vast quantities of grain were sold for export in the Middle Ages. Little remains of the old buildings in **Fishamble Street**, where Molly Malone was born and Handel conducted the first performance of *Messiah* to raise funds for the Rotunda Hospital. The **Liberties** was the name given to the area farther south and west, which lay outside the jurisdiction of the medieval city; here the buildings vary from 17C high-gable houses built by French Huguenot refugees to 19C mansion flats and 20C housing estates.

▶ *From the south side of O'Connell Bridge walk upstream along Aston Quay.*

Liffey Footbridges

The popular name for the delicate cast-iron footbridge, opened in 1816 as the Wellington Bridge, is the **Ha'penny Bridge** ✶, so-called because of the ½d toll levied until 1919. It now has a companion, the **Millennium Bridge**.

▶ *Opposite the Ha'penny Bridge turn away from the river through the arch.*

Merchants' Hall *(Wellington Quay)* was designed by Frederick Darley for the Merchants' Guild, also known as the Fraternity of the Holy Trinity, the first of Dublin's 25 guilds; the arched passage through the building leads into Temple Bar.

Temple Bar

The area between the river and Dame Street, now known as Temple Bar (28 acres/11ha) takes its name from Sir William Temple, Provost of Trinity (1628–99), who owned land which included a sand bar on the south bank of the river. A stroll through its medieval network of narrow streets and courts reveals a variety of old buildings – Georgian houses, warehouses and chapels – restored and converted to new uses,

H.Champollion/MICHELIN

Liffey Bridge

interspersed with new purpose-built property. Derelict sites have been converted into open spaces – Temple Bar Square, Meeting House Square and Central Bank Plaza among the banks and insurance offices of Dame Street. This astonishingly successful case of urban renewal, has produced a **cultural district** with venues for entertainment and "alternative" shops, restaurants, hotels and residential areas. Eustace Street is now home to two national institutions – the Irish Film Centre and the National Photographic Archive; the **Temple Bar Information Centre** *(18 Eustace St)* provides details of what's on and when.

▶ *Walk west up Dame Street. Either walk past City Hall into Lord Edward St and turn left into Werburgh St. Or turn left into Dame Lane, walk past Dublin Castle, past Dubh Linn Garden and the Chester Beatty Library; continue west along Ship Street and turn right into Werburgh Street.*

St Werburgh's Church

◷ *Open by appointment, Mon–Fri 10am–4pm. Key from 8 Castle St.* ☎ *01 4783710.* The 1715 church replaced an early 12C one; it was remodelled in 1759 after a fire and has one of the city's most elegant Georgian interiors. The British authorities, nervous after the 1798 rebellion, insisted on the removal of the spire overlooking the Castle courtyard. One of the most distinguished of the rebels, Lord Edward Fitzgerald, was secretly buried in the vaults; his captor, Major Henry Sirr, is buried in the churchyard.

▶ *Walk south down Werburgh St into Bride St; turn right into Upper Kevin St, right into St Patrick Close, past Marsh's Library and the Cathedral (◷ see Inner Dublin); turn right again into Patrick St.*

The arches on the east side of **St Patrick's Park** form a literary parade of Dublin-born writers, with their dates

DUBLIN

Adelaïde Rd	BT 3	Morehampton Rd	BT 108
Alfie Byrne Rd	CS 5	Mount St Upper	BT 112
Bath Ave	CT 9	Palmerston Park	BT 123
Benburb St	BS 15	Phibsborough Rd	BS 132
Berkeley Rd	BS 16	Rathmines Rd Upper	BT 135
Botanic Rd	BS 19	Ringsend Rd	CT 139
Canal Rd	BT 30	Sandford Rd	BT 151
Clanbrassil St	BT 40	Shelbourne Rd	CT 157
Conyngham Rd	AS 48	Shrewsbury Rd	CT 159
Denmark St	BS 52	South Circular Rd	AS 162
Donnybrook Rd	CT 54	St Agnes Rd	AT 141
Dorset St	BS 55	St Alphonsus Rd	BS 144
Drimnagh Rd	AT 57	St John's Rd West	AS 147
Eglinton Rd	CT 63	Suir Rd	AT 168
Grand Parade	BT 72	Terenure Rd East	BT 172
Inchicore Rd	AT 79	Thomas St West	BT 174
Infirmary Rd	AS 81	Victoria Quay	BS 178
James St	BT 84	Western Way	BS 184
Leeson St Upper	BT 94	Wolfe Tone Quay	BS 195
Macken St	BST 99		

Ceol	BS	V
Guinness Storehouse	BT	M⁷
Kilmainham Gaol Museum	AT	M⁶
National Concert Hall	BT	T
Phoenix Monument	AS	L
Portobello Hotel	BT	Q
Shaw Birthplace	BT	W
St Stephen's Church	BT	X
Waterways Visitor Centre	CT	K
Wellington Monument	AS	N

and major works; three won a Nobel Prize for Literature.

▶ *Continue north up St Patrick St; turn left into Back Lane.*

Tailors' Hall★

The Tailors' Hall (1703–07) is the only surviving guild-hall in Dublin. The Great Hall has a stage, a handsome marble fireplace and a minute gallery with a wrought-iron railing: the building is now used by *An Taisce*, the Irish National Trust.

▶ *Return to St Patrick St and continue to the south end.*

There is a fine view of **Christ Church Cathedral** (⮌ *see Inner Dublin*) and the covered bridge linking it to the old Synod Hall which now houses Dublinia.

▶ *Walk west along High St.*

St Audoen's Church

(Dúchas) ⮌ ⏰ *Open May–Oct, 9.30am–5.30pm (4.45pm last admission).* ☏ *01 6770 088. www.heritageireland.ie/en.*
The old church (now Anglican) was founded by the Anglo-Normans and dedicated to St Audoen of Rouen in France. The west doorway is 12C, the nave is 13C. **St Audoen's Gate** (1275), leading to the river, is one of 32 gates in the Norman city walls.

▶ *Turn right into Cook St and left into Winetavern St; walk down to the river and look across to Inns Quay.*

Four Courts

⏰ *Open Mon–Fri 10am–1pm, 2pm–4pm, subject to official business.* ☏ *01 872 5555.*
The building (1785) accommodating four major courts – Chancery, King's Bench, Exchequer and Common Pleas – was begun by Thomas Cooley and completed by James Gandon. It was

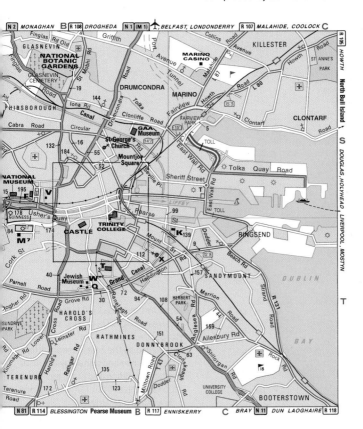

DUBLIN

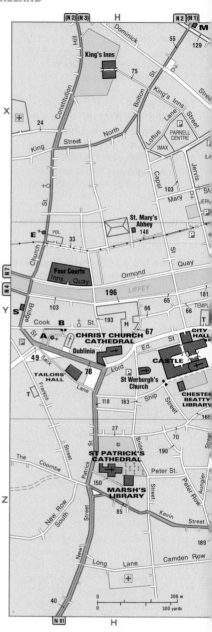

seized by the rebels in 1916 and again by anti-Treaty forces. On the first occasion it escaped serious damage but in 1921, it was shelled by the Free State army from across the river and mined by the insurgents; the building and the ir-replaceable national archives from 1174 it contained, were virtually destroyed.

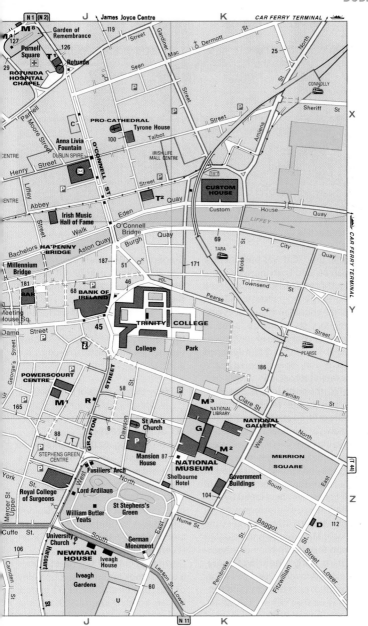

> ▶ Turn right and walk along Wood Quay and Essex Quay.

> ▶ Continue along the quays to return to the Ha'penny Bridge.

On the corner of Essex Quay and Parliament Street stand **Sunlight Chambers**, built as the headquarters of Lever Brothers with coloured terracotta friezes telling the story of soap.

North Bank

In the Middle Ages, the Viking settlement by the Liffey, known as Oxmantown, was dominated by **St Mary's**

Sunlight Chambers

Abbey. In the 17C it was built up on a grid plan around Oxmantown Green, now Smithfield. The Hospital and Free School of King Charles II was founded in 1670 for the education of poor boys who wore military-style blue uniforms; in 1773 the **Bluecoat School** was housed in Blackhall Place in a building designed by Thomas Ivory, now occupied by the Incorporated Law Society.

By the 18C, the north bank had become the most fashionable residential district of Dublin, centred on O'Connell Street, then known as Gardiner's Mall. No-one today would describe O'Connell Street as fashionable but it retains its generous dimensions and remains a vital part of the city centre. Farther north, the site of Parnell Square was developed by Bartholomew Mosse to raise money for his maternity hospital, which occupied the south side. Many of the once-elegant Georgian terraces in the neighbourhood, particularly **Mountjoy Square**, have passed through neglect and decay to demolition or restoration and conversion. **St George's Church** (1802–14), where the Duke of Wellington married Kitty Pakenham in 1806, was designed by Francis Johnston with a marked similarity to St Martin's-in-the-Fields in London.

Two of Dublin's major theatres are located on the north bank. The **Gate Theatre** was founded in 1928 by Hilton Edwards and Micheál MacLiammóir. The earlier **Abbey Theatre**, now a national institution, was founded in 1904 by Lady Gregory and W B Yeats as part of the Irish literary revival. In 1924 it became the first state-subsidised theatre in the English-speaking world, and for a while its productions continued to cause controversy, even riots, notably with the plays of Sean O'Casey. The original theatre building was destroyed by fire in 1951.

▶ *From the north side of O'Connell Bridge walk up O'Connell St.*

O'Connell Street★

This broad, elegant thoroughfare was laid out by Luke Gardiner in the 18C as a tree-lined mall and later converted into a narrow residential square. Renamed Sackville Street, it developed into the most important street in 18C Dublin; later it was extended south to Carlisle Bridge (1794) and renamed after O'Connell in 1922.

Down the centre of the street stands a row of **monuments** by John Foley of *(south to north)* Daniel O'Connell; William Smith O'Brien (1803–64), the leader of the Young Ireland Movement sentenced to death for treason in 1848; Sir John Gray, who organised Dublin's water supply; James Larkin (1876–1947), founder of the Irish Transport and General Workers' Union (1909); Father Theobald Mathew of the 19C temperance movement.

The **GPO building**★ with its Ionic portico was designed by Francis Johnston in 1814. It was the headquarters of the rebels in the Easter Rising in 1916 and still bears scars of the fighting.

Erected in 2003, the **Spire of Dublin** was the brainchild of Ian Ritchie Architects. This impressive stainless steel needle-like sculpture, topped by a beacon, measures 120m high, seven times the height of the GPO building. It replaced the much abused **Anna Livia Fountain**. This in turn occupied the site of Nelson's Pillar (1808), which was damaged by an IRA bomb in 1966 and as a result demolished. The head of the statue of Nelson can be seen nearby at the Dublin Civic Museum. The fountain has been relocated to Croppy Memorial Gardens facing Collins Barracks.

▶ *Turn right into Talbot Street.*

(St Mary's) Pro-Cathedral★

Open Mon–Sat, 7.30am–6.45pm (Sat 7.15pm), Sun 9am–1.45pm, 5.30pm–7.45pm ☎01 8745441. www.procathe dral.ie.

Dublin's most important Roman Catholic church was built in 1821 in the style of a Greek temple with a Doric portico and a dome. Its monumentality contrasts with its rather cramped setting, but Protestant interests kept it away from its intended site on O'Connell Street. In 1851 John Newman made his profession of faith to Cardinal Cullen in this church. The Palestrina Choir was endowed in 1902 by Edward Marty; one of its early members was John McCormack.

Opposite, stands **Tyrone House**, an elegant mansion, designed by Richard Castle in 1741 and now occupied by the Department of Education.

▶ *Return to O'Connell St.*

Parnell Square

Rutland Square was renamed in honour of **Charles Stewart Parnell**, whose statue stands at the road intersection. The south side of the square is taken up by the elegant lying-in hospital designed by Richard Castle in 1752 for Dr Bartholomew Mosse (1712–59). The **Rotunda Hospital Chapel**★ (*open Wed 10am–noon, on application in writing; ☎01 8730700*) is an exuberant Rococo creation, decorated with superb stuccowork by Bartholomew Cramillion and carved mahogany woodwork by John Kelly.

Funds for the hospital were raised from entertainments given in the **Rotunda** (1764), designed by John Ensor – now a cinema, or in the **Assembly Rooms** (1786), designed by Richard Johnston – now the Gate Theatre. Yet more fundraising was done in the walled **pleasure gardens** (*Dúchas; ♿ open May–Sept 9.30am–8pm, Oct –Apr 11am–7pm (4pm, Nov–Feb); ☎office–01 647 2498, garden–01 874 3074*) in the centre of the square, laid out with a wilderness, temples of refreshment and a terrace where music was played – known as the Orchestra. The surrounding houses were completed in the 1770s and inhabited by peers, bishops and members of Parliament.

The north end of the square has been converted into a **Garden of Remembrance** designed by Daithí P Hanly; the gates incorporate Celtic motifs, the central sculpture by Oisín Kelly echoes Yeats' poem *Easter 1916* and the mythological transformation of the Children of Lir into swans. The broken spears in the mosaic reflect the Celtic custom of

Charles Stewart Parnell

R Holzbachova, Ph Benet/MICHELIN

throwing weapons into water after a battle.

The site is significant because it was here that plans for the Easter Rising (1916) were hatched *(plaque on the north side)* and the rebels were held overnight.

▶ *On the north side of the square are the Dublin Writers' Museum and the Hugh Lane Gallery (see Inner Dublin). Turn right into Granby St. Turn left into Dorset St and right into Henrietta St.*

King's Inns

The building where barristers used to live and study was started in 1795 and completed in 1827. It is the last great public building designed by James Gandon and the dining room is the only Gandon interior to survive.

▶ *Return to Dorset St; turn left and right into Dominick St Lower; turn left into Parnell St and right into Moore St.*

A lively **street market** is held here at the heart of a busy shopping district.

▶ *Turn right into Henry St and left into Liffey St to return to the Ha'penny Bridge.*

Phoenix Park★★

The largest enclosed urban park in Europe (1 752 acres/709ha) derives its name from the Gaelic for clear water *(Fionn Uisce)*. The land, confiscated from Kilmainham Priory in 1543 by the Crown, was enclosed in 1662 by the Duke of Ormond who introduced a herd of fallow deer which still roam the Fifteen Acres (actually approximately 300 acres/121ha).

The southeast gate is flanked by the **Wellington Monument**, designed by Sir William Smirke in 1817, and the **Peoples' Garden** sloping to a small lake. From here Chesterfield Avenue, lit by gas lamps, leads to the **Phoenix Monument**, erected by Lord Chesterfield in 1745. To the south stands the residence

of the Ambassador of the USA and the **Papal Cross** marking the visit of Pope John Paul II in 1979.

In 1882, at the height of agitation over the Land Act, the newly appointed Chief Secretary, Lord Frederick Cavendish, and the Under-Secretary, Thomas H Burke, the intended victim, were stabbed to death while walking in the park near the Vice-Regal Lodge by the "Invincibles", members of an extremist Fenian sect. All this and more is told in the **Phoenix Park Visitor Centre**. *(Dúchas)* Open mid-Mar–Oct, 10am–6pm (5.30pm mid- to end Mar and Oct); Nov–mid-Mar, Sat– Wed 10am–5pm. Last admission 45min before closing; Sun 1hr before closing. €2.90 016770095. www.heritage ireland.ie/en.

Dublin Zoo★   Kids

9.30am (10.30am Sun)–6.30pm (dusk Oct–Feb). Last admission 1hr before closing. €14. 01 474 8900. www. dublinzoo.ie.

Founded in 1830, Dublin Zoo is set in attractive parkland (30 acres/12ha). Besides being a showcase, the zoo is actively involved in breeding pro- grammes with other zoos and is under constant development. The **World of Cats** has snow leopards, lions and other felines; the **World of Primates** has vivacious monkeys and sad-faced orang-utans. Arctic foxes and snowy owls inhabit **Fringes of the Arctic**, while the lakes and their banks provides a habitat for water fowl, flamingoes, penguins and sealions. **City Farm** and **Pets Corner** are especially popular with children.

Aras an Uachtaráin

Open by guided tour only, (1hr) Sat 10.15am–4.30pm (3.30pm in winter). Closed 24–26 Dec. and New Year week- end. Tickets available from Phoenix Park Visitor Centre. 01 677 0095. www. president.ie.

The **official residence** of the President of Ireland, formerly Vice-Regal Lodge, was built (1751–54) as a private house by Nathaniel Clements and in 1815 acquired its Ionic portico by Francis Johnston.

Sights

Inner Dublin

Trinity College Old Library★★★

Entrances in College Green and Nassau St. ♿ ⏰ *Open all year Mon–Sat, 9.30am–5pm; May–Sept, Sun 9.30am–4.30pm; Oct–Apr, Sun noon–4.30pm.* ⏰ *Closed 21 Dec–2 Jan.* €8 *College tour (30min, including the Colonnades and Book of Kells): mid-May–Sept 10.15am–3.40pm, every 40min (no tours Sun at 1.35pm or 3.40pm) from the Front Arch.* €5. *Joint ticket with Library €10.* ☎ *01 896 1661. www.tcd.ie/library.*

The austere building (1712–32) was designed by Thomas Burgh, Chief Engineer and Surveyor-General of Her Majesty's Fortifications in Ireland. The library acquired its books by purchase or donation until 1801, when it became a copyright library, receiving copies of every book published in the Commonwealth. Since then the increased pace of acquisition has required new buildings: the Reading Room built in 1937 and the Berkeley Library designed by Paul Koralek in 1967. Until 1892 the ground floor was an open colonnade designed to protect the books from damp; in 1992 part of it was converted to provide two galleries: The Colonnades for annual themed exhibitions, and the Treasury.

Treasury★★★

This gallery displays the great treasures of Trinity College Library. The **Book of Kells**, the most famous of them, is an illuminated manuscript of the four Gospels in Latin on vellum, produced c 800 and kept at Kells until the 17C. The **Book of Durrow** (c 700) is another illustrated manuscript of the Gospels in a simpler style. The **Book of Armagh** (c 807) contains the complete text of the New Testament in Latin, as used by the Celtic Church, as well as the lives of St Patrick and St Martin and the Confession of St Patrick. The **Book of Dimma** contains both the Gospels and some liturgical text; its silver shrine dates from c 1150.

Long Room★★

Above the entrance door at the top of the stairs are the **arms of Elizabeth I**, a relic of the original college. The **Long Room** (209ft/64m x 40ft/12m) is lined with bookcases. The original flat ceiling was replaced in the mid 19C by the present higher wooden barrel vault to provide more shelving. The 29-string **Irish harp** (c. 15C, restored) made of willow, is the oldest in Ireland; it was found in Limerick in the 18C.

Long Room, Old Library, Trinity College

R Holzbachova, Ph Benet/MICHELIN

Wedgwood Room, Dublin Castle

Chester Beatty Library★★★

Dublin Castle Precinct, Dubh Linn Garden; entrance in Dame Lane or Ship St. &. ⊙Open May–Sept, 10am(11am Sat, 1pm Sun)–5pm; Oct–Apr, Tue–Sun, 10am (11am Sat, 1pm Sun)–5pm. ⊙Closed 1 Jan, Bank Hol Mon, Good Fri, 24–26 Dec. ✗ ☎01 4070750. www.cbl.ie.

This fabulous collection of Islamic and Far Eastern manuscripts and artworks was bequeathed to the nation by Sir Alfred Chester Beatty (1875–1968), an American businessman who was made the country's first honorary citizen. Among the **Arabic**, **Persian and Turkish manuscripts** are over 270 copies of the **Koran**, some with illuminations by great master calligraphers. The **Biblical material** consists of Syriac, Armenian, Ethiopian and Coptic texts, also early Western Bibles and Books of Hours. Of international importance are the biblical papyri dating from the early 2C to 4C.

The **Japanese and Chinese collection** includes paintings and prints of the highest quality, including Japanese woodblock prints which influenced 19C European art. In addition, there is a large collection of snuff bottles, *netsuke*, jade books and rhinoceros-horn cups. The **Western European collection** contains many important printed books as well as prints by Dürer, Holbein, Piranesi, Bartolozzi and many others.

Dublin Castle★★

Entrances in Dame Lane and Ship St. (Dúchas) &.⚲ Open by guided tour only, (45min) including State Apartments, Chapel Royal and Undercroft), 10am (2pm Sat–Sun, Bank Hols)–4.45pm. ⊙Closed 1 Jan, Good Fri, 25–26 Dec. ⊛ €4.50 ✗ ☎01 645 8813. www.dublincastle.ie.

Between 1204 and 1922 Dublin Castle represented British rule in Ireland. People under suspicion languished in its prisons; traitors' heads were exhibited on spikes over the gate. Embedded within the tight-knit urban fabric of the city, the Castle changed over the centuries from a formidable fortress to an administrative complex of almost domestic character. By the 19C the Lord Deputy usually resided at Vice-Regal Lodge in Phoenix Park, staying at the Castle only for the few winter weeks of the Castle Season, which was a glittering round of levées, balls and receptions. The Castle is now one of the symbols of Irish statehood, its sumptuous State Apartments used to receive foreign dignitaries and other important ceremonial occasions.

Its construction began 30 years after the Anglo-Norman landing in Ireland, when King John ordered a castle to be built on the high ground southeast of the existing town, a site protected on two sides by the River Poddle. The original structure expanded into a rough quadrangle with a round tower at each corner on the site of the present Upper Yard. In 1684 much of the medieval castle was destroyed by fire. New apartments designed by Sir William Robinson were completed in 1688 but most of them were replaced in the middle of the 18C. The Castle's two courtyards now have an essentially Georgian appearance, with the Powder Tower as the most visible reminder of its medieval origin, even though it too was much altered in the early 19C.

State Apartments

Upper Yard. The upper floor on the south side was built between 1750 and 1780 but the interiors have been much modified subsequently. The **Grand Staircase** and the **Battleaxe Landing** lead to a suite of sumptuously furnished and decorated interiors overlooking Castle Green and the wall named after Queen Victoria, built to protect the royal gaze from the sight of the adjoining stables. In 1916, one room served as a prison for James Connolly, one of the leaders of the Uprising. There is Sheraton, Regency and Louis XIX furniture, fine plaster or painted ceilings, and modern, colourful carpets from Killybegs. The **Throne Room** has ovals and roundels with deities probably painted by the Venetian Giambattista Bellucci in the early 18C, portraits of Viceroys in the **Picture Gallery** are set off by superb Venetian chandeliers, and the **Wedgwood Room** has paintings attributed to Angelica Kauffmann (1741–1807) and black Wedgwood plaques.

Many glittering balls were held in Ascendancy times in St Patrick's Hall built in the mid-18C and named after the Order of the Knights of St Patrick, an order instituted by George III in 1783. Crests, helmets and banners hang above the stallplates recording the names of the members of the Order, while the ceiling is a glorification of the relationship between Britain and Ireland, painted by Vincenzo Valdré (1742–1814), an Italian who came to Ireland in 1774 with the Viceroy, the Marquess of Buckingham, for whom he had worked at Stowe.

Castle Hall

The dignified two-storey building *(closed)* on the north side of the upper yard was designed c 1750 by Thomas Ivory for the Master of Ceremonies. It incorporates the **Bedford Tower**, named after John Russell, Duke of Bedford and Lord Lieutenant, and built on the base of the west tower of the original castle gate. Four days before the state visit of Edward VII and Queen Alexandra in 1907 the Crown Jewels were stolen from the Office of Arms in the Bedford Tower; they have never been recovered.

Flanking Castle Hall are two gates surmounted by statues by Van Nost: *Fortitude* on the west gate and *Justice* on the east gate, which was the sole entrance until the west gate was opened in 1988 and a new bridge built; the fountain and pool recall the old moat. A figure of Justice stands atop the Tower; Dublin wags liked to point out that her back is turned to the city and that her scales dipped unevenly in wet weather; holes were eventually bored in the outer pan to allow the rainwater to drain away.

Powder Tower Undercroft

Lower Yard. Excavations beneath the Powder Tower have revealed parts of the Viking and Norman defences – a 13C arch and relieving arch in the **Old City Wall** which enabled boatmen to enter the moat to deliver goods to the postern gate.

Church of the Most Holy Trinity

This fine example of a Regency Gothick building was designed by Francis Johnston and consecrated in 1814. Before reconsecration as a Roman Catholic sanctuary (1943) the building served as the Chapel Royal, on the site of an earlier, smaller church. The exterior is decorated with over 100 heads carved in Tullamore limestone by Edward Smyth and his son John; the interior plasterwork is by George Stapleton and the woodwork by Richard Stewart. The Passion of Christ panels in the east window are composed of old Continental stained glass. The arms of all the Viceroys from 1172 to 1922 are represented in the galleries, gallery windows, and on the chancel walls.

National Museum (Archaeology)★★

Kildare St. ♿ ⏱*Open Tue–Sun 10am (2pm Sun)–5pm.* ⏱*Closed Good Fri, 25 Dec.* *Guided tour (45min) at frequent intervals.* *€2.* ✗ *01 677 74444. www. museum.ie/ archaeology.*

The Kildare Street branch of the National Museum was purpose-built in 1890 to display treasures from the national archaeological collections. A short video contextualises the masterpieces of Irish art now on show in **The Treasury**★★. Precious objects range in date from the Bronze Age to the 15C and include: a model boat in gold from the Broighter Hoard (1C); the Loughnashade Trumpet (1C BC); the Ardagh Chalice (8C); the Tara Brooch (8C); the Shrine of St Patrick's Bell in bronze, gold and silver (c 1100); the "Cathach", a book shrine made to contain the Psalter of St Columba (Colmcille) (12C–15C); the Kavanagh Charter Horn of ivory and brass, the only surviving object associated with Irish kingship (12C–15C).

The section on **Prehistoric Ireland** has a reconstruction of a passage tomb as well as the huge Lurgan Longboat from around 2500 BC. **Ireland's Gold** displays a gleaming array of artefacts, some from hoards preserved for millennia in the Irish boglands.

Among the objects shown in **Viking Ireland** are items from the Viking settlement at Wood Quay in Old Dublin: iron, bone, wood utensils, clothing and ornaments. St Manchan's Shrine, a spectacular reliquary, is one of several ecclesiastical treasures on display in the section entitled **The Church**.

The small but exquisite objects from **Ancient Egypt** are dramatically lit. **Irish Glass** has an excellent range of this craft in which the country has long excelled.

National Gallery★★

Kildare St, Merrion St or Clare St. (Dúchas) ♿ ⏱*Open daily 9.30am (noon Sun)– 5.30pm (8.30pm Thu).* ⏱*Closed Good Fri, 24–26 Dec.* *Guided tour: Jul–Aug, daily 3pm; rest of year, Sat 3pm, Sun 2pm, 3pm, 4pm.* ✗ *01 661 5133. www.nation algallery.ie.*

Ireland's National Gallery, inaugurated in 1864, has one of the finest collections of art in Europe. By the Merrion Street entrance stands the statue of William Dargan (1799–1867), a railway magnate and the promoter of the Irish Industrial Exhibition of 1853 which included a Fine Art Hall, and it is these works that formed the founding collection. Other benefactors have included Sir Hugh Lane, Sir Henry Vaughan, and G B Shaw, whose donation included royalties from *My Fair Lady*. The Milltown Rooms were built to house the Milltown Collection. The latest addition is the controversial Millennium Wing, a striking stone-clad edifice providing a spacious new entrance area and space for loaned exhibitions from abroad.

Understandably, the gallery's collection of Irish art is outstanding, with examples by the country's major painters and sculptors from the 17C to the 20C, displayed alongside select items of furniture. There are fascinating topographical pictures, portraits, and a whole room devoted to the work of Jack B Yeats (1871–1957), who ably captured the colour and spirit of contemporary life in Ireland and its landscapes, as did, of course, his brother, W B Yeats. The gallery's British paintings include works by Hogarth, Wilson, Gainsborough, Reynolds and Romney; lovely watercolours by Bonington and Crome. There is an important Italian collection ranging from early altarpieces to paintings by Fra Angelico, Mantegna and Titian and a superbly dramatic Caravaggio, *The Taking of Christ*. French art is represented by Claude and Poussin, by several artists of the Rococo, and a number of Impressionists. Outstanding among the Dutch paintings is the tranquil *Woman Reading a Letter* by Gabriel Metsu, matched by works by Vermeer, Ruisdael and Hobbema. The Spanish collection is substantial, with pictures by El Greco, Velazquez, Murillo, Zurbaran, and Goya.

Christ Church Cathedral★★

♿ ⏱*Open Jun–Aug, Mon–Fri 9am–6pm; rest of year, 9.45am–5pm (winter) 6pm (spring/autumn).* ⏱*Closed 26 Dec.* *€6.* *01 677 8099. www.cccdub.ie.*

Like the Castle, Christ Church Cathedral became a symbol of the Ascendancy, and the Romanesque/Early English building is still the seat of the Anglican Bishop of Dublin and Glendalough and the Metropolitan Cathedral of the Southern Province of the Church of Ireland, second only to Armagh. Largely rebuilt in the 19C by George Scott, it is nevertheless an important link to the city's very earliest days, being the successor to the wooden church built in 1038 by Dunan, the first Bishop of Dublin, on land provided by Sitric, the Viking King of Dublin. Soon after 1170 this building was replaced by a stone church built on the orders of Strongbow, Richard de Clare, Earl of Pembroke. . A number of medieval features survived the 19C rebuilding: the elegant **Romanesque south door** overlooking the ruins of the Chapter House, the **brass eagle lectern**, and some of the original encaustic tiles in the Chapel of St Laud. Hanging on the chapel wall *(right)* is a casket containing the heart of St Laurence O'Toole, the second Archbishop of Dublin. In the south aisle is the "**Strongbow**" **monument;** though the effigy in chainmail is certainly not the great Anglo-Norman commander, the half figure beside it may well belong to the original tomb. "Strongbow's tomb" was frequently specified in legal contracts as the place of payment. Of all the Cathedral inte-

St Patrick's Cathedral

R Holzbachova, Ph Benet/MICHELIN

riors, the 12C Norman **crypt** *(access in the south aisle)* is perhaps the most evocative. It has been used for services, has been let to shopkeepers and used for burials until the mid 19C.

St Patrick's Cathedral★★

&. Open Mon–Sat 9am–6pm (5pm Sat, Nov–Feb). Sun, Mar–Oct 9am–11.45am; 12.45pm–3pm; 4.15pm–6pm. Nov–Feb 10am–11am, 12.45pm–3pm. Closed 1 Jan and 25–26 Dec. €5. 01 475 4817. www.stpatrickscathedral.ie.

Jonathan Swift (1667–1745)

Swift was born in Dublin in 1667 and educated at Kilkenny and Trinity College, Dublin. In 1689 he became Secretary to Sir William Temple of Moor Park in England but failed to secure advancement. Back in Ireland he was ordained (1694) and appointed as prebendary of Kilroot, near Carrickfergus, where he wrote his first book, *A Tale of a Tub*, a satire on "corruptions in religion and learning", published in 1704 together with *The Battle of the Books*. He went back to England but, on Temple's death in 1699, returned to Ireland. He became Vicar of Laracor, south of Trim (1701) and was appointed Dean of St Patrick's Cathedral in 1713.

Today, Jonathan Swift is best remembered for *Gulliver's Travels,* despite all that he wrote on church matters, politics and Ireland – including the wickedly satirical *A Modest Proposal* (1729) – for disposing of unwanted babies. His *Journal to Stella*, a collection of intimate letters, was addressed to Esther Johnson; according to some she and Swift were married in the Deanery garden but they never lived together.

Swift spent one-third of his income on the poor and saved another third which he bequeathed for the founding of a hospital for the insane. At the end of his life he suffered from Ménière's disease and lost the use of many of his faculties.

John Comyn, appointed Archbishop of Dublin in 1181, objected to being subject to the laws and regulations of the City Provosts. He moved his seat out of the city jurisdiction to the site of a holy well used, according to tradition, by St Patrick to baptise converts. His church was promoted to a cathedral and rebuilt in the Early English style in the mid-13C, with a tower added a century later.

The cathedral is forever associated with **Jonathan Swift** (*see 'Jonathan Swift' box*), its Dean from 1713 to 1745. His tomb is marked by a bronze plaque in the floor near the main door, beside it that of his friend "Stella". Swiftian memorabilia includes his death-mask and a replica of his skull (in the bookcase). Swift wrote his own epitaph; he also composed an epitaph for the black marble tomb of the **Duke of Schomberg** (*north choir aisle*), and put up a plaque (*south transept*) to his faithful servant Alexander McGee.

The vaulted **baptistery** in the southwest corner of the nave was probably the entrance to the original church. The 13C floor tiles, transferred from the south transept in the 19C restoration, have been copied throughout the cathedral. The huge and splendid **Boyle Monument** (1632), erected by the great Earl of Cork in memory of his second wife Catherine, is adorned with no fewer than 16 polychrome figures.

In the north aisle stands a fine statue by Edward Smyth of the Marquess of Buckingham, Viceroy and first Grand Master of the **Order of St Patrick;** until 1871 the cathedral was the chapel of the Order, hence the banners and escutcheons. In the north transept stands the old door of the Chapter House; the hole was cut in 1492 so that the Earl of Kildare could "chance his arm" in a conciliatory gesture to Black James Ormond who had taken refuge in the Chapter House; they had quarrelled because Ormond had been appointed Lord Deputy in place of Kildare.

Marsh's Library★★

St Patrick's Close. Open Mon, Wed–Fri, 10am–1pm, 2pm–5pm, Sat 10.30am–1pm. €2.50. 01 454 3511. www.marshlibrary.ie.

The building in St Patrick's Close was designed in 1701 by Sir William Robinson to house the first public library in Ireland. A portrait of the founder, Archbishop Narcissus Marsh, hangs above the stairs. The dark oak bookcases, surmounted by a mitre, divide the long room into seven bays. Beyond the office are three "cages" where precious books can be consulted. The total of 25 000 books is composed of four individual collections.

Bank of Ireland★★

Foster Place. Open Tue–Fri 10am–4pm (5pm Thu). guided tour, Tue 10.30am, 11.30am, 1.45pm. Closed Bank Hols. 01 677 6801.

Ireland was governed from this elegant building in Foster Place from when it was completed (1728) until 1800, when the Act of Union abolished the country's jurisdiction and transferred it to Westminster. Several eminent architects contributed to its appearance – Sir Edward Lovett Pearce, James Gandon, and Francis Johnston, who converted it for use by the Bank of Ireland in 1803. The old House of Commons is now the banking hall. The **House of Lords** is still largely intact, with a magnificent coffered ceiling, a great chandelier of Irish glass, an oak mantelpiece to a design by Inigo Jones, and splendid 17C Flemish tapestries depicting the Battle of the Boyne and the siege of Londonderry.

In the **Story of Banking** a short video and display of currency, bank notes and an old money cart form part of an excellent interpretation of the role of the Bank of Ireland in the commercial development of the country, since its establishment in 1783.

Newman House★★

St Stephen's Green South. Visit by guided tour only (40min), Jun–Aug, Tue–Fri, 2pm–4pm on the hour; otherwise by appointment. €5. 01 716 7422 or 475 7255.

The two 18C town houses named after Cardinal Newman honour the memory of the first Rector of University College, which started here in 1854. Almost intact, they provide an insight into the 18C city. The smaller house was designed by Richard Castle in 1738 and retains many original features like the glazing bars he devised. The splendid stucco figures of Apollo and the Muses are by the Lafranchini brothers. The larger house dates from 1765; the Bishops' Room has a portrait of Cardinal Newman and his Rector's Chair, while the staircase is decorated with lovely Rococo plasterwork by Richard West. An antiques-and-collectibles fair is held here every other Sunday.

Custom House★★

Custom House Quay; entrance in south front. ⏱*Open mid-Mar–Oct: Mon–Fri, 10am–12.30pm; Sat–Sun and Bank Hols, 2pm–5pm. Nov–mid-Mar: Wed–Fri, 10am–12.30pm; Sun, 2pm–5pm.* ✆*€1.* ☎*01 888 2538.*

The Custom House, with its long façade and central dome, is one of the great landmarks of Dublin. It was designed by James Gandon, completed in 1791, and restored after being set on fire by anti-Treaty forces at the beginning of the Civil War in 1921. The **Visitor Centre** in the ceremonial vestibules behind the south portico, offers a detailed and fascinating history of the building, Gandon's career and the work of the government offices which were housed there.

Outside on the quay beside the River Liffey stands the **Famine Memorial**: six bronze figures by Rowan Gillespie personify the mixed emotions – ranging from despair through suffering to hope – of the many victims of the Great Famine.

Hugh Lane Gallery of Modern Art★

Parnell Square, North. ♿⏱*Open Tue–Sun 10am (11am Sun)–6pm (5pm Fri–Sun).* ⏱*Closed Good Fri, 25 Dec.* 🍴 ✆*€7 Francis Bacon Studio; €3.50 Tue morning.* ☎*01 222 5550. www.hughlane.ie.*

The extensive collection of late-19C and 20C works by Irish and Continental artists supplement the works acquired by **Sir Hugh Lane** (1875–1915), who drowned on the *Lusitania*. The building, a three-storey mansion of Portland stone and granite, flanked by curved screen walls, was designed in 1762 by Sir William Chambers for an earlier connoisseur, **James Caulfield**, 1st Earl of

Newman House

Charlemont, who also built the Marino Casino.

There are works by several Impressionists, Corot and Courbet, and contemporary pieces by the likes of Christo who swathed the pathways of St Stephen's Green. The most interesting room, however, is probably the one reserved for works by Irish artists. *Lakeside Cottage* (c 1929) is a landscape by Paul Henry; *The Rescue of the Prison Van at Manchester* by Maurice MacGonical dramtically portrays a famous Fenian incident from 1867. One room is devoted to Roderic O'Conor (1860–1940), a friend of Gauguin, who reflects the influence of colleagues, like Seurat and Van Gogh.

City Hall★

Dame St. ⏱*Open 10am (2pm Sun) –5.15pm (5pm Sun).* ⏱*Closed Good Fri, 25–26 Dec.* ✆*€4.* ☎*01 222 2222. www. dublincity.ie.*

This magnificent edifice, one of the finest public buildings in Dublin, built in 1769–79 by Thomas Cooley as the Royal Exchange, marked the arrival in Ireland of the neo-Classical style. When economic activity declined after the 1800 Act of Union, the building lost much of its purpose, and in 1852 it was bought by the City Corporation. During the **Easter Rising** of 1916 it was occupied by the insurgents; from the roof they commanded the approaches and main gate of Dublin Castle but after about three hours the regular soldiers regained command of the Upper Yard.

The splendid domed **rotunda** has early 20C frescoes illustrating aspects of city history. **The Story of the Capital**, a lively introduction to Dublin's past, is housed in the vaulted basement: this excellent multi-media exhibition complements Dublinia, exploring the post-medieval history with plans, photographs, old film, artworks and precious objects like the Civic Sword presented by Henry IV around 1409.

Number Twenty Nine★

Open Tue–Sun, 10am (1pm Sun)–5pm. Closed Good Fri, 2 weeks at Christmas. €5. 01 702 6165. www.esb.ie/main/about_esb.

This 18C terrace house evocatively re-creates domestic life in Dublin in the Georgian era. It is decorated throughout with appropriate furniture, carpets, curtains and paintings, and is crammed with the paraphernalia of everyday living. Among the wealth of objects are a wine cistern designed by Francis Johnston and a curved belly-warmer.

Statue of James Joyce

Dublin Writers' Museum

Parnell Sq North. Open daily 10am (11am Sun, Bank Hols)–5pm (6pm Mon–Fri, Jun–Aug). €7. 01 872 2077. www.writersmuseum.com.

The Irish writers associated with the city of Dublin – Jonathan Swift, Oscar Wilde, Bernard Shaw, James Joyce, Samuel Beckett, WB Yeats, Synge, O'Casey, Flann O'Brien, Brendan Behan and Patrick Kavanagh to name just the best known – are remembered with personal items, photos, portraits, busts, manuscripts and copies of their major works. The museum also traces the written tradition in Ireland from the illuminated manuscripts of the Celtic Christian church, such as the Book of Kells, to the present day. Temporary exhibitions are held in the elegant reception rooms, readings and workshops in the children's section. The museum occupies two Georgian terrace houses with **elegant stucco ceilings**★; the one in the library is by Michael Stapleton. Alterations made in 1891–95 by Alfred Darbyshire for George Jameson include the addition of stained-glass windows bearing the Jameson monogram, four female figures representing Music, Literature, Art and Science, and, in the first-floor saloon, a series of painted door panels by Gibson and an ornamental colonnade and gilded frieze.

James Joyce Centre

35 North Great George's St. Open Tue–Sat, 10am–5pm. Closed Bank Hols. €5. Guided tours available, Joyce's Dublin, Sat at 11am, 2pm. €10. 01 878 8547. www.jamesjoyce.ie.

The centre promotes the life and work of James Joyce by hosting talks, tours of the house and walks through the north inner city. As a boy, Joyce lived nearby in Fitzgibbon Street and attended Belvedere College *(Denmark St)*. The restored terrace house, built in 1784 by Francis Ryan, once served as the town house of Valentine Brown, Earl of Kenmare; the very fine **plasterwork**★ is mostly by Michael Stapleton. Joyce family portraits line the staircase.

F Vidal/MICHELIN

Dublinia & The Viking World [Kids]

High St. ⓖ Open Apr–Sept, 10am–5pm; Oct–Mar 11am (10am Sat–Sun, Bank Hols)–4pm. Last admission 45 mins before closing. ⓖ Closed 17 Mar, 23–26 Dec. €6. ☎01 679 4611. www.dublinia.ie.

This entertaining interactive exhibition provides a sensory experience of the medieval city. There are tableaux, live costumed figures, a superb model of the Dublin of around 1500, a mock-up of part of an important archeological excavation along the Liffey and key finds, and a reconstruction of the face of a medieval Dubliner, whose skeleton was found nearby. It is housed in the Synod Hall of Christ Church Cathedral *(High Street)*, with which *it is* linked by an arch.

Civic Museum

South William St. ⓖ Open Tue–Sat 10am–6pm, Sun 11am–2pm. ⓖ Closed Christmas ☎01 674 4999 or 4998.

The history of Dublin can be traced in the old City Assembly House with displays of maps, prints, postcards, photographs, relics of old buildings and a set of Malton's views of Dublin (1792–99).

St Michan's Church

Church St. ⓖⓖ Open Mar–Oct, Mon–Fri 10am–12.45pm, 2pm–4.45pm. Nov–Feb Mon–Fri 12.30pm–3.30pm. Sat all year 10am–12.45pm. ⓖ Closed Christmas and Bank Hols. €4. ☎01 872 4154.

The first church on the site was probably built by the Danes as St Michan is thought to be a Danish saint. The present church dates from 1095 but gained its present appearance in 1686. While the **interior** boasts the early 18C organ played by Handel and **vaults** containing their **mummified corpses** preserved for over 300 years by the dry air and constant temperature.

St Mary's Abbey

(Dúchas). ⓖ Open mid-Jun–mid-Sept, Wed and Fri, 10am–5pm (4.15pm last admission). ☎01 833 1618; wwwheritage ireland.ie/en.

Founded by Benedictines but taken over by Cistercians, St Mary's was the richest monastery in the Pale and the meeting place for the Council of Ireland.

It was here in 1534 that Silken Thomas renounced his allegiance to Henry VIII, thereby setting off the Kildare Revolt. All that remains of the abbey are the **Slype** and the rib-vaulted **Chapter House**, which now contains a reconstruction of the 15C cloister arcade (recovered in 1975 from a 17C building in Cork Street) and information about the foundation, architecture and history of the abbey and the Cistercian way of life.

Parliament

Visit by guided tour only (30min), Mon–Fri, 10.30am–3.30pm by arrangement through your embassy. Contact Events Desk for more information. ☎01 618 3781. www.oireachtas.ie.

The two houses **(Dáil Éireann and Seanad Éireann)** meet in **Leinster House**, which was designed in 1745 by Richard Castle for the Duke of Leinster and converted to house the republican parliament in 1922. Visitors are admitted to the public gallery when the house is in session *(Tue–Thu)*.

Government Buildings

Upper Merrion St. Visit by guided tour only (40mins), Sat 10.30am–1.30pm. Tickets required (no charge), available from National Gallery, Merrion Sq West. ☎01 619 4116. www.taoiseach.gov.ie.

This imposing structure in Edwardian Baroque, opened in 1911 by George V, was the last major public building project completed in Dublin under British rule. Until 1989 parts of the building were occupied by Trinity College. Modern furniture and a fascinating range of contemporary art provide a fitting workplace for government committees and the Prime Minister *(Taoiseach)*.

Natural History Museum

Closed until further notice for refurbishment. Merrion Street Upper. ☎01 677 7444. www.museum.ie/ naturalhistory.

A barely altered example of a Victorian museum, the building's pillared hall and galleries are as fascinating as their contents, which include three skeletons of the Great Irish Deer, now extinct. The specimens, still exhibited in the original display cabinets cover` complete range of creatures ever to have lived in Ireland.

National Library

Kildare Street. ♿🕐*Open Reading Room Mon–Wed 9.30am–9pm, Thu–Fri 9.30am–5pm, Sat 9.30am–1pm. Exhibitions (main building) Mon–Wed 9.30am–7.45pm, Thu–Fri 9.30am–4.45pm, Sat 9.30am–12.45pm. Exhibitions (2–3 Kildare Street) Mon–Wed 9.30am–8.30pm, Thu–Fri 9.30am–4.30pm, Sat 9.30am–12.30pm.* 🕐*Closed Bank Hols, Good Fri, 22 Dec–2 Jan.* ✕. ☎*01 603 0311. www.nli.ie.*

Opened in 1890 this classical-style building mirrors the National Museum opposite. Its attraction for visitors lies in its first-class free **exhibitions** –two of which are staged at a time, in the modern part of the main building and in the adjacent 2–3 Kildare Street address, respectively – and in the classic domed reading Room of the Library (portrayed in *Ulysees*). There is also a **Genealogy Room** where visitors in search of their roots can seek advice.

Northside

National Museum (Decorative Arts & History) ★★

Collins Barracks, Benburb Street. 🕐*Open Tue–Sat, 10am (2pm Sun)–5pm.* 🕐*Closed Good Fri, 25 Dec.* 🚶*Guided tour (45min) at frequent intervals.* ☜€2. ✕. 🅿. ☎*01 677 7444. www.museum.ie/ decorative.*

The great barracks which once housed 3 000 men and 1 000 horses, was commissioned in 1700 by King William III. Thomas Burgh designed a "plain and useful, without any unnecessary ornament" complex which, in its day, was the largest institution of its kind in the British Isles, a progressive alternative to the contentious practice of billeting soldiers on the population. Today, the buildings have been converted for use by the National Museum for displays of decorative arts and history.

The **West Block** shows an enthralling array of special treasures – 25 highly varied pieces grouped together under the heading of **Curators' Choice**; these might be a rare astrolabe from Prague, an elongated late-13C or early-14C wood statue of St Molaise and Bow figurines

made by Thomas Frye, or modelled by his fellow London Irishmen.

The **South Block** displays Irish country furniture and woodcraft *(third floor)* from the Baroque to Modern era, including fascinating examples of late-19C Neo-Celtic pieces inspired by objects like the Tara Brooch discovered in 1850; scientific instruments *(second floor)*; Irish silver from the early 17C to the present day *(first floor)*.

Marino Casino★★

Off Malahide Rd, Marino. (Dúchas) 🚶*Visit by guided tours only, May–Oct, 10am–5pm (6pm Jun–Sept); Feb–Apr and Nov, Sat–Sun and Bank Hols noon–4pm (5pm Apr). Last admission 45min before closing.* 🕐*Closed 1 Jan, 25–26 Dec.* ☜€2.90. 🅿☎*01 833 1618. www.heritage ireland.ie/en.*

The charming Palladian villa, designed by Sir William Chambers in 1765, was built in the grounds of Marino House (demolished 1921), the country seat of James Caulfield, Earl of Charlemont, who had met Chambers on the Grand Tour (1746–54). The centrally-planned French neo-Classical casino is built of Portland stone; 12 Doric columns support a frieze and cornice topped by pediments, statues and urn-shaped chimneys. The sculpture is by Simon Vierpyl and Joseph Wilton.

The interior contains four state rooms, decorated with elaborate plaster ceilings and inlaid floors using eight different kinds of wood, and four small bedrooms on the upper floor.

National Botanic Gardens★★

Botanic Rd, Glasnevin. (Dúchas) ♿🕐*Gardens: open 9am–6pm (4.30pm, late Oct–early Feb). Glasshouses close 5pm (5.45pm Sat–Sun).* 🚶*Guided tours available (☜free) Sun, noon, 2.30pm.* 🅿✕. ☎*01 804 300, or 857 0909. www. botanicgardens.ie.*

The gardens were started in 1795 on a 48acre/19ha site beside the Tolka River. The splendid Victorian glasshouses include the **Curvilinear Range** (1843–69), designed by Richard Turner, and the **Great Palm House** (1884). There is a delightful **walk** along the river from the **rose garden**, through the **peat** garden and the **bog garden** beside the ornamental pond to the **arboretum**. Further specimens in the rock garden, cactus house and fern house account for the 20 000 species grown here.

Glasnevin Cemetery★

Finglas Rd, Glasnevin. ✎ *Visit by guided tour only (90min), from main gate, Wed, Fri 2.30pm.* ☎ *01 830 1133. www.glas nevin-cemetery.ie.*
Europe's largest cemetery (120acres/ 49ha) is the resting place of over a million people, nearly all Roman Catholics: anonymous paupers, cholera victims, and historical figures including Eamon De Valera, Daniel O'Connell and Michael Collins.

Old Jameson Distillery

Bow St, Smithfield Village. &. ✎ *Visit by guided tour only, 9.30am–6pm (last tour 5.30pm).* ○*Closed Good Fri, Christmas hols.* ☞ *€11.* ✗. ☎ *01 807 2355. www. jamesonwhiskey.com.*
Part of the old distillery has been converted to show current and earlier methods of production of whiskey (note the e in the spelling).
A video (*8min*) is followed by a tour of a kiln and barley store; the mystery of worts and wash-backs in the process is explained. The tour ends in the bar where visitors are invited to take part in a whiskey tasting.

Chimney Viewing Tower

o━ *Closed until further notice for refurbishment. Smithfield Village.* ☎*01 817 3800.*
The chimney (175ft/60m), constructed in 1895 as part of the Jameson Distillery, is now flanked by a glass-walled lift and crowned by a glass observation platform – fine views of the city, the bay and the mountains to the south.

GAA Museum

Croke Park, St. Joseph's Avenue, off Clon- liffe Rd. ○*Open Mon–Sat, 9.30am (noon Sun)–5pm (6pm Jul–Aug); match days, open to Cusack stand ticket holders only.* ○*Closed 1 Jan, 24–28, 31 Dec.* ☞*€5.50.* ✎*Museum and stadium guidedtour available (daily on the hour).* ☞*€9.50.* ✗. ☎*01 819 2323. http://museum.gaa.ie.*

Croke Park is the home of the national games of Ireland – hurling and Irish football. The museum traces the development of the **Gaelic Athletic Association** and its influence on the sporting, cultural and social traditions of Ireland. Computers provide highlights of past games; visitors can test their speed of reaction and high-jumping ability or try hitting the *sliothar* with a *camán* in the practice nets.

Southside

Kilmainham Gaol Museum★★

Inchicore Rd, Kilmainham. (Dúchas) &. ✎ *Visit by guided tours only (1hr). Apr–Sept, 9.30am–6pm (last tour 5pm). Oct–Mar: Mon–Sat, 9.30am–5.30pm (last tour 4pm); Sun 10am–6pm (last tour 5pm).* ○*Closed 24–26 Dec.* ☞ *€5.30.* ✗. [P]. ☎ *01 453 5984. www.heritageireland. com/en.*
The struggle for political independence is excellently presented in the prison where so many Irishmen were incarcerated for offences against the Crown – United Irishmen, Young Irelanders, Fenians, Invincibles, and participants in the Easter Rising. Collections of souvenirs, photographs, letters and press cuttings illustrate the many incidents and rebellions from 1796 to 1924 and

Office of Public Works

Kilmainham Gaol

their socio-political contexts. The **tour** includes the Central Hall (1862) containing 100 cells, the chapel, individual cells in the 1798 corridor, and the exercise yards also used for executions. The New Gaol, erected in 1792, consisted of a central range flanked by an east and a west courtyard divided into exercise yards; one contains Erskine Childers' boat, **Asgard** (*see 'Guns for Independence' box*).

Irish Museum of Modern Art

Military Rd, Kilmainham. Open Tue–Sun, 10am (10.30, Wed; noon Sun, Bank Hols)–5.30pm (5.15pm last admission). Closed 29 Mar. . 01 612 9900. www.imma.ie.

The museum presents 20C Irish and international art, and allied theatrical and musical performances. Its exciting and wide-ranging programme includes exhibitions of major 20C art and promising contemporary talent.

The museum is housed in **Royal Kilmainham Hospital**★★, the earliest-surviving Classical building in Ireland. It was commissioned by the Duke of Ormond, James Butler of Kilkenny, who was appointed Viceroy in 1669 on his return from exile in France, and modelled on Les Invalides in Paris. The architect was William Robinson, Surveyor-General, who designed four ranges of buildings (1680–84) to provide accommodation for 300 old soldiers, the last of whom left in 1929.

Guns for Independence

In July 1914, 900 German rifles and 25 000 rounds of ammunition for the Irish Volunteers were landed at Howth from the *Asgard*, the yacht belonging to Erskine Childers a committed Republican, influenced by the time he had spent at Glendalough, his mother's childhood home, which he loved passionately. Strongly opposed to the Anglo-Irish Treaty which partioned the country, he was arrested in 1922 by the Free State government for possessing a revolver, and executed; his novel *The Riddle of the Sands* has been made into a film.

The **Great Hall**, now hosts concerts and government receptions; the ceiling of the **Chapel**, is made of papier maché. *(Dúchas) Visit by guided heritage tour only, early Jul–mid-Sept, Tue–Sun and Bank Hols, noon–5.30pm. call for tour charge. . 01 612 9900. www.heritage ireland.ie/en.*

Rathfarnham Castle★

3mi/5km south of Dublin by N 81 and R 115. (Dúchas). Closed for refurbishment, may open for limited period 2008, call for details. 01 493 9462. www.heritageireland.ie/en.

The magnificent but forbidding exterior gives no hint of the elegant 18C interior designed by Sir William Chambers and James "Athenian" Stuart. The rectangular central keep with four flanker towers was built c 1593 by Adam Loftus, a Yorkshireman who became Archbishop of Dublin. The castle was abandoned in the early 20C, then used as a Jesuit seminary; its splendid interiors, remodelled in the 1770s for Henry Loftus, are currently undergoing painstaking restoration.

Guinness Storehouse★

Crane Market St, off Thomas St. Visit by guided tour only (1hr), 9.30am–5pm (7pm Jul–Aug). Closed Good Fri, 24–26 Dec. €14 (€12.60 online). . 01 408 4800. www.guinness-storehouse.com.

The tour provides a complete survey of the Guinness production process and the 140-year history of the family firm. In Thomas Street, next to the main brewery gate, is the house built by Arthur Guinness in the 18C. The tour ends at the 7th-floor Gravity Bar where visitors receive a complimentary pint of Guinness and can enjoy uninterrupted panoramic views across Dublin.

Drimnagh Castle

Long Mile Rd. Tours Wed, Sat, Sun noon–5pm. Last tour 4pm. €4. 01 450 2530.

Drimnagh is a 13C moated castle with a medieval Great Hall and vaulted undercroft, flanked by a battlemented tower. It boasts a formal 17C garden with box hedges, lavender bushes and herbs.

Patrick Pearse (1879–1914) – Teacher, Barrister, Poet, Activist

James Pearse, a stone carver from England, kindled his son's love of English literature while his great-aunt, Margaret, stimulated an interest in the Irish language. Patrick joined the **Gaelic League**, campaigned for the use of Gaelic in schools and set up his own boy's school. Prominent names – WB Yeats, Patrick MacDonagh and Padraic Colum – attended pupils' theatrical productions. Over the years his pride in all things Irish evolved into more active political engagement. In November 1913 he joined the Irish Volunteers and in February 1914 he the IRB. He took a prominent part in the Easter Rising and was executed at Kilmainham Gaol on 2nd May 1916. His brother William was executed the following day.

The Shaw Birthplace

33 Synge St.
🕐 *Open May–Sept Mon–Tue, Thu–Fri 10am–1pm and 2pm–5pm; Sat–Sun, Bank Hols, 2pm–5pm.* ✆€7. ☎*01 475 0854. www.visitdublin.com.*
The modest house, where **George Bernard Shaw** (1856–1950) was born and spent his early years, is furnished in the style of the mid 19C.

Irish Jewish Museum

Walworth Rd.
🕐*Open May–Sept Sun, Tue, Thu 11am–3.30pm; Oct–Apr Sun 10.30am–2.30pm.* ☎*01 490 1857. www.visitdublin.com.*
Set in a former synagogue, this museum was opened by Chaim Herzog, President of Israel and son of the first Chief Rabbi of Ireland. It displays material on the history of Irish Jews from the 11C.
The **synagogue** upstairs retains ritual fittings.

Pearse Museum

4.5mi/7.2km S of Dublin by N 81.
In Terenure fork left. In Rathfarnham bear left to Bray; turn first right onto Grange Rd; after 0.5 mile/0.8km turn right onto Sarah Curran Ave. 10min there and back on foot from the car park by the footpath parallel with the road. (Dúchas) ⚠*Closed until mid-2008 for renovation.* ☎*01 493 4208 www.heritageireland.ie/en.*
The house (1797) was acquired by the Pearse brothers (👓*see 'Patrick Pearse' box*) in 1910 for their boys' school, to encourage Irish culture and develop talents free from the pressure of exams.

Excursions

The Ben of Howth ★

North side of Dublin Bay by the DART (Raheny Station for North Bull Island) or by the coast road and R 105.
Ben of Howth, on the north side of Dublin Bay, shelters North Bull Island, originally a mere sandbank covered at high tide, which has grown to its present size (3mi/4.5km long) and continues to increase in width seawards, since the Bull Wall was built in the late 18C to protect Dublin harbour from silting up.

North Bull Island

♿🕐*Open Mon–Thu, 10.15am–1pm, 1.30pm–4.30pm; Fri 10.15am–1.30pm; Sat–Sun 10am–1pm, 1.30pm–5.30pm (4.30pm Oct–Mar).* 🕐*Closed Easter, Christmas.* ☎*01 833 8341.*
The exhibition on the wildlife and natural habitats of the island underline the significance of the **nature reserve** where wildfowl and wading birds spend the winter, and where some 30 000 shore birds take daily refuge from the high tide covering their feeding grounds in Dublin Bay. The island has two golf courses and several lovely beaches.

▶ *Continue by road or rail to Howth.*

Howth

The picturesque village clings to the steep north face of the headland. At its heart are the ruins of **Howth Abbey** (St Mary's) and the splendid tomb of a late-15C knight and his lady.
St Mary's Abbey: key from Mrs O'Rourke, 13 Church St.

Howth Harbour

The harbour (1807–09), which now shelters sailing and fishing boats, was the packet boat station from 1813 until Dún Laoghaire took over in 1833.

Offshore lies **Ireland's Eye** (*boats depart from East Pier; open May–Sept,10.30am–6pm on demand;* €10; 086 8459154; www.islandferries.net), a bird sanctuary, where 6C Christians built a church.

West of the village is Howth Castle Demesne (*private*), a medieval keep with a 15C gatehouse.

Next to the castle (closed to the public) is the **National Transport Museum of Ireland** (*open Jun–Aug, Mon–Sat 10am–5pm; Sept–May, Sat–Sun 2pm–5pm; Closed Bank Hols;* €3; ; 01 832 0427; www.national transportmuseum.org), a comprehensively labelled collection of horse-drawn or motorised, commercial and military vehicles.

Dún Laoghaire

South side of Dublin Bay by the DART or by N 31.

Dún Laoghaire (pronounced Leary), the main port of entry to Ireland from Great Britain, has become an attractive residential area, with the amenities of a seaside and boating resort. It grew from a small fishing village into a busy port through the growth of trade with Britain in the 18C and is named after Laoghaire, the High King of Ireland in the 5C, who built a fort here.

For 100 years the port was known as **Kingstown** in honour of **George IV**, who landed here in September 1821; an **Obelisk**, erected in memory of the king's visit to Ireland, stands on the waterfront south of the harbour.

National Maritime Museum of Ireland

Haigh Terrace. Closed. 01 280 0969. www.visitdublin.com.

Housed in the Mariners' Church (1835–60) on the south side of Moran Park, this small collection belies its name and consists largely of model ships.

James Joyce Museum

0.5mi/0.8km east by the coast road to Sandycove. Open Mar–Oct 10am–1pm, 2pm–5pm(6pm Sun, Bank Hols); or by appointment. €7.25. 01 280 9265. www.visitdublin.com.

The Martello Tower (1804) on the point at Sandycove now houses a **Joyce Museum:** first editions, letters, photos, his death-mask, piano, guitar, cabin trunk, walking stick, wallet and cigar case. Joyce stayed there for six days in 1904 as the guest of the writer Oliver Gogarty, who had rented the tower from the government. The upper room, the location of the breakfast scene in *Ulysses*, is furnished appropriately, while the **view** from the roof embraces Dún Laoghaire Harbour (*northwest*), the coast to Dalkey Island (*southeast*) and the Wicklow Mountains (*southwest*).

Dalkey Village

1mi/1.6km S of Dún Laoghaire.

Dalkey (pronounced Dawkey), now designated a Heritage Town, was once a walled town with seven fortified buildings. **Bulloch Castle** by the shore was built in the 12C by the monks of St Mary's Abbey in Dublin to protect the harbour. Two late-medieval tower houses survive in the heart of the village. One is **Archbold's Castle**, which stands opposite the graveyard of the ruined **St Genet's Church**, which may date from the 8C. The other is **Dalkey Castle and Heritage Centre** which comprises a 15C fortified town house (called Goat Castle) offering splendid views from the battlements; Dalkey Town Hall (1893); the 10C St Begnet Church and graveyard; an exhibition area with excellent displays on local history; an art gallery and gift shop. &. ⊙ *Open Apr–Dec, 9.30am (11am Sat–Sun, Bank Hols)–5pm.* ⊛€6. ☎*01 285 8366. www.dalkeycastle.com.*

Many writers, including James Joyce, have associations with Dalkey; as a child (1866–74) George Bernard Shaw (1856–1950) lived in Torca Cottage on Dalkey Hill and learnt to swim at Killiney beach. Recent local luminaries include Maeve Binchey and film director Neil

Dalkey Island and Vico Road

Jordan. Offshore lies **Dalkey Island**, which is now a bird sanctuary.

From the coast road south of Sorrento Point there is a magnificent **view**★★ of Killiney Bay extending south to Bray Head.

The park covering the south end of Dalkey Hill was opened to the public and includes a **nature trail** which winds through trees and over the heath to an **obelisk**, built by John Mapas in 1742 to provide work for his tenants. From here there are **panoramic views**.

DUNDALK

POPULATION 25 762

At the head of Dundalk Bay, midway between Dublin and Belfast, Dundalk (Dún Dealgan) is one of the country's largest urban centres, with a harbour and a range of industries. In medieval times it was fortified by the Anglo-Normans, who used it as a base for incursions into the Gaelic strongholds of Ulster; subsequent repeated attacks and sieges have left little of its early heritage intact. Nevertheless it makes a good centre for exploring the many attractions of the nearby coast and countryside.

- **Information:** Jocelyn St. ☎042 933 5484. www.eastcoastmidlands.ie.
- ▶ **Orient Yourself:** Dundalk is served by the main road (N 1) north up the coast to the border with Northern Ireland, and bypassed by the motorway (M 1)
- ◔ **Also See:** BOYNE VALLEY, DROGHEDA, KELLS, MOURNE MOUNTAINS, NEWRY.

Walking Tour

Dundalk was comprehensively re-planned in Georgian times by its then owner, James, 1st Earl of Clanbrassil. To the south of the bridge over the Castletown River *(Church St)* stands

one of the few reminders of the place's medieval past, the 14C tower of **St Nicholas' Church** (Anglican); the church was rebuilt in 1707 and later given a spire by Francis Johnston.

The **Courthouse** *(south)* is a formidably austere neo-Classical structure with a

Doric portico, designed by Park and Bowden in 1813.

An elaborate porch-screen *(Roden Place – east)* leads to **St Patrick's RC Cathedral**, modelled on King's College Chapel in Cambridge; the sanctuary and the side chapels are richly decorated with mosaics.

County Museum

Jocelyn St. ○*Open Mon–Sat (Oct–Apr, Tue–Sat) 10.30am–5.30pm. Sun, Bank Hols 2pm–6pm.* ≈*€3.80.* ☎*042 932 7056. www.louthcoco.ie.*

A restored 18C warehouse houses a clear and comprehensive review of local history (archaeological finds, farming and industry, the port and railway) through audio-visual presentations, touchscreens, films and graphics.

Driving Tours

Cooley Peninsula

The Cooley Peninsula is a mountainous granite promontory, providing magnificent landscapes and seascapes – *(south)* over Dundalk Bay and – *(north)* over Carlingford Lough to the glorious outline of the Mourne Mountains in Northern Ireland. This is excellent walking country and features in many a legend; in particular it is associated with Cuchulain, the hero of the epic tale *The Cattle Raid of Cooley (Táin bo Cuainlge).*

Fine sandy beaches stud the edge of Carlingford Lough.

▷ *From Dundalk take N 1 N and R 173 E.*

Proleek Dolmen★

Ballymascanlon Hotel. 20min return on foot through the yard and along the tarmac path between the fields.

A massive capstone (40 tons/47 tonnes) on two supports dates from 3000 BC; according to legend the wish will be granted of anyone who can make three pebbles land on the top. Nearby is a wedge-shaped gallery grave.

▷ *Continue E and turn left into the mountain road north to Omeath.*

Windy Gap★

The road climbs towards Carlingford Mountain (1 932ft/587m). Beyond the site of the Long Woman's Grave *(plaque)* the road enters the aptly named **Windy Gap**, a narrow pass between rocky crags; fine view south over Dundalk Bay. Farther north there is a **viewpoint** overlooking the mouth of Newry River at Warrenpoint and the Mourne Mountains rising from the eastern shore.

Omeath

Once a Gaelic-speaking fishing village, Omeath is now a little resort with a rocky shoreline, where one can savour freshly caught seafood. In summer jaunting cars carry fares to the outdoor Stations of the Cross at the monastery of the Rosminian Fathers, and the Carlingford Lough Ferry plies across the border to Warrenpoint.

▸ *From Omeath take the coast road R 173 S.*

Carlingford★

Viking and Norman monuments add to the charm of this attractive resort at the foot of the Cooley Mountains, facing the Mourne Mountains across Carlingford Lough (marina and boat trips). Carlingford Oysters are a local delicacy with an international reputation.

Local history is traced on great triptychs in the **Carlingford Heritage Centre** (🕐 *open Mon–Fri 10am–12.30pm, 2pm–4pm;* 🕐 *closed Bank Hols;* ⊕ €3; ☎042 9373888; www.carlingfordheritage centre.com), housed in the deconsecrated Anglican church, which is the starting point for a guided tour of the town centre.

Spanning the main street is the **Tholsel**, a gateway, once three storeys high, where Parliament is said to have promulgated laws for the Pale.

South of the town square stands a 15C fortified house *(right)* decorated with Celtic mouldings; although it is known as the **Mint**, there is no proof that the local mint, founded in 1467, ever operated there. Overlooking the harbour is **Taaffe's Castle**, a late-15C square tower fortified with machicolations, crenellations, arrow slits and murder holes; the vaulted basement may have been a boat-house since the tide used to reach the foundations. It was built by the Taaffe family, created Earls of Carlingford in 1661. The ruins of **King John's Castle** stand on a bluff north of the harbour commanding the entrance to Carlingford Lough; the western bailey was probably built by Hugh de Lacy, before King John's visit in 1210; the eastern apartments were added in 1261.

Between the Fane and the Dee

▸ *From Dundalk take R 171 SW to Louth.*

Patrick Kavanagh Centre

Patrick Kavanagh

St Mochta's House★

It is hard to believe that little Louth was once the centre of the 11C/12C Kingdom of Oriel. In a field behind the ruins of a Franciscan friary (14C–15C) stands a stone oratory with a **corbelled roof**, which has been much restored; it is said to have been built in a night as a resting place for St Mochta who died in 534.

▸ *From Louth take the minor road N via Chanonrock to Inniskeen.*

Inniskeen

The village is the birthplace of **Patrick Kavanagh** (1904–67), poet, author and journalist, who is buried in the old churchyard; his life and work are sympathetically presented in the **Patrick Kavanagh Centre** (🕐 *open Tue–Fri 11am–5pm, Sat 2pm–5pm. Sun, Jun–Sept 2pm–5pm;* 🕐 *closed mid-Dec–mid-Jan;* ⊕€5; ☎042 937 8560; www.patrickkavanaghcountry.com), alongside information about the local history. The remains of a round tower mark the site of a 6C monastery founded by St Daig beside the Fane River.

▸ *From Inniskeen take the road W to Carrickmacross.*

Carrickmacross

Known today as a good angling centre, the town grew up round a castle built by the Earl of Essex, to whom the land was granted by Elizabeth I. For two centuries it has enjoyed a reputation for hand-made lace: the **Carrickmacross Lace Gallery** (*Market Square at* *the north end of the main street;* ⏰*open Mon–Fri 9.30am–5.30pm (4.30pm Fri);* ⏰*closed Bank Hols, 25 Dec–1 Jan;* ☎042 966 4176; www.carrickmacrosslace.ie) displays examples of the local "mixed lace", composed of cambric patterns applied to machine net and embellished with point stitches and loops.

The Roman Catholic church (1866) was designed by JJ McCarthy, with stained glass (1925) by Harry Clarke.

▶ *From Carrickmacross take R 179 SW to Kingscourt.*

Dún A' Rí Forest Park★

The forest park, until 1959 part of the Cabra estate, is set in a valley beside the Cabra River. A **nature trail** and four signposted **walks** provide access to the red deer enclosure, a waterfall downstream from Cromwell's Bridge, a wishing well, Cabra Cottage – the Pratt family mansion until Cabra Castle *(east)* was built in 1814 – a ruined flax mill, an ice house and the ruins of Fleming's Castle (1607) – named after an Anglo-Norman family who lost their land for supporting James II.

▶ *From Kingscourt take R 165 SE via Drumcondra; at the crossroads turn left into N 52.*

Ardee (Baile Átha Fhirdhia)

The name means the Ford of Ferdia. On the east side of the main street stand two fortified buildings: **Hatch's Castle**, a late-medieval fortified house, and **Ardee Castle**, built in 1207 by Roger de Peppard, although much of the present building dates from the 15C. In the 17C the castle was granted to Theobald Taaffe, Earl of Carlingford.

ENNIS

POPULATION 15 333

Known as the "Banner County", Co Clare has a long history of dogged nationalism, the veritable heartland of Irish traditional music. There is evidence of both in the little county town of Ennis with its narrow winding streets and colourful shopfronts. Harriet Smithson, the wife of Hector Berlioz, was born in Ennis; her father was the manager of the first theatre built in the town in the late 18C.

- 🛈 **Information:** Arthurs Row. ☎065 682 8366. www.visitennis.ie.
- ▶ **Orient Yourself:** Ennis (Inis) bestrides the junction of N 8, N 85 and N 68 mid-way between Limerick and the Burren.
- 👣 **Also See:** ADARE, THE BURREN, KILLALOE, KILRUSH, LIMERICK, TRALEE.

A Bit of History

Royal Origins – Ennis is proud of its distinguished beginnings. Its origin can be traced back to the 13C, when the O'Brien family, kings of Thomond and descendants of the great Brian Ború, built their royal residence nearby. Because of its central position Ennis became the county town of Clare during the shiring of Ireland in the reign of Elizabeth I.

In 1610 the town was granted permission to hold fairs and markets; two years later it received a corporation charter from James I.

Famous Statesmen – Two of the outstanding figures in Irish political history are commemorated in the town. In 1828, the election by an overwhelming majority of **Daniel O'Connell** as MP for Clare led directly to Catholic emancipation the following year. Nearly a century later, **Eamon de Valera** was elected to Parliament in 1917; he served as Member for the county until 1959.

A modern statue to him stands before the old Courthouse (1850), a neo-Classical building with a pedimented Ionic portico *(Galway Road N18)*.

© World Pictures/Photoshot

Ennis Friary

Sights

Ennis Friary★

(Dúchas) ♿🕐*Open Easter–Oct 10am–6pm (5pm Oct).* ✆€1.60. ☎065 682 9100. *www.heritageireland.ie/en.*
The Friary was founded by an O'Brien in the 13C, and by the 14C had become one of Ireland's foremost institutions of learning, with over 600 students as well as hundreds of friars. Now a picturesque ruin, it has a superb east window but is most noteworthy for its sculpture. An **Ecce Homo** shows Christ with the Instruments of the Passion. St Francis is depicted with stigmata. The Creagh tomb (1843) in the chancel consists of five carved panels showing the Passion, taken from the MacMahon tomb (1475), and figures of Christ and the Apostles from another tomb.

Clare County Museum

♿🕐*Open Jun–Sept 9.30am–5.30pm (9.30am–1pm Sun). Oct–May, Tue–Sat 9.30am–1pm, 2pm–5pm.* ☎065 682 3382. *www.clarelibrary.ie.*
Housed in an imaginatively redesigned former convent school, the *Riches of Clare* exhibition traces the history of this particularly distinctive county via four themes – Earth, Power, Faith and Water – using a variety of state-of-the-art techniques to interpret the carefully selected range of items on display. Among them is a *shelagh-na-gig* (a carved graphic representation of a woman displaying her genitalia), a gorgeously carved panel from the wreck of an Armada galleon, and a striking banner of 1917 celebrating the election victory which confirmed Sinn Fein as a force to be reckoned with and Eamon De Valera, who represented East Clare for three decades, as a major political figure.

Cathedral

The Roman Catholic Cathedral, dedicated to St Peter and St Paul, was built between 1831 and 1843 in a Tau-cross (letter T) shape; the tower with its spire was added 1871–74.

Address Book

ENTERTAINMENT

For a taste of the Middle Ages, book a **medieval banquet** in **Knappogue Castle** or head out to **Bunratty Folk Park** Corn Barn to the Traditional Irish Night of music, song and dance. (*www.shannonheritage.com*)

TRACING ANCESTORS

Clare Heritage Centre
(see Excursions).

The Brendan Voyage

St Brendan the Navigator was a sea-faring monk who, in the 6C, set sail for the New World from Brandon Creek, at the foot of Brandon Mountain on the Dingle Peninsula.

His account of the voyage, *Navigatio*, written in medieval Latin, was long thought to be fanciful until, in 1976, Tim Severin built the *Brendan* and proved that the earlier voyagers *could* have reached America several centuries before Christopher Columbus. The 20C adventure, which substantiates the 6C narrative, is retold in *The Brendan Voyage*.

Excursions

Dromore Wood

8mi/13km north by N 18 (signed) to Barefield. (Dúchas) ♿🕐*Forest Park: Open daylight hours. Visitor Centre: July–early Sept 10am–6pm.* ☎*065 6837166. www. heritageireland.ie/en.*

This nature reserve (1 000 acres/400ha) provides various animal habitats, including lakes, limestone pavement and turloughs, river, fen and semi-natural woodland; among the examples of human habitation are ruins of the 17C O'Brien castle.

Dysert O'Dea★

6mi/10km N by N 85, R 476; after 4mi/ 6.4km turn left; after 1mi/1.6km turn right. 🕐*Open May–Sept,10am–6pm.* ⊕*€4.* 🚻. ☎*065 683 7401 or 7794 in off season.*

This monastery was founded by St Tola in the 8C, and the site has a number of evocative remains, albeit of later date. A great battle raged here in 1318, when the O'Briens routed the Anglo-Norman Richard de Clare, thereby delaying English control of Clare for two hundred years. There is an **archaeology centre** and a small **museum** devoted to the prehistoric and later culture of the neighbourhood, housed in a 15C tower house with a murder hole above the entrance.

In a neighbouring field *(access on foot or by car)* stands the late-12C **White Cross of Tola**: by this date, large fig-ures carved in high relief had replaced the exuberant organic ornamentation. This example shows the Crucifixion and a bishop. The site also has the stump of an 11C **round tower**, and fragments of an 11C **church**.

Clare Heritage Centre★

8.5mi/14km north by N 85 and R 476 at Corrofin. ♿🕐*Museum: Open Apr–Oct 9.30am–5.30pm.* ⊕ *€ 4. Genealogy Centre: Mon–Fri 9am–5.30pm.* 🕐*Closed Good Fri, 25 Dec.* 🚻. ☎*065 683 7955. www.clareroots.com.*

The centre, housed in the former Anglican church, illustrates life in Co Clare in the 19C, highlighting the exodus of some 100,000 inhabitants after the Famine. An intriguing section of oak trunk is marked with the dates of historic events. The centre also provides access to its extensive genealogical records.

Clare Abbey

1mi/1.6km southeast by R 469; turn right before the railway station, then left; park at the corner; 0.5mi/0.8km on foot over the level crossing and right.

Down by the River Fergus stand the substantial ruins of an Augustinian friary founded in 1189 by Dónall Mór O'Brien, last king of Munster.

Quin Franciscan Friary★

6.5mi/10.5km southeast by R 469; in Quin turn left. 🕐*Open late-May–late Sept Wed–Mon, 10.30am (11.30am Sat–Sun)– 6pm.* ☎*091 844084.*

The extensive ruins of the friary, built c 1430 by Sioda McNamara, include the **cloisters**, the tower and the south transept. The remains of an earlier ruined Norman castle (1280–86) include three round towers, erected over of an even earlier monastery.

Knappogue Castle★

8mi/13km southeast by R 469. ♿🕐*Open May–Sept 9.30am–5pm (4.15pm last admission – subject to change).* ⊕ *€7.* ☎*061 368103. Medieval banquets: Apr– Oct 6.30pm* ⊕ *€52–€54.50.* ☎*061 360 788. www.shannonheritage.com.*

This massive tower house, the seat of the McNamara family from 1467 to 1815 has been beautifully restored and furnished, and the gardens and orchards replanted and restored to their former splendour.

Craggaunowen Centre★
11mi/18km southeast by R 469 (sign). ♿🕐*Open mid-Apr–mid-Oct 10am–6pm (5pm last admission).* ✆€8.50. 🖂. ☎061 367 178. www.shannonheritage.com. Craggaunowen recreates aspects of Ireland's past with the restoration and re-constructions of earlier forms of dwelling houses, farmsteads, hunting sites and other features of everyday life during the Pre-historic and Early Christian eras. As well as a ringfort, a *togher* (wooden marsh track) the arti-

ficial island of a crannóg there is also a reconstructed 15C castle.

A highlight is The **Brendan**, a replica wood-and-leather *curragh*, sailed across the ocean in 1976 by Tim Severin order to prove that St Brendan did at least have the means to have made his claimed crossing of the Atlantic (*See box*). Note the patch where the leather hull was holed by an ice floe. A **tower house** is used to display items from Hunt's extensive antiquarian collection (more can be found in the Hunt Museum in Limerick).

On the estate live Wild Boar (*Porcus sylveticus*) and early breeds of Soay sheep.

ENNISCORTHY

POPULATION 3 788

The market town of Enniscorthy (Inis Córthaidh) occupies an attractive site on the steep slopes of the River Slaney at its tidal limit. Historically, the town played a key role in the 1798 rebellion. Castle and cathedral dominate a townscape that has scarcely changed since the 19C. Local events are commemorated in the 1798 memorial *(Market Square)* showing Fr Murphy leading the uprising, while the 1916 Easter Rising is marked by Seamus Rafter, a local commander *(Abbey Square)*. The surrounding country is well suited to the growing of soft fruit, celebrated at the Strawberry Fair in early July.

- **Information:** 1798 Visitor Centre, Mill Park Road. ☎054 37596. www.iol.ie/~98com.
- **Orient Yourself:** Enniscorthy sits on the junction of the N 11, running between Dublin and Wexford, and the N 30 to Enniscorthy and New Ross.
- **Also See:** NEW ROSS, WEXFORD, WICKLOW MOUNTAINS.

A Bit of History

Monastic Foundation – The origins of Enniscorthy go back to the 6C, when St Senan arrived from Scattery Island to found a monastic settlement at Templeshannon, on the east bank of the Slaney River. From the 12C the monastery's fortunes were controlled by the Normans, who ruled from their castle until the 15C when the MacMurrough Kavanaghs clan gained control. In the late 16C, Queen Elizabeth I appointed Sir Henry Wallop and Philip Stamp to put an end to local rule.

Commercial Development – Commercial exploitation in Elizabethan times: trees were felled and the timber was exported to France and Spain through Wexford; Philip Stamp set up an ironworks, which survived until the 1940s, and brought many English families to settle in Enniscorthy, which expanded across the River Slaney. At the close of the 18C, several distillery and brewery businesses were launched; by 1796 Enniscorthy had 23 malthouses.

Today, the main concerns revolve around bacon curing, fruit growing, cutlery and potteries.

Address Book

POTTERIES

Carley's Bridge Potteries – Ireland's oldest pottery. *N30, Enniscorthy to New Ross.* ☎054 35149 for visiting details.
Hillview Pottery – *Carley's Bridge Open Mon–Sat 9am–5.30pm, Sun 2pm–5.30pm.* ☎053 923 5443.
Badger Hill Pottery – produces Jack O'Patsy hand-thrown stoneware, ovenware, tablewear and ornamental pots. *Ballinavary. Open Wed–Sun, Bank Hols 10am–1pm, 2pm–5pm.*

Kiltrea Pottery – *3.5mi/5.5km, off the Kiltealy Road (R702).* Handthrown pottery and terracotta. *Open Mon–Sat, 10am–1pm, 2pm–5.30pm.* ☎053 923 5107. www.kiltreapottery.com.

SPORTS AND LEISURE

Greyhound racing – Show Grounds, Enniscorthy. ☎053 92 33172. *Most Mon and Thu €6.* 🅿

Sights

National 1798 Visitor Centre

South of town centre. ♿ 🕐*Open Apr–Sept 9.30am (2pm Sat–Sun)–5pm (last admission); Oct–Mar, Mon–Fri 9.30am–4pm.* ☜*€6.* 🚻. ☎054 37596. *www.iol.ie/~98com.*

The visitor centre was opened to mark the bicentenary of the 1798 uprising and to study the birth of popular democracy in Ireland. The rebellion, particularly the three weeks of disruption in Co Wexford, is presented in vivid detail; parallels are made with contemporary events in France and America and the emergence of modern political parties are reviewed. The highlight is the stirring virtual recreation of the battle of Vinegar Hill (♿*see 'Vinegar Hill' box*).

Vinegar Hill

21 June 1798 is the most (in)famous date in the history of Enniscorthy. Following the rebellion that year, centred mostly in Co Wexford and Co Wicklow, the insurgents, known as the pikemen after their weapons, made their last stand on Vinegar Hill, which they held for nearly a month. The 20 000 insurgents, accompanied by many women and children, were faced by an equivalent number of government troops led by General Lake; the armed men killed in the battle were far outnumbered by the defenceless civilians killed by the army. The defeat at Vinegar Hill marked the end of the 1798 rebellion.

Enniscorthy Castle★

With its four corner towers, the castle owes its present formidable appearance to a 1586 rebuilding of the original stronghold probably erected by Raymond le Gros, who led the first Anglo-Norman soldiers into the town in 1169. After many years in the hands of the MacMurrough clan, the castle became Crown property; Elizabeth I granted it to her favourite poet, Edmund Spenser, who spent a mere three days here before escaping its chilly walls. The **Wexford County Museum**★ displays items relating to the 1798 rebellion, the 1916 Easter Rising and aspects of local history. ☞*Closed for renovation, expected to reopen 2009.* ☎054 35926.

St Aidan's Cathedral

This fine Gothic Revival Roman Catholic church is one of several built by Pugin (1843–46); much of the stone came from the ruined Franciscan friary in Abbey Square.

Excursions

Ferns★

8mi/13km NE of Enniscorthy by N 11.
The modest village was once capital of the province of Leinster and the royal seat of the MacMurroughs: as the significant **ruins** will testify. The tower and part of the north wall are vestiges of the abbey founded in the 12C by the King of Leinster, Dermot MacMurrough Kavanagh. The 13C **castle**, one of the best of its kind in Ireland, has a

Enniscorthy Castle and its reflection over the River Slaney

Bord Fáilte, Dublin

rectangular keep and circular towers; the first-floor **chapel** has a fine vaulted ceiling. (*Dúchas*) ♿ ⏰ *Grounds: open throughout the year. Castle: open May–Sept 10am–6pm.* ☕. ☎054 66411.

Bunclody
12mi/19km N of Enniscorthy by N 11 and N 80.
The town is attractively sited on the River Clody, a tributary of the Slaney, at the north end of the Blackstairs Mountains. The broad central mall is bisected by a stream that falls in steps. The Church of the Most Holy Trinity, consecrated in 1970, was designed by E N Smith. Bunclody was the last bastion in Co Wexford of the Irish language, commonly used until a century ago.

Mount Leinster★
17mi/28km N of Enniscorthy by N 11 and N 80. In Bunclody take the minor road W; after 4mi/6.4km turn left onto the summit road; it is 0.25 mi/0.4km to the peak.

From the summit (2 602ft/793m) on a clear day, there are great views over southeast Ireland: Wexford and Wicklow; the Welsh mountains across St George's Channel.

Altamont Garden
25mi/40km north by N 11 and N 81; turn right (sign) into minor road. ♿ ⏰ *Open 9am–7.30pm (or dusk);tel or see website to confirm.* ☎059 915 9444. www.alta montgarden.com.
The formal and informal gardens have many specimen trees, an arboretum and a small garden with species of flowers normally found growing in Ireland's marshy bogs. The lake was dug out by hand to provide employment during the Famine.

On the horizon rise Mount Leinster *(south)* in the Blackstairs Mountains, and the Wicklow Mountains *(northeast)* across the River Slaney.

FINGAL★

The area north of Dublin, which re-adopted the ancient name of Fingal in 1994, consists of rich farmland fringed by a long coastline. The seaside resort of **Skerries** has several beaches, a colony of grey seals and a fishing harbour where famous Dublin Bay prawns are landed. **Portmarnock**, another popular resort, is known for its long sandy Velvet Strand and its championship golf course. In the Middle Ages Fingal formed part of **The Pale** (*see TRIM*) and contains several historic sites, elegant parks surrounding old stately homes and the charming dormitory town and seaside resort of Malahide.

- **Information:** Main Street ☎01 840 0077. www.fingal-dublin.com.
- **Orient Yourself:** Fingal is the northern sub-division of County Dublin, which includes the city of Dublin and the adjacent suburbs from Balbriggan in the north to Lucan and Brittas in the west and Killiney in the south.
- **Also See:** BOYNE VALLEY, DROGHEDA, DUBLIN, KELLS, TRIM.

Sights

Malahide Castle★★

8.5mi/13km north of Dublin by R 107 or by M 1 and R 106. Open all year Mon–Sat 10am–5pm; Apr–Sept Sun and Bank Hols 6pm; Oct–Mar Sun and Bank Hols 11am–12.45pm, 2pm–5pm. ∞ €7. ✕. ☎01 846 2184. www.malahidecastle.com.

The castle was the home of the Talbot family for nearly 800 years, the great demesne was the prize awarded to Richard Talbot who came to Ireland with Henry II in 1177. Built around the original 14C tower, the castle has been picturesquely extended: the Great Hall dates from the 15C, the reception rooms, some furniture and wonderful **Rococo plasterwork** date from the 18C. It is still highly atmospheric, hung with portraits from the National Portrait Collection. The *Battle of the Boyne* by Jan Wyck in the **Great Hall** recalls the story that 14 Talbot cousins, all Jacobites, breakfasted at Malahide on the morning of the battle, and were killed in the fighting.

The **Talbot Botanic Gardens** (19 acres/7.5ha with 4 acres/1.5ha of walled garden) were largely created by Milo, the last Lord Talbot, between 1948 and 1973,

Malahide Castle

M Ivory/MICHELIN

who indulged his passion for plants from the southern hemisphere. The result is a superb collection of trees and shrubs arranged around luscious lawns.

The **Fry Model Railway Museum** (⏱open Apr–Sept, Mon–Thu, Sat 10am–1pm, 2pm–5pm, Sun, Bank Hols 1pm–5pm; €7.25; ☎01 846 3779; www.visitdublin.ie, www.malahidecastle.com) displays model engines and rolling stock made by Cyril Fry of Dublin; there is also information on the development of railways in Ireland and a huge O-gauge model railway incorporating replicas of various railway stations.

Tara's Palace and Childhood Museum (⏱open Easter–Sept Mon–Fri 10.45am–4.45pm, Sat–Sun and Bank Hols 11.30am–5.30pm; €2; ☎01 846 3779; www.visitdublin.ie) features one of the world's finest dolls houses, which re-creates the grandeur and elegance of three great 18C Irish mansions in miniature.

Newbridge House★

10mi/16km north of Dublin by M 1 and a minor road east to Donabate. Tour (45min) Apr–Sept: Tue–Sat 10am–1pm, 2pm–5pm; Sun, Bank Hols noon–6pm. Oct–Mar, Sat–Sun & Bank Hols, noon–5pm. €7 (House); €3.80 (Farm). ☎01 843 6534/6530. www.fingalcoco.ie.

George Semple's early-18C Georgian country house, on the edge of Donabate, is set in extensive grounds, and is one of the finest remaining examples in Ireland of a landscaped park. It has been the home of the Cobbe family since c 1740 when it was built for Charles Cobbe, who came to Ireland in 1717 as Chaplain to the Lord Lieutenant, and rose to become Archbishop of Dublin (portrait in the hall). Much of the interior has remained unchanged for centuries: some original furniture was made by Dublin craftsmen; the **stucco** and **plasterwork (**18C–early 19C) is superb. The **Red Drawing Room**, added c 1760, preserves the wallpaper, curtains and carpet fitted in 1820. The family **museum** (1790), decorated in Chinese style is intriguing, crammed with souvenirs, trophies, and exotica brought back from foreign travels.

Traditional Farm – A museum of traditional rural life is presented in the outbuildings – dairy (19C), dwelling,

carpenter's shop, forge, stables and coach house. Domestic animals live in the paddocks; the large walled garden was converted to an orchard during the Second World War.

Ardgillan Castle

22mi/35km north of Dublin by M 1 and a minor road east to Balbriggan. ⏱Open Apr–Sept, Tue–Sun & Bank Hols, 11am–6pm; third week Dec–Jan, Sun, 2pm–4pm. Rest of year, Wed–Sun & Bank Hols, 11am–pm. Guided tour available. €6. ☎01 849 2212. www.iol.ie/~cybmanmc.

On the coast north of Skerries stands the Georgian country house acquired in 1737 by the Taylor family, descendants of Thomas Taylor, a professional surveyor, who had come to Ireland from Sussex in 1650 to work on the **Down Survey**.

The elegant interiors contain mementoes and furniture of the Taylor family. Kitchens, larder and scullery occupy the extensive basement, and on the upper floor there is a excellent exhibition on the Down Survey. Beyond the rose gardens are the walled gardens, laid out with lawns, flowers and vegetables in geometric plots. The west front is screened by Irish yew trees.

Skerries Mills

20mi/32km north of Dublin by M 1 and R 127. Visit by guided tour only, 10.30am–4.30pm (3.30pm Oct–Mar ⏱Closed Good Fri, 20 Dec–1 Jan. €6. ☎01 849 5208. www.skerriesmills.org.

The Down Survey

The confiscation and redistribution of almost half the land in Ireland during the Cromwellian Settlement involved the preparation of accurate maps: these were provided by **Sir William Petty** and his team of surveyors over 13 months (1655–6). This exercise, known as the Down Survey, has no connection with Co Down, but was so called because the results were set down on maps rather than in the more usual tabulated form. Several sets of maps were individually drawn and coloured; while at sea between Dublin and London in 1707 the Petty set was captured by the French.

This rare survival of 17C–19C industrial technology comprises a watermill, two windmills (one with five sails and one with four), mill races, a mill pond and a wetlands. The mills have been restored to working order.

Swords (Sord)
8mi/14km north of Dublin by M 1.
The bustling county town has a history going back to the 6C when St Columba founded a monastery on a low hilltop now marked by the Anglican church, a 9C **round tower** and a 12C **Norman tower**. At the northern end of the town stand the substantial remains of **Swords Castle** (&open Mon–Fri 10am–noon, 1pm–4pm (Fri 3pm); 01 890 5629; www. fingalcoco.ie), the summer palace of the Archbishops of Dublin.

Lusk Heritage Centre
13mi/21km north of Dublin by M 1 and R 127 to Lusk. (Dúchas) Open mid-Jun–mid-Sept, Fri 10am–5pm (4.15pm last admission). €1.20. 01 843 7683.
The tower of an Anglican church, which incorporates an earlier round tower, houses a display about the 5C monastery founded here and its star feature, the magnificent 16C effigy tomb of Sir Christopher Barnewall and his wife Marion Sharl, almost unique in Ireland at this early date (1589).

GALWAY ★★

POPULATION 57 241

The largest town in the west of Ireland bestrides the Corrib River as it enters Galway Bay. Galway (Gaillimh) has grown from a medieval core of narrow streets into a buzzing cathedral and university city sustained by modern industries and a thriving port. It is also well placed as a centre for excursions westwards into the wild mountainous country of Connemara while east and south lies the fertile Galway plain. This location, together with the city's own dynamic character, draws cosmopolitan crowds of visitors to its busy streets, which take on an almost Mediterranean air when the summer sun contrives to shine.

- **Information:** Forster Street; 091 537 700. Salthill; 091 520 500. www.galway.net. Tuam; 093 25486 *or* 24463; www.tuam-guide.com.
- **Orient Yourself:** Galway is located roughly half way along the west coast at the head of Galway Bay with Connemara north and The Burren south. Due west are the Aran Islands, and then America! Take the O'Neachtain Galway Sightseeing open-top hop-on hop-off bus tour to get your bearings (€11, pay on the bus or at the tourist office).
- **Especially for Kids**: Atlantaquaria, Glengowla Mine.
- **Don't Miss:** One of Galway's major festivals; Lough Corrib.
- **Also See:** ARAN ISLANDS, ATHENRY, THE BURREN, CONG, CONNEMARA.

A Bit of History

City of the Tribes – The Anglo-Normans were attracted by the sheltered anchorage strategically located midway along Ireland's western coast. The city was founded on the east bank of the river in the 12C by the de Burgo (later Burke) family, who encouraged immigration from England and Wales. Defensive walls were built and Galway prospered on trade with France, Spain and the West Indies. As an Anglo-Norman enclave in the midst of an often hostile region, the city excluded the native Irish who had their own settlement outside the walls. Cromwell called this oligarchy of Anglo-Norman families who controlled the city from the 15C onwards "the Tribes of Galway" and the name lives on. Prosperity did not, however, survive the religious disputes of the Reformation and their political consequences. After two lengthy sieges – by the Cromwellians in

Galway Bay

The Irish romance of Galway Bay is famously alluded to in the Pogues' evergreen Christmas song *Fairytale of New York,* in the line, *the boys of the NYPD choir were singing Galway Bay.* This is most probably a reference to the traditional song *Galway Bay* by Arthur Colahan :

If you ever go across the sea to Ireland,
Then maybe at the closing of your day,
You will sit and watch the moon rise over Claddagh
And see the sun go down on Galway Bay.

1652 and by William of Orange's forces in 1691 – Galway went into decline.

The Claddagh – Long before the arrival of the Normans, an Irish-speaking community with its own traditions and elected leader, known as the King, thrived in a fishing village on the west bank of the Corrib River. Its name – the Claddagh – derived from the Gaelic *cladach* meaning a rocky or pebbly shore. The men fished by night, and the women sold the catch on the Spanish Parade. The picturesque scattered whitewashed thatched cottages were replaced in the 1930s by a modern housing scheme. The Claddagh finger ring, formed by a heart held by two clasped hands, is popular throughout Ireland.

Gaelic Galway – The city adjoins the most extensive Gaelic-speaking region in Ireland: the Aran Islands, Connemara and the Joyce Country. The 19C revival of interest in the language drew many visitors to the region; two of the oldest Gaelic summer schools were founded at the turn of the century at Spiddal *(west)* and Tormakeady on the west shore of Lough Mask. Since the establishment of the Republic, the Gaelic character of the region has been reinforced: University College, Galway, founded in 1849 as Queen's College, was made a bilingual institution in 1929. Today it is an important centre for Gaelic culture with a state-sponsored Irish Theatre *(Taibhdhearc na Gaillimhe)* launched by Micheál Mac Liammóir and his partner Hilton Edwards. In 1969 the offices of the Gaelic Development Authority were moved to Furbogh (Na Forbacha – *5mi/8km west of Galway by R 336)* and in 1972 Gaelic Radio began operating from Costelloe (Casla – *further west by R 336).*

Literary Galway – Galway city and its environs have produced or fostered several literary personalities: Patrick O'Connor (1882–1928) wrote short stories in Gaelic, Nora Barnacle (1884–1951) lived in Bowling Green and married James Joyce, who with Frank Harris (1856–1931) were natives of the city. Violet Martin, the second half of the Somerville and Ross partnership, lived at Ross House on the west shore of Lough Corrib. In 1896 Edward Martyn, who lived at Tullira Castle in south Galway, introduced William Butler Yeats to Lady Gregory; they co-founded the Irish Literary Theatre, which later became the Abbey Theatre in Dublin.

Walking Tour

Eyre Square

The focal point of the modern city, Eyre Square was officially renamed the **Kennedy Memorial Park** after the US President visited Galway in 1963, but its original name has always been in common use. The square underwent a major redevelopment, completed 2006, and incorporates a major shopping and leisure centre.

There are several monuments: the **Browne doorway** removed from a wealthy merchant's 17C town house; cannons from the Crimean War presented to the Connaught Rangers; and a statue of **Liam Mellows**, a Sinn Féin politician who took part in the 1916 Easter Rising and was executed by the Free State army during the Civil War.

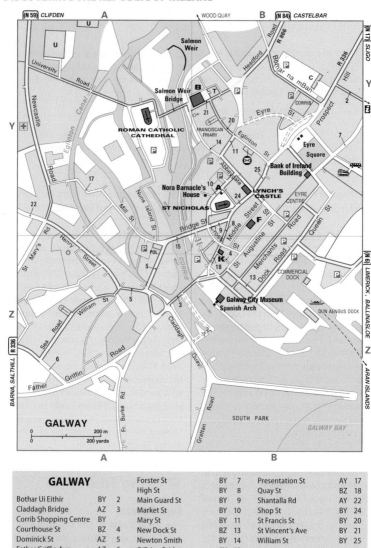

GALWAY

▶ *From Eyre Square turn left into William Street.*

Lynch's Castle

This splendid 16C mansion belonged to the most powerful of the 14 "tribes". The grey stone façade has some fine carved gargoyles, hood mouldings over the windows, and medallions with the family crest (the lynx) and one with the arms of Henry VII.

▶ *Continue into Shop Street.*

St Nicholas' Church★

The collegiate church dedicated to St Nicholas of Myra, the patron saint of sailors, is said to be the largest medieval church in Ireland still in use today. Recent research claims that Christopher Columbus visited the church in 1477, during a stay in the area probably prompted by

Address Book

♿ *For coin ranges, see the Legend on the cover flap.*

GETTING AROUND

Galway Airport at Carnmore
(3.7mi/6km SE of Galway via the N17).
☎091 755 569. www.galwayairport.com.

SIGHTSEEING

Boat trips to Lough Corrib
(♿see Driving Tour) – Corrib Cruises operates various options between Cong, Inchagoill Island, Oughterard and Ashford Castle. ☎092 46029 or 46292 or 091 552808. www.corribcruises.com. Services to the **Aran Islands** by air (☎091 593 034, www.aerarannislands.ie) and by sea (☎091 568 903. www.aranislandferries.com).

WHERE TO STAY

◯◯**Adare Guest House** – *9 Father Griffin Place.* ☎91 582 638. Adare@iol.ie. This three-storey guesthouse west of the river Corrib lies in a quiet residential area near Wolf Tone Bridge. A cheery breakfast room and modern bedrooms with orthopaedic beds and pine furniture make for a relaxing stay.

◯◯**Spanish Arch Hotel** – *Quay Street.* 20rm. ☎091 569 600. www.spanisharch hotel.ie. Former 16C Carmelite convent in times past: busy hotel with organic restaurant and popular bar featuring live music nightly including traditional Irish music sessions.

◯◯◯◯**The G Hotel** – *Wellpark,* ☎091 865200. www.theghotel.ie Designed by renowned milliner, Philip Treacy, a native of Galway, this ultra-glamorous luxury boutique hotel was the talk of Ireland when unveiled in 2006 and remains one of Ireland's most beautiful and trendy places to stay. Its restaurant, Riva (◯◯◯◯), offering contemporary Italian cuisine with some international favourites, is equally sensational.

WHERE TO EAT

◯◯**Nimmo's/Ard Bia**– *Spanish Arch, Long Walk.* ☎87 236 8648 or 091 539 897. www.ardbia.com. This personally run award-winning cafe-restaurant with a bohemian edge has recently moved a few yards but is still located in the heart of the city in the "Latin Quarter". Good value, refreshingly simple, un-fussy dishes utilising quality local produce.

ENTERTAINMENT

Druid Theatre – *Flood Street.* ☎091 568 660. www.druidtheatre.com. Ground-breaking productions of classic and new dramatic works.
Irish Theatre (An Taibhdhearc na Gaillimhe), *Middle Street.* Stages Irish productions (music, singing, dancing and folk drama). ☎091 563600/562024. www.antaibhdhearc.com (in Gaelic only).

SPORTS AND LEISURE

Galway Bay Sailing Club – ☎091 794 527. www.gbsc.ie. Cruiser sailing, dinghy sailing, windsurfing.
Bow Waves Sailing & Powerboat School – ☎091 560 560. www.bow waves.com. Power and sail.

EVENTS AND FESTIVALS

Galway is famous as Ireland's festival town, with more events than any other provincial town and of a quality and size that rival even the largest festivals in Dublin and Belfast.

For details of the **Oyster Festival**, the **Hookers Regatta Festival** (a hooker is a type of local boat), the famous **Arts Festival** the **Jazz Festival** and the children's **Baboro Festival** ♿ see Calendar of Events.

In addition to these events is **Galway Races** (*seven consecutive days starting from the last Monday in July. www.galwayraces.com*). One of the world's top horse-racing meetings it features Ladies Day Mad Hatters Day and all sorts of other race-related fun

Rather more laid back is the **Film Fleadh** (*July, www.galwayfilmfleadh.com*) and the **Galway Early Music Festival** (*mid May, www.galway earlymusic.com*).

Spanish Arch, Galway

R Holzbachova, Ph Benet/MICHELIN

the legendary voyage of St Brendan to the New World (👆*see ENNIS*).

The **exterior** has gargoyles and carved mouldings; the **interior** includes a medieval water stoup, a font and numerous tombstones.

Around the corner on Market Street, behind the church, is the city's famous **Lynch Memorial**, on the site of the old jail. It commemorates the drastic action of Judge James Lynch. In the 1490s, in a fit of jealousy, his son, Walter, murdered a Spaniard who was a guest in their household. This was a heinous crime, given the duty of care, and Walter was sentenced to death. However the boy was very popular locally and an appeal was made on his behalf by the townsfolk, who refused to execute him. His father consequently took the law into his own hands and hanged Walter himself, from the jail window. A skull and crossbones carved into the stone below the window marks the spot. It is claimed that this is where the term "lynching" originated.

▶ *Walk round to the north side of the Church and into Mary Street.*

Nora Barnacle's House

🕐*Open mid-May–mid-Sept Mon–Sat 10am–1pm, 2pm–5pm.* 👝€2.50 ☎091 564 743. www.norabarnacle.com.

Nora Barnacle, the wife of James Joyce, lived in this Cottage before she moved to work in Dublin, where she met and married Joyce; letters, souvenirs, photos.

▶ *Walk south along Mary Street; continue into Cross Street; turn right into Quay Street and left at the end.*

Spanish Arch

The arch, recalling the city's links with Spain, may have been part of a bastion, incorporating four blind arches, one of which was opened in the 18C to give access to a new dock beside Eyre's Long Walk. Part of the medieval **town wall** (20yd/20m long) is visible on the south side, as are the tidal quays of 1270.

Galway City Museum

👆🕐*Open year-round daily 10am–5pm (closed Sun–Mon Oct–May).* ☕. ☎091 536 597. www.galwaycity.ie.

This striking modern complex, opened in 2006, is home to imaginative exhibitions relating to the history of Galway City. Suspended in the atrium is the Galway City hooker (local fishing boat), *Máirtín Oliver*. Other highlights are the city corporation Irish-made **sword and mace**★ and the statue by Albert Power RHA of **Patrick O'Connor** (Padraic O Conaire 1882–1928) and a rare 17C altar piece.

▶ *Return to the south end of Quay Street; turn left into a narrow lane; turn left into Bridge Street; turn right into Nuns Island Street.*

Roman Catholic Cathedral★

The huge neo-Romanesque cathedral, dedicated to Our Lady Assumed into Heaven and St Nicholas, was designed by John J Robinson in 1957 and defies all the precepts of architectural modernism. It is built of black Galway "marble", the local limestone. Above the altar in St Nicholas' Chapel *(east transept)* are early-17C carved stone plaques, rescued during the Cromwellian troubles from St Nicholas' Church.

Kirwan's Lane

Just off Quay Street, this is one of Galway's last remaining late-medieval lanes and has been recently redeveloped as a residential area. It was here that the Galway MP Richard Martin built a 100-seater theatre for his actress wife in 1783. Among the many famous people who trod the boards was the great republican patriot, Wolfe Tone.

Salmon Weir Bridge

The bridge was built in 1818 to link the old prison (1802–1939) on the cathedral site, with the **County Courthouse** (1812–15) where the Franciscan Abbey stood. Upstream is the **salmon weir**; beyond are the pontoons of the late 19C viaduct of the old Galway-Clifden railway.

Atlantaquaria   Kids

&. ⓒ*Open Mon–Fri 9am–5pm, Sat–Sun 9am–6pm.* ⓒ*Closed occasionally Nov–Feb Mon–Tue for tank maintenance.* ⬤*€9; child €5.50.* ▭. ☎*091 585 100. www. nationalaquarium.ie.*
On the seafront promenade of Salthill, this is Ireland's National Aquarium, home to the country's largest display of indigenous marine and fresh water life. Highlights are the touch pools and (in a quite separate area) conger eels, weighing up to 30kg.

Excursions

Annaghdown Church and Priory
12mi/20km north of Galway via the N 84; in Cloonboo turn left to Annaghdown.
St Brendan of Clonfert founded this convent for his sister: the existing 15C Cathedral incorporates earlier decorated stonework, including a fine doorway and window (c 1200).
The middle church is the oldest part (11C or 12C). The ruined priory *(west of the graveyard)* is a good example of a fortified monastery, built c 1195.

Tuam
20mi/32km northeast of Galway via the N 17.
The tiny city of Tuam, boasting two cathedrals, is the ecclesiastical capital of Connaught and the market centre for northern Co Galway. In the 12C, when the O'Connor kings of Connaught were High Kings of Ireland, it was virtually the capital of the whole country. Its present layout, with all the streets converging on the central diamond, dates from 1613, when it was given borough status by King James I.

St Mary's Cathedral ★ stands in a walled enclosure, on the site of a monastery founded late in the 5C by Jarlath. The original cathedral dates from 1130, most of the present building however, including the hexagonal spire (200ft/61m), is the result of a neo-Gothic rebuild by Sir Thomas Deane (1860) around parts of the 12C Irish-Romanesque red sandstone chancel. The shaft of a high cross in the north aisle is inscribed with prayers for an O'Connor king.

The 14C building east of the cathedral, badly damaged by the Cromwellians, has been restored to its original castellated style to serve as a Synod Hall.

West of the town centre, Irish yews grow among the tombstones of **St Jarlath's Churchyard** and around the ruins of the 13C parish church, dedicated to Tuam's patron saint.

A 17C corn mill on a tributary of the Clare River *(west of North Bridge)* houses the **Mill Museum** (ⓒ*open May–Oct Mon–Fri 10am–5.30pm;* ⬤*donation requested;* ☎*093 24141, www.tuam-guide.com)* with three sets of mill-wheels driven by an undershot spur wheel. A video provides an insight into the history of Tuam and its locality.

The cruciform neo-Gothic **Roman Catholic Cathedral of the Assumption** (*093 24250 www.tuamparish.com* was one of the first major Roman Catholic places of worship to be built in the 19C, initiated in 1827, a year before the Emancipation Act set off a wave of church construction. Funds were subscribed by the local inhabitants, regardless of denomination. Its profusion of spikes and spires prompted one 19C tourist to memorably describe the sight of the cathedral as putting him "in mind of a centipede or a scorpion thrown on its back and clawing at the sky". The Stations of the Cross are 17C, the modern stained glass is from the Harry Clarke Studios.

Knockmoy Abbey★
20mi/32km northeast of Galway via the N 17 and N 63. In Knockmoy village turn left. After crossing the river turn right and park by the cemetery (15min walk there and back).

Set in fields on the north bank of the River Abbert are the substantial ruins of an abbey founded in 1189 for the Cistercians of Boyle by Cathal O'Connor, king of Connaught. The church, with nave, a transept with two chapels and **chancel**, has some fine stone carving and a 13C tomb niche. A grill protects a rare **fresco** (1400) of the medieval legend of the Three Live Kings (dressed for hawking), and the Three Dead Kings (the inscription reads "We have been as you are, you shall be as we are").

Driving Tour

Lough Corrib★★
17mi/27.5km northwest of Galway via the N 59.

Lough Corrib, the second-largest lake in Ireland (36mi/58km long), is dotted with islands and **drumlins**, including Inchagoill island, the site of a 5C monastery.

▶ *From Galway take the N 59 ; after 16mi/26km turn right (signposted).*

Aughnanure Castle★
5min wak (there and back) from the car park. (Dúchas) ⟶Tours (45 min) mid-Mar through Oct 9.30am–6pm (last admission 5.15pm). ⟶€2.90. ☎091 552 214. www.heritageireland.ie/en.

These formidable ruins of a tower house and bawn, probably built by Walter de Burgo, are defended but also undermined by the Drimneen River. The circular **watch tower** is all that remains of the original bawn wall. Most of the **Banqueting Hall** has collapsed into the river leaving the east wall with its Decorated windows. The **keep** rises through six storeys from a battered base to Irish-style crenellations with a machicolation on each side. From the roof there is a fine view of Lough Corrib.

▶ *Continue northwest on the N 59.*

Oughterard (Uachtar Ard)★
This attractive town on the west shore is famed for its excellent fishing.

The road north runs parallel to the shore to **Curraun** *(8mi/13km there and back)* where the **view**★★ of the lake and its backdrop of mountains is truly spectacular.

Beyond Oughterard *(2 mi/3km on N59)* you come to Ireland's only show mine, the **Glengowla Mine** (Kids ⟶*Underground tours, 55min, Mar–Nov 10am–6pm or 5.30pm in low season, every 20min in high season; ⟶€8. ☎091 552021 or 552360. http://glengowla.goegi.com).* This silver and lead mine reaches down 70ft/20m, and is complete with its original timbers and many other features. Mining started in 1851 and was suspended in 1865. During that short period, 545 square metres was "stopped" to produce 390 tonnes of lead containing 28 kilograms of silver. The underground tour explores large marble chambers and caverns studded with lead and silver pyrite, veins of calcite and quartz in addition to other precious materials. On the surface, the powder magazine, blacksmith's workshop and the agent's cottage have been restored and contain items rescued from the mine. A hand windlass and a horse-gin have been reconstructed.

GLENDALOUGH ★★★

POPULATION 1 695

This once-remote valley among the Wicklow Mountains where St Kevin sought solitude, and later founded a great monastery, has long been a place of pilgrimage. It continues to be one of Ireland's most popular sites and today attracts over one million visitors each year. Despite this, the "Glen of the Two Lakes" (Gleann Dá Locha) is one of the most evocative of all Irish monastic sites, both for the beauty of its setting and for the array of buildings left over from the early days of Christianity in Ireland.

- **Information:** ☎0404 45325/45352. www.heritageireland.ie/en.
- ▶ **Orient Yourself:** Glendalough stands 30mi S of Dublin in the Wicklow Mountains and can be reached by the coast route (M 11 and N 11 S to Ashford and R 763 to Annamoe, R 755 S to Laragh and R 756 W or by the inland route (N 7, N 81 and R 756); slower but more scenic routes take the road through the Sally Gap (R 115) or via Enniskerry, Roundwood and Annamore (R 117, R 760, R 755and R 756). From Dublin take **St Kevin's Bus Service**, which departs from Dawson St. on the north side of St Stephen's Green, daily 11.30am, returns 4.30pm (5.40pm Sun all year, and Sat Jul–Aug). ☞Return €18. ☎01 281 8119. www.glendaloughbus.com.
- ☺ **Don't Miss:** A tour of the monastic site. Bring a picnic; there is no food available on site.
- ☖ **Also See:** ATHY, KILDARE, WICKLOW MOUNTAINS.

A Bit of History

The monastery founded by St Kevin flourished long after his death (c 617), drawing pilgrims deterred from journeying to Rome by war and conflict: seven pilgrimages to Glendalough were said to be the equivalent of one to Rome. Despite repeated raids and destruction by the Vikings and Irish, the monastery enjoyed a golden age in the 10C and 11C, a period of Celtic revival. Glendalough also prospered under St Laurence O'Toole (1128–80), who became abbot in 1153 and Archbishop of Dublin in 1163. Decline began in the 13C and an English attack in 1398 caused much destruction. Dissolution followed during the reign of Henry VIII but the pilgrimages continued until disorderly behaviour caused their suppression in the 1860s.

The two lakes at Glendalough, once one stretch of water, are set in a beautiful valley shaped by an Ice Age glacier descending from the Wicklow Mountains. The splendidly-wooded southern shore of the Upper Lake, associated with St Kevin, is particularly striking, with cliffs (100ft/30m) dropping precipitously into the dark waters of the lake. For many years the area was mined, so the woods were cut to smelt the lead, zinc, iron, copper and silver ores. The Miners' Road, which runs along the northern shore of the lake to a deserted mining village at the top of the valley, provides the best view of St Kevin's Bed and the ruins of Temple-na-Skellig.

Walking Tour

The spacious modern **visitor centre** (*Dúchas ☖ ⊙open 9.30am–6pm (5pm mid-Oct–mid-Mar). Last admission 45min before closing. ⊙Closed 24–27 Dec. ☞ €2.90*) presents various displays including a fine model, based on Glendalough, of a typical medieval monastery complex. Old photographs show the site before and after restoration; a video narrates the history of monastic Ireland.

Monastic Site ★★★

The ruins of the later monastic settlement, east of the Lower Lake, form the most important part of the Glendalough

The Recluse and the Blackbird

St Kevin – Probably born sometime in the mid-6C, the young Kevin soon attracted attention for his ability to work miracles, but entrusted to the care of clerics, he instead sought solace from Nature, living in the hollow of a tree above the Upper Lake at Glendalough. Although he returned to his studies, he remained bewitched by Glendalough. The monastery in the lower part of the valley flourished under his leadership, until he retreated once more to the wilderness, living in complete solitude probably somewhere above the Upper Lake (Temple-na-Skellig). One story tells how a blackbird laid her egg in his hand as he stood in ascetic contemplation, his arms outstretched in the shape of the Cross, forcing him to remain there standing still *"in the sun and rain for weeks, until the young are hatched and fledged and flown."* (Seamus Heaney, *St Kevin and the Blackbird*).

site, approached through the gateway, an unique example to a monastic enclosure. Set in the wall just beyond the first of two arches is a great slab of mica schist with an incised cross, probably marking the point at which sanctuary would be granted to those seeking it.

The **Round Tower**★★ (100ft/30m high) is an iconic landmark probably constructed in the early 10C. It would have served as a six-storeyed storehouse, bell-tower, look-out and refuge: note how its entrance is some way above the ground (12ft/4m), and how the thick walls (3ft/1m at the base) taper slightly towards the top.

The roofless **Cathedral**★★, once the focal point of the community, continues to be a substantial presence on the site, its nave one of the widest of early Irish churches. Built in stages, perhaps from the late 10C, it consists of a nave and chancel with a small sacristy. Note the nave pilasters, the west doorway and south windows. A gravestone against the north chancel wall is carved with crosses and inscriptions in Irish; an adjacent slab has outstanding scroll designs.

St Kevin's Cross, the early, undecorated Celtic high cross (12ft/3.5m high) is the best preserved.

St Kevin's Church★★ is an early 11C Irish oratory with a high-pitched roof of overlapping stones. Its alternative popular name – St Kevin's Kitchen – was perhaps prompted by its unusual circular chimney-like tower or the scullery-like sacristy.

St Saviour's Priory★

The Priory (*east of the Lower Lake by the Green Road*) is said to have been founded by St Laurence O'Toole, Abbot of Glendalough, but may be earlier in

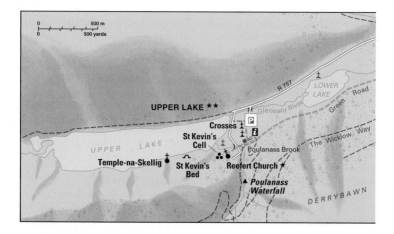

Glendalough

origin. The buildings (reconstructed in 1875), now enclosed in a forestry area, include a church nave and chancel with fine carving typical of the Irish Romanesque style.

Upper Lake★★

1.5mi/2.5km on foot west of the Visitor Centre by the Green Road, or 0.5mi/0.8km on foot from the Upper Lake car park. ⚠The way up to St Kevin's Cell is very steep in places.
The **crosses**, which originally marked the boundary of the monastic site on the east shore, were later used by pilgrims as Stations of the Cross.

Reefert Church★, set above the lake among oaks and hazels, is deemed to be the traditional burial place of kings, and maybe of St Kevin.

The roofless late 10C church has a plain but beautiful chancel arch, nave windows and an imposing granite doorway with sloping jambs.

Nothing remains of **St Kevin's Cell** save for a ring of foundation stones, colonised by three oak trees. His lonely abode was probably built with corbelled stones on the pattern of the beehive dwellings on Skellig Michael.

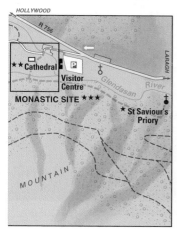

**St Kevin's Bed and
Temple-na-Skellig** *(○━No access.)*
The tiny cave known as **St Kevin's Bed**
(30ft/9m above the lake) was probably
a Bronze Age tomb. For as long as it was
believed to be where St Kevin would
come to pray and fast, it attracted pilgrims to Glendalough; after landing at
Temple-na-Skellig by boat, they would
walk along the lake shore and up the
steps hewn in the cliff, to be helped, one
by one, into the "bone-rock bed of the
austere saint" (Richard Hills).

The first church at **Temple-na-Skellig**
(about 20ft/6m above the lake) may
date from the time of St Kevin, though
the present ruins are probably 12C. The
huts of the earliest monastic community
are thought to have been in the raised
enclosure west of the church.

National Park Information Centre
Call in here to obtain information on the
various waymarked walking routes in
the valley (○*Open 10am–6pm or dusk
☎0404 45425*). Close by a path follows
the Lugduff Brook steeply upstream
to the lovely **Poulanass Waterfall** in
the woods.

KELLS★

POPULATION 2 183

This little market town, a designated Heritage Town in the valley of the River
Blackwater, owes its fame to the wonderful illuminated manuscript now in the
library of Trinity College.
Of the monastery from which the Book of Kells was taken there remain some
fascinating relics, while the town itself boasts a courthouse and a church designed
by the Georgian architect Francis Johnston.

- **Information:** Kells Heritage Centre, Navan Road.
  ☎046 9247840. www.meathtourism.ie.
- **Orient Yourself:** Kells is situated in the Irish Midlands, NW of Dublin on N 3.
- **Don't Miss:** The Round Tower and carved High Crosses.
- **Also See:** BOYNE VALLEY, CAVAN, DROGHEDA, DUNDALK, MULLINGAR, TRIM.

A Bit of History

The Book of Kells – The monastery at
Kells (Ceanannas Mór) was founded by
St Columba in the 6C. In the 9C his relics
were brought here by monks fleeing the
Viking raids on Iona. Even here they were
not secure and Kells itself was attacked
by the Vikings, by the native Irish in
the 12C, and by the Scotsman, Edward
Bruce in the 14C. The great illuminated
manuscript may have been produced at
Kells or brought here from Iona. In 1007
it was stolen from the sacristy but found
two months later minus its gold ornament. During Cromwell's campaigns, it
was taken to Dublin for safe keeping,
and presented to Trinity College in 1661
where it has stayed ever since.

UPPA/Photoshot/Trinity College, Dublin

Book of Kells

Sights

Round Tower and
High Crosses★★
St Columba's Church, Market Street.
♿ ⏰*Church open daily outside service times.* 🚶*Tours by arrangement with TIC.*
🅿 ☎*046 9247840, kellsheritagecentre@ eircom.net.*
Parts of the monastery survive in the grounds of **St Columba's Anglican Church**.
The **round tower**, built before 1076, has lost its conical cap, but still rises to an impressive height (100ft/30m). A number of well-weathered heads adorn the doorway.
Next to the tower stands the **South Cross**, considered to be from the 9C. The lively biblical scenes, among the interlacing, foliage, birds and animals include Daniel in the Lions' Den, the Three Children in the Fiery Furnace, Cain and Abel and Adam and Eve; the Sacrifice of Isaac, St Paul and St Antony in the desert, David with his harp, the miracle of the loaves and fishes, the Crucifixion and Christ in Judgement. South of the church stands an unfinished cross with raised panels ready to be carved and the Crucifixion.
Detailed information about the monastery, the crosses, the Kells Crozier (in the British Museum) and the Book of Kells is displayed in the gallery of the church.

St Columba's House★
⏰*Key available: enquire at the Heritage Centre.*
Higher up the lane stands a beautifully preserved ancient stone oratory with a steep corbelled stone roof, probably from the 11C/12C. The original entrance is visible in the west wall; the intervening floor is missing; between the ceiling vault and the steep roof there is a tiny chamber *(access by ladder)*.

Kells Heritage Centre
Old Courthouse, Navan Road. ⏰*Open May–Sept, Mon–Sat 10am–5.30pm, Sun, Bank Hols noon–6pm; Oct–Apr Mon–Sat 10am–5pm.* 👓€4. ☎ *046 9247840. kellsheritagecentre@eircom.net.*
If you have not had the opportunity to see the real thing, the centre holds a per-

Dark Ages Missionary
St Kilian was born in the 7C in Mullagh, Co Cavan and was educated at the monastic school in Rosscarbery in Co Cork. As a pilgrim for Christ, he went to Würzburg in Franconia to make Christian converts. Legend has it that he disapproved of the local ruler, Gozbert (one of his converts) marrying his brother's wife. As a result he had St Kilian beheaded. In 782 his remains were moved to Marienberg.

fect (modern) copy of the Book of Kells. Artefacts on loan from the National Museum, touch screens, models and a video all shed light on the monastery and history of the locality.

Excursions

St Kilian's
Heritage Centre, Mullagh
8mi/13km north of Kells by R 164. ⏰*Open Easter–Oct Tue–Fri 10am–6pm, Sat–Sun, Bank Hol Mon 2pm–6pm.* 👓€3. ☎*046 9242433.*
The centre celebrates the life of St Kilian (640–689), born in Mullagh, the "Apostle of the Franks" and patron saint of Würzburg. North of Mullagh stands a

Round Tower and High Cross

Address Book

SHOPPING

Loughcrew Studio, Loughcrew Gardens (⚘ see Excursions) – Furnishings, carpets, fabrics; showrooms and workshop.

EVENTS AND FESTIVALS

Opera in Loughcrew Gardens – Two performances under canvas in late July, plus **Jazz** in late June. ☎49 85 41356. www.loughcrew.com.

O'Carolan Harp Festival – This festival of traditional music is held annually at Nobber (9mi/15km NE by N 52 and R 162). Late-Sept/early-Oct Fri–Sun. ☎46 905 2115. www.nobberfest.com.

ruined church known as Kilian's church (Teampall Ceallaigh). People still pray at his holy well, although formal observances ended early in the 19C.

Castlekeeran High Crosses

5mi/8km west of Kells by R 163; after 3mi/5km turn right at the crossroads. Through the farmyard and across the field and stile.

The graveyard has three undecorated early crosses which pre-date the scriptural crosses at Kells; beside the yew tree stands an Ogham Stone. They mark the site of an early monastery which grew up around the hermitage of Kieran, a monk from Kells.

Ballinlough Castle Gardens

3mi/5km W of Kells by R 163 to Ballinlough. ♿☉Open May–Sept Sat–Sun, noon–6pm by arrangement. ⬅€6. ☎046 9433268, www.ballinloughcastle.ie.

Set in extensive parkland, Ballinlough Castle (not open) has been continuously inhabited by the O'Reilly/Nugent family since the Middle Ages. Its present appearance reflects the late 18C idea of what a castle should look like. Its complex of walled gardens, rescued from dereliction, are expertly planted for maximum contrast.

Loughcrew Historic Gardens

15mi/24km from Kells by R 163 and R 154 and a minor road west to Millbrook. ☉Open Apr–Sept 12.30pm–6pm; Oct–Mar Sun, Bank Hols 1pm–5pm. ⬅€7. ⬚. ☎049 85 41356; www.loughcrew.com.

The gardens are an extraordinary palimpsest of ruins, earthworks, and ancient avenues, once owned by the Plunkett family – including Saint Oliver Plunkett. Around the church (roofless) extends the skeleton of an early 17C formal garden with an avenue of venerable yew trees leading to a medieval motte. Close by are the foundations of the original Loughcrew House, replaced in the early 19C by an imposing neo-Classical mansion devised by Charles Cockerell, which has also disappeared, although its portico survives as a folly beyond the gardens.

Loughcrew Cairns★

15mi/24km west of Kells by R 163. Beyond Ballinlough bear right onto R 154. After 3mi/4.6km turn left; after 0.5mi/0.8km turn left again onto a narrow rough road. (Dúchas) ☉Open mid-Jun–Aug 10am–6pm. ☎01 647 6916/6915. www.heritageireland. ie/en. ⬚Steep climb to Cairn.

Far less famous than the Neolithic tombs of the Boyne valley, the passage graves prominently sited on the Loughcrew Mountains, are almost as impressive. The cemetery covers the adjoining peaks, Cairnbane East and Cairnbane West, and Slieve na Calliagh (908ft/277m). There are at least 30 graves, some of which have been excavated, most dating from 2500–2000 BC. In 1943, however, excavations in Cairn H on Cairnbane West uncovered objects bearing Iron Age La Tène style decoration. Inside **Cairn T** (120ft/37m in diameter), the largest grave, lies a cruciform chamber, a corbelled roof and concentric circles, zigzag lines and flower motifs some of the most beautiful examples of Neolithic art in Ireland. During the Vernal and Autumn Equinox crowds gather at dawn in Cairn T to watch sunlight enter the chamber and illuminate the inside of the tomb.

KENMARE ★
POPULATION 1 420

This small market town, designated a Heritage Town, proclaims itself "The Jewel on the Ring of Kerry". It is charmingly set in a horseshoe of mountains at the point where the Roughty River widens into the long sea-inlet known as the Kenmare River. Kenmare (Neidín) is a popular tourist centre, with a wide range of hotels and restaurants and elegant shops (jewellery, linen, delicatessen, books) catering for visitors from many countries, many of whom use it as a starting point for explorations of the Beara and Iveragh peninsulas.

- **Information:** Fair Green, Kenmare; ☎064 42615 (seasonal). Glengariff; ☎027 63084 (seasonal). www.kenmare.com.
- **Orient Yourself:** Kenmare is located on N 71, a scenic road between Killarney and Glengarriff, and is a good place to stay while exploring Co Kerry.
- **Don't Miss:** Glen Inchaquin Park and the Ring of Beara.
- **Also See:** BANTRY, CORK, KILLARNEY.

Town Centre

Kenmare is an 18C planned town shaped like a cross, sponsored by the first Marquess of Lansdowne.

Its two streets, lined with neat stone houses, meet at a triangular space intended to serve as a market-place and now a park. The town's real origin, however, goes back to the energetic Sir William Petty (1623–87), organiser of the Down Survey (*see FINGAL*) who encouraged immigration from England and Wales, founded ironworks, and astutely acquired property to the extent that he eventually owned around a quarter of Kerry.

Kenmare Heritage Centre

&. ⊙ *Open Easter–Oct, 9.15am–5pm (9am–7pm mid-Jun–Aug)* ☎064 41233. The centre traces the history of Kenmare, originally called Nedeen (*Neidín* in Irish), the local impact of the Famine and the story of the Nun of Kenmare, a member of the community which established the lace-making industry in the 19C.

Lace and Design Centre

⊙ *Open mid-Apr–Oct, 10am–1pm, 2.15pm–5.30pm; Nov–Apr by appointment, Mon–Sat 10.30am–1.30pm. Lace-making demonstrations.* ☎064 41491/42636. www.kenmarelace.ie. Displays of lace and lace-making.

H Champollion/MICHELIN

Kenmare

Address Book

♨*For coin ranges, see the Legend on the cover flap.*

GETTING AROUND

Garinish Island – Ferries *operate from Glengariff Mar–Oct.*
Blue Pool Ferry. €10. ☎027 63333. www.bluepoolferry.com.
Harbour Queen Ferry. ☎27 63116. www.harbourqueenferry.com. €12.
Note that there is also a €3.70 landing fee to visit the island.
Dursey Island Cable Car – *Operates from Ballaghboy year-round, Mon–Sat 9–11am, 2.30pm–5pm, 7pm–8pm; Sun 9–10.30am, 1pm–2.30pm, 4pm–5pm (Jun–Aug only), 7pm–8pm. Arrive 30min before departure.*
Bere Island Ferry – *Operates from Castletownbere and Bere Island third week Jun to third week Sept. Call for price and times.* ☎27 75009. www.bereisland ferries.com.
Driving tours – Kenmare Coach and Cab Co offer day trips round the Ring of Kerry, Ring of Beara and Garinish/Glan-gariff. *Jun–Aug 10am–5pm €25.* ☎064 41491. www.kenmarecoachandcab.com.

WHERE TO STAY

⊜⊜**The Rosegarden** – *0.75mi W by N 71 on N 70 (Sneem Road).* ☎064 42288. www.euroka.com/rosegarden. Open Mar–Oct. 8rm. Meals ⊜⊜. It would be hard to find more immaculately kept accommodation. The Dutch owners provide old-school hospitality; the bedrooms are colourful, bright and cheerful. A simple dinner menu is also provided.
⊜⊜ **Sea Shore Farm** – *Tubrid. 1mi. W by 71 on N 70 (Sneem Road). 6rm.* ☎064 41270. www.kenmare.eu/seashore. Open Mar–mid-Nov. This farmhouse B&B is set in grounds of 32 acres/13ha with excellent views of the river and Caha mountains. Comfortable bedrooms come in different colour schemes and bathrooms have power-showers.
⊜⊜⊜ **Sallyport House** – *0.25mi S on N 71.* ☎064 42066. www.sallyporthouse. com. Open Apr–Oct. 5rm. No children under 13. This elegant country house is laid out with lawns and trees, overlook-ing the harbour and with panoramic views of Kenmare Bay and surrounding mountain; impressive breakfast and very comfortable bedrooms. Antique pieces throughout.

WHERE TO EAT

⊜⊜ **D'Arcy's Oyster Bar and Grill** – *Main Street.* ☎064 41589. Closed Mon. Housed in a former bank this town-centre restaurant with rooms (⊜⊜) specialises in seafood on a Modern Irish menu. Striking contemporary bedrooms.
⊜⊜ **Packies** – *Henry Street.* ☎064 41508. Closed Sun and 24 Dec–Feb. One of the town's established buzzing dinner spots, with its flagstone flooring adding to the character. The menu fea-tures traditional Irish country cooking, adds a touch of contemporary cuisine and complements it with relaxed and welcoming service.
⊜⊜ **Mulcahys** – *16 Henry Street.* ☎064 42383. www.kenmarerestaurants. com/mulcahys. Closed Tue. The decora-tion of this modern restaurant features an assortment of Eastern banners and sculptures. The fusion of interna-tional cuisine with an oriental touch, particularly Japanese, using fresh Irish produce, makes for an eclectic menu.
⊜⊜**The Lime Tree** – *Shelburne Street.* ☎064 41225. www.limetreerestaurant. com. Open Apr–Oct. This elegant building has been converted from a 19C schoolhouse with such warm hospitality and outstanding modern Irish cooking, that few guests consider truancy. Local artists' work is for sale in the upstairs gallery.

SPORTS AND LEISURE

The Beara Way – Rarely rising above 1115ft/340m, these old roads and tracks form a loop (122mi/196km) round the Beara Peninsula that may be walked with moderate ease.

EVENTS AND FESTIVALS

Queen of the Sea Festival – Held in Castletownbere *(early Aug).*

Stone Circle

The prehistoric circle comprises one central stone and a ring of 15 upright stones.

Excursion

Glen Inchaquin Park★★

8mi/14km SW by R 571 and left turn into a single-track lane (5mi/8km). ◷*Open year round dawn–dusk.* ◉€4. ⌣.☎*064 84235 www.neidin.net/gleninchaquin.*
The lane leads into a remote landscape of mountains and lakes, clear streams, glorious sessile oak woodland and wild flowers (laid footpaths). At the head of the glen there is a farmhouse by a spectacular braided waterfall. The views down to the Kenmare River and McGillycuddy Reeks are spectacular.

Driving Tour

Ring of Beara★★

Round trip of 85mi/137km – 1 day.

The Beara peninsula projecting some 30mi/48km into the Atlantic, has some wild and beautiful mountain, moorland and coastal scenery.

▹ *From Kenmare take N 71 S and turn left beyond the Kenmare River.*

Caha Pass

Work on the Kenmare-Glengarriff road began around 1839, cutting across the **Caha Mountains**, providing great **views** of Glengarriff and Bantry Bay.

Glengarriff (An Gleann Garbh)★

Little more than a high street, Glengarriff has been a resort of international renown since the mid 19C, famed for its mild climate and exotic flora. The **Eccles Hotel**, built in 1833 as a coaching stage, accommodated Queen Victoria on her visit to south western Cork, and George Bernard Shaw wrote part of *St Joan* here en route to Garinish Island.
There are pleasant walks along the wooded shore of the Blue Pool in the northwest corner of Glengarriff Harbour.

Kenmare Lace

Kenmare lace is needlepoint lace introduced from Italy in the 17C. It is particularly difficult because it is worked in needle and thread (linen rather than cotton), according to designs drawn on parchment or glazed calico and outlined with skeleton threads: these are later removed, as is the backing. Raised point is created by using buttonhole stitches over cords or horsehair.

The best view of Glengarriff is from **Shrone Hill** (919ft/280m *southwest*).

Ilnacullin (Garinish Island) ★★

Access by Garinish Island Ferry (☞ see Address Book). (Dúchas) ◷*Open Mar–Oct, 10am–6.30pm (Sun from noon/1pm). Shorter hours Mar, Oct; longer hours Jun–Aug: see website for times.* ▧*Hiking trail (1hr 45min).* ◉€3.70. ⌣.✗.☎*027 63040. www.heritageireland.ie/en.*
Ilnacullin (or Ilaunacullin), also known as Garinish Island, (or Garnish Island), lies in Glengarriff Harbour. The English landscape designer Harold Peto turned it into a meticulously planned 37 acres/15ha garden for the Belfast-born MP, Annan Bryce. Italianate formality and Classical pavilions contrast well with the austere mountain backdrop and with the lush planting of exotic species. A path leads to the **Martello Tower**, which at 135ft/41m above sea-level is the highest point on the island.

Bamboo Garden

Glengarriff. ◷*Open daily 9am–7pm.* ◉€5. ⌣.☎*027 63975 or 63570. www.bamboo-park.com.*
The bamboo is ideally suited to the climate, so 30 different species and 12 types of palm thrive here. There are fine views of Glengarriff Harbour and Bantry Bay from the Tower and waterfront.

▹ *From Glengarriff take R 572 west; in Adrigole turn right (sign) to the Healy Pass.*

Healy Pass★★

The road is particularly steep near Glanmore Lake.

Opened in 1931, the road climbs through a series of tortuous hairpin bends *(7mi/11km)* to the summit; on a clear day there are **views**★★ of both shores of the peninsula.

The **Healy Pass** was named after Tim Healy, born in Bantry in 1855. Healy was a Nationalist MP at Westminster (1880-1916) before being appointed the first Governor-General of the Irish Free State (1922): at a presentation in the Anchor Bar, Bantry, on his retirement as Lord Chief Justice of Ireland, he was invited to choose a leaving present – he requested the bridleway over the mountains be improved.

Derreen Gardens★

Open Apr–Oct, 10am–6pm (Aug Fri–Sun only). ∞€6. ☕. ☎064 83588, www. castlesgardensireland.com/derreen-garden.html.

These lush mature gardens were planted by the fifth Lord Lansdowne beside Kilmakilloge Harbour, an inlet on the south shore of the Kenmare River. The woodland is richly underplanted with azaleas and rhododendrons, and rare New Zealand tree ferns.

▶ *Take R 571 W for 8mi/12.9km to the Ballycrovane junction.*

Ballycrovane Ogham Pillar Stone

∞ *Donation to enter the field.* In a field stands the tallest pillar stone in Ireland (15ft/5m high); the Ogham inscription – MAQI-DECCEDDAS AVI TURANIAS – of the son of Deich descendant of Torainn – was probably added later.

▶ *Continue W to Eyeries.*

Eyeries

This typical Irish mountain settlement is renown for its soft tangy cow's cheese.

▶ *Take R 575 W on the coast to Allihies.*

Allihies

The peninsula became known for its rich **copper mines**★, worked by a predominantly Cornish workforce, and bestowing prosperity on 19C Allihies. Old engine houses and spoil heaps are visible among the many invisible dangerous abandoned mineshafts. The **Allihies Copper Mine Museum** was opened in 2007 (*open Mon–Wed 10am–5pm, Thu–Fri 10am–pm, 2pm–5pm. Sat–Sun noon–5pm. WInter, Sat–Sun only, noon–5pm.* ☕.

Ballydonegan Strand *(1mi/1.6km south)* is a beautiful golden sand beach made of crushed stone from the mines.

▶ *Continue S on R 575; after 2.5mi/4.2km turn right onto R 572.*

Garnish Bay (Garinish Bay)

At low tide, you can walk from the tiny hamlet to **Garnish (Garinish) Island**, a good vantage-point for **views**★ *(north)* of the Iveragh Peninsula and *(northwest)* of the Skellig Islands.

▶ *Continue W to Dursey Island.*

Dursey Island

Access by cable-car (see Address Book).

The island's isolation was broken when Ireland's only cable railway was strung across the strait in 1970, capable of carrying six passengers, or a cow and its minder! Dursey, 4mi/6km long, has one village, Kilmichael, one road, and large nesting colonies of birds.

▶ *Return E; after 1.5mi/2.4km turn right to Crow Head.*

Crow Head

The bleak headland provides a fine view of Mizen Head *(south)* and the Skellig Islands.

▶ *Continue E on R 572; after 6mi/9.7km a road turns left to the Slieve Miskish Mountains (suitable only for climbers). After 1mi/1.6km turn right to Dunboy Castle (0.5mi/0.8km).*

Dunboy Castle

Surrounded by woods are the remains of this star-shaped castle, the last O'Sullivan stronghold to resist the English in 1602. Nearby is the vast shell of Puxley's Castle, part French château, part Italian villa, burned down by the IRA in 1921. It was built by the Puxley family from their Beara copper mines wealth. The history of the family and the mines inspired Daphne du Maurier to write *Hungry Hill*.

▶ *Continue east on R 572 to Castletownbere.*

Castletownbere

The town prospered in the early 19C when rich copper deposits were discovered at Allihies but was badly affected by the potato famine. By the late 19C, it had become an important fishing port: today fish processing is a substantial industry.

▶ *Pass the ferry to Bere Island. Take R 572 east to return to Glengarriff and N 71 north to return to Kenmare.*

KILDARE★

POPULATION 4 278

Kildare (Cill Dara) is intimately associated with the nearby Curragh; the extensive plain covered in short springy turf and famous for horse racing and breeding. This neat little county, cathedral and Heritage town, traces its origins to the 5C religious community founded by St Brigid and St Conleth, which was one of the few convents for women in the Celtic period.

🛈 **Information:** Market House. ☎045 530672. www.kildare.ie/kildareheritage. www.eastcoastmidlands.ie.
▶ **Orient Yourself:** Kildare is situated on the main road (N 7) leading southwest from Dublin to Limerick.
⊛ **Don't Miss:** A visit to the Irish National Stud.
⚿ **Also See:** ABBEYLEIX, ATHY, MAYNOOTH, MULLINGAR, ROSCREA, TULLAMORE, WICKLOW MOUNTAINS.

Sights

Cathedral★

🕔*Open Mon–Sat 10am–1pm, 2pm–5pm. Sun 2pm–5pm.* ⊛*Cathedral €1.50, Round Tower €4.*

Kildare Cathedral is a late-19C building incorporating 13C sections, a medieval stone font, stained-glass windows, and a number of tombs with effigies, including the superb figure of Bishop Wellesly dating from around 1539.

Beside the cathedral stands a **round tower** (108ft/30m high – the tallest scalable tower in Ireland) which has been substantially restored in recent years. Opposite, a small road leads to **St Brigid's shrine** and **well**.

Kildare Heritage Centre

♿🕔*Open May–Sept, Mon–Sat 9.30am–5.30pm; Oct–Apr, Mon–Fri 10am–5pm.* ⊛ *€1.* ☎*045 530672. www.kildare.ie/kildareheritage.*

The history and heritage of Kildare are clearly described by video and story boards in the beautifully restored 18C Market House, which also acts as the tourist office.

Address Book

SIGHTSEEING

Canal Barge trips in summer from the **Old Canal Hotel**, Robertstown (⚿*see Excursions; call for details,* ☎*045 890 450*); cruisers for hire from **Lowtown Marina**.

SPORTS AND LEISURE

The **Curragh Racecourse** hosts all five Irish Classic **horse races** including The Irish Derby and 16 other racedays. ☎*045 441205. www.curragh.ie.*

Penned thoroughbred at the Irish National Stud

Excursions

Irish National Stud and Japanese Gardens★★

1mi/1.5km SE of Kildare (sign) at Tully. ♿ ⊙Open mid-Feb–23 Dec, 9.30am (10am from mid-Nov) to 5pm. Last admission 3.30pm. ⬦Guided tours of Stud available (35min). ✆€10. ⎚. ☎045 52 1617. www.irish-national-stud.ie.

Lord Wavertree, a wealthy Scotsman from a brewing family, began breeding horses at Tully in 1900; in 1915 he gave his stud to the British Crown and it continued as the British National Stud until it was handed over to the Irish Government in 1943.

The **Irish Horse Museum** traces the story of horse racing in Ireland and contains the skeleton of Arkle, an outstandingly successful racehorse during the 1960s. A stroll down the **Tully Walk** is a good idea to see any mares and foals that might be out and about, and In the main yard, a video shows "Birth of a Foal", made on the Stud.

The grounds contain a large lake, created by **Eida**, and the ruins of the **Black Abbey**, founded as a preceptory of the Knights Hospitaller of St John after the Anglo-Norman invasion of Ireland in 1169. According to tradition it is connected by a tunnel (1mi/1.5km) to Kildare Cathedral. When the abbey was suppressed in the mid 16C, it passed into the possession of the Sarsfield family, of which **Patrick Sarsfield** was leader of the Irish at the Siege of Limerick.

Among the most ambitious of their kind outside Japan, the **Japanese Gardens** were created for Lord Wavertree between 1906 and 1910 by the Japanese gardener Eida and his son Minoru. The main garden depicts the story of the life of man, beginning with the **Gate of Oblivion** and the **Cave of Birth**, continuing across the bridges of engagement and marriage to the **Hill of Ambition** and the **Well of Wisdom**. Formerly the concluding feature, the **Gateway to Eternity** now leads into the **Garden of Eternity** (1974) and onto the **Zen meditation garden** (1976) where visitors might pause for contemplation.

St. Fiachra's Garden, which celebrates the patron saint of gardeners re-creates the type of natural environment to that which inspired the spirituality of the monastic movement in Ireland during the 6C and 7C. Seeking to capture the power of the Irish landscape in it's rawest state, this rock and water garden is within a natural setting of woodlands, wetlands, lakes and islands and features monastic cells of fissured limestone surrounded by water.

Bog of Allen Nature Centre

12mi/19km N by R 401 and R 414 at Lullymore. ♿ ⊙Open Mon–Fri, 10am–5pm (occasional Sun, call for dates) ⊙Closed Bank hols and Christmas. ✆€5. ⎚. ☎045 860133. www.ipcc.ie.

Bog Allen is the largest complex of raised bog in Ireland. As the visitor centre will tell you, 90 per cent of this fragile ecosystem has been lost through drainage and mining over the past four centuries.

Hill of Allen
6mi/10km N by R 415.
The summit of a 19C tower (676ft/206m) provides **views** of the vast Bog of Allen stretching west to the Shannon.

Robertstown (Inis Robertaig)
10mi/16km N by R 415.
The village is strategically located where the Grand Canal divides bound for Waterford and the Shannon. The waterfront is dominated by the stately red-brick Grand **Canal Hotel**, built in 1803 to serve the passengers on the flyboats.

Punchestown Standing Stone
15mi/24km E by N 7 to Naas and R 411.
North of the famous racecourse stands a granite long stone (20ft/6m high) which is thought to date from the early Bronze Age.

Kilcullen
7mi/11km east by R 413.
The **Hide Out Bar** has a bizarre relic: the black and withered right arm of prize-fighter Dan Donnelly (1786–1820), who won a spectacular bout on the The Curragh on 13 December 1815.

KILKENNY

POPULATION 8 507

Kilkenny (Cill Chainnigh) is Ireland's outstanding medieval city, set on the banks of the River Nore and dominated by the castle and cathedral. Narrow alleys, known locally as slips, recall the medieval street pattern. The city's historical legacy, splendidly expressed in any number of well-restored ancient buildings, is matched by a strong cultural and artistic tradition.

- **Information:** Shee Alms House, Rose Inn Street. ☎056 7751500. www.kilkennytourism.ie/eng. www.southeastireland.com.
- **Don't Miss:** Castle, Design Centre, St Canice's Cathedral, Jerpoint Abbey.
- **Organising Your Time:** Kilkenny is a good base to explore southeast Ireland.
- **Also See:** ABBEYLEIX, CAHER, CASHEL, CLONMEL, ENNISCORTHY, NEW ROSS, ROSCREA.

A Bit of History

Capital of the Kingdom of Ossory – The city is named after St Canice, the 6C founder of a church here, in what was, from the 2C to the 12C, the capital of the Gaelic Kingdom of Ossory, mainly ruled by the MacGiolla Phadruig family who constantly struggled for the kingship of Leinster.

Statutes of Kilkenny – Following the Anglo-Norman invasion (12C), Kilkenny quickly assumed strategic and political importance as a major venue for Anglo-Irish parliaments. Under Anglo-Norman rule, the native clans and the invaders lived alongside each other in relative harmony despite frequent incomprehension. Over the centuries, the Anglo-Norman families, led by the dominant Butler clan, integrated into the native Gaelic culture, adopting their dress and language, and intermarrying. Not unnaturally, this process displeased the authorities in Dublin and England: so in 1366, the **Statutes of Kilkenny** were passed by Parliament to prohibit the Anglo-Normans from intermingling with the Irish; but it was too late, and the new laws were ignored.

Confederation of Kilkenny – The height of Kilkenny's authority (1642–48) came when the Confederation of Kilkenny functioned as an independent Irish parliament, representing both the old Irish and the Anglo-Irish

Irish pipers

Roman Catholics. When this body split, the Anglo-Irish sided with the English Viceroy, and the Old Irish looked to Pope Innocent X for support. The Old Irish, led by Owen Roe O'Neill, were eventually defeated; following Cromwell's siege of Kilkenny in 1650, the Irish army was permitted to march out of the city.

Nationalist Tradition – Kilkenny has always had a strongly nationalistic tradition and played a key role in the movement for independence early in the 20C. **William T Cosgrave**, the first president of the Executive Council, was a steadfast leader in the young Free State, acting as Sinn Féin member for Kilkenny at Westminster and then in the Irish Parliament *(Dáil)*.

Walking Tour

Among the vestiges of the old town, there is the 16C **Shee Alms House**, once used as a hospice, now the tourist office (⏱*Open Mon–Fri 9.30am–6pm, Sat 10am–6pm.* ☎*056 7751500*) and the 18C **Tholsel**, a former toll house, customs house, courthouse and guild hall, now the town hall.
Grace's Courthouse (also known as **Grace's Castle**) stands above the remains of a castle (1210), which served as a prison in the 16C and then a courthouse in the 19C.

▶ *Walk up Rose Inn Street and turn right into High Street.*

Rothe House★
⏱*Open Apr–Oct, Mon–Fri 10.30am–5pm; Sat 10.30am–1pm, 2pm–5pm; Sun 3pm–5pm. Nov–Mar Mon–Sat 10.30am–4.30pm.* ⏱*Closed 24 Dec–first week Jan.* ⏺*€4. Combined ticket with St Canice Cathedral (not inc Round Tower).* ⏺*€7. Genealogy service.* ☎*056 772 2893; www.rothehouse.com.*

With its splendid Tudor facade, this is the only remaining town house of the Renaissance period in Ireland. Built in 1594 by a local merchant, John Rothe, it was used in the 17C as a meeting place by religious and political leaders during the Kilkenny Confederation, then in the 19C by the nationalist Gaelic League. It now houses the local museum featuring an entertaining rotating programme of local exhibits.

▶ *Continue N along Parliament Street over the bridge; cross Dean Street and take the steps up to the Cathedral.*

St Canice's Cathedral★★
♿⏱*Open Jun–Aug, 9am (2pm Sun)–6pm. Apr–May and Sept, Mon–Sat 10am–1pm, 2pm–5pm, Sun 2pm–6pm. Oct–Mar, Mon–Sat 10am–1pm, 2pm–4pm. Sun 2pm–4pm.* ⏺*€4 Cathedral; €3 Round Tower. Combined tickets: Cathedral/Round Tower €6; Cathedral/Rothe House €7.* ☎*056 776497. www.stcanices cathedral.ie.*

This 13C Early Gothic cathedral is thought to stand on the raised site of St Canice's 6C church. It is best approached by St Canice's Steps *(SE)* laid out in the early 17C when damage inflicted by Cromwell (who stabled horses in the nave) necessitated repairs.
There are many fine tombs: most notably that in black Kilkenny marble of Piers Butler, Earl of Ormond and Ossory (died 1539) and his wife Margaret Fitzgerald; her effigy has a finely jewelled and embroidered girdle. The oldest tomb (13C) bears part of the original dog-tooth ornament. The oldest tombstone is the **Kyteler slab**, inscribed in Norman French in memory of Jose Kyteler, probably the father of Dame Alice Kyteler, who was tried for witchcraft in 1323.
In the graveyard stands a **round tower** (100ft/30m high), built between 700 and

1000, which gives an overall view of Kilkenny and its surrounding countryside (Ⓢ*usually closed Oct–Mar. Min age 12 years old*).

▷ *From Parliament St turn left into Abbey St, through the medieval* **Black Freren Gate**.

Black Abbey★

The **medieval church**, founded c 1225 for the Dominicans and repressed in 1543, served as the city's courthouse from the 17C. It was re-consecrated in the 19C. The interior is lit by fine early-14C traceried windows and a lovely alabaster carving of the Most Holy Trinity beside the altar from c 1400 despite the inscription. In the graveyard are 10 stone coffins dating from the 13C and 14C.

Castle

Kilkenny Castle and Park★★

(*Dúchas*)Ⓓ♿♨☕*Visit by guided tours only, Jun–Aug 9.30am–7pm; Sept 10am–6.30pm; Apr–May 10.30am–5pm; Oct–Mar 10.30am–12.45pm, 2pm–5pm. Last admission, 1hr before closing.* Ⓢ*Closed Good Fri and Christmas hols.* ◉€5.30 ☕.✕. ☎056 77 21450. www.heritage ireland.ie.

The castle, built by William the Earl Marshal (1192–1207) overlooks the River Nore. Uniquely among Irish castles, it

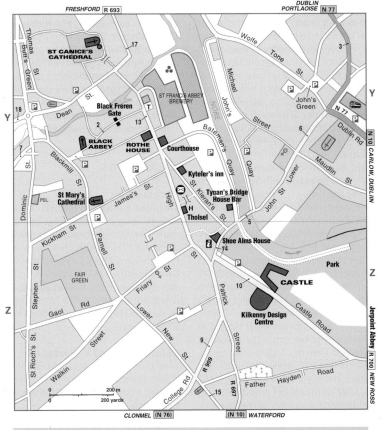

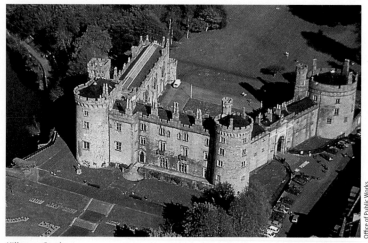

Kilkenny Castle

Office of Public Works

was a nobleman's residence: the seat of the Butler family, Earls and Dukes of Ormond, who dominated the southeast of Ireland. Much of the medieval fabric remains, including three of the four corner towers, though it was acquired by the state in 1967 to save it from dereliction. Today, after much restoration, the great stronghold provides a window on the lifestyle of the Anglo-Irish aristocracy.

The most imposing interior is the 19C Long Gallery hung with Gobelin tapestries and family portraits, with a hammerbeam roof decorated with pre-Raphaelite neo-Celtic motifs.

In the basement is the **Butler Gallery** (&⊙*open daily. Jun–Aug 9.30am–6pm, Sept 10am–6pm, Oct–May 10.30am–5pm (closes Oct–Mar 12.45pm–2pm). ☎056 77 61106. www.butlergallery.com)*, which displays 19C–20C Irish art and visiting contemporary art exhibitions.

Housed in the monumental 18C stable buildings of the castle the **Kilkenny Design Centre** (&⊙*open as castle. ☎056 772 2118; www.kilkennydesign. com)*, is a major retail outlet for high-quality souvenirs and provides accommodation for a variety of craftspeople; it was set up in the 1960s as a focal point for improvement in the design of ceramics, textiles, furniture and jewellery. It also incorporates a very good self-service cafe-restaurant.

Also in the old stables is **The National Craft Gallery** (&⊙*Open 10am (Apr–Dec Sun 11am)–6pm. ☎056 77 61804. www. ccoi.ie)*, Kilkenny's newest exhibition space, which stages exhibitions of some of the finest contemporary craft and design from Ireland and abroad.

The extensive **park** (50 acres/20ha) has formal gardens and woodlands.

Excursions

Thomastown
11mi/18km S of Kilkenny by R 700.
Little twisting streets converge on the main street close to the old bridge over the Nore, half-obliterated by its modern concrete deck. **The (Ladywell) Water Garden** (&⊙*open Mar–Nov 9.30am–5pm; ⊙closed Public Hols; ⊜donation requested; ⊡; ☎056 772 4690)* is an intricate mixture of trees, shrubs and aquatic plants.

Kilfane Glen and Waterfall★
14mi/23km S of Kilkenny by R 700 and N 9 N from Thomastown. ⊙Open Jul–Aug 11am–6pm. ⊜€6. ☎056 7724558. www. kilfane.com.
This wonderful, unusual Romantic creation from the late 18C nestles in a wooded ravine, with more formal contemporary gardens and modern sculpture added later – including an installation by the American artist, James Turrell,

Address Book

♿*For coin ranges, see the Legend on the cover flap.*

SIGHTSEEING

Guided walking tour of the medieval town. *Operates 4 times daily May–Oct (twice Sun). €6. Call TIC for details.*

WHERE TO STAY

⊜⊜ **Shillogher House** – *Callan Road, Southwest.* ☎056 776 3249. *www. shillogherhouse.com. 6rm.* More modern than its gables at first suggest, this is a redbrick purpose-built guesthouse facing a landscaped lawn which includes modern en suite bedrooms kept spotless by affable hosts.

⊜⊜ **Blanchville House** – *Dunbell, Maddoxtown, Southeast. 6rm. Open Mar–Oct.* ☎056 772 7197. *www.blanch ville.ie.* Follow the tree-lined drive to this restored Georgian country house in quiet farmland. A firelit drawing room and charming bedrooms furnished with antiques and family heirlooms make this experience complete.

⊜⊜⊜⊜ **The Hibernian** – *1 Ormonde Street. 43rm, 3 suites.* ☎056 777 1888. *www.kilkennyhibernianhotel.com.* Part Georgian hotel, set in a former bank within sight of Kilkenny Castle, this classically proportioned haven houses understated, modern bedrooms, a spacious bar in dark wood with long tan sofas and a comfortable restaurant with both traditional appeal and modern dishes (⊜⊜⊜).

WHERE TO EAT

⊜⊜ **Zuni** – *26 Patrick Street.* ☎056 772 3999. *www.zuni.ie.* The building's origins as Kilkenny's first cinema are reflected in the original façade and contrast with the stylish and modern interior, following its recent conversion into the city's trendiest restaurant, mixing modern Irish cuisine with Mediterranean, Middle Eastern and Asian influences. 13 very elegant modern bedrooms (⊜⊜).

SHOPPING

In addition to the craft outlets in the Castle stables a number of craft studios are grouped in **Bennetts-bridge** *(7mi/11km south),* including **Nicholas Mosse**, housed in an old flour mill, which offers a variety of craft work, including pottery made on the premises *(www.nicholasmosse.com).* For hand-blown glass, where the craftsmen can be seen at work, visit **Jerpoint Glass Studio** *(south of Stoneyford on the Thomastown road. www.jerpointglass.com).*

SPORTS AND LEISURE

The magnificent estate of **Mount Juliet** (1 400 acres/567ha) offers many sporting facilities, the star attraction being a golf course designed by Jack Nicklaus. Other activities include horseriding, archery, clay target shooting, angling and a spa.*www.mountjuliet.ie.*

EVENTS AND FESTIVALS

Kilkenny Arts Festival – One of the most important arts events in Ireland, featuring classical music, visual art, theatre, literature, children's arts and outdoor events *(mid-Aug. www.kilkenny arts.ie).*

Smithwick's Cat Laughs Comedy Festival – Rated the best comedy festival in the world featuring comedians from Ireland and abroad at venues across town *(late May–early Jun. www.thecatlaughs.com).*

---

inviting visitors to contemplate the sky. Precipitous walks, steps and bridges, a waterfall and a delightful thatched cottage orné set in a grassy glen, testify to the Power family's interest and love of the landscape since the 1790s.

The ruined church in the village contains a famous effigy, the **Cantwell Knight**★, a fine carving of a Norman nobleman, placed upright in the roofless nave.

Jerpoint Abbey★★

12mi/19km S of Kilkenny by R 700 and N 9 S from Thomastown. (Dúchas) ♿◷*Open Jun–mid-Sept, 9.30am–6.30pm; mid-Sept–May 10am–5pm (4pm Nov–Feb).*

Jerpoint Abbey

Bord Fáilte, Dublin

🕐*Closed Christmas week.* ⮠€2.90. ☎056 7724623. www.heritageireland.ie/en.
A sturdy tower with its stepped Irish battlements rising over the Little Arrigle River is a landmark for the ruins of what was once one of the country's foremost Cistercian monasteries.

Cistercian monks from Baltinglass in Co Wicklow (🕯*see ATHY*) arrived here in 1180, and constructed their own complex on an earlier Benedictine house. In the mid-13C there were 36 monks and 50 lay-brothers; after the Dissolution (1540), the monastery, its farm buildings, fisheries, and considerable estates, passed to the Earl of Ormond.

Jerpoint is of sufficient importance to warrant a **visitor centre**, with a small exhibition devoted to medieval stone carving in the region.

The abbey **church** has the classic Cistercian cruciform plan. The transepts, which belong to the original late-12C construction, have two chapels each. In the **chancel** are splendid effigies of two bishops, one believed to be Felix O'Dulany, first abbot of Jerpoint and bishop of Ossory (1178–1202). On the north wall are remains of a 15C–16C wall painting showing the heraldic shields of Jerpoint's main benefactors.

The columns of the 14C or 15C **cloisters** (restored) bear remarkable carvings of animals, saints, knights and ladies in contemporary attire and armour.

Kells Priory★
8mi/13km S of Kilkenny by R 697.
The tranquil remains of this priory by the Kings River are some of the largest and most spectacular ruins in Ireland. Founded in 1193 by Geoffrey de Marisco with four Augustinian canons from Bodmin in Cornwall, the priory suffered repeated attacks; the extensive (5 acres/2ha) site is enclosed by a curtain wall with towers and a gateway.

Edmund Rice Heritage Centre
Callan; 10mi/16km SW of Kilkenny by N 76. ♿🕐*Open Apr–Sept, 10am–6pm.* 🕐*Closed Good Fri, 25 Dec.* ☎056 77 25993.
Edmund Ignatius Rice (1762–1844), was the founder of the Christian Brothers; a teaching order that has played an important role in Irish education. This complex with its visitor centre and chapel is built around the his cottage **birthplace**. The kitchen has a stone-flagged floor, open hearth and spinning wheel, as in Rice's day: the other rooms are similarly preserved with furniture of the period.
In the town of Callan there are substantial remains of a 15C Augustinian priory.

Bród Tullaroan
10mi/16km W of Kilkenny by a minor road. 🕐*Open Jun–Aug Mon–Fri 10am–4pm; otherwise call to confirm. Irish story telling/music nights (min party size, 20 people).* ⮠€4. 🍴. ☎056 77 69202.
The "Pride of Tullaroan" heritage centre, set in deep countryside, is devoted to the memory of **Lory Meagher**, the "prince of hurlers" who dominated the sport in Co Kilkenny in the 1920s and 1930s. The thatched farmhouse where he was born and lived has been restored and furnished to evoke the period around 1884, the year in which the Gaelic Athletic Association was founded by Lory's father among others. The **Museum of Hurling** presents the fascinating local history of the sport.

Kilcooly Abbey
21mi/32km NW of Kilkenny by R 693;
from Urlingford take R 689 S for
3.5mi/5.5km; 500yd/0.5km on foot
from parish church car park.
The substantial ruins of this Cistercian abbey, founded c 1200, include a massive tower and a cloister; note the carved effigy of a knight. In the field stands a large dovecot.

Dunmore Cave★
7mi/11km N of Kilkenny by N 77
and N 78. (Dúchas).
Visit by guided tour only (1hr), mid-Jun–mid-Sept, 9.30am–6pm; mid-Mar–mid-Jun, mid-Sept–Oct, 9.30am–5pm; Nov–Mar Sat–Sun, Bank Hols 10am–5pm (last admission 1hr before closing, 3pm Nov–Feb). €2.90. ☏056 7767726. www.heritageireland.ie/en.

Beneath the isolated Castlecomer limestone outcrop is this large cave encrusted with stalagmites and stalactites. The visitor centre explains the site's geology and history. The 10C tale of a horrible massacre by Vikings seemed partially confirmed when 40 or so human skeletons were found in 1973, adding to the Viking remains, coins, brass buckles and delicate silverwork of North African origin recovered in the 1880s.

Castlecomer
11.5mi/19km N of Kilkenny by
N 77 and N 78.
The village was laid out in Italian style by Sir Christopher Wandesforde in 1635; his family mined coal in the region for three centuries. There is no more coal-mining, but plenty of mementoes are preserved at the Coal Mine Lounge pub.

KILLALA ★
POPULATION 713

Killala (Cill Ala) is a quiet seaside resort overlooking Killala Bay at the mouth of the River Moy, and Bartragh Island, a narrow sandbank. It has a sandy beach, and plenty of sports facilities. The harbour warehouses are a reminder of its importance in the past, most notably as it was here that the French first halted when they invaded in 1798. To the west of the town lies North Mayo, one of the most remote and least inhabited regions of Ireland. In fine weather the bog gleams gold in the sun but when the sky is overcast the landscape is bleak. Nevertheless this apparently unwelcoming land was an important human habitat in Neolithic times, and traces of its occupation are still to be seen.

▯ **Information:** Ballina. ☏096 70848.
▶ **Orient Yourself:** Killala lies on R 314 north of Ballina (N 59 west of Sligo).
◔ **Also See:** KNOCK, SLIGO, WESTPORT.

Visit

St Patrick's Cathedral
The present Anglican **cathedral** was erected in 1670 by Thomas Ottway, Bishop of Killala, using stone from the ruined medieval cathedral, including the south doorway and Gothic east window. The great 12C **round tower**, built of limestone (84ft/25m high) and recapped in the 19C, is all that remains of the monastery founded by Muiredach, the first bishop of Killala, who was appointed by St Patrick in the 5C.

There is also a 9C **souterrain** with many chambers (*unfenced*).

Driving Tours

North Mayo Coast
25mi/40km.

The northern coast of Co Mayo confronts the Atlantic with a line of dramatic sea cliffs, broken only by **Broad Haven**, a wide bay of sandy coves, narrow sea-inlets and tiny habitations, enclosed by

Address Book

🜚 *For coin ranges, see the Legend on the cover flap.*

WHERE TO STAY

🍽️🍽️**Downhill Inn** – *Sligo Rd, Ballina. 1mi E off N 59.* ☎*096 73444. www.down hillinn.ie. Closed 1 week at Christmas. 45rm. Restaurant*🍽️. This family owned purpose-built hotel on the outskirts of town offers clean and comfortable accommodation. Bedrooms are warmly decorated and uniform in size.

SPORTS AND LEISURE

All sorts of water sports can be found around Killala Bay. There is salmon fishing in the River Moy and in the Deel River at Crossmolina, and canoeing on the Moy River at Foxford.

The **seaweed baths** at Inishcrone (🜚 *see Moy Estuary Driving Tour*) are a must. Children enjoy **Waterpoint Leisure Centre** (*www. waterpoint.ie*) which not only has seaweed baths, but water flumes and other family activities.

Benwee Head (829ft/253m – *east*) and **Erris Head** (285ft/87m – *west on the Belmullet Peninsula*). Inland the country is largely covered in Atlantic blanket bog (400sq mi/1 036sq km): its turf is extensively harvested by machine to fuel the power station at Bellacorick, which is supplemented by wind turbines.

▶ *From Killala take R 314 N; cross the river, turn right; climb the stile into the field (left).*

Breastagh Ogham Stone

The stone (8ft/2.5m high), probably a Bronze Age standing stone, is marked with the linear Ogham script that is only partially legible.

▶ *Continue to the crossroads; right.*

Rathfran Abbey

The 13C Dominican friary by the shore was burned down in 1590 by Sir Richard Bingham, the English Governor of Connaught, in the course of one of his destructive forays. Little remains of the cloisters and out-buildings but the long rectangular church is still largely intact. Note the panel over the west door depicting the Crucifixion.

▶ *Return to the crossroads; turn right; continue N via Carrowmore, Killogeary and Rathlackan. Turn right to Downpatrick Head.*

Downpatrick Head

The projecting headland is undermined by the sea which comes up through a **blow hole** *(fenced off)*. Just offshore stands Dunbriste, a rock stack surmounted by a prehistoric earthwork,

---

The Year of the French, 1798

In August 1798 a force of 1 067 French revolutionaries under General Humbert landed at Kilcummin in Killala Bay and Humbert appointed John Moore as President of the Provisional Government of Connaught in Killala; as the French advanced inland they were joined by enthusiastic but ill-equipped Irishmen.

Their first success was at Ballina; then they met General Lake and his vastly superior force of militia and yeomanry. Although outnumbered, General Humbert routed his opponent and the ignominious retreat of General Lake's cavalry became known as the **Races of Castlebar**. At Carrignagat, they had their third victory. Humbert moved southeast hoping to avoid the English army and join up with the United Irishmen but the latter had been defeated; he was defeated at Ballinamuck, near Longford. The French were taken prisoner; the Irish were hanged as traitors.

The 1798 Rebellion was re-enacted in Killala in 1981 for the film version of Thomas Flanagan's historical novel, *The Year of the French*.

SLIDE FILE, Dublin

Killala Harbour

probably detached from the mainland in 1393. The views are superb, taking in *(E)* Benbulben and the Dartry Mountains north of Sligo, *(SE)* the Ox Mountains (Slieve Gamph), *(SW)* the Nephin Beg Mountains, *(W)* the cliffs to Benwee Head and the Stags of Broadhaven offshore.

▶ *Continue to Ballycastle; R 314 NW.*

Céide Fields★

(Dúchas) ⌖ ⬤ Visit by guided tour only (1hr), mid-Mar–Nov 10am–5pm (6pm Jun–Sept). Last tour 1hr before closing. ⌖ Be sure to dress warmly and wear walking shoes. ⬤ €3.70. ⬤ ☎096 43325, www.heritageireland.ie/en.

Most of North Mayo is covered by blanket bog, a desolate and seemingly unwelcoming landscape that conceals fascinating evidence of settled and productive prehistoric occupation. Using iron probes and bamboo markers, archeologists have mapped several square miles of fields laid out by the Neolithic people who lived near the Céide Cliffs over 50 centuries ago and who were contemporaries of the tomb builders of the Boyne Valley.

In fact these are not only the most extensive Stone Age monument in the world, but the stone walled fields, extending over thousands of acres are almost 6 000 years old, are the oldest known in the world.

The centrepiece of the strikingly modern **visitor centre** is a large, twisted 4 400 year old Scots pine found in the vicinity; displays explain the geology and evolution of the bog reaching depths of 13ft/4m. Parts of a primitive plough and postholes suggest how the Stone Age farmers might have cleared the land of primeval forest and piled stones to create enclosed fields and houses.

A bonus is that the centre is located beside **spectacular cliffs** and rock formations and a viewing platform is positioned on the edge of the 110m high cliff.

Moy Estuary
20mi/32km.

The coast road around the estuary of the salmon-rich River Moy passes close to the exceptionally picturesque ruins of two 15C Franciscan establishments, and continues to North Mayo's largest town, Ballina, and Inishcrone beyond.

▶ *From Killala take the coast road S.*

Moyne Abbey★
The extensive remains of the Franciscan friary at Moy include cloisters, sacristy, chapter-house, kitchen, refectory, church, and splendid six-storey tower. It was inhabited by the friars until the close of the 18C.

▶ *Continue S; on reaching the Rosserk River turn left.*

Rosserk Abbey★

The abbey on the Rosserk River, a tributary of the Moy, was the first Franciscan house to be built in Ireland, and its ruins are some of the best preserved in the country. Among the decorative features to survive, note the west door of the church and the carved piscina in the chancel, carved with a round tower, angels and the instruments of the Passion. From the cloisters, stairs lead up to the dormitories and refectory. Rosserk also suffered grievously at the hands of the ruthless Sir Richard Bingham.

▶ *Return to the T-junction and turn left; continue S.*

Ballina

Busy Ballina, the largest town in North Mayo offers good salmon fishing on the River Moy. The **Cathedral of St Muredach** on the east bank was built in the 19C next to the ruins of a late-14C Augustinian **friary**.

▶ *From Ballina drive through Castleconor, for 9mi/14km.*

Inishcrone (Enniscrone)

This is a popular family seaside resort on the east coast of Killala Bay. The local speciality is a traditional Irish seaweed bath at the elegant Edwardian **Kilcullen Seaweed Baths** (⏱open May–Oct 10am–9pm, Nov–Apr noon–8pm (Sat–Sun 10am). ✆€20; ☕; ☎096 36238; www.kilcullenseaweedbaths.com), a fine way of relaxing, and said to relieve rheumatism and arthritis.

KILLALOE★

POPULATION 972

Killaloe (Cill Dalua) is delightfully sited on the west bank of the Shannon, at a point where the river, emerging from Lough Derg, is forced into a relatively narrow channel, constricted by the Arra Mountains to the east and Slieve Bernagh to the west. Killaloe is a pretty village and a designated Heritage Town, with steep narrow streets, a cathedral, and an ancient stone bridge. It is also a watersports centre of international importance.

- **Information:** The Bridge, Killaloe; ☎061 376866. Connolly Street, Nenagh; ☎067 31610. www.shannonregiontourism.ie. www.shannonheritage.com.
- ▶ **Orient Yourself:** Killaloe is just off the main road (N 7) between Limerick and Nenagh, at the south end of Lough Derg.
- **Also See:** BIRR, CASHEL, ENNIS, LIMERICK, ROSCREA.

Sights

St Flannan's Cathedral★

The Dónall Mór O'Brien's austere, aisleless **cathedral** of 1185, on the site of a monastery founded in the 6C by St Molua and dedicated to his successor, was rebuilt in 1225 in the Romanesque/Gothic transitional style you see today. Its outstanding features include an elaborately carved 12C **Romanesque doorway**, a 12C High Cross from Kilfenora in the Burren, and a cross shaft carved c 1000 bearing a unique dual

inscription in both **Ogham** and **Viking Runic script**.

Beside the cathedral stands the vaulted nave of **St Flannan's Oratory**, a little 12C Romanesque church incorporating a loft beneath its steeply sloping stone roof.

St Molua's Oratory

The oratory beside the Roman Catholic church at the top of the hill, was built c 1000 on Friar's Island in the Shannon; it was transferred here when its original location was submerged by the hydroelectric scheme in the 1920s.

Killaloe Brian Ború Heritage Centre

⚐⏱*Open May–Sept 10am–6pm (last admission 5.30pm).* ✎€3.20. 🅿. ☎*061 376866. www.shannonheritage.com.* Displays trace the history of Killaloe from the birth of Brian Ború, High King of Ireland (1002–14), through many years of fishing and cruising, to the Civil War and local modern projects such a the building of the Ardnacrusha Dam.

Driving Tours

Lough Derg

▷ *From Killaloe take R 463 N; after 1mi/1.6km turn right into a track (0.5mi/0.8km).*

Béal Ború Earthwork

This large circular earthwork surrounded by a deep ditch and a grove of beech and pine trees is set immediately above the Lough Derg shoreline. From its name, which means "Pass of the Tributes", Brian Ború took his title.

▷ *Continue N on R 463.*

Tuamgraney

The village is known as the birthplace of the novelist, Edna O'Brien. At the south end of the village stands a 15C tower house and St Cronan's Church (Anglican), which is believed to be the oldest church in continuous use in Ireland or Great Britain. The west portion with its lintelled doorway dates from c 969; the east end of the building is 12C; note the Romanesque windows. It now houses the **East Clare Heritage Centre** (⚐⏱*open Jun–Oct 10am–12.30pm, 1.30pm–5pm;* 🔍*guided tour available;* ✎€4; ☎ *061 921351; www.eastclare heritage.com)*, which documents local history, including the life and times of Brian Ború.
The **Memorial Park** *(330yd/300m W of the village)*, is planted with indigenous trees and shrubs to commemorate the victims of the Great Famine of 1845–52.

▷ *Continue N on R 463 to Mountshannon.*

Holy Island★

The island with its extensive and evocative remains of a 7C monastery is a good excuse for a short trip on Lough Derg. As well as the remains of no fewer than six churches, there is a **round tower** (80ft/24m high) and a curious **bargaining stone** with a hollow channel through which men would shake hands to seal an agreement.

Mountain Drive

▷ *From Killaloe take R 463 S; in O'Briensbridge cross the river; in Montpelier turn right to Castleconnell.*

Castleconnell★

The well-kept small village by the Shannon offers excellent salmon fishing and riverside walks beneath the trees.

▷ *From Castleconnell drive E on a minor road (crossing N 7); turn left onto R 503; E of Newport turn right (sign); car parks both sides of the river.*

Clare Glens★

The Clare River descends in a series of lovely **waterfalls** through wooded glens.

▷ *Continue S on minor road to Murroe; turn in through the park gates.*

Glenstal Abbey
🕐 *Grounds open daily* ☎ *061 386103; www.glenstal.org.*
Impressive grounds and lakes surround the castle now used as a Benedictine monastery and school *(private)*. The modern **church** is known for its surrealistic decor and for the Ikon Chapel in the crypt.

▸ *Return to R 503 and continue E. At the crossroad near Inch turn left onto R 497. Drive N via Dolla to Nenagh.*

Nenagh
Little survives of the **Anglo-Norman castle**★ built c 1200 save the colossal circular keep (100ft/30m high), the finest in the country, and the 13C hall (restored).

Nenagh, a substantial garrison town in the 19C, is now the county town and commercial centre of Tipperary North Riding. The 13C Franciscan friary, one of the most important in Ireland, was dissolved in Elizabethan times; only the church wall stands.

▸ *From Nenagh take R 494 W. Beyond Portroe turn left (sign) into minor road.*

Graves of the Leinstermen
The group of prehistoric stones on the west face of Tountinna (1 512ft/461m) may be one of the first inhabited places in Ireland. There are commanding **views**★ over much of Lough Derg to Slieve Bernagh.

▸ *Continue along minor road. Turn left into R 494. In Ballina turn right to Killaloe.*

KILLARNEY ★★
POPULATION 8 809

Tourists have been coming to Killarney (Cill Airne) for more than two hundred years, entranced by its glorious setting of lakes, luxuriant vegetation, romantic ruins and meticulously managed demesnes. All around are rugged mountains including the Macgillycuddy's Reeks, which culminate in the highest peak in Ireland, Carrauntoohill (3 414ft/1 041m). No visit to the area is complete without making the classic trip into the Gap of Dunloe, a formidable breach rammed by a glacier through the heart of the mountains.

🛈 **Information:** Beech Rd; ☎064 31633. Waterville; ☎066 9474646. www.corkkerry.ie. www.killarneyonline.ie.
▸ **Orient Yourself:** Killarney is an ideal touring centre on the N 22 between Cork and Tralee, not far from Farranfore Airport *(north by N 22).*
🕾 **Don't Miss:** The Gap of Dunloe and Killarney National Park, the Ring of Kerry and Skellig Islands.
🕑 **Also See:** DINGLE PENINSULA, KENMARE, TRALEE.

A Bit of History

The monastery founded on the little island of Innisfallen in the 7C became a centre of learning, where the *Annals of Innisfallen*, one of Ireland's earliest historical chronicles, was composed. The area was subsequently governed by the O'Donoghues, McCarthys, and O'Sullivans, who were displaced by Elizabethan settlers like the Brownes and Herberts. It was in the 18C that Thomas Browne, the 4th Viscount Kenmare (1726–95), planned the present neat town of slated houses and shops. He also introduced linen and woollen manufacturing and beautified the surroundings by planting trees and providing seats and belvederes. Over time, streams of visitors came, including poets, painters and writers – Shelley found Killarney more impressive even than Switzerland, Macaulay thought Innisfallen "not a reflex of heaven, but a bit of heaven itself"; on the other hand, Charlotte Brontë had the misfortune to be thrown from her horse while exploring the Gap of Dunloe and Thackeray was dismayed by the throngs of touts and guides. Killarney's tourist vocation was confirmed with the visit of Queen Victoria in 1861. In 1932 the Muckross estate was presented by its American owners to the nation as the Bourn Vincent Memorial Park, becoming the core of the present National Park, Ireland's first.

Walking Tour

Killarney town is thronged with visitors crowding its streets, bars, hotels and shops. Focal points include Market Cross, the intersection of Main Street, High Street and New Street, and Kenmare Place, where the jaunting cars wait for passengers.

A prominent spire (285ft/87m high) marks **St Mary's RC Cathedral**★ designed by Augustus Pugin. Although work began in 1842, it was not consecrated until 1855 as the building was used to provide shelter to famine victims between 1848 and 1853. It was adapted for the new liturgy in 1972–73.

The Early-English **St Mary's Anglican Church**, built in 1870 contains a stained-glass window reproducing Holman Hunt's *Light of the World*. Among its memorials, there is one to the Revd Arthur Hyde, great-grandfather of Douglas Hyde, first president of Ireland.

Kerry Poets' Memorial

The personification of Ireland as a beautiful woman *(speir bhean)* was created in 1940 by Seamus Murphy to commemorate Co Kerry's four best-known Gaelic poets – **Pierce Ferriter**, a poet, soldier and musician from the Dingle Peninsula, who refused to submit to the Cromwelli-

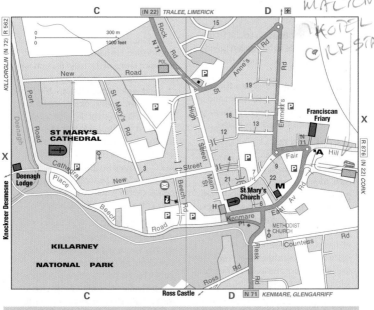

Address Book

For coin ranges, see the Legend on the cover flap. All Accommodations close during winter, except where stated.

GETTING AROUND

Valentia Island-Renard Point
Car Ferry – ☎066 94 76141. www. corkkerry.ie. Operates Apr–Sept, daily 8.30am–10.30pm.

Skellig Islands Ferry – ☎066 94 72437/087 23 95470. www.skelligislands. com. From Portmagee Pier to the Skellig Islands (45min) daily at 10am (return at 3pm), weather permitting. ☞€40. Reserve two days in advance.

Kerry (Farranfore) Airport – ☎066 976 4644. www.kerryairport.ie. Flights to Dublin, Manchester, Stansted, Luton and Frankfurt.

SIGHTSEEING

There are **information centres** at Muckross House and at Torc Waterfall (*summer only*). The **National Park** may be explored on foot, by boat or by bicycle. **Walks** are waymarked at Ross Castle, Muckross House and through the Gap of Dunloe.

There are **boat trips** on Lough Leane, from Ross Castle to Innisfallen Island, or as part of the trip through the Gap of Dunloe.

Jaunts in a horse-drawn **jaunting car** are available from the southern end of the Main Street, or from Kate Kearney's Cottage, or from Muckross House.

WHERE TO STAY

☞**Kingfisher Lodge** – *Lewis Road.* ☎064 37131. www.kingfisherkillarney. com. 10rm. Friendly and comfortable guesthouse, three minutes walk from the centre. Bedrooms are clean and neat, in co-ordinated pastel colours, with the quieter ones at the back of the house. All have large showers.

☞**Hussey's Townhouse** – *43 High Street.* ☎064 37454. 5rm. Relax in the first floor lounge, with its quiet reading area, or mix with the locals in the snug bar at the front of this town house. Bedrooms are compact, cosy and well-kept and all have en-suite shower rooms.

☞ **Redwood** – *Rockfield, Tralee Rdoad, 3mi N on N 22.* ☎064 34754. www. redwoodkillarney.com. 6rm.

Very comfortable accommodation to the north of the town, surrounded by several acres of farmland; decorated throughout to a very high standard and featuring antiques and interesting artworks. Spacious sitting room and conservatory. Very good value.

☞☞**Old Weir Lodge** – *Muckross Road.* ☎064 35593. www.oldweirlodge.com. Closed 23–29 Dec. 30rm. The emphasis is on comfort and space at this elegant property just south of the town centre. There are two stylish lounges and a roomy breakfast room with conservatory extension. Immaculate bedrooms in warming hues.

☞☞ **Fuchsia House** – *Muckross Road.* ☎064 33743. Closed Jan–Feb. 9rm. A small hotel with the feel of a country house, from its antique furnished and individually designed bedrooms to the comfortable sitting room and well-tended back garden. Home-made breakfast produce.

☞☞ **Kathleens Country House Hotel** – *Tralee Road, 2mi N on N 22.* ☎064 32810. www.kathleens.net. 17rm. Surrounded by glorious countryside but only 1 mile (1.6 km) from town, Kathleens is charming and comfortable with pretty bedrooms overlooking the garden. The ebullient Kathleen is one of the main reasons why guests keep returning each year.

☞☞☞**Coolclogher House** – *Mill Road.* ☎064 35996. www.coolclogherhouse. com. 5rm. Play Lord of the Manor by staying at this imposing Victorian Italianate mansion standing proudly in 68 acres/27ha of parkland within walking distance of the National Park. Sympathetically restored yet retaining a period charm. A 180-year old camellia is the centrepiece of the conservatory.

WHERE TO EAT

☞**The Laurels** – *Main Street.* ☎064 31149. www.thelaurelspub.com. One of the best of the town's many pubs. Live music, a bustling atmosphere and palpable sense of tradition. The menu offers an extensive selection of favourites from Irish stew to home-made burgers and good pizzas.

☞☞**The Cooperage** – *Old Market Lane.* ☎064 37716. www.cooperagerestaurant. com. This stylish slate-floored town centre bar-restuarant is lit by eye-catching modern chandeliers. Modern Irish and European cooking with early-bird specials.

🍴🍷**The Old Presbytery** – *Cathedral Place.* ☎*064 30555. Closed Tue (Mon–Wed Nov–Mar).* A more recent addition to the town's restaurant scene, opposite St Marys Cathedral. Spread over two floors serving imaginative Modern Irish cuisine.

TAKING A BREAK

O'Connor's – *7 High Street.* ☎*064 30 200.* This recently restored family-owned watering hole is the real deal. There's a welcoming atmosphere, home-made soup and sandwiches and traditional music on Thu–Mon.

SHOPPING

High Street – The main shopping district of the town and where to find the majority of pubs and restaurants. The perfect place for local souvenirs, from jewellery to linen and glassware.

Quills Woollen Market – *Market Cross, High Street.* ☎*064 32 277. Open daily 9am (11am Sun) to 6pm (later in summer).* A family business established in 1939. Spread over two floors, with a large collection of authentic, and typically Irish, goods, ranging from Donegal tweeds and Aran handknits to linen and individually designed pieces of jewellery.

Avoca Weavers – *Moll's Gap.15mi/24km S by N 71.* Set in a striking location, this branch of the famous Irish retailer sells their usual stylish and fashionable woollen clothing plus lots of other household items, all made to high quality traditional standards. There's a good cafe-restaurant here too.

Kerry Woollen Mills – *Beaufort; 5mi/8km W by N 72; 4mi/6km turn right at sign; after 1mi/1.6km turn left and then right.* ☎*064 44122. www.kerrywoollen mills.ie.* Woollen goods have been produced at the mill here for over 300 years; rugs and blankets for people and horses, tweeds for clothes and furnishings, scarves and shawls, knitwear and knitting yarn, from traditional to cutting- edge designs.

ans in 1652 and was hanged in 1653 in Killarney; **Geoffrey O'Donoghue of the Glens** (1620–78), who was Chieftain of Glenflesk and lived in Killaha Castle, southeast of Killarney; **Egan O'Rahilly** (1670–1728), the greatest of the four poets, who was educated in the bardic tradition and gave his allegiance to the Brownes, as the McCarthys were unable to act as his patrons; **Owen Roe O'Sullivan** (1748–84), who led a roving life as a hedge schoolmaster in winter and an itinerant labourer in summer, as well as serving in the British army and navy; to the delight of Admiral Rodney he wrote a poem in English about the Admiral's victory over the French at Dominica in 1782.

Franciscan Friary

The friary, built in 1860 in a style similar to Muckross Friary (👁*see Killarney National Park Driving Tour*), contains a stained-glass window *(entrance hall)* by Harry Clarke.

Local Driving Tours

① Gap of Dunloe★★

There are various ways of exploring the Gap. 👁*Gap of Dunloe Tours operate mid-Mar–Oct. Depart by bus from Killarney at 10.30am to Kate Kearney's Cottage; either travel by pony trap (€20 extra) or walk (2.5hrs) through the Gap to Lower Brendans' Cottage (lunch extra); boat trip across the three lakes at 2pm; return by bus to Killarney at 4p.m. Tours must be booked in advance; take a rain jacket* 🚌*Bus and boat €20.* ☎*064 30200. www.gapofdunloetours.com.*

By car: from Killarney take N 72 W; after 4mi/6km turn left and continue to Kate Kearney's Cottage, hire a pony and trap or continue on foot before returning to the car park. Boat trips only possible if booked as part of a tour with Dunloe Gap Tours.

By bicycle: make a round trip by hired cycle either via the lakes (cycles are

Cycling Killarney

Cycling is an excellent way to see the National Park, particularly around Muckross House. Hire a bike from one of the many outlets in town (the tourist office will give you details).

Within easy pedalling distance of the centre are Ross Castle and Muckross House (though in opposite directions). Cycling lanes go for most of the way to Muckross House (don't forget that you must cycle anti-clockwise around the lake).

carried aboard a special boat), via the Kerry ay (involving some pushing) or via Moll's Gap.

The jarvies (jaunting car drivers) plying for hire throng the roadsides and the forecourt of **Kate Kearney's Cottage**, (&⟲ open daily 10am until late; ☎064 44236; www.katekearneyscottage.com); originally an old coaching inn kept by Kate, who served *poteen* to 19C tourists; the cottage now serves 20C hospitality including traditional Irish nights.

This excursion, through a deep and narrow rock-strewn gorge, is one of the highlights of a visit to Ireland for many people. The initial crowd of pony traps, riders, cyclists and walkers soon thins out; it is less crowded towards the end of the day, and can be entered from the Black Valley to the south. The U-shaped glacial breach (1 500ft/457m deep) is traversed by a narrow track which winds up a series of hairpin bends, past several mountain tarns, to cross a stream before

Jaunting car

R Holzbachova, Ph Benet/MICHELIN

reaching the ruins of a Royal Irish Constabulary strongpoint. Most traffic turns back on reaching the Head of the Gap (794ft/242m). As the track descends into the Gearhameen Valley, where red deer graze, there is a fine view of the Upper Lake, bordered by native oakwoods and backed by Mangerton Mountain (2 756ft/838m).

2 Killarney National Park★★★

Tour of 30mi/48km.

S of Killarney by N 71. **Killarney National Park** (39sq mi/101sq km· *Dúchas;* &⟲ *visitor centre open mid-Mar–Oct 9am–6pm (7pm Jul–Aug); last admission 1hr before closing;* ⬜; ✗; ☎064 31440, www.heritageireland.ie/en; http://homepage.eircom.net/~knp) embraces the three lakes – Lower (Lough Leane), Middle (Muckross Lake) and Upper, which are linked by the Long Range River – the foreshore and the mountain slopes south and west. The original nucleus of the Muckross Estate is now complemented by Knockreer, Ross Island and Innisfallen, formerly part of the Kenmare Estate. Blanket bog on the higher land contrasts with Ireland's largest remaining area of ancient oak woodland, and examples of mature yews, alder carrs, and, arbutus (or strawberry tree) which flourishes in the exceptionally mild climate. The special character of the park was given international recognition in 1981 when it was designated as a UNESCO Biosphere Reserve. An audio-visual show in the visitor centre showcases the Park.

Knockreer Demesne
Footpath to Ross Castle.
The grounds of Knockreer House extend westwards from Killarney to the shore of Lough Leane; the entrance from the town is marked by a thatched cottage, **Deenagh Lodge** *(tea room).*

Ross Castle★
1mi/1.6km S by N 71 and a minor road W (sign). Boat trips to Innisfallen Island. (Dúchas) ⟶ *Visit by guided tour only (40min,) Jun–Aug, 9am–6.30pm; Apr –May, Sept–Oct 10am–6pm (5pm Apr,*

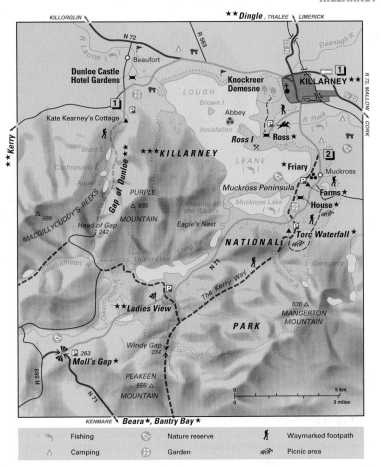

Map legend:

⌇	Fishing	🌲	Nature reserve	🚶	Waymarked footpath
Λ	Camping	🌸	Garden	🏞	Picnic area

Oct). Last admission 45min before closing. **⊙***Closed 24–26 Dec.* ⊛*€5.30.* ☎*064 35851. www.heritageireland.ie/en.*

The well-restored castle, the last in Munster to hold out against Cromwellian forces (1652) until attacks were mounted from armed boats, was built on the shore of Lough Leane in the 15C by one of the O'Donoghue Ross chieftains. A fortified bawn reinforced by circular flanking towers surrounded the rectangular keep. The four floors have been restored using medieval techniques and furnished in styles appropriate to the early-15C to late-16C period.

The promontory, known as **Ross Island**, dotted with copper mines from the early 19C, extends into Lough Leane. Access is along a profusion of tree- and flower-lined avenues. There are fine views of Lough Leane and the islands.

No trace remains on **Innisfallen** of the 7C monastery once so renown as a centre of learning, but the luxuriantly wooded island still harbours evocative remains of a later abbey with a fine Romanesque doorway.

Muckross Friary (Abbey) ★

⊙*Open mid-Jun–early Sept 10am–5pm.*
Muckross Friary was founded for the Franciscans in 1448 and took 59 years to build. The mid-15C nave and choir, broad central tower and south transept were erected c 1500.

The 22-arch cloisters and the domestic offices were constructed in four phases. The three-storey building north of the choir probably contained the Sacristy and the Sacristan's lodging.

SLIDE FILE, Dublin

Muckross Gardens

Muckross House, Garden and Traditional Farms★

(Dúchas) ♿ 🕐*House and gardens: open daily year-round 9am–5.30pm (6pm Jul–Aug)* 🕐*Closed Christmas hols.* 🕐*Farms: open Jun–Sept 10am–6pm. May 1pm–6pm. Mar, Apr, Oct Sat–Sun and Bank Hols 1pm–6pm. Last admission 1hr before closing.* 🚌*House/farm: €5.75; house and farm €9.50.* ☕. 🍴. ☎ *064 31440. www.muckross-house.ie.*

The Elizabethan-style **Muckross House** in Portland stone was built in 1843 for the Herbert family. Many rooms are reflect the taste of the early 20C: the drawing room, library and dining room are all lavishly decorated. The basement is devoted to regional crafts.

The **Traditional Farms** are a showpiece of early 20C Irish rural life. Animals inhabit the yards and fields and the buildings, from large farmhouse to labourer's cottage, are appropriately furnished with dressers, presses and settle-beds. Indoors, turf fires burn in the hearths and the staff, in period costume, demonstrate the work of a country housewife in the days before electricity and other modern amenities came to the Irish countryside.

The **Muckross Peninsula**, which divides Lough Leane from Muckross (Middle) Lake, contains one of the finest yew woods in Europe and are crossed by nature trails.

Torc Waterfall★

The **cascade** (60ft/18m) is one of the highest in Ireland. The viewpoint *(173 steps)* provides a fine view of the lakes.

Ladies View★★

Climbing over the hills to Kenmare, the N17 enables visitors to enjoy some of the finest panoramas over the Killarney landscape without the need to scale a mountain. Queen Victoria was particularly impressed by the prospect of Macgillycuddy's Reeks and the island-studded Upper Lake, little has changed since she and her entourage came this way in 1861.

Moll's Gap★

The pass (863ft/263m) provides *(north)* a striking view of the Gap of Dunloe in Macgillycuddy's Reeks and *(south)* a glimpse of the Kenmare River.

Driving Tour

Ring of Kerry★★

126mi/203km – 1 day.

The Iveragh peninsula is endowed with a spectacular high mountains, rocky bays, sandy beaches and dramatic seascapes. The **Ring of Kerry** is the road (N 70) that skirts the entire coastline between Killorglin and Kenmare. This great scenic drive *can* be completed in a single day but only a more measured trip of several days is sufficient to do justice to the wonderful, ever-changing succession of landscapes.

▷ *From Killarney take N 72 NW. Most coach tours on this route travel from north to south; passing is difficult as the coast road is narrow. After 4mi/6km turn left.*

Dunloe Castle Hotel Gardens
🕐*Open May–Sept.* 🛏. ✗. ☎*064 44111. www.dunloecastlehotel.com.*
Passing the modern 5-star hotel, luxuriant gardens, partly enclosed by grey stone walls, extend to the ruins of the old castle, its 13C tower house overlooking the River Laune and the River Loe with a clear view of the Dunloe Gap. An award-wining botanic collection consists of exotic specimens including the Killarney Strawberry tree, South African lilies, Australian gums, New Zealand cabbage trees and cherries, Japanese maples, North American dogwood, Chilean fir trees, South American fuchsias, Chinese swamp cypress and the "Headache" tree with aromatic leaves.

▷ *Return to N 72; NW to Killorglin.*

Killorglin (Cill Orglan)
The town is best known for the **Puck Fair** *(August)* when a large local billygoat is enthroned on a chair in the town square during three days and nights of revelry.

▷ *Continue W on N 70; turn left to Caragh Lake; right and left to Lickeen.*

Lough Caragh★
The road along the west shore affords views of the lake, renown for salmon and trout fishing; southeast rise the Macgillycuddy's Reeks (3 414ft/1 038m).

▷ *Return to N 70 and continue W; in Caragh Bridge turn right.*

Cromane Strand
The long spit of sand shelters the shallows known as Castlemaine Harbour.

▷ *Continue W on N 70; west of Glenbeigh take the minor road W across the bridge to Rossbeigh Strand.*

Rossbeigh Strand
The long strand (3mi/5km) is backed by a small hamlet; there are good walks in Rossbeigh Woods.

▷ *Continue W on N 70; in Kells turn right onto the minor road to Kells Bay (lovely beach) or continue W on N 70.*

Cahersiveen (Cathair Saidhbhín)
The native town of Daniel O'Connell by the Valentia River, dates from the early 19C. The **O'Connell Memorial Church**, built in 1888 of Newry granite with dressings of local black limestone, lacks the intended tower – rejected by the church authorities as too elaborate, but approved by Pope Leo XIII.

▷ *Take the minor road N towards Cooncrome harbour; after crossing the river turn left (2mi/3.2km).*

Cahergall Fort
The walls of this massive stone fort are stepped on the inside: within are two drystone buildings, a beehive hut and a rectangular house.

▷ *On foot continue W; turn right into a private road.*

Lough Caragh, Ring of Kerry

B. Kaufmann/MICHELIN

Leacanabuaile Fort

This partly reconstructed prehistoric drystone fort was inhabited during the Bronze and Iron Ages; from the top ramparts there are excellent **views**★★ of the coast.

▶ *Return to Cahersiveen and continue W on N 70. To visit Valentia Island EITHER turn right to Renard Point and take the ferry to Knight's Town (⚓see Address Book) OR continue on N 70, turn right onto R 657 to Portmagee and cross the bridge over the Portmagee Channel.*

Valentia Island

The island is a small (7mi/11.3km x 2mi/3.2km), but an important landmark, mentioned in the shipping forecasts. In 1858, less than 2 000mi/3 219km from Newfoundland, Valentia was the eastern terminal for the first transatlantic telegraph cable.

Knight's Town, a quiet little harbour settlement, consists of a single street. A steep narrow road north of the church leads up to a disused slate quarry – good views of Beginish Island and Doulus Head extend from the hill.

The western extremity of island is marked by **Bray Tower**, a 16C stone watchtower with views *(south)* to the Skellig Islands and *(north)* to the Dingle Peninsula. The stone-clad, grass-roofed building by the bridge linking Valencia to the mainland, houses the **Skellig Experience** (&⚓open Apr–Nov 10am–6pm, last admission 5.15pm (7pm Jun–Aug, last admission 6pm); ⚓€5, inc 2hr boat trip, departs daily, weather permitting, at 3pm) €27.50; ⚲;✗;☏066 9476306. www.skelligexperience.com) – an imaginative exhibition about the extraordinary character of the Skellig Islands: the monastery, lighthouses, wildlife and underwater sealife.

Skellig Islands★★

These bare and rocky islands, 10m/16km offshore, rise dramatically above the Atlantic. Little Skellig *(no landing allowed)* is a nature reserve with bird colonies (kittiwakes, razorbills, guillemots, shearwaters and gannets). The larger island, Skellig Michael, now a World Heritage Site, can be accessed, weather permitting, by boat. Its remote position on the westernmost edge of the known world was chosen as a monastic site in the 6C by St Finian; in 11C/12C the remaining residents moved to more congenial quarters at Ballinskelligs on the mainland. The well-preserved ruins – church, two oratories and six beehive huts – survive, perched precipitously above the sea on a narrow platform.

▶ *From the island take the bridge over the Portmagee Channel to Portmagee (An Caladh); turn right to take the coast road S up behind Glanearagh (1 044ft/318m) to St Finan's Bay. Continue S on R 567.*

Ballinskelligs (Baile an Sceilg)

This Irish-speaking village has a minute harbour and long strand (4mi/6km).

▶ *Continue E on R 567; at the junction turn right onto N 70.*

Waterville (An Coireán)

The little resort, built on an isthmus between **Lough Currane** and the sea, has a long promenade (0.5mi/0.8km). Photographs of Charlie Chaplin's frequent visits hang in the foyer of the Butler Arms Hotel, once redolent of 1950s splendour.

Derrynane National Historic Park★★

(Dúchas).&⚓Open May–Sept, Mon–Sat 9am–6pm, Sun 11am–7pm; Apr and Oct, Tue–Sun 1pm–5pm; Nov–Mar, Sat–Sun 1pm–5pm. ⚓€2.90. ⚲. ☏066 9475113. www.heritageireland.ie/en.

The demesne formerly belonged to **Daniel O'Connell** (1775–1847), the great champion of Catholic emancipation, known as the Liberator. The **park** (298 acres/121ha) which borders Derrynane Bay includes a bathing beach, a bird sanctuary and Abbey Island *(accessible at low tide)*. The south and east wings of the slate-fronted **house** are presented as they were when built by O'Connell in 1825 – there are family portraits, original furniture and mementoes. The centrepiece of the drawing room *(first floor)* is the elaborate **table** presented to O'Connell when he was an alderman of Dublin Corporation. The chapel was built by O'Connell in 1844 in thanksgiving for his release from prison; and includes the huge triumphal chariot, in which he was paraded through Dublin.

▶ *Derrynane take N 70 E; in Castlecove turn left at Staigue Fort House hotel.*

Staigue Fort★

⌂*Narrow road;* ⌦*€0.20 donation requested "for trespass".* ♿⌚*Exhibition Centre open Easter–Sept from 10am.* ⌦*Call for prices and times.* ☎*066 75127. www.sneem.net/staiguefort.*
This restored 2 000-year-old drystone fort is one of the finest of its kind in Ireland. It was built as a centre of communal refuge probably before the 5C.

The walls (18ft/5m high and up to 13ft/4m thick) are stepped on their interior face. The entire fort is surrounded by a bank and ditch. There is a video presentation in the Exhibition Centre.

▶ *Continue E on N 70 for 3 mi/5 km.*

Sneem (An Snaidhm)★

This attractive village is set at the head of the Sneem Estuary. Monuments to Cearbhall O'Dálaigh (1899–1976), former President of Ireland, who lived in Sneem, have been erected in the two large grass-covered squares. The **Anglican Church** is a charming small building dating from 1810.

▶ *Continue E on N 70 to Kenmare and then on N 71 N to return to Killarney.*

KILRUSH★

POPULATION 2 740

Overlooking the sheltered waters of the Shannon estuary, the second-largest town in County Clare retains something of the character it had when laid out by the Vandeleur family in the 18C. In the 19C Kilrush (Cill Rois) prospered as a port, and became the favourite summer resort of prosperous people from Limerick. Today it is a designated Heritage Town and a gateway to the beaches and cliffs of the Loop Head peninsula. There is a modern marina and colourful horse fairs are often held in the main square. In summer families of bottle-nosed dolphins can be seen in the Shannon Estuary.

🛈 **Information:** Frances Street; ☎065 905 1577. Kilkee; ☎065 9056112.
▶ **Orient Yourself:** Kilrush is SW of Ennis by N 68 and a few miles W of Killimer on the north bank of the River Shannon (Shannon Ferry Terminal).
♿ **Also See:** ADARE, ENNIS, LIMERICK, TRALEE.

Visit

Vandeleur Walled Garden

Ferry Road. ⌚*Open Apr–Sept 10am–6pm (Oct–Mar, Mon–Fri 10am–5pm). Last admission 45min before closing.* ⌦*€5.* ☕. ☎*065 90 51760, www.vandeleur walledgarden.ie.*
The Vandeleurs, a family of Dutch origin, settled in Kilrush in 1688 and were responsible for building the town in the 18C but they acquired an unenviable reputation as harsh landlords in the 19C. These magnificent woodlands (420 acres/168ha) and the old walled

garden, redesigned, revived and first opened to the public in 2000, are what remain of the Vandeleur family seat.

Excursions

Scattery Island★

Accessible by boat from Kilrush (♿see Address Book).
In the 6C the island 2mi/3km out in the estuary was chosen as the site of a monastery by St Senan. Legend relates that the saint had first to rid it of a terrible monster; more certain is the monastery's

Address Book

GETTING AROUND

Shannon Car Ferry – *From Killimer; 5.5mi/8.8km E of Kilrush.* ☎*065 90 53124. www.shannonferries.com.* Carries vehicles and passengers to Tarbert on the south shore of the Shannon Estuary.
Ferry to Scattery Island – *From Kilrush Creek Marina. Apr–Oct.* ☎*065 90 51327.*

SIGHTSEEING

Dolphin watch trips – depart from Kilrush Creek Marina. (☜€20. ☎*065 90 51327. www.discoverdolphins.ie.)* and from Carrigaholt *(☜€22. ☎065 90 58156; www.dolphinwatch.ie).*

Both operators: Jun–Aug; also Apr–May & Sept–Oct, subject to demand and weather.

SPORTS AND LEISURE

Beaches at Cappa and Brew's Bridge.
Marina at Merchant's Quay in Kilrush with 120 berths, a boatyard and yachts for hire.
Fishing in the Shannon Estuary and off the Atlantic Coast.

---

fate at the hands of the Vikings, who raided it on more than one occasion. There are evocative ruins of five medieval churches, but the most imposing structure is the tall (115ft/33m) **round tower**, with its doorway, unusually, at ground level.

West Clare Railway

4mi/6.4km NW of Kilrush by N 67 opposite Clancy's pub in Moyasta. ⏰*Open mid-Mar–Sept 10am (noon, Sun)–6pm. Check website foe schedule.* ☜€6. ☜. ☎*065 9051284. www.westclarerailway.ie.*

Alongside the restored station house visitors can take a ride on a restored 1.5 mi/2km section of the West Clare Railway, which once ran between Ennis and Kilkee.

Kilkee (Cill Chaoi)

8.5mi/13.5km NW of Kilrush by N 67.
This seaside resort is set on Moore Bay with a long promenade embracing a wide horseshoe-shaped sandy beach. Horse races are held on the sands at low tide on the last weekend in August. The Duggerna rocks at the entrance to the bay are accessible at low tide.

Kilkee Beach

Loop Head Peninsula

West of Kilrush and Kilkee the land forms a peninsula, terminating in Loop Head. The treeless landscape is divided into fields by earthbanks rather than the hedges or flagstones found farther inland.

On the south coast, **Carrigaholt Tower House** was built in the 16C by the McMahon family, who once controlled the peninsula. From the top of the tower there are fine **views** south to the north Kerry coast *(3mi/5km)*.

The north coast is much wilder, with spectacular cliffs, stacks and puffing holes. Near Moneen a huge natural arch, the **Bridge of Ross**★ *(sign)*, formed by the action of the sea, is visible from the edge of the cliffs.

Loop Head is surmounted by the lighthouse (277ft/84m above sea-level) which was built on the headland in 1854. It is the third light on the site; the first, built in about 1670, was one of four stone-vaulted cottage lights which had a coal-burning brazier on a platform on the roof.

KINSALE★★

POPULATION 2 007

Pretty little Kinsale (Cionn Tsáile), a designated Heritage Town on the broad estuary of the River Bandon, has had a long history as a harbour town, then as a favoured resort, with charming narrow lanes and neat Georgian houses stepping up the hillside overlooking the water. In recent years Kinsale has become particularly fashionable, with a gastronomic reputation that is celebrated annually with a food festival.

- ⓘ **Information:** Pier Road; ☎021 4772234. Ashe Steet, Clonakilty; ☎023 33226. www.corkkerry.ie. www.kinsale.ie.
- ▶ **Orient Yourself:** Kinsale, situated south of Cork city and Cork Airport, is easily reached by N 27 and R 600.
- Kids **Especially for Kids:** The West Cork Model Railway Village at Clonakilty.
- Ⓒ **Also See:** COBH, CORK, SKIBBEREEN.

A Bit of History

Kinsale was founded in the late 12C by the Anglo-Normans, but only really enters the history books in 1601 when a Spanish force occupied the town, a long way from their ally Hugh O'Neill, fighting the English in far-off Ulster. Kinsale was besieged by an English army, who were besieged in their turn by O'Neill after an exhausting march from the north. The combined Irish/Spanish forces should have easily defeated their enemy but the Spaniards watched from the walls as O'Neill was routed. This defeat marked the beginning of the end of the old Gaelic order and clan system; until the end of the 18C no native Irish were to settle within its 13C walls. In 1641 the town sided with Cromwell and so was spared much damage.

Similar lack of success attended James II who landed at Kinsale in March 1689 in an attempt to regain his kingdom. After the Battle of the Boyne he returned to exile in France from Duncannon in Waterford Harbour.

During the 17C Kinsale flourished as a shipbuilding port for the Royal Navy, which constructed *HMS Kinsale* here in 1700. The 18C trend towards larger ships rendered the docks obsolete.

Sights

Kinsale Regional Museum★

🕐*Open Wed–Sun, 10.30am–5pm.* ☎021 4777930. *http://homepage.eircom.net/ ~kinsalemuseum.*

The museum in the late-17C town hall with distinctive Dutch gables, has

Address Book

🪙For coin ranges, see the Legend on the cover flap.

SIGHTSEEING

Historic Kinsale Walking Tours – *Guided tours (1hr) Apr–Oct, daily 11.15am. €8. Start from outside the Tourist Office. ☎021 477 2873. For more tours see www.kinsale.ie/acwalk.htm.*

Kinsale Harbour Scenic Cruises ☎021 4778946; www.kinsaleharbourcruises. com. €12.50. Cruises operate daily.

WHERE TO STAY

◡–◡◡ **Rivermount House** – *Barrells Cross 4mi NE. ☎021 477 8033. www.rivermount.com. 6rm.* This large dormer bungalow guest-house in a quiet hillside spot enjoys sweeping views over the garden and the River Bandon. Beaches and a golf coourse are nearby

◡◡**Glebe Country House** – *Ballinadee. ☎021 477 8294. 4rm. Meals by arragement* ◡◡. The spacious gardens of this ivy-covered 17C former rectory provide many of the ingredients for the kitchen. A peaceful setting with the church steeple peeping over the trees. Individually decorated bedrooms with antiques aplenty.

◡◡**Desmond House** – *42 Cork Stret. ☎021 477 3575. www.desmondhouse kinsale.com. 4rm.* The owners of this centrally located Georgian townhouse are proud of the extensive breakfasts they lay on for their guests. Bedrooms are large, well equipped and offer excellent value.

◡◡**Kilcaw Guesthouse**– *1mi E on the R 600. ☎021 477 4155. www.kilcawhouse. com. 7rm.* A custom-built luxury guest-house in seven acres/3ha of land. The breakfast room has a farmhouse feel while the sitting room, with its open fireplace, offers a restful sanctuary.

◡◡ –◡◡◡ **Chart House** – *6 Denis Quay. ☎021 477 4568. www.charthouse-kinsale.com. 4rm.* An elegant, Georgian guesthouse with cosy, quaint ambience. There is a splendid breakfast room and bedrooms that boast antique beds with crisp white linens.

WHERE TO EAT

◠**Dalton's** – *3 Market Street. ☎021 477 7597. Closed Good Fri, 2 weeks in Aug, and 25 Dec.* 🍽. The emphasis at this pub is firmly on the food (especially seafood) with a menu that blends international influences garnered from the owner's experiences abroad.

◠**Kinsale Gourmet Store and Seafood Bar** – *Guardwell. ☎021 477 4453 (bookings not accepted). www. irelandwide.com/fish/gourmet. Closed Sun Dec–Feb.* Half shop, half restaurant, this friendly, informal and busy seafood spot is fresh and full of fish, but be sure to arrive early or be prepared to queue. Choose your fish from an impressive selection behind the counter or from the menu and grab a seat inside or out on the pavement terrace.

◠**Max's** – *Main Street. ☎021 477 2443 Closed Tue Nov–Mar.* Quaint and inti-mate with exposed beams, wood floor-ing and a small conservatory extension. The menu is French with an Irish accent and features carefully sourced local produce with deft use of herbs.

◡◠**Toddie's** – *Kinsale Brew Co, The Glen. ☎021 4777769. www.toddies.ie.* Set above the local brewery, Toddie's features a delightful terrace. The interior is relaxed with lots of glass and artwork. Comprehensive modern menus.

◡◠**The Vintage** – *Main Street. ☎021 477 2502.* The oak beams add to the palpable sense of history while the cosy bar and candlelight add to the intimate atmosphere. The traditional menu features local produce; seafood and oysters are the house speciality.

SPORTS AND LEISURE

Good facilities for yachting and deep-sea fishing.

EVENTS AND FESTIVALS

The Kinsale Food Festival is held in October when visitors sample the delights created by the international chefs of the Kinsale Good Food Circle.

many relics of old Kinsale, including several royal charters. The great hall is associated with the famous inquest on the victims of the *Lusitania* (see 'The Lusitania' box). The exhibition room displays a variety of items: Kinsale-made lace which, like the Kinsale cloak, was popular for over a century; footwear and cutlery belonging to "The Kinsale Giant", **Patrick Cotter O'Brien** (1706–1806), who made a lucrative career on the English stage – who lived in Giant's Cottage *(private)* in Chairman's Lane.

Kinsale Harbour

St Multose Church (Anglican)★
The original church was built about 1190 and dedicated to St Multose or Eltin, the patron saint of Kinsale, who lived in the 6C. The massive square tower has a 12C Romanesque doorway with zig-zag decoration; a statue of St Multose stands in a niche over the west door. Inside are various interesting 16C tombstones.

Desmond Castle
(Dúchas). Open mid-Apr–Oct 10am–6pm. Last admission 5.15pm. €2.90. 021 477 4855. www.heritageireland. ie/en. www.desmondcastle.ie.
The three-storey tower house was built in the late 15C or early 16C by the Earls of Desmond as a custom-house. During the siege of Kinsale it served as a magazine; in 1641, it served as a gaol for French and other foreign prisoners. It now houses a **Museum of Wine** reflecting the days when Kinsale was a port, and highlights several Irish families connected with winemaking in France, Spain, Australia and the USA.

Excursion

Kinsale Harbour★
There is a pleasant walk *(1.5mi/2.4km)* along the east bank of the Bandon estuary to **Summercove** where English ships landed guns and supplies for their army during the siege of Kinsale (1601–02). From the graveyard of St Catherine's Anglican Church there are extensive **views**★ across the harbour.
Charles Fort★ *(Dúchas; up the hill;* visit by guided tour (1hr) only, 10am–6pm (5pm Nov–mid-Mar); last

admission 5.15pm; €3.70; ; 021 477 2263), was begun about 1670 and remained in use until 1922. The vast star-shaped stronghold is a typical example of Baroque fortification, and is the largest structure of its date in Ireland. Many of the buildings surrounding the quadrangle of greensward are derelict but the old ordnance-store houses a good interpretive exhibition.
From the fort there are extensive **views** of Kinsale harbour, guarded on the west side by **James Fort**, built 1604 *(cross the bridge over the Bandon River and turn left; 0.5mi/0.8km on foot from the carpark).* Only the central tower, blockhouse and portions of the defensive walls are still partially intact.
The harbour entrance is protected by the headland, **Old Head of Kinsale** *(from the river bridge take R 600 W and R 604 S).* On the top of here stand the ruins of a 15C fort. The road stops just short of the modern lighthouse.

The Lusitania
On the seabed *(12mi/19km S)* lies the wreck of the great transatlantic liner *Lusitania*, torpedoed by a German submarine on 7 May 1915 on her way from New York to Liverpool; her sinking changed the climate of opinion in the United States and prepared the way for the American declaration of war on Germany two years later. Among the 1 500 who lost their lives was Sir Hugh Lane, the wealthy art collector who established the Hugh Lane Gallery of Modern Art in Dublin.

Kinsale at night

Driving Tour

Carbery Coast★

38mi/61km W of Kinsale by R 600.

Timoleague★

www.timoleague.ie.
The village on the Argideen estuary is dominated by a ruined **Franciscan friary**★, founded in 1320 and plundered by Oliver Cromwell in 1642. The extensive ruins include the cloisters and the outer yard, and the ruins of a 12C leper hospital.

Courtmacsherry★

3mi/5km detour E by R 601. This attractive village is a fine base for walking and deep-sea fishing; footpaths lead through the trees to Wood Point, or to a pebble beach at Broadstrand Bay.

▶ *From Timoleague take R 600 W. Before the junction with N 71, turn left (sign).*

Lios-na-gCon

Visit by guided tour only, summer, daily, noon–4pm. €5. 08 7785 2238. http://liosnagcon.com.
The 10C Ringfort of the Hound has been restored according to recent archaeological excavations.
The souterrain is intact; the enclosing ditch and bank are well preserved and give a wide **view** of the surrounding country.

Clonakilty (Cloich na Coillte)

023 33380. www.clonakilty.ie.
This market town, founded in 1598, renowned for its Gaelic traditions and its **black puddings**, was recently voted the country's best emerging rural tourism destination.
The town centre is distinguished by **Emmet Square**, with its central garden and tall Georgian houses.
A locally celebrated water pump, known as the Wheel of Fortune *(corner Connolly St and Lower Lamb St)*, was provided by the Earl of Shannon in 1890. Many renovated shopfronts have attractive Gaelic lettering.
The **West Cork Regional Museum**★ *(open May–Oct; Enquire at house next door if the museum is closed; Donation requested; ; 023 33115)*, in the converted schoolhouse, traces local history with special emphasis on the War of Independence and on Michael Collins, who was born at Sam's Cross *(3mi/5km west).*
The **West Cork Model Railway Village** *(open year-round (may close for maintenance Jan, see website) 11am–5pm (Jul–Aug 10am); Christmas Hols, phone to confirm; Village: €7 (child €4.25); Village and train ride: €11 (child €6.25); ; 023 33224; www.modelvillage.ie),* which portrays life (in miniature) as it was in the 1940s, is a delight for young and not-so-young visitors.
The peninsula known as **Inchydoney Island** *(3mi/5km S by the causeway road),* has a series of lovely sandy beaches; the large grass-covered spit of land jutting south into the sea is known as the "Virgin's Bank".

▶ *From Clonakilty take N 71 W.*

Rosscarbery

This small village at the head of a narrow inlet has an enormous quadrangular square and a much-restored 12C Romanesque building, **St Fachtna's Cathedral** (Anglican), with an elaborately-carved west doorway.
That great evangeliser of the Germans, St Kilian was educated here at the monastic school, founded in AD 590 by St Fachtna, bishop and abbot, before

setting out on his mission to Würzburg; two centuries later, that city repaid the compliment by sending one of its monks, St James, to found a Benedictine community in Rosscarbery.

▷ *From Rosscarbery take R 597 W towards Glandore; after 4mi/ 6.4km turn left to the Drombeg Circle (sign).*

Drombeg Stone Circle★

This is probably the most impressive of the 60 stone circles built in prehistoric times in west Cork.

It has 14 evenly-spaced stones which form an enclosed circle (30ft/9m in diameter); usually the number of stones was uneven. Of similar antiquity is the nearby cooking pit.

▷ *Continue W on R 597 to Glandore.*

Glandore★

The original Irish name for this small village, Cuan Dor meaning the "harbour of the oaks", alludes to the days when extensive woodland covered much of west Cork.

The semicircular harbour faces two minute islands in the estuary called Adam and Eve; old sailing directions told sailors to "avoid Adam and hug Eve".

Somerville and Ross

Castletownshend in West Cork was once a stronghold of the Anglo-Irish Ascendancy: a perfect subject for the novelists Edith Somerville and Violet Martin, second cousins, known as **Somerville and Ross**. The success of *Some Experiences of an Irish RM* (1899) prompted *Further Experiences of an Irish RM* (1908) and *In Mr Knox's Country* (1915). More serious issues appear in *The Real Charlotte* (1894); but *The Big House at Inver* (1925), written by Edith after Violet's death, is perhaps the best. Both lie buried in St Barrahane's Church graveyard.

▷ *Cross the river to Union Hall; take the road via Rineen to Castletownshend.*

Castletownshend★

The steep Main Street of this tiny village descends to the water's edge where a small pier offers fine views across the lovely Castle Haven estuary. **St Barrahane's Church** (Anglican) is attractively set at the top of four flights of steps *(50)* at the foot of the Main Street; the colourful Nativity Window was designed by Harry Clarke.

©Joe Gough/Dreamstime.com

Drombeg Stone Circle

KNOCK

POPULATION 575

Until the late 19C Knock (An Cnoc) was a quiet little village set on a wind-swept ridge – the Irish word 'cnoc' translates into English as 'hill' – in the middle of a vast and inhospitable bog. Today, it has become one of the world's great Marian shrines, attracting 1.5 million pilgrims a year, many of them during Knock Novena week in August, when the Statue of the Virgin is carried in procession in the grounds to celebrate the anniversary of the Apparition.

- **Information:** Knock Village. ☎094 9388 193. www.irelandwest.ie.
- ▶ **Orient Yourself:** Knock is 44mi/71km north of Galway on the R 329.
- **Don't Miss:** Museum of Country Life, Turlough Park.
- **Also See:** BOYLE, CONG, SLIGO, STROKESTOWN, WESTPORT.

Sights

Church of the Apparition

The south gable of the church where the Apparition was seen (*see 'The Apparition at Knock' box*) is now protected by glass, as early pilgrims used to take away pieces of the wall plaster, believing it to have miraculous powers.

Basilica of Our Lady, Queen of Ireland★

The huge hexagonal church (over 48 000 sq ft/4 500sq m), was designed by Dáithí P Hanly to hold 12 000 people, and consecrated in 1976. The external ambulatory has 12 pillars of red Mayo granite and 32 pillars of stone from each of the 32 counties of Ireland. Inside hangs a large Donegal hand-knotted tapestry of the apparition, designed by Ray Carroll. The central space accommodates the high altar; the rest is divided into five chapels dedicated to the Sacred Heart, St John the Evangelist, Our Lady of Knock, St Joseph and St Columba. The partition walls hold replica church windows from each of the four provinces of Ireland.

Folk Museum

⏷○*Open May–Oct 10am–6pm, Nov–Apr noon–4pm.* ○*Closed 25–26 Dec.* ⊙€4. ⊑ ℗. ☎094 938 8100. www.knock-shrine.ie.

A modern building, bearing the shields of the four provinces of Ireland – Ulster, Connaught, Leinster, Munster – houses a well-presented display illustrating the development of the Knock shrine; life in

The Apparition at Knock

One wet August evening in 1879 two village women said they saw Mary, Joseph and St John bathed in light against the south gable of the church. Another 13 people, aged 6 to 75, were called to share the vision. A church commission examined all the witnesses and accepted their account. Pilgrims came in droves, cures of the sick and disabled were reported. In 1957 the church was affiliated to the Basilica of St Mary Major in Rome and special indulgences were granted to pilgrims. On the centenary of the apparition, in 1979, Pope John Paul II paid the first papal visit to Ireland.

Address Book

GETTING AROUND

Ireland West Airport Knock, Charlestown, Co Mayo. 9mi/14.5km northeast of Knock by N 17. ☎094 9368100. www.knockairport.com.

SHOPPING

Foxford Woollen Mill – (*see Inland Mayo*).

SPORTS AND LEISURE

Castlebar International 4 days Walks – Held late Jun–early July. www.castlebar4dayswalks.com.

the west of Ireland in the 19C; the Papal visit in 1979 and the life and achievements of Msgr James Horan, parish priest (1963–87).

Driving Tour

Inland Mayo
Round trip of 86mi/139km.

▷ *From Knock take the R 323 N via Kiltimagh; in Bohola turn left onto the N 5 to Turlough.*

Museum of Country Life★★
🕐*Open Tue–Sun 10am–5pm (2pm Sun).* 🕐*Closed Good Fri, 25 Dec.* ☕. 🅿. ☎1 6777 444. www.museum.ie/countrylife. Some 50,000 items from the National Museum's collections are displayed in a Victorian Gothic mansion and a stunning, purpose-built four-storey curved, stone-clad block blended with the terraced landscape of Turlough Park. The richly varied collections eschew any hint of sentimentality to present traditional life in the Irish countryside until the late 20C. The displays address the physical realities of the countryside, the unremitting cycle of work, the home, the role of women, the community, folklife and folklore.

The imposing ruin of a medieval Fitzgerald stronghold guards the approach to the park. The hilltop on the far bank of the Castlebar River is marked by a fine round tower and a roofless church marking the site of a monastery founded by St Patrick.

▷ *Continue west on the N 5.*

Castlebar
This is the county town and commercial centre of Mayo, set on the Castlebar River. It is best known as being the place where the French General Humbert and his Irish peasant allies put a far superior British force to ignominious flight in 1798 in an episode gleefully referred to thereafter as the "Castlebar Races". Another famous local rebel was John Moore, the leader of the short-lived "Republic of Connaught". He was captured at Castlebar, died in prison and is buried by the 1798 memorial in **The Mall**.

▷ *From Castlebar take the L 134 north; on the outskirts of the town turn left onto the minor road towards Burren and Windy Gap. Continue north and turn left onto the R 315; 3mi/5km beyond Lahardaun turn right.*

Errew Abbey★
20min there and back on foot across the fields.
The scant ruins of an Augustinian abbey (1413) enjoy a picturesque **site** on a spit

---

Michael Davitt (1846–1906)

Davitt was born during the Great Famine. When aged four, his family was evicted for non-payment of rent and emigrated to Lancashire in England. Five years later, he was working in a woollen mill; a bad accident there meant his right arm had to be amputated. He went to a Wesleyan School; at 16 he was employed in a printing business, following evening classes in Irish history at the Mechanics' Institute. He joined the Fenian movement, rose to be secretary in Northern England and Scotland until he was arrested and imprisoned for seven years for smuggling arms.

He returned to Co Mayo (1878) and helped tenants to get better treatment from the landlords. Then he persuaded Parnell to join the movement, and the Mayo Land League was formed in Daly's Hotel in Castlebar on 16 August 1879. The Irish National Land League was formed in October. During the ensuing Land War, Davitt and others were arrested under the Coercion Act (1881). On his release, Davitt abandoned the spotlight to work as a reformer, teacher, writer and social thinker, defending the rights of agricultural labourers and trade unionism.

He helped to form the GAA and travelled widely. His books – *Leaves from a Prison Diary* (1885), *The Fall of Feudalism in Ireland* (1904), and other writings examine working conditions in Australia and South Africa.

of land pointing into Lough Conn. A 13C church with trefoil windows pre-dates the cloister buildings.

▶ *Return through Lahardaun; continue S on R 315; left in Pontoon. Continue east to the R 318 and turn right.*

Foxford Woollen Mills

🕐 *May–Oct 10am–6pm (noon Sun), Nov–Apr 10am–6pm (2pm Sun).* ⛔ *Last tour 5.30pm.* 🎫 *€9.* ✕ 🅿. 📞 *094 925 6756. http://foxford.mayo-ireland.ie/ WoolMill.htm.*

The mills were set up by the Irish Sisters of Charity in 1890. The nuns are no more, but the famous Foxford blankets, rugs and tweeds continue to be sold. A presentation about the history of the mill is followed by a self-guided tour of the 1930s machinery and a view of the many stages of production. The mills also hold two art galleries.

▶ *Take the N 58 south to Straide.*

Michael Davitt Memorial Museum

♿🕐 *Open daily 10am–6pm.* 🎫 *€3.50.* 🅿 📞 *094 903 1022.*

The remarkable Republican reformer Michael Davitt (👉 *see 'Michael Davitt' box*) was born and buried in Straide.

▶ *Continue on the N 58, turn left onto the N 5; in Bohola turn right onto the R 321; in Kiltimagh take the R 323 to return to Knock.*

LIMERICK★★

POPULATION 52 039

Astride the River Shannon at its lowest fording point, Limerick (Luimneach) is the main administrative and commercial centre of the mid-west region and the fourth largest city in Ireland. Its three historic quarters are still quite distinct: medieval Englishtown on King's Island defended by one of the most formidable castles in Ireland; Irishtown, forming the modern city centre; and the Georgian district of Newtown Pery, laid out on a grid pattern during the 18C. The atmosphere created by a particularly turbulent past, with extremes of wealth and poverty, marked Limerick deeply but today the city, with its modern university, new industries and proximity to Shannon Airport, is a more welcoming place than it has ever been.

🛈 **Information:** Arthurs Quay. 📞 061 317 522. www.visitlimerick.com.

▶ **Orient Yourself:** Limerick is 62mi/100km south of Galway, on the N 20.

👁 **Don't Miss:** The Hunt Museum and an excursion to Bunratty Castle.

👣 **Also See:** ADARE, ENNIS, KILLALOE, KILRUSH.

A Bit of History

City of Sieges – In 922 Vikings from Denmark sailed up the Shannon, landed at Great Quay (now Long Dock), and established a base on King's Island from which they plundered the rich agricultural hinterland. For over a century the town was repeatedly attacked by Irish forces until Brian Ború, High King of Ireland, sacked it and banished the settlers. In 1194, the Normans seized control of the region, raising the great fortress of King John's Castle, building city walls, and peppering the countryside with hundreds of strongholds.

In 1642 Limerick was besieged by the Cromwellians, followed by a momentous siege after the Battle of the Boyne in July 1690, when James II had fled to France and the defeated Jacobites withdrew to Limerick. Eventually, under the bold leadership of Patrick Sarsfeld, the Williamites abandoned their siege at the end of August. The following year another Williamite army led by General Ginkel returned to the attack while an English fleet blockaded the Shannon.

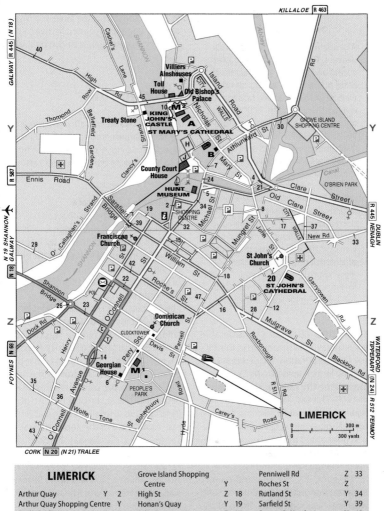

Sarsfield sued for peace which was granted on surprisingly generous terms by the **Treaty of Limerick**. The Irish were given safe conduct to France and Roman Catholics in general were guaranteed various rights and privileges, including the freedom to practise their religion. Ratification of the treaty by the Irish Parliament was, however, only partial and the Penal Laws enacted from 1695 were seen by Roman Catholics as a betrayal.

Sarsfield's Ride

A gentleman of Old English, Catholic descent, **Patrick Sarsfield** showed daring and effective generalship. In early August 1690, acting on information from a deserter, he slipped out of the city with 600 cavalry, and headed north, then east, fording the Shannon upstream of Killaloe Bridge, which was held by the Williamites. After travelling south through the Silvermine Mountains, he intercepted the Williamite siege train at Ballyneety *(18mi/30km south of Limerick); the noise of its destruc-* tion reached the city. With this coup Sarsfield had bought time but not victory. After negotiating the Treaty of Limerick he and 10 000 Irish soldiers known as "Wild Geese", left for France. Sarsfield died in battle in 1693, fighting for Louis XIV.

18C to 20C – Despite a considerable agrarian revolt in the region in the 18C, the City Corporation decided that Limerick no longer needed to be fortified, so most of the city walls were demolished in 1760. The 18C also marked the last flowering of the old Irish culture. As the Great Famine and subsequent emigration devastated the local population in the 1840s, Gaelic ceased to be the vernacular language of Limerick.

In the early 20C the city and county became strongholds of nationalism and working-class radicalism. Three of the leaders of the 1916 Easter Rising came from the Limerick district, including **Eamon de Valera** (1882–1975), Prime Minister *(Taoiseach)* and President of the Republic.

Limerick Lace

Lace making was introduced to Limerick in the 1820s by the English and reached its peak in the 19C when 900 girls were employed locally.

The elaborate Celtic patterns were outlined on machine-made cotton net in thin or thick thread and filled in with decorative stitches.

In 1919, at the start of the three-year War of Independence, a general strike took place to protest against British military rule.

Walking Tour

As **King's Island** was almost encircled by the Shannon and the Abbey River, it was an obvious site for the Vikings and Normans to establish their settlements.

St Mary's Cathedral★

www.cathedral.limerick.anglican.org.
This transitional Romanesque Anglican cathedral, founded in 1168 by Dónall Mór O'Brien, King of Munster, is the oldest surviving building in Limerick. Parts of the king's palace are incorporated in the original cruciform church.

The 15C black oak choir stalls and splendid carved misericords are unique in Ireland; the high altar reredos was carved by the English father of Patrick Pearse (🔥 *see DUBLIN*) ; the north transept contains the fine 15C **Arthur Memorial** *(below the window)* commemorating the cathedral Treasurer Geoffrey Arthur (d 1519), and a small rectangular lepers' squint *(right);* the south transept contains the 15C Galway-Bultingfort tomb.

Farther along Nicholas Street are seven Tuscan columns, bricked up to form a wall, all that remains of the Old Limerick Exchange, built in 1673.

▶ *Turn down Bridge Street and cross Matthew Bridge.*

Hunt Museum★★

🔥🕐*Open year-round Mon–Sat 10am–5pm (2pm Sun).* 🕐*Closed Good Fri, 24–26 Dec, 1 Jan.* 👓 *€7.75.* ✗. ☎*061 312 833. www. huntmuseum.com.*
The 18C Custom House designed by Italian architect Davis Duchart provides a fitting home for this outstanding collection of art and antiquities amassed during the life of John and Gertrude Hunt. The expertly selected items span every age and include works of every scale. Highlights include the wooden carved *Apollo – Genius of the Arts*, a small

Address Book

For coin ranges, see the Legend on the cover flap.

GETTING ABOUT

Shannon International Airport – ☎061 712 000. www.shannonairport.com.

SIGHTSEEING

Walking Tours – *Angela's Ashes* tour, based on the popular novel by Frank McCourt about the wretched life of the poor in Limerick during his childhood. Depart from tourist office, Arthur's Quay. *Call for times and prices.* ☎061 327 108. www.visitlimerick.com.

WHERE TO STAY

Carrig House – *2 Meadowvale, Raheen, 2.75mi southwest of town.* ☎061 309 626. 3rm. This immaculately kept, purpose-built welcoming guesthouse offers compact colourfully decorated en-suite bedrooms.

Clifton House – *Ennis Rd. 1.25mi NW on R 587.* ☎061 451 166. Closed 21 Dec–2 Jan. 16rm. Simple well-priced accommodation, set in 1 acre of landscape gardens, a 15min walk from town.

Clonmacken House – *Clonmacken Rd, off Ennis Rd. 2.5mi NW by N 18 turning right at Clonmacken roundabout.* ☎061 327 007. 10rm. This modern well-kept guesthouse is a 5-min drive from the city centre Pretty little garden, and a quiet position.

Jurys Inn Limerick – *Lower Mallow St.* ☎061 207 000. http://limerickhotels. jurysdoyle.com. In the heart of Limerick city, close to all the main business and shopping areas. Jurys Inns offers bright, spacious rooms, which can accommodate up to three adults or two adults and two children. Some overlook the River Shannon; those at the rear are quietest.

WHERE TO EAT

Brûlées – *Corner Mallow/Henry Street.* ☎061 319 931. Closed Sun, Mon. Split between three floors of a Georgian house, with the aproned owner providing the attentive service and his wife the Modern Irish cooking, which emphasises local produce. Plenty of daily specials and local fish.

TAKING A BREAK

Dolans – *Dock Road.* ☎061 314 483. www.dolanspub.com. Probably the best known pub in the region. It offers a comprehensive menu specialising in seafood but what really draws the crowds is the live music (and comedians) at the end of the week, featuring a variety of traditional and folk, rock and blues, all staged in Dolan's Warehouse, specially built for gigs.

Schooners – *Steamboat Quay, Dock Road.* ☎061 318 147. Boasts a super location beside the Shannon with a terrace in summer to watch the boats go by. Live concerts are held at the end of the week.

ENTERTAINMENT

Belltable Arts Centre – ☎061 315 871. www.belltable.ie. This multi-functioning arts centre houses a 250-seat theatre/cinema (Limerick's only city centre cinema), a 50-seat balcony studio (for occasional poetry and small performances), a visual arts gallery and restaurant which serves throughout the day.

SHOPPING

Arthur's Quay Shopping Centre – *Arthur's Quay* – ☎061 419 888. Housing more than 30 stores, this centre has several boutiques where you will find hand-knit and machine-made sweaters and clothing by Irish designers in linen, tweed and cotton.

Limerick Lace is now rare, though a few people still hand-make the delicate fabric on request. Enquire at the tourist office.

Irish Dresden – *Dromcolliher, 34mi/ 56km north of Limerick. Open Monday to Friday 9am–1pm and 2- 4.30pm (closed Bank Holidays and first 2 weeks Aug)* ☎063 83236.www.irishdresden. Visitor Centre and guided tours of factory.

17C Italian mould blown emerald green glass jug with gilt metal mounts

Hunt Museum

bronze *Horse*, attributed to Leonardo da Vinci, and a startling self-portrait by Robert Fagan (c 1745–1816), a painter of the English school, and a dealer in antiquities in Rome. The archaeological collection is drawn from ancient civilisations in Egypt, Greece and Rome, as well as Irish treasures such as the Cashel Bell and Antrim Cross. The Jewellery Gallery displays the Mary Queen of Scots Cross. Religious Art is dramatically exhibited in the Treasury: among the silver and precious stones is a Greek coin, traditionally thought to be one of the "Thirty Pieces of Silver" given to Judas Iscariot.

▶ *Walk over the pedestrian bridge, past the County Court House (1809) and back to Nicholas Street.*

Limerick Museum/Jim Kemmy Municipal Museum★

&⊘*Open Tue–Sat 10am–1pm, 2.15pm–7pm.* ⊘*Closed Bank Hols.* ☎*061 417 826. www.limerickcity.ie/CityMuseum.*
The Limerick museum gives a comprehensive account of the city and its history. An excellent collection of 18C silver, tambour, needlepoint and tape **lace** recall important Limerick crafts. The brass-topped limestone **Nail** from the Old Exchange was used to settle commercial transactions – hence the expression "paying on the Nail". Finds from excavations in the Abbey River are also displayed.

King John's Castle★

&⊘*Open May–Sept 9.30am–5.30pm, Mar–Oct 9.30am–5pm, Nov–Feb 10am–4.30pm. Last admission 1hr before closing.* ⊘*Closed Good Fri, 24–26 Dec.* &≈€9. ☎*061 711 200. www.shannonheritage.com.*
This was once the most important Norman stronghold in the west and remains a fine example of medieval fortification (1200–16). Instead of a keep, it has massive round towers protecting the gateway; the walls would originally have been taller to withstand siege machines, but in 1611, the towers and the wall-walks were lowered to accommodate cannons, and the diamond-shaped gun bastion was added. The history of the castle and the city is retold in the **visitor centre**.
Reproductions of war engines are displayed in the courtyard. The sentry walk on the battlements provides good views of the Shannon, the city and its surroundings.

Bishop's Palace

⊘*Open by arrangement.* ☎*061 313 399. www.limerickcivictrust.ie.*
The oldest-surviving dwelling in the city, the Palace was designed in the Palladian style by Francis Bindon (c 1690–1765), a native of Limerick. It now houses the Limerick Civic Trust. Limerick is unusual in having two sets of almhouses: the **Villiers Almshouses** (1826), north of the castle, were built in the Bishop's Palace garden by James Pain for 12 poor Protestant widows with an annual income of £24. The **Corporation Almshouses**, also known as the 40-shilling (£2) Almshouses for 20 widows were erected by the Limerick Corporation in 1691.

Thomond Bridge

The Gothic-style **Toll House** with castellated parapets dates from 1839 when the bridge was rebuilt.
The **Treaty Stone** *(on the west bank of the river)*, is a block of limestone on which the 1691 Treaty of Limerick is said to have been signed; it was moved here in 1865

King John's Castle

from outside Black Bull Pub, where it had been used as a mounting-block.

Sights

The old Irish quarter on the south bank of Abbey River, outside the walls of the English Town, now forms the **town centre** of modern Limerick. The district to the south is a fine example of 18C town planning with broad parallel streets lined with **red-brick terraces** – named **Newtown Pery** after Edmond Sexton Pery (1719–1806), Speaker of the Irish House of Commons.

People's Park
♿ ⏱ *Open Mon–Fri 10am–4pm (last admission).* 💲€5. ☎061 3141 30. *www.limerickcivictrust.ie/georgian.*
The focal point of the Newtown Pery district was built by the Pery Tontine Company in 1838.
The **Georgian House**★ at No 2 Pery Square has been restored as a splendid example of Georgian architecture and décor. It also houses the **Carrol Collection** of family heirlooms and military memorabilia dating between the late 1700s and the 1920s.
The military careers of five generations of this remarkable family start with the legendary exploits of Major-General Sir William Parker Carrol in the Peninsular War and progress through the Boer War and both World Wars.
The recently extended **Limerick City Gallery of Art** (♿ ⏱ *open Mon–Fri 10am –6pm (7pm Fri), Sat 10am–1pm;* ☎061 407 100; *www.limerickcity.ie/LCGA)* holds the National Collection of Contemporary Drawings as well as a growing collection of leading 18C–20C Irish art (Sean Keating, Jack B Yeats and Evie Hone) and visiting exhibitions.
At **St Saviour's Dominican Church**, stands the 17C statue of Our Lady of Limerick. This was brought from Flanders in 1640 and presented to the Dominicans as a mark of atonement by a Limerick merchant, whose uncle had sentenced the Irish politician and soldier Sir John Burke to death for allowing a priest to say Mass during a time of severe religious persecution.

Milk Market
The open area, on the corner of Ellen Street and Wickham Street, accommodates a bustling Saturday market, where home-grown local produce has been traded since 1830: today it is the gourmet area of Limerick. **William Street** and **O'Connell Street** are prime shopping areas. The **Franciscan Church** (1876–86) with its fine Corinthian portico, was extended in 1930 with a richly decorated apse.

John Square★
The square, laid out in 1751, is bordered by terraces of three-storey houses once occupied by wealthy citizens. On the fourth side, stands **St John's Church** (1843). The neo-Gothic Roman Catholic **St John's Cathedral**★ on the edge of what was the old Irish town dates from

The First Limerick

The origin of the term limerick in poetry, meaning a five-line poem, usually witty, sometimes rude, and originally popularised by Edward Lear, is obscure. In the 18C a rustic school of Gaelic poetry flourished along the banks of the River Maigue. **Aindrias Mac Craith**, a local schoolmaster was possibly jointly responsible for the invention of the limerick; in playful poetic conflict with a fellow-poet and tavern-keeper, one Seán Ó Tuama, he wrote:

O'Toomey! You boast yourself handy
At selling good ale and brandy,
But the fact is your liquor
Makes everyone sicker
I tell you that, I, your friend Andy.

1861. The spire (280ft/85m), completed in 1883, is the tallest in Ireland.

Excursions

Cratloe Woods House

5mi/8km W by N 18. &⚲*Open Jun–mid-Sept 2pm-4pm by appointment.* ⊜€5. ☎*061 327 028.*

The house (1600) is a rare example of the Irish long house, albeit altered. The interior displays furniture and fascinating souvenirs of the owners, direct descendants of Brian Ború and the O'Briens, the leading family of the region. **Cratloe Wood** at the foot of Woodcock Hill incorporates a lake and forest walks.

Bunratty Castle & Folk Park★★

7mi/11km W by N 18. &⚲⬤Castle open by guided tour only, Apr–Oct 9am–5.30pm (6pm Jun–Aug); Dec–Mar 9.30am–5.30pm. Last tour 4pm ⚲Folk park: same hours. Last admission 45min to 1hr 15min

"Crom Abu"

The battle cry of the Earls of Kildare derives from their castle at Croom on the River Maigue.

before closing; Irish Night: Apr–Oct 7pm;. Medieval banquet: year-round nightly 5.30pm, 8.45pm (reservation required). ⚲Closed Good Fri, 24–26 Dec. ⊜€15 Castle and Folk Park. Medieval banquet €57.50. Irish night €47.95. ☎061 711200. www.shannonheritage.com. www.bunrattycollection.com.

The most splendid **tower house** in Ireland commands a formidable position on the main road between Limerick and Ennis, at the point where the Bunratty River flows into the Shannon Estuary. It was built in 1460 by the powerful O'Brien family on the site of earlier fortifications. In the 1950s, it was restored to its 16C state to display the superb Gort collection of furniture and tapestries from the 14C–17C. In the evenings medieval-style banquets are held in the Great Hall which has a fine **oak roof**.

The **Folk Park** is a very convincing re-creation of country life, set at the turn of the century when traditional practices were dying out. There is a blacksmith's forge, flour mill and houses of different regional types – a mountain farmhouse and a more elaborate thatched Golden Vale farmhouse. The **Village Street** contains 19C shops: a pawnbroker, pub, post office, hardware shop, grocery store, draper's and printing workshop equipped with hand-set type and a hand-operated press. The whole park is staffed by costumed characters.

Bunratty House, built in 1804, is a local adaptation of the Georgian box house so common in Ireland. In its farmyard is displayed the **Talbot Collection of agricultural machinery**.

Driving Tour

Maigue Valley

▶ *From Limerick take the R 512 south; after 8.5mi/13.6km bear left.*

Lough Gur

Set among low hills, horseshoe-shaped Lough Gur is the largest water body in Co Limerick and the area around the lake is one of the longest-inhabited districts in Ireland. It has an exceptional wealth

Eamon de Valera

Eamon de Valera (1882–1975), born in New York to a Spanish father and Irish mother, was largely brought up by his uncle near Kilmallock. One of the leaders of the 1916 Rising De Valera only escaped execution because of his American birth. He was imprisoned by the British, then later also spared by the Free State authorities after siding with the Republicans in the Civil War. He founded the Fianna Fáil party in 1926, became Prime Minister *(Taoiseach)* in 1932, and kept Ireland neutral in the Second World War. Between 1959 and 1973 he served as President of the Republic, steadfastly nationalist in his politics but conservative when deciding how Ireland should develop.

of stone circles, standing stones, burial chambers and cairns. Artefacts, relics and models of stone circles and burial chambers, are on display in the thatched hut housing the **Lough Gur Visitor Centre**★ (♿🕐*open daily May–Sept 10am–6pm; €5; ☎061 711200; www. shannonheritage.com)*, which also screens a video illustrating the life of Neolithic people in this region.

▷ *Return to the T-junction; turn left onto the R 512; continue south via Holycross and Bruff.*

Kilmallock★

Kilmallock developed around the 7C abbey founded by St Mocheallog, to become the seat of the Fitzgeralds and a pre-eminent town in the province of Munster, with town walls, a castle and four gates. In 1568 it was burnt down to prevent it from being taken by the English; a century later, after Cromwell's departure, its extensive walls had gone and many of its buildings lay in ruins; it suffered again in the Williamite wars and never regained its former status.

By the river stand the ruins of the 13C Dominican **Kilmallock Abbey**★. A fine transept window and part of the tower (90ft/27m high) survive. At the entrance to the abbey is a small town **museum** (🕐*open 11am–3pm; ☎063 91300)*.

The walls and arches of the nave and south transept of the 13C Roman Catholic **Collegiate Church**★, dedicated to St Peter and St Paul, are largely intact; the tower is part of an ancient round tower. A substantial section of the medieval **Town Walls** can be seen between the Collegiate Church and **Blossom's Gate** – the only one of five still standing. The **King's Castle**, a 15C tower house, occupies the site of an earlier fortress built to guard the Loobagh valley. During the Parliamentary Wars (1645–51) it was used as an arsenal by the Irish and later as a hospital by the Cromwellians.

▷ *From Kilmallock take the R 518 west to Bruree.*

Bruree

The **De Valera Museum** (♿🕐*open 10am–5pm (2pm Sun); call for dates; ☎063 90 900)*, in the old school between the ancient six-arch bridge over the River Maigue and the old mill, celebrates the former President of the Republic with displays of his school copy-books and a desk carved with his initials.

▷ *From Bruree take the minor road north; in Athlacca bear left to Croom; take the minor road east to Monaster (Manister).*

Monasteranenagh Abbey★

The impressive ruins beside the River Camoge are those of a Cistercian monastery, colonised by monks from Mellifont, founded in the 12C by Turlough O'Brien, King of Thomond, as a mark of thanksgiving for defeating the Danes in the Battle of Rathmore in 1148.

LISMORE ★

POPULATION 715

No bigger than a village, but a designated Heritage Town, this idyllic little place on the banks of the salmon-rich River Blackwater was once a great centre of medieval learning. It still has a cathedral, but the dominant landmark is the castle overlooking the lovely wooded valley.

- **Information:** Lismore Heritage Centre. ☎058 54975. www.discoverlismore.com.
- ▶ **Orient Yourself:** Lismore (Lios Mór) is situated on the south bank of the River Blackwater roughly half way between Waterford 41mi/66km northeast and Cork 34mi/54km southwest.
- **Also See:** CAHER, CLONMEL, COBH, CORK, MALLOW, MIDLETON, YOUGHAL.

A Bit of History

The monastery, founded by **St Carthach** in the 7C, became one of Europe's most distinguished universities with some 20 seats of learning and religion until 978, when the Danish Vikings raided the town and burned the monasteries. Lismore was still sufficiently important, however, for Henry II to receive the submission of Irish chiefs here soon after his landing in Ireland in 1171. A prosperous town developed around the castle built in 1185 by King John. In 1589 it came in to the possession of Sir Walter Ralegh. The present castle (private) is one of the most spectacular in Ireland, rebuilt by Sir Joseph Paxton (of Crystal Palace fame) who was then gardener to the Duke of Devonshire, the castles's new proprietor. It is a theatrical neo-Tudor fantasy looking out over the valley of the River Blackwater. In the mid-20C the castle was home to Adele Astaire, sister of the great dancer Fred, and wife to the then owner Lord Charles Cavendish.

Sights

Lismore Castle Gardens★

⟐⟁Open 17 Mar–Sept 11am–4.45pm. ⟐€7. ☎058 54424.
The gardens are set in seven acres within the 17C outer defensive walls and have spectacular views of the Castle and surrounding countryside. They are divided into two sections, comprising the 17C walled garden and the lower garden. The lower garden, known as the Pleasure Grounds, was laid out c 1850, although the Yew Walk where, traditionally, Edmund Spenser (⟐see MALLOW) composed part of The Faerie Queene, is much older. Yew, beech and box hedges screen flower and vegetable beds, Paxton's greenhouses date from 1858. The Broghill Tower (SW corner) provides a fine view. Contemporary sculpture by the likes of Anthony Gormley, Emily Young, David Nash and, Marzia Colonna) add a modern twist to this immaculate landscape. A new contemporary art gallery has also opened in the West Wing of Lismore Castle (same ticket as gardens).

St Carthage's Cathedral (Anglican)★

Surrounded by a picturesque graveyard shaded by yews and lime-trees, the parish church is redolent of Lismore's long history. The existing building, the fourth on the site, is largely the result of a rebuild ordered by Sir Richard Boyle in 1633; the **ribbed ceilings** were added by Sir Richard Morrison (c 1820), and the fine **tower** and **ribbed spire** (1826) by the Payne brothers of Cork. Note the fine stained-glass window donated by Sir Edward Burne-Jones, the pebbles from the Isle of Iona (Scotland) in the floor of St Columba's Chapel, and the elaborate **table-tomb** of 1548.

St Carthach's Church (Roman Catholic)

Designed by WG Doolin in 1881, this is one of the most outstanding Lombardo-Romanesque churches in Ireland, richly detailed and built of red sandstone with white limestone dressings and a detached bell-tower.

Facing the west entrance to the church is a fine row of 19C artisans' cottages.

Lismore Heritage Centre

🕐 *Open year-round Mon–Fri 9.30am–5.30pm. May–Oct also Sat–Sun 10am (noon Sun)–5.30pm. Video show.* ✆€5. ☎*058 54975. www.discoverlismore.com.*
The Old Courthouse provides an audio-visual history of Lismore, an exhibition gallery on the town and the life and works of **Robert Boyle**, the father of modern chemistry, who was born in Lismore Castle.

Excursion

The Gap★
10mi/16km north via the R 688.
Beyond the Blackwater valley, rise the Old Red Sandstone Knockmealdown Mountains (2608ft/795m). The Lismore-Caher road follows the lush valley before climbing to the scenic V Gap with its magnificent **views**★. On the north slopes of Sugar Loaf mountain (2 144ft/653m) stands **Grubb's Grave**, the burial cairn of a local Quaker called Samuel Grubb who died in the 1920s; the sugar-loaf construction enabled him to be buried upright overlooking his estates.

LONGFORD

POPULATION 6 393

The market centre for the surrounding agricultural area, Longford (An Longfort) lies on the Camlin River amid pleasant if undistinguished scenery, a few miles from where the Shannon broadens out into Lough Ree. Co Longford has important literary associations with Oliver Goldsmith (Lough Ree) and Maria Edgeworth (at Mostrim), and it was at Ballinamuck (10mi/16km north) that the last engagement of the 1798 rebellion was fought, when General Humbert's French troops and Irish volunteers were defeated by the English under General Lake.

- 🛈 **Information:** Dublin Street. ☎043 43 42577. www.longford.ie.
- ▶ **Orient Yourself:** Longford stands on the N 4 roughly half way between Dublin, 73mi/118km southeast and Sligo 51mi/82km northwest.
- 🎯 **Also See:** ATHLONE, CARRICK-ON-SHANNON, MULLINGAR, STROKESTOWN.

Visit

St Mel's Cathedral
Longford's principle landmark is the monumental neo-Classical Roman Catholic cathedral with its vast Ionic portico supporting a richly sculpted pediment and tall octagonal bell-tower capped with a dome – designed by John Keane in 1840.

The greatest treasure of the **Diocesan Museum** *(right transept)* is **St Mel's Crozier** (10C), a stick of yew encased in bronze inset with studs and decorated with animal motifs, foliage and interlacing, found at old St Mel's Church in Ardagh (🎯*see Excursions*) in 1860. St Mel was a nephew of St Patrick.

Excursions

Carrigglas Manor
3mi/5km east of Longford on the R 194. www.carrigglas.ie.
This castellated neo-Gothic mansion was built in 1837 for Thomas Lefroy,

Address Book

LOCAL ART
Michael Casey of Newtowncashel is an artist in bogwoods, ancient tree roots uncovered during peat-harvesting. Keep an eye open for some of his works, which stand round the village green in Newtowncashel on the east bank of Lough Ree.

Travels in Goldsmith Country

The country around Lough Ree is where the poet, playwright, historian and naturalist **Oliver Goldsmith** (c 1731–74) spent the first 20 or so years of his life, visiting relatives and going to school in Elphin, Mostrim, Athlone and Lissoy.

In **Ardagh** he experienced the plot of his play *She Stoops to Conquer*, by mistaking the big house for the village inn. The site of his first boyhood home at **Pallas** is marked by a statue by Foley. Until 1731 his father was Rector of **Forgney** church, which contains a stained-glass window depicting "sweet Auburn".

After her husband's death in 1747, Goldsmith's mother lived in **Ballymahon** on the Inny River. It was in **Tang** that Goldsmith first went to school near the mill. The pub, known as **The Three Jolly Pigeons**, preserves the name of the inn in Goldsmith's play *She Stoops to Conquer*.

Lissoy Parsonage, now in ruins, was the house where the Goldsmith family lived from 1731 to 1747; **Lissoy** village is recalled as "sweet Auburn" in his poem *The Deserted Village*.

Lord Chief Justice of Ireland and youthful admirer of Jane Austen, who may have used him as the model for the hero of *Pride and Prejudice,* Mr Darcy. The Manor is presently being restored and converted into 19 5-star hotel suites.

The woodland garden, planted with a rich variety of species, was inspired by the great Victorian designer, William Robinson, its avenue and Palladian courtyards were designed by James Gandon (who also created The Customs House and Four Courts in Dublin); and the magnificent Victorian Gothic manor house is by Daniel Robertson, who was responsible for the famous Italian Gardens at Powerscourt. A startling new contemporary addition to the estate is **Carrigglas Hotel**, a luxurious 96-room hotel, spa and leisure complex. It features a stunning glazed atrium, grassed roofs and glazed façades. A championship golf course has also recently opened.

Ardagh
7mi/11km south east of Longford on the N 4 and R 393.

The charming little estate village was largely rebuilt in the 1860s by Lady Fetherstone, who lived at Ardagh House. The ruins of a simple stone church, St Mel's Cathedral, are said to stand on the site where the saint was buried.

The **Ardagh Heritage Centre** (🕐*open Mon–Sat 9.30am–5.30pm;* 🚫*closed Bank Hols;* ☎*043 42577*) traces the history of the locality from the pre-Christian era, through the internal rivalries of the local O'Farrell tribe, and the 1619 Plantation to the present.

Corlea Trackway
10mi/16km S of Longford by the N 63 and R 397; in Kenagh turn right (sign).(Dúchas). ♿🕐*Open Apr–Sept Mon–Sat 10am–6pm. Last admission at 5.15pm.* 🍽. ☎*043 22386. www.heritageireland.ie.*

The centre interprets an Iron Age track that was built in the year 148 BC across the boglands of Longford, close to the River Shannon. The ancient trackway *(togher)*, consisted of a series of oak planks secured by pegs, wide enough to carry wheeled vehicles across the

Maria Edgeworth

Maria Edgeworth (1767–1849) was the eldest daughter of Richard Lovell Edgeworth, a wealthy eccentric with an interest in science who had four wives and 22 children, and who installed heating in Tullynally Castle. She is best remembered as a pioneer of regional and historical novels: *Castle Rackrent* (1800), *The Absentee* (1812) and *Ormond* (1817) are about Irish life. Apart from a few school years in England, she spent her whole life at the family home in Mostrim, also known as Edgeworthstown *(8.5mi/14km east)*.

Corlea Trackway

bog, sinking under the weight over time. A 59ft/18m long section of the preserved timber trackway – the largest of its kind to have been uncovered in Europe – discovered in the 1980s, is displayed under cover, The story of its discovery and its preservation are the subject of a video; the accompanying exhibition sets it in its Iron-Age context.

MALLOW★

POPULATION 6 434

The busy market town of Mallow (Mala) in Co Cork is built at a major crossroads, attractively sited above the River Blackwater, sometimes described as the "Irish Rhine". A faint air of nostalgia pervades, the place recalling the glory days when it was the foremost spa in Ireland, frequented by the notorious "Rakes of Mallow", (see 'The Rake's Last Resort' box) who today would no doubt be keen patrons of the local racecourse.

- **Information:** Bridge St. ☏022 42222. www.mallow.ie.
- ▶ **Orient Yourself:** Mallow is 21 mi/33km north of Cork via the N 20.
- **Also See:** COBH, CORK, LISMORE, MIDLETON.

A Bit of History

Mallow had a late 12C Anglo-Norman castle, built perhaps by King John, that was replaced by a 16C mansion *(in ruins just inside the gates of Mallow Castle)* as a seat for Sir John Norreys, Lord President of Munster. In 1688, the town was granted a charter by King James II. A spa developed in the 18C after the discovery of a natural hot spring. As the spa declined in the early 19C, the town became a centre of great political activ-

Steeplechasing

The **steeplechase** had its origin in Ireland, when huntsmen set wagers with each other on who would be the first to reach a prominent landmark. The first such contest took place from Buttevant in 1752, with the steeple of the Anglican Church as the starting point of a race to St Leger Church near Doneraile (4.5mi/7km).

The Rake's Last Resort

The curative properties of Mallow water, said to be good for purifying the blood, were discovered in 1724. It was not long in becoming a popular spa with a fast reputation; its male patrons infamous as the **Rakes of Mallow**.

Living short but merry lives,
Going where the devil drives,
Having sweethearts, but no wives…

From April to October, visitors would take the waters; in the evening, there was dancing and cards; balls, meetings and gatherings were held in the Long Room as was the fashion in Bath, Tunbridge Wells and Scarborough.

ity, in part because two eminent Nationalists were born here: **Thomas Davis** (1814–45), the Protestant patriot and unchallenged leader of the Young Ireland movement; the noted MP **William O'Brien** (1852–1928). Mallow also has literary connections with **Anthony Trollope**, a resident for some years *(Davis St)*; with **Canon Patrick Sheehan**, the former parish priest at Doneralle (1895–1913) who became one of Ireland's most prolific and popular authors of the late

19C and early 20C *(born at 29 O'Brien St)* and with Elizabeth Bowen, author of The Last September (1929), Seven Winters (1942) and Bowen's Court (1942).

Sights

St James's Church★

Mallow's Anglican church is a fine example of Gothic Revival architecture, built in 1824 by the English-born Pain brothers from Cork. Substantial ruins remain of the former medieval church of St Anne's, badly damaged in the Williamite wars, in which Thomas Davis was baptized in 1814.

Spa House

Visit by guided tour only (20min) Mon–Fri 9am–5pm. ☏022 43610.
The Tudor-style complex housing the pump-room, reading room and baths, was built in 1828 by Charles Jephson. Unfortunately all traces of the spa have now vanished and the present use of the building (now in the hands of the Energy Agency) is to house an exhibition related to geo-thermal technology.

Clock House

This four-storey timber-framed building flanked by a clock tower was erected c 1855 by an amateur architect, supposedly enthused by an Alpine holiday!

Church of the Resurrection

J R Boyd Barratt's Catholic church (1966–69) is shaped like an open fan; the Stations of the Cross are of Tyrolean oak; the stained glass is by the Murphy Davitt Studios of Dublin.

Excursions

Buttevant Friary★

7mi/11km N of Mallow by N 20.
The ruins of the Franciscan friary (1251), stand beside the River Awbeg next to St Mary's Roman Catholic Church. The building, used until recently as a place of burial, has two crypts, one above the other; the chancel walls are still largely intact.

Stained glass window, Church of the Resurrection

P Thebault/MICHELIN

Iconoclast and Creator; the Poet Laureate

A leading light of early modern English, **Edmund Spenser** was also a zealous advocate for the colonisation of Ireland and the destruction of Irish culture. In 1586 a perpetual lease of the lands and castle of Kilcolman, plus a tower house near Doneraile, was granted to Edmund Spenser, who held a post in the Dublin Court of Chancery.

During his years at Kilcolman Spenser received Sir Walter Raleigh and wrote poetry – the fourth, fifth and sixth books of *The Faerie Queen*, the *Amoretti* (love sonnets about his second wife) and his *Veue of the State of Ireland*. Although he had little sympathy for the Irish, the beauty of the landscape pervades his work. During the Rising in 1598 the castle was burned by insurgents and some of Spenser's manuscripts may have perished, including a seventh book of *The Faerie Queen*.

Doneraile Wildlife Park★

*6mi/10km NE of Mallow by N 20
and R 581.*

⟲♿Open mid–Apr–Oct Mon–Fri 8am–
8pm, Sat–Sun & Bank Hols 9am–8pm.
Oct–mid-Apr Mon–Fri 8am–5pm, Sat–
Sun & Bank Hols 9am–5pm. ☎087 251
5965. www.heritageireland.ie.

The walled Doneraile demesne (395 acres/160ha) is noted for its herds of red, fallow and sika deer. Wooded areas and ornamental lakes punctuate the gently rolling landscaped parkland around **Doneraile Court**, built c 1700 and remodelled in the early 19C (the house will be opened to the public in the future, following completion of necessary restoration and safety works).

A stone vault and spiral staircase are all that remains of **Kilcolman Castle**, once the residence of the English poet **Edmund Spenser** (👜see 'Poet Laureate' box).

Annes Grove Gardens★

*11mi/18km E of Mallow via the N 72;
in Castletownroche turn left onto the
minor road.*

♿⟲Open 17 Mar–Sept Mon–Sat 10am–
5pm, Sun 1pm–6pm. ✎€6. ☎022 26145.
www.annesgrovegardens.com.

These woodland gardens, surrounding an 18C house overlooking the River Awbeg, include a fine collection of rhododendrons and magnolias, rare trees and shrubs. Winding paths lead to a cliff garden and an extensive river garden; 19C hedges in the walled garden enclose herbaceous borders and water gardens.

Longueville House

*3mi/5km W of Mallow by N 72; turn right
at sign. www.longuevillehouse.ie.*

Now a luxury hotel this magnificent house, built in 1720, boasts an imposing dual staircase hung with political portraits featuring many of the great men who fashioned the course of Irish history from the 18C to the 20C. In the courtyard at the rear there is a mature **maze**. The estate (500 acres/202ha) includes a **vineyard** (3 acres/1.2ha), the only one in Ireland, which produces grapes that make a Riesling-type wine.

Kanturk (Ceann Toirc)★

*13mi/21km west of Mallow on
the N 72 and R 576.*

This small market town has three great **bridges** spanning the River Dalua and River Allua erected in 1745, 1760 and 1748: the latter, a four-arch Metal Bridge built by Sir Edward Tierney.

The striking French Gothic church at the western end of the town is dedicated to the Immaculate Conception.

South of Kanturk is a ruined **castle**★ *(take the R 579)* dating from 1609. It was intended by the local chieftain, MacDonagh MacCarthy, to be the largest mansion ever to belong to an Irish chief but was stopped by the English Privy Council on the grounds that "it was much too large for a subject (of the English Crown)".

MAYNOOTH

POPULATION 8 528

Maynooth is synonymous with the great seminary, which for more than two hundred years, has prepared priests for the Roman Catholic Church. Today it is a growing commuter and university town, with rail and motorway connections to Dublin.

▶ **Orient Yourself:** Maynooth is 18 mi/30km west of Dublin on the Grand Canal, and main roads out of the capital; it is now bypassed by the M 4.
ⓖ **Also See:** DUBLIN, FINGAL, KILDARE, MULLINGAR, TRIM.

Sights

Maynooth Castle

ⓘ*Open Jun–Sept daily 10am–6pm; Oct Sat–Sun & Bank Hols only, 10am–5pm. Access to the keep by guided tour only, last tour 1hr before closing.* ☎01 628 6744. www.heritageireland.ie/en.

The ruins of the 12C Fitzgerald castle predate the period when the Earls of Kildare reached pre-eminence serving as Lord Deputy from 1471 to 1534. During this time Maynooth was effectively the political capital of Ireland. In 1535, following the Silken Thomas rebellion of 1534, it was successfully besieged by the royal forces and Thomas was spirited away to London to be executed. In 1656 the castle was abandoned in favour of a new residence at Carton House.

Maynooth College

The college, now part of the National University, is laid out around two spacious courtyards: the first dates from the early 19C, the second is one of Pugin's finest Gothic Revival projects, completed in mid-century despite the Great Famine and inadequate funding. The Chapel with its tall spire and splendid oak choir stalls are by Pugin's pupil, JJ McCarthy.

The preceding College of the Blessed Virgin Mary, founded by a Fitzgerald in 1518, was suppressed a mere 17 years later after town and castle were seized by royal forces. During the Penal period, Roman Catholic priests had to be educated abroad; this changed during the French Revolution as continental seminaries were suppressed and the government became anxious to propriti-

ate local Catholic opinion by opening a seminary in Ireland. St Patrick's College was founded in 1795 with some refugee French priests on the academic staff. Since then, it has educated countless churchmen who have served congregations throughout the British Empire where Roman Catholics far outnumbered Protestants, most notably across India, China and Africa. In 1966, the first lay students were admitted.

The history of the college, the town and district is presented in the **Visitor Centre**, which organises guided tours of the Chapel, Stoyte House, the Pugin building and the gardens. The **National Science Museum** (ⓘopen May–Sept Tue, Thu 2pm–4pm, Sun 2pm–6pm; Oct–Apr by appointment; ⓔ€4; ☎01 708 3576; www.nuim.ie/museum) displays scientific and ecclesiastical artefacts.

Excursion

Castletown House★★

Celbridge; 4mi/6.4km SE of Maynooth by a minor road. (Dúchas) ⓖ*Visit by guided tour (1hr) only 17 Mar–mid-Nov Tue–Sun & Bank hol Mon 10am–5pm Apr–Oct); last tour 4.45pm.* ⓘ*Castletown may be closed at very short notice for Government business.* ⓔ€4.50. ✕⌂. ☎01 628 8252. www.heritageireland.ie/en. www.castletown.ie.

At the time of its completion in 1722, this great Palladian mansion was the largest private house in Ireland, setting a precedent for scores of other palatial residences. The final result, facing south over the Liffey valley to the Wicklow Mountains, consists of

Stained glass window in Maynooth College depicting Jesus with Joseph and Mary in his father's workshop

©JoeHoughton/Bigstockphoto.com

a 13-bay central block by the Italian architect Alessandro Galilei, linked by curving colonnades to two pavilions designed by Sir Edward Lovett Pearce: all built for William "Speaker" Connolly (⚹ see 'Speaker Conolly' box), reputedly the richest commoner in Ireland.

Work on Castletown's sumptuous interiors spanned two generations. The original decorative scheme, using only local wood and stone, is preserved in the **Brown Study** (tall and narrow oak doors and pine panelling).

In 1758, aged just 15, Lady Louisa Lennox married into the family and her touch is evident throughout the house. The Lafranchini brothers transformed the stairwell with exuberant stuccowork, Sir William Chambers gave the ground-floor rooms a neo-Classical decor, the **print room** was hung with Old Master prints, and the magnificent **Long Gallery** was modelled on Pompeii and provided with hand-blown chandeliers from Venice.

Castletown Follies

The extraordinary **Castletown Obelisk**, also known as the **Conolly Folly** (*visible from the windows of the Long Gallery and from the Maynooth–Castletown road*), north of the house, comprises two tiers of arches designed by Richard Castle;

it was erected in memory of Speaker Conolly by his wife, in part to provide employment during the severe winter of 1739.

The **Wonderful Barn** (*private*) which closes the northeast vista (*3mi/5km east via the R 403 and R 404*) was built in 1743. The conical structure, with an external spiral staircase and four diminishing brick domes, was used for drying and storing grain.

Lodge Park Walled Garden and Straffan Steam Museum

5mi/8km south of Maynooth on the R 406. 🕐*Open Jun–Aug, Wed–Sun & Bank Hols 2pm–6pm. Engines steamed up on Sun.* 🎟€7.50. ☕. ☎01 6273155 (in season) or 01 6288412. www.steam-museum.ie.

The restored 18C garden attached to a Palladian house (*private*) built in 1773 provides a strong contrast to the Gothic Revival church used by the engineers of the old Great Southern & Western Railway, transferred from Inchicore near Dublin: today, it holds the **Model Hall** in which a fascinating collection of over 20 18C–20C locomotives are displayed. In the **Power Hall** is an array of engines that once powered mills, distilleries and breweries, and a steamship.

"Speaker" Conolly

William Conolly (1662–1729) was a lawyer of humble origins from Ballyshannon, who made a fortune by shrewd dealing in forfeited estates after the Battle of the Boyne.

Member of Parliament for Donegal in 1692, Commissioner of the Revenue in 1709, he was elected Speaker of the Irish House of Commons in 1715, becoming one of the country's most powerful politicians.

Coolcarrigan Gardens
10mi/16km south west of Maynooth.
♿🕒*Limited opening Apr–May & Jul–Oct, phone or see website for dates.* ☎€8. ☎*045 863 527. www.coolcarrigan.ie.*
The parkland laid out in the 19C has been enriched by subsequent planting. Roses and herbaceous borders add colour to the formal gardens near the handsome Victorian house. The **glasshouse** hosts a vine, a passion flower, peaches and nectarines. At the end of the **woodland walk** *(30min)* there is a fine view across the Bog of Allen. The **church** (1881), surrounded by a moat and approached through a lych gate, is in the Hiberno-Romanesque revival style and decorated with stained glass.

MIDLETON

POPULATION 3 266

Incorporated in 1670, Midleton (Mainistir An Corann) is a pleasant old market town, set in the rich fertile plain of East Cork. Its greatest draw is the Jameson Irish Whiskey distillery.

- 🛈 **Information:** Jameson Heritage Centre. ☎021 461 3594.
- ▶ **Orient Yourself:** Midleton is situated on the N 25, between Cork and Youghal.
- ☾ **Also See:** COBH, CORK, KINSALE, YOUGHAL.

Visit

Old Midleton Distillery
♿✉*Visit by guided tours only, Mar–Oct 10am–5pm (tours on demand); Nov–Mar: at 11.30am, 1pm, 2.30pm, 4pm.*🕒*Closed Good Fri and Christmas hols.* ☎€12.50. ✕. ☎*021 461 3594. www.jameson.ie.*
The Jameson Irish Whiskey distillery was built in 1975 alongside the old buildings that once accommodated a woollen mill and barracks. The tour begins with a video presentation on the history of the distillery. Then follows a visit to the old buildings including the Distiller's cottage, the drying kiln, the great storehouse and the giant waterwheel of 1852 which at one stage powered five pairs of millstones and all of the distillery machinery. Today it still turns the cogs and wheels in the Mill Building. Most impressive of all is the **largest copper pot still** (1825) in the world (capacity 33 000 gallons/1 485hl). Finally there are the oak casks in which the spirit was matured and the tour concludes, naturally, with a whiskey tasting.

Excursions

Cloyne
5mi/8km south via the R 630 and R 629.
Three people are particularly associated with the cathedral village of Cloyne: Christy King, the greatest ever hurler; **George Berkeley** (1684–1753), the bishop of what was once a vast diocese, and St Colman (522–604) who founded a local monastery, of which only a tiny oratory and 10C **round tower** (100ft/30m high) remain next to the restored 14C **Cathedral**★. Bishop Berkeley, was a highly regarded and original philosopher who also devoted himself to practical matters such as good farming practice; though his attempt to found a

Midleton Distillery

SLIDE FILE, Dublin

college in America came to nothing, he is honoured by Berkeley in California.

Barryscourt Castle

4mi/6.4km W by N 25 and R 624. (Dúchas) ♿ 🔊 *Visit by guided tour (1hr) only, Jun–Sept 10am–6pm. Last admission 5.15pm.* 👓€2. 🔲✕🅿. ☎*021 488 2218. www.heritageireland.ie.*

This ruined medieval castle, surrounded by a bawn (a defensive wall surrounding an Irish tower house, whose original purpose was to protect livestock during an attack) is strategically sited on the main route from Cork to Waterford. Its name is derived from Philip de Barri of Manorbier in Wales, who arrived c 1180 in the early days of Anglo-Norman Ireland. A more famous descendent was **Gerald of Wales** (c 1146–1233), known as Giraldus Cambrensis, who travelled with Prince (later King) John and published accounts of the country and of its conquest by Henry II.

Both the First floor Main Hall and the Second Floor Great Hall have been extensively restored with fittings and furnishings reinstated to an original 16th century design and a herb garden has been reinstated in the bawn.

Address Book

SHOPPING

Stephen Pearce Pottery. Visit the original Old Pottery at Ballycotton Bay or the newer Stephen Pearce Gallery, in the grounds of Shanagarry Castle. *www.stephenpearce.com*

SPORTS AND LEISURE

Safe beaches and coves dot the coast south of Midleton from Roche's Point eastwards to Knockadoon Head. **Trabolgan Holiday Village**: *Roche's Point. ☎21 466 1551. www.trabolgan. com)* has a tropical themed indoor swimming pool, plunge pool, sauna, solarium, fitness centre, tennis, par-3 golf, 10-pin bowling and many adventure sports.

There is sailing in Ballycotton Bay, at Roche's Point and in Cork Harbour, angling from the shore or on the lake. The area also boasts golf courses, pleasant walks notably in **Rostellan Wood** on the shore of Cork Harbour. *(6mi/9.7km south east via the R 630)* or along the **cliff-top** from Roche's Point to Ballycotton overlooking Ballycotton Bay and the lighthouse on Ballycotton Island *(11mi/18km south east via the R 630 and R 629).*

MONAGHAN

POPULATION 5 628

Monaghan (Muineachán) is the commercial centre and the county town of Co Monaghan, once part of the original province of Ulster, projecting into Northern Ireland as far as the Blackwater River. Previously ruled by the McMahon clan, the area was settled by the British in the early 17C and Monaghan town was given its charter in 1613. Its mostly Scottish Presbyterian citizens established a thriving linen industry in the 18C. In the 19C the building of the Ulster Canal and the Ulster Railway brought further benefits, and the town still bears the imprint of these prosperous times, with dignified grey limestone buildings lining its narrow streets.

- **Information:** Market House. ☎047 81122. www.monaghantourism.com.
- **Orient Yourself:** Monaghan is on N 2, 58mi/92km southwest of Belfast.
- **Also See:** CAVAN, ENNISKILLEN, NEWRY.

Sights

St Macartan's (Roman Catholic) Cathedral

This splendid Gothic Revival landmark was built in 1892, of local limestone, with a soaring spire (250ft/76m) by JJ McCarthy. The exterior is extravagantly decorated with Carrara marble statues of saints and bishops; the spacious interior is contained by a splendid **hammerbeam roof** and ornamented by modern **tapestries** illustrating the Christian life and the life of St Macartan, one of the earliest Irish saints.

Town Centre

The elegant grey limestone **Market House** (1792) was designed by Samuel Hayes, an amateur architect. Church Square *(east)* forms a dignified ensemble, with the **Courthouse** (1830), a handsome Classical building still bearing the scars of the Civil War, and **St Patrick's Anglican Church** (1831), a charming example of Regency Gothic style. East of Church Square is the **Diamond**, the original market place which was set against the north wall of the 17C castle (long demolished). The **Rossmore Memorial**, an elaborate neo-Gothic drinking fountain (1875), honours the 4th Baron Rossmore.

Museums

Two elegant early 19C terrace houses in Hill Street accommodate the **County Museum** (♿🕐*open Mon–Fri 11am–5pm (noon Sat); ☎047 82928, www.monaghan.ie*). It features exceptional displays on the region and its history, including linen and lace-making but the museum's greatest treasure is its 12C–14C **Cross of Clogher**.

The **St Louis Heritage Centre** (🕐*open Apr–Oct Thu–Sun 2pm–4.30pm; ☎047 83529*) tells the story of the Order of St Louis, founded in France in 1842, and its nuns who came to Ireland in 1859. There is a **crannóg** (an ancient island which was once settled) in Spark's Lake in the convent grounds.

Excursions

Rossmore Forest Park

2mi/3.5km S of Monaghan by N 54 and R 189.

Only the foundations of the Rossmore residence remain, though the Earls' **mausoleum** (♿🕐*open 9am–8pm, 6pm in winter; ☎047 81968*) still stands in the grounds of the desmesne, now a Forest Park landscaped with woods and water.

Clones

12mi/19km SW of Monaghan by N 54.

Right on the border with Northern Ireland, Clones (pronounced as two syllables) is a pleasant market town renowned for its angling. It is a typical Ulster plantation settlement, with a long history stretching back to a monastery founded by St Tighernach in the 6C, of which a **round tower**, **monolithic shrine** and a 12C **church** survive. The **high cross** (c 10C) standing in the central Diamond, below the Anglican church (1822), may also be contemporary with the monastery.

The **Ulster Canal Stores** now hosts a display of **Clones lace**, a crochet lace with individual motifs connected by areas of Clones knot.

Lough Muckno Leisure Park

15mi/24km SE of Monaghan on the N 2 to Castleblaney.

Lough Muckno, the largest and loveliest of the lakes in Co Monaghan is surrounded by a wooded park (91 acres/37ha) threaded with **nature trails**. The park was originally the desmesne of Sir Edward Blaney, King James I's Governor of Monaghan, whose name lives on in Castleblaney, the little town overlooking

B Lynch/Bord Fáilte, Dublin

Clones Lace

the lake's western shore. A later Blaney built the Georgian **Courthouse** and, in 1808, the Anglican church. In the late 19C Blaney Castle was bought by Thomas Hope, a London banker, who renamed it Hope Castle; his name too lives on as the owner of the ill-omened Hope Diamond, now in the Smithsonian Institution.

MULLINGAR

POPULATION 8 040

Mullingar (An Muileann Gcearr), the county town of Westmeath, is an important agricultural market in the middle of prime cattle country.

🛈 **Information:** Market House. ☎044 93 48650. www.midirelandtourism.ie.

▶ **Orient Yourself:** Mullingar is 50mi/80km northwest of Dublin via the M 4.

Kids Just for Kids: Belvedere House adventure playground.

👁 **Also See:** ATHLONE, BIRR, KELLS, KILDARE, LONGFORD, TRIM, TULLAMORE.

A Bit of History

In the 2C AD a royal residence topped **Uisneach Hill** *(6mi/9.6km W by R 390)*, an ancient druidic sanctuary where the Celts held their rituals. The **Catstone** marks the meeting point of the five provinces of ancient Ireland. When the Normans arrived in the 12C, they constructed stone castles and several mottes and baileys across the region; a Corporation was established in Mullingar. In the 16C under Henry VIII, Meath was divided in two: Mullingar became the county town of Westmeath, its prosperity assured by good communications with Dublin – the Royal Canal (1790s), the Midland & Great Western Railway

A Literary Family

The talented **Pakenham** family includes Lord Longford, a Socialist peer, his wife Elizabeth who writes biographies, their son, Thomas Pakenham, an author, and their daughters Antonia Fraser, another biographer, and Rachel Billington, a novelist.

Address Book

SHOPPING

Mullingar Pewter Ltd. – *go 5mi/8km east of Mullingar on the N 4; after 4mi/6km bear left towards Killucan to The Downs. Open Mon–Fri 9.30am–6pm, Sat 10am–5.30pm. Last tour Fri 12.30pm.* ☏*044 934 8791. www.mullingarpewter. com.* Here you can watch the moulding, soldering, turning, polishing and blackening, and, of course, purchase the finished articles in the showroom.

SPORTS AND LEISURE

Fishing and sailing on Lough Ennell. Greyhound Racing in Mullingar.

(1848), and the main Dublin–Sligo road which ran through town until the bypass was built. In 1825 a prison and a handsome courthouse were erected in Mount Street, with the space between used for public hangings.

During his student days **James Joyce** came to Mullingar, where his father was reorganising the electoral rolls: hence the reason it features in *Ulysses* and *Stephen Hero*.

Visit

Cathedral of Christ the King

The main landmark is the Roman Catholic cathedral set in parkland that stretches down to the Royal Canal, with its tall twin towers (140ft/43m), designed by Ralph Byrne in a "last flamboyant fling... of Classicism" (J Sheehy), dedicated in 1939. The portico tympanum **sculptures** of Portland stone are by Albert Power, a pupil of Rodin. The chapel **mosaics** are by the Russian artist Boris Anrep.

The **museum** *(upstairs – ask the Verger)* displays a letter written by Oliver Plunkett, his vestments and other church-related artefacts.

Excursions

Belvedere House and Gardens★

3.5mi/5.6km south on the N 52. ♿☉*Open daily: House May–Aug 10am–5pm, Mar–Apr & Sept–Oct 10.30am–7pm, Nov–Feb 10.30am–4.30pm. Gardens May–Aug 10am–5pm.* ⬮*€8.75, child €4.75.* ⬮. ✕. ☏*044 934 9060. www.belvedere-house.ie.* The beautiful landscape park above Lough Ennell is graced by an elegant villa (1740) probably designed by Richard Castle as a fishing lodge for Robert Rochfort, the first Earl of Belvedere. The house has been restored to its original appearance, complete with finely-carved wood work and Rococo plasterwork ceilings; the furnishings are in period. The **visitor centre** gives a detailed history of the estate and owners, including the mountaineer Colonel Charles Howard-Bury (♿*see 'Tales of the Yeti' box*).

The **gardens** include three terraces overlooking the lake. The **woodland walk** *(2mi/3km)* is dotted with various **follies** including an octagonal gazebo, a Gothick arch, an ice house, and two stone bridges over the stream. The **Jealous Wall** (148ft/45m high), is described as "Ireland's biggest folly", and was designed as a mock-Gothic ruin, erected c 1760, either to hide the stables or to blot out the view of Tudenham House (now in ruins) where his estranged brother George lived.

Dining Room, Belvedere House

Derek Cullen/Bord Fáilte, Dublin

Multyfarnham Franciscan Friary★

*8mi/13km N of Mullingar via the N 4;
in Ballynafid turn right.*

The Stations of the Cross are represented by life-size figures among the trees.

Taghmon Church

*7mi/11.5km north of Mullingar via the N 4
and R 394; in Crookedwood turn right.*

By the stream, on the site of a monastery founded by St Fintan Munna, stands a fortified church; the four-storey tower contains living accommodation. Note the two sculpted heads facing out from the north and west walls.

Tullynally★

*15mi/24km north: R 394 to Castlepollard
and R 395 west.* ♿⏱*Gardens: open May
& Jun Sat–Sun & Bank Hols 2pm-6pm, Jul–
mid-Aug daily 2pm–6pm. Castle open to
pre-booked groups only.* Ⓡ*€6.* ⛳*.*☎*044
966 1159. www.tullynallycastle.com.*

Tullynally, the seat of the Pakenham family since 1655, bristles with turrets and crenellations above the treetops of the extensive grounds. The original fortress with massive walls (10ft/3m thick) was converted early in the 18C into a country house, Gothicised by Francis Johnston and extended by Sir Richard Morrison. The interiors reflect the 19C love of all things medieval: it has a **Great Hall** and an octagonal dining room covered with wallpaper designed by Pugin for the House of Lords. The family coach is parked in the courtyard.

By 1760 the early-18C formal layout of canals and cascades had been replaced by naturally landscaped **gardens**; the terraces date from Victorian times when tennis and croquet were popular. Two Coad stone sphinxes (1780) guard the huge walled **kitchen garden** with its Regency glasshouses and avenue of Irish yews.

A **forest walk** leads past a waterfall to the lower lake and **views** of the castle.

Fore Abbey★

*15mi/24km north on the R 394 to
Castlepollard and the R 195 east,
then turn right.*

This ancient monastic site is one of the loveliest in the country. The extensive ruins – church, cloisters, chapter house, refectory, kitchen and columbarium – belong mostly to the Benedictine abbey founded in 1200, but **St Fechin's Church** is named after the founder (d 665) of the earlier 11C–12C complex. In 1436 the buildings were fortified to protect them from attack by the native Irish.

The Abbey's various features have traditionally been known as the **"Seven Wonders of Fore"**, described in miraculous terms. The "monastery in a bog" (the **abbey** itself), raised on firm ground in the middle of marshland; "water that will not boil" from **St Fechin's Well;** a "tree that will not burn", the three branches of which represented the Trinity; the "stream that flows uphill" to drive the "mill without a race" appeared when the saint beat his crozier on the ground; the "hermit in the stone" was Patrick Beglen, the last anchorite in Ireland, who in the 17C languished in a medieval watchtower, later incorporated into a **chapel mausoleum** for the Nugent family; and finally the "stone raised by St Fechin's prayers" is the huge lintel over the west doorway of the church, which proved too heavy for the masons to lift into place and had to be wafted aloft by the power of prayer!

NEW ROSS

POPULATION 5 012

Far inland on the tidal River Barrow, this thriving place was once the country's principal port; ocean-going ships still dock at the broad quayside opposite the substantial warehouses and tall houses reminiscent of the 19C. Its history, however, can be traced back to the 6C. Narrow streets, many linked by footpaths and flights of steps, rise steeply from the riverside to Irishtown, site of the ancient monastic settlement on the heights above. Very much a working town, New Ross (Ros Mhic Treoin) is an ideal place from which to explore the attractive scenery of the Barrow valley upstream to Nore, and downstream to the Hook Head Peninsula.

- ⓘ **Information:** The Quay; ☎051 421857. www.newrosstourism.com. Hook Head; ☎051 421 857.
- ▶ **Orient Yourself:** New Ross is 14mi/23km northeast of Waterford.
- ⓖ **Also See:** CLONMEL, ENNISCORTHY, KILKENNY, WATERFORD, WEXFORD.

A Bit of History

New Ross was founded below the site of St Abban's late 6C–early 7C monastery, in about 1200 by William le Marshall, Earl Marshal of Ireland, and his wife, Countess Isabelle de Clare, daughter of Strongbow. The first bridge across the River Barrow was built in 1211 and in 1265 the first town walls were constructed. New Ross prospered but by the end of the 17C Ireland's premier harbour was Waterford.

In 1649, mindful of the massacre suffered by Wexford, the Catholic garrison prudently surrendered the town to Cromwell. In the 1798 rebellion the town was successfully defended against the insurgents, who suffered thousands of casualties. In 1832, a cholera epidemic swept through the region claiming 3,000 lives.

In Search of American Emigrants

The Dunbrody Famine Ship offers access to a fascinating database compiled from the original passenger lists of ships, which sailed from Ireland and the UK in the 19C. Insert any name you like into the database and in a matter of seconds you can see how many people of this name sailed to the USA, how old they were, what ship they travelled on and which port they arrived at.

By the mid 19C New Ross had re-established substantial trading links, with ships sailing to the Baltic and across the Atlantic, some carrying emigrants fleeing the Famine.

Walking Tour

Dunbrody Famine Ship★

ⓢ *Open daily by guided tour (50 mins) only, year-round daily 9am–6pm (Oct–Mar 5pm). Last tour 1hr before closing.* ⓢ*€7.50.* ☎*051 425 239. www.dunbrody. com.*

The *Dunbrody* is a splendid replica of a 458 tonne three-masted barque (176ft/54m long). The original freighter, built in Quebec by an Irish shipwright for a New Ross merchant, ferried emigrants mainly between 1845 and 1851.

After a 9min introductory audio visual introduction you will be greeted by your "emigrants", (costumed actors) tour hosts who re-enact the terrible conditions endured on a trip to New York in 1849. A fascinating exhibition evokes the achievements of members of the Irish diaspora. Joining the multitudes of Irish fleeing the Great Famine was Patrick Kennedy who departed the port of New Ross on a wet day in 1848 to set sail for the United States; his descendants were to become one of the world's most famous families (ⓖsee *Downstream from New Ross*).

▶ *Walk up Mary Street.*

Tholsel
Corner of South Street and Quay Street.
🕐*Open by appointment Mon–Fri 9am–5pm.* ☎*051 421 284.*

The neo-Classical building with a tower topped by a weather-vane, was erected in 1749 and rebuilt in 1806 after the ground subsided. The front façade is by William Kent, pupil of Sir Christopher Wren. It now houses the local council, its volumes of corporation minutes collected since the 17C, the mace of Charles II (1699) and the charter of James II (1688).

▶ *Continue up Mary Street.*

St Mary's Church★
The early-19C Anglican church was built on the site of the nave and crossing of what was probably the largest parish church in medieval Ireland, part of the abbey founded by William le Marshall and his wife (1207–20). Besides the ruined chancel, there are a number of striking late-13C and early-14C effigies.

▶ *Walk back down Mary Street turn left into Bewley St and right into Michael Street.*

Roman Catholic Parish Church
The building with its high ceiling and Corinthian columns echoes St Mary's Church *(adjacent)*; its completion was delayed by the cholera epidemic in 1832.

▶ *Leave by the rear entrance. Walk up Cross Lane; turn right into Neville Street.*

Town Walls and Gates
At the junction stands the Three Bullet Gate *(left)*, through which Cromwell entered the town in 1649, and the Mural Tower erected in the 14C. The substantial remains of the Maiden Gate are 15C.

▶ *Walk down William Street. Turn right into Priory Street and left into Marsh Lane to return to the Quay.*

Excursions

Upstream from New Ross

Graiguenamanagh★
11mi/18km north of New Ross via the N 30, R 700 and R 705.

The commercial quays of Graiguenamanagh ("granary of the monks") occupy a particularly attractive stretch of the River Barrow, overlooked by the heather-covered summit of Brandon Hill (1694ft/516m). The township is dominated by the restored ruins of Duiske (pronounced Dooishka) Abbey, established here in the early 13C by William le Marshall for the Cistercians.

Duiske Abbey★★
Despite having been suppressed in 1536, the abbey continued to function for years after. The tower collapsed in 1774 and most of the precincts were subsequently built over. The most outstanding feature of the restoration is the high-pitched church roof, constructed from unseasoned timbers of oak and elm secured with pegged wooden joints. Note the superb effigy of the Knight of Duiske (c 1300), cross-legged, sword-seizing; his identity remains a mystery. The **Abbey Centre** (🕐*open Mon–Fri 10am–5pm;* ☎*059 972 4238)* houses a museum for examples of the Abbey plate and other items; a gallery shows works by contemporary artists on Christian themes.

Inistioge★
10mi/16km north of New Ross via the N 30 and R 700.

Inistioge (pronounced Inisteeg), a famously picturesque village, is set on the west bank of the Nore, spanned by a splendid 18C 10-arch bridge.
The ruins of the 13C **castle**, once the borough courthouse, flank the tree-lined **square**. On the west side next to the ruined Tholsel is a real curiosity, the **Armillary Sphere**, a device said to have been invented by Eratosthenes in 250 BC to demonstrate the movements of the earth and moon. The 19C almshouse was built by a member of the Tighe family, who resided at Woodstock. The

Roman Catholic church contains early stone carvings, apparently illustrating the legend of the mermaid being taken from the River Nore in 1118. Up the lane is **St Colmcille's Well**.

Adjoining the Anglican Church are the tower, nave and Lady Chapel of the **Augustinian priory**, founded in 1210. **Woodstock Forest Park** (*1mi/1.6km south west of Inistioge*) includes walks, an old tiled Japanese garden and a conical dovecot.

Downstream from New Ross

Dunganstown

4mi/6.4km south of New Ross via the R 733 and the minor road west.

The **Kennedy Homestead** (&open *Jul–Aug daily 10am–5pm; May–Jun & Sept Mon–Fri 11.30am–4.30pm; €5; ☎051 388 264; www.kennedyhomestead. com*), where the great-grandfather of John F Kennedy, President of the USA (1961–63) was born in 1820, and still in family hands, now displays photographs and souvenirs of the President's visit in 1963, including the wreath he laid on the graves of the leaders of the 1916 Easter Rising at Arbour Hill in Dublin.

Kennedy Arboretum★

7.5mi/12km south of New Ross off the R733. (Dúchas)& Open daily from 10am: May–Aug until 8pm; Apr & Sept until 6.30pm; Oct–Mar until 5pm. Closed 25 Dec, Good Fri. €2.90. ☎051 388 195. www.heritageireland.com.

Opened in 1968 to honour John F Kennedy, the arboretum is divided into plant collection, forest plots and mountain heathland. Various lovely walks meander through the estate (667 acres/252ha), and a scenic road winds to the summit of Slieve Coillte from where extensive views extend over farmland, the Hook Peninsula and mountains.

Kilmokea Country Manor Gardens★

10mi/15km south of New Ross via the R 733 and a minor road west. Open Mar–Nov daily 10am–6pm. €6. ☎051 388 109. www.kilmokea.com.

Within the earthen ramparts of what was probably an Early Christian monastic foundation stands a handsome Georgian glebe house (now a luxury guesthouse); its assorted gardens, among the most exquiste in Ireland, were developed over half a century.

Dunbrody Abbey★

10mi/16km south of New Ross via the R 733. Open May–mid-Sept 10am–6pm. €2; €4 Maze, pitch & putt. ☎051 388 603. www.dunbrodyabbey.com.

Close to the village of Clonmines, a deserted medieval borough with remains of tower houses, a fortified church and Augustinian priory, are the handsome ruins of the abbey built in 1182 by Cistercian monks from St Mary's Abbey in Dublin. The roofless but well-preserved cruciform abbey church, pleasantly set above an inlet of the river Barrow, has a low turreted tower and six transept chapels with slender single-light windows. After the Dissolution, the abbey passed to the Etchingham family who erected a fortified dwelling Dunbrody Castle. Long demolished, on its site is now a visitor centre and the Castle garden houses an intricate **yew hedge maze**. Made with 1 500 yew trees, and gravel paths, it is one of only two full size mazes in the Republic of Ireland.

Ballyhack Castle

(Dúchas) Open mid-Jun–mid-Sept daily 10am–6pm. Last admission 5.45pm. ☎051 389 468. www.heritageireland.com.

Overlooking the ferry crossing to Passage East on the west bank of Waterford Harbour is an imposing 15C–16C tower house. The site originally belonged to the Knights Templar, then to the Knights Hospitaller before being acquired by the Earl of Donegall.

Address Book

GETTING AROUND

Waterford Harbour Ferry – *Operates between Passage East and Ballyhack daily, 7am (9.30am Sun and Bank Hols) to 10pm (8pm Oct–Mar)* ⚓ €6.50. *Single journey per car, return €9.50 ; €2 pedestrian.* ☎051 382 480, 382 488.

ENTERTAINMENT

The Galley Cruising Restaurant – *Gourmet and ecological trips on the local rivers – Cruises Apr–Oct from New Ross (North Quay to Inistioge, towards St. Mullins or downriver depending on tide). and Waterford (Afternoon Tea trip at 3pm from Quay (beside bus station) to Cheekpoint, Ballyhack, Passage East or New Ross). Cruise only prices from €8; cruise with lunch from €20; afternoon cruise €10 with afternoon tea; evening cruise with dinner from €38.* ☎051 421 723, www.rivercruises.ie.

SPORTS AND LEISURE

Beaches at Duncannon; scuba-diving at Slade; riverside walks in Inistioge; bird-watching In spring and autumn on the Hook Head Peninsula, where over 200 species have been recorded.

Duncannon

Duncannon Fort★ was first selected for defensive purposes by the Anglo-Normans in the 12C. In 1588, as part of the precautions against the Spanish Armada, the fortress was strengthened and assumed its present star-shaped form with a dry moat (3 acres/1.2ha). In 1690 both James II and William III took ship from Duncannon following the Battle of the Boyne. A **maritime museum** (♿🕐*open Jun–Sept daily 10am–5.30pm;* 👣*guided tours available 10.30am, 12.30pm, 2pm, 3pm, 4.30pm;* ⚓€3 (€5 *with tour);* ☕; ☎051 389 454; www. duncannonfort.com) charts the maritime history of the Wexford coast, one of the most dangerous coastlines in Ireland.

Tintern Abbey★

5mi/8km E of Duncannon by R 737, R 733 and R 374 to Saltmills. (Dúchas) ♿🕐*Open mid-Jun–Oct 10am–6pm (Oct 5pm). Last admission 5.45pm.* ⚓€2.10. ☕. ☎051 562 650. www.heritageireland.com.
This ruined Cistercian abbey, a daughter house of Tintern Abbey in Monmouthshire, was founded in 1200 by William le Marshall in thanks for his safe crossing from England in a violent storm.

Hook Head Peninsula

The remote beaches and distinctive landscapes have long drawn holiday-makers to this spot, bounded to the west by Waterford Harbour and to the east by Bannow Bay. The pleasant little resort of **Fethard** was originally founded by the Anglo-Normans, whose first expedition to Ireland landed in 1169 at Bannow Island.

Slade is a tiny fishing village, with a double harbour, popular for scuba-diving. On the pier are the remains of 18C salthouses where sea water was evaporated to make salt. Beside them stood **Slade Castle**, a tower house (15C–16C) and house (16C–17C) built by the Laffan family.

Hook Head Lighthouse (👣*tower open by guided tour only: Mar–Oct daily 11am–5pm (Jun–Aug 9.30am–6pm), Nov–Feb Sat–Sun & hols only 10am–5.30pm; Visitor Centre open year-round from 9.30am; closes 6pm Jun–Aug, 5.30pm May–Sept, 5pm rest of year;* ⚓€6; ☕; ☎051 397 055/4, www.thehook-wexford.com) has served sailors and shipping for 800 years, apart from a short closure during the 17C, and is thought to be one of the oldest operational lighthouses in the world. It was automated in 1996. The first cylindrical keep (82ft/25m) with its vaulted chambers was built by the Normans in the early 13C to aid navigation up Waterford Harbour to their port at New Ross.

PORTUMNA ★

POPULATION 984

The little township of Portumna (Port Omna), meaning the port of the oak, is a major crossing point on the River Shannon where it enters Lough Derg, the lowest and most attractive of the Shannon lakes. Occupying part of the shoreline, Portumna Forest Park has a deer herd, nature trails, a marina and an observation tower; the bird life, both migratory and resident, is abundant.

▶ **Orient Yourself:** Portumna lies 40mi/65km southeast of Galway and 46mi/74km northeast of Limerick. It is situated at the north end of Lough Derg on N 65 between Borrisokane and Loughrea and R 489 and R 353 between Birr and Gort. The road bridge over the Shannon is raised at regular intervals to allow the passage of vessels on the river.

◔ **Also See:** ATHENRY, BIRR, CLONMACNOISE, KILLALOE (LOUGH DERG).

Visit

Portumna Castle★

(Dúchas) ♿ ◷ *Ground floor and formal gardens only: open mid-Mar–Oct, 10am–6pm. Last admission 45min before closing.* ⊚*€2.10.* ☎*090 974 1658. www.heritage ireland.com.*

This early 17C castle was for centuries the seat of the Burke family. Long derelict but now restored to its full splendour, it is a handsome example of the sophisticated, semi-fortified residence that replaced the tower houses and castles of medieval times. The first house was accidentally burnt out in 1826 and abandoned; its replacement, designed by Sir Thomas Deane, was also burned down, deliberately this time, during the Civil War.

The approach passes through a series of formal gardens. The Gothic Gate houses an exhibition telling the story of the castle and its occupants; the 17C walled kitchen garden is planted with fruit trees, flowers, herbs and vegetables.

South of the castle stand the ruins of **Portumna Priory**, originally a Cistercian chapel granted to the Dominicans by O'Madden, the local chieftain.

Portumna Castle

Office of Public Works

Adjacent to Portumna on the northern shore of Lough Derg is **Portumna Forest Park** with forest and lakeside walks and observation points. Along the nature trail is a viewing tower.

Excursions

Clonfert Cathedral★

17mi/27km north east of Portumna via the N 65, R 355, R 356 via Eyrecourt and a minor road east. 🔑*Key available from the house to the right of the cathedral.*
The original 12C church was built on a monastery founded in 563 by St Brendan the Navigator. It is justly famous for its great **west doorway**★★, a masterpiece of Hiberno-Romanesque decoration in red sandstone, aptly described as "the apogee of the Irish Romanesque mason's love of ornamentation" (P Harbison). Friezes of heads and triangles, fantastical motifs and animal heads are contrived in one harmonious whole; the sixth order dates from the 15C, as do the tower, south transept and sacristy.

The grounds *(through the rear church-yard gate; turn left)* contain an ancient **yew walk**, probably planted by the monks in the shape of a cross. The ruined **Bishop's Palace** belonged to Sir Oswald Mosley from 1951 to 1954, when it was destroyed by fire. The charming circular oratory serves the Emmanuel Retreat House.

Meelick Franciscan Friary

7mi/11km north east of Portumna via the N 65, R 355 and a minor road east.
The friary, built in the 15C overlooking the Shannon, has been restored for worship. Most of the walls, the west door and two arches in the south wall are original. A short walk *(0.5mi/1km east)* leads to Meelick Weir and Victoria Lock, the largest lock on the Shannon.

Lorrha

6mi/10km E of Portumna by R 489 via Portumna Lifting Bridge and minor road S.
The tiny village contains no fewer than three ruined churches. The west front of the Anglican church has a 15C doorway carved with a pelican vulning (pecking at her breast); its predecessor was the monastery founded by St Ruadhán (d 845), a disciple of St Finian of Clonard. **St Ruadhan's Church** is the 15C building with an ornate west doorway, handsome east and west windows and a vaulted sacristy. By the Roman Catholic church, are the remains of a church that formed part of a Dominican priory founded by Walter de Burgo c 1269.

De Burgo – de Burgh – Burke

The origins of the name Burke can be traced to the Norman de Burgo. In 1193 William de Burgo, came to Ireland with Prince John and married the daughter of Donal Mor O'Brien, king of Thomond (1185); their son was made Lord of Connaught. In 1265, Walter de Burgo was created Earl of Ulster. In the 14C Portumna Castle was owned by a descendant of Richard, Lord of Connaught, who adopted the name de Burgh, and was made Earl of Clanrickard (1543).

John, the 9th Earl, fought with the Jacobites and was taken prisoner at Aughrim (1691); 12 years later he redeemed his property for £25 000. When Hubert de Burgh Canning (1832–1916) died, the title passed to the Marquess of Sligo and the land went to Henry Lascelles, 6th Lord Harewood who married the daughter of George V and Queen Mary.

ROSCREA ★

POPULATION 4 170

Laid out on the steep banks of the Bunnow River, the prosperous agricultural town of Roscrea (Ros Cré) nestles between the Slieve Bloom Mountains to the north and Devils Bit Mountain to the south. It has also been nominated a Heritage Town. Ancient roadways converge on the 7C site of a monastery started by St Cronan, and where, in early 13C, the Anglo-Irish had a strategic castle built.

▶ **Orient Yourself:** Roscrea is 76mi/123km southwest of Dublin via the M 7 and 46mi/74km northeast of Limerick on the E 20.

 Also See: ABBEYLEIX, ATHY, BIRR, KILKENNY.

Sights

Roscrea Castle

(Dúchas). Open mid-Mar–Oct 10am–6p; Nov–mid-Dec 9.30am–4.30pm. Last admission 45 mins before closing. Restored period gardens open at all times. €3.70. 050 521 850.

Dominating the centre of the town is the 13C **castle**, an irregular polygonal enclosure contained by curtain walls and two D-shaped towers. The medieval gatetower was embellished with gables and chimneys in the 17C.

Damer House ★ is an elegant three-storey furnished house started in 1715 by Joseph Damer, a member of a Plantation family which came to Ireland in 1661; when he died in 1720, he was deemed to be the richest man in Ireland. On completion, the house was used by the Anglican Bishop of Killaloe. Today, the rooms display exhibitions relating to local history.

Blackmill, the mill built in 1722, is dedicated to providing information about **St Cronan's Church and Round Tower**, the remains of the monastery sacked no fewer than four times in the course of the 12C, which was plundered for building stone in the 19C and further destroyed when the main Dublin-Limerick road was completed. Little survives other than the west façade of the 12C church, a 12C **high cross** and the 8C round tower (60ft/18m high) which lost its conical cap in 1135 and suffered further damage during fighting in 1798.

Franciscan Friary

The present Roman Catholic church of St Cronan is approached through the bell-tower of the original 15C friary. The east and north walls of the earlier chancel and part of the nave arcade have been incorporated into the modern church.

Excursions

Monaincha Abbey

1mi/1.6km west via the N 7 and a minor road from the roundabout.

An exquisite 12C ruin with its finely carved doorway and chancel arch stands on a raised isolated site, which was an island until the bog was drained in the late 18C. In Early Christian times this was a famous retreat associated with various saints, notably St Cronan, which grew to be a major pilgrimage centre in the Middle Ages.

Devil's Bit Mountain

15mi/24km south of Roscrea via the N 62.

Legend has it that the gap at Devil's Bit Mountain was scooped out by the devil to form the Rock of Cashel, in reality it was caused by glaciers. An easy climb to the summit (1 577ft/479m) is rewarded by extensive views over the Golden Vale.

SKIBBEREEN

POPULATION 1 926

This attractive and prosperous little market town owes its existence to Algerian pirates, who raided the neighbouring settlement of Baltimore in 1631, capturing some of the English settlers. As a result the others fled inland and set up two settlements of which Skibbereen (Sciobairín) was one. The town suffered severely during the 19C famine but today it is a lively spot – with many good restaurants (ironically) – from which to explore the beautiful coastal scenery and Lough Hyne.

- **Information:** North St. ☎028 21766. www.skibbereen.ie.
- **Orient Yourself:** Skibbereen stands on the southwest Cork coast road (N 71) where it crosses the River Ilen a few miles inland, 52mi/83km SW of Cork.
- **Also See:** BANTRY, CORK, KINSALE.

Visit

Skibbereen Heritage Centre

🕐 Open mid-Mar–Oct Tue–Sat 10am–6pm (daily Jun–mid-Sept) 10am–6pm. ☞€6. ☎028 40900. www.skibbheritage.com.

Located in the old gas works **The Great Famine Commemoration Exhibition** is a sombre reminder that the Skibbereen area was one of the worst affected by the Irish Potato Famine. Newspapers of the day depicted Skibbereen as being symbolic of the destitution and hardship caused by the failure of the crop and between 8,000 and 10,000 unidentified souls are buried in a single Famine Graveyard at Abbeystrewery near Skibbereen. More cheerfully the Heritage Centre also interprets beautiful **Lough Hyne**, offers guided walks (Tue, Sat 6.30pm) and a genealogy resource.

Address Book

👜 For coin ranges, see the Legend on the cover flap.

SIGHTSEEING

Baltimore–Sherkin Island Passenger Ferry – 8 return journeys from 9am to 8.30pm from Baltimore; 9.45am to 8.45pm from Sherkin ☎028 20125. www.baltimore-ireland.com.

Baltimore–Cape Clear Island Ferry – Operates daily (weather permitting); times available by phone or website. Return €12. ☎087 282 4008. www.capeclearferry.com.

West Cork Coastal Cruises – Operates from Baltimore to Cape Clear Island and from Cape Clear to Schull (Fastnet Rock) Jun–Aug, twice daily. Baltimore to Cape Clear (45min) 11.30am, 5.30pm; Cape Clear to Schull 3.30pm; Schull to Cape Clear 2.30pm; Cape Clear to Baltimore 10.30am, 4.30pm; return €12.50. ☎028 39153, 087 268 0760 (mobile). www.westcorkcoastalcruises.com

WHERE TO STAY

👜 **Stanley House** Colla Road, Schull. 4 rms. ☎028 28425. www.stanley-house.net. Modern but characterful house in an elevated position with excellent bay views.

ENTERTAINMENT

West Cork Arts Centre (North Street, Skibbereen) – Regular arts events, films and contemporary art exhibitions Open Mon–Sat, 10am–6pm. ☎028 22090. www.westcorkartscentre.com

SPORTS AND LEISURE

Sailing at Baltimore (temporary marina in summer) and Schull.

Baltimore

SLIDE FILE, Dublin

Excursions

Liss Ard

2mi/3km south of Skibbereen on the R 596.
&. ⏰ *Open May–Oct Mon–Fri 10am–4.30pm.* ⏰*Closed Bank Hols.* ☏*028 40000 www.lissard.com. www.lissardresort.com.*
This beautiful estate, home to a Georgian and a Victorian country manor, both used as retreats, is managed to encourage the natural flora and fauna to flourish. A series of isolated contemplative areas allow day visitors to enjoy the peace and tranquility of the place, most notably the extraordinary **Crater**, designed by James Turrell (b 1943) – the American artist who is world-renowned for his works on the theme of 'Light – to be appreciated by spectators lying on the stone structures at the bottom of the crater. The dome-effect that is created in the elliptical frame is a remarkable experience.

Lough Hyne Nature Reserve

6mi/10km southwest of Skibbereen via the R 595 and a minor road south.
⚠*Beware of sea urchin spines if moving about barefoot.*
Set among low hills, this unpolluted saltwater lagoon is a marine nature reserve, with a unique ecosystem; over 60 species have been recorded, including the redmouth goby, otherwise only found in Portugal.

Baltimore

8mi/13km southwest of Skibbereen on the R 595.
This picturesque fishing village faces a myriad of islands offshore in sheltered Roaring Water Bay. There is always boat traffic animating the horizon. Overlooking the piers are the ruins of an early-17C fortified house. On the breezy headland *(1mi/1.6km south)* stands **Lot's wife**, a medieval rocket-shaped, white painted beacon.

Sherkin Island★

Access by ferry (⛴ see Address Book).
The island is home to the remains of an O'Driscoll stronghold, a ruined friary, some lovely beaches, and a marine research station.

Cape Clear Island

Access by ferry (⛴ see Address Book).
Great colonies of guillemots, cormorants, shearwaters, petrels and choughs attract ornithologists to this remote, rock, Ireland's southernmost inhabited island. Whales, turtles, sharks, seals and dolphins can be seen in the waters around here. The tiny settlement of **Cummer** is the last bastion of Irish in west Cork.

Driving Tour

Mizen Peninsula
*Tour of 35mi/56km west of
Skibbereen – allow 1 day.*

▶ *From Skibbereen take the N 71 west.
After 10mi/16km turn left.*

Ballydehob
The main street, lined with brightly
painted houses slopes steeply down to
Roaring Water Bay. The 12-arch railway
bridge, part of the Schull and Skibbereen light railway which closed in 1947,
has been converted into a **walkway**.

▶ *Take the minor road north up to
Mount Gabriel and Schull.*

Mount Gabriel
It is a stiff climb to the aircraft tracking
station at 1 339ft/408m. During the
Bronze Age, copper was mined here in
large quantities.

▶ *Take the road south to Schull.*

Beyond the pass there is a fine **view**★★
of Roaring Water Bay and Schull.

Schull (Skull)★
*Ferries to Baltimore and Cape Clear Island
(see Address Book).*
The name of this pretty little market
town, meaning "school," comes from a
monastic centre of learning (10C). Schull
is home to the Republic's only **planetarium** (*starshow (45min): Jun–Aug Mon
& Sat 8pm; Jul–Aug also Wed & Fri 4pm;
Sept first and second Sun 5.30pm; €5;
☎028 28315).*

▶ *Continue west; in Toormore turn
left onto the R 591 to Goleen and
Crookhaven. Turn right (sign) at the
entrance to the village of Goleen.*

Crookhaven
The little resort of Crookhaven was once
a busy fishing harbour where mailboats
stopped en-route to America and the
West Indies, copper was shipped from
nearby Brow Head, and Marconi's transatlantic telegraph station was put into
operation in 1902.

"Keeping an eye on the Czar of Russia"

In the 1890s a leader in the *Skibbereen Eagle* remarked that the paper
was "keeping an eye on the Czar of
Russia." The comment, outrageously bombastic for a small provincial
newspaper, was picked up by the
international wire services and
went around the world. Still quoted
today, it turned out to be the most
famous line ever written in an Irish
newspaper. The files of the old
Eagle may be inspected by appointment at the offices of the *Southern
Star* newspaper in Ilen Street.

▶ *Take the minor road along the
east side of Barley Cove.*

Barley Cove
The deep inlet lined with a **sandy
beach** between the cliffs makes this a
fine holiday resort, especially popular
with surfers.

▶ *Cross the causeway at Barley Cove
and turn left to Mizen Head.*

Mizen Head
*10min steep descent on foot
from car park.*
The storm-battered cliffs of Mizen
Head mark the southwesternmost tip
of Ireland. In 1910 the Irish Lights fog
signal station was built on Cloghnane
Island; access is via a reinforced concrete
footbridge constructed with some dif-
ficulty because of the extreme exposure.
Crossing the chasm 150ft/46m above
the Atlantic swell can be a thrilling experience in wild weather. The **Mizen Head
Signal Station Visitor Centre** (*open
daily mid-Mar–Oct 10.30am–5pm (Jun–
Sept 6pm), Nov–mid-Mar Sat–Sun 11am–
4pm; €6; ; ☎028 35115/35225, www.
mizenhead.net)* presents the work of
the station and of lighthouse keep-
ers, local marine life – dolphins, seals,
basking sharks and whales and seabirds
– wrecks, the famous Fastnet Yacht Race
and the building of the Fastnet Rock
Lighthouse *(SE – 9mi/14km).*

SLIGO★★

POPULATION 17 786

Sligo (Sligeach) is a busy market town and an important shopping and cultural centre for much of the northwest of Ireland. It stands on the River Garavogue, which drains Lough Gill into the sea. One of its greatest assets is its beautiful and varied surrounds – green and wooded valleys, lofty mountains, sandy seashores, and an exceptional wealth of prehistoric monuments. Sligo and its surroundings are intimately associated with the Yeats family: the portrait painter John B Yeats, the artist Jack B Yeats, and the poet William Butler Yeats (1865–1939).

- **Information:** Aras Reddan Temple St. ☎071 916 1201. www.sligotourism.ie.
- ▶ **Orient Yourself:** Sligo is the hub of several major roads, 40mi/64km southwest of Donegal.
- **Don't Miss:** Lough Gill.
- **Also See:** BOYLE, DONEGAL, ENNISKILLEN, KILLALA, KNOCK.

A Bit of History

A Turbulent Past – In 807 Sligo was plundered by the Vikings. Following the Norman invasion in the 13C it was granted to Maurice Fitzgerald. Over the following 200 years, its possession by the O'Conors was disputed by the O'Donnells.

A fort was built by the Cromwellians. Patrick Sarsfield reinforced the defences so that Sligo was one of the last places to capitulate after the Battle of the Boyne (1690). The Battle of Carrignagat (1798) was fought south of the town.

Yeats' Country

In their youth, the Yeats brothers spent many of their summer holidays with their Pollexfen cousings at Elsinore Lodge on Rosses Point, watching their grandfather's ships in the bay from the top of the warehouse now known as the Yeats Watch Tower. Jack Yeats once remarked that he never did a painting without putting a thought of Sligo in it. The countryside and its rich legendary associations, continued to inspire William throughout his life, recording in verse his visits to Lissadell House on Drumcliff Bay; he is buried at Drumcliff.

A Prosperous Port – In the 18C and 19C Sligo developed into a busy trading port from which many emigrants set out for the New World. Buildings from that period include the warehouses by the docks, the Courthouse (1878), and the Italianate City Hall (1865). The stone lookout turret, known as the **Yeats Watch Tower** *(no public access)*, marks the warehouse owned by W B Yeats's mother's family, the Pollexfen dynasty of Sligo merchants and sea traders.

Sligo Today – Sligo has a lively cultural scene: theatre, music and high-profile art installations at the Model Arts Centre; festivals stud the calendar; the Yeats Memorial Building hosts a famous summer school devoted to the work of the poet and his family. All this urban bustle contrasts strongly with the unspoilt countryside beyond, its fine sandy beaches at Strandhill and at Rosses Point, where there is also a championship golf course.

Sights

Sligo Abbey★

(Dúchas) ⏱ *Open mid-Mar–Oct daily 10am–6pm. Nov–mid-Dec Sat–Sun only 9.30am–4.30pm.* ⊙€2.10. ☎071 914 6406. www.heritageireland.ie.
The ruins on the south bank of the Garavogue River occupy the site of a Dominican friary, founded by Maurice Fitzgerald

Address Book

For coin ranges, see the Legend on the cover flap.

GETTING AROUND

Sligo Airport – ☎071 916 8280. www.sligoairport.com.

SIGHTSEEING

Walking Tour – *Operates Jun–Sept.* ☎071 9161201.

Wild Rose Water Bus – *Operates mid-Jun–Sept, from Doorly Park and Parke's Castle, particularly to the Isle of Innisfree (€6.35). Apr, May, Oct, limited sailings. Check website or call for details.* ☎071 9164266; 087 25988 869 (mobile). www.roseofinnisfree.com

There are also boat trips offshore to **Inishmurray** from Mullaghmore *(north of Sligo). 15 passengers minimum.* ☎071 9166 124 (Lomax Boats).

WHERE TO STAY

Ard Cuilinn Lodge – *Drumiskabole, 3mi SE of Sligo.* ☎071 91 62925. *4rm.* Quiet, semi-rural location with views of the surrounding hills, five minutes drive from the town centre. The three well-kept bedrooms overlook the garden. Local smoked salmon and scrambled egg are a breakfast speciality.

Benwiskin Lodge – *Shannon Eighter, 1.25mi N of Sligo. 4rm.* ☎071 914 1088. The décor is bright and cheery at this modern guesthouse and character is provided by the interior furnishings, handcrafted by the owner.

Tree Tops – *Cleveragh Rd, 0.25mi S of Sligo by Dublin road.* ☎071 9160160. www.sligobandb.com. *5rm.* An unassuming house in a residential area made special by the warmth and

hospitality of the owner. Bedrooms are cosy and comfortable.

WHERE TO EAT

Montmartre – *Market Yard.* ☎071 9169 901. Broad range of cooking styles but the atmosphere and style of the room have a strong Gallic accent, from the pictures of French landmarks on the walls to the helpful mesdemoiselles providing the service.

ENTERTAINMENT

The **Hawk's Well Theatre** – ☎071 9161526. www.hawkswell.com. A wide range of shows, including drama, children's theatre, contemporary and classical dance, opera, jazz, roots and pop music, comedy and pantomime.

SHOPPING

Sligo Crystal – *10mi/16km north at Grange. Open Jun–Sept Mon–Fri 9am–9pm, Sat–Sun 10am–7pm. Oct–May Mon–Sat 9am–6pm.* ☎071 43440. Factory and showrooms with guided tours; watch craftsmen producing hand-cut crystal.

SPORTS AND LEISURE

Strandhill is good for wind-surfing but bathing can be dangerous.
Rosses Point *(An Ros)*, a sandy peninsula projecting into Drumcliff Bay, provides a championship golf course and two beautiful sandy beaches for bathing and wind-surfing.

EVENTS AND FESTIVALS

Yeats Annual Winter School – Weekend in February of lectures and a tour of Yeats Country

---

c 1252, damaged by an accidental fire in 1414; the refurbished buildings (1416), spared by Queen Elizabeth on condition that the friars became secular clergy, were torched in 1641 by the Parliamentary commander Sir Frederick Hamilton. The nave contains an elaborate altar tomb honouring the O'Creans (1506); a 15C rood screen across the 13C chancel containing the 17C O'Conor monument. North of the church are the 13C sacristy and chapter-house and extant parts of the 15C **cloisters**.

Model Arts and Niland Gallery★

Closed until Spring 2009 for redevelopment.

This contemporary arts centre of national importance includes the **Niland Collection of Modern Irish Art** featuring some 200 paintings by such notable artists as Jack B Yeat, George Russell, Maurice

McGonigal, Norah McGuiness, Estella Solomons, Paul Henry, Augustus John and Seán Keating.

Yeats Memorial Building

🕐 *Open: Yeats Exhibition year-round Mon–Fri 10am–5pm☎071 9142693. www. yeats-sligo.com.* 🕐 *Open: Sligo Art Gallery, for exhibitions only, Mon–Sat 10am–5.30pm.* ☎ *071 9145847. www.sligoart gallery.com.*

Sligo's most famous family is featured in **The Yeats Exhibition** which outlines the Yeats family genealogy, the people and places which were a major influence on the life and career of W B Yeats, the man as well as the poet. In the same building is the **Sligo Art Gallery** and the Yeats River Café.

County Museum

♿🕐*Open Jun–Sept Tue–Sat 10am– noon, 2pm–4.50pm; Oct–May Tue–Sat 2pm–4.50pm.* ☎*071 9141623.*

The old manse (1851) houses the **Yeats Memorial Collection** of manuscripts, photographs and letters; local antiquities and a large painting *"1916"*, showing Countess Markiewicz and fellow-insurgents surrendering outside Dublin's College of Surgeons.

St John's Cathedral

🕐*Open Jul–Aug 10am–2pm. http://sligo cathedral.elphin.anglican.org.*

This unusual structure was designed in 1730 by Richard Castle, and altered in 1812. A brass tablet *(north transept)* commemorates the mother of WB Yeats, Susan, who was married here; the tomb of her father, William Pollexfen, lies near the main gates.

Cathedral of the Immaculate Conception

The highlight of this uninspired neo-Romanesque building (1874) are the 69 stained-glass by Loblin of Tours in France, best seen in the early morning or evening light.

Driving Tours

Sligo Peninsula

Strandhill marks the end the peninsula assaulted by Atlantic breakers (*good surfing but hazardous bathing*). Here too is Sligo's little airport, but the area's particular attraction are its outstanding prehistoric monuments.

Carrowmore Megalithic Cemetery★

3mi/5km SW of Sligo by a minor road. (Dúchas)♿ 🕐 *Open mid-Mar–Oct 10am–6pm.* ☞ *€2.10.* ☎*071 916 1534. www.heritageireland.ie.*

Carrowmore is the largest Stone Age cemetery in Ireland, having over 60 passage graves, dolmens, stone circles and one cairn marking the largest grave. The most ancient dates from 3200 BC, 700 years earlier than Newgrange. A **visitor centre** contains an exhibition about Stone Age man and the excavations.

▷ *7mi/11km W of Sligo by R 292. After 6mi/10km bear left; park after 1mi/1.6km; 1hr 30min there and back on foot to the summit.*

Knocknarea★

The approach road climbs up "The Glen", a natural fault in the limestone providing a haven for rare plants. On the summit of **Knocknarea** (1 076ft/328m) is a massive heap of stones (197yd/180m round), visible for miles and providing a fine **view**★★ on a clear day. According to tradition, and W B Yeats, this contains a passage grave and tomb of Medb/Maeve, Queen of Connaught in 1C AD; however, it is more likely that she was buried at **Rathcroghan** near Tulsk, Limerick.

Lough Gill★★

Round tour of 30mi/48km E of Sligo – half a day.

Lough Gill is one of Ireland's loveliest lakes, dotted with islands, fringed by shoreline woodlands, picturesquely set against looming limestone mountains.

Parke's Castle

▷ *Take the N 4 south; after 0.25mi/0.4km bear left to Lough Gill.*

Tobernalt

The holy well shaded by trees marks an old Celtic assembly site where a summer festival (Lughnasa) was celebrated in August.

▷ *Continue on the shore road; at the T-junction turn left onto the R 287.*

Dooney Rock Forest

The top of Dooney Rock offers superlative views of the lake and Benbulben.

▷ *At the crossroads turn left; after 2mi/3.2km turn left; 2mi/3.2km to car park.*

Innisfree

W B Yeats was especially drawn to this tiny island (💧*see Address Book*), immortalised in his poem *Lake Isle of Innisfree*.

▷ *Return to the R 287, continue east.*

Dromahair

This attractive riverside village sits between the shell of Villiers Castle (17C) and a ruined abbey.

Creevelea Abbey

Park behind the Abbey Hotel; 6min there and back on foot across the bridge.
An avenue of evergreens beside the Bonet River leads to the ruins of a Franciscan friary which was founded in 1508.

▷ *Continue on the R 287.*

Parke's Castle★

(*Dúchas*). 🕐*Open mid-Mar–Oct 10am–6pm.* ⌕€2.90. ☕ *(summer).* ☎*071 916 4149. www.heritageireland.ie.*
The extensively restored fortified plantation mansion, apparently sitting on the lough waters, was built in 1609 by the Englishman Capt Robert Parke on the site of Sir Brian O'Rourke former home. The bawn wall enclosing the yard once supported the less substantial thatched outbuildings; note how the water-level must have been higher (10ft/3m) in the 17C. A **sweat house** (an early sauna) has been hollowed out in the wall by the shore. A video presentation provides an overview of the area's history.

▷ *Continue west on the R 286, after 7mi/11.3km turn left.*

Hazelwood

Striking views of the lake are to be enjoyed from the trails through the woods; the Palladian house *(private)* was designed by Richard Castle in 1731.

Yeats' Tomb , Drumcliff

▶ *Continue west on the R 286 to return to Sligo.*

Benbulben
Round-trip of 44mi/71km N of Sligo – Allow 1 day.

The dramatic silhouette of Benbulben, a limestone table mountain with a west-facing escarpment like the prow of a dreadnought, dominates the country for miles around.

▶ *From Sligo take the N 15 north.*

Countess Markievicz

The most remarkable member of the Gore-Booth family was Constance (1868–1927), the wife of the Polish artist, impresario and boulevardier Casimir Markievicz, who lived in Dublin and Paris.

The couple drifted apart as Constance devoted herself to the Nationalist cause. While Casimir fought on the Allied side in World War I, Constance took part in the Easter Rising. Condemned to death and later reprieved, she was the first woman elected to the House of Commons in Westminster, though she never took her seat.

Drumcliff★
Fans of **William Butler Yeats** are regular visitors to the churchyard at Drumcliff, where his great-grandfather had been rector, to pay tributes to the poet. Yeats died in the south of France in 1939, and was buried here in accordance with his wishes. The gravestone carries an enigmatic epitaph he composed himself : *Cast a cold eye On life, on death Horsman, pass by!*
The site beneath Benbulben (1 730ft/526m) by the Drumcliff River was chosen by St Columba for the foundation of a monastery in c 575. Its **round tower** was damaged by lightning in 1396; the **high cross** (c 1000) features biblical carvings.

▶ *Make a detour left via Carney.*

Lissadell House
House open by guided tour (40min) only, on the hour, year-round daily 10.30am–6pm. Last tour at 5pm. €6. *Countess Markievicz Exhibition (same hours).* €5. *Walled garden: open Jun–Sept 10.30am–4pm.* €5. *Alpine garden: open mid-Jul–late Sept 10.30am–4.30pm.* €5. *Combined admission all areas €12.* ✗ ☎071 916 3150. *www.lissadellhouse.com. www.constancemarkievicz.ie.*

Standing on the north shore of Sligo Bay surrounded by woods, this austere neo-Classical house owned by the Gore-Booth family (until 2003), descended from the Englishman Captain Gore, who settled in the district in the reign of Elizabeth I. Sir Robert Gore-Booth, for whom the house was built in 1830, was almost bankrupted by efforts to relieve the distress of his tenants during the Famine. W B Yeats was a visitor here, enchanted by the house's atmosphere and entranced by Constance, the Countess Markievicz (◖see 'Countess Markievicz' box).

▶ *Leave the grounds by the north gate; turn left; after 1mi/1.6km turn left to Raghly.*

Ardtermon Castle

Standing within its bawn wall is the restored fortified dwelling built by a member of the Gore family in the early 17C. The entrance is flanked by two round towers; the staircase is contained in a semicircular projection at the rear.

▶ *Return to the N 15, continue north.*

The road passes **Streedagh Point**, a sand bar (3mi/5km) lying parallel with the shore, where three ships from the Spanish Armada went down; survivors were killed by English troops; together over 1 300 men perished.

▶ *In Cliffony turn left to Mullaghmore.*

Mullaghmore

The village shelters on the east side of the rocky headland pointing north into Donegal Bay, grouped around the stone-walled harbour, built in 1842 by Lord Palmerston before his splendidly picturesque neo-Gothic **Classiebawn Castle** (1856) was completed on the exposed west shore.

Inishmurray

11mi/18km offshore; boat from Mullaghmore Pier and from Rosses Point.
St Molaise founded a settlement on this little island in the 6C. The remains of the monastery include the Women's Church (*Teampall na mBan*); rectangular and "beehive"-style dwellings; the Men's Church; souterrains and stone altars. Elsewhere on the island are pillar stones which may be pre-Christian, 57 inscribed stone slabs and 16 Stations of the Cross, spaced around the rocky perimeter. The island has a long history of human habitation – one decorated container found here has been dated to 2000 BC – and not until 1948 did the last islanders leave.

▶ *Return inland bearing left at the first fork and right at the second. At the crossroads turn left onto the N 15.*

Creevykeel Court Cairn★

This well-preserved Late Stone Age court tomb (c 2500 BC), consists of an open court and a double burial chamber surrounded by a wedge-shaped mound of stones. Two other chambers, entered from the side, are probably later.

▶ *At the crossroads turn left inland.*

Gleniff Horseshoe Scenic Drive

This short loop road (*6mi/10km*) makes a fascinating incursion into the upland landscapes of the Darty Mountains between **Truskmore** (2 120ft/644m), and Benbulben.

▶ *Turn left onto the minor road. After 6mi/9.5km turn left onto the N 15; before reaching Drumcliff turn left onto a minor road.*

Glencar Waterfall★

Access path right; 5min return by foot.
The waterfall tumbles over the rocks to a sheer drop (50ft/15m). The wind howling in from the Atlantic sometimes blows up the spray (*the cataract smokes upon the mountain side… that cold and vapour-turbaned steep.* W B Yeats).

▶ *Continue east. At the junction turn right onto the N 16 to return to Sligo.*

STROKESTOWN★

POPULATION 568

A particularly fine example of an estate village and now a Heritage Town, Strokestown (Béal Na Mbuillí) has a broad main street running up to the fanciful Gothic arches of the entrance to Strokestown Park House. Lived in by its founding family until 1979, the house gives an intriguing picture of the life led by a prominent family of the Anglo-Irish Ascendancy. The surrounding district is rich in relics of earlier Irish society.

- 🛈 **Information:** Abbey St, Roscommon. ☎090 662 6342. www.irelandwest.ie. www.visitroscommon.ie.
- ▸ **Orient Yourself:** Strokestown is on the N 5, the main road leading northwest from Longford, 13mi/20km northeast of Roscommon.
- ♿ **Also See:** ATHLONE, BOYLE, CARRICK-ON-SHANNON, KNOCK, LONGFORD.

A Bit of History

Confiscated from its original owner, O'Connor Roe, part of whose bawn survives in the building now housing the restaurant, land at Strokestown was granted to Capt Nicholas Mahon (d 1680), a Cromwellian officer; the estate was later extended to secure his support for Charles II. As they prospered, successive members of the Mahon family rebuilt or extended the house begun by Nicholas Mahon. In 1800, Maurice Mahon accepted a Union peerage, becoming Baron Hartland of Strokestown, despite his father having been a bitter opponent of the Act of Union. In 1845, as the Great Famine began, the property passed to Major Denis Mahon, who acquired an unenviable reputation as a heartless evictor of his destitute tenantry, more than 3 000 in total, many of whom perished aboard the notorious "coffin ships" sailing to America. On 2 November 1847 in broad daylight, while riding in an open carriage, he was shot dead by two assassins; that evening, bonfires were lit in celebration on the nearby hills.

Visit

Strokestown Park House and Famine Museum★

♿*House guided tour only, 17 Mar–Oct 10.30am–5.30pm. House and garden.* ◉*€12.50; garden only, €8.* ✕. ☎*071 963 3013. www.strokestownpark.ie.*

The house, a fine Palladian mansion designed by Richard Castle in the 1730s, consists of a central three-storey block with a pillared portico, linked by curving corridors to the service wings. The well-preserved interiors give an impression of a comfortable and sociable rather than ostentatious life. As well as spits and a trio of ovens for baking, roasting and smoking, the great **kitchen** has a dresser filled with Belleek pottery and is overlooked by a gallery from which the housekeeper could supervise her underlings.

The **Walled Gardens** have been restored; the larger pleasure garden (4 acres/1.6ha) is embellished with a magnificent Edwardian pergola and

Famine pot, Strokestown Famine Museum

long herbaceous border; the smaller Georgian fruit and vegetable garden contains the original glasshouses used to cultivate grapes, peaches and figs.

The **Famine Museum** in the stable yard, presents a comprehensive, detailed and balanced account of the Great Famine, based on State archives and the Strokestown estate records, used by Cecil Woodham-Smith for her book *The Great Hunger*. References to the family, the estate and their history are put in their mid-19C context.

Driving Tour

Cruachan District

▶ *From Strokestown take the R 368 northy to Elphin and follow signs.*

Elphin Windmill

Visit by guided tour only Jul–Aug 10am–6pm, Sept–Jun Mon–Fri 2pm–6pm, Sat–Sun 10am–6pm. Phone to confirm. €5. ☎086 400 2765.

This early 18C windmill (restored) is the only one of its kind in the west of Ireland: what is unusual about it, is its conical thatched roof and sails made to face the wind by means of cartwheels running on a circular track.

▶ *From Elphin take the R 369 west; turn left onto the N 61 ; in Tulsk turn right onto the N 5 to Rathcroghan.*

Cruachan Aí Visitor Centre

Open Jun–Oct Mon–Fri 9am–6pm, Sat–Sun 10am–6pm (1pm Sun). Nov–May Mon–Sat 9am–5pm. €5. ☎071 963 9268. www.cruachanai.com.

On the banks of the little Ogulla River, this sensitively designed structure hosts fascinating display about the area's extraordinary field monuments which have long fascinated archeologists and antiquarians but whose precise function and meaning is only now being unravelled.

The Centre abuts a ringfort and the motte of an Anglo-Norman style castle, but the majority of the monuments – Bronze Age tumuli, ring-barrows, souterrains, field systems and ceremonial avenues – are spread widely over a broad and fertile landscape which has been grazed since Neolithic times, featuring in the country's most compelling myths, legends and history. According to the *Táin Bó Cúailgne* saga, it was from here that Queen Medb/Maeve set out on the great Cattle Raid of Cooley, and the kings of Ireland were buried here before Tara became the favoured royal cemetery in the first century AD. The kings of Connaught were inaugurated on the summit of the hill at Carnfree, the last such ceremony taking place as late as 1641.

▶ *Continue northwest on the N5 for 9mi/14km.*

Douglas Hyde Interpretative Centre

Open May–Sept Tue–Fri 2pm–5pm, Sat–Sun 2pm–6pm. ☎0907 70016.

The Anglican Church in Portahard, Frenchpark, where his father was Rector, is now devoted to the life of Douglas Hyde (1860–1949), first President of the Irish Republic (1938–45). Unusually for one of Anglo-Irish origin, Dr Douglas Hyde was an Irish scholar and a passionate collector of Irish poetry and folk tales. As president of the Gaelic League, his efforts were directed to the preservation of Gaelic as the national language of Ireland and the promotion of Irish literature.

▶ *Take the minor road south via Cloonfad and Fairymount and the R 361 to Castlerea. Turn right onto the N60, then right again.*

Clonalis House★

Open to non-residents by guided tour only (45min), Jun–Aug Mon–Sat 11am–4pm. €7. ☎094 962 0014. www.clonalis.com.

Address Book

TRACING ANCESTORS

County Roscommon Heritage & Genealogy – *Mon–Fri* ☎071 963 3380. www.roscommonroots.com.

Clonalis is the seat of the O'Connor Don (Don means king or leader), one of the most ancient of Irish dynasties with an ancestry leading back to Federach the Just in AD75. The Italianate house, overlooking the River Suck, was designed in 1878 by the English architect Pepys Cockerell. Today it offers luxury accommodation in the mainhouse and self-catering in the cottages.

The well-furnished house is a monument to the O'Connors in Ireland and abroad: one member founded the city of Tucson in Arizona. There is a great library of books and archived documents (correspondence from Louis XIV, Samuel Johnson, Daniel O'Connell, Gladstone, Douglas Hyde), portraits, costumes, uniforms, and the standard borne at the coronation of George V in 1911 by Denis O'Connor, the first member of an Irish Gaelic family to be so honoured. There is also the harp of the famous blind bard Turlough Carolan' who often played for the O'Connors.

Two relics from the Penal Period are displayed in the **chapel:** an altar from a secret chapel, and a special chalice.

▶ *Take the N 60 southeast; after 2.5mi/4km turn left to Ballintober.*

Ballintober Castle

The ruined castle was inhabited well into the 19C. The high walls, fortified by a polygonal tower at each corner and originally surrounded by a moat, enclose a large rectangular courtyard. Two projecting turrets guard the entrance gate. In 1652 the castle was captured by the Cromwellians but in 1677 it was returned to the O'Connor Don, by whose ancestors it was built c 1300.

▶ *Take the R 367 south ; turn right onto the N 60. In Ballymoe turn left and left again onto the minor road to Glinsk.*

Glinsk Castle

The four-storey ruin suggest a fine fortified house, built by the Burkes c 1618–30.

▶ *Continue SE through Creggs and on R 362. Before joining N 63, turn left and left again onto a private drive.*

Castlestrange Stone★

In a field *(right)* is a rounded granite boulder decorated with a curvilinear Celtic-style La Tène design from 250 BC.

▶ *Turn left onto the N 63 towards Roscommon.*

Roscommon Dominican Friary

This ruined friary, established in 1253, still has an effigy of its founder, Felim O'Connor, his feet resting on a dog; below is a panel with vigorous carvings of well-armed mail-clad gallow glasses, the fearsome mercenary warriors imported from the west of Scotland in the 14C.

▶ *Continue on the N 63 to Roscommon.*

Roscommon

The county town, an important market in the middle of rich cattle and sheep country, is named after St Comán, first Bishop of Roscommon and abbot of Clonmacnoise. He founded a monastery of Augustinian canons in Roscommon, elements of which may be incorporated into the Anglican church. The history of the monastery, the town and the district is illustrated in the **Roscommon County Museum** (&⊙*open Jun–Aug Mon–Sat 10am–5.30pm; Sept–May Mon–Fri 10am–4pm; ☎090 6625613)* housed in a former Presbyterian chapel.

▶ *North of town on the N 61. 2min on foot from the car park across a field.*

Roscommon Castle★

The impressive ruin of an enormous Norman castle, built in 1269 by Robert de Ufford and originally protected by a lake or swamp suggests it had massive walls, and round corner bastions. The mullion windows were inserted by Sir Nicholas Malby, Governor of Connaught; it was destroyed largely by Cromwellian troops.

TRALEE

POPULATION 19 056

At the head of its bay, the county town of Kerry is a flourishing, workaday place with a range of traditional and modern industries. Not particularly oriented to tourism, it is nevertheless an important gateway to the Dingle peninsula, treating its visitors to an ambitious and informative evocation to the "Kingdom of Kerry". It is also the home of the country's National Folk Theatre, which attracts hopefuls from the Irish diaspora for the annual "Rose of Tralee" festival.

- **Information:** Ashe Memorial Hall ☎066 712 1288. www.tralee.ie.
- **Orient Yourself:** Tralee is situated at the neck of the Dingle Peninsula, between Dingle, 31mi/52km west, and Limerick, 64mi/106km northeast.
- **Especially for Kids:** Crag Cave.
- **Also See:** ADARE, DINGLE PENINSULA, KENMARE, KILLARNEY.

A Bit of History

Desmond Stronghold and Denny Fief

– Tralee (Trá Lí) grew around the Anglo-Norman castle built by John Fitzgerald in 1243. His descendants, the Earls of Desmond became one of the most powerful Old English clans, "more Irish than the Irish" and deadly rivals of the Ormonds. The Geraldine/Fitzgerald line came to an end in 1583 when the 15th Earl, who had rebelled with Spanish and Papal help, was betrayed and executed; his head was displayed on a spike at the Tower of London. Tralee and the Desmond estates were granted to Sir Hugh Denny whose family held sway here for 300 years.

The town suffered badly in the wars of the 17C and now has a largely 18C and 19C character. Strongly nationalistic in outlook, Tralee became an important centre of opposition to British rule in the late 19C/early 20C.

Sights

Kerry County Museum★

&. ⊙ Open daily May–Oct 9.30am–5.30pm; Nov–Apr Tue–Sat 9.30am–5pm, Bank Hols & Sun 10am–5pm. ⊙Closed 24–27 Dec ≈€8. ☑ 🅿. ☎066 712 7777.

Begin your visit at this excellent museum with the introductory audio-visual **Kerry the Kingdom**. The **Medieval Experience** recreates the sights, sounds and smells of the town in the Middle Ages and the **Knights Hall** further explores this period. Learn about local man **Tom Crean**, and his expeditions and bravery in Antarctica. The main galleries displays a wide-ranging array of historical artefacts and scale models.

The surrounding **town park** contains the ruins of the **Geraldine castle**.

Tralee Bay

H Champollion/MICHELIN

Tralee & Dingle Railway

&. ⏱*Operates May–Sept. For times and fares contact the Tourist Office on ☎066 712 1288. www.tdlr.org.uk.*

The Tralee & Dingle Railway, serving the disparate communities of the Dingle peninsula closed in 1953, but the centenary year of its construction was marked in 1991 by the re-opening to passenger traffic of the first stretch *(1.5mi/2.4km)* of the narrow-gauge (3ft/1m) line between Tralee and Blennerville. The train is composed of three original carriages drawn by No 5, last of the original steam locomotives.

Excursions

Blennerville Windmill★

2mi/3.2km S of Tralee via R 559. &. ⏱*Open Apr–Oct 10am–6pm.* ☞*€5.* ✗. ☎066 712 1064.

The white-painted five-storey (60ft/18m high), windmill built by the local landlord, Sir Rowland Blennerhassett, c 1800 and derelict by 1880, is again in working order; as long as there is wind in the sails, grain is ground to produce flour. Helpful staff are on hand.

The **Emigration Exhibition** illustrates the experience of the many thousands who left Ireland for America in the 19C. Its centrepiece is the **Jeanie Johnston Commemorative Quilt** designed by a group of local women to commemorate the emigrant barque *Jeanie Johnston* that made sixteen Trans-Atlantic trips and never lost a crewmember or passenger. The design incorporates the ship in Blennerville with a group of emigrants on the quay waiting to board it.

Crag Cave★   Kids

11mi/18km E of Tralee via N 21 to Castleisland (Oileán Ciarraí); take the minor road N for 1mi/1.6km (sign). ☞*Cave open by guided tour (30min) only; mid-Mar–Oct 10am–5.30pm (6pm Jul–Aug). Visitor centre and adventure playground 10am–6pm.* ⏱*Closed Mon–Tue Jan–Feb.* ☞*€12, child €5 (Crazy Cave €8 for 2hrs play; combination ticket with Cave tour €11.* ✗. ☎066 714 1244. www.cragcave.com.

The limestone caves (4 170yd/3 813m), discovered in 1983, are thought to be over a million years old. A short descent *(62 steps)* leads to the tunnels and chambers of the show cave (383yd/350m) with stalactites, stalagmites, columns, curtains, drip stones and flow stones.

The **Crazy Cave** Indoor Adventure Centre is one of the biggest in the region and is an ideal place for little ones to let off steam on a rainy day. There is also an outdoor play area, a good quality shop and an excellent café/restaurant.

Driving Tour

North Kerry

Drive of 87mi/140km.

▶ *From Tralee take the R 551 north and the R 558 west, then the minor road north to Ardfert.*

Ardfert Cathedral★

(Dúchas). ⏱*Open Easter weekend, early May–Sept, Oct Bank hol weekend (Sat–Mon) 9.30am–6pm.* ☞*€2.10. ☎066 7134 711. www.heritageireland.ie.*

Ardfert was established as a missionary base as early as the 5C. Under the Normans Ardfert became a borough, far more important than Tralee, though the lack of a harbour led to its eventual eclipse; two major ecclesiastical ruins have survived from this period.

The **cathedral** was built c 1150 and destroyed by fire in the 17C but its

Blennerville Windmill

walls still rise to the eaves. The south transept (15C) contains an exhibition on the history of the building and the two adjacent small churches, which are decorated with interesting sculptures. Standing among the fields, **Ardfert Friary**, a Franciscan house, was founded in 1253 and substantially rebuilt in 1453; much of the tower and chancel are still intact.

▷ *Continue N on R 551.*

Banna Strand★

The vast stretch of sandy beach (5mi/ 8km) was one of the locations used in the filming of *Ryan's Daughter* (&see *Planning Your Trip*) in 1968. A memorial at the entrance commemorates Sir Roger Casement (1864–1916), who landed on the beach on 21 April 1916 from a German submarine with a consignment of arms for the Easter Rising ; he was recognised, arrested and subsequently executed.

▷ *Continue north on the R 551.*

Rattoo Round Tower★

The exceptionally well-preserved round tower and the ruined 15C church mark the site of an abbey founded in 1200 for the Knights Hospitaller.

Rose of Tralee

Every August the town is host to the famous International Rose of Tralee Festival which attracts visitors, particularly emigrants, from all parts of the world. Any girl of Irish descent is eligible for the title. This long-running beauty show lasts for 5 days and includes a family carnival, fashion show and concerts: www.roseof tralee.ie.

▷ *Continue north on the R 551; detour along the coast road via Kilcoly, Beal and Astee.*

Ballybunnion

This rather old-fashioned little seaside resort has amusement arcades and several fine beaches; it is also noted for its therapeutic seaweed baths.

▷ *Continue north and east on the R 551; just before Ballylongford turn left into a minor road.*

Carrigafoyle Castle★

Once the principal seat of the O'Connor clan, who ruled most of north Kerry, the castle, originally on an island, was destroyed by Cromwellian forces. One of the flanker towers is fitted out as a dove-

Address Book

ENTERTAINMENT

National Folk Theatre of Ireland (Siamsa Tíre) – ☎066 712 3055. www. siamsatire.com. Founded in 1974, this theatre company draws on the rich local Gaelic tradition to evoke the seasonal festivals and rural way of life in past centuries. The ultra-modern theatre building is shaped like a ringfort.
St John's Theatre and Arts Centre, Listowel (☎068 22590. www.stjohns theatrelistowel.com) hosts a lively programme of drama, dance, music and art. It also holds the Listowel tourist information office.

SHOPPING

Crafts – Visit the Blennerville craft workshops (&see *Excursions*).

SPORTS AND LEISURE

Beaches – Tralee Bay (west and north).
The **Aqua Dome** (*open Jul–Aug daily 10am–10pm, Sept–Jun Mon–Fri 10am–10pm, Sat–Sun 11am–8pm; €12, €10 child; ☎066 712 9150; www.discover kerry.com/aquadome*) is a bit dated, but fun for a rainy day visit with the little ones.
Seaweed baths at Ballybunnion.
Horse races at Tralee and Listowel during the festivals. **Greyhound racing** every Tuesday and Friday at Tralee.

cot. A spiral staircase leads to the top of the tower (80ft/29m high) for extensive **views** of the Shannon estuary.

▷ *Return to the R 551 and continue east; in Ballylongford turn left to Saleen.*

Lislaughtin Abbey

This Franciscan foundation dates from the 15C; the church has an attractive west window and three well-preserved sedilia.

▷ *Continue east to Tarbert.*

Tarbert

Tarbert Bridewell (◐*open daily Apr–Oct 10am–6pm.* ◉€5. ☐. ☎068 36 500) has been converted into an exhibition describing, through wax tableaux in the courtroom and cells, the rough justice in force in Ireland 1828–31.

A **woodland walk** leads through the grounds of 17C **Tarbert House** (◐*open May–Jul, call for days and times;* ◉€8; ☎068 36198) – visited by such notable guests as Winston Churchill, Jonathan Swift, Benjamin Franklin, Charlotte Brontë and Daniel O'Connell – and continues along the wooded shore to Tarbert Old Pier.

▷ *From Tarbert take the N 69 south.*

Listowel (Lios Tuathail)

17mi/27km N of Tralee by N 69.

The literary reputation of this Heritage Town, and the area in general, is celebrated in **Writers' Week**, Ireland's longest running literary festival, held annually in May/June with an international reputation: *www.writersweek.ie.*

The **Seanchaí Kerry Literary and Cultural Centre** (♿◐*open daily Jun–Sept 9.30am–5.30pm, Oct–May Mon–Fri 10am–4pm.* ◉€5; ✗*Mon–Fri;* ☎068 22212; www.kerrywritersmuseum.com) honours the principal writers and storytellers of Co Kerry with displays of texts and video screenings. Seanchaí, pronounced "shan-a-key" comes from the Irish language and means 'Storyteller'.

▷ *Continue south on the N 69 to return to Tralee.*

TRIM ★

POPULATION 1 740

Straddling the Boyne by an ancient ford, little Trim (Baile Átha Troim), **a designated Heritage Town, is dominated by the ruins of its castle, the largest in Ireland, a medieval monument to match the great prehistoric structures farther down the valley. Other imposing remains recall Trim's important role as a stronghold and ecclesiastical centre on the outer edge of the Pale established by the Anglo-Normans.**

▯ **Information:** Castle St ☎046 943 7227. www.meathtourism.ie.

▷ **Orient Yourself:** Trim is situated on the River Boyne, 10mi/16km southwest of Nava and 28mi/45km northwest of Dublin on the R 154.

☺ **Don't Miss:** Trim Castle.

☼ **Also See:** BOYNE VALLEY, FINGAL, KELLS, MAYNOOTH, MULLINGAR.

Visit

Trim Castle ★★

South bank; access through the Town Gate or along the river bank from the bridge. (Dúchas). ◐*Open daily 10am–6pm (5pm Nov–Easter).* ☞*Castle keep visit by guided tour (45min) only.* ◉€3.70.

Site is extremely busy in summer so come early. ☎046 943 8619. www.heritage ireland.ie.

This magnificent medieval castle overlooks the meadows beside the Boyne, whose waters fed the now-dry moat. An outer curtain wall with gatehouses and several towers encloses a broad grassy

H Champollion/MICHELIN

Trim Castle

space dominated by the formidable **keep** (1225) with its two great halls and sleeping accommodation above.

The first stronghold here was built in 1172, in the early days of the Anglo-Norman conquest by Hugh de Lacy, but was soon attacked and destroyed by the native Irish. Rebuilt, it served as King John's headquarters on his sojourn in Ireland and is often called King John's Castle. Protected by two drawbridges and a barbican, the Dublin Gate served as a prison, where the young prince who was to become Henry IV was held prisoner by Richard II. The castle was attacked by Cromwell's troops, who left a breach in the river wall; an adjacent stretch of wall collapsed in 1839, in the course of a storm known as the Big Wind.

Across the river stands a stone arch, the medieval **Sheep Gate**, a fragment of the town's medieval walls; tolls were levied here on flocks bought and sold at the great sheep fairs.

Yellow Steeple

North bank; access from the High St.

The ruined late-14C tower, which gleams in the sun, marks the site of **St Mary's Abbey**, an Augustinian community, founded by St Malachy of Armagh in the 12C near the point where St Patrick landed in the 5C and converted Foitchern, the son of the local chieftain and later first Bishop of Trim. Many pilgrims were attracted to the abbey by Our Lady of Trim, a wooden statue with a reputation for effecting miracles, which disappeared in the Cromwellian period.

In 1425 the west cloisters of the abbey were converted by Lord Lieutenant Talbot into a fortified house, **Talbot's Castle**, which bears the Talbot coat of arms on the north wall. After the Reformation the house became a Latin School, later attended by the young Duke of Wellington, sometime MP for Trim, whose family home was at Dangan *(southeast)*. Unlike many other members of the Ascendancy, the Iron Duke was not particularly proud of his origins, famously denigrating his Irishness by declaring "because a man is born in a stable, it does not make him a horse".

Cathedral

1mi/1.6km east at Newtown Trim.

Among the graves of Newtown Cemetery is a **tomb** bearing the recumbent figures of Sir Luke Dillon, in his Renaissance armour, and his wife, Lady Jane Bathe, in an Elizabethan gown. Separated by a sword, they are referred to as "the jealous man and woman", Lady

The Pale

In Medieval times the Irish living outside Anglo-Norman jurisdiction were "beyond the Pale", from the Latin *palus* for a stake, as applied to a fence (made from palings). The settlement, under Henry II (1154–89), comprised Louth, Meath, Trim, Dublin, Kilkenny, Tipperary, Waterford and Wexford; by the late 15C, as English control weakened, the Pale included Louth, Meath, Dublin and Kildare.

Jane supposedly having deceived her husband with his brother. People leave pins on the tomb in the belief that their warts will disappear.

Farther west are the lovely ruins of a **cathedral**, built early in the 13C to replace the church at Clonard *(southwest)*, which was burned by the Irish at the end of the 12C. To the southwest, further remains are those of a priory, two walls of its refectory still standing next to the 14C kitchen.

Crutched Friary

1mi/1.6km E at Newtown Trim.

On the south bank of the Boyne are the ruins of a 13C hospital built by the Crutched Friars, an order of mendicant friars who wore a cross on their habits. The buildings consist of a keep with several fireplaces, a ruined chapel with a triple-light window and the hospital and stores beside the river.

Excursion

Bective Abbey★

5mi/8km NE by R161 (T26); after 4mi/6.4km turn right. Park beyond the abbey near the bridge.

The impressive and extensive ruins stand in a field on the west bank of the Knightsbrook River. The abbey, one of the earliest Cistercian houses in Ireland, was founded in 1150 by the King of Meath, Murcha Ó Maolsheachlainn, and dedicated to the Blessed Virgin; its abbot was a member of the Parliament of the Pale and Hugh de Lacy was buried here in 1195. Little remains of the 12C buildings. The **cloisters**, the tower and the great hall in the south wing date from the 15C when the buildings were altered and fortified.

The film *Braveheart* (1996) was partly shot among these ruins and at Dunsoghly Castle.

TULLAMORE

POPULATION 9 221

Bustling Tullamore (Tulach Mhór) has been the county town of Offaly since 1833. Otherwise undistinguished, the place still has something of its late 18C/early 19C character, when much rebuilding took place and when the construction of the Grand Canal brought the town a measure of prosperity.

- **Information:** Tullamore Dew Heritage Centre. ☎057 935 2617.
- ▶ **Orient Yourself:** Tullamore is 62mi/100km due west of Dublin, on the Grand Canal, just south of the Dublin–Athlone road (N 6).
- **Also See:** ABBEYLEIX, ATHLONE, ATHY, BIRR, KILDARE, TRIM.

Visit

Tullamore Dew Heritage Centre

⟳Open daily May–Sept 9am–6pm, Oct–Apr 10am–5pm. Sun (year-round) noon–5pm. €6. 　 ☎057 9325015. www.tullamore-dew.org.

A golden drop of *Tullamore Dew* whiskey or *Irish Mist* awaits in the bar but first it is worth discovering the history of Tullamore, particularly of the distillery, founded in 1829 by Michael Molloy. In

1887 Daniel E Williams, who had been steeped in whiskey production since joining the staff at the age of 15, became general manager and gradually acquired overall control of the business. He used his own initials to provide a brand name – *Tullamore Dew* – for the distillery's pot still whiskey and from that flowed the advertising slogan – *Give every man his Dew*. In the 1950s, when sales were low, the distillery began to produce *Irish Mist*, a whiskey-based liqueur, inspired by a

Durrow High Cross

The **Book of Durrow**, an illuminated manuscript now in Trinity College Library, Dublin, was produced at the abbey founded in 556 by St Columba at Durrow *(4mi/7km N of Tullamore by N 52)*. In 1186 the abbey church was pulled down by the Anglo-Norman Hugh de Lacy, an act of sacrilege which so outraged a local man that he cut off the intruder's head. The *Book* survived despite being used by a farmer to cure his sick cattle, touching them with it after soaking it in water.

The site of the abbey *(private property)* is a gloomily romantic place, with a ruined 18C church, a holy well, a cemetery with 9C to 11C grave slabs, and above all a fine 10C **high cross**. Its east face shows the Sacrifice of Isaac together with Christ in Glory flanked by David with his harp *(left)* and David killing the Lion *(right)*; the west face shows the Crucifixion and associated events.

traditional Irish recipe for heather wine made with pot still whiskey, herbs and heather honey.

Excursions

Locke's Distillery Museum

Kilbeggan; 7.5mi/12km N of Tullamore via the N 52.   *Visit by guided tour (40min) only. Apr–Oct 9am–6pm, Nov–Mar 10am–4pm.* €6. *0506 32134. www.lockesdistillerymuseum.com.*

On the west bank of the River Brosna stand the extensive buildings of the distillery (1757–1953) established by John Locke, possibly the oldest licensed pot distillery in Ireland. The process of distill-

Locke's Distillery

Bord Fáilte, Dublin

Address Book

TRACING ANCESTORS
Irish Midlands Ancestry *Bury Quay, Offaly. Open Mon–Fri 9am–1pm and 2pm–4pm.* 05 06 21421. *www. offalyhistory.com.*

ing whiskey is explained and much of the original equipment is still in place: three sets of millstones for grinding barley; the mash tuns (known as kieves) for making wort; the huge wooden vats (washbacks) for fermentation; the hogsheads for maturing the whiskey; coopers' tools; the under-shot water-wheel, and the steam engine which replaced it when the water-level was too high or too low.

Clara Bog

7mi/10km NW of Tullamore by N 80; in Clara take a minor road south; car park at the end of a short causeway. *Visitors should not stray from the causeway unless accompanied by a knowledgeable guide.*

This raised bog (1 640 acres/665ha; 23ft/7km maximum depth) is one of the finest and largest of its kind remaining in Ireland and is of international interest. In 1987 it was designated a National Nature Reserve. It has a diverse flora, including at least 10 different bog mosses; in wet areas carnivorous plants, like sundews and bladderworts, entrap unwary insects.

WATERFORD★

POPULATION 42 540

The harbour city of Waterford (Port Láirge) continues to benefit from its superb location on the tidal River Suir inland from its confluence with the River Barrow and the vast stretch of sheltered water known as Waterford Harbour. Waterford glassware has become a global brand and the city enjoys a prosperity rooted in a mercantile and manufacturing tradition going back to its foundation by Vikings in the 9C. Many memories of this long history are preserved in the mile-long quayside, the close-packed streets and the surviving sections of the once extensive City Walls★ that enclosed the town. The watchtower (35ft/10m high) surveys a well-preserved section on the south side near John's River. As well as the Norman extensions, which are mostly 13C, there are traces of the 9C and 10C Danish walls, including the sallyports in Reginald's Bar near Reginald's Tower.

🛈 **Information:** The Granary, Merchant's Quay; ☎051 875 823.
Waterford Crystal Visitor Centre; ☎051 332 585. www.southeastireland.com.
www.waterfordtourism.org.

▶ **Orient Yourself:** Waterford is situated on the country boundary with County Wexford on the major coast road between Wexford, 37mi/60km east and Cork 75 mi/120km west.

👁 **Also See:** CLONMEL, NEW ROSS, WEXFORD, YOUGHAL.

A Bit of History

The Danish Vikings sailed up the Suir in 853, establishing a settlement which they called *Vadrefjord* (meaning weatherhaven). Despite constant warfare with the local Irish, the Danes retained control of Vadrefjord until 1169 when the Anglo-Norman Earl of Pembroke (Strongbow) fought his way into the town, subsequently marrying the King of Leinster's daughter in Reginald's Tower.

Under Anglo-Norman rule Waterford became the second most important town in Ireland after Dublin with a reputation of fierce loyalty to the English king. In 1649 Waterford was unsuccessfully besieged by Cromwell but it fell to his general, Ireton, the following year.

Waterford Crystal

Famous Sons

Thomas Francis Meagher (1822–67) was a wealthy lawyer, who joined the Young Ireland Uprising. For his part in the rising at Ballingarry in Co Tipperary he received a death sentence, which was commuted to transportation to Tasmania. From there he escaped to the USA where he founded the Irish Brigade and fought in the American Civil War.

William Hobson (1783–1842), who was born in Lombard Street near The Mall, be-came the first Governor of New Zealand.

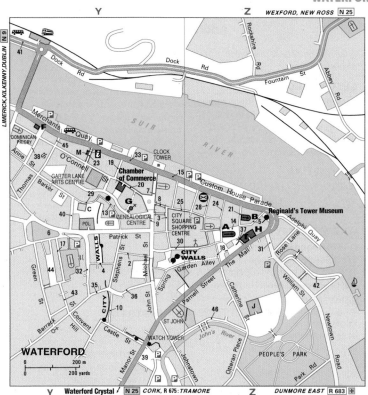

Walking Tour

Reginald Tower

(Dúchas) & Open Easter–Oct 10am–
5pm (Jun–Sept 6pm); Nov–Easter Wed–
Sun 10am–5pm. Closed Christmas
period. €2.10. 051 304 220. www.
heritageireland.ie.

The stone fortress in a commanding
location overlooking the River Suir, was
built by the Vikings in 1013 as part of
the town's defences, then strengthened
by the Anglo-Normans. Its four floors,
linked by a spiral stair built within the
thickness of the walls, contain displays
about tower.

Many distinguished families of Waterford
are buried within the precincts of the
ruined **French Church** (access through
Reginald Tower – on request).

Originally a Franciscan foundation, built
in 1240, then a hospital, this was where

345

Address Book

For coin ranges, see the Legend on the cover flap.

GETTING AROUND

Passage East Car Ferry – ferry across Waterford Harbour from Passage East *(southeast of Waterford via the R 683)* to Ballyhack. ☎*051 382 480, 382 488; http://homepage.eircom.net/~passferry.*

SIGHTSEEING

Walking Tours – ☎*051 873 711 (before 5pm), 051 851 043. (after 5pm). www.iol. ie/~mnoc/wktour.html.*

WHERE TO STAY

Diamond Hill – *Slieveroe.* ☎*051 832 855. www.stayatdiamondhill.com. 18rm.* Set 2km from town, Diamond Hill is set in 2 acres of delightful mature gardens for which the owners have won awards. The house itself is modern and rather bland.

The Anchorage – *9 The Quay* ☎*051 854 302. 14rm.* Simple, clean and straightforward accommodation on the edge of the city and priced fairly. The rooms at the front have views of the quay and the river while those at the back tend to be quieter.

Avondale – *2 Parnell Street, Dunmore East.* ☎*051 852 267. www. staywithus.net.* Personally run, clean and friendly terraced town house, two minutes walk from the town centre. Bedrooms are tidy, come in a variety of shapes and sizes and are sensibly priced.

Coach House – *Butlerstown Castle, Cork Rd.* ☎*051 384 656. http://www.iol. ie/~coachhse. 7rm.* Large stone-built house of Victorian origins that lies in the grounds of the ruins of Butlerstown Castle. Decorated with period furniture sitting alongside modern facilities.

Foxmount Country House – *Passage East Road, 4.5mi southeast.* ☎*051 874 308. www.foxmountcountry house.com. 5rm.* Ideal for escaping the pressures of modern metropolitan life, this charming 17C country house is surrounded by a working dairy farm. Elegantly fitted bedrooms look out over the mature gardens; award-winning breakfasts. Very good value.

Three Rivers – *Cheekpoint. 7mi east.* ☎*051 382 520. 4rm.* This recently refurbished purpose-built guesthouse enjoys a peaceful setting and excellent views with the garden and lounge overlooking the estuary, and river views from several rooms.

Waterford Castle Hotel and Golf Club – *The Island, Ballinakill. 2.5mi east* – ☎*051 878 203.www.waterford castle.com/. Restaurant (*). Catch the private ferry to reach this luxury resort set around an imposing 15C castle on its own 300 acre/121ha island on the River Suir. Granite arches, gargoyles, oak panelling, log fires and tapestries all add to this authentic baronial experience. Amenities include a spa, championship golf course, horse-riding and other country pursuits.

WHERE TO EAT

McAlpin's Suir Inn – *Cheekpoint.* ☎*051 382 220. www.mcalpins.com.* This pretty and immaculately kept inn on the harbour-front in a charming village has served the local fishermen for almost 300 years. Hand-written daily changing menu of tried-and-trusted favourites.

Azzurro at The Ship – *Dock Road, Dunmore East.* ☎*051 383 141. www. azzurro.ie.* One of Waterford's most successful restaurateurs has given a Mediterranean makeover to this ivy-clad pub in a picturesque fishing village.

The Wine Vault – *High Street.* ☎*051 853 444.* Wine is the speciality of this bistro set in a converted 15C wine warehouse with an impressive number of varieties available by the glass. The menu mixes the classical with the more modern.

ENTERTAINMENT

Garter Lane Arts Centre – *O'Connell Street.* ☎*051 855 038. www.garterlane.ie.* Regular art exhibitions, recitals, world music, comedy, dance and theatrical productions.

Theatre Royal – *The Mall.* ☎*051 874 402. www.theatreroyalwaterford.com.* Waterford's leading mainstream drama theatre (*see Walking Tour*).

SHOPPING

The main shopping streets are Barronstrand Street, which runs inland from the Clock tower in the Quay, and the neighbouring streets (see Sights).

SPORTS AND LEISURE

Beaches and bathing at Tramore and at Woodstown south of Passage East and south of Duncannon Fort on east shore of Waterford Harbour.
Splashworld – ☎051 390 176. Ireland's premier water leisure centre.
Greyhound Racing.

EVENTS AND FESTIVALS

Waterford International Festival of Light Opera – Held annually last two weeks of September at the Theatre Royal. ☎051 874402.
Spraoi – the best of national and international street art and world music staged over three days around August Bank Holiday. www.spraoi.com
Waterford Arts Festival (Imagine) – Live performances, music, exhibition, film and special workshops Spans a week in late Oct–early Nov. www.waterfordartsfestival.com.

TRACING ANCESTORS

Waterford Heritage Genealogical Service – Jenkin's Lane. Open Mon–Fri 9am–5pm (2pm Fri). ☎051 876 123. www.iol.ie/~mnoc.

---

the Huguenots of Wexford worshipped between 1693 and 1815.

City Hall and Theatre Royal

The **City Hall**, originally the city exchange, is a stately edifice designed by John Roberts in 1788. The building incorporates the 1876 **Theatre Royal** (☎051 874 402. www.thetheatreroyalwaterford.com); its Victorian decor is rare in a theatre in Ireland. The three-tier horse-shoe design (seating capacity 650) rises to an impressive dome; the specially designed Waterford Crystal chandelier was presented in 1958.

Christ Church Cathedral

♿ ◷Open Easter to Oct 10am (noon Sun) to 5pm. Tours at 11.30am, 3pm. ◷Closed Bank Holidays. Donations welcome. ☎051 858 958. www.christchurchwaterford.com.
The present building was designed by John Roberts (1714–96) in the 18C English Classical style; it was completed in 1779. In 1891 the galleries and square pews were removed. Within is a model of the original Viking church (1050–1773); among the monuments from the medieval church, is one of James Rice, showing his body a year after his death with signs of decay and vermin; two monuments by John van Nost to the Fitzgeralds and to Susanna Mason.

Medieval Waterford

When the City Square Shopping Centre was built, 12 layers of housing were found resting on Viking foundations. Stones mark the site of St Peter's church (12C), the earliest example of an apsed church in Ireland. The mural depicts the area c 1100.

St Patrick's Church

As it was built during the Penal Period, the church was deliberately constructed to resemble a house from the outside.

Chamber of Commerce

The fine Georgian building (1795) was designed by John Roberts, a noted 18C Waterford architect.

Sights

Waterford Crystal★

1.5mi/2.5km south by N25. ♿ Factory visit by guided tour (1hr) only: Mar–Oct daily 8.30am–4.15pm; Nov–Feb Mon–Fri 9am–3.15pm. €8. ☎051 332 500. www.waterfordvisitorcentre.com.
Waterford Glass was first produced in 1783 and the factory has grown to be the largest glassworks in the world. Tours begin with a film about the story of glass in Ireland and continue through the different stages of production.

Waterford Treasures

Waterford Treasures★
The Granary. &. ⏰*Open daily: Apr–Sept 9.30am–6pm (9pm Jun–Aug), Oct–Mar 10am–5pm.* ⬤€4. ☎051 30 4500. www. waterfordtreasures.com.

The old grain store houses a fascinating display of Viking and medieval finds from local excavations: a plan of a Viking house, the city charters and regalia, plus interactive displays, video.

Driving Tour

Waterford Coast
From Waterford take the R 683.

Passage East

▶ *Take the car ferry across Waterford Harbour to Ballyhack.*

Built originally around a fort, the fishing village Of Passage East sits beneath a high escarpment with small squares narrow streets and brightly painted houses; there are no fewer than three quays.

▶ *Continue south on the R 685.*

Geneva Barracks
On the west shore of Waterford Harbour stand the remains of an extraordinary project undertaken by the government in 1793. The four walls (each 0.25mi/0.4km long) were intended to enclosed a new town to house Swiss immigrants, who would set an example to the locals with their metalworking skills and Protestant work ethic. The project failed, and the buildings became a barracks, notorious for the atrocities committed in 1798 against the rebels held there.

▶ *Continue south on the R 685; turn left into a minor road.*

Dunmore East★
This Breton-style fishing village comprises several thatched cottages clustered around attractive little coves. There are forest walks beside the Ballymacaw Road *(0.25mi/0.4km west).*

▶ *Take the R 684 and R 685 west via Clohernagh.*

Tramore (Trá Mhór)
9mi/14.5km S of Waterford by R 675.
Tramore is one of Ireland's main holiday resorts, equipped with a large amusement park (50 acres/20ha), a water park and a long sandy beach (3mi/5km) overlooking Tramore Bay.

There are fine walks along the Doneraile cliffs *(south).* Great Newtown Head *(west)* across the bay, is marked by three early-19C navigational pillars; the **Tramore Metal Man** is an extraordinary cast-iron figure (14ft/4m high), with pale blue jacket and white trousers, erected in 1823 as a warning to shipping.

▶ *Take the R 675 north to return to Waterford.*

WESTPORT★★

POPULATION 4 253

Westport (Cathair Na Mart), a designated Heritage Town, occupies an attractive site on the meandering Carrowbeg River and is an excellent centre for touring the west coast of Mayo. The town was planned and built c 1780, with more than a touch of Georgian elegance and charm, for the local landlord, John Denis Browne, of Westport House, one of Ireland's great country houses. Until the arrival of the railway in the 19C, Westport Quay was a busy port lined with imposing 18C warehouses.

- **Information:** James Street. ☎098 25711. www.visitmayo.com. www.westporttourism.com.
- ▶ **Orient Yourself:** Westport is at the western extremity of the N 5, part of the national road network, 36mi/48km west of Knock International Airport and 50 mi/80km north of Galway.
- **Especially for Kids:** Westport House family attractions.
- **Don't Miss:** Westport House, Ballintubber Abbey, and the scenic drive around the Murrisk Peninsula.
- **Also See:** CONG, CONNEMARA, KNOCK.

Sights

Town Centre★

The focal point of this neat Georgian town is the **Octagon**, where the weekly market is held. From here James Street descends to the river past the **tourist office and Heritage Centre** with informative displays and splendid models of the town and the nearby holy mountain of Croagh Patrick.

The leafy North and South Malls follow the river, spanned by three bridges. In South Mall is **St Mary's Church**, rebuilt in the 20C as a spacious, basilica-like structure, with stained glass by Harry Clarke and Patrick Pye. By contrast, **Holy Trinity Church** is a neo-Gothic building, with a pencil spire and an interior decorated with ornate mosaics illustrating scenes from the Gospels.

Westport House★★   Kids

House & Gardens open daily Easter–Oct 11.30am–5.30pm. Family attractions: Easter week, Suns in May (see website for

Westport House Staircase

Bord Fáilte, Dublin

Address Book

For coin ranges, see the Legend on the cover flap.

SIGHTSEEING

Clare Island Ferry – *Operates from Roonagh Quay (20min) Jul–Aug, 6 times daily; May, Jun and Sept, 4 times daily. There and back €15.* ☎*086 8515003; 098 25265/25212 (winter); www.clareislandferry.com*

WHERE TO STAY

Ashville House – *Castlebar Rd. 2mi E on N 5.* ☎*098 27060. http://homepage. eircom.net/~ashville. Mar–Oct. 9rm.* This guesthouse is a couple of miles outside of town but is worth it for the tennis court, large garden and suntrap terrace. Wood-floored throughout with two of the bedrooms on the ground floor. A warm welcome is assured.

Augusta Lodge – *Golf Links Rd. 0.5mi N off N 59.* ☎*098 28900. www.augusta lodge.ie. Closed 1 week at Christmas. 10 rm.* There' a clue in the name. Not only is this guesthouse close to the local course but the owner has his golfing memorabilia displayed in the lounge along with a wall-mounted map highlighting all of Ireland's courses. He even has his own putting green next door.

The Wyatt Hotel – *The Octagon.* ☎*098 25027. www.wyatthotel.com. Closed 23–27 Dec. 49rm. Restaurant.* Contemporary comfort in the very centre of the town. Its busy bar is a popular local spot and the restaurant provides a menu featuring assorted influences from around the world. Bedrooms are modern and comfortable.

Atlantic Coast – *The Quay. 1 mi W by R 335.* ☎*098 29000. www. atlanticcoasthotel.com. Closed 24–25 Dec. 84rm. Restaurant.* Originally an 18C mill, converted into a modern and well-equipped hotel and overlooking Clew Bay and Croagh Patrick. Bedrooms are roomy and stylish while the top floor restaurant offers contemporary cuisine. Up-to-the-minute leisure club.

Delphi Lodge – *Leenane. 8.25mi NW by N 59 on Louisburgh Rd.* ☎*095 42222. www.delphilodge.ie. Closed 20 Dec–6 Jan. 12rm. Restaurant.* Dwarfed by the surrounding mountains and nestling by the lake, this Georgian sporting lodge boasts an unrivalled setting and is much loved by holidaying fishermen. Communal dinner around the large polished table allows guests the chance to discuss the one that got away.

WHERE TO EAT

Matt Molloy's – *Bridge St.* ☎*098 26655. www.mattmalloy.com.* The eponymous Matt Molloy is a member of the celebrated Irish folk band, The Chieftains, and live music plays a big part in this town centre pub. Its smoky, lively, noisy and the authentic Irish pub experience.

Lemon Peel – *The Octagon, Leenane.* ☎*098 26929. www.lemon peel.ie. Closed 24–26 and 31 Dec and Mon. Booking essential.* Klimt prints and appropriately lemon hued walls decorate this narrow little restaurant in the town centre. The chef owner often comes out of his kitchen to greet the regulars. Lively, informal feel with an eclectic mix of influences on the menu.

Linenmill – *The Demesne, off Newport Rd.* ☎*098 29500. www.linenmill.ie. Closed Good Fri , 25–26 Dec, Mon, Tue, Sun dinner.* Part of a new development to the west of town, comprising of a museum of the textile industry, a shop selling fabrics and home decoration and a roomy, bright restaurant. Accomplished modern cooking; try the daily changing seafood dishes.

SHOPPING

Linen Mill & Museum – *See Where to Eat.*

SPORTS AND LEISURE

Sailing, fishing, walking and horse riding; sandy beaches to the southwest (Silver Strand).

The Brownes of Westport

Twelve generations of Brownes have lived at Westport, all documented in the 400 year family archive. The family is descended from Sir Anthony Browne of Cowdray Castle in Sussex, whose younger son John came to Mayo in the reign of Elizabeth I. The first house was built by Col John Browne (1638–1711), a Jacobite bankrupted by the Williamite victory, married to the great-great-granddaughter of Grace O'Malley. Their grandson, John Browne (1709–76), was brought up an Anglican to avoid the Penal Law sanctions, ennobled as Earl of Altamont.

John Denis (1756–1809) was made Marquess of Sligo at the time of the Act of Union in 1800. The 2nd Marquess, Howe Peter (1788–1845), a friend of Lord Byron, returned from a tour of Greece in 1812 with the two columns from the doorway of the Treasury of Atreus in Mycenae; in 1906 they were presented to the British Museum.

other days) & Jun–Aug daily 11.30am–5.30pm. ⬛ House & Gardens €11.50. House and attractions: €21.50, child €16.50. 🖂. ☎098 25430/27766. www.westporthouse.ie.

The house is the work of several architects: Richard Castle designed the east front (1730), Thomas Ivory was responsible for the south elevation (1778), and James Wyatt added the west front c 1780; the columns on the south date from 1943. The lake was created in the 18C by damming the Carrowbeg River. and the garden terraces were built in the early 1900s.

A **tour** of the interior reveals an elegant decor with several distinctive features – the Pompeian frieze and cloud-painted ceiling in the drawing room commissioned by the 2nd Marquess in about 1825; a collection of **family portraits** in the Long Gallery; doors made of mahogany from the family estates in Jamaica; Waterford glass finger bowls; 18C silver dish rings and a unique **centrepiece** of bog oak and beaten silver; the **Mayo Legion Flag** brought to Mayo in 1798 by General Humbert; an **oak staircase** by James Wyatt and **marble staircase** installed by Italians; The Holy Family by Rubens; 200-year-old wallpaper in the **Chinese Room**. The basement **dungeons** of the O'Malley castle, originally on this site, now turned into an attraction for children.

The old **walled garden**, containing a mulberry tree planted in 1690, now houses an **animal and bird Park**. Other **family attractions** include slides, a flume ride, indoor soft play area, a gal-

leon to clamber aboard, and pitch and putt, A **craft shop** is located in the Farmyard Buildings Holiday Centre, there are fishing and rowing **boats** and swan pedaloes on the lake and a diesel train in the grounds.

Clew Bay Heritage Centre

♿🕐Open Apr–May & Oct Mon–Fri 10am–2pm, Jun–Sept Mon–Fri 10am–5pm, Sun (Jul–Aug only) 3pm–5pm. ⬛€3. ☎098 26852. www.museumsofmayo.com/clew bay.htm.

This small museum on Westport Quay is endearingly cluttered with items relating to local history and colourful characters associated with the area: the pirate Grace O'Malley (♿see 'Pirate Queen' box), John MacBride (1868–1916), executed in Kilmainham Gaol for his part in the Easter Rising, and William Joyce, who broadcast from Germany as Lord Haw-Haw during the Second World War.

Excursion

Ballintubber Abbey★★

13mi/20km SE of Westport by R 330; after 11mi/18km turn left. ♿🕐Open year-round daily 9am–midnight. 🔊Tours by arrangement. ⬛€4. ☎094 9030 934. www.ballintubberabbey.ie.

Mass has been celebrated continually for over 750 years at this wonderful Romanesque abbey. Founded in 1216 by Cathal O'Conor, king of Connaught, for a community of Augustinian canons, the abbey lost most of its conventual buildings when it was sacked in 1653 by the Cromwellians who destroyed its timber roof. Note, however, the 13C west door and window, and 13C piscina with a carved head in the Lady Chapel. The de Burgo chapel (now the Sacristy) contains the tomb of Theobald Burke, Viscount Mayo, who was murdered in the locality in 1629.

The **Cloisters** are in ruins but elements have survived of the 13C Treasury and Chapter House and of the warming room with under-floor heating ducts and an external fireplace. The abbey is the rallying point for the revived pilgrimage *(20mi/32km)* to Croagh Patrick.

Driving Tours

Murrisk Peninsula★★
51mi/82km south of Westport – 1 day.

On leaving Westport Quay the road skirts the wooded shore, crossing the Owenee River at Belclare where the O'Malley chiefs (*see 'Pirate Queen' box*) had their seat.

▶ *From Westport take the R 335 west; after 5.5mi/9km turn right.*

Murrisk Abbey
By the shore are the ruins of an Augustinian Friary founded by the O'Malleys in 1457 and suppressed in 1574, although a chalice was made for the monastery by the son of Grace O'Malley (*see 'Pirate Queen' box*), Theobald, in 1635.

▶ *Return to the R 335.*

Croagh Patrick★
2hr on foot to the summit.

The distinctive conical mass of Ireland's sacred mountain (2 503ft/763m) dominates Clew Bay and its countless islands. According to legend all the snakes in Ireland plunged to their death when St Patrick rang his bell above the mountain's steep southern face. In his honour up to 100,000 pilgrims, some of them barefoot, climb the stony slopes to the summit on the last Sunday in July ("Reek Sunday"). Traditionally the climb was completed by torchlight, possibly an echo of the old Celtic festival of Lughnasa. Recent excavations have shown that the narrow plateau at the top was occupied by a pre-Christian hillfort, then by a Early Christian oratory; the present one dates from 1905. The superlative panorama of sea and mountains is ample reward for the rigour of the climb, best begun from the **Croagh Patrick Information Centre** (&open 17 Mar–May 10am–6pm, Jun–Aug 10am–7pm, Sept–Oct 11am–5pm, Nov–17 Mar (call for times); ✕; ☎098 64114; www.croagh-patrick.com), which gives essential background information on the mountain as well as useful tips on the ascent *(2hr)*.

On the opposite side of the road to the Centre, John Behan's startling modern sculpture of a "cofffin ship" constitutes the **National Famine Monument**, unveiled by former President Mary Robinson in 1997.

▶ *Continue west on the R 335.*

Granuaile, the Pirate Queen

Granuaile, also known as **Grace O'Malley** (1530–1603), gained fame for resisting English rule as a female pirate. From her strongholds in Clew Bay, where the many islands made pursuit difficult, she commanded a fleet of privateers who preyed upon ships in Galway Bay, imposing pilot charges or confiscating cargoes. She had two sons and a daughter from her first marriage to Donal O'Flaherty, who owned castles at Ballynahinch and Bunowen in Connemara. Her brief marriage (1566) to Iron Richard Burke gave her Carrigahowley Castle, where she brought up her youngest son, Theobald Burke. In 1574 she successfully repelled an English attempt at besieging the castle.

In 1593 she sailed to Greenwich to petition Elizabeth I for the release of her brother and son, Theobald Burke, who was later made Viscount Mayo by Charles I in 1627.

SLIDE FILE, Dublin

Bunlahinch Clapper Bridge

Louisburgh

The central octagon of this charming little 18C town on the Bunowen River was laid out by the 1st Marquess of Sligo, whose uncle Henry had fought against the French at the Battle of Louisburgh in Canada.

The **Gronwaile (Granuaile) Heritage Centre** (🕐open Jun–Sept 10am–6pm; ⊚€4; ☎098 66341) traces the family tree of the O'Malleys, the history of the clan and their territory, and the life of Grace O'Malley, "the Pirate Queen" (👤 see 'Pirate Queen' box).

▷ *Take the road south towards Killadoon. Make a detour west to Roonagh Quay for the ferry to Clare Island.*

Clare Island

Clare Island Ferry (👤 see Address Book). Bicycles for hire at the island harbour. www.clareisland.org.

Bounded by 300ft/90m cliffs and rising to 1512ft/461m at the summit of Mount Knockmore, the massive bulk of Clare Island commands the entrance to Clew Bay. Grace O'Malley spent her childhood in the castle by the quay; she may be buried in the Carmelite friary which was founded on the island by the O'Malleys in 1224, although the ruins are of later date. The sandy beach near the harbour is safe for bathing and used for water sports. Traditional Irish music is played in the island pubs.

▷ *Return to the road to Killadoon and continue south.*

Killeen

A cross-inscribed stone stands in the northwest corner of the graveyard.

▷ *Turn right at the crossroads; after 0.5mi/0.8km turn right and park.*

Bunlahinch Clapper Bridge★

Beside a ford stands an ancient clapper stone footbridge of 37 arches constructed by laying flat slabs on stone piles.

▷ *Return to the crossroads. Either go straight across or turn right to make a detour (10mi/16km there and back) to Silver Strand.*

Silver Strand

The vast sandy beach (2mi/3.2km) is sheltered by dunes.

▷ *Return to the crossroads and turn right.*

Altore Megalithic Tomb

Beside the road *(left)* overlooking Lough Nahaltora are the remains of a wedge-shaped gallery grave.

▷ *At the T-junction turn right onto the R 335.*

Doo Lough Pass★

The road, constructed in 1896 descends from the pass to **Doo Lough** (2mi/3.2km long), which is enclosed by the **Mweelrea (Muilrea) Mountains** (2 668ft/817m) *(west)* and the **Sheeffry Hills** (2 504ft/761m) *(east)*; at the southern end of the lake rises Ben Gorm (2 302ft/700m).

Delphi

The 2nd Marquess of Sligo renamed his fisheries on the Bundorragha River near Fin Lough after visiting Delphi in Greece.

Aasleagh Falls★

At the narrow head of the fjord the Erriff River gushes over a broad sill of rock.

▷ *Turn right onto the N 59.*

Killary Harbour★

The harbour is a magnificent fjord, a narrow arm of the sea (13 fathoms/24m deep) extending inland *(8mi/13km)* between high rock faces; it broadens out opposite Leenane on the south shore.

Clew Bay

Drive of 25mi/40km – allow half a day.

▷ *From Westport take the N 59 north.*

Newport

The charming little angling resort is dominated by its disused railway viaduct (1892), now converted into an unusual walkway across the Newport River. The broad main street climbs the north bank to the pink granite Irish-Romanesque St Patrick's Church (1914) which contains a particularly spectacular **stained-glass window** by Harry Clarke.

▷ *Continue north on the N 59; after 1mi/2.4km turn left.*

Burrishoole Abbey★

By a narrow inlet where the waters of Lough Furnace drain into the sea, lie the ruins of a Dominican Friary, founded in 1486.
A squat tower marks out the church. The east wall is all that remains of the cloisters. In 1580 the friary was fortified and garrisoned by the English under Sir Nicholas Malby.
Burrishoole was an important port before the Normans came, but was abandoned when Westport harbour was developed.

▷ *Continue north on the N 59; after 2.5mi/4km turn left.*

Carrigahowley Castle (Rockfleet)

This 15C/16C four-storey tower house is built on flat rocks beside a sea-inlet commanding Clew Bay. The living room was on the fourth floor separated from the lower storeys by a stone vault. In 1566, its owner, Richard Burke, married Grace O'Malley (see 'Pirate Queen' box).

▷ *Take the N 59 east; after 1mi/1.6km turn left.*

Furnace Lough★

A narrow switchback road loops north between Lough Furnace and Lough Feeagh. Where the waters of Lough Feeagh run over the rocks into Furnace Lough, there is a salmon leap where the numbers of fish moving up and down stream are monitored. There is a **view** north to Nephin Beg (2 065ft/628m).

▷ *Continue west on N 59 and R 319.*

Achill Island★

Achill Island, approached by a bridge from the Corraun peninsula is Ireland's largest (36 223 acres/14 659ha) – a wonderful mixture of sandy bays and spectacular cliffs dominated by two peaks, Slievemore (2 204ft/671m) and Croaghaun (2 192ft/667m). Once poor and remote, its economy dependent on emigrants' remittances, the island's fortunes waxed as it attracted artists and writers such as the painter Paul Henry and the German Nobel Prize winner Heinrich Böll. Today, tourism, stimulated by the excellent conditions for surfing, boating and sea angling has brough prosperity.
On the shore of Achill Sound south of the bridge stand the restored ruins of **Kildavnet (Kildownet) Church** (c 1700), which contains Stations of the Cross in Gaelic, and is dedicated to Dympna, an

Killary Harbour

Irish saint who sought shelter on Achill in the 7C.

Kildavnet (Kildownet) Castle, a square four-storey 15C **tower house**, commanding the southern entrance to Achill Sound, was one of the strongholds of the redoubtable Grace O'Malley; there are traces of a boat slip and the original bawn.

Trawmore Strand has a splendid sandy beach backed by cliffs. **Keel** is the main resort; at the southeastern end of its long beach the cliffs have been sculpted into bizarre forms. **Keem Strand** too has a lovely sandy shore, sheltered by the great mass of Croaghaun, whose northwestern face plunges spectacularly seaward forming one of the most awesome sea-cliffs in Europe, best viewed by boat.

Between Keel and the little north coast resort of **Doogort** are the remains of abandoned settlements.

WEXFORD ★

POPULATION 9 533

The county town and the commercial centre of the southeast region, Wexford (Loch Garman), set on the south bank of the River Slaney where it enters Wexford Harbour, is a place of great antiquity, first granted a charter in 1317. It is a designated Heritage Town with a strong cultural tradition and is famous for its annual international opera festival.

- **Information:** Crescent Quay; ☎053 912311. Kilrane, Rosslare Harbour; ☎053 9233 232. www.southeastireland.ie. www.wexfordtourism.com.
- ▶ **Orient Yourself:** Wexford lies in the southeast corner of the country, 37mi/60km east of Waterford. The ferry terminal at Rosslare Harbour (5mi/8km southeast) provides passenger and car ferry services from Ireland to South Wales and the ports of northern France.
- ⚲ **Also See:** ENNISCORTHY, NEW ROSS, WATERFORD, WICKLOW MOUNTAINS.

A Bit of History

The site of Wexford was noted by Ptolemy in his 2C AD map but the town's history really began when the Vikings arrived in 950, naming their settlement *Waesfjord* (the harbour of the mud-flats). Following the Anglo-Normans invasion (1169) Wexford was captured and the first Anglo-Irish treaty

Address Book

For coin ranges, see the Legend on the cover flap.

GETTING AROUND

Environmental and sightseeing trips around the Saltee Islands from Kilmore Quay. Reef and wreck fishing. *Operates Apr–Oct (12 person maximum). Call for rates.* ☎053 912 9704, mobile 087 254 9111.

SIGHTSEEING

Walking Tours – Enquire at the Tourist Information Office.

WHERE TO STAY

McMenamin's Townhouse – *3 Auburn Terrace, Redmond Road.* ☎053 914 6442. www.wexford-bedand breakfast.com. 6rm. Sympathetic decoration, antiques and original fireplaces add to the charm and period feel of this late Victorian townhouse. The bedrooms have original wash-stands and wrought iron or half tester beds. Homemade breads, marmalade and jams.

Whitford House Hotel – *New Line Road. 2km west of town.* ☎053 91 43444. www.whitford.ie. 36rm. Luxury bedrooms, many with private balconies or patios, a health and leisure club, fine dining (☺☺), a children's lawn, pool and playground means that all the family are happy here.

Ferrycarrig Hotel – *Ferrycarrig, 4.5mi north west.* ☎053 91 20999. www.ferrycarrighotel.com. 102rm. Restaurant ☺☺. This imposing hotel is idyllically set on River Slaney and its estuary with each of its stylish, contemporary rooms enjoying the view.

A health club, a Beauty Lodge, Kids Club hand either fine dining or summer bar-becues are reasons why this has hotel has won family-friendly awards.

ENTERTAINMENT

Wexford Arts Centre – *Open Mon–Sat 10am–6pm, Sun noon–4pm.* ☎053 91 23764. www.wexfordartscentre.ie. Con-certs, plays and art exhibitions are held throughout the year at this recently refurbished centre. Good restaurant.

SHOPPING

The majority of shops are in Main Street – North and South.

SPORTS AND LEISURE

Beaches at Rosslare (south) and Curracloe (north).

EVENTS AND FESTIVALS

Wexford Festival Opera– *High Street* – ☎053 9122400. www.wexfordopera. com. *Open mid-Oct–early Nov, Mon–Fri 9am–5pm; performances Sat–Sun.* This Opera Festival is inspired by a long-established love of opera in Ireland and it provides many young singers with an opportunity to start a career. The annual event, lasting 18 days in late October includes three produc-tions and over 50 events. The festival has gained an international reputation for the quality of its performances and for its policy of specialising in rare or unjustly neglected operas. In 2006 the 1832 **Theatre Royal** was demolished to make way for the **Wexford Opera House**, which cost 33milllion euros to build and seats 750, giving the Wexford Festival Opera a new home.

was signed at Selskar Abbey. In the 13C the earthen ramparts of the Norse town were replaced by stone walls.

In 1649 Cromwell entered Wexford; Selskar Abbey was destroyed and hun-dreds, possibly thousands of citizens were massacred in the market place. During the rebellion of the United Irish-men in 1798 Wexford was held for a month by the insurgents, some of whom treated their opponents with extreme

cruelty. It was then recaptured with even more bloodshed by Crown forces.

In the 19C, led by local shipping com-panies, Wexford built up a strong mari-time trade. Silting of the harbour and competition from Waterford led to its decline in the early 20C but the town's proximity to the harbour at Rosslare and its vibrant cultural life have more than compensated for this in recent years.

Walking Tour

Crescent Quay

Wexford's long quayside and prom-enade, facing the broad and tidal River Slaney, is relieved by the curve of Crescent Quay; a statue honours John Barry, a native of Co Wexford, who became senior commodore of the US Navy in 1794.

▷ *From Crescent Quay walk inland along Henrietta St; turn right into Main St.*

Main Street★

The commercial centre of Wexford is a long and narrow winding pedestrian-ised street, fronted by grey slate build-ing typical of the area, and shops that retain their traditional 19C design and style of country town establishments.

St Iberius' Church★

🕐*Open year-round daily 10am–4pm (occasionally 3pm in winter).*
The Anglican church stands on an ancient Christian site, formerly at the water's edge. The present Georgian church dates from 1760. The Venetian façade is mid-19C.

Bull Ring

The scene of Cromwell's devastating massacre in 1649 is marked by the **Bull Ring**, once used for bull baiting, a pas-time popular in 12C/13C Wexford.
The **1798 Memorial** shows the bronze figure of a pikeman, a dramatic work by Oliver Sheppard (1864–1941), designer of many patriotic monuments.

▷ *Continue along Main Street North.*

Selskar Abbey

Only the outer walls and square tower remain of the abbey, founded c 1190 by the Anglo-Norman nobleman Sir Alex-ander de la Roche on his return from the Crusades. In 1170–71 Henry II, king of England, spent time in Ireland, partly to assert his authority over the ambitious Strongbow, partly perhaps to escape the opprobrium following the murder of Thomas à Becket, and it was at Selskar that he passed the whole of Lent in 1171 doing penance for the assassination of his archbishop.

West Gate Heritage Centre

🕐*Open Feb–Dec Mon–Sat 10am–5.30pm.* ▧*Audio-visual €3.* 🅿 . ☎*05391 46506.*
The West Gate is the only one of the five original fortified gates still stand-ing; it was built by Sir Stephen Devereux c 1200 and closed to traffic in the late 16C. There is an audio-visual presenta-tion of the town's history and Norman rooms in the tower give access to a bat-tlement walk to Selskar Abbey. Walking tours (1hr) of the city depart from here at 10.30am and 2.30pm *(€5)*

▷ *Walk south on Abbey St and High St; turn right into Rowe Street Upper.*

Twin Churches★

The **Church of the Immaculate Con-ception** *(Rowe Street)* and the **Church of the Assumption** *(Bride Street – south)* were both designed by Augustus Pugin in an almost identical Gothic style; their towers are the same height (230ft/70m) and their foundation stones were laid on the same day in 1851.

▷ *From Rowe Street Upper, turn left into School Street.*

Franciscan Friary★

🕐*Open 9.30am–5.30pm (1.30pm Sun).* ☎*053 9122758.*
The church founded by the Franciscans in 1230 was confiscated in 1540 at the Dissolution of the Monasteries but returned in 1622. The present church (restored) has an attractive stucco ceil-ing and works by contemporary Irish artists, including **The Burning Bush Tabernacle** sculpted by Brother Ben-edict Tutty of Glenstal Abbey.
In 2007, after 750 years in residence at Wexford, a lack of vocations meant that the Franciscans could no longer sustain themselves here. The Friary has been taken over by the Grey Friars brother-hood.

▷ *Continue south via School Street and Roches Road; turn left into Bride Street then left into Main Street South.*

Excursions

Rosslare (Ros Láir)

10mi/16km S of Wexford via the N 25.
The popular seaside resort and ferry port has a fine beach (6mi/10km) with ample sporting facilities.

Lady's Island

11mi/18km south of Wexford via the N 25 and a minor road from Killinick.
This former centre of pilgrimage developed around an Augustinian friary and Norman castle.

Tacumshane Windmill (*Key available from shop next door, leave a donation if possible*) built in 1846, was restored complete with sails in the 1950s.

Tacumshin Lake attracts flocks of wintering wildfowl.

Kilmore Quay★

15mi/24km SW Wexford, N 25 and R 739.
This fishing village retains some of its 19C character, notably where the houses are thatched. The *Wooden House* pub has a fine collection of historic photographs.

The **maritime museum** (*open Jun–Sept noon–6pm; €4; 053 912 1572*) housed in the former *Guillemot* lightship, contains artefacts relating to Wexford seafaring: maps, antique compass and binnacle, a whale's backbone and a large-scale model of *HMS Africa*, sister ship to Nelson's *Victory*.

Saltee Islands★

Boat trips from Kilmore Quay; 3mi/4.8km.
The Great and Little Saltee Islands (each about 0.5mi/0.8km long) form Ireland's largest bird sanctuary (gannets, guillemots, puffins).

Irish Agricultural Museum, Johnstown Castle★★

5mi/8km southwest of Wexford via the N 25. Open Apr–Nov daily 9am–5pm (11am Sat–Sun & Bank Hols). Dec–Mar Mon–Fri 9am–12.30pm & 1.30pm–5pm. €6. 053 91 71247. www.irish agrimuseum.ie.

The Johnstown estate was donated to the Irish State in 1945. **Johnstown Castle** (*closed to the public*), designed by Daniel Robertson, houses an agricultural research centre.

The park (50 acres/20ha) contains **ornamental grounds** with over 200 species of trees and shrubs, three ornamental lakes, walled gardens and hothouses. The well-presented **Agricultural Museum** displays obsolete farming machinery. The transport section includes tub traps, a late-19C jaunting car, carts, traps and harness; corn winnowing machines and old tractors. There are reconstructions of a cooperage, a harness-maker's workshop, a blacksmith's forge and a carpenter's shop; a re-creation of 19C Irish rural living and a display of fine Irish country furniture. The **Famine Exhibition** is a thorough, science-based interpretation of the causes, effects and aftermath of the Great Famine (1845–49), with re-creations of a rural home and a soup kitchen.

Irish National Heritage Park★

Ferrycarrig. 2.5mi/4km NW of Wexford via the N 11. Open 9.30am–6.30pm (subject to seasonal change; check with centre). €8. 053 9120733. www.inhp.com.

Some 9,000 years of Irish history are brought to life by 16 separate sites, linked by a trail. The **Stone Age**, 7000–2000 BC, is represented by a Mesolithic camp site, an early Irish farmstead and a portal dolmen. The **Bronze Age** is illustrated by a cist burial chamber and a stone circle. The Celtic and early-Christian ages are represented by an early-Christian monastery, an **Ogham stone** showing the earliest form of writing in Ireland, and a **crannóg**, an artificial island protected by a palisade. The horizontal watermill is a reconstruction of a Co Cork mill dating from 833. The round tower is a replica, built in 1857 to commemorate Wexford men killed in the Crimean War (1854–56). The only real historic relic is the Norman earthworks and fortifications, built by Robert FitzStephen in 1169. Other exhibitions cover the Great Potato Famine (1845–47) and Harry Ferguson and his tractors.

Wexford Wildfowl Reserve

3mi/5km north of Wexford via the R 741. (Dúchas). Visitor Centre open daily year-round 9am–5pm. Closed 25 Dec. 091 9123129. www.heritageireland.ie.

H Champollion/MICHELIN

Curracloe Beach

For eight months of the year most of the world's population of Greenland white-fronted geese winters on the north shore of Wexford Harbour. Exhibitions and an audio-visual introduce the reserve to visitors.

Curracloe★
6mi/9km N of Wexford, R 741 and R 742. Thatched cottages, glorious sand dunes and seemingly endless sandy beaches (7mi/11km) overlook Wexford Bay.

WICKLOW MOUNTAINS★★

The Wicklow Mountains, south of Dublin, provide high peaks and spectacular views, lakes, reservoirs and waterfalls, open moorland and verdant valleys, some landscaped into elegant gardens. The rolling heights are covered in peat bog where the rivers form broad shallow treeless corridors; on the harder schist they create deep and narrow wooded gorges, like Dargle Glen, Glen of the Downs and Devil's Glen. In the past the mountains were even wilder and far less accessible than today and served as a refuge for outlaws and rebels; some of the 1798 insurgents found sanctuary here for several years, prompting the construction by the British of the Military Road. The mountains fall eastwards to the shingle ridge and sand dunes of the coast, with its string of resorts: Bray, Greystones, Wicklow and Arklow.

- **Information:** Fitzwilliam Sq, Wicklow; ☎0404 69117. Arklow; ☎0402 32484. www.wicklownationalpark.ie. www.eastcoastmidlands.ie.
- ▶ **Orient Yourself:** The Wicklow Mountains extend south from Dublin for about 30m/48km as far as Arklow. Between the coast road (N 11) and the inland road (N 81) there is a network of steep and narrow country roads providing magnificent views of the lakes and moorland.
- **Especially For Kids:** Powerscourt Waterfall, National Sea Life Centre, Bray, Clara Lara Fun Park.
- **Don't Miss:** Powerscourt, Russborough.
- **Also See:** ATHY, DUBLIN, ENNISCORTHY, KILDARE, MAYNOOTH, GLENDALOUGH.

Driving Tours

Inland

Powerscourt★★
♿⚓*House and gardens: open year-round daily 9.30am–5.30pm (garden close at dusk in winter). Ballroom & Garden Rooms close year-round Sun 1.30pm; May–Sept Mon 1.30pm. ⚓House & Gardens closed 25–26 Dec. ⚓Gardens €8, waterfall €5, house and exhibition free. ✕. ☎01 204 6000. www.powerscourt.ie.*

Restored after a terrible fire in 1974, the Palladian mansion designed by Richard Castle in 1730 looks out over a

Address Book

For coin ranges, see the Legend on the cover flap.

GETTING AROUND

St Kevin's Bus Service from Dublin to Glendalough – *Operates daily 11.30am, 6pm, Sun and Bank Hols, 11.30am, 7pm from Dublin (north side of St Stephen's Green) via Bray and Roundwood. Single €13; there and back €20. www.glendaloughbus.com.*

SIGHTSEEING

Wicklow Mountains National Park Information Point by the Upper Lake *(open May–Aug daily 10am–6pm, Apr & Sept Sat–Sun only 10am–5pm)* and Visitor Centre at Glendalough (*see GLENDALOUGH*). *℡0404 45245. www.wicklownationalpark.ie.*

WHERE TO STAY

Glendalough River House – *Rathdrum. 4rm. ℡0404 45577. www. glendaloughriverhouse.ie.* Late 17C farmbuilding beside a meandering river provides quiet and cosy accommodation. Surrounded by 10 acres of woodland so plenty of choice for walkers. Simple but spotless pine-furnished bedrooms.

Keppel's Farmhouse – *Ballanagh. 2mi south of Avoca. 5rm. ℡0402 35168. www.keppelsfarmhouse.com.* Farmhouse on a dairy estate dating back to 1880 with far-reaching views of countryside. The atmosphere is relaxed and tranquil and breakfast is a predictably hearty affair.

Ballyknocken House and Cookery School – *Glenealy, 3mi south of Ashford. 7rm. ℡0404 44627. www. ballyknocken.com. Restaurant .* This Victorian guesthouse, elegantly furnished with antiques, has charming romantic bedrooms, some with Victorian baths and brass beds. Food is so important here that a School of Cookery has been recently established by Catherine Fulvio who appears on Irish cookery programmes and Discovery Channel.

WHERE TO EAT

Fern House Cafe (Avoca Weavers) – *℡01 274 6990. www. avoca.ie. Lunch only.* In the charming setting of Glencormac House gardens (*see Inland Driving Tour, Kilmacanogue*), choose from table service – high quality Italian-influenced cuisine, or self service () from salads, quiches, local wild salmon etc.

Ballymore Inn – *Ballymore Eustace. ℡045 864 585. www.ballymoreinn. com.* A characterful pub in the middle of town. Choose from the Back Bar or (slightly more formal) restaurant. The food in both is imaginative with an eclectic range of international and Irish dishes using local ingredients.

SHOPPING

Avoca Weavers – Very popular, ever fashionable woollen goods and clothes household accessories, glassware, ceramic, jewellery, foodstuffs and more available at the mill in Avoca or at the shop in Kilmacanogue.

Glendalough Woollen Mills – *Laragh. ℡040 445156. www.glendalough woollenmills.com.* Factory outlet shop with tea rooms.

Kildare Outlet Village – *Kildare. ℡045 520 501. www.kildarevillage.com.* Discounted international designer brands.

SPORTS AND LEISURE

Clara Lara Fun Park Kids, *Vale of Clara – Open May (Sat–Sun only), daily Jun–Aug 10.30am–6pm. €10 (some extra charges). Max age 12 years old. ℡0404 46164; www.claralara.com.* Some 50 acres of outdoor activities for young-children – assault course, adventure playgrounds, go-karts, radio-controlled boats, bathing, boating and fishing, picnic meadows.

Wicklow Way – *www.wicklowway.com.* This long-distance footpath (82mi/ 132km), starts in Marlay Park in Rathfarnham, in the southern suburbs of Dublin, passes near Powerscourt, Lough Tay and Lough Dan, Glenmacnass, Glendalough, Glenmalur and Aghavannagh and finishes in Clonegal in Co Carlow (access at Moyne, Bridgeland and Kilquiggin). The trail, consisting of forest tracks, bog roads and mountain paths, crosses mountains, switches back and forth through river valleys and presents glorious views. Tackle as little or as much as you like of the trail!

Powerscourt Estate

Powerscourt Gardens

magnficent landscaped park with grassy terraces, stone stairways, antique statuary, fountains, woodland and specimen trees, set against the backdrop of mountains beyond, including the near-perfect cone of Great Sugar Loaf (1 654ft/503m).

In the house an exhibition brings to life the rich history of the estate, while the double height Georgian ballroom has been restored and hosts weddings and corporate events. The house is also now home to several high quality shops specialising in Irish design in gifts, clothes, and furniture.

The estate is named after Eustace le Poer, a Norman knight. In 1609 the land was granted to Sir Richard Wingfield by James I, who made him Viscount Powerscourt. In 1961 the estate was sold to Mr and Mrs Slazenger.

The **gardens** may have first been laid out by Richard Castle. They were then added to by successive viscounts, mostly in the course of the 19C. In 1843 the 6th Viscount employed the architect Daniel Robertson to design the terraces. The 7th Viscount added the superb wrought-iron gates and much of the statuary, some of it brought from Europe, some of it specially commissioned, like the Triton Fountain in the lake, which spews a jet of water 100ft/30m into the air. Many of the ornamental trees were planted at this time, among them numerous superb

conifers. New features continued to be added in the early 20C, among them the Pepper Pot Tower and the jungle-like Japanese Gardens, created in 1908 on reclaimed bogland.

▶ *Take the R 760 south; after 2mi/3.2km turn right (signposted); at the crossroads drive straight on for 2mi/3.2km to Valclusa.*

Powerscourt Waterfall★★ Kids

&⃝*Open 9.30am–7pm (10.30am–dusk rest of year).* ⃝*Closed 2 weeks up to 26 Dec.* ⊛€5. ▭ *(summer only).*☎*01 204 6000. www.powerscourt.ie.*
5min on foot from car park to waterfall; ☺*Climbing the rock face is dangerous.*
Part of the Powerscourt estate, the highest waterfall in Ireland is formed

---

Military Road

After the 1798 Rebellion the British Government built a military road running south from Dublin through some of the most rugged and isolated parts of the Wicklow Mountains. The original barracks in Glencree now house **The Glencree Centre for Peace and Reconciliation**, an organisation which seeks to promote reconciliation between people of different religious traditions on both sides of the border.

Bord Fáilte, Dublin

Drawing Room, Russborough

by the Dargle River, which plunges (400ft/122m) in a spray of thick white spume down a jagged grey rock face in a horseshoe of hills. This is a popular picnic spot with pleasant walks and nature trails by the river, and a good play area for children.

Killruddery★

&. ⏰ *Gardens: open Apr Sat–Sun and May –Sept daily 1pm–5pm. House May–Jun andSept daily 1pm–5pm.* ⟨⟩ €10; *gardens only,* €6. ☎01 286 3405. *www. killruddery.com.*

The **formal gardens** at Killruddery were designed by a Frenchman in 1682 for the Earl of Meath, whose descendants still inhabit the house. The gardens are a fascinating rarity, a particularly complete example of the kind of formality which went out of fashion in the following century, when most desmesnes were landscaped (or re-landscaped) in an informal, naturalistic manner.

The major features are a pair of parallel canals (550ft/168m long), the **Long Ponds**, prolonged by the **Lime Avenue** leading uphill to the 18C park. The **Angles** consists of a number of intersecting walks lined with high hedges; the wilderness of trees is bisected by broad walks; a bay hedge encloses the **sylvan theatre**, while the **beech hedge pond** consists of two concentric circular beech hedges, surrounding a round pond (60ft/18m in diameter) and a fountain.

The **house**, which dates from the 1650s, was considerably remodelled in the 1820s in neo-Tudor style by Richard and William Morrison. The west front is enhanced by a lovely conservatory with a domed roof and an ornamental octagonal dairy. Above the stableyard entrance is a clock and striking mechanism, both operated by water power and built by members of the family in 1906–09.

Kilmacanogue

The headquarters of the acclaimed **Avoca Weavers** (⏰ *open year-round*

Russborough's Stolen Treasures

Russborough's magnificent painting collection has proved too great a temptation to thieves not once, but twice. In 1974 a gang including the British heiress Rose Dugdale broke in and took 19 pictures worth £8m, using them in a vain attempt to get IRA prisoners in England transferred to Belfast. On this occasion all the paintings were swiftly found by the police. In 1986 another raid, this time by professional criminals, netted £30m worth of pictures. Their fame made them almost impossible to sell and most, but not all, have been subsequently recovered.

daily 10am–6pm; ☏01 286 7466; Fern House Cafe, reservations advisable in summer; ☏01 274 6990; www.avoca.ie) stands on the site of **Glencormac House**, built in 1864 by James Jameson of the famous whiskey family. The grounds contain various rare species of tree – a weeping cypress, Blue Atlantic cedars, several Wellingtonias, various types of eucalyptus and pine and 13 yew trees which are said to be 700 to 800 years old and originally formed part of an avenue leading to Holybrook Abbey. Such is the popularity of Avoca that there are two cafes (both with terrace) to accommodate the many shoppers who come for the high-quality Irish designed Avoca range of goods, plus a gourmet foodhall and a garden nursery.

Russborough★★★

House open by guided tour (45 min) only each hour 10am–5pm. Easter Sun, Mon and every Sun until end Apr, May–Sept daily, Oct Sun & Bank Hols. €10, child €5. Maze €2. ☏045 865239. This is one of the grandest country houses in Ireland, a Palladian palace in Wicklow granite facing a lake which mirrors the mountains rising to the east. Commissioned in 1742 by Joseph Leeson, heir to a brewing fortune, it is the masterpiece of the architect Richard Castle, its central block reaching far out into the landscape via curving colonnades, side pavilions, walls, archways and minor buildings.

Leeson – later Earl of Milltown – is depicted in stucco over the door linking the staircase and entrance halls; he was a great traveller and collector and, when his line died out at the end of the 19C, his paintings passed into the ownership of the National Gallery in Dublin.

The outstanding features are the almost incredibly rich **stucco ceilings** by the Lafranchini brothers and their pupils. The thick and heavy stuccowork on the staircase is by a less accomplished hand. Gorgeous stucco panels frame exquisite seascapes by Vernet, now back in place after being sold in 1926.

Sally Gap★★

The crossroads on the Military Road offers splendid views of the surrounding blanket bog on the Wicklow Mountains.

Loughs Tay and Dan★

Scree slopes plunge directly into the dark waters of Lough Tay, which is linked to Lough Dan by the Cloghgoge River.

Roundwood

The village (780ft/238m above sea-level) consists of little more than a broad main street lined with pubs and craft shops; a pub and a café both claim the honour of being the highest in Ireland.

Annamoe

There are pleasant walks beside the Annamoe River. It was here, at the age

Glenmacnass

H Champollion/MICHELIN

of seven, in 1720, that Laurence Sterne (the author of *Tristram Shandy*) fell into the mill race but emerged unscathed.

Glenmacnass Waterfall★
The mountain river streams dramatically down an inclined rock face.

Wicklow Gap★★
The road west from Glendalough to Hollywood follows the course of the medieval pilgrims' path, **St Kevin's Road**, through the Vale of Glendasan. Where the modern road loops northeast, hikers may follow the old direct route (*2mi/3km*) closer to Lough Nahanagan. The motor road rejoins the old route to pass through the Wicklow Gap between Tonelagee (2 686ft/816m *north*) and Table Mountain (2 302ft/700m *west*).

Devil's Glen★
The Vartry River makes a spectacular **waterfall** (100ft/30m) by cascading into the Devil's Punchbowl, a deep basin in the rock. There are **walks** in the immediate vicinity and good views of the coastline.

Mount Usher Gardens★
&⊙*Open Mar–Oct 10.30am–6pm (cafe and shopping courtyard year-round).* ⊕€7. ⌓. ☎0404 40116. www.mount ushergardens.ie.
Set on the outskirts of Ashford village, the natural-style gardens (20 acres/8ha), which are planted with over 5 000 species, many sub-tropical, are renowned for the collections of eucryphia and eucalyptus. They were laid out in 1868 by Edward Walpole, a member of a Dublin linen-manufacturing family, and totally restored following severe flood damage in 1986.
Two suspension bridges lead to the woodland walks on the east bank of the River Vartry, which has been attractively developed with the addition of weirs.

Samuel Hayes
Avondale was inherited by the Parnell family from Samuel Hayes, a plantsman, whose Chippendale bureau is on display in the house. In 1788 Hayes presented a bill to Parliament "for encouraging the cultivation of trees" and in 1904 Avondale became the national forestry training centre.

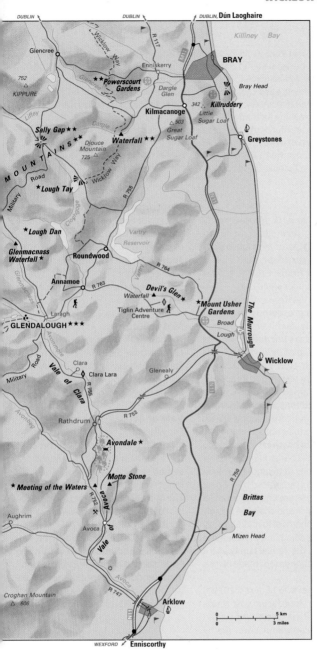

Vale of Clara
The road, which follows the lushly wooded course of the Avonmore River, links Laragh, a natural junction of roads and glens, to the attractive village of Rathdrum.

Glenmalur★
The road beside the upper reaches of the Avonbeg River ends in a remote and desolate spot at the northeast foot of Lugnaquilla, Ireland's second-highest mountain (3 039ft/926m high).

The Uncrowned King of Ireland

Charles Stewart Parnell (1846–91) entered Parliament in 1875. He became Vice-President of the Home Rule Confederation of Great Britain and President of the Land League, campaigning for tenants' rights to their homesteads. He travelled regularly to America and Canada to raise funds and was so well received there that he was dubbed the "uncrowned king of Ireland". In 1882 he founded the National League to campaign for Home Rule.

The life and career of one of the greatest political leaders in Irish history ended in tragedy however when in 1886 he became the third party in a bitter high-profile divorce case, involving a Mrs Kitty O'Shea. Parnell refused to resign; his party split and he died in October 1891 four months after marrying Kitty.

Avondale★

Park: Open to dusk. House open 17 Mar–Oct daily 11am–6pm. Last admission at 5pm. Closed Mon (open Bank Hol Mon) Mar–Apr & Sept–Oct; Good Fri. Car park: €5; House: €6. . *0404 46111. www.heritageisland.com.*

The Avondale estate was the home of the Parnells, a prosperous Protestant landlord family, and it was here that **Charles Stewart Parnell** (*see 'The Uncrowned King of Ireland' box*), was born. The two-storey neo-Classical **house** has been restored to its appearance during Parnell's lifetime when it was much used for social occasions. It was designed in 1759 by Samuel Hayes; there is Coade stone ornamentation by the **Lafranchini brothers** in the dining room. The life of Charles Parnell, the history of his family in Ireland, his role in 19C Irish politics, are traced by a video. Among the furniture and memorabilia are Parnell's stick and chair (he was 6ft 3in/1.9m tall), photos of Parnell and Kitty O'Shea, her wedding ring of Avonmore gold mined by the Parnell family, and a set of folding library steps made of Irish bog oak.

The **forest park** (512 acres/207ha) covers a steep slope facing east across the Avondale River. The oldest surviving trees – two gigantic silver firs by the river as well as oaks, beeches and larches – were planted by Samuel Hayes in the 18C. The stump of a beech tree, planted nearly 250 years ago, has its rings delineated in relation to subsequent historical events. There are several trails and woodland walks along the banks of the Avonmore River and along the Great Ride.

Meeting of the Waters★

The confluence of the rivers Avonbeg and Avonmore is set amid the forests of south Co Wicklow; it was here, that Thomas Moore (1779–1852) is said to have celebrated the "valley so sweet" in his poem *The Meeting of the Waters* of 1807.

Motte Stone

The name of the large glacial boulder is derived from the French word for half (*moitié*), as it used to mark the half-way point between Dublin and Wexford before the advent of mileposts.

Vale of Avoca

The village of Avoca has attracted visitors in great numbers, since it was chosen as the setting for the hugely popular television series, *Ballykissangel*. There are forest walks in the wooded river valley. **The Mill at Avoca Village** (*open year-round daily 9am–6pm; winter 5.30pm;* ; *0402 35105, www.avoca.ie*) was founded in 1723 and is therefore the oldest surviving business in Ireland. Visitors flock in large numbers to watch the traditional production methods used t make the famous Avoca textiles (*see Address Book, Shopping*).

Coast

Bray

Bray is an old-established resort with a sand and shingle beach at the south end of Killiney Bay. As the southern terminus of Dublin's DART suburban railway line, in recent years it has become a fashionable commuter haven from the capital.

The public park on Bray Head provides a fine **view** of the coastline. Local history is traced through photographs, maps and artefacts in the **Heritage Centre**. (♿⏰*Open Mon–Fri 9.30am–1pm, 2pm–4.30pm (5pm Jun–Aug), Sat 10am–3pm;* ✉*€3;* ☎*01 286 6796*) also home to a tourist information office.

On the sea-front, the **National Sea-Life Centre** (Kids ♿⏰*open May–Sept daily 10am–6pm; Oct–Apr Mon–Fri 11am–5pm, Sat–Sun & Bank Hols 10am–6pm;* ✉*€10.50, child €7.90;* ✋*buy tickets online for significant discounts;* ☎*01 286 6939,www.sealife.ie, www.heritageisland. com*) presents more than 30 displays populated by over 90 species of marine and freshwater creatures and Ireland's largest collection of sharks.

Greystones

This resort has developed from a fishing village with a harbour flanked by shingle beaches.

The Murrough

0.5mi/0.8km north of Wicklow.
A long shingle beach (3mi/5km) backed by a broad grass bank is flanked by the sea and the **Broad Lough**, a lagoon noted for wildfowl and golden plover.

Wicklow

At the eastern foot of the mountains, the harbour town of Wicklow is the main commercial centre for the area as well as the county town and a Heritage Town. The Vikings established a 9C port which developed into a major trading centre. The statue of a pikeman in the Market Square represents all those who fought in nationalist uprisings.

The **Halpin Memoria** commemorates Captain Robert C Halpin (1836–94), a native of the town, who commanded the *Great Eastern*, the ship built by Brunel which laid the first transatlantic telegraph cable.

Black Castle, which stands on a rocky promontory immediately south of the harbour, was built in 1176. The ruins form a fine vantage point for **views** over the town and the coast of north Co Wicklow.

The 18C **Anglican Church** has an onion-shaped copper cupola, donated in 1777, and incorporates a 12C Irish-Roman-esque doorway. The interior contains a fine king-post roof and a 12C font. In the grounds of the parish priest's house are extensive ruins of a **Franciscan friary**, founded by the Fitzgeralds in the 13C.

Wicklow's Historic Gaol Kids

♿💬*Visit by guided tours only (1hr), every 10 mins, 17 Mar–Oct daily 10am–6pm. Last admission 5pm.* ✉*€7.30, child €4.50.* 🍴 ☎*0404 61599. www.wicklows historicgaol.com.*

This formidable stone-built prison dates from 1702, the time of the Penal Laws, and was used as a prison until 1924. It now houses elaborate exhibits and actors which bring to life its history of rough justice. A warder inducts visitors into the ghastly conditions; British soldiers ponder how to crush the 1798 Rebellion (many of the participants were tried in this building); local gentleman-rebel Billy Byrne awaits his execution; the life of convicts in the 19C, both here and in Australia, is evoked, and so on.

Brittas Bay

This long sandy beach (3mi/5km), backed by dunes, is one of the most popular resorts on the east coast.

Arklow

Founded by the Vikings, on the Avoca estuary, Arklow is a seaside resort, an important east-coast fishing harbour and a base for Ireland's main fleet of coastal trading ships. The most famous product of the local boatyards is **Gypsy Moth III**, the yacht in which Sir Francis Chichester sailed around the world in 1967. There are pleasant walks by the harbour and along the south bank of the river.

The **Maritime Museum** (♿⏰*open year-round Mon–Fri 10am–1pm & 2pm–5pm, Sat (May–Sept only);* ✉*€5;* ☎*0402 32868*) displays exhibits connected with Ireland's maritime history and traces the development of local commercial shipping since the 1850s. **Arklow Rock** *(2mi/3.2km south)* provides a fine **view** of the coastline.

YOUGHAL ★

POPULATION 5 630

Nowadays an attractive seaside resort with miles of fine beaches along the lovely estuary of the River Blackwater, the ancient harbour town of Youghal (pronounced Yawl) looks back on a long and colourful history, attested to by a fine array of old buildings and the country's most extensive system of defensive walls, enough to merit the title Heritage Town.

- ▮ **Information:** Heritage Centre, Market Square. ☎024 20170. www.youghal.ie.
- ▶ **Orient Yourself:** Youghal lies on the coast road 46mi/74km west of Waterford.
- ⊛ **Don't Miss:** St Mary's Collegiate Church.
- ⏱ **Also See:** COBH, CORK, CLONMEL, LISMORE, MIDLETON, WATERFORD.

A Bit of History

The name comes from the Irish for yew tree, a reminder that the town's hinterland was once richly wooded. In the 9C the site was occupied by the Danish Vikings, who used it as a base to plunder the rich lands along the River Blackwater and to raid other settlements along the south coast. The Anglo-Normans arrived at the end of the 12C; strategically placed for the landing of forces from England and always vulnerable to the threat of invasion from France and Spain, Youghal became one of Ireland's most strongly defended seaports, enclosed by impressive town walls.

In the late 16C, while mayor of Youghal, **Sir Walter Ralegh** introduced the tobacco and potato plants into Ireland.

He later sold his extensive estates to another Englishman, Richard Boyle (1566–1643), an unscrupulous speculator in confiscated lands who became the richest individual in Ireland and was ennobled as the 1st "Great" Earl of Cork. In 1649 Youghal's garrison prudently went over to Cromwell, who overwintered here with his army.

Despite its prosperity as one of Ireland's leading ports, for much of the 18C the town was riven by conflict between the dominant Protestant minority and the underprivileged Roman Catholic majority. In the latter part of the 19C some 150 sail-powered schooners traded from here; sailors from Youghal could recognise one another throughout the ports of the world by their distinctive whistle.

Youghal Harbour

H Champollion/MICHELIN

The town's sailing tradition declined early in the 20C with the silting-up of the estuary and the building of steam-powered freight ships.

Walking Tour

Youghal Heritage Centre

&♿⏰ *Open year-round Mon–Fri 9am–5.30pm, Sat–Sun 9.30am–5pm.* ☎024 20170. www.youghal.ie.

The old Market House now houses the Tourist Information Office and an exhibition on the history of Youghal.

In the Market Square stands a memorial commemorating the *Nellie Fleming*, the last of the old Youghal sailing vessels. The pub on the corner, **Moby Dick's**, displays many photographs taken during the filming of *Moby Dick* on location in Youghal during the summer of 1954.

▶ *Walk inland along a side street; turn right into South Main Street.*

Clock Gate★

The unusual four-storey building straddling the Main Street was constructed by the corporation in 1777 to replace the Iron Gate, also known as Trinity Castle, part of the walls. The new tower was used as the town gaol until 1837; such was the state of insurrection in the late 18C that it soon became overcrowded; rebels were hanged from the windows as an example to the rest of the populace.

▶ *Walk though the Clock Gate and continue north along South Main Street.*

Benedictine Abbey

Left side of the street.

All that remains of the abbey is the east gable wall pierced by a moulded Gothic doorway with ornamental spandrels; in the passageway are the arched piscina and square aumbry from the original church. The abbey was founded in 1350 and used by Cromwell as his winter headquarters in 1649–50.

The Red House

Left side of the street.

This fine example of early-18C Dutch domestic architecture creates a marked contrast with its neighbours. The red brick façade with white stone quoins is surmounted by a triangular gable and a steep mansard roof. It was designed in 1710 for the Uniacke family by a Dutch architect-builder Claud Leuvethen.

Address Book

♿*For coin ranges, see the Legend on the cover flap.*

SIGHTSEEING

Guided walking tour of Youghal – *Operates Jun–mid-Sept daily at 11am or by appointment (1hr).* ☎024 92447.

WHERE TO STAY

◎**Ardsallagh Lodge** – *N25 towards Waterford; just past the Blackwater River Bridge.* ☎024 93496. www.waterford houseireland.com. *Also known as the Waterford House, this comfortable guesthouse offers river and sea views.*

◎**Glenally House** – *Copperalley – 1mi north.* ☎024 91623. www.glenally. com. *Meals◎. The owners have successfully combined contemporary styles and bold, rich colours with the original features of this peaceful Georgian house, set in 7 acres of private grounds. Guests can enjoy carefully prepared meals 'en famille'.*

WHERE TO EAT

◎◎◎ **Aherne's Townhouse and Restaurant** – *163 North Main Street.* ☎024 92424. www.ahernes.net. *12rm.* ◎◎◎ *Lovers of seafood have made this family-run business a landmark since its opening in the 1960s. The artwork in the dining room is available to buy and the luxurious bedrooms are all thoughtfully decorated.*

SPORTS AND LEISURE

Beaches at Ardmore.
Greyhound Racing at Youghal.

Tynte's Castle
Right side of the street. This 15C battlemented building has a device over the front door for pouring boiling oil on rebels and other unwelcome visitors. Once on the waterfront, it is now 200yd/182m from the river.

Almshouses
Left side of the street. The Elizabethan almshouses, still used for residential purposes, were erected in 1610 by the Earl of Cork, who provided "five pounds apiece for each of ye six old decayed soldiers or Alms Men for ever".

▶ *Turn left into Church Street.*

Also used for residential purposes is the neighbouring former Protestant **asylum**, dated 1838, now called Shalom House.

St Mary's Collegiate Church★★
It is probable that the first church on this site, a wooden building, was erected by followers of St Declan of Ardmore in c 400. The present early-13C edifice is one of Ireland's most impressive ancient churches. It replaced an 11C Danish-built church destroyed in a great storm soon after its construction. During the late-15C wars, the forces of the Earl of Desmond occupied the building and removed the roof of the chancel. Large-scale restoration, including the re-modelling of the chancel, took place between 1851 and 1858. The church contains a large collection of **grave slabs** and **effigies**, including some from the 13C and 14C with Norman-French inscriptions. None remotely match the monument in the south transept erected by the 1st Earl of Cork to himself. This superbly pretentious house-size structure shows him reclining nonchalantly beneath his family tree, surrounded by his wives, children, and mother-in-law.

Town Walls★
Partially accessible from the churchyard. Youghal has the best-preserved town walls in Ireland, their extent even greater than the city walls of Londonderry. They were built in the 13C and extended in the 17C; large sections are still in excellent condition, although only three of the 13 medieval towers remain. The portion restored in the 19C with a turret and a cannon is accessible from the churchyard; the sentry walk provides a fine **view** of the town and the harbour. The full length of the walls is best seen from the outside *(Raheen Road).*

Excursion
30mi/48km.

▶ *From Youghal take the N 25 east; beyond Kinsalebeg turn right into a minor road via Moord to Ardmore.*

Whiting Bay★
The bay, which is flanked by Cabin Point and Ardoginna Head, is very isolated but

St Mary's Collegiate Church

©David Morrison/Dreamstime.com

offers fine **views** *(SW)* across Youghal Bay to Knockadoon Head.

Ardmore★

The many attractions of this pleasant little resort include a lovely sandy beach, wonderful cliff walks, and a fascinating architectural heritage evoking the era of St Declan, a predecessor of St Patrick. Declan, who died early in the 5C, seems to have studied in Wales and is said to have sailed across St George's Channel to Ardmore together with a huge stone. The stone (in fact a glacial boulder) is still here, on the beach, and by tradition it offers a cure for rheumatism to anyone agile enough to crawl beneath it! There is also a holy well associated with the saint.

The site of Declan's original monastic foundation overlooking the sea is marked by the exceptionally fine **round tower**★ (97ft/29m) which is among the best preserved of its kind and probably dates from the 12C. Adjacent, the outstanding feature of the ruined **cathedral**★ (10C–14C) is the exterior **arcade**★ of sunken panels on the west gable; nearly all the panels are filled with vigorously carved but much weathered sculptures similar in style to those found on high crosses dating from the 10C. Nearby, a small building probably dating from the 5C settlement of Ardmore by Declan is known as **St Declan's Oratory**, thought to be the Saint's final resting place.

The long distance footpath called **St Declan's Way** runs for almost 100km from here to Cashel; a shorter local walk offering superb sea views, is from the Cliff House Hotel to Ram Head.

▶ *Take the coast road east to Mine Head and Helvick Head.*

Ringville (An Rinn)

This small village is the centre of an Irish-speaking area, the **West Waterford Gaeltacht**; there are excellent **views**★ across Dungarvan harbour.

Helvick Head★

1mi/1.6km east of Ringville.
Helvick Harbour, a small but busy port backed by a row of fishermen's cottages,

---

A Dog's Life

In a career of 37 races, **Master McGrath**, a locally-bred greyhound, was beaten only once. Between 1868 and 1871 he won the Waterloo Cup in England three times and is commemorated in the only monument in Ireland to a dog *(2mi/3.2km NW of Dungarvan by R 672)*.

---

shelters below the headland which, despite its modest height (230ft/82m), provides outstanding **views**★ of the coastline.

Cunnigar Peninsula

1mi/1.6m west of Ringville.
The sandy spit of land extending into Dungarvan harbour shelters a wealth of birdlife and may be walked from end to end *(1.5mi/2.4km)*.

Dungarvan

18mi/29km east by N 25.
This thriving seaside resort occupies an attractive **site** astride the Colligan estuary overlooking the broad bay known as Dungarvan Harbour. It is flanked by the Drum Hills *(south)* and the Monavullagh and Comeragh Mountains *(north)*.

King John's Castle, built by the king in 1185, not long after the Anglo-Norman invasion, consists of a large circular **keep** surrounded by fortified walls, much modified in subsequent centuries.

The **Waterford County Museum** (🕐*open Mon–Fri 9.30am–5pm;* ☎*058 45960; wwwwaterfordcountymuseum. org)*, housed in the old Town Hall, has a nautical theme; local shipwrecks are well documented, especially the *Moresby* which went down in Dungarvan Bay on 24 December 1895 with the loss of 20 lives.

On the east bank of the river are the ruins of a 13C **Augustinian priory** which was founded by the McGraths, who also built the 12C or 13C **castle**, of which only the west wall still stands. The walk on the seaward side of the graveyard provides fine **views**★ across Dungarvan Harbour south to Helvick Head.

Giant's Causeway
H Champollion/MICHELIN

ANTRIM

POPULATION 20 878

The former county town of Co Antrim (Aontroim), traditionally known for its linen-spinning, is linked to Belfast by rail and motorway and expanded rapidly in the last decades of the 20C. Located on the Six Mile Water, a fine trout stream, the town's greatest asset is its proximity to the broad waters of Lough Neagh. Antrim was attacked during the 1798 Rebellion by a force of 3 500 United Irishmen under Henry Joy McCracken, a Belfast cotton manufacturer, who was defeated and subsequently hanged.

- **Information:** 16 High Street, Antrim. ☎028 9442 8331. www.antrim.gov.uk.
- **Orient Yourself:** Antrim is situated on the shore of Lough Neagh, 20mi/32km north west of Belfast via the M2.
- **Also See:** ANTRIM GLENS, BELFAST, CARRICKFERGUS, LOUGH NEAGH.

Walking Tour

Pogue's Entry Historical Cottage

East end of the main street. ♿⏱*Open Jul–mid-Sept Thu–Fri 2pm–5pm, Sat 10am–1pm and 2pm–5pm, Sun 2pm–5pm.* ☎ *028 9448 1338 (call to check opening times).*

This simple cabin was where Alexander Irvine (1863–1941), the son of a cobbler, spent his childhood. Irvine became a missionary in the Bowery in New York; his book, *My Lady of the Chimney Corner*, is about his mother's struggle against poverty.

Antrim Castle Gardens

West end of the main street.

Beyond the Market Place and the Court House (1726), a magnificent Tudor gate leads to the former demesne of the Clotworthys, ennobled as Lords Massarene in the 17C. Their castle burned down in 1922 but the formal garden survives, best viewed from the Norman motte. The garden is a rare example (unique in Ulster) of a Dutch-style landscape, with ornamental canals, a cascade, geometric parterres and high pleached (formally trained) hedges of lime and hornbeam.

Round Tower★

From the High Street 10min on foot north along Railway Street and Station Road.

Among the trees of Steeple Park stands a fine example of a round tower (90ft/27m), one of the best preserved in Ireland, probably built c 900 as part of an important 6C monastery, that was abandoned in 1147.

Excursions

Patterson's Spade Mill

5mi/8km SE by A 6 via Templepatrick. (NT). ♿➷*Open by guided tour only 2pm–6pm: St Patrick's Day weekend (Sat–Mon). Easter Week (daily). Apr–Jun & Sept Sat–Sun. Jul–Aug Wed–Mon. All Bank Hols and public hols.* ➷*£4.09.* ☎*028 94433619. www.nationaltrust.org.uk.*

The only surviving working water-powered spade mill in the British Isles was founded in 1919; five generations of Pattersons worked at the mill until 1990. The tour includes all the stages involved in producing spades in the traditional way completed by two men. Beside the mill are the ruins of associated industrial buildings.

Ballance House

11mi/17km south via the B 101, A 26 and A 30 to Glenavy. ⏱*Open Apr–Sept Sun, Wed, Bank Hols, 2pm–5pm or by appointment.* ⏱*Closed 12 Jul.* ➷*£3.* ☎*028 9264 8492. www.ballance.utvinternet.com.*

This is the birthplace of John Ballance (1839–93), who emigrated to Birmingham and then to New Zealand, where he became a journalist and rose to be the first Liberal Prime Minister. Partly furnished in mid-19C style, the house is

D Gilbert/National Trust Photographic Library

Finishing Shop, Patterson's Spade Mill

a fascinating museum devoted to the Ulster-New Zealand connection.

Templetown Mausoleum

Templepatrick; 5mi/8km east of Antrim on the A 6. Park at the end of the drive. (NT). ⓞ*Open 11am–6pm.* ☎*028 97510721.*
A walled graveyard encloses the mausoleum, a triumphal arch designed by Robert Adam in the Palladian style c. 1770 for Sarah Upton in memory of her husband Arthur. Tablets honour subsequent generations of Uptons entitled Viscount Templetown.
The name Templepatrick derives from an earlier church dedicated to St Patrick who is supposed to have baptised converts at a nearby Holy Well in about 450.

Slemish Mountain

16mi/26km north east on the A 26 to Ballymena, A 42 east and B 94; after 1mi/1.6km turn left; after 3mi/4.8km turn right (Carnstroan Road); after 0.25mi/0.4km turn right. From the car park 1hr there and back on foot.
The distinctive profile of the Slemish Mountain (1 437ft/438m) rises abruptly from the flat landscape of the Ballymena plain. On St Patrick's Day (17 March) it is a place of pilgrimage since tradition has it that **St Patrick** spent six years here in captivity herding swine for the local

chieftain Miluic. The fine **view** takes in the ruins of Skerry Church *(northwest)*, the burial place of the O'Neills, supposed to be founded by St Patrick himself.

Arthur Cottage

17mi/27km north west via the A 26 to Ballymena and B 62 to Cullybackey. Cross the river and turn sharp right onto a narrow lane. ⓞ*Open Easter–Sept Thu–Sat 10.30am–4pm.* ⓞ*Closed 12 Jul.* ⬤*£2.50.* ☎*028 2563 5900. www.ballymena.gov. uk/tourism.*

At the end of the lane stands an isolated one-storey cottage; from here the father of Chester Alan Arthur, 21st President of the USA, emigrated in 1816 to Vermont where he became a Baptist clergyman. His son was one of more than a dozen US Presidents with Ulster roots. Traditional crafts, local agricultural and domestic implements, a display on Chester Alan Arthur's family and 19C emigration from Ireland are on show in the summer; especially atmospheric on 'baking days' (high summer).

Gracehill
11mi/18km north west via the A 26 to Ballymena and the A 42.
This attractive Georgian village was laid out by a group of Moravian settlers from Bohemia fleeing religious persecution. Begun in 1759, the community built a central square, a church, the minister's house and communal houses for single men and women. The boarding schools for girls and boys acquired an enviable reputation far outside their locality. Men and women sat on separate sides in church and were buried in separate sections of the graveyard.

GLENS OF ANTRIM★★★

A drive up the Antrim Coast offers a great variety of scenery: seaward are attractive villages, long flat strands, steep basalt or limestone cliffs, and a distant prospect of the Mull of Kintyre in Scotland; inland are the glens created by the tumbling mountain streams that descend from the uplands of heath and bog, now punctuated by forestry plantations. In the glens, where the underlying sedimentary rocks are exposed, the farms are arranged like ladders climbing the valley sides so that each has a share of the good land near the river and of the poorer upland pasture.

- **Information:** Ballycastle; ☎028 20762024. Narrow Gauge Road, Larne, ☎028 2826 0088. www.larne.gov.uk. www.moyle-council.org/tourism. www.causewaycoastandglens.com.
- **Orient Yourself:** The A 2 runs along the Antrim coast between Larne and Ballycastle at the foot of the nine Glens of Antrim.
- **Don't Miss:** Excursions to Glenariff Forest Park and its waterfall, and Murlough National Nature Reserve to admire the view from Benmore, and a hair-raising walk across the Carrick-a-rede Rope Bridge.
- **Especially for Kids**: Carfunnock Country Park, Carrick-a-rede Rope Bridge.
- **Also See:** CARRICKFERGUS, GIANT'S CAUSEWAY, PORTRUSH.

A Bit of History

This once isolated area was the least anglicised part of the country, accessed by an old coastal track. The first road dates from 1832 when the Grand Military Road from Carrickfergus to Portrush was built along an ancient raised beach, and on a ledge blasted from the basalt and chalk rock.

Two narrow-gauge railway lines (3ft/1m) were laid in the 19C to carry the increasing output of the Glenariff mines in operation from the late 1860s. The Glenariff Iron Ore & Holding Co line ran from Inverglen down Glenariff to the southeast end of Red Bay, where the bed of the track is still visible..The other, from Ballymena up the Clogh Valley to Retreat (1876) was never extended farther because of the steep gradient down Glenballyemon to the coast; it closed in 1930.

Driving Tour

Larne to Ballycastle
70mi/113km – Allow 1 or 2 days.

Larne

The southern gateway to the Glens of Antrim, Larne is a busy port with a regular ferry service to Cairnryan in Scotland and Island Magee (a peninsula on the east coast of Co Antrim). Larne has been a regular landing point since the 9C when the Vikings arrived and Edward Bruce sailed here from Scotland to secure an Irish crown in 1315. 25,000 German rifles and 3 million rounds of ammunition were unloaded in Larne in April 1914 and rapidly distributed to the Ulster Volunteers; clear evidence of the local determination to resist Home Rule by all possible means.

On Curran Point stand the ruins of **Olderfleet Castle**, a square four-storey tower house, one of three built in the early 17C to protect the entrance to the lough. The **Chaine Memorial Tower** honours James Chaine, a local MP and benefactor.

▶ *From Larne take the A 2 north.*

Carnfunnock Country Park Kids

◷*Open 9am–dusk (9pm Jul–Aug). Most family attractions Easter–Oct;* ▭*;* ☎*028 28270541 (Easter–Oct). Larne TIC;* ☎*028 28260088; www.larne.gov.uk.*

In a lovely setting of green hills dropping down to the sea north of Drains Bay village, the Park (473 acres/190ha) was once a private demesne. Original remaining features including the walled garden, lime kilns and icehouse. A whole host of family attractions include a Northern Ireland-shaped **maze**, a 9-hole golf course and putting green, miniature railway, bouncy castle, trampolines, mini cars etc…

▶ *Continue north on the A 2.*

Ballygally Castle, now a hotel (*www. hastingshotels.com*), was built in 1625 by James Shaw; the twin bartizans (overhanging, wall-mounted turrets) are original but the sash windows were introduced later. Inland rises a natural

amphitheatre, Sallagh Braes; the fine walk above the Braes along the plateau edge *(access via Carncastle and Ballycoose Road)* forms part of the Ulster Way.

▶ *Continue north on the A 2.*

Glenarm Village

This attractive little port is the oldest village in the Glens. The main street runs inland past the 19C barbican gateway of **Glenarm Castle** *(private)*, the seat of the Earl of Antrim, which was begun in 1606 and re-modelled in the Elizabethan style by William Vitruvius Morrison early in the 19C.

The **Forest Park** at the top of the street provides a view of the castle, and there are pleasant walks by the stream in the upper woodlands beyond the belt of conifers.

▶ *Return to A 2; turn left onto b97.*

The road runs up **Glenarm**, the southernmost of the Antrim Glens, passing through open farmland with views of Glenarm Forest on the far side of the valley. At the top of the glen, the unmistakable outline of Slemish Mountain can be seen due south.

▶ *At the T-junction turn right onto the A 42. Turn left onto the A 2.*

Carnlough

A large sandy bay makes this an attractive seaside resort. Until the 1960s,

Away with the Fairies

Between Knockacarry and Glenaan is **Glencorp**, which translates as the glen of slaughter/bodies. The derivation of this is uncertain but "The Fairy Hill" on the east slope of Glencorp is called Tieveragh famous locally as being the home of the fairies or the "little folk" who are said to emerge in processions on the last day of April (known as May eve). Only believers can see them!

limestone was quarried above the town and was transported by rail to the tiny harbour (now full of pleasure-boats). The low bridge, former courthouse and adjoining clock tower, were built by the Marquess of Londonderry in 1854.
Beyond Garron Point lies **Red Bay**, backed by the distinctive steep-sided, flat-topped silhouette of Lurigethan (1 154ft/352m).

Glenariff★

The "**Queen of the Glens**", Glenarrif comprises broad lush pastures enclosed between steep hanging crags.
Waterfoot village lies at the mouth of the Glenariff River. On the headland, above the road tunnel, stand the ruins of Red Bay Castle, built by the Norman Bisset family.

Waterfall, Glenariff Forest Park

▶ *From Glenariff take the A 43 inland. Alternatively if you want to take the spectacular glen walk to the Forest Park from here, there is an entrance to the Park from Waterfoot on the main Coast Road.*

Glenariff Forest Park★★

&.◐Open 10am–dusk. ⌔£4 per car, £1.50 pedestrians. ⌕. ☏028 2955 6000.
This beautiful forest (2 298 acres/930ha) comprises areas of woodland, peat bog, rocky outcrops lakes and rivers. The visitor centre provides information about the Antrim Glens and has excellent displays on local wildlife, the 19C iron ore and bauxite mines and their railways.
The **Ess na Larach waterfall**★★ *(1hr there and back on foot from the north side of the car park)* tumbles through a wooded gorge created by the Glenariff River.

▶ *Continue south west on the A 43; at the junction turn right onto the B 14.*

Cushendall

Cushendall stands at the meeting point of three glens. Its landmark red sandstone Curfew Tower was built as a watchhouse in 1809 by Francis Turnly of the East India Company.

▶ *Take Layde Road, the steep coast road going north to Cushendun.*

Layd Old Church

The ruins of the church stand in a graveyard romantically sited by a swiftly flowing stream which plunges directly into the sea. Between 1306–1790 it served as a parish church; note the MacDonnell memorials in the graveyard.

▶ *At the T-junction in Knocknacarry turn left onto the B92 and left onto the A 2.*

▶ *After 1.5mi/2.4km turn right onto Glenaan Road. Turn left onto a lane; 20min there and back on foot.*

Ossian's Grave

The figure of Ossian appears in a number of guises in Irish lore; one of them as an early Christian warrior-bard, the son of

Finn McCool, whose legendary feats are recounted in the Ossianic Cycle. Revived in the work of the 18C poet James McPherson, Ossian became a hero to the Romantic writers of the late 18C/early 19C, particularly in continental Europe. Whoever he was, it seems very unlikely that he found his last resting place here; Ossian's Grave is in fact a Neolithic court tomb, enclosed in an oval cairn.

▷ *Continue west up the glen.*

In **Glenaan**, the Glenaan River flows down from the slopes of Tievebulliagh *(south)* where Neolithic men once made axe heads from the hard porcellanite rock.

▷ *At the crossroads turn right onto Glendun Road to Cushendun.*

Glendun★, the Brown Glen, is the wildest of the nine glens; its river is noted for sea trout and salmon fishing. The viaduct was designed by Charles Lanyon in 1839.

Cushendun

The houses of this picturesque village cluster at the southern end of a sandy beach flanked by tall cliffs. The village owes its distinctive and rather fey character to Sir Clough Williams-Ellis, the playful architect of Portmeirion in North Wales, who worked here for Ronald McNeill, the first (and only) Lord Cushenden. There are terraces of small white houses around a square, a number of slate-hung cottages, and a neo-Georgian mansion, Glenmona Lodge, which stands in a pine grove facing the sea.

▷ *Take the steep and narrow road north. After 5mi/8km fork right onto Torr Road.*

Torr Head is a low promontory, crowned by a look-out post – the nearest point on the Irish mainland to the Scottish coast (12mi/19km), enjoying spectacular views over to the Mull of Kintyre.

▷ *Continue north west along the coast road; after 2.5mi/4km turn right.*

Murlough National Nature Reserve★★★

1mi/1.6km to the upper car park; smaller car park lower down the cliff face. ○*Information Centre: Open Jun–mid-Sept 10am–6pm; mid-Mar–May, Sat–Sun only 10am–6pm.* ○*£2.50 per car.* ☎*028 43751467. www.nationaltrust.org.uk.*

This is the most beautiful bay on the Antrim coast, set in the lee of **Fair Head** (Benmore) at the foot of steep and towering cliffs, and overlooked by the rounded peaks of the Mourne Mountains to the south.

The stone cross is a memorial to Sir Roger Casement. The waymarked footpaths from the lower car park lead north to some long-abandoned coal mines before returning along the shore past the remains of the miners' cottages and the ruins of Drumnakill Church; south past an old lime kiln, through a wood to avoid Murlough Cottage *(private)* and ends at Benvan farmhouse. A second path goes along the clifftop to windblown **Fair Head** (Benmore) from where there are glorious **views**★★★ of Rathlin Island *(north)* and the Mull of Kintyre *(northeast)*, before cutting across the rough and often wet ground of the plateau, past a **crannóg** in Lough na Cranagh *(right)*, farm buildings at Coolanlough, to reach Lough Fadden *(left)*.

A boardwalk from the car park through the dunes to the **beach**, a long arc of sand several miles long. An information centre and toilets are located in the car park and are open throughout the summer months.

▷ *Return to the coast road; turn right to Ballycastle.*

Bonamargy Friary

The remains of a Franciscan friary (c 1500) sit by a stream, surrounded by Ballycastle golf course. The ruined church has a vault containing remains of several MacDonnells, descended from the Scottish MacDonalds who fought with the McQuillan clan for possession of this part of Ireland. By contrast, the McQuillans produced a nun, Julia, known for her piety; the round-headed cross in the nave is thought to mark her grave, placed here so that even in death she could practise humility, walked on by the feet of worshippers.

▶ *On the edge of Ballycastle turn left onto the B 15; after 0.25mi/0.4km bear right to Dunamallaght Road.*

Glenshesk

The road overlooks the Glenshesk River and skirts the southern edge of Bally-castle Forest. From Breen Bridge, at the foot of Knocklayd Mountain, runs the waymarked **Moyle Way**, a spur of the Ulster Way long-distance footpath.

▶ *Take the B15 west.*

Only the base of the **Armoy Round Tower** (30ft/9m) remains, sited in the graveyard of St Patrick's Church, built in 460 by the monastery founded by Olcan, a disciple of St Patrick.

▶ *At the crossroads take the minor road north. Turn right onto the A 44 to Ballycastle.*

Ballycastle

This attractive little market town backed by Knocklayd Mountain, has many amenties – a long sandy beach, angling and golf and summer festivities. A stone memorial by the harbour, recalls the

Carrick-a-rede Rope Bridge

H Champollion/MICHELIN

wireless link between Ballycastle and Rathlin Island set up in 1898 by Marconi and his assistant George Kemp.

▶ *From Ballycastle take the B15 west. After 5mi/8km turn right to Larry Bane Bay and Carrick-a-rede Rope Bridge.*

Carrick-a-rede Rope Bridge★★★   Kids

(NT) From the car park 30min there and back on foot. ◷Open Mar–Oct, 10am–6pm (7pm late May–Aug). ☞£3.36, child £1.81 ☎028 2076 9839. www.national trust.org.uk.

This precarious looking (but very safe) bridge was traditionally erected by salmon fishermen every spring to get to their fishery. As the migrating salmon head for their spawning grounds in the River Bush or River Bann, they are deflected north by the island (*Carrick-a-rede* means Rock-in-the-Road) straight into the nets.

The bridge (66ft/20m long) sways with each footfall over the spectacular rock-strewn water (80ft/25m below) and a warden ensures that a maximum of 8 people only ever cross at one time.

Rathlin Island★

Access by boat from Ballycastle (◖see Address Book).

The island is separated from Ballycas-tle by Rathlin Sound (5mi/8km wide). Rathlin is treeless, pitted with shallow lakes and divided into fields by drystone walls. It is surrounded by tall white cliffs where seabirds breed. From the shel-tered harbour, three roads radiate to the outlying homesteads and lighthouses. The traditional occupations are fishing and farming, supplemented in the past by smuggling and now by tourism.

In the 6C St Columba nearly lost his life off Rathlin when his boat was trapped in a whirlpool. In 1306, according to tradi-tion, it was while taking refuge in one of the island's many caves that Robert the Bruce received his famous lesson in perseverance from a spider.

ARMAGH★★

POPULATION 14 265

Ireland's ecclesiastical capital stands on hills surrounded by pleasant countryside and prosperous fruit orchards, planted originally by English settlers who came to populate the early 17C plantation of Ulster. The town with its many fine Georgian buildings is dominated by its two cathedrals, the seats of Ireland's Anglican and Roman Catholic archbishops.

- **Information:** 40 English St. ☎028 3752 1800. www.visitarmagh.com.
- ▶ **Orient Yourself:** Armagh lies between Lough Neagh and the border, 50mi/80km south west of Belfast via the M 1.
- **Kids Especially for Kids:** Land of Liliput at St Patrick's Trian, Armagh Planetarium, Tayto Potator Crisp Factory.
- **Also See:** DUNGANNON, MONAGHAN, LOUGH NEAGH, NEWRY, SPERRIN MOUNTAINS.

A Bit of History

Armagh, from *Ard Macha* meaning Macha's Height, alludes to the legendary pagan queen who built a fortress on the central hill. Although the major pre-Christian power centre of Ulster was nearby at Navan Fort, Armagh acquired new prominence after Navan's destruction in AD 332. St Patrick arrived in Armagh (c 445) and made it the centre of the new religion, declaring that his new church should take precedence over all other churches in Ireland. In the following centuries Armagh developed into a leading centre of learning: it was here that the famous 9C manuscript, the *Book of Armagh*, now in Trinity College Library, Dublin, was produced; in the 12C, the great Archbishop St Malachy was based here and Armagh's reputation grew such that an ecclesiastical Synod decreed (1162) that only those who had studied at Armagh could teach theology elsewhere in Ireland. The school was dissolved at the Reformation.

Walking Tour

The Mall★

This distinctive long stretch of grass with a pavilion and cricket pitch bordered by elegant terraces is, to say the least, an unusual Irish urban feature. From the 8C it was common grazing land, used for horse racing, bull-baiting and cock-fighting until such activities were stopped by Archbishop Robinson in 1773.

The Classical-style **Courthouse**, at the north end, was designed in 1809 by Francis Johnston. The former **Sovereign's House** now houses the **Royal Irish Fusiliers Museum**★, (🕐*open Mon–Fri 10am–12.30pm & 1.30pm–4pm; 🕐closed Christmas and New Year; ☎028 37522911; www.discovernorthernireland.com*) with a splendid collections of flags and standards, uniforms, medals, weapons, silver, portraits and paintings relating to the five units raised in 1793 to fight the French.

Beresford Row was designed by John Quinn between 1810 and 1827.

Architectural Elegance

During peaceful times in the 18C and early 19C, farming and commerce flourished; Armagh acquired some fine buildings under the patronage of its Anglican Primate: Richard Robinson, later Lord Rokeby, Archbishop from 1765.

Robinson restored the cathedral, built himself a fine palace, commissioned a library and other public buildings, started the observatory, and beautified the Mall. He was also the patron of Francis Johnston (1761–1829), a native of Armagh, who he helped to become one of Ireland's leading architects.

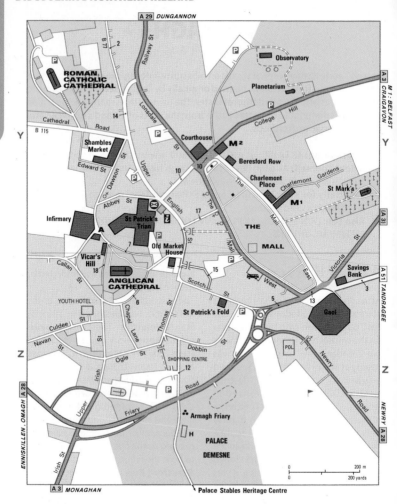

Palace Stables Heritage Centre

Charlemont Place, one of the finest Georgian terraces (1827), was designed by Francis Johnston as was the Ionic portico gracing the **Armagh County Museum★** (◷open Mon–Fri 10am–5pm, Sat 10am–1pm & 2pm–5pm; ☎028 3752 3070; www.armaghcountymuseum.org.uk). Up the long tree-lined drive stands Johnston's **St Marks Church** (1811). The old **gaol** at the end replaced barracks.

St Patrick's Fold

The house, which is thought to stand on the site of St Patrick's first church in Armagh, was designed in 1812 for Leonard Dobbin, MP for Armagh (1833–38), by Francis Johnston.

Old Market House

A technical school now occupies the former two-storey Market House, commissioned in 1815 by Archbishop Stuart from Francis Johnston.

St Patrick's Anglican Cathedral★

⏰*Open year-round daily 10am–5pm (4pm Nov–Mar).* Guided tours Jun–Aug 11.30am, 2.30pm. ☎028 3752 3142. *www.stpatricks-cathedral.org.*

The core of the cathedral on its hilltop site is medieval, although its present plain Perpendicular Gothic appearance is the result of works conducted by Archbishop Robinson in 1765, and by Archbishop Beresford (1834–37) when it was clad in sandstone and had its steeple demolished.

Inside, note the outstanding collection of 18C monuments by eminent masters such as Roubiliac, Rysbrack, Nollekens and Chantrey. Outside, note the grotesque medieval stone heads and sundial (1706).

When King Brian Ború and his son, Murchard, were killed at the Battle of Clontarf (1014), on the north side of Dublin Bay, they were buried according to the king's wishes at Armagh *(north transept).*

The terrace of small houses known as **Vicar's Row** on the west side of the cathedral close was begun in about 1720 to accommodate female clergy dependants.

Armagh Public Library

⏰*Open Mon–Fri 10am–1pm and 2pm–4pm.* ☎028 375 23142. *www.armaghrobin sonlibrary.org.*

Thomas Cooley's library, founded by Archbishop Robinson (1771), bears a Greek inscription which translates as "the healing of the mind". Besides many ancient books and manuscripts, the library has a copy of *Gulliver's Travels* annotated by Swift, the Rokeby Collection of 18C engravings, and a range of historical maps, including a complete set of 1838 Ordnance Survey Maps of the 32 counties of Ireland.

George Ensor's 1774 **infirmary** opposite (still in use), was also founded by Archbishop Robinson.

▷ *Turn right into Abbey Street.*

St Patrick's Trian　　　　Kids

⏰*Open Sept–Jun Mon–Sat 10am–5pm, Sun 2pm–5pm; Jul–Aug Mon–Sat 10am–5.30pm, Sun 2pm–6pm.* ⏰*Closed 12 July.* ⏴£4.50 ☎028 3752 1801. *www.saint patrickstrian.com.*

The name of this modern attraction derives from the ancient division of Armagh City into three distinct districts, or 'Trians'. They were known as Trian Mor (to the south and west), Trian Masain (to the east) and Trian Sassenach or Saxon (to the north). The city today has an Eng-

Cricket in the Mall

SLIDE FILE, Dublin

Ceiling, St Patrick's Roman Catholic Cathedral

lish Street, Irish Street and Scotch Street which roughly mark the boundaries of these Trians.

It offers interactive displays on **The Armagh Story**, as related in the supposed voice of 18–19C architect Francis Johnston; **Patrick's Testament - The Book of Armagh** explored through touch-screen computers and hands-on exhibits and **Land of Lilliput** (narrated with the help of a 20 foot giant!) about Jonathan Swift's *Gulliver's Travels*. Swift was a frequent visitor to Co Armagh, where he had several friends.

The Shambles
Archbishop Beresford's meat market (1827) was designed by Francis Johnston.

▶ *From Dawson Street turn left into Cathedral Road.*

St Patrick's RC Cathedral★
🕒*Open 10am–5pm (4pm Nov–Mar).* 🥾*Guided tours Jun–Aug Mon–Sat 11.30am–2.30pm. www.armagharch diocese.org.*

The twin-spired 19C Roman Catholic cathedral stands up 44 steps, flanked by statues of Archbishop Crolly and Archbishop McGettigan, under whom it was built. It is a striking Gothic Revival structure, occupying the most prominent position available, an expression of growing Catholic confidence, built

with the proceeds of countless collections and raffles, and contributions from royalty and the Pope.

Construction began in 1840, in the Perpendicular style of Thomas J Duff, but the Great Famine halted progress until 1854, delaying completion in 1873 but allowing a change to the Decorated style favoured by JJ McCarthy.

The **interior** is lavishly and colourfully decorated with a painted vaulted roof, stained-glass windows and wall mosaics; the spandrels honour Irish saints. The sanctuary was renovated in 1981–82 by the architect, Liam McCormick.

Sights

Palace Demesne
Friary Rd. 🕒*Open Easter Mon & Tue 11am–5pm; Apr–May & Sept Sat 10am–5pm, Sun noon–5pm (May Bank Holiday Sat–Sun noon–6pm, Mon 10.30am–5.30pm); Jun–Aug Mon–Sat 10am–5pm, Sun noon–5pm.* 🥾*Last tour 4pm.* 🕒*Closed 12 Jul.* 💷*£5.* ✕. ☎*028 3752 1801. www. visitarmagh.com.*

Between the 17C and the 20C the Palace Demesne served as the state residence of the Anglican Archbishop of Armagh. The **Palace Stables Heritage Centre** re-enacts life in the palace on 23 July 1786 when Arthur Young, the famous agricultural improver, and other guests were entertained by Archbishop Richard

Robinson. Costumed interpreters ensure visitors have a memorable experience. The **Primate's Chapel** commissioned by Richard Robinson, is a superb example of Georgian neo-Classical architecture bgun by Thomas Cooley 1770 and completed in 1786 by Francis Johnston. It contains very fine carved oak panelling and an ornamental plaster ceiling. The long ruin of the 13C Franciscan **Armagh Friary** is typical.

Armagh Planetarium [Kids]

College Hill. Open Mon–Sat usually 11.30am–5pm (check website for programme). Evening shows last Thu each month, 7pm and 9pm. Tickets must be collected from reception at least 30 mins before show commences. £6, child £5. Booking essential. Under-16s must be accompanied by an adult. 028 3752 3689. www.armaghplanet.com.

Recently refurbished with the latest digital technology, the Planetarium offers full-colour 3-D 360° star shows projected over its entire huge dome (50ft/15m in diameter).

In the grounds the **Observatory**, founded and endowed in 1789 by Archbishop Robinson is one of the oldest meteorological stations in the British Isles.

Excursions

Navan Fort★

2mi/3.2km west of Armagh on the A 28. Visitor Centre open Jun–Aug Mon–Sat 10am–5pm (noon Sun); Apr–May and Sep, Sat 10am–5pm, Sun noon–5pm. Fort open year-round freely accessible. Closed 12 Jul. £5. 028 3752 1801. www.visitarmagh.com.

In the late Bronze Age this impressive earthwork, surrounded by sacred places and settlement sites, was the most important place in Ulster, thought to be synonymous with Emain Macha, the capital of legendary Ulster, mentioned in the **Ulster Cycle** (*see Myths and Lore in Introduction*). The multi-media displays in the **Visitor Centre** evoke the world of the Celts and pre-Christian Ireland; archaeological research about the fort and its associated Neolothic sites charts

Address Book

For coin ranges, see the Legend on the cover flap.

WHERE TO STAY

Armagh City Hotel – *2 Friary Road. 82rm. 028 3751 8888. www. armaghcityhotel.co.uk.* Modern hotel with large bedrooms, healths centre and pool, bar with live bands.

TRACING ANCESTORS

Armagh Ancestry – *38a English St. Mon–Fri 11am–4pm. 028 3752 1802.*

their evolution. The fort itself *(5min on foot from the Visitor Centre)* consists of a massive circular bank and inner ditch around a hill with a high mound on top, flanked by a low circular mound surrounded by an infilled ditch.

The Argory★

(NT) 10mi/16km north of Armagh via the A 29 and a minor road right. House open May–Sept Sat–Sun 2pm–5.30pm (Jul–Aug daily). Grounds open year-round daily 10am–4pm (6pm May–Sept). House £5, grounds £3.50 per car. 028 8778 4753. www.nationaltrust. org.uk.

This handsome neo-Classical country house built around 1824 is little changed since the early years of the 20C, and a tour of the house is a fascinating evocation of an ancient family home. The most extraordinary single object is the cabinet **barrel organ** of 1820, still in full working order.

Navan Fort

Road Bowls

The ancient Irish sport of road bowling is still played on Sundays in Co Armagh and Co Cork. A heavy iron ball (28oz/794g; 7in/18cm) is hurled along a stretch of quiet winding country road in as few throws as possible; the ball may hurtle through the air at shoulder height. Betting is heavy.

The **Gardens**, which extend to the Blackwater River, comprise old roses set in box-lined beds, a sundial dated 1820, yew tree arbours, Pleasure Grounds, a Garden House, a Pump House and a lime tree walk.

Ardress House

7mi/11km NE of Armagh on the B77. (NT) ♿ⓘ*Open mid-Mar through Sept Bank Hol Mons, St Patrick's Day & weekends 2pm–6pm.* ☎*£4.* ☎*028 8778 4753. www. nationaltrust.org.uk.*

Ardress is a simple 17C manor house enlarged and embellished in the 18C. It was inherited by the architect, George Ensor, on his marriage in 1760.

The house displays glass from Dublin, Cork and Belfast, and some fine furniture, including Irish Chippendale chairs. The symmetry and proportions of the elegant **drawing room** are enhanced by the delightful stuccowork of Michael Stapleton.

The cobbled **farmyard** with its central pump is surrounded by farm buildings equipped with antiquated implements including baskets and bee hives.

Dan Winter's Cottage

6mi/10km NE of Armagh via the the A 29 and B 77 to Loughgall. ⓘ*Open year-round Mon–Sat 10.30am–5.30pm. Sun 2pm–5.30pm.* ☎*028 3885 1344. http:// orangenet.org/winter.*

On 21 September 1795, following the affray later called the "Battle of the Diamond" at **Dan Winter's House** *(3mi/5km NE)*, the victorious Protestant Peep O'Day Boys retired to celebrate

their triumph at **Jim Sloane's pub** *(half way up the main street)*. It was here that the Orange order was instituted, dedicated to sustaining the "glorious and immortal memory of King William III". The pub's long and narrow room is overflowing with mementoes of the Order: sashes, caps, waistcoats, banners, guns and pikes used in 1795.

Tayto Potato Crisp Factory 📷Kids

11mi/18km Eeastof Armagh via the A 51; factory entrance next to the police station on entering Tandragee. ☎☎*Factory tours, ihr 30min, must be booked, min. age 5yrs old: Mon–Thu 10.30am & 1.30pm, Fri 10.30am only.* ⓘ*Closed all public holidays.* ☎*£5, child £3.* ☎*028 3884 0249. www. tayto.com.*

The factory is installed in Tandragee Castle, overlooking the town, built in 1837. The factory tour starts in the warehouse and follows the route of the potato on its journey of transformation into neatly packed wavy golden crisps,

Gosford Forest Park

7mi/11km south east of Armagh via the A 28 to Markethill. ⓘ*Open daily 10am– sunset.* ☎*Charges on board at entrance.* ☎*028 3755 1277.*

Now in the care of the Forest Service, the park was formerly the demesne of the Acheson family, the Earls of Gosford. The present castle *(private)*, a huge pseudo-Norman pile designed by Thomas Hopper in 1819, was built at the same time as the **arboretum** was planted with exotic trees. The **walled gardens** contain a brick **bee house** with niches to protect the straw hives from damp. The **Gosford Heritage Poultry Collection** *(www.forestserviceni.gov. uk/gosford-leaflet-06.pdf)* aims to preserve rare native poultry breeds once common in the 18C.

Dean Jonathan Swift was a frequent visitor, hence **Swift's Well** and the **Dean Swifts Chair**, an artificial sun trap created by making a semicircular hollow protected by a yew hedge in a south-facing bank.

BANGOR

POPULATION 52 437

Looking out over Belfast Lough at the northern end of the Ards Peninsula, Bangor (Beannchar) is Northern Ireland's foremost seaside resort, well stocked with Victorian hotels and guest houses. By contrast it began as one of Ireland's most important monastic settlements, reformed in the 17C as a Plantation town. Today it largely serves as a dormitory town for Belfast commuters.

- **Information:** Tower House, 34 Quay Street. ☎028 9127 0069. www.northdown.gov.uk.
- ▶ **Orient Yourself:** Bangor is situated 15mi/24km east of Belfast via the A 2.
- **Don't Miss:** Ulster Folk and Transport Museum, and a trip to the beach.
- **Organising Your Time:** Allow at least 2 days, you will need a full day to explore the Ulster Folk and Transport Museum.
- **Especially for Kids:** Bangor Beach and Crawfordsburn Country Park' beach.
- **Also See:** BELFAST, MOUNT STEWART, STRANGFORD LOUGH.

A Bit of History

Bangor Abbey, founded by St Comgall in 558, became one of the most famous abbeys in western Christendom, sending its missionary monks to found monasteries in Ireland and abroad. In the 9C Comgall's tomb was desecrated in Viking raids; Malachy, appointed abbot in 1124, built a stone church and introduced the Augustinian Order; in 1542 the abbey was dissolved.

On the accession of James I in 1603, Bangor was granted to Sir James Hamilton, later Viscount Clandeboye, who created a town with settlers from his native Ayrshire. In 1620 he was granted a warrant to establish a maritime port including the nearby creeks. In 1689 the Duke of Schomberg landed at Groomsport; his army of 10 000 men probably coming ashore at Bangor or Ballyholme. The Duke spent a night with the Hamiltons before setting off to the Battle of the Boyne, where he was killed.

In 1710 Sir James's estates passed by marriage to the Ward family of Castle Ward on Strangford Lough. Two generations later Col Robert Ward improved the harbour, promoted the textile industry and founded a boys' school. Bangor's role as a seaside resort, complete with pier, started with the arrival of the railway in 1865.

Walking Tour

Old Custom House and Tower

The Custom House (now the Tourist Information Centre) was built by Sir James Hamilton in 1637 with financial assistance from the Crown, in the Scottish Baronial style with flanking watchtowers, a crow-stepped gable and a quarter-round corbelled turret.

Bangor Abbey Church

The 14C tower is the only section to survive the dissolution of Bangor Abbey in 1542.

North Down Museum★

Open year-round Tue–Sat, Bank Hol Mon and Mon during Jul–Aug 10am–4.30pm. Sun 2pm–4.30pm ☕ 🅿. ☎028 9127 1200. www.northdown.gov.uk/heritage.

The Centre is housed in part of Bangor Castle, a fanciful mid-19C exercise in Elizabethan-Jacobean revival style. An exhibition of evocative artefacts and models celebrates Bangor's eventful past and development into a popular seaside resort. There is also an informative section promoting the 15mi/26km coastal walk.

Address Book

For coin ranges, see the Legend on the cover flap.

SIGHTSEEING

Bangor Bay Cruise – *MV Blue Aquarius, Bangor Marina* ☎07779 600 607. *www.bangorboat.com. Daily in summer 2pm. £5 cruises, £14 fishing trips.*

Belfast Lough Cruise –*146 Killaughey Rd.* Daily sea fishing trips, pleasure cruises, day trips to the Copeland Islands (Jun–Sep) from Donaghadee Harbour. ☎028 9188 3403. www.nelsonsboats.co.uk

WHERE TO STAY

Cairn Bay Lodge – *278 Seacliffe Road. 1.25mi East. 5 rm.* ☎028 9146 7636. *www.cairnbaylodge.com.* A detached Edwardian house, sympathetically decorated with feature wood panelling. The sitting room is particularly attractive while the dining room overlooks the beautifully landscaped gardens with panoramic views of Ballyholme Bay. Beauty therapy; gourmet breakfast.

Shelleven House – *59–61 Princetown Road. 11rm.* ☎028 9127 1777. *www.shellevenhouse.com.* A large Victorian terraced house with the bedrooms at the top of the house, many enjoying views over the town or sea. Neat, traditionally decorated bedrooms.

WHERE TO EAT

Coyles Bistro – *44 High Street.* ☎028 9127 0362. *www.coylesbistro.co.uk.* Beautifully decorated in the Arts & Crafts style with a wide range of bistro favourites at reasonable prices Coyles use as much local produce and fish as possible.

Donegans – *37 High Street.* ☎028 91463928. *This rural-themed pub, with turf-burning ranges, serves traditional Irish food including pleanty of seafood dishes. Regular live music.*

Grace Neill's – *33 High Street, Donaghadee.* ☎028 91884595. *www.graceneills.com.* The oldest pub in Ireland (1611), full of atmosphere; traditional and contemporary cooking.

SPORTS AND LEISURE

Safe sandy beaches, sea-water swimming pool, marina (560 berths), waterfront fun park, golf course.

Excursions

Crawfordsburn Country Park [Kids]

7mi/11km W of Bangor by B 20. (HM)
Park open daily Apr–Oct 9am–8pm (4.45pm Oct). Visitor centre daily 10am–5pm. Grey Point Fort Apr–Sept Wed–Mon 2pm–5pm, Oct–Mar Sun only 2pm–5pm. ☎028 9185 3621. *www.ehsni.gov.uk/Crawfordsburn.*

Situated on the southern shores of Belfast Lough, the picturesque village and its coastal country park are named after the Crawford family from Scotland who bought the estate in 1674.

The Country Park is full of variety, featuring over 2 mi/3.5km of coastline, often rugged and rocky, but also including the two best beaches in the Belfast area. There is a deep wooded glen with an impressive waterfall at its head, a pond and wildflower meadows with excellent views over the Lough. The history of the estate and its flora and fauna are comprehensively illustrated in the **Park Centre**, equipped with interactive displays for children.

The **glen walk** *(30min there and back on foot)* passes the old salmon pool before dipping under the handsome railway viaduct of 1865. Upstream is the waterfall which was used to power corn, flax and saw mills, and from 1850 to generate electricity to light the glen.

Grey Point Fort *(Coastguard Avenue, accessible by footpaths within the Country Park – 1hr there and back)* commands the sea approaches to Belfast and was manned during both World Wars by the Royal Artillery. Panels outline its history (1907–63) and a solitary six-inch gun, a gift from the Government of the Republic of Ireland, is mounted in one of the massive reinforced concrete gun emplacements.

Ulster Folk and Transport Museum★★ Kids

Cultra, Holywood. 8mi/13km west of Bangor via the A 2. ♿🕐*Open Mar–Sept Mon–Fri 10am–5pm (6pm Jul–Sept), Sat 10am–6pm, Sun 11am–6pm. Oct–Feb Mon–Fri 10am–4pm, Sat 10am–5pm, Sun 11am–5pm. Nov–Jan outlying rural area closes 4pm. Last admission 1hr before closing.* ⊜*£5.50 for each collection, £7 combined ticket.* ✕. ☎*028 9042 8428. www.uftm.org.uk.*

This is one of the most extensive and interesting museums in the whole of Ireland. Bisected by the busy coast road, one section is dedicated to the folk collection, the other to transport.

Rectory , Ulster Folk Museum

Folk Museum

A vast open-air museum is installed in a series of old buildings transferred from the Ulster countryside where traditional trades, practices and crafts are demonstrated. Costumed staff narrate the story of each structure and explain how the equipment was used for weaving, spinning, agricultural work and cooking.

The dwellings, furnished as they would have been at the end of the 19C, range from a one-room farmhouse shared between the family and their cows, to a substantial 17C farmhouse with panelled walls. Working premises include a flax-scutching mill, a spade mill, a weaver's house and more. The **village** is composed of a school, a market-cum-courthouse, a church and a rectory, together with two terraces of urban cottages including a shoemaker's workshop and a bicycle repair shop.

In the **Gallery** *(three floors)* the traditional Ulster way of life is illustrated with original domestic, industrial and agricultural implements.

Transport Museum

Examples of virtually every kind of wheeled vehicle used in Ireland in the last two centuries is displayed in its social context.

In the **Irish Railway Collection**, fascinating wall panels evoke the sometimes idiosyncratic history of the railways powered by the beautifully restored engines and carriages; note the wonderful *Maeve (Maebh)*, the most powerful ever to run on Irish rails.

The **Road Transport Galleries**, richly furnished with all types of transport memorabilia, display two-wheelers through the ages. Buses include a lovingly rebuilt 1973 Daimler Fleetline, and No 2 of the Bessbrook and Newry Tramway Co, built in 1885 and still carrying passengers in the 1940s. The final gallery is devoted to *The Car in Society*, and ranges from an 1898 Benz Velo Confortable, the oldest petrol vehicle in Ireland to the legendary **De Lorean motor car** (made famous in the *Back to the Future* movies) produced in Belfast in 1981 by the short-lived De Lorean company. The **Dalchoolin Transport Galleries** present a miscellany of exhibits – shoulder creels and wooden sledges, carts and jaunting cars; horse-drawn vehicles and ships.

The **X2 Flight Exhibition** is an exciting, interactive exhibition, exploring the history and science of flight, including the important role played by local pioneers. You can "test fly" a range of exhibits, including a full-motion flight simulator ride.

The **Titanic Gallery** honours the great ill-starred liner, built at the famous Harland and Wolff shipyard in Belfast.

Somme Heritage Centre

3mi/5km south of Bangor via the A 21. 🕐*Open Apr–Jun & Sept Mon–Thu 10am–4pm, Sat noon–4pm; Jul–Aug Mon–Fri 10am–5pm, Sat–Sun noon–5pm. Oct–Mar Mon–Thu 10am–4pm. First Sat of each month noon–4pm.* 👣*Last tour 1hr before closing.* 🕐*Closed 20 Dec–mid-Jan.*

©Robert Mayne/istockphoto.com

Ballycopeland Windmill

NITB, Belfast

✆*£4.25.* ☎*028 9182 3202. www.irish soldier.org. www.heritageisland.com.*
With the outbreak of the First World War (1914), many Irishmen put aside their political differences and volunteered for service in the British army. Irish units suffered terrible losses in the Somme offensive of 1916: 5,000 men from the Ulster Division were killed in the first two days alone. The Centre commemorates the sacrifices made in battle with a "time tunnel" and an uncanny re-creation of the trenches complete with terrible sights and sounds.

Groomsport
1.5mi/2.5km east by the coast road.
This is an attractive little seaside resort and fishing village complete with sandy beaches. Two original fishermen's dwellings, **Cockle Row Cottages** (☉*open daily last weekend May–early Sept 11.30am–5.30pm;* ☎*028 9127 1200, www. northdown.gov.uk/heritage)* now illustrate life for a fisherman and his family at the turn of the last century. There is entertainment staged every weekend from 2pm–4pm.

Donaghadee
7mi/11km E of Bangor on the B 21.
Picturesque winding streets lead to the **parish church** which dates from 1641. The huge harbour, now full of leisure craft, was built in 1820 to accommodate the mail ships, which were transferred to Larne in 1849. From the 16C to 19C Donaghadee–Portpatrick was the most popular route between Ireland and Scotland as it is the shortest crossing (21mi/34km). The Norman **motte** near the shore was probably raised by William Copeland, a retainer of John de Courcy; it is crowned by a stone building (1818) providing a fine **view** of the Copeland Islands and the coast of Galloway.

Copeland Islands
Accessible by boat from Groomsport or Donaghadee.
The nearest and largest island was inhabited until the 1940s. A modern lighthouse was built on Mew Island in 1884. **Lighthouse Island** is now a wildlife sanctuary in the care of the National Trust, populated by buzzards, golden eagles, resident seals, dolphins, porpoises, basking sharks, minke whales, killer whales.

Ballycopeland Windmill★
10mi/16km SE of Bangor, 1mi/1.6km west of Milisle village on the B172. ☉*Open Jul–Aug Tue–Sun 10am–6pm (2pm Sun).* ☎*028 918 61413. www.ehsni.gov.uk.*
In the late 18C, when grain was grown extensively in the Ards Peninsula, the landscape was thickly dotted with windmills. This rare survivor at Ballycopeland was probably built between 1780–90 and worked until 1915. The complex includes the mill, back in working order; the miller's house with an explanatory display; a dust-house and kiln.

Ards Peninsula
Extending south from Bangor to Ballyquintin Point, the Ards peninsula encloses the broad waters of Strangford Lough. This is one of the best grain-producing regions of Ireland.
The breezy **coast road** follows the bare shoreline, past sandy beaches and occasional rocky outcrops. **Portavogie** shelters one of Northern Ireland's three fishing fleets. The southern end of the peninsula presents an austere landscape of marsh and heath.

BELFAST★★

POPULATION 279 237

Few cities have such a splendid natural setting; Belfast (Béal Feirste) stands at the mouth of the River Lagan at the point where it discharges into the great sea inlet of Belfast Lough which is sheltered on both sides by hills; to the west rises the formidable basalt escarpment of Cave Hill and Black Mountain. One of the great industrial and commercial cities of the Victorian era, the capital of Northern Ireland has survived thirty years of Troubles. Today's fragile peace has encouraged a tidal wave of new building and a vibrant cultural life without equal in the rest of the province. Half a million people live within a few miles of the city centre, a third of Northern Ireland's population.

- **Information:** Belfast Welcome Centre, 47 Donegall Place. ☎028 9024 6609. www.gotobelfast.com. There are information desks at both airports.
- ▶ **Orient Yourself:** Belfast is set on the shores of Belfast Lough. For an overview of the city take the City Sightseeing open-top bus tour.
- **Don't Miss:** Ulster Museum. Belfast Zoo. A tour of the Murals.
- **Organising Your Time:** Allow 2–3 days.
- **Especially for Kids:** Belfast Wheel, W5 (Odyssey Complex), Belfast Zoo.
- **Also See:** ANTRIM, BANGOR, CARRICKFERGUS, LISBURN.

A Bit of History

Norman Castle to Industrial City – Belfast takes its name from a ford by a sandbank *(bealfeirste* in Irish) where the Anglo-Norman John de Courcy built a castle after his invasion of Ulster in 1177. Development only came in the early 17C when a quay was built and trade diverted from Carrickfergus. The city was settled by hard-working Scottish Presbyterians, followed later by industrious Huguenot refugees who brought new techniques to the burgeoning linen industry. Cotton spinning was introduced in 1777, shipbuilding in 1791; by the early 19C, industry was booming; the population multiplied fifteenfold, from under 25,000 to 350,000 over to generations. General engineering flourished, as did distilling, rope-making and tobacco products, but it was the great shipyards that gave the city its distinctive industrial character, with Harland and Wolff – builders of the *Titanic* – becoming the United Kingdom's largest construction and repair yard. In the 20C, Short Brothers produced the Sunderland flying boat and the first VTOL jet; their airstrip in the docks is now used by George Best Belfast City Airport.

Dissent and Division – The predominance of the Presbyterian Church, its cultural links with Scotland and its commercial wealth, underpinned Belfast's early reputation as a centre for intellectual activity and articulated independence. Belfast had the first printing press in Ireland (c 1690) and published the first Irish newspaper, the *Belfast News Letter*

Belfast City Hall

Ph Hurlin/MICHELIN

Address Book

👛*For coin ranges, see the Legend on the cover flap.*

ARRIVING

Belfast International Airport – flights to several European and UK destinations. ☎028 9448 4848. *www. belfastairport.com.*18 mi/29km north west of Belfast. Airport Express 300 bus shuttles to and from the city centre every 10 mins, journey 30–40mins. *£6 one-way, £9 return.*

George Best Belfast City Airport – flights to the UK, Jersey Cork, Paris, Rennes, Salzburg, Geneva, Chambery. 2mi/3km north east of city centre. ☎028 9093 909. *www.belfastcityairport. com.* Metro Bus 600 to and from the city centre every 20–30min, journey 10–15 mins. *£1.30 one-way, £2.20 return.* Bueses from both airports terminate at the Europa Bus Centre.

SIGHTSEEING

City Sightseeing Belfast – *Open-top hop-on hop-off* bus tours operate from Castle Place. *Operate year-round Mon–Fri every 30–60mins, Sat–Sun 20–40mins 10am–4.30pm (Nov–Feb 4pm).* ☎028 9045 9035. *www.belfastcity sightseeing.com.*

Black Taxi Service – Guided personalised tours (👛*see 'The Murals of Belfast' box*).

There are various **themed walking tours** of the city, including:
Historic Belfast – *Wed, Fri, Sat (also Sun, Jun–Sept) 2pm, meet Belfast Welcome Centre.* 🚶*£6.* ☎028 9024 6609. *www.gotobelfast.com.*

Bailey's Historical Pub Tour of Belfast – *Sat (May–Oct) at 4pm and Thu at 7pm , meet upstairs at Crown Liquor Saloon, Great Victoria Street.* ☎028 9268 3665 *(Judy Crawford).* 🚶*£6.*

WHERE TO STAY

🛏🛏**Ash Rowan Town House** – *12 Windsor Avenue. 5rm.* ☎*028 9066 1758.* Close to the Ulster Museum and a good range of restaurants, this Victorian bed and breakfast house has a real traditional feel and period charm, and offers no less than nine gourmet breakfasts! It was once home to Thomas Andrews, designer of the Titanic.

🛏🛏**Benedicts of Belfast** – *7–21 Bradbury Place. Shaftsbury Square.* ☎*028 9059 1999. www.benedictshotel. co.uk.* Fashionable boutique hotel with themed bar hosting live music shows and popular restaurant. Excellent value.

🛏🛏**Madison's Hotel** – *59–63 Botanic Ave nue. 35rm.* ☎*028 9050 9800. www. madisonshotel.com.* Madison's proximity to the university ensures a lively atmosphere and the hotel contributes by having its own nightclub. Bright contemporary bedrooms, bar and restaurant.

🛏🛏**The Old Rectory** – *148 Malone Road. 5 rm.* ☎*028 9066 7882. www. anoldrectory.co.uk.* Charming little place in quiet suburbs (10-min bus-ride to city centre) serving award-winning breakfasts.

🛏🛏**Jurys Inn** – *Great Victoria Street.* ☎*01 607 5000. http://belfasthotels. jurysinns.com.* Friendly smart comfortable medium-sized chain hotel in the heart of the city - ask for one of the side room which overlook the lawns of the "Inst"school, and also have views to the hills

🛏🛏🛏**The Crescent Townhouse** – *13 Lower Crescent. 11rm.* ☎*028 9032 3349; www.crescenttownhouse.com.* This regency house in the University Quarter has been converted into a stylish boutique hotel. The bar has a Gothic feel with oak panelling and the highly rated brasserie offers imaginative dishes in a lively atmosphere.

🛏🛏🛏**Malmaison** – *34–38 Victoria Street.* ☎*028 9022 0200. www.mal maison-belfast.com. 64rm.* The Belfast outpost of this highly popular chain offers accommodation in a converted former seed warehouse, combining original features such as iron pillars and beams with the best of contemporary design. (Do note the setting is on a very busy road however). Excellent restaurant.

🛏🛏🛏🛏**Merchant Hotel** – *35–39 Waring Street.* ☎*028 9023 4888 www. themerchanthotel.com.* This intimate and sumptuous 5-star hotel, set in the buzzing Cathedral Quarter, occupies a magnificent Grade 1 listed property, formerly the headquarters of the Ulster Bank, built in 1860. It has been sensitively restored to its original splendour and is now regarded as one of the top hotels in Northern Ireland. The domed Great Room Restaurant, used for à la carte dining and traditional afternoon teas is breathtaking.

WHERE TO EAT

Cayenne – *7 Lesley House, Shaftesbury Square.* ☎028 9033 1532. *www.therankingroup.com.* Very stylish with impressive modern artwork. Lively atmosphere, well-priced menu featuring contemporary cuisine with an Asian twist.

Ginger – *7 Hope Street, Great Victoria Street.* ☎028 9024. 4421. *www.ginger.ie.* Busy and unpretentious little place, tucked away in a parade of shops. Ample choice from the blackboard menu of daily specials, with influences from all around the world.

Nick's Warehouse – *35–39 Hill Street.* ☎028 9043 9690. *www.nicksware house.co.uk.* Set in an old Bushmills warehouse on a cobbled street in the fashionable Cathedral Quarter, downstairs has the buzz, upstairs is slightly more formal. Nick oversees a busy kitchen producing carefully prepared modern cooking. Excellent wine list.

Oxford Exchange – *First floor, St Georges Market, Oxford Street.* ☎028 9024 0014. *www.oxfordexchange.co.uk.* Overlooking St George's Market., its glass roof ensures the room is bright and airy. The open-plan kitchen speciality is chargrilled fish and meats.

Deanes – *36–40 Howard Street.* ☎028 9033 1134. *www.michaeldeane. co.uk.* The city's premier restaurant provides original and accomplished fusion cooking, discreet and professional service in elegant minimalist surroundings.

PUBS & BARS

Bittle's Bar – *103 Victoria Street* – ☎028 903 11 088. This cosy local, dating from 1861 is well worth a look, with fine paintings of Belfast heroes by pub regular, Joe O'Kane, and friendly locals.

Cafe Vaudeville – *35 Arthur Street.* ☎028 9043 9160. *www.cafevaudeville. com.* Outrageously decorated highly theatrical Art Nouveau bar set in a neo-Classical former bank building: good food and drink, albeit at high prices. Unmissable!

Kelly's Cellars – *30 Bank Street* – ☎028 9032 4835. This 1720 pub, one of the oldest in the city, tucked away in the financial district, is an atmospheric antidote to the homogeneous modernity of the surrounding development.

Kitchen Bar – *16–18 Victoria Street.* ☎028 903 24 901. Reputedly opened in 1859 (but recently relocated a few yards), this bar is celebrated for its live traditional Irish music. Comprehensive drinks selection.

Madden's – *Berry Street.* ☎028 9024 4114. Low-ceilinged, dark and atmospheric, Madden's is a genuine local's local, known for its live blues and traditional folk music.

Pats Bar – *19–22 Princes Dock Street.* ☎028 9074 4524. Century-old atmospheric pub set in the docklands. Wednesday is traditional music night.

Robinson's – *38–40 Great Victoria Street.* ☎028 902 47 447. *www.robinsons bar.co.uk.* Established in 1895, rebuilt in the 1990s, Robinson's houses five very different venues in one large Victorian building from traditional boozer to bistro restaurant, hip lounge, gin palace and industrial-chic nightclub.

Rotterdam Bar – *54 Pilot St* – ☎028 907 46 021. *www.rotterdambar.com.* By day this dockside bar with open fires is an oasis of calm. It is transformed at sundown with live music: blues, salsa, folk, jazz. Good choice of spirits.

The Crown Liquor Saloon – *46 Great Victoria Street.* ☎028 9024 9476. The city's most famous pub (⚑see *Walking Tour*).

The Morning Star – *17 Pottinger's Entry.* ☎028 9023 5986. *www.themorningstar bar.com.* Classic Victorian gin palace: the downstairs bar has its original mahogany counter, terrazzo floor and snob screens. The pub is famed for its food, great value at lunchtime.

The John Hewitt – *51 Donegall Street* ☎028 902 33 768. *www.thejohnhewitt. com.* Although less than a decade old this pub in the Cathedral District has a genuine community feel and a real pedigree already. Good food, art gallery, live gigs and, with its log fire and

Crown Liquor Saloon

long counter, ensures that the art of conversation is alive and well.

Whites Tavern – *2–4 Winecellar Entry.* ☎*028 9024 3080. www.whitestavern. co.uk.* Dating from 1630 Whites claims to be the oldest tavern in Belfast and certainly feels that way with peat-burning fires and historical artefacts liberally dotted around its whitewashed stone walls. Traditional folk music and honest "pub grub" on offer.

ENTERTAINMENT

Belfast Waterfront Hall – *2 Lanyon Place.* ☎*028 903 334 455. www.waterfront.co.uk.* Excellent venue attracting top Irish and intenational acts (💧*see The Laganside).*

The Empire – *40–42 Botanic Avenue.* ☎*028 902 49 276. www.belfastempire. com.* Contemporary music, tribute bands ,and The O'Malley Experience , a top-quality display of traditional Irish music and dance.

The Grand Opera House – *Great Victoria Street.* ☎*028 9024 1919. www.goh.co.uk* Recently endowed with a new extension, Belfast's leading venue for theatre, musicals and opera goes from strength to strength

The Odyssey – *2 Queen's Quay.* ☎*028 9045 0055. www.theodyssey.co.uk.* The place for seeing Ice Hockey and visiting musical superstars (💧*see The Laganside)* as well as home to a 10-pin bowling alley and Bar Seven nightclub.

Ulster Hall – *Bedford Street.* ☎*028 9032 3900. www.ulsterhall.co.uk.* Superb Victorian venue recently refurbished to the tune of over £7 million. Pop concerts, sporting events and a regular venue for the Ulster Orchestra.

SHOPPING

St George's Market – *12–20 East Bridge Street. Open Fri -Sat.* Belfast's finest market (💧*see Walking Tour).*

Victoria Square – *Victoria Square. www.victoriasquare.com.* Stunning new mall (💧*see City Centre).*

PUBS

The Spaniard – *3 Skipper Street.* ☎*028 9023 4488. www.the spaniardbar. com.* Charming quirky tiny bar in the Cathedral Quarter serving up tapas, live music and DJs, and a good dose of the craic.

McHugh's Bar – *29–31 Queens Square.* ☎*028 9050 9999. www.mchughsbar. com.* Set in the oldest building in the city, dating back to 1711 McHugh's is famous for its music and food. Don't miss having a peek at its famous political chessboard!

Other historical pubs in the city centre well worth a visit are:

The Deers Head (*Garfield Street);*
The Duke of York (*Commercial Court);*
The Front Page (*Donegall Stret, Union Street);* **The Garrick** (*Chichester Street);*
The Harbour Bar(*Ann Street);*
Hercules Bar (*Castle Street).*

EVENTS AND FESTIVALS

Titanic Festival –last week Mar. *www.belfastcity.gov.uk.*

Cathedral Quarter Arts Festival – *1–11 May. www.cqaf.com.*

Festival of Fools – International Street Theatre and comedy. 1–5May. ☎*028 9023 6007. www.foolsfestival.com.*

Belfast City Carnival –last Sat June. *www.gotobelfast.com.*

Feile an Phobail – Music and dance. 1st to 2nd Sun Aug.*www.feilebelfast.com.*

Belfast Festival at Queen's –3 weeks mid-Oct–early Nov. Claimed to be Britain's second largest arts festival (after Edinburgh). ☎*028 9097 1034. www.belfastfestival.com*

in 1737 – the oldest morning paper in the British Isles.

It was in Belfast in 1791 that Wolfe Tone helped to found the Society of United Irishmen; in 1792 they published the *Northern Star*, a newspaper which expressed radical opinion and first promoted the idea of the Irish nation, which, in Tone's words, would "substitute the common name of Irishman in place of… Protestant, Catholic, and Dissenter". To the dismay of the United Irishmen, their ideals, which had sharpened existing divisions, did not survive the failed 1798 Rebellion. The overwhelmingly Presbyterian city of the late 18C changed as spectacular industrial growth began employing large numbers of Catholics drawn from all over Ireland in the 19C, settling in the **Falls Road** area of the city, between the predominantly Protestant working-class districts of Sandy Row and **Shankill Road**.

During The Troubles these names became synonymous with extremes of sectarianism and violent conflict. Today they are still divided by sectarian loyalties but now attract visitors by the busfull, who come to view the murals.

Centre Walking Tour

Donegall Square★

The hub of Belfast is Donegall Square: a vast rectangle of grass and gardens peopled with statues, laid out around the City Hall. On sunny summer days every square inch of grass is taken up by picnicking office workers and visitors.

Facing onto the square are a variety of handsome Victorian buildings, notably **Yorkshire House** with roundels containing low-relief heads of famous men and deities *(south side)*; the elegant block commissioned for **Scottish Provident** (1899–1902) designed by the Belfast architects, Young and Mackenzie *(west side)*; an old pink stone linen warehouse (1869) *(north side)*, and the **Linen Hall Library**, (🕑*open Mon–Sat 9.30am–5.30pm (1pm Sat);* 🕑*closed Bank Hols;* ☕; ☎028 9032 1707, www.linenhall.com) founded in 1788 as the Belfast Library and Society for Promoting Knowledge: it has a delightfully old-fashioned interior with great views onto the Square where you can escape the bustle of the city with a newspaper and a cup of coffee. Its modern annexe contains various material relating to The Troubles and there is a genealogy section.

City Hall★

�*Closed until 2009.* ☎028 9027 0456. www.belfastcity.gov.uk.

The great neo-Renaissance Portland stone building with its copper-covered dome and corner towers was designed by Sir Brumwell Thomas and completed in 1906, at a time when Belfast was at its zenith of industrial and commercial might, to mark its city status granted by Queen Victoria in 1888.

Highlights of the **interior** include the grand staircase; a mural of the founding of the city and its principal industries painted by John Luke; a sculpture by Patrick MacDowell (1790–1870), a native of Belfast, of the Marquess of Donegall (1827–53), who devoted the proceeds of his music and poetry to good works; the Council Chamber, panelled in hand-carved Austrian oak; the Reception Hall displaying the original Charter of Belfast granted by James I on 27 April 1613; the Banqueting Hall; and the shields of the Provinces of Ireland in the stained glass of the Great Hall.

The Belfast Wheel   Kids

The wheel may be moved and re-erected near the Odyssey Complex in 2009. ♿ 🕑*Open year-round Sun–Thu 10am–9pm, Fri 10am–10pm, Sat 9am–10pm.* 💷*£6.50, child £4.50.* 🖱*10 per cent discount when booking online.* ☎028 903 10607. www. worldtouristattractions.co.uk.

Jump aboard one of the 42 fully enclosed, climate-controlled capsules and as you are gently lifted to a height of 200ft/60m above the dome and towers of adjacent City Hall, you can enjoy spectacular views of the city.

Adjacent to the wheel is the **Titanic Memorial**, sculpted by Thomas Brock, which pays tribute to 22 Ulstermen who lost their lives on the ship. Ironically this included the elite 9-man Harland and Wolff "Guarantee Group", all expert in their fields who were sent on each maiden voyage in case of problems.

▶ *From the north west corner of Donegall Square, walk west along Wellington Place and cross the road.*

Royal Belfast Academical Institute

⊶ *Closed to the public.*
The inter-denominational boys' school, known as "Inst", on College Square, was probably designed by Sir John Soane (1814).

▶ *Continue left and cross the road.*

Church House

♿ 🕐 *Assembly Hall open for viewing-normal office hours subject to functions, enquire at the reception desk.* ☎*028 9032 2284. www.presbyterianireland.org.*
The headquarters of the Presbyterian Church in Ireland was designed by Young and Mackenzie (1905), Belfast architects, in the 15C Gothic style of a Scottish baronial castle. The massive 131-ft/40-m high Clock tower, inspired by St Giles' Cathedral in Edinburgh, contains a peal of 12 bells.
Church House was extensively renovated in 1992 and he ground floor is now a shopping mall while the administrative offices of the Church are on the upper floors. At the heart of the building is the 1,300 seater Assembly Hall, entered on the first floor with its all round gallery and pipe organ.

Grand Opera House

Designed by the theatre architect Frank Matcham and opened in 1894, this gorgeous building has a gilt-and-red-plush interior to match its exuberant facade. Its famous neighbour, the **Europa Hotel**, once held the unenviable title of "most bombed hotel in Europe", thanks in no small part to it being a base for journalists covering The Troubles. Happily, because warnings were always given, no-one was killed here. There is a wonderful story involving The Europa's first general manager, Harper Brown, who received an MBE (Member of the British Empire) medal from The Queen for keeping the hotel open. Mr Brown was so determined to remain open for business that on one occasion when the IRA came in with a bomb and left it in the lobby, he picked it up and thew it outside in the car park. The bomber saw what happened and, in turn, brought it back in. The redoubtable Mr Brown carried it straight back out again, at which stage the bomber gave up and left!

Crown Liquor Saloon★

(NT). ♿ 🕐 *Open year-round Mon–Sat 11.30am–11pm, Sun 12.30pm–10pm.* ☎*028 9027 9901. www.crownbar.com.*
The Victorian interior of this famous city landmark is richly decorated with coloured glass, coloured and moulded tiles, arcaded mirrors and polished marble. Carved animals top the doorposts of each of the 10 elaborately carved and panelled Snugs or Boothes, lettered from A-J. In these you will find gun metal plates for striking matches, and an antique bell system (this used to be very common in Victorian Houses where servants were employed), which alerts bar staff when drinks are required.
The ornate ceiling is supported on hexagonal wooden columns with feathered ornament. Inspired by his travels in Spain and Italy, Patrick Flanagan built the public house as a railway hotel in 1885; it is now owned by the National Trust.

▶ *Turn left into Amelia Street and walk eastwards along Franklin Street. Turn right into Alfred Street.*

St Malachy's Church★

The austere fortified exterior of this red-brick crenellated Roman Catholic church (1844) gives no hint of the ornate interior enclosed by white stucco fan vaulting inspired by Henry VII's Chapel in Westminster Abbey.

▶ *Return to the junction; turn right into Sussex Place; walk along Hamilton Street and into East Bridge Street; turn left and walk north along Oxford Street.*

St George's Market

🕐 *Open Fri 6am–1pm, Sat 9am–3pm www.belfastcity.gov.uk/markets.*
Built between 1890 and 1896 this is the oldest covered market in Ireland and one of the best markets in the British Isles. It sells a variety of products, includ-

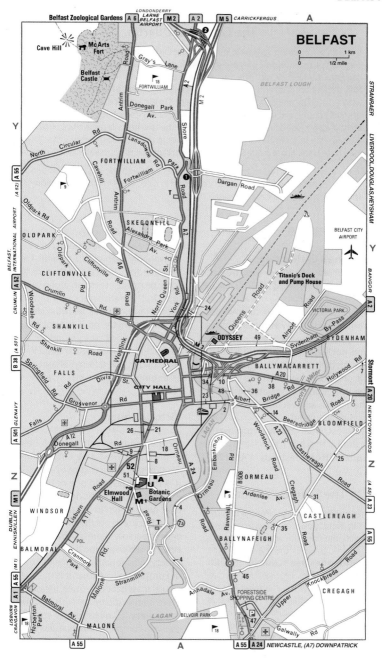

BELFAST

0   1 km
0   1/2 mile

ing food, clothes, books and antiques and on every Friday morning boasts the largest indoor fish market in Ireland with 23 seafood stalls. The Saturday morning Farm & Speciality Food Market offers a wide range of local high quality specialist food products.

▶ *The front entrance of the market is May Street. This leads west (with your back towards the river) back to Donegall Square.*

The Cathedral Quarter

The area surrounding St Anne's, known as The Cathedral Quarter is the city's up and coming cultural hotspot. Bars and pubs include the smart Northern Whig, The Parliament, The John Hewitt, The Spaniard while restaurants include the trail-blazing Nick's Warehouse, recently joined by now joined by Ba Soba Noodle Bar and Opium with its intimate and exotic oriental ambience. On the artistic theme there are a host of small commercial galleries and The Black Box with its experimental theatre. The areas is also a nightclub mecca with arguably the two best places in town, Milk and Kremlin (the latter is one of the top gay venues in the UK). Most recently the 5-star Merchant Hotel has indicated its more mainstream seal of approval to the Quarter.

Each May the Quarter hosts a cutting edge festival, with the emphasis on bringing arts to unorthodox places: poetry readings in cafe;, plays in pubs, exhibitions in shops, a circus on the street.

City Centre

St Anne's Cathedral★

⏲ *Open Mon–Fri 10am–4pm, weekend for services only.* ☏ *028 9032 8332. www. belfastcathedral.org.*

Belfast's Hiberno-Romanesque Anglican Cathedral (1899–1981) by Sir Thomas Drew, suffered many delays in construction, not least because, like much of the city, it is built on waterlogged and unstable ground. It contains a fine Chapel of the Holy Spirit, consecrated in 1932 on the 1500th anniversary of St Patrick's mission to Ireland.

The most remarkable and controversial feature of the church however is its new **Spire of Hope**, installed in April 2007.

The Seamen's Church

From the Lagan Weir, instead of turning right (towards Waterfront Hall), walk the opposite way along the riverbank, towards the ferries, and the **Sinclair Seamen's Church**★ (⏲ *open Wed 2pm–4pm.* ☏ *028 9071 5997)* dating from 1857. The charming interior of this Venetian-style harbourside church was refurbished on a maritime theme. Early 19C shipyard workers, dockers and sailors would have felt at home in its ship-like interior, with its pulpit shaped as a ship's prow, flanked by navigation lights, ship's binnacle font and the bell of *HMS Hood* calling worshippers to service. The imposing Victorian block next door is the Belfast Harbour Commissioners Office.

This relentlessly modern very slender titanium and stainless-steel clad spike, is invariably likened to a gigantic knitting needle. The base section of the spire protrudes through a glass platform in the Cathedral's roof directly above the choir stalls, allowing visitors to view it from the nave. In total it rises 300ft/100m above the ground.

To the side of the cathedral stand three large buoys, taken from Belfast Lough as a reminder of the city's seafaring history.

Victoria Square

Completed in March 2008, this spectacular shopping centre in the heart of the city covers some 800,000 sq ft /75,000 sq m. At a cost of over £400m it is the biggest and one of the most expensive property developments ever undertaken in Northern Ireland. The attraction is not the 100-plus shops and restaurants (there is also a multiplex cinema) which are mostly of the chain variety to be found in any major British or European city. Rather it is the spectacular glass geodesic dome, measuring 115ft/35m in diameter, with its **viewing gallery** (⏲ *admission free but ticket required, from the information desk below the dome; www.victoriasquare.com*), which not only gives a panorama over the city rooftops, but offers vertiginous views down into the complex itself. At night the dome glows blue, a new city landmark. By contrast just outside the complex, on the river side, is the eye-catching bright yellow ornate Victorian **Jaffe Memorial Fountain**.

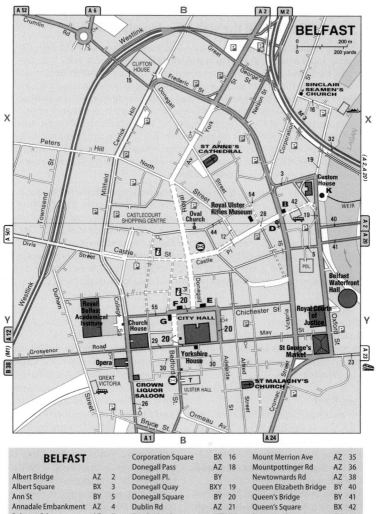

The Laganside★

The River Lagan heads north-south through Belfast with the city centre to the east, and across the water the former docklands area - great swathes of deserted and derelict former industrial land. This now hosts one of the biggest urban renewal projects in Europe, akin to the redevelopment of the London Docklands, albeit on a much smaller scale, and in a few years time

Politics off the wall? The Murals of Belfast

These mean streets were once feared no-go areas for the police and even the army. Today however, in a situation that would have been unthinkable a decade ago, the Shanklin and Falls Road are now prime tourist areas. Visitors flock to see their Murals. These giant works of street art/propaganda vary in subject matter from romanticised portrayals of Irish myths and legends (tailored to a political message) to a rather unflattering representation of the late Queen Mother; a hero-ic representation of IRA hunger-striker and MP, Bobby Sands, to chilling pictures of hooded gunmen. Perhaps the most memorable is the mural, nicknamed with typical Belfast black humour, "The Mona Lisa". It depicts a gunman whose rifle is pointing towards the viewer. No matter where you move to (in view of the gun-man) you are always looking down the barrel.

The Belfast City Sightseeing bus tour takes in both the Shanklin and Fall Road and gives you a good idea of the murals. If you want to learn more take Black Cab Tour (in a London-style taxi cab). These will tell you all about the city and are particu-larly good on the areas once dominated by The Troubles. (☎028 9087 5978, 07765 401 090, Billy Scott). Another option is the **Coiste Political Tours** of Republican West Belfast, accompanied by a guide from the ex-prisoner community (✆tours Mon–Sat 11am, Sun 2pm from Divis Tour £8 ☎028 9020 0770, www.coiste.ie). Do bear in mind however that by their very nature Coiste tours are politically biased.

---

it is envisaged that this new "**Titanic Quarter**" will be home to shop, offices, housing and leisure facilities. With a few exceptions however, it is presently a huge building site.

East Bank

The riverside is approached along the High Street - before it was filled in, huge ships once sailed up here, as far as Bridge Street - and ends at the 113-ft/35-m high **Prince Albert Memorial Clock Tower**.

This was built 1867–79 in honour of Queen Victoria's consort (even though he never visited Belfast) and is famous for its lean - 4ft/1.25m off the vertical, due to the fact that it was built on land reclaimed from the river. Its sinking piles have recently been shored up however.

To the left, approaching the Lagan is the handsome classical **Custom House** (*closed to the public*) on Donegall Quay. This too is Victorian, built 1854–57 by Charles Lanyon, designer of many of Bel-fast's finest buildings. Novelist Anthony Trollope once worked here as a survey-or's clerk. In front of the building stands a statue of an orator, a reminder that in the 19C this large square was a "Speak-er's Corner", a place of free speech where all sorts of debates were held in the open air. The square is empty most days and reserved for festivals.

Across the busy Oxford Street/Donegall Quay road is the riverfront and **Lagan Weir**, marked by **Big Fish** a 32-ft/10-m long blue ceramic-mosaic salmon by John Kindness, one of Northern Ire-land's leading contemporary artists. The "scales" of the fish is a cladding of ceramic tiles decorated with texts and images relating to the history of Belfast. It was commissioned in 1999 to celebrate the regeneration of the River Lagan and, appropriately, the river is now clean enough for salmon to swim in. The adjacent building, formerly the Lagan Lookout Visitor Centre, awaits a new tenant. A few yards to either side of here, river boat trips depart featur-ing Titanic-related sites(☎028 90 330844 www.laganboatcompany.com)

Walk along the river bank and on the junction with the bridge is another striking new modern (large wire) sculp-ture of a ponytailed woman standing on a sphere. Her title is **The Angel of Thanksgiving and Reconciliation**, though locals refer to her as "the doll on the ball."

Beyond is **Belfast Waterfront Hall** (☎ 028 9033 4400, www.waterfront. co.uk), a major concert and arts venue, conference centre and city landmark, opened in 1997 as a flagship of redevelopment. It is well worth a visit, even outside performances, and includes a brasserie, overlooking the water.

Opposite the Hall the massive Portland stone **Royal Courts of Justice** (1929–33) scene of many a serious case in Belfast's recent troubled history strikes a more sombre note.

West Bank (Titanic Quarter)

Towering above the old dockyards the iconic massive yellow gantry cranes of the Harland and Wolff shipyard, "Samson" and "Goliath", both distinctively marked H and W, are visible from many points in the city (tour guides joke that this is for the benefit of visitors and stands for "Hello and Welcome"). Each crane has a span of 460ft/140m and can lift loads of up to 840 tonnes to a height of 230ft/70m, making a combined lifting capacity of over 1,600 tonnes, one of the largest in the world. The dry dock below *is* the largest in the world, measuring 1824 ft/556m by 93m/305ft.

At its peak Harland & Wolff employed 35,000 men in shipbuilding.

Today it employs only around 500 people and no longer build ships. Instead it is involved in overhaul, re-fitting and ship repair, as well as the construction and the repair of offshore equipment such as oil platforms.

Odyssey Complex   Kids

Open W5: year-round Mon–Sat 10am–6pm (during school term Mon–Thu 5pm), Sun noon–6pm. Last admission 1hr before closing. £7, child £5. P (charge). 028 9046 7700. www.theodyssey.co.uk. www.w5online.co.uk. IMAX: 028 9046 7000; www.belfastimax.com.

This huge complex is Belfast's landmark Millennium project. The centrepiece is the **Odyssey Arena** auditorium, capable of housing up to 10,000 spectators who come to see musical superstars and spectacular productions. It is also the home of the very successful Belfast Giants ice hockey team. The complex also houses Ireland's only **IMAX cinema**, showing giant-scale 2-D and 3-D films; and the family-friendly **W5 (**who, what, where, when, why) interactive Discovery Centre. As well as 160 interactive

exhibits, experiments and activities (build a house, dance to music, tug of war challenge, explore space, beat the lie detector, touch the sound wall, use professional microscopes, play invisible instruments, light up lasers, optical illusion, bring robots to life, study nature's shapes produce your own animated film etc…) it hosts regular large-scale exhibitions.

SS Nomadic

Queens Quay. Open daily late May–Sept 10.30am–5.30pm. £5. Mon–Fri in Innovation Centre. no tel number, contact by e-mail via www.nomadicpreservationsociety.co.uk.

The last surviving White Star vessel afloat , the SS Nomadic is a First & Second Class Tender, whose function it was to carry the wealthiest passengers onto RMS Titanic. Launched in 1911. After a long service as a tender, troop carrier and latterly, as a floating restaurant in Paris, she fell derelict and was due to be scrapped in 2006. She received a last-minute reprieve however, is now undergoing restoration and is open to visitors.

Titanic's Dock and Pump House

Guided tours late Mar–Oct Wed, Sat & Sun 2pm. £3.50. Outside of these hours visitors are still welcome to visit to view and walk along the Dry-Dock and view the exterior of the Pump House and HMS Caroline. 028 90737813. www.nisp.co.uk.

Work began in 1904 on the 880ft/268m long dock, whose walls were 18.5ft thick and which had 332 massive keel-blocks of cast iron to support the weight of the great liners it would hold. At the same time a large outfitting wharf was constructed nearby and the surrounding water was dredged to a depth of 32 ft. Despite its size, the dock still had to be extended so its first ship, Olympic, could enter in April 1911.

It was here that the ships' engines, boilers and superstructure would be added and work completed on their luxurious cabins and rooms. In October 1911, Titanic had to be moved from the dock to the wharf to allow repairs to be completed on Olympic, which had been involved in a collision. The delay pushed

Botanic Gardens, Belfast

back the date of Titanic's maiden voyage nearly three weeks. Had she sailed on time, it is very doubtful the world's most famous ship would have encountered the fateful iceberg. For more information on the Titanic's connection with Belfast visit *www.titanicinbelfast.com.*

University District

The area south of the city centre is dominated by Queen's University and the "Golden Mile" lined with busy pubs, bars and all kinds of places to eat, drink and while the night away. In between, clustered around the university are pleasant Georgian and Victorian suburban streets, the Botanic Gardens and the province's most important museum.

Ulster Museum★★

○━*Closed until 2009.* ☎*028 9038 3000. www.ulstermuseum.org.uk.*
The national museum and art gallery of Northern Ireland is housed in a modern building (1972) appended to premises built in 1929 in the Botanic Gardens. The varied collections give an excellent overview of the province, its capital and their place in Ireland.

ⓖ *It is best to take the lift to the fourth floor and descend through the galleries.*

The **Art Galleries** enclose a small collection of pre-1900 British and Continental painting by JMW Turner (1775–1851)

and portraits by Sir Joshua Reynolds (1723–92), George Stubbs (1724–1806) and Pompeo Batoni (1708–87). The two charming views of the Giant's Causeway by Susanna Drury (c 1740) were largely responsible for popularising the extraordinary natural landscape. Works by Irish artists – Hugh Douglas Hamilton (1740–1808), Joseph Peacock (c 1783–1837), Sir John Lavery (1856–1941), Roderic O'Conor (1860–1940), Sir William Orpen (1878–1931), Andrew Nicholl and Richard Dunscombe Parker – or on Irish subjects are periodically presented alongside furniture in the **Irish Gallery**.

The **Craft Galleries** document developments in glass, ceramics (Belleek pottery, silver (17C to 19C), jewellery (16C to 20C), textiles and dress (18C to 20C) that include collections of lace, embroidery and household linen.

A skeleton of the extinct Giant Irish Deer dominates the excellent **Geology of Ireland** gallery dedicated to the Irish Flora and Fauna and Living Sea.

Human activity from the Prehistoric Era to the Middle Ages is traced through artefacts excavated from archaeological sites: the **Shrine of St Patrick's Hand**★, a 14C or 15C silver-gilt hand studded with glass and rock crystal and stamped with animal figures; a Bronze Age cauldron and a pair of horns which still produce a musical note; early Iron Age sword scabbards decorated in the "Celtic" style; an early Christian brooch. Pride of place goes to the **Spanish Armada treasure**★★, excavated from shipwrecks on the Irish coast: cannon and shot, a gold salamander set with rubies, gold chains, rings and crosses and coins.

The **Local History (16C-20C)** galleries have a "Made in Belfast" section devoted to industry in the northeast of Ireland; a section for coins minted up to 1690 and another on the Post Office displaying the portable desk used by **Anthony Trollope** to write his novels.

The **Textile Gallery** explores the process of turning flax into linen, the traditional industry most intimately associated with Ulster.

Botanic Gardens

Open dawn to dusk (Palm House and Ravine house close earlier). in adjacent leisure centre. 028 90320202. www.belfastcity.gov.uk.

At the University Road entrance to the gardens stands a statue of Lord Kelvin (1824–1907), a native of Belfast, who invented the absolute scale of thermodynamics, the Kelvin Scale. The gardens (28 acres/11ha) slope gently to the River Lagan: they were originally laid out for the study of plants by the Botanic and Horticultural Society, but since 1895 they have been a public park.

The beautiful cast-iron and curvilinear glass **Palm House**★, one of the earliest of its type, was designed by Charles Lanyon and completed in 1840. It was constructed by Richard Turner, who later collaborated with Decimus Burton on the construction of the Great Palm House at Kew. The dome was added in 1852.

The **Tropical Ravine House** is an extension of the older Fernery established in 1887 by the curator, Charles McKimm. In 1900 a stove section was added; two years later the lily pond was created over the boiler house.

Queen's University

Queen's College, Belfast, was incorporated in 1845 and established as a university in 1908. The red-brick Tudor-style building by Charles Lanyon is reminiscent of Magdalen College in Oxford.

Elmwood Hall, now an examination hall, is the Italianate building with an arcaded façade in polychromatic freestone which was designed in 1862 by John Corry as a Presbyterian Church.

University Square is an attractive mid-Victorian terrace with fanlights over the front doors and magnolia trees in the gardens – now occupied by the Faculty of Arts.

Excursions

Belfast Zoo ★★ Kids

5mi/8km north of Belfast via the A 6.
Open late Mar–Sept 10am–7pm (last admission 5pm). Oct–late Mar 10am–4pm (last admission 2.30pm). £8.10, child £4.30. 028 9077 6277. www.belfastzoo.co.uk.

Queens University, Belfast

©Robert Mayne/istockphoto.com

The Zoological Gardens, which opened in 1934, are home to more than 1,200 animals and 140 species, the majority of these are critically endangered in the wild. Set in the former Hazlewood Gardens, the zoo eschews cages and enclosures wherever possible instead it surrounds the animals by dry ditches or water-filled moats. There are spacious green areas for the big cats (including white tigers and Barbary Lions), various types of deer (including bongos) and kangaroos. An aquatic complex houses penguins, sea-lions and polar bears. Other visitor favourites include elephants, giraffes and gorillas. A large walk-through **aviary** enables visitors to look for free-flying birds in the trees and the latest attraction is **The Rainforest House** is a walk-through exhibition with tropical landscaping and a constant temperature of 27 degrees.

Belfast Castle

4mi/6.4km N of Belfast by A 6. Turn left into Innisfayle Park to Belfast Castle.
🕐*Open (functions permitting) 9am–10pm (6pm Sun).* ✕. ☎*028 9077. 6925. www.belfastcastle.com.*
In a superb location on the lower slopes of Cave Hill, this great mansion in Scottish Baronial style was built for the Donegall family in 1867–70 by WH Lynn; the external Baroque staircase was added in 1894.
At an elevation of 400ft it offers a tremendous panorama of the city and is a favourite place for weddings.
The **Cave Hill Visitors Centre** is divided into four separate rooms. One room tells the story of people on the hill, from Stone Age up to current times; another looks at the natural setting, views both of and from the hill, geology and wildlife. A compact audio visual room shows an 8 minute presentation entitled 'Watching Over Belfast', the story of Belfast Castle and Cave Hill, while the fourth room has been set up as a 1920s style bedroom where a bride-to-be prepares for her wedding. A collection of photographs illustrates the changing fashions in weddings at the castle since 1940s to the present day.

The castle also features the **Cave Hill Adventurous Playground** (🕐*open year-round Sat–Sun, daily Apr–Sept: see website for times.* 🎫*£1.80. Max age 14)* plus formal gardens and waymarked trails to the **Cave Hill Country Park**.

Cave Hill

4mi/6.4km N of Belfast by A 6.
Accessible on foot from Belfast Castle, the Zoological Gardens and various other points across town.
North of Belfast rears the black basalt cliff with a profile likened to Napoleon, known as Cave Hill (1 182ft/360m), which marks the southern end of the Antrim plateau. The headland, which is separated by a deep ditch from the rest of Cave Hill, is marked by an ancient earthwork, known as **McArts Fort** which has served as a watchtower providing refuge to the native Irish hounded by Vikings and Anglo-Normans. In 1795 Wolfe Tone and his fellow United Irishmen spent two days and nights in the fort planning the independence of Ireland. Fine views extend over Belfast and the lough to County Down and Strangford Lough *(southeast)*, Lough Neagh and the Sperrin Mountains *(west)*.

Stormont

4mi/6.4km east of Belfast via the A 20.
🕐*Grounds: Open dawn to dusk. Members of the public can watch Plenary Sittings from the Public Gallery Mon from noon, Tue from 10.30am.* ☎*028 9052 1362. www.niassembly.gov.uk.*
The Northern Ireland Parliament, a plain white Classical building designed by A Thornley, stands prominently on a hill surrounded by rolling parkland. Parliament met regularly from 1932 until 1972 when direct rule from Westminster was imposed. In 1999 it became the meeting place of the new Northern Ireland Assembly which due to constant political wrangling and disagreement has endured several years of suspension and resumption. However following the historic meeting in 2007 between Dr Ian Paisley (the leader of the DUP) and Gerry Adams (the leader of Sinn Fein) at Stormont, the Northern Ireland Assembly was restored on 8 May 2007. **Stormont Castle** *(right)* accommodates other government offices.

CARRICKFERGUS

POPULATION 22 786

Atop its basalt promontory, the largest and best-preserved Norman castle in Ireland dominates this pleasant seaside town (Carraig Fhearghais) on the north shore of Belfast Lough. A broad promenade runs along the front, between the bathing beach and the Marine Gardens; and a marina packed with yachts and fishing boats now occupies the harbour where, until the development of Belfast, there was a thriving port. The district has nurtured three literary figures: Jonathan Swift wrote his first book at nearby Kilroot, while William Congreve and Louis MacNeice lived in Carrickfergus as children.

- **Information:** Museum and Civic Centre, 11 Antrim Street. ☎028 9335 0350. www.carrickfergus.org. www.causewaycoastand glens.com.
- ▶ **Orient Yourself:** Carrickfergus is 10mi/16km north of Belfast via the A 2.
- **Don't Miss:** The Castle.
- **Also See:** ANTRIM, ANTRIM GLENS, BELFAST.

A Bit of History

The name Carrickfergus (Rock of Fergus), refers to the ruler of the ancient kingdom of Dalriada, Fergus Mór, who was shipwrecked in c 531. The castle was built late in the 12C by the Anglo-Norman, John de Courcy, and completed by Hugh de Lacy c 1240. Its strength and strategic position conveyed the idea that it was the key to Ulster, indeed to Ireland. In 1315 it was captured after a year-long siege by Lord Edward Bruce from Scotland. The English recaptured it and held it for the next 300 years, withstanding many attacks by the local Irish and by invading Scots troops.

In 1688 the castle and the town were held for James II by Lord Iveagh but were captured in 1689 by Schomberg. On 14 June the following year William of Orange landed in Carrickfergus harbour on his way to the Battle of the Boyne.

In February 1760 the town was briefly occupied by a French naval detachment, then in 1778 the American privateer John Paul Jones in his vessel *Ranger* attacked *HMS Drake* in an offshore engagement; Belfast folk, many of whom sympathised with the American Revolution, gathered in boats to watch the spectacle.

Sights

Carrickfergus Castle★★

(HM) ⅊ ⏰ *Open Apr–Sept Mon–Sat 10am–6pm; Sun noon–6pm (2pm Apr–May & Sept); Oct–Mar Mon–Sat 10am–4pm, Sun 2pm–4pm. Last admission 30 minutes before closing.* ✆£3. ☎028 93351273. www.ehsni.gov.uk.

Commanding the seaward approach to Belfast, the great stronghold makes a splendid picture. Initially, it occupied just the tip of the basalt promontory but was extended over the years, protected by the sea on all sides but one.

The once circular **gatehouse towers** built at the same time as the Outer Ward,

Carrickfergus Castle

P Thebault/MICHELIN

405

were cut back some time after the Elizabethan period. The **outer ward** was probably built by Hugh de Lacy between 1228 and 1242, to enclose the whole promontory and make the castle less vulnerable to attack. Originally it probably contained living quarters but these were replaced in the 19C by ordnance stores supporting gun platforms.

The wall enclosing the **middle ward**, now partly reduced to its foundations, was built to improve the castle's defences soon after it had been successfully besieged by King John in 1210.

The castle's nucleus was the **inner ward**, enclosed by a high curtain wall, built by de Courcy between 1180 and 1200. The **keep** provided living quarters. Life in the castle is recreated by a large model at the time of Schomberg's siege (1689), a video *Feasts and Fasts* in the Banqueting Hall, and with period costume on the top floor.

Standing sentinel over the harbour in front of the castle, the bronze statue of **King William III** was commissioned to mark the Tercentenary of the landing of the king. At barely 5ft tall the king strikes a very slight figure though this is believed to be historically accurate.

Carrickfergus Museum

&🕐*Open year-round Mon–Sat 10am–6pm, Sun 1pm–6pm. Oct–Mar closes 5pm.* ☎*028 9335 8049. www.carrickfergus.org.* Carrickfergus claims to be the most archaeologically explored town in Northern Ireland and the finds on display here provide a rich glimpse into life in the town from the Medieval period onwards, using a range of media, including audio-visual presentations and hands-on interactives.

The Gallery features special and touring exhibitions.

St Nicholas' Church★

John de Courcy provided Carrickfergus with a church as well as a castle. Centuries of turbulence left the building in a poor state; in 1614 it was heavily restored. The west tower, initiated in 1778, was completed in 1962 as a memorial to both World Wars. In the north transept is a fine marble and alabaster monument to Sir Arthur Chichester (1563–1625)who as Governor of Carrickfergus played a prominent and particularly ruthless role in the subjugation of Ulster, who fathered the great landowning Donegall dynasty.

Flame! The Gasworks Museum of Ireland

🕐*Call for visiting details.* ☎*028 9336 9575.* This is Ireland's sole surviving coal gasworks and is one of only three left in the British Isles. Opened in 1855, it supplied Carrickfergus with gas until 1965 and was closed in 1987. It is now fully restored. Ascend the working gasholder for panoramic views of the town.

North Gate and Town Walls

Between 1607 and 1610 Carrickfergus was enclosed with defensive walls and ditches by Sir Arthur Chichester, who by this time had been elevated to the rank of Lord Deputy of Ireland. The big arch of the North Gate is still largely 17C despite repairs and alterations; the pedestrian arch and crenellations are 19C. A good stretch of wall survives to the east in Shaftesbury Park.

Excursions

Andrew Jackson Centre

2mi/3.2km N of Carrickfergus via the A 2; turn right onto Donaldsons Avenue. 🕐*Open Apr–Oct Mon–Fri 10am–1pm & 2pm–6pm (4pm Apr–May & Oct). Sun, afternoons only.* ☎*028 933 58049.* The Jackson family emigrated from Carrickfergus in 1765; their son, Andrew, born two years later, went on to become the 7th President of the United States. The Jackson homestead has long since disappeared but close to where it stood, this restored 17C single-storey cottage with its earthen floor preserves the family memory and traces the Ulster-American connection. The adjoining **US Rangers Centre** presents the story of the elite American force, formed in Northern Ireland in June 1942, to spearhead the invasions of the World War II.

Dalway's Bawn

6mi/10km north of Carrickfergus.
By the side of the road south of Bally-carry *(left)* stand the remains of a bawn (a defensive wall surrounding an Irish tower house) and three towers c 1609.

Whitehead

5.5mi/9km north east of Carrickfergus.
This little seaside resort, sheltered between the cliffs of White Head and Black Head has a pebble beach backed by a promenade and two golf courses. The **Railway Preservation Society of Ireland** (☎028 2826 0803, www.rpsi-online.org) has a unique collection of steam locomotives and coaches, and operates steam rail tours to all parts of Ireland during the summer season.

Island Magee

6mi/10km north of Carrickfergus via the A 2.
Although not strictly an island, this peninsula (7mi/11km long) feels quite detached from the mainland. The road *(B 90)* provides fine views across Larne Lough. At the northern end of the peninsula, standing incongruously in the front garden of a private house, is the **Ballylumford Dolmen**⋆, a Neolithic burial monument, consisting of four stones supporting a capstone. From the sandy shores of **Brown's Bay**, you can watch the maritime traffic to and from Larne. Farther south are **The Gobbins**, precipitous cliffs (2mi/3.2km) from which the local inhabitants were flung into the sea in 1641 by the soldiers from the garrison in Carrickfergus.

Glenoe Waterfall

12mi/20km north of Carrickfergus.
The gorge is so deep and so well screened by trees that this well-known waterfall can be heard long before it is seen. The double cascade pours into a deep pool before flowing on under an old stone bridge through the village.

DOWNPATRICK

POPULATION 10 113

Historic Downpatrick (Dún Pádraig) owes the first part of its name to a pre-Christian fort (*dún* in Irish), built on the prominent site now occupied by the cathedral, but the town is famous above all for its associations with the patron saint of Ireland. Traditionally held to be St Patrick's burial place, it developed into an ecclesiastical city with many religious foundations. Despite losing its status as a county town in 1973, Downpatrick is still a busy market centre serving the surrounding agricultural area, which to the south is known as the Lecale Peninsula.

- **Information:** 53a Market Street. ☎028 4461 2233. www.armaghanddown.com.
- ▶ **Orient Yourself:** Downpatrick sits between the Mourne Mountains and Strangford Lough, 23mi/37km south of Belfast via the A 7.
- **Especially for Kids:** Seaforde Gardens and Tropical Butterfly House.
- **Also See:** LISBURN, MOURNE MOUNTAINS, STRANGFORD LOUGH.

A Bit of History

As well as the hill now crowned by the cathedral, Downpatrick boasts a second mound, in fact a great Iron Age earthwork, known as the **Mound of Down**, which rises from the marshy levels north of the town. The tree-covered mound sheltered an urban settlement destroyed by the Norman knight, de Courcy, in 1177 as a first step in his conquest of East Ulster. In the 18C, when Downpatrick was the administrative centre for the whole county, great improvements were made to the physical appearance of the town by the Southwell family, who had acquired the demesne of Down through marriage to Lady Betty Cromwell, the last of the line to whom the land had been granted by James I in 1617. Until modern times Downpatrick was almost entirely surrounded by water and marshy ground, its narrow medieval thoroughfares – English, Irish and Scotch Streets – converging on the town centre where the market house once stood.

Walking Tour

Saint Patrick Centre

&🕙*Open Apr–Sept Mon–Sat 9.30am–6pm (5.30pm Apr–May & Sept), Sun 1pm–6pm (5.30pm Apr–May & Sept); Oct–Mar, Mon–Sat 10am–5pm. Last admission 1hr 30 min before closing.* £4.90. ✗. ☎028 44619000. www.saintpatrickcentre.com.

The story of Ireland's patron saint is told by a series of interactive displays which also features the impact of Irish missionaries in Europe.

Its **Grove Gallery** is a showcase for local, regional and national Irish art sand crafts including paintings, sculpture, print, textiles, ceramics and jewellery.

English Street

The red-brick Venetian Gothic Assembly Rooms (1882) were designed by William Batt of Belfast. The **Customs House** *(no 26)* was built in 1745 by Edward Southwell. The Clergy Widows' Houses *(nos 34–40)* date from 1730 and 1750, but were altered in the early 19C. The low two-storey edifice *(right)*, was originally conceived to hold prisoners, its vaulted cells were converted in 1798 into the **Downe Hunt Rooms:** they house records from 1757. The Courthouse (1834) is the sole section of the new prison complex to survive.

Down County Museum★

&🕙*Open Mon–Fri 10am–5pm, Sat–Sun 1pm–5pm.* ☎*028 4461 5218. www.down countymuseum.com.*

The old Down County prison was built between 1789–96 was where Thomas Russell,. When the prison moved, these premises were taken over by the South Down Militia, then by the army until the mid 20C.

The display in the former **Governor's House** in the centre of the courtyard traces the history of Co Down from 7000 BC and describes the local wildlife.

A **Son et Lumiere show (***shown at regular intervals throughout the year*) dramatises episodes from the history of the gaol and its prisoners.

The show is projected on to the wall of the cell block and features the stories of its most famous prisoners including Thomas Russell, the United Irishman, hanged here in 1803.

The Mall

To avoid the deep dip between the Cathedral and English Street, in 1790. the road was raised some 15ft/5m. Well below road level stands the **Southwell Charity**, a school and almshouses founded in 1733 by Edward Southwell, the Secretary of State for Ireland, who by his marriage in 1703 became Lord of the Manor of Down.

Opposite are the **Judges' Lodgings** *(nos 25 and 27)*, two late Regency houses built soon after 1835.

P Thebault/MICHELIN

St Patrick's Tomb

Down Cathedral★

Open Mon–Sat 9.30am–4.30pm, Sun 2pm–5pm. Donation requested. 028 4461 4922. www.downcathedral.org.

No traces of the monastic complex founded by St Patrick survive, although a round tower stood on the site until 1780. In the 12C, John de Courcy replaced the incumbent Augustinians with a community of Benedictine monks from Chester, rebuilt the abbey church and interred the supposed relics of St Patrick, St Colmcille and St Brigid here, changing the dedication to St Patrick and renaming the town Downpatrick to please the native Irish. This building was destroyed by Edward Bruce in 1316 and its replacement was built by the English in 1538. The present building largely dates from the early 19C, built using the stone on site, and incorporating the chancel of the abbey church. The original dedication to the Holy and Undivided Trinity was restored in 1609 by James I.

Inside, there are various remarkable features: the granite font was once used as a watering trough, two unusual figures in ecclesiastical robes flank the Chapter Room door, the choir screen is unique in Ireland, the splendid Georgian Gothic organ was given by George III. Outside, in the graveyard, south of the cathedral, stood a stone bearing the names of the three saints said to be buried in the same plot; this was replaced in the early 20C by a great slab of granite, simply inscribed with the name Patrick.

Excursions

▶ *From Downpatrick take the minor road east for 2mi/3.2km to Saul.*

St Patrick's Memorial Church

The hilltop site, where St Patrick is said to have made his first Irish convert (*see 'St Patrick's Saul' box*), now accommodates a church, built of Mourne granite in 1932 to commemorate the 1 500th anniversary of St Patrick's landing near Saul, designed in the Celtic Revival style by Henry Seaver of Belfast incorporating a characteristic Irish round tower.

There are few traces of the original medieval abbey, but its graveyards hold two cross-carved stones and two small **mortuary houses**.

St Patrick's Saul

When St Patrick returned to Ireland in 432 to convert the people to Christianity, his ship was carried by the wind and tide into Strangford Lough, and up the River Slaney, now a mere stream, to land near Saul. He converted the local chief, Dichu, who gave him a barn (*sabhal* in Irish, pronounced Saul) to use as a church.

St Patrick grew attached to Saul and returned there to die in 461; some records even state he was buried in Saul, rather than in Downpatrick.

Slieve Patrick

3mi/4.8km east of Downpatrick. 15min there and back on foot to the summit.

A statue of St Patrick was erected on the top of the hill in 1932 to commemorate the 1 500th anniversary of his landing near Saul. The path up to an open-air altar is marked by the Stations of the Cross. From the top there is a fine **view** over the surrounding countryside and the drumlin islands of Strangford Lough.

St Tassach's (Raholp) Church

4mi/6.4km east of Downpatrick.

The ruins of this 10C/11C church stand on the spot where Bishop Tassach is said to have administered the last sacrament to St Patrick.

Struell Wells★

2mi/3.2km south east of Downpatrick.

A popular place of pilgrimage from the 16C until the 1840s, these Wells were once pagan places of worship (streams and springs were important to the Celts)but are now strongly associated with Saint Patrick.

The site, in a secluded rocky hollow by a fast-flowing stream, comprises five buildings: an unfinished 18C church; a circular Drinking Well with a domed roof built on a wicker supporting arch; a rectangular Eye Well with a pyramidal corbelled roof; a Men's Bath-house, with a stone roof and a dressing room with seats next to the bath; and a Women's Bath-house without a roof – its dressing room is in the men's bath-house.

Although the oldest of these buildings dates only from c 1600, there is written reference to a chapel on the site in 1306.

Ardglass★

7mi/11km S of Downpatrick by b1.

Little Ardglass is attractively located in a natural harbour, home to one of the province's fishing fleets. In the 15C it was an Anglo-Norman enclave, the busiest port in Ulster, protected from the native Irish by numerous fortified buildings. The finest of those standing is **Jordan's Castle** *(HM ◷ open Jul–Aug Tue, Fri, Sat, Bank Hols 10am–1pm; Wed–Thu 2pm–6pm; ☎028 905 43034)* an early-15C tower house overlooking the harbour, which, in the Elizabethan era, withstood a three-year siege under its owner, Simon Jordan, until relieved by Mountjoy in June 1601. It was restored in 1911 by FJ Bigger, a solicitor and antiquarian from Belfast, and now houses his collection of antiquities.

Playing Golf in Ardglass

King's Castle and Isabella's Tower are predominantly 19C. A row of fortified warehouses along the harbour front is now the clubhouse of the local golf course.

Killough

7mi/11km S of Downpatrick by b176.
A broad central avenue runs through this peaceful village on the edge of a deep sea-inlet. In the 17C it was known as Port St Anne after Anne Hamilton, whose husband, Michael Ward of Castle Ward, developed the port to facilitate the export of lead and agricultural products from his estates.

St John's Point

10mi/16km S of Downpatrick via the B176, A 2 and a minor road.
The ruins of a 10C/11C pre-Romanesque church mark the site of an early monastery. A lighthouse stands on the southernmost point of the Lecale Peninsula.

Ballynoe Stone Circle

▶ *3mi/5km south of Downpatrick. Park opposite the old railway station (east); 6min there and back on foot by the track (west) between the fields.*

Low close-set stones encircle an oval mound which contained a stone cist at either end in which cremated bones were found (1937–38), probably built by the late-Neolithic Beaker people c 2000 BC.

Clough

6mi/10km south west of Downpatrick via the A 25.
North of the crossroads stands a stone tower (13C with later additions) surmounting an Anglo-Norman earthwork castle, which was once enclosed by a wooden palisade.

Loughinisland Churches

5mi/8km west of Downpatrick via the A 2 and a minor road north.
Three ruined churches stand on what was originally an island overlooking the lake. The middle one is the oldest (13C); the largest is 15C; the third bears the date 1636 over the door, but may be earlier. The initials PMC stand for Phelim MacCartan, whose family owned property in the area and are probably buried here.

Seaforde Gardens and Tropical Butterfly House   Kids

9mi/14.5km west of Downpatrick via the A 25 and A 2 north.
Open Easter–Sept Mon–Sat 10am–5pm, Sun 1pm–6pm. Garden: £3.50, Butterfly House and garden £6. Child £2.30/ £3.50. ☎028 4481 1225. www.seaforde gardens.com.
The gardens are situated in the historic demesne of Seaforde, which has been a family home for almost 400 years.
The old walled garden, dating from the 18C or possibly earlier, has been revived with a large hornbeam **maze** and a **tropical butterfly house**. The Pheasantry is a deep dell planted with great rhododendrons and exotic trees. Across the lawns and parallel with the maze are two avenues of Eucryphias. The garden also holds the National Collection of Eucryphias with over 20 varieties grown here. These white or pink Southern hemisphere trees are one of the glories of the garden in late summer and autumn.

Downpatrick & Country Down Railway

See website for dates and times of operation. ☎077 9080 2049, or 028 4461 5779 (10am–2pm Mon, Wed & Fri only). www.downrail.co.uk.
Steam locomotives from the 1920s and '30s, or diesels from the '60s carry passengers in 50–100 year old carriages from Downpatrick to the tranquil ruins of Inch Abbey approximately 2 mi/3km away.
There are also guided tours of exhibitions and workshop. Real enthusiasts can book a day's experience on the footplate, driving a diesel train, or firing and driving a steam locomotive.

DUNGANNON

POPULATION 9 190

On its hilltop site , Dungannon (Dún Geanainn) was for centuries a main residence of the O'Neill clan, one of the great families of Gaelic Ulster. Nowadays it is the busy hub of a rich dairying and fruit-growing district, and a manufacturing centre of some importance. One of its oldest industries, textiles, has brought international fame to the Moygashel linen company (founded in 1875).

- **Information:** Killymaddy Centre, Ballygawley Road. ☎028 8776 7529. www.dungannon.gov.uk. www.flavouroftyrone.com.
- **Orient Yourself:** Dungannon is 11mi/18km north of Armagh on the A 29.
- **Also See:** ARMAGH, LOUGH NEAGH, SPERRIN MOUNTAINS.

A Bit of History

Plantation Town

Under by the O'Neills, Dungannon was little more than a collection of huts grouped round Castle Hill; but early in the 17C English and Scottish settlers started developing a modern town. A charter was granted in 1612; When the native Irish rebelled in 1641, the settlers' buildings were burned and their farms and orchards destroyed; the population dropped to 130. A new plantation followed the restoration of peace in 1653. After the Battle of the Boyne (1690) Dungannon expanded rapidly; in 1692 the town was purchased by Thomas Knox, whose expansionary regime coincided with the development of the coalfields at Drumglass and the digging of the local canal.

Sights

The Linen Green

🕐 Open year-round Mon–Sat 10am–5pm. ✕. ☎028 8775 3761. www.thelinen green.com.
One of Dungannon's oldest industries is recalled with this designer outlet shopping village built on the site of the former Moygashel linen mill. For non-shopper the Moygashel Linen Visitors' Centre, provides historical interest. Moygashel's history began c. 1795 when Huguenot settlers established the Irish Linen weaving company, weaving some of the finest linens in the world. Their ancestors, the Webb family, came to own the famous Moygashel Weavers.

They were taken over by Ulster Weavers in the late 20C and in 2005 the factory at Moygashel closed.,

Tyrone Crystal

1.5mi/2.5km from Dungannon on the Killybrackey Road (A 45) towards Coalisland. ♿ ☎➤Factory tours (45 mins) Mon–Fri 11am, noon, 2pm (booking requested). Sat: audio-visual tour only, 9am–5pm.☎£5. ☐. ☎028 9772 5335. www.tyronecrystal.com.
Tyrone Crystal opened in 1971, exactly 200 years after an earlier glasshouse had started production on the same premises at Drumreagh, Newmills (north). The nascent enterprise faced closure in the recession of the late 1970s but local financial support was found and the factory moved here in 1990.
The **tour** takes visitors through the various stages of production to the cut and polished product on sale in the shop.

Excursions

Coalisland

4mi/6.4km north east of Dungannon via the A 45.
The landscape around Coalisland is still scarred by the industries which once flourished here. Coal was dug from bellpits as early as the 17C but severe faulting problems led to the closure of the last mine in 1970. The other industries included weaving, milling and a fireclay works; the Coalisland Canal had the first inclined plane to be built in the British Isles.

Fallow deer, Parkanaur Forest Park

NITB, Belfast

Parkanaur Forest Park★

*4mi/6.4km west of Dungannonon
via the A 4.*

The park's herd of **white fallow deer** are direct descendants of a white hart and doe given by Elizabeth I in 1595 to her goddaughter, Elizabeth Norreys, who married Sir John Jephson of Mallow Castle. The former Burgess family estate boasts several unusual specimen trees, notably two parasol beeches with branches like corkscrews. The woodland is being developed as an oak forest; walks and nature trail thread through the formal Victorian Garden, by the stone archway and stone bridge on the Torrent River. The farm buildings (1843) contain a display of forestry machinery.

Donaghmore

5mi/8km N of Dungannon via the B 43.

In the centre of this quiet village stands an ancient sandstone cross (AD c 700–1000), associated with a former abbey, and composed of two different crosses. New and Old Testament scenes ornament the faces.

Castlecaulfield

*5mi/8km NW of Dungannon
via the A 4 and a minor road north.*

The stark ruins are those of a Jacobean **mansion** built (1611–19) by an ancestor of the Earls of Charlemont, Sir Toby Caulfield, who commanded Charlemont Fort and whose arms appear over the gatehouse, an earlier structure defended with murder holes above the main door.

Bloody Battlefields

Two important military engagements involving the O'Neills took place south of Dungannon. At the **Battle of the Yellow Ford** on the River Callan in 1598 Hugh O'Neill defeated the English forces under Sir Henry Bagnall; only about 1 500 Englishmen out of over 4 000 survived.

In 1646 the **Battle of Benburb** at Derrycreevy, the Scottish army of General Monroe was outmaneuvered by Owen Roe O'Neill and 3 000 Scots were killed.

Although burned by the O'Donnells in 1641, the Caulfields continued in residence until the 1660s.

Moy

5.5mi/9km south of Dungannon via theA 29.

This attractive Plantation town was laid out in the 1760s by James Caulfield, Earl of Charlemont, modelled on Marengo in Lombardy, which he had visited while on the Grand Tour. The broad central green was once the site of the great monthly horse fairs which lasted a whole week. From here, the road slopes down to the Blackwater River past the screen and entrance gates to Roxborough Castle (destroyed by fire in 1921), the 19C seat of the Earl of Charlemont. The Blackwater marks the boundary between Armagh and Tyrone, and formed the front line in 1602 between territory held by the rebellious Hugh O'Neill and his English opponents, who fortified it with a great star-shaped stronghold. Most of the fort was burned down in 1922, though the gatehouse still stands at the end of a short avenue of trees.

Benburb

7mi/11km south of Dungannon via the A 29 to Moy and then west on the B 106.

The ruins of **Benburb Castle** *(access on foot from priory grounds or just inside priory entrance)* occupy a dramatic rocky ledge above the River Blackwater, which tumbles through the tree-lined gorge (120ft/37m below). The castle, which was built by Sir Richard Wingfield in 1611, replaces an earlier O'Neill stronghold.

Simpson-Grant Ancestral Home

11mi/18km west of Dungannon via the A 4; before Ballygawley turn left to Dergenagh.

🕐 *Open year-round daily 10am–4pm.* ☎*028 8775 0311.*

This 17C homestead once belonged to John Simpson, maternal great-grandfather of Ulysses S Grant, 18th President of the USA (1869–77), who commanded the Union Army during the American Civil War.

Errigal Keerogue Cross

16mi/25km west of Dungannon via the A 4; 1mi/1.6km west of the Ballygawley roundabout turn right to Errigal Keerogue (sign); at the crossroads in Ballynasaggart continue west; after 2mi/3.2km turn right.

In the graveyard stands a **high cross**. Two yew trees grow in the ruins of the medieval church, thought to be a Franciscan foundation (1489) replacing an earlier monastery associated with St Kieran.

Augher

18mi/29km west of Dungannon via the A 4.

This beautiful stretch of the Blackwater River provides good fishing. On the north side of the lake stands Spur Royal, now a hotel, built on the site of a 1615 stronghold.

Clogher

20mi/32km W of Dungannon by A 4.

Clogher claims to be the oldest bishopric in Ireland, supposedly founded in the 5C by St Macartan or Macartin, a disciple of St Patrick. The present **Cathedral**★ (🕐 *open by appointment;* ☎*028 6634 7879, http://clogher.anglican.org)*, is an austere mid-18C Classical structure with a squat tower, but it preserves some early relics: a 7C **stone cross** *(outer porch)*, thought to be a sundial for timing the services of the Celtic church; the **Golden Stone** *(inner porch)* – a famous oracle in pagan times, known in Irish as **Clogh-Oir**, which may be the origin of the name Clogher.

Knockmany Passage Grave★

21mi/34km west of Dungannon via the A 4 and north on the B 83; 1.5mi/2.4km north of the crossroads turn right onto a track. Car park; 20min there and back on foot.

The cairn on its hilltop site commands a superb view south over Knockmany Forest into the Clogher Valley. In 1959 a concrete bunker and skylight were built to protect it from the weather but the stones of the burial chamber are visible through the grill: the decoration of circles, spirals and zigzags is typical of passage grave art.

ENNISKILLEN

POPULATION 11 436

The principal town of Co Fermanagh (Inis Ceithleann) is a lively commercial and cultural centre, occupying a strategically important island site between Lower and Upper Lough Erne. In the 17C it was one of the main strongholds of the 17C Plantation of Ulster; nowadays it makes an ideal base for exploring Lough Erne, the Shannon–Erne Waterway, the Fermanagh lakes and the Sperrin Mountains. Nearby are two of Ireland's most magnificent country houses, Castle Coole and Florence Court.

- **Information:** Wellington Road. ☎028 6632 3110. www.fermanagh.gov.uk. www.fermanaghlakelands.com.
- ▶ **Orient Yourself:** Enniskillen is situated between Upper and Lower Lough Erne, 50mi/80km west of Dungannon by the A 4 and 12mi/19km from the border.
- **Don't Miss:** Castle Coole, Florence Court , Marble Arch Caves and Lough Erne.
- **Especially for Kids:** Marble Arch Caves.
- **Also See:** CAVAN, DONEGAL, SLIGO, SPERRIN MOUNTAINS.

Walking Tour

In 1688 the **East Bridge** replaced the drawbridge built by the planters on the site of an old ford in 1614. The **Courthouse** *(left)*, with its Classical portico, was radically remodelled in 1821–22 by William Farrell of Dublin. William Scott's **Town Hall** (1898) and splendid clock overlooks The Diamond.

In the **Buttermarket** *(turn right along Church Street)* the 19C courtyard buildings have been converted into a craft and design centre (*see Address Book*). **St Macartin's Anglican Cathedral** was completed in 1842 although the tower is earlier. The French Gothic Revival **St Michael's Roman Catholic Church** (1875) lacks a spire. Down by the **West Bridge** (completed in 1892) are the Old Militia Barracks (1790) and Enniskillen Castle.

Sights

Enniskillen Castle

♿ ⏰*Open Jul–Aug Sat–Mon 2pm–5pm, Tue–Fri 10am–5pm; May–Jun & Sept Mon & Sat 2pm–5pm, Tue–Fri 10am–5pm; Oct–Apr Mon 2pm–5pm, Tue–Fri 10am–5pm. Bank Hols 10am–5pm.* ⊜£2.95. ☎028 6632 5000. www.enniskillencastle.co.uk. Until the 18C Enniskillen castle was surrounded by water from the Erne. Built in

the 15C as a stronghold for the powerful Maguire family (then rulers of Fermanagh) the castle defended the strategic route between Ulster and Connaught across the formidable Erne. In 1607 it was granted to the planter Captain William Cole, whose family later moved to nearby Florence Court. Cole laid out the town and made good damage to the castle; Enniskillen held out against the native Irish uprising in 1641 and against Jacobite attacks in 1689.

The castle exhibitions unravel the history of the region.

This historic site houses two museums, **Fermanagh County Museum** and

The Cole Family

The Coles came to Ireland from Devonshire in the reign of Elizabeth I. They lived first at Enniskillen Castle and then at Portora Castle.

Sir John Cole (1680–1726) settled at Florence Court, named after his wife, Florence Wrey, a wealthy heiress from Cornwall. Their son, John Cole (1709–67), made Lord Mount Florence in 1760, built the present central block; the wings were added by his son, William Willoughby Cole (1736–1803), later Viscount and Earl of Enniskillen, who went on the Grand Tour in 1756–57.

The Corrys of Coole

John Corry, a Belfast merchant, originally from Dumfriesshire, purchased the manor of Coole in 1656 and in 1709 built a new house near the lake incorporating parts of an early-17C castle. In 1741 the estate passed to Armar Lowry-Corry, created 1st Earl of Belmore in 1797, who commissioned Wyatt to design the present house; his son, the 2nd Earl of Belmore, was responsible for the interior decoration and the Regency furnishings.

Regimental Museum of the Royal Inniskilling Fusiliers, the prestigious regiment formed in the late 17C. However the latter is housed in the Keep which is closed for most of 2008 while undergoing a major refurbishment.

The Fermanagh Museum has displays on the history, landscapes and wildlife of the county, while the keep, which incorporates parts of the original 15C fortress, deals with the evolution of the castle and the fortunes of the Maguires.

The **Curved Range** displays information about the ancient monuments and castles of Fermanagh, and the pilgrim's trail to Devenish Island.

Forthill Park

🕒Cole's Monument open Apr–Sept 1.30pm–3pm. 🖼 £1.

Enniskillen's town park is named after the star-shaped fort built here in 1689 during the Williamite Wars. It has a delightful oriental-looking cast-iron Victorian **bandstand**. The centre of the fort is now occupied by **Cole's Monument**, erected between 1845–57, in memory of General the Hon Sir Galbraith Lowry Cole (1772–1842), brother of the 2nd Earl

The 1987 Bombing

For many outsiders the name Enniskillen still conjures up the dreadful memory of Remembrance Day 1987 when an IRA bomb killed 11 people and injured 61 others as they gathered to commemorate the dead of the two world wars.

of Enniskillen of Florence Court, and a close friend of the Duke of Wellington. Within the fluted Doric column a spiral stair (180 steps) climbs to a platform providing great **views** of the area.

Excursions

Castle Coole★★★

(NT) SE of the town centre by A 4.
♿🕒Grounds: open 10am–8pm (4pm Nov–Mar). 👣House open by guided tour only, Sat–Mon around 17 Mar 1pm–6pm; Easter Weekend–Mar daily 1pm–6pm; Jul–Aug daily noon–6pm; Jun Fri–Wed 1pm–6pm; Apr–May & Sept Sat–Sun only 1pm–6pm; All hols 1pm–6pm. 🖼£5. 🍴.🅿(charge). ☎028 6632 2690. www.nationaltrust.org.uk.

Among great oaks and beeches and overlooking its lake, this superb neo-Classical house is perhaps the finest building of its kind in the whole country. It was completed to designs by James Wyatt in 1798 for the **Corry** family, Earls of Belmore, who lived here until the house passed into the hands of the National Trust in 1951. Built, decorated and furnished without apparent regard to expense, it has been comprehensively restored to something like its original glory.

The **exterior** consists of a central block containing the formal rooms, flanked by single storey colonnaded wings with the family accommodation. The pale Portland stone which lends the facade its particular distinction was imported from the far-off Dorset quarry via Ballyshannon, where a special quay had to be built. So as not to interfere with the harmony of the composition, the stable yards added in 1817 by Richard Morrison were built out of sight below the level of the house and linked by tunnel. Lord Belmore's coach, built in 1863 was used until the 1940s to fetch guests from the station.

The spacious feel and sense of proportion in the **entrance hall** are repeated throughout the house. **James Wyatt**'s scheme of decoration and furnishings is best seen in the **library** and in the **dining room**, where little has changed since Wyatt's day. The **oval Saloon**, the most important room in the house, is

State Bedroom, Castle Coole

decorated with elaborate plasterwork; the curved mahogany doors veneered with satinwood, are hung on pivots. Wyatt specified the ceramic stoves which have the same decorative motif as the friezes.

Between 1807 and 1825 some interiors were refurbished by Preston, one of the leading upholsterers of the period; his more flamboyant style is evident in the colours of the hall, staircase and first-floor landing; the hangings and furniture in the drawing room and the saloon and the **Bow Room**. The gold and scarlet decoration and furnishing of the **State Bedroom** were in anticipation of George IV's visit to Ireland in 1821.

Florence Court★★

8mi/13km S of Enniskillen by A 4, A 32 and W by a minor road. (NT) ◐Grounds: open 10am–8pm (4pm Nov–Mar). ☛House open by guided tour only, Sat–Mon around 17 Mar 1pm–6pm; Easter Week-end–Mar daily 1pm–6pm; Jul–Aug daily noon–6pm; Jun Wed–Mon 1pm–6pm; Apr–May & Sept Sat–Sun only, 1pm–6pm; all hols 1pm–6pm. ⊚£5. ⊡ P. £3.50. ☎028 6634 8249. www.nationaltrust.org.uk.

County Fermanagh's second great country house stands surrounded by parkland at the foot of Cuilcagh Mountain. Faced in attractive greyish-gold stone, the original three-storey house, probably designed in the 1740s, is flanked by seven-arched colonnades and canted pavilions, which were probably designed in the 1770s by Davis Ducart, a Sardinian,

who spent most of his working life in Ireland. The property was transferred, largely unaltered, to the National Trust in 1955.

The interior is charmingly decorated with family portraits, photographs, drawings and other memorabilia, but the glory of Florence Court is the exuberant **Rococo plasterwork**, some of it restored after a fire in 1956.

The **Pleasure Grounds** were mostly planted by the 3rd Earl early in the 19C. The walled garden retains some of its original features, although lawn now replaces the vegetable plots.

Since 1975, the estate grounds have been developed as **Florence Court Forest Park**. In the woodlands southeast of the house stands the famous **Florence Court Yew**, also known as the Irish Yew, a columnar-shaped freak, which can be reproduced only by cuttings as seedlings revert to the common type. There are several trails signposted with coloured indicators; the most challenging extends to moorland *(9hr there and back on foot)* and the top of Cuilcagh Mountain (2 198ft/670m).

Marble Arch Caves European GeoPark★★ 🅺🅸🅳🅢

11mi/18km south of Enniskillen via the A 4, A 32 and west by a minor road. ☛Open by guided tour only (75 mins, comfortable shoes and sweater recommended): mid-Mar–Sept 10am–4.30pm (5pm Jul–Aug); booking recommended in high season. ◐Closed after heavy rain. ⊚£8, child £5.

P Thebault/MICHELIN

Lough Erne

🍵. ☎028 6634 8855. www.marblearch caves.net.

This spectacular cave system was formed in a bed of Dartry limestone by three streams on the northern slopes of Cuilcagh Mountain, converging underground to form the Cladagh River which emerges at the Marble Arch and flows into Lough Macnean Lower.

The **reception centre** presents an exhibition on caving and a video *(20min)*, covering the same ground as the tour. The **cave tour** includes a short boat trip on an underground lake into a fantastic subterranean decor of stalactites, stalagmites, columns, flow stones, cascades, draperies and curtains, with picturesque names such as the Porridge Pot, Streaky Bacon, Cauliflowers, Tusks and Organ Pipes. The longest stalactite (7ft/2m) is named after Edouard Martel, a famous French cave scientist who explored the caves in 1895.

The **nature reserve** consists of the wooded Cladagh gorge created by the collapse of caves eroded by the river.

Portora Royal School

This famous school was founded in 1608 by James I at Lisnakea *(south)*. In 1643 it moved to Enniskillen and in 1777 to a site near **Portora Castle** (17C), which was partially destroyed by an explosion caused by schoolboys in 1859. Among its pupils were Oscar Wilde and Samuel Beckett.

A path *(1hr there and back on foot)* along the east bank links the **Marble Arch** and the **Cascades**, where more water gushes forth.

Lough Erne★★

Wet and wooded, the Fermanagh Lakeland was once the remotest part of a remote province, described by an early 16C traveller as "full of robbers, woods, lakes and marshes". Nowadays it is more accessible, much frequented by fishermen and increasingly popular for water-based activities, though its vast extent is such that it rarely feels crowded. Fed by the River Erne (50mi/80km long), Lough Erne is divided into two by the narrows around Enniskillen; the Upper Lough is a watery labyrinth of islands and twisting channels, while the glorious expanse of Lower Lough Erne has a more orderly assemblage of islands and a greater share of attractions exploiting its maximum width of 5mi/8km.

Lower Lough Erne
Round tour of 66mi/106km – 1 day.

▷ *From Enniskillen take the A 32 north; after 3mi/5km turn left to Trory Point.*

Devenish Island★
Access by ferry (🚗 see Address Book).
Devenish was chosen as the site for a monastery in the 6C by St Molaise. Dev-

Address Book

For coin ranges, see the cover flap.

GETTING AROUND

Devenish Island Ferry – *Operates Apr - Sept at 10am, 1pm, 3pm, 5pm. Check with TIC for other times.* www.ehsni.gov.uk

SIGHTSEEING

Lough Erne Cruises – there are sveral operators offering cruises on the lough and inland waterways: visit *www.ferm anaghlakelands.com (click on cruising).*
Upper Lough Erne Cruises *(1hr 30min)* depart from the Share Centre in Lisnakea *(east shore of Upper Lough Erne).*
The principal marinas are on Lower Lough Erne at **Kesh** *(east shore)* and on Upper Lough Erne at **Bellaneck** *(west shore)* and **Carrybridge** *(east shore).*

WHERE TO STAY

Cedars –*Irvinestown – 10mi/16km N of Enniskillen. 10rm.* ☎*028 686 21493. www.cedarguesthouse.com.* Situated beside Castle Archdale, amid beautiful Fermanagh countryside, this converted period-styled 19C rectory offers a good choice of cheery individual rooms and an attractive bar and bistro.

WHERE TO EAT

Ferndale Country House Restaurant – *139 Irvinestown Road, Cross, Ferndale. 2.5mi north via the A 32.* ☎*028 6632 8374.* Sophisticated country house restaurant where the chef owner combines robust Irish cooking with subtle modern influences picked up from his Antipodean travels.

MacNean House & Restaurant –*Blacklion, Co Cavan.* ☎*071 985 3022. www.macneanrestaurant.com.*

The proprietors took inspiration from extensive travel and research in London, Paris, Australia, New Zealand and Thailand and the menu reflects advocacy of local and artisan producers and seasonal and traceable produce.

SHOPPING

Buttermarket Craft & Design Courtyard. *www.thebuttermarket.com.*
Belleek Pottery – *See Lower Lough Erne Driving Tour.*
Sheelin Irish Lace Museum & Shop – Bellanaleck. All shop items are handmade antique lace. *Museum open Apr–Oct 10am–1pm & 2pm–6pm.* £3. ☎*028 6634 8052. www.irishlacemuseum.com.*

SPORTS AND LEISURE

Fermanagh Lakeland Tourism – provide information on all amenities – boat hire, boat charters, fishing facili- ties and angling licences. ☎*028 6632 3110. www.fermanaghlakelands.com*
Melvin Angling Centre – ☎*028 686 58194.*
Belleek Angling Centre – ☎*028 686 58181.*
Lakeland Canoe Centre, Castle Island, Enniskillen – ☎*028 6632 4250.*
Lakeland Forum – Sports and leisure centre. *www.fermanagh.gov.uk.*
Share Village – the largest outdoor activity centre in Ireland, particularly good for disabled visitors: canoeing, yaghting, archery etc. *www.sharevillage.org.*

EVENTS AND FESTIVALS

Lady of the Lake Festival in Irvines- town in mid-July: drama, childrens' entertainment, fishing competition.

astated by the Vikings, frequently caught up in local feuds, and burnt down in the 12C, it nevertheless survived until early in the 17C. The picturesque remains enjoy a lovely lakeside setting; while a **visitor centre** (*open Apr–Sept 10am– 5pm; £3 including boat crossing; ☎028 68621588; www.ehsni.gov.uk*) traces the history of the monastery.

Nearest to the jetty are the ruins of the **Lower Church** (Teampull Mór), begun in the early 13C and later extended. The mortuary chapel to the south was built for the Maguire family. The smallest and oldest building, **St Molaise's House**, dates from the 12C although it is based on an earlier wooden church.

Devenish Island

St Mary's Priory dates from the 15C although the tower is later. A most unusual 15C **high cross** stands in the graveyard.

▶ *Continue north on the B 82, along the east shore of the lake.*

Castle Archdale Country Park★

🕙*Park: open year-round daily 8.30am–dusk. Museum and Countryside Centre: Jul–Aug & May Bank Holidays daily 10am–6pm; Easter–Jun & Sept Sat–Sun only, 10am–6pm. ☎028 6862 1588. www. ehsni.gov.uk/Archdale.*

The fortified residence built in the early 17C by the Archdales, an English planter family from East Anglia, has long since been abandoned, but their fine arboretum, 19C pleasure grounds, a cold bath and sweat house, and an old walled garden live on.

The former outbuildings house a Countryside Centre with a display of agricultural implements. A caravan park occupies the site of the Second World War base used by the British and Canadian flying boats which patrolled the North Atlantic sea lanes, overflying neutral Ireland on the way.

The park has extensive and wonderfully diverse woodlands harbouring a variety of wildlife, while the ruins of **Old Castle Archdale** near the northeast entrance include the original gateway of the bawn.

White Island★

🕙*Open Jul–Aug daily 10am–5pm; Jun, Sept, Sat–Sun & Bank Hols only, 10am–5pm. ☜£3. ☎028 6862 1892.*

Within a large pre-Norman monastic enclosure stand the remains of a 12C church with a handsome Romanesque doorway. Speculation continues to surround the eight 9C/10C **stone figures** set against the north wall: while definitely Christian, they have something of the pagan about them and include a particularly lewd example of a *sheilagh-na-gig* (female grotesque displaying its genitals).

Belleek Parian Ware

The pottery was founded in 1857 by John Caldwell Bloomfield, shortly after he inherited Castle Caldwell and felt the need for more income. Being a keen amateur mineralogist, he discovered all the ingredients to make pottery – feldspar, kaolin, flint, clay, shale, peat and water power were available on the estate. At first only earthenware was produced; Parian ware was refined over 10 years and won a Gold Medal in Dublin in 1865.

▶ *Continue north by the scenic route; north of Kesh bear left onto the A 47. Near the western end of* **Boa Island** *park beside the road and follow sign to cemetery (about 550yd/500m there and back on foot).*

Janus Figure★

In an overgrown graveyard, sits this squat and ancient stone figure with two faces, staring eyes and crossed arms, possibly from the Iron Age.

▶ *Continue west on the A 47.*

Castle Caldwell Forest Park

An important bird sanctuary, the forest covers two long fingers of land at the western end of Lough Erne The ruined planter's castle (1612) was once owned by the Caldwells. In 1770, family members were being entertained aboard a boat by a fiddler whose inebriated state caused him to fall overboard and drown. He is commemorated by the **Fiddler's Stone** at the park entrance.

▶ *Continue west on the A 47.*

Belleek Pottery

🕐*Open Visitor Centre: Jan–Feb Mon–Fri 9am–5.30pm; Mar–Jun Mon–Fri 9am–6pm, Sat 10am–6pm, Sun 2pm–6pm; Jul–Oct Mon–Fri 9am–6pm, Sat 10am–6pm, Sun noon–6pm; Nov–Dec Mon–Fri 9am–5.30pm, Sat 10am–5.30pm. ⚐Pottery tours: (30min) every 30min, Mon–Fri 9.30am–12.15pm, 1.45pm–4pm (last tour Fri 3pm). 🕐Closed 21/22 Dec–3 Jan, 17 Mar, no tours on Bank Hols. ⚐£4. ✕. ☎028 6865 9300. www.belleek.ie.*

The village stands at the point where the waters of the Erne flow swiftly westward in a narrow channel to enter the sea in Donegal Bay.

The **Belleek Pottery**, and its distinctive Parian ware, has an international reputation. The **Guided Pottery Tour** begins where the slip is moulded and trimmed and continues through the stages to completion and sale in the Visitor Centre.

The Erne Gateway Centre exhibition **ExplorErne** (🕐 *open Mar–Nov daily 10.30am–6pm; ☕; ☎028 6865 8866)*

Janus Figure, Boa Island

B. Kaufmann/MICHELIN

introduces visitors to the history, landscapes and ecology of the Lough, from legendary beginnings to the harnessing of its waters to generate hydroelectric power.

▶ *Leave Belleek eastbound on the A 46. After 10mi/16km turn left.*

Tully Castle★

(HM)

🕐*Open Easter–Sept daily 10am–6pm. ☎028 6862 1588. www.ehsni.gov.uk.*

The ruins of a fortified planter's house, built in 1613 by Sir John Hume from Berwickshire were left when the castle was captured and abandoned in the rising of 1641. The partially paved bawn is protected by walls and corner towers with musket loops; the rest has been transformed into a 17C-style garden. The three-storey house has a vaulted room on the ground floor containing the kitchen fireplace, an unusually large staircase leading to a reception room on the first floor and a turret stair to the floor above. An abandoned farmhouse, a short stroll from the Castle, has been restored as a Visitor Centre.

▶ *Return to the A 46, immediately turn right onto the B81 and then second right to the Lough Navar Scenic Drive. After 3mi/5km turn right opposite Correl Glen.*

GIANT'S CAUSEWAY★★★

Perhaps the strangest but also the most spectacular of Ireland's scenic attractions, the 40 000 basalt columns of the Giant's Causeway have inspired legend, intense scientific debate and endless wonder. Today the Causeway is a World Heritage Site, the annual destination of hundreds of thousands of visitors. It is the focal point, but by no means the only attraction, of the "Causeway Coast" which stretches eastward from the resort of Portrush.

- **Information:** Causeway Visitor Centre, 44 Causeway Rd, Bushmills. ☎028 2073 1852. www.giantscausewaycentre.com. www.causewaycoastandglens.com.
- ▶ **Orient Yourself:** The Giant's Causeway is on the coast road, A 2, between Portrush and Ballycastle on the north Antrim coast.
- ⏲ **Also See:** ANTRIM, GLENS OF ANTRIM, LOUGH NEAGH, PORTRUSH.

A Bit of History

The Giant's Causeway is the most dramatic geological feature along this coastline. It is the result of a great volcanic eruption some 60 million years ago that impacted on this part of northeast Ireland, western Scotland (producing Fingal's Cave), the Faroe Islands, Iceland and Greenland, when lava exuded through cracks in the chalk mantle, solidifying into layers of hard basalt. The distinctive mass of geometric forms caused during cooling has created a variety of polygonal (four-, five-, six-, seven-, eight- and even nine-sided) columns.

The Causeway was first publicised in 1693 by the Royal Society; then, in the mid 18C, the Dublin artist Susanna Drury painted a pair of topographical views (now in the Ulster Museum) provoking great speculation among geologists.

Legends relating to the Causeway describe it as the work of giants, often in the form of the Ulster warrior Finn McCool. One story relates how he fell in love with a Scottish giantess and constructed a land-bridge to reach her. In another he builds the causeway to fight with another giant from over the water, the fierce Benandonner. However Finn flees when he discovers that his rival is bigger than him, dresses as a baby in the cot and waits. When Benandonner arrives to fight, he

finds only Finn's wife and "baby". Seeing the size of the "baby" Benandonner panics at how big the adult Finn really must be, and races back to Scotland, tearing up the causeway behind him!

Walking Tours

①Giant's Causeway★★★

(NT) ⏲ ⏲*Causeway: open daily. Shuttlebus.* ⟜ *£1 each way. Visitor Centre year-*

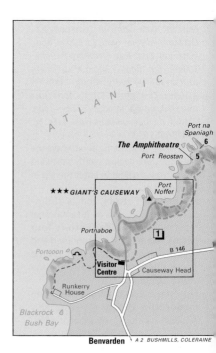

Address Book

ACCESS AND CLIFF WALKS

From the Visitor Centre to the Causeway takes 10min on foot: in summer there is a shuttle bus service.

Observe the warning signs: freak waves can break over the rocks.

To view the Causeway from above, walk through the Giant's Gate into Port Noffer and climb up the Shepherd's Path (1hr – 2mi/3km) and continue along the top to the Visitor Centre. Alternatively, from Port Noffer, go up the path (steep steps) to Benbane Head and walk back along the cliff top path (5mi/8km – 2hr). If you have time, it is worth continuing east along the cliffs (2hr) to Dunseverick Castle (B 146). *Proper walking shoes are recommended.*

---

round daily from 10am (closing times vary according to season). 👁 £1. ☕. 🅿 *(£5)*. Before you begin exploring the site see the video and exhibition in the Visitor Centre. The Causeway proper extends from the foot of the cliffs into the sea like a sloping pavement, divided into sections by the sea: the Little Causeway, the Middle Causeway and the Grand Causeway. The columns themselves are split horizontally, forming concave and convex surfaces. Certain features have acquired fanciful references: the **Wishing Well** is a natural freshwater spring in the Little Causeway, and the **Giant's Gate** carries the coastal path through the **Tilted Columns**. East across Port Noffer the columns (40ft/12m) of the **Organ** are visible in the cliff face.

Causeway Coast Way ②

The headland known as Aird Snout gives a bird's-eye view of the Causeway, while from Weir's Snout to the west, there is a view across Port Ganny *(east)* to the Causeway and down into Portnaboe *(west)* where a volcanic dyke, known as the Camel's Back, is visible.

It is well worth escaping the crowds by walking to the headland. After Port Noffer comes Port Reostan, where the curved columns of the **Harp** are set in a natural **amphitheatre**. The next headland has the **Chimney Tops**, three

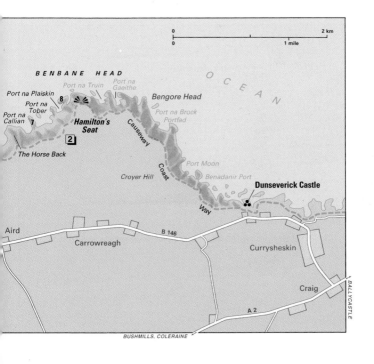

The Giant's Causeway

NITB, Belfast

rock stacks formed by the second lava flow. The path enters Port Na Spaniagh where the *Gerona*, part of the Spanish Armada, was wrecked in 1588 with no survivors. Beyond the next headland, the Horse Back, lies Port na Callian; the farther promontory is the **King and his Nobles**, its figures apparently riding in from the sea. After skirting two bays, the path climbs up past the **Horseshoe** *(left)* to Benbane Head and **Hamilton's Seat**. The spectacular **view**★★ extends over the rocks to the mountains of Donegal, Rathlin Island and Mull of Kintyre.

Excursion

Dunseverick Castle

Accessible by B 146 from Bushmills; on foot by narrow cliff top path from the Visitor Centre at Causeway Head (5mi/8km).
On their craggy promontory, separated from the mainland by two defiles, the scanty ruins of Dunseverick recall the ancient kingdom of Dalriada which included Antrim and Argyll in Scotland. This was a strategic spot on the road from the Hill of Tara to the sea, and lands beyond.

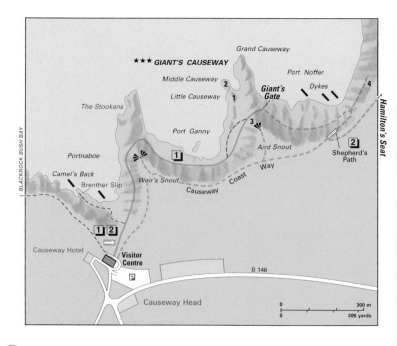

LISBURN

POPULATION 42 110

Lisburn (Lios Na Gcearrbhach) is a sizeable industrial and commercial town, now conjoined with Belfast's southwestern urban sprawl. It stands on the River Lagan at the very heart of Ulster's linen-manufacturing district, and in the 19C produced half the linen woven in the province. The Huguenot Louis Crommelin made Lisburn his headquarters when he was appointed Linen Overseer of Ireland by William III. In 1707 most of the town was destroyed by fire, save for the Assembly Rooms at the top of the market square.

- 🗊 **Information:** 15 Lisburn Square. ☎028 9266 0038. The Square, Hillsborough ☎028 9268 9717. www.visitlisburn.com.
- ▶ **Orient Yourself:** Lisburn is 8 mi/13km south west of Belfast on the A3 Armagh Road.
- ⏱ **Also See:** BELFAST, NEWRY, DOWNPATRICK, STRANGFORD LOUGH.

Sights

Irish Linen Centre and Lisburn Museum★

♿⏱*Open Mon–Sat 9.30am–5pm.* 🗩; 🍴. ☎028 92663377. www.lisburn city.gov.uk.

Lisburn's Market House now displays exhibitions about the local linen industry, past and present. In the Middle Ages Irish flax was exported to England to be woven; in the 17C English and Scottish weavers helped establish looms in Ireland, largely under the direction of Crommelin, whose portrait hangs in the main hall. There are live demonstrations of spinning and weaving, a re-creation of a family at work in a late-18C–early-19C spinner's cottage, and a vivid reconstruction of the weavers' toil in "Webster's," a hypothetical 19C mill, where conditions were tough.

Christchurch Cathedral

The cathedral is a fine example of the Gothic style adopted by the Planters (1623, reconstructed in 1708); in the graveyard *(south side)* is the Crommelin tomb.

Lisburn Castle Gardens

⏱*Open year-round daily 8am–8pm.* 🍴*Meet at Lisburn Musem (1hr).*

North of the cathedral is the Castle Gardens, recently restored, enclosed within the surviving walls of the 17C castle.

Old Cannon in Liburn Castle Gardens

©Robert Mayne/iStockphoto.com

Walled Garden, Rowallane Gardens

Excursions

Hillsborough★

2.5mi/5km S of Lisburn by minor roads.
This charming little town acquired its
Georgian aspect under Wills Hill (1718–
92), Marquess of Downshire (from 1789).
Hillsborough is famous locally for its
September Oyster Festival,

Hillsborough Castle

*Open by guided tour only, May–
Jun, Sat every half hour 10.30am–4pm.
£5. ☎028 9268 1309. www.nio.gov.uk.*
This neo-Classical red-brick building
with a magnificent 18C wrought-iron
screen was the former residence of the
Governor of Northern Ireland. Since 1972
it has been the official residence of the
Secretary of State and is used for state
functions, most importantly, for discus-
sions on the Anglo-Irish Agreement.

Hillsborough Courthouse

*Open Mon–Sat 10am–7pm, Sun 2pm–
7pm (closes 4pm daily Oct–Mar). ☎028
9023 5000. www.ehsni.gov.uk.*
The 18C Courthouse houses the tourist
office and temporary exhibitions. A fixed

exhibition shows courtroom proceed-
ings through the ages.

Hillsborough Fort★ *(same hours)* was
built c 1630 to command the chief roads
in Co Down, on instructions from Col
Arthur Hill, who gave his name to the
town. The fort is laid out as a square
(270ft/82m x 270ft/82m) with a spear-
shaped bastion at each corner to provide flanking fire from heavy cannon.
Wills Hill later added the delightful
gazebo over the northeast entrance and
miniature Gothic fort in the northwest
rampart.
The central ditch is part of a circular
trench revealed by excavations (1966–
69) that prove the site was occupied
from c 500–1000.
St Malachy's Anglican Church (1662)
was endowed with its towers and spire,
Irish oak furnishings and box pews by
Wills Hill in 1760–73.

Rowallane Gardens★

*10mi/16km east of Hillsborough: B 178 to
Carryduff, B 6 to Saintfield, then A 7 S. (NT).
Open year-round daily 10am–8pm
(4pm mid-Sept–mid-Apr). £4.36. ☎028
97510131. www.nationaltrust.org.uk.*

Sir Richard Wallace

From 1873 to 1885 the MP for Lisburn was Sir Richard Wallace, owner of the Wallace Collection in London, whose mansion, built in imitation of Hertford House in
London, stands opposite the entrance to the Castle Park.

The gardens (52 acres/21ha) are renowned for their azaleas and rhododendrons and were planted by Hugh Armitage Moore, who inherited the estate in 1903. Over the years, he turned the drumlins with their light acid soil into a series of natural gardens, seeding wild flowers to attract butterflies. The pleasure grounds behind the house (National Trust headquarters) extend in a great grass sweep to a small pond.

Driving Tour

Lagan Valley
9mi/14.5km – half a day.

The River Lagan meanders between Lisburn and Belfast, through highly fertile country, before discharging into Belfast Lough. A succession of woods and landscaped estates now form the magnificent **Regional Park**. The **Lagan Canal**, was built to bring coal from Coalisland via Lough Neagh to Belfast and under the Lagan Navigation Company, founded in 1843, it became Ulster's most successful waterway; it declined in the 1930s and was closed in 1958.

▶ *From Lisburn take the A 1 north; in Hilden turn right (signposted).*

Hilden Brewery Visitor Centre
⊙*Open Tue–Sat 10am–5pm.* ⌇*Guided tours (40min): 11.30am, 2.30pm.* ⊛*£4.50.* ✕*.* ☎*028 9266 3863. www.hildenbrewery. co.uk.*
The brewery is Ireland's oldest independent brewery and one of only two real-ale brewers in Ireland. It occupies a Georgian house once visited by William Wordsworth. An exhibition in the restaurant covers the history of beer, Hilden Village and the brewery building.

▶ *Continue N on A 1; right under the railway bridge onto B 103 to Lambeg.*

Lambeg
This attractive village, with a delightful suspension bridge, has given its name to the huge painted drums, introduced to Ireland from the Netherlands by

William III's army, which are played on the Orange Day parades.

▶ *Continue on the B 103 to Drumbeg.*

Drumbeg Church
Picturesque little Drumbeg has a church on a knoll, reached via a magnificent lych gate and path shaded by yews. The present cruciform church (1870) with a shallow apsidal chancel has an interesting wooden roof.

▶ *Continue north on the B 103.*

Dixon Park
These famous rose trial grounds (11 acres/ 4ha) contain some 30 000 roses set in a park with woods, meadows and a tranquil Japanese garden. The final judging of the trial roses takes place during **Belfast Rose Week** (mid July).

▶ *Continue north on the B 103. At the roundabout turn right onto the dual carriageway and right again.*

Malone House
♿⊙*Open year-round daily 9am–5pm (–11 Sun).* ☎*028 9068 1246. www.malone house.co.uk.*
In 1603 James I granted the Barnett demesne to Sir Arthur Chichester, whose descendants became the Earls of Donegall, one of the country's great landed families which once owned Belfast itself. Since Sir Arthur's day, three houses have occupied the hilltop overlooking the Lagan crossing: the present one was probably designed by William Wallace Legge, who later bought the lease of the whole demesne. It is now owned by the City of Belfast, and used for meetings, conferences and lectures.

Spanning the Ladan is the **Shaw's Bridge** (1711), which replaced an oak bridge built by Captain Shaw in 1655 to enable Cromwell's cannon to cross the river.

▶ *On leaving the park turn right; after crossing the bridge turn right; take the road along the south bank to Edenderry (signposted).*

Edenderry

Five terraces of red-brick cottages and a chapel down by the river form part of a fascinating 19C industrial village built for the workers of the local weaving mill.

▶ *Return to the last T-junction; turn right onto Ballynahatty Road; after 1mi/1.6km turn right (signposted "Giant's Ring").*

Giant's Ring

The Ring is a huge circular bank of gravel and boulders (600ft/183m in diameter) around a megalithic chambered grave. Its true purpose is unknown; in the 18C it was used as a racecourse.

LONDONDERRY/DERRY ★

POPULATION 72 334

Northern Ireland's second city, close to the border with the Republic, is pleasantly sited on the River Foyle, surrounded by the Sperrin Mountains (southeast) and the wild heights of Donegal (west and north). Almost uniquely in the British Isles, it has kept its defensive walls, erected in the early 17C when the ancient Irish settlement of Derry became a key stronghold in the English Plantation of Ulster and was renamed Londonderry (Doire). A powderkeg during the Troubles, the city has since undergone something of a revival, with renewed economic growth, vibrant commercial activity, and an emphasis on tourism.

▪ **Information:** 44 Foyle Street. ☎028 7126 7284. www.derryvisitor.com.
▶ **Orient Yourself:** Ireland's northernmost tip, near the border and Co Donegal.
◉ **Don't Miss:** A tour of the city walls.
◔ **Also See:** BUNCRANA, DONEGAL COAST, DONEGAL GLENS, PORTRUSH, SPERRIN MOUNTAIN.

A Bit of History

Monastic Foundation – According to tradition, the monastery at Derry (from *Doire* meaning "oak grove") was founded in 546 by St Columba. Between 1565–1600, Derry was occupied by the English. During the four-month rebellion of Sir Cahir O'Doherty in 1608, his forces attacked and captured Derry but could not sustain their momentum after his death at Kilmacrenan in Donegal.

The Irish Society – Under the scheme for the colonisation of Ulster with settlers from Britain, The Honourable The Irish Society was constituted by Royal Charter in 1613 to plant the County of Coleraine, now known as County Londonderry. Most of the land was parcelled out to the 12 main livery companies of London but the towns of Derry and Coleraine were retained by the Society, which still uses its income from fisheries and property to support projects of general benefit to the community.

Siege of Londonderry – In the uncertainty created by James II's flight to France and William of Orange's landing in Devon, 13 Derry apprentices locked the city gates against the Jacobite regiment led by the Earl of Antrim sent to garrison the town in December 1688. The citizens declared for William and received an influx of supporters although food supplies were low. In March James II landed in Ireland with an army of 20 000 and in April besieged the city, erecting a boom across the river which held the relief ships at bay for seven weeks. The Scottish commander of the city, Robert Lundy, favoured capitulation to what seemed an overwhelming force but advocates of resistance deposed him and took command. On 10 July a shell bearing terms for surrender was fired into the town by the besiegers; the defenders raised a crimson flag on the Royal Bastion to signify "No surrender", a slogan which continues to resonate with Northern Ireland's Protestant population. The siege lasted 15 weeks during which the 30 000 people crammed within the walls were reduced to eating cats, dogs, mice, rats and leather; thousands died of starvation. On 28 July 1689 the boom was broken and the relief ships sailed through to the quay. Three days later the Jacobite army retreated.

Sectors of the City – The character of the Plantation city changed drastically in the 19C. Migrants flocked here from all over Catholic Ireland, and by 1900 Protestants were a minority, though careful management of the boundaries of electoral districts and the allocation of public housing continued to deny Catholics control of the city council. While the traditional industry of shirt-making employed many women, male unemployment was rife, and housing conditions – notably in the Catholic Bogside district – were among the worst in the United Kingdom. The city erupted

Lundy

When the Scottish Col Lundy advised the citizens of Londonderry to avoid bloodshed and destruction and surrender to the superior Jacobite army, he utterly underestimated their fighting spirit. In his stead, Major Henry Baker and the Reverend George Walker rallied their fellow-Protestants and organised their brave resistance. Ever after, the term "Lundy" has been synonymous with cowardice and treachery, and the wretched colonel's effigy is ceremoniously burned during the Apprentice Boys' annual parade in August.

into riot in 1968, the "Battle of the Bogside" erupted in 1969, and on 30 January 1972 – Bloody Sunday, paratroopers shot dead unarmed 14 civilians in the violent aftermath of a banned protest march. In the years since, despite relative calm, sectarian boundaries have become more pronounced, with Protestants tending to withdraw from the west bank of the Foyle and settle in the Waterside district on the east bank.

Walking Tour

City Walls and Gates★★

&. ⏰ *Walls open daily.* *Guided walking tour (90min) from tourist information centre Jul–Aug Mon–Fri 11.15am &*

Halloween Street Parade in Londonderry

NITB, Belfast

Ferryquay Gate

3.15pm. Sept–Jun Mon–Fri 2.30pm. £6 (inc St Columb's Cathedral). ☎028 7137 7577.

The walls (1mi/1.6km long) enclosing the Plantation town were erected between 1613 and 1618 by the Irish Society. Their near-perfect preservation is remarkable, given that they have sustained more than one siege, and their vulnerability to gunfire from warships in the Foyle. A walk around the walls past gateways, bastions, watch-towers and artillery pieces makes for a fine introduction to the city.

▶ *Join the wall walk on the east side by Newmarket Street: walk clockwise.*

Ferryquay Gate was slammed shut by the 13 Apprentice Boys in the face of the Jacobite troops at the start of the 1688/89 siege.

The present triumphal arch replacing the original **Bishop's Gate** was erected to mark the centenary anniversary of the siege in 1789: it provides a good view down **Bishop's Street Within**, the city's most distinguished thoroughfare with its cluster of fine late 18C/early 19C buildings including the red-brick Bishop's Palace (Freemasons' Hall) built by the Earl Bishop, the Greek Revival Courthouse, the Irish Society's headquarters (1764) and elegant Deanery.

The Royal Bastion, overlooking Bogside, is the point where Col Michelburn hoisted the crimson "No Surrender" flag at the beginning of the great siege. The **Apprentice Boys' Hall** stands on the site of the original Shambles.

From **Butcher's Gate**, Butcher Street leads into **The Diamond**, the characteristic focal point of a Plantation town where four main thoroughfares meet in front of the Town Hall, in this case replaced by a war memorial. Beyond Butcher's Gate on the right is the **Fifth Province**.

The northernmost corner is marked by the entrance to the **Tower Museum**. The **Shipquay Gate**, surmounted by five cannon used to defend the city during the siege, straddles another thoroughfare up towards the Diamond.

Within the Walls

St Columb's Cathedral★

☾Open Apr–Sept Mon–Sat 9am–5pm; Oct–Mar 9am–1pm & 2pm–4pm. Sun for services only. £2. Guided tours £1.50. ☎028 7126 7313. www.stcolumbs cathedral.org.

The fortified Plantation city was speedily provided with a formidable battlemented late-Perpendicular cathedral, planned in 1613, started in 1628 and completed in 1634. It was the first cathe-

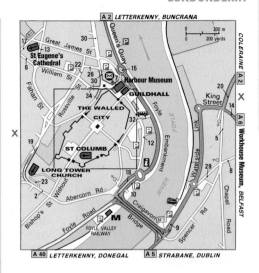

LONDONDERRY

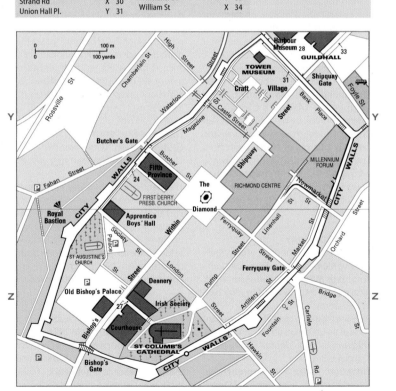

dral to be built in the British Isles since the Reformation. The 191ft/58m spire was added in the early 19C. Probably its most striking feature is the superb open-timbered **nave roof** supported on corbels carved to represent the Bishops of Derry from 1634 to 1867, and the Revd George Walker, city governor

The Guildhall from the City walls

during the Siege. In the porch stands the **mortar shell** containing terms for surrender which was fired into the city during the Siege; windows in the Choir Vestry *(right)* depict the Closing of the Gates (1688), the Relief of the City (1689) and the Centenary Celebrations (1789). The splendid 18C mahogany Chinese Chippendale **bishop's throne** was probably given by the flamboyant Earl Bishop. On the chancel arch above the pulpit is a **Cross of Nails**, a gift from Coventry Cathedral signifying peace and reconciliation. The **chapter house** dates from 1910 and houses a miscellany of historical objects *(for access ask the Verger)*.

Tower Museum★

○*Open Oct–Jun Tue–Sat 10am–5pm; Jul–Aug Mon–Sat 10am–5pm, Sun 11am–3pm; Sept Mon–Sat 10am–5pm.* ☜*£4.* ☎ *028 7137 2411. www.derrycity.gov. uk/museums.*

Excellent displays of artefacts, wall panels and a video explain the story of the shipwreck of *La Trinidad Valencera* in Kinnagoe Bay.

Elsewhere, there are comprehensive displays relating to the **Story of Derry**. From the top of the tower there is an extensive view over the inner city and the Foyle.

Beyond the Walls

Long Tower Church★

○*Open year-round daily 9am–8.30pm (summer 9pm).* ☎*028 7126 2301.*

The oldest Roman Catholic church in Derry (1784–86) has an lovely Rococo interior with extensive steeply sloping galleries. It stands on the site of Templemore, a great medieval church built in 1164 alongside the Long Tower (10C) which survived an explosion in 1567. From the churchyard there is a fine view of the Royal Bastion.

Guildhall★

♿○*Open Mon–Fri 9am–5pm.* ○*Closed Bank Hol Mon.* ☎*028 71377335. www.derry city.gov.uk/guildhall.htm.*

The late-Gothic Guildhall with the corner clocktower was erected in 1890 with a loan from the Irish Society. It was severely damaged by fire in 1908 and by bombs in 1972. A reproduction of Follingby's painting of the Relief of Derry graces the marble-faced vestibule. The numerous stained-glass windows by Ulster craftsmen, make up a visual history of the city, with London scenes on the stairs and early views of Derry in the Great Hall.

Harbour Museum

○*Open Mon–Fri 10am–1pm, 2pm–5pm.* ☎*028 7137 7331. www.derrycity.gov.uk/ museums.*

The grandiose 19C building, which once hosted meetings of the Londonderry Port and Harbour Commissioners, is now a museum with paintings, models and maritime memorabilia. The dominant exhibit is the largest curragh ever built, constructed in 1963 to recreate the legendary voyage of St Columba to Iona.

St Eugene's Cathedral

○*Open year-round daily 9am–8.30pm (summer 9pm).* ☎*028 7126 2894.*

Northwest of the city centre, between a district of elegant Georgian terraces and the green peace of Brooke Park, stands the Roman Catholic Cathedral dedicated to St Eugene in 1873 by Bishop Keely. The building was designed in the Gothic revival style by JJ McCarthy in 1853 and completed with a cross on the top of the spire in 1903.

Foyle Valley Railway Centre

Open early Jul–Aug Tue–Sat 10am–4.30pm. www.derrycity.gov.uk.
Londonderry was once the focal point of no fewer than four railway companies, including the Londonderry and Enniskillen, "possibly the least efficient if not the most dangerous railway ever to operate in Ireland" and the County Donegal Railway, the most extensive of all the Irish narrow-gauge systems (125mi/200km). The Centre has steam engines, coaches, an old goods wagon, signals, signs and luggage. Excursion trains drawn by diesel car (1934) operate beside the Foyle.

Workhouse Museum★

Open Sat–Thu 10am–4.30pm. 028 7131 8328. www.derrycity.gov.uk/museums.
The city workhouse at 23 Glendermott Road, designed by George Wilkinson, opened in 1840 with 800 inmates. Today it servers as a library and museum acknowledging the important role played by the city in the Second World War, notably in the Battle of the Atlantic; upstairs recreates the grim 19C workhouse conditions.

Museum of Free Derry

55–61 Glenfada Park. Open year-round Mon–Fri 9.30am–4.30pm. Apr–Sept also Sat 1pm–4pm; Jul–Sept also Sun 1pm–4pm. £3. 028 71360880. www.museumoffreederry.org.
This intriguing museum is an archive focusing on the civil rights era of the 1960s and the Troubles during the 1970s; artefacts and documents explain the unrest in the Bogside area, the repercussions of Bloody Sunday and the effects on the local community.

MOUNT STEWART★★★

A celebrated landscaped park and dramatic views across Strangford Lough help make this palatial mansion one of Ireland's premier visitor attractions.

- **Information:** 028 4278 8387. www.nationaltrust.org.uk.
- **Orient Yourself:** Mount Stewart on the eastern shore of Strangford Lough is 5mi/8km SE of Newtownards by A 20.
- **Also See:** BANGOR, DOWNPATRICK, STRANGFORD LOUGH.

Walking Tour

(NT) Formal gardens: open daily: last three weeks Mar 10am–4pm, Apr–Oct 10am–6pm (8pm May–Sept). £4.86. House: open by guided tour only: Mar, Apr & Oct Sat–Sun noon–6pm. Easter week daily noon–6pm. May Wed–Mon 1pm–6pm, Jun daily 1pm–6pm; Jul–Aug daily noon–6pm; Sept Wed–Mon 1pm–6pm. Houses open noon every weekend. House tour and gardens £6.36. Temple of the Winds: open Easter Sat–Mon & Apr–Oct, Sun 2pm–-5pm.

Soldiers and Statesmen

Mount Stewart owes its name to the Scottish family who settled on the banks of Strangford Lough in 1774. They acquired vast fortunes from substantial property holdings, including their immensely profitable coal mines in northern England. Robert Stewart was made Marquess of Londonderry in 1816, but his elder son, Lord Castlereagh (1769–1822), is better known having served as leader of the House of Commons and attended the Congress of Vienna in 1815 as Foreign Secretary. The family's eminence was maintained in part by entertaining the British Establishment in London, across England and at Mount Stewart, rallying support for the Unionist cause.

Italian Garden

Gardens

The old demesne acquired by the Stewarts was soon landscaped with fine parkland trees, including a number of exotic species planted by Edith, Lady Londonderry. Having consulted Sir Edwin Lutyens and Gertrude Jekyll, she laid out a series of formal gardens that effectively link the house with its surroundings.

The huge Irish yews by the house overlook the geometrical **Italian Garden**; the **Dodo Terrace** is ornamented with droll stone animals bearing nicknames that allude to Lady Edith's London set. The **Spanish Garden** echo the ceiling pattern in the **Temple of the Winds**. The **Sunk Garden** honours Gertrude Jekyll with its orange, blue and yellow-flowering plants. The **Shamrock Garden** celebrates Ireland with a topiary harp and Red Hand of Ulster bed.

The parkland beyond is planted with exotic trees and shrubs. The hill overlooking the artificial **lake** (1846–48), provides a superb **view** over Strangford Lough. A genuine miniature Japanese pagoda stands beside the **Ladies' Walk**, an old path to the dairy and kitchen gardens.

The Londonderrys' sumptuous **residence** was built in two stages; the west wing in 1805 (George Dance), the main part 1825–35 (William Vitruvius Morrison).

The interior is richly furnished with family portraits, Irish and English furniture, a collection of porcelain and Classical sculpture.

Temple of the Winds

Inspired by the Temple of the Winds in Athens, this pleasure pavilion, designed by James "Athenian" Stuart in 1783, stands on a mound with a fine prospect of Strangford Lough and Scrabo Hill (topped by a tower commemorating the 3rd Marquess of Londonderry). The elegant banqueting room has a superb inlaid floor echoing designs in the ceiling. The gloomy servants' quarters, unusually, are underground.

J Cornish/National Trust Photographic Library

MOURNE MOUNTAINS★★

The highest granite peaks in Northern Ireland rise dramatically from the sea and plain of Co Down to Slieve Donard, and extend westwards to Carlingford Lough and north into rolling foothills. The Kingdom of Mourne, the strip of land between the mountains and the sea, is a region of small fields divided by drystone walls where for centuries a life of farming and fishing continued largely undisturbed by external events. Nowadays the mountains and coast are a favourite holiday area, with good beaches and lovely scenery enjoyed by hill walkers and climbers.

- **Information:** 10–14 Central Promenade, Newcastle; ☎028 4372 2222. 28 Bridge Street , Kilkeel; ☎028 41762525; www.downdc.gov.uk.
- ▶ **Orient Yourself:** The Mourne Mountains are bounded by the Newry–Downpatrick road, A 25, and the coast road, A 2.
- **Don't Miss:** Castlewellan Forest Park.
- **Also See:** DOWNPATRICK, DUNDALK, NEWRY.

Inland

Murlough National Nature Reserve
2mi/3.2km E of Newcastle by A 2. (NT)
🕐Park: dawn to dusk. Information Centre: Jun–Sept 10am–6pm; 17 Mar–May, Sat–Sun & Bank Hols 10am–6pm. Jun–Sept1 daily 10am–6pm. ☜£2.70 per car. ☎028 43751467.
The magnificent sand dunes between the Carrigs River and Dundrum Bay, which reach a height of 100ft/30m, provide sanctuary to migratory birds and a broad range of plants. There are traces of early human habitation, including an ancient tripod **dolmen** (8ft/2.5m high). The reserve also contains an excellent beach.

Dundrum Castle★
4mi/6.4m east of Newcastle on the A 2; in Dundrum turn left uphill to car park. (HM).
🕐Open Apr–Sept Tue–Sun 9am–6pm (2pm Sun); Oct–Mar Sat only, 10am–4pm. ☎028 9054 3034. www.ehsni.gov.uk/dundrum.
The ruins north of the town show how the castle's strategic position and natural defences were supplemented by an impressively deep rock-cut ditch. Building was probably initiated by John de

Mourne Mountains

Address Book

For coin ranges, see the Legend on the cover flap.

SIGHTSEEING

Mourne Countryside Centre – *87 Central Promenade, Newcastle.* Provides information and organises a programmme of hill walks in the summer months, including the **Mourne International Walking Festival** *(last weekend in Jun)* which starts from Newcastle or Warren Point ☎028 4372 4059

WHERE TO STAY

The Cuan – *Strangford. 9.5mi/ 15km north west.* ☎028 4488 1222. *www.thecuan.com.* Well located for Strangford Lough, golfing, sailing and walking, this comfortable guesthouse with an established restaurant will suit most needs.

Slieve Croob Inn – *Castlewellan, 5.2mi north. 7rm.* ☎028 4377 1412. *www. slievecroobinn.com.* Modern rusticised hotel with exposed timbers. The bedrooms are simple yet pleasantly decorated. Self-catering cottages available.

SPORTS AND LEISURE

There are bathing beaches at Newcastle and Cranfield.

Castle and Islands Park, *Newcastle.* – Swings, slides, Slippery Dip, 9-hole pitch and putt course, tennis, boating.

Tropicana – *Newcastle. Open Jul–Aug daily.* Heated outdoor sea-water pools, giant water slide, bouncy castle etc.

Coco's Indoor Adventure Playground, *Newcastle.* – Snake slides, free fall, assault course and soft play activity area ☎028 43726226

Soak Seaweed Baths –*Newcastle* ☎028 43726002 – *www.soakseaweedbaths.co.uk.* Pamper yourself with a revitalising steam bath with seaweed.

EVENTS AND FESTIVALS

The **Boley Fair**, traditional sheep fair, in Hilltown *(Tuesday after 12 July). www.boleyfair.com.*

The **Maiden of Mourne Festival** in Warrenpoint *(early Aug). www.maidenofthemournes.com*

Fiddlers' Green Festival – Folk festival at the picturesque town of Rostrevor *(last week in July).* ☎028 4173 8738. *www.fiddlersgreenfestival.com.*

Courcy c. 1177, so that the approach to the Lecale peninsula and Strangford Lough could be defended. There is an unusual circular keep (fine views from the parapet) and Lower Ward, added between the 13C and 15C, enclosing the remains of a once-grand house built by the Blundell family in the 17C.

Tollymore Forest Park★

Open 10am–dusk. *£4 per car. www.forestserviceni.gov.uk.*
The main mansion at the heart of this vast landscaped demesne straddling the salmon-rich River Shimna is long gone, but several follies and bridges are preserved in the province's first Forest Park (1955). There is a hermitage, the extravagantly decorated Gothic and Barbican Gates, and the church-like Clanbrassil Barn (now an **information centre**); trails thread past splendid specimen trees, and through an avenue of Himalayan cedars, an azalea walk, and con-

ifer plantations. The local fauna includes foxes, otters, badgers, red squirrels and pine martens, moths, butterflies and many birds.

Castlewellan Forest Park★★

4mi/6.4km N of Newcastle by A 50. *Open 10am–dusk.* *£2 pedestrian, £4 car. www.forestserviceni.gov.uk.*
Castlewellan, a spacious and elegant little market town was laid out in 1750 around its two squares by the Earl of Annesley.
The **forest park** is based on the demesne developed by the Annesley family from the mid-18C, its splendid tree collection forming the basis of the national **arboretum**. The Annesleys, descendants of an Elizabethan army captain, were successors in this part of Ulster to the Magennis clan, who lost their landholdings after the 1641 rising. The core of the estate is not so

much the Scottish baronial style castle built in granite and now used as a conference centre, but the superb **Annesley Gardens**, enclosed by a wall and ornamented by two fountains. The mile-long lake provides excellent fishing, while along its shores a 3mi/5km **Sculpture Trail** features pieces created from natural materials. There is an icehouse on the south shore and a pagan standing stone, now covered with Christian symbols, on the north bank. From the highest point, Slievenaslat (8 96ft/273m) provides magnificent views of the Mourne Mountains. The largest and longest permanent hedge maze in the world, the **Peace Maze** was opened in 2001.

Legananny Dolmen

11mi/18km N of Newcastle via the A 50 and side roads from Castlewellan.

The dolmen consists of a huge slanting capstone delicately balanced on three unusually low supporting stones. It is sited in a theatrical setting on the southern slope of Slieve Croob (1 745ft/532m) with a magnificent view of the Mourne Mountains.

Brontë Centre

1.5mi/2.5km north of Rathfriland, off the B 25 in Drumballyroney (signposted). Open 17 Mar -late Sept Fri–Sun & Bank Hols noon–4.30pm. £3. 028 4062 3322. www.banbridge.com.

The hamlet's little white schoolhouse and church now function as an interpretative centre for the life and work of **Patrick Brontë** (see 'Brontë Country' box)and his three famous daughters. A signposted tour, **The Brontë Homeland Drive** starts at Drumballyroney Church and School near Rathfriland, ten miles south of Banbridge. It is well-signposted along the 10-mile/16-km route which highlights other sites in the area associated with the family.

Drumena Cashel and Souterrain★

A good number of Early Christian farm enclosures, or cashels, have survived in the Mourne Mountains. This well-preserved example consists of an oval

---

Brontë Country

Among the rolling northern foothills of the Mourne Mountains stands the ruined cottage *(plaque)* where Patrick Brunty (O'Pronitaigh), the father of the famous literary sisters, Charlotte, Emily and Anne, was born in 1777.

He may have changed his name to Brontë before leaving Ireland in 1802 (to study theology at Cambridge) inspired perhaps by Lord Nelson who was made Duke of Brontë (1799), after a place in Sicily, by Ferdinand, King of Naples, in recognition of his assistance in recapturing Naples from the French.

---

space encircled by a drystone wall, containing the foundations of a house and a T-shaped underground tunnel, called a souterrain, which can be entered.

Silent Valley Reservoir★

Visitor Centre: Open daily Jun–Aug, & Bank hols in Apr, May, Sept, 11am–6.30pm. £3 car, £1.50 pedestrains. Shuttle to/from Ben Crom £1.20 return. . www.newryandmourne.gov.uk.

The Mourne Mountains have few natural lakes, so the reservoirs supplying Belfast and Co Down since 1933 have altered the landscape, many would say for the better.

The Silent Valley scheme on the Kilkeel River took 10 years to complete, and holds 136 million cubic metres of water. The catchment is protected by the extraordinary 22mi/35km linear **Mourne Wall**, beautifully constructed in rough mountain granite between 1910–22, providing seasonal relief work to as many as 2000 local men.

There is a pleasant walk *(2hr there and back on foot)* to the dam which provides a superb **view**★ of the reservoir below Slieve Binnian (2 441ft/744m). From the east end of the dam the path continues north to **Ben Crom Reservoir** (3mi/4.8km), while the path at the opposite end returns down the valley past **Sally Lough**, through a grove of conifers and over a wooden footbridge spanning the Kilkeel river.

Spelga Pass and Dam★

From the dam there is a wonderful **view** north over the foothills of the Mourne Mountains to the rolling hills of Co Down. The reservoir (which provides fine angling for brown trout) flooded the summer pastures, known as Deer's Meadow, in 1959.

Crocknafeola Forest

This small coniferous forest stands beside the road which traverses the Mourne Mountains from north to south skirting the west face of Slieve Muck (2 198ft/670m).

Driving Tour

Along the coast

Newcastle

The town "where the mountains of Mourne sweep down to the sea", as immortalised in verse by Percy French, began to develop in the early 19C when seaside holidays became fashionable. From the tiny harbour a long promenade of hotels, shops and amusement arcades face onto the long sandy beach of Dundrum Bay.

The town's Roman Catholic church (1967), **Our Lady of the Assumption**, is a modern circular structure with striking stained glass.

Donard Park on the banks of the Glen River, is a good point from which to start the steep but steady climb to the summit of **Slieve Donard**, named in honour of Donard, a local chieftain supposedly converted to Christianity by St Patrick.

▶ *From Newcastle take the A 2 south.*

Bloody Bridge

It is thought that the name for this scenic bridge comes from an incident at the time of the 1641 uprising when a group of government prisoners, en-route to be exchanged for captured rebels, was murdered by a soldier called Russell after he suffered a panic attack.

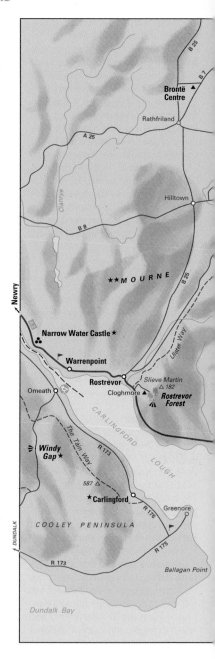

Annalong

From the A 2 turn south by the police station towards the shore.

Annalong's early-19C restored **corn-mill★** (&⃝ *open Apr–Sept Wed–Mon 2pm–6pm;* ⊖*£2.15;* ☎*028 4376 8736, 0773 952 7036 for tours*) is driven by a

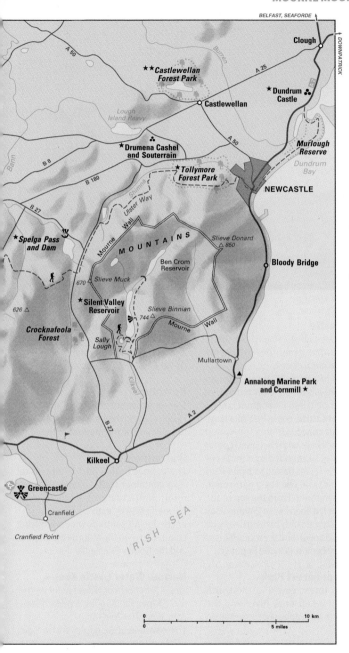

back-shot breast-shot water-wheel and is the last of some 20 mills in the Kingdom of Mourne which once milled wheat and oats or scutched flax. The Exhibition Room describes the history of milling.

Kilkeel

The little town is full of interest, with stepped pavements and different levels, but its true colours are really seen when the boats of Northern Ireland's largest fishing fleet land their catch at the quayside.

Narrow Water Castle

Greencastle

(HM). ⏲*Open Jul–Aug Tue, Fri–Sun 2pm–6pm, Wed–Thu 10am–1pm.* ☎*028 9181 1491. www.ehsni.gov.uk.*

The ruins of a mid-13C Anglo-Norman stronghold are set on a low outcrop of rock extending into Carlingford Lough. The **Royal Castle**, consisting of a large rectangular keep within a four-sided walled enclosure with D-shaped corner towers, was surrounded by a moat cut in the rock. It was besieged by Edward Bruce (1316) and used as a garrison in Elizabethan times. From the top of the keep there is a fine view to Cranfield Bay (which has good sandy bathing beach, up Carlingford Lough and the mountains of the Cooley Peninsula in the Republic.

Rostrevor Forest Park

The pine forest covering the south bank of the Kilbroney River and the steep northwest slopes of Slieve Martin (597ft/182m), is ideal for walking – to the **Cloghmore**, a great glacial boulder, and to the **viewpoint**★ high above Rostrevor Bay.

Rostrevor

This attractive little town on Carlingford Lough enjoys a temperate climate allowing palm trees and mimosa to thrive.

Warrenpoint

The town is both a port equipped to take container traffic, and a pleasant resort, with a vast central square, used for markets and festivals, and a promenade facing south down Carlingford Lough between the Mourne Mountains and the Cooley Peninsula.

Narrow Water Castle Keep★

2mi/3.2km north of Warrenpoint on the A 2. ⏲*Open Jul–Aug Tue, Fri–Sat 10am–1pm, Wed–Thu 2pm–6pm.*

The castle keep occupies a strategic position on a promontory commanding the narrows at the mouth of the Newry River where it enters Carlingford Lough. It was built in the 1650s as an English garrison at the cost of £361 4s 2d. Although restored, it is an excellent example of a **tower house** complete with **bawn**. The Elizabethan Revival castle *(private)* is only open for private receptions.

> ## Warrenpoint Massacre
>
> In 1979 Narrow Water was the scene of the largest single loss of life for the British Army since the Second World War when 18 soldiers were killed by two IRA bombs.

LOUGH NEAGH ★

Ten rivers converge on this broad and tranquil lough, which is the largest body of fresh water in the British Isles (153sq mi/400sq km). It is drained by just one of these, the Lower Bann, which flows north to discharge into the sea just downstream from Coleraine. Despite its size, the lake is never more than 50ft/12m deep, and has little impact on the surrounding flat countryside. Only in Antrim Bay is the shore lined with woodland; elsewhere it is low and marshy, virtually roadless, and sometimes infested with (non-biting) midges.

Together with its tiny northern neighbour, Lough Beg, Lough Neagh is a site of international importance for wintering wildfowl, and nature reserves have been established on many of its islands.

- **Information:** Lough Neagh Discovery Centre. ☎028 3832 2205. www.oxfordisland.com. www.discoverloughneagh.com.
- ▶ **Orient Yourself:** Lough Neagh lies 15mi/24km W of Belfast There is no continuous shore road, only a few points where minor roads reach the water's edge.
- **Also See:** ANTRIM, ARMAGH, BELFAST, LISBURN, SPERRIN MOUNTAINS.

Excursions

In clockwise order from the south-east.

Lough Neagh Discovery Centre
South shore; Oxford Island; sign at Junction 10, M 1. ♿⊙Open Apr–Sept 10am–6pm (7pm Sun); Oct–Mar 10am–5pm. ✕. ☎028 3832 2205. www.oxfordisland.com.
This modern centre provides information on the wildlife and history of the lake; great views from the mezzanine level of the restaurant. Five hides and several footpaths provide ample opportunity to watch out for birds.

Peatlands Park
South shore; sign at Junction 13 on M 1. ♿⊙Open 9am–9pm (5pm Oct–Easter). Info centre and narrow-gauge railway:
open weekends & Bank Hols noon–5pm. ⊙railway £1. ☎028 3885 1102. www.ehsni.gov.uk.
This old hunting park is the best place in the North to learn about Ireland's long relationship with peat: the **narrow-gauge railway** provides a scenic tour of the site; **turf cutting** by hand and machine is demonstrated at the outdoor turbary station, while the **bog garden**, two small lakes, an orchard and woodland provide nature lovers with a place to enjoy the unusual flora and fauna.

Maghery
Sited where the River Blackwater enters the lough, the village has a lakeside country park from which Coney Island, a densely wooded island, can be visited by boat.

Lough Neagh Discovery Centre

NITB, Belfast

Inside the Empire of the Eel

The waters of Lough Neagh and its tributaries teem with every kind of freshwater fish: rudd, roach and pike, pollan (freshwater herring) and the rare dollaghan (a kind of salmon-trout). There are giant pike in Lough Beg, bream in the Blackwater, trout and salmon in the Bann. But the lough is particularly famous for its eels which hatch far away in the Sargasso Sea, and swim across the Atlantic to the Bann to spend 12–14 years in the lough before heading back to their birthplace to die. Many, however, are caught and exported from the cooperative fishery at Toome to connoisseurs abroad, who relish them both smoked or unsmoked.

Ballyronan

West shore. The little marina, lake shore and beach are a great draw.

Kinturk Cultural Centre

&. ⏱*Open daily 2pm–5pm, 7.30pm–11pm.* ✆*£1. Boat trips and guided tours.* ✕. ☏*028 8673 6512.*
Learn about the long-established local eel industry (⏱*see 'Inside the Empire of the Eel' box*).

Ardboe Cross★

East of Cookstown via the B 73.
The finest high cross of its kind in Ulster stands in an evocative spot at the entrance to a graveyard around the ruins of a 17C church. It is decorated with biblical scene, probably carved in the 10C to mark the site of Ardboe Abbey, founded around the 6C, associated with St Colman. From Ardboe Point is an extensive **view**★ of Lough Neagh, Slieve Gallion and the Sperrin Mountains, Slemish, Divis Mountain and the Mourne Mountains.

Bellaghy Bawn

North shore; in Bellaghy(HM). ⏱*Open Easter–Aug daily 10am–6pm; Sept–Easter Mon–Sat 9am–5pm, including Bank Hols.* ⏱*Closed Xmas–New Year.* ✆*£2.* ☏*028 7938 6812. www.ehsni.gov.uk/bellaghy.*
This 17C fortified house and bawn was built by the Vintners' Company in 1619; its exhibition relate to local history, the Ulster Plantation and the poetry of Seamus Heaney, born nearby in 1939. Much of Heaney's work, notably his *Lough Neagh Cycle* is marked by the memories of the local people and landscapes.

Address Book

GETTING AROUND

The Loughshore Trail, a relatively flat route, ideal for cycling and walking, is composed of 128mi/206km miles of quiet lanes, which run alongside or close to the lough shore. It forms Route 94 of the National Cycle Network and incorporates a short section of Route 96 by Lough Beg. *www.loughshoretrail.com.*

SIGHTSEEING

Lake Cruises are available from **Kinnego Marina** on the south shore. *Master McGra takes 12 passengers Apr–Oct Sat–Sun afternoons. Prior booking essential.* ☏*028 3832 7573 or 077 7481 1248.*
The are also cruises from **Sixmilewater Marina** in Antrim. Occasionally there is also a **Bann cruise** between Antrim and Castlerock *(35mi – 6/7hr).*

SPORTS AND LEISURE

Watersports are available at the marinas at Antrim, Ballyronan and Kinnego and at the Craigavon Watersports Centre.
There is an **RSPB reserve** at Portmore Lough (southeast) and **nature reserves** at Reas Wood in Antrim, at Oxford Island, at Peatlands Park, at Washingbay Wetlands near Dungannon and at Randalstown Forest.
Fishing Permits are available from tackle shops and from the Fishery Conservancy Board in Portadown. ☏*028 3833 4666. www.fcbni.com.*
Permits and **gillie services** for the Lower Bann are available from Bann System Ltd, Coleraine ☏*028 7034 4796. www.bannsystem.com.*

NEWRY

POPULATION 21 633

Newry (An Tiúr) occupies a commanding position in the "Gap of the North" or Moyry Gap, between the line of hills that separates Ulster from the plains of Meath. A location that has brought destruction and prosperity to the place, as armies marched through on their way north or south. In the 18C Newry was linked by canals to Lough Neagh and to the sea at Carlingford Lough, becoming for a while the busiest port in the North. Those days are long gone but its road and railway links to both Belfast and Dublin enable shoppers to come from both sides of the border.

- **Information:** Bank Parade ☎028 30268877. www.newryandmourne.gov.uk.
- **Orient Yourself:** Newry is 37mi/60km south west of Belfast.
- **Also See:** ARMAGH, DUNDALK, MONAGHAN, MOURNE MOUNTAINS.

A Bit of History

Newry's history began with the foundation in 1157 of a Cistercian abbey. Turbulent times have erased most of the old town, including the castle built by the Anglo-Norman John de Courcy, and all the strongholds that succeeded it. In the 16C, the abbey accommodated Sir Nicholas Bagenal, Marshal of Ireland, who built St Patrick's Church (1578) on the hill to the east of the town centre: the first Anglican church to be built in Ireland, bearing its founder's coat of arms in the porch.

In 1731 work began here on the first inland canal in the British Isles, linking Newry via fourteen locks to Lough Neagh. Thirty years later, a ship canal was dug to provide the town with an outlet to Carlingford Lough and the Irish Sea. The town prospered from the trade in linen, coal, building stone and emigrants, as the Georgian town houses and multi-storey quayside mills testify. In 1956, the inland canal was closed and the ship canal became redundant when modern port facilities were provided downstream at Warrenpoint. Today it provides for recreational use.

Sights

Newry Cathedral

Newry has been the seat of the Roman Catholic diocese of Dromore since about 1750. Its cathedral, designed by Thomas Duff in 1825 and dedicated to St Patrick and St Colman, was the first Roman Catholic cathedral to be built in Ireland following the Act of Emancipation. Inside, it is vivid with stained glass and colourful mosaics.

Newry and Mourne Museum

♿ⓘ *Open year-round Mon–Fri 10.30am–1pm, 2pm–4.30pm.* ☎028 30266232.
The modern Arts Centre beside the Town Hall straddles the river and thus has one foot in Co Armagh and one in Co Down. The museum deals competently with the archeology and history of the area. It has a lovely early 18C panelled room recalling prosperous times, and Nelson's cabin table from *HMS Victory*.

Excursion

Cullyhanna

15mi/24km west of Newry by the B 30 and north by the A 29 and a minor road (left). ⓘ *Open Mon–Fri 1pm–5pm. Bank Hols 10am–6pm.* ✉*£2.50.* ☎028 30868757. *www.ofiaichcentre.co.uk.*
The **Cardinal O'Fiaich Centre** is devoted to the life of Tomás O'Fiaich (d 1990), a local boy who became Cardinal-Primate of all Ireland. It charts his career as student, priest, professor, scholar with recorded interviews, video and personal memorabilia.

Driving Tour

Slieve Gullion★
Round tour of 27mi/43.5km – 1 day.

This "enchanted mountain", together with its attendant circle of lesser heights, known as the Ring of Gullion, dominates the countryside to the west of Newry. It is intimately associated with the legendary Cuchulain, hero of the epic *The Cattle Raid of Cooley (Táin bo Cuainlge)* and is rich in prehistoric remains.

▶ *From Newry take the A 25 west; after 1.5mi/2.4km turn right onto the B 133 to Bessbrook.*

Bessbrook
This early and fascinating example of a planned industrial village has terraces of granite-built, slate-roofed cottages neatly ranged round three sides of two grassy squares. The settlement, complete with churches, schools, shops and a community hall (but significantly, no pub), was built in 1845 by the Quaker linen manufacturer John Grubb Richardson for his flax workers. Bessbrook later inspired the Cadbury family to build the far larger model settlement of Bournville near Birmingham.

Kilnasaggart Stone

P Thebault/MICHELIN

▶ *From Bessbrook take the B 112; turn right onto the A 25. West of Camlough village turn left onto the B 30.*

Cam Lough
From the road there is a fine view of the narrow lake in its deep trough between Camlough Mountain (1 417ft/423m) and Slieve Gullion.

▶ *At the crossroads turn left onto a narrow road along the west side of Cam Lough.*

Killevy
An ancient graveyard, overhung with beech trees, surrounds the ruins of two **churches**, standing end to end. The eastern building is medieval; the western one is earlier (12C) although the west wall, which is pierced by a doorway below a massive lintel, may be 10C or 11C. A granite slab in the northern half of the graveyard is said to mark the grave of St Monenna (also known as Darerca and Bline) who founded an important early nunnery here in the 5C. This later became an Augustinian convent until it was suppressed in 1542. A path north of the graveyard leads to a holy well.

▶ *Continue south for 1.5mi/2.4km; turn right onto the B 113.*

Slieve Gullion Forest Park★
8mi/13km Scenic Drive. ⚠*Beware steep gradients and difficult bends.*
The pines, larches and spruce of the Forest Park clad the lower slopes of the southwest face of Slieve Gullion. The visitor centre housed in old farm buildings provides information about the park and displays old hand tools.
After climbing through the forest, the Scenic Drive emerges on the open slopes of Slieve Gullion; on the left is an extensive view over the treetops; on the right is the path, waymarked in white, to the top of the south peak of Slieve Gullion (1 894ft/573m) marked by a cairn; another cairn crowns the lower north peak. The Drive swings left downhill and doubles back along the southwest slope, through the trees and rocks, to a

viewpoint★ overlooking a section of the **Ring of Gullion**.

▶ *At the exit turn right onto the B113 and immediately turn left. After 1.5mi/2.4km turn right; after 1mi/1.6km park at the T-junction.*

Kilnasaggart Stone

Most of Ireland's cross-decorated pillar-stones are in the west of the country but this granite example (7ft/2.15m high) in its hedged enclosure *(across two fields)* is the earliest dateable one of its kind, its crosses carved around AD 700. The pillar itself, which marks the site of an Early Christian cemetery, may in fact be much older, a prehistoric standing stone converted to a new use. It also bears an inscription in Irish stating that the site was dedicated under the patronage of Peter the Apostle by the son of Ceran Bic, Ternohc, who died c 715.

▶ *Return to the B 113; turn right towards Newry; after 5mi/8km turn left to Ballymacdermot Cairn (sign).*

Ballymacdermot Cairn

Beside the road *(right)* on the south slope of Ballymacdermot Mountain are the remains of a Neolithic court grave: two burial chambers with an antechamber and a circular forecourt enclosed in a trapezoidal cairn. Fine **views** extend southwest across the Meigh plain to Slieve Gullion and the Ring of Gullion.

▶ *Continue for 1mi/1.6km.*

Bernish Rock Viewpoint★★

The view sweeps over Newry to the Mourne Mountains on the eastern horizon.

▶ *Return downhill to Newry.*

PORTRUSH

POPULATION 5 703

Easily accessible by road and rail from Belfast, Portrush has been one of the North's most popular seaside resorts since early Victorian times, the natural qualities of its sandy beaches and the nearby coastline are now supplemented by a host of man-made attractions. The town is laid out on a little peninsula which ends in Ramore Head, a notable haunt of bird watchers.

🛈 **Information:** Dunluce Centre, Sandhill Drive; ☎028 70823333. Railway Rd, Coleraine; ☎028 70344723. www.causewaycoastandglens.com.

▶ **Orient Yourself:** Portrush is situated 58mi/94km northwest of Belfast and 36mi/58km northeast of Londonderry, between Portstewart and Ballycastle, on the A 2 coast road.

🞉 **Don't Miss:** Dunluce Castle, Gortmore Viewpoint and Magilligan Strand.

Kids **Especially for Kids:** Dunluce Centre, Leslie Hill Open Farm.

🕭 **Also See:** GIANT'S CAUSEWAY, LONDONDERRY, LOUGH NEAGH, SPERRIN MOUNTAINS.

Visit

Dunluce Centre   Kids

♿🕘*Open 15–17 Mar noon–5pm; Easter week & Jul–Aug daily 10am–6pm; Apr–Jun & Sept–Oct Sat–Sun only, noon–5pm. ⛁Combined ticket £8.50; individual facilities £4.25, £4.50, £2. ☎028 7082 4444. www.dunlucecentre.co.uk.*

This large family entertainment complex includes Ireland's only "4-dimensional" motion simulator, Treasure Fortress, a large soft-play adventure area and a viewing tower which offers a superb panoramic view of Portrush.

Close by, **The Coastal Zone** (🕘*open Easter weekend, Jun Sat–Sun, Jul–Aug daily 10am–5pm; ⓟ; ☎028 7082 3600; www.ehsni.gov.uk*), located in an old

Ph Hurlin/MICHELIN

Dunluce Castle

Victorian bath-house, provides an introduction to the ecology and marine life of the locality; visitors can observe the denizens of the seabed from within the "wreck" of the Nautilus.

Driving Tours

East of Portrush
7.5mi/12km.

▷ *From Portrush take the A 2 east.*

Dunluce Castle★★

(HM) ◷Open year-round daily 10am–5.30pm (4.30pm Oct–Mar). ✆£2. ☎028 2073 1938; www.northantrim.com.
There can be few more romantic sights than the jagged outline of ruined Dunluce Castle, perched on its isolated rock stack 100ft/30m above the sea. For years it was the seat of the Irish branch of the Scottish MacDonnell clan, known as "Lords of the Isles"; the most notable leader was Sorley Boy MacDonnell, a constant irritant to both the native Irish and the English. Despite the use of artillery, the latter failed to expel him permanently from Dunluce, and his descendants were eventually made Earls of Antrim. In the 17C they modernised the castle to provide more comfortable accommodation but when the kitchen collapsed into the sea, they abandoned it.

Beyond the drawbridge and the late-16C gatehouse with its Scottish-style turrets and crow-step gables, stand the two 14C towers and south wall. The upper yard is dominated by the 17C **great hall**, built in grandiose style with bay windows on the west front. The cobbled **lower yard** is surrounded by service buildings including the bakery. From here there is a superb **view** of the Causeway Coast.

▷ *Continue east on the A 2.*

Key to the Causeway

West of Portrush the coast is interrupted by the Bann estuary; beyond is a long sand dune extending into Lough Foyle. East of the town, more sand dunes give way to strangely weathered and cave-riddled limestone cliffs, and the extraordinary volcanic rock formations of the Giant's Causeway. This geologically important section of the north Antrim Coast has been designated as a National Nature Reserve. Detailed analysis of the rocks at Portrush provided the key to the long-standing riddle about the origin of such features as the Giant's Causeway.

Bushmills Distillery

Factory open by guided tour only, Mar–Oct Mon–Sat 9.15am–5pm (last tour at 4pm); Mar–Jun & Oct Sun noon–5pm. Jul–Sept Sun 11.30am–5pm. Closed Good Fri afternoon, 4 & 12 Jul, Christmas and New Year. No children under 8 on tour. Tour £6, other areas free. Charge reduced Fri afternoon and during July when no production is in process. 028 2073 3218. www.bushmills.com.

The most prominent feature in the village is the distinctive caps of the Bushmills Distillery kilns. The original licence to distil was granted to Sir Thomas Phillips in 1608, although references to a local distillery date back to 1276. Water drawn from St Columb's Rill, a tributary of the River Bush which rises in peaty ground, is used to produce two blended whiskeys and one malt.

The tour includes the main stages in the production of whiskey: mashing, fermentation, distillation, maturing in oak casks, blending and bottling. Tasting takes place in the Potstill Bar; a small museum has been created in the old malt kilns.

Inland from Portrush

15mi/24km.

▶ *From Portrush take the A 29 inland to Coleraine.*

Coleraine

At the head of the Bann estuary, Coleraine is Co Londonderry's second largest town, now an important shopping and commercial centre for the area, and home to the province's second university (1968). The main attractions are the river and its estuary, the quayside, occasional regattas, a large-scale marina, and a bird sanctuary.

▶ *From Coleraine take the B 6 7 east via Ballybogy for 5.5mi/9km.*

Benvarden★

Open Jun–Aug Tue–Sun & Bank Hols noon–5.30pm. £3.50. 028 2074 1331. www.benvarden.com.

Benvarden House, home of the Montgomery family since 1798, opens its garden and grounds to the public every summer. One of Ireland's most attractive walled gardens (2 acres/0.8ha), parts of which may date back to the original fortified enclosure, it features rose beds, a formal hedged garden, a vinery and a pergola walk. Beyond are

Limestone cliffs of the White Rocks stretch from Curran Strand to Dunluce Castle

Address Book

For coin ranges, see the cover flap.

SIGHTSEEING

Portrush Puffer – Road-driven tourist train. *Operates Jul–Aug, Mon–Sat every half hour 11am–1.30pm, 2pm–7.pm, Sun 2pm–7pm – £2.50. www.translink.co.uk.*

Open Topper – Open-top bus rides along the Causeway Coast between Coleraine and Giant's Causeway via Portstewart, Portrush, Bushmills, Portballintrae (bus route 177) Jul–Aug. Hopper fare £4.80.
Translink ☎028 703 25400

Excursions by boat – To visit the caves in the limestone cliffs at **White Rock** *(east)*, and to **The Skerries** , a chain of offshore islands densely populated by sea birds.

WHERE TO STAY

Glenkeen Guest House – *59 Coleraine Road. 10rm ☎028 7082 2279.* Well-priced guest house accommodation on the main road into town. Personally run, well-kept house with spacious en-suite bedrooms.

WHERE TO EAT

The Harbour Bistro – *The Harbour. ☎028 7082 2430. www.ramorerestaurant.com.* Smart contemporary bar/bistro serving a wide-ranging menu of grilled meats, chicken and fish. Its neighbouring sister establishment the **Ramore Wine Bar** *(☎028 7082 4313).* is a relaxed and informal bar, with a similar atmosphere and smaller bistro menu.

SPORTS AND LEISURE

Sandy beaches at Portballintrae, Portrush, Portstewart, Castlerock and Magilligan Strand (Benone).

---

neatly laid out kitchen gardens, with Victorian hothouses and the old gardener's bothy. A wild garden and azalea walk lead down to the River Bush, which is spanned by a Victorian stone and cast-iron bridge, rare of its type in Ireland.

▷ *Return to Ballybogy. Turn left onto B 62 towards Ballymoney; from the by-pass roundabout follow the sign.*

Leslie Hill Open Farm Kids

Open Jul–Aug daily 11am–6pm (2pm Sun). Jun Sat–Sun 2pm–6pm. Easter–May Sun & Bank Hols 2pm–6pm. £3.50. ☎028 276 66803. www.lesliehillopen farm.co.uk.

This mixed-farming estate has been in the ownership of the same family since the mid-18C, so its buildings and implements provide a vivid picture of farming evolution. A track leads to the walled garden with its pit-house, hot wall, and the remains of the heating arrangements for growing peaches. Children enjoy the horse-drawn vehicles, an adventure playground, and the chance to feed some of the animals.

West of Portrush
20mi/32km.

▷ *From Portrush take the A 2 west.*

Portstewart

Less exuberant than Portrush, Portstewart was a fashionable watering place in the 19C and has kept something of its Victorian atmosphere. It has a picturesque harbour and the very prominent O'Hara's Castle, a Gothic-style mansion (1834) transformed into a Dominican college. From the promenade, paths lead west along the cliffs to Portstewart Strand *(2mi/3.2km)*. Regular exhibitions are held at the Flowerfield Arts Centre.

▷ *Continue west on the A 2 via Coleraine; 1mi/1.6km beyond Articlave at the Liffock crossroads turn left.*

Hezlett House
Castlerock, on the NW corner of the cross-roads. (NT). Admission by guided tour (40min) only: usually Jul–Aug Wed–Sun & Bank Hols - call for details. £2.72. ☎028 2073 1582. www.nationaltrust.org.uk.

The Flamboyant Earl Bishop

Known as the Earl Bishop, **Frederick Augustus Hervey**, **Bishop of Derry** (1730–1803), was also an unusually enlightened prelate, an advocate of church reform and a supporter of emancipation for Dissenters. He became the 4th Earl of Bristol on the death of his brother. Bad health dictated long spells on the Continent, where many a Hotel Bristol is named after him. A flamboyant character, fabulously rich, he was arrested by Napoleon's police as a spy, and enjoyed a particularly scandalous affair with the mistress of the King of Prussia: he was described as "a bad father, a worse husband, very blasphemous in his conversation, and greatly addicted to intrigue and gallantry".

A passionate builder, traveller and collector of art and antiquities, he is responsible for Ickworth Place in Suffolk and a palatial residence at Ballyscullion on Lough Beg (never completed; its portico now fronts St George's Church in Belfast). **Downhill Castle** was designed in 1772 by his favourite architect, Michael Shanahan, to house his huge art collection: largely destroyed by fire in 1851.

Hezlett House, built in 1691 probably as a clergyman's residence, is a long, single-storey thatched cottage with battered, rough-cast walls, an attic and cruck truss roof. It was taken over by the Hezlett family in 1761.

Visitors are led through the kitchen, pantry, dining room, bedrooms and parlour and into the attic, where the servants slept. Furnishings date from the 19C and include balloon chairs (with holes for women's bustles) and prayer chairs, allowing women to kneel in hoop skirts. A small museum shows Victorian farming implements.

▶ *Continue west on the A 2.*

Downhill Demesne★

(NT) ◷*Open Easter week and Jul–Aug daily 10am–5pm. St Patrick's Day weekend, Apr–Jun & Sept–Nov, Sat–Sun 10am–5pm.* ◌*£2.09.* ℙ *(charge).* ☎*028 7084 8728. www.nationaltrust.org.uk.*
Even though the castle is now a roofless shell the demesne still reflects the personality of its flamboyant creator, **Earl Bishop Hervey** (ℓ *see 'The Flamboyant Earl Bishop' box*). From the imposing **Bishop's Gate** a charming glen planted with flowers and shrubs, a path leads up to the cliff top from where there is a splendid **view** of the coast.
The romantic much-photographed **Mussenden Temple**★ erected as a memorial to his cousin, Mrs Mussenden, clearly suggest the Earl Bishop's taste. This elegant Classical rotunda perched precariously on the very edge of the high cliffs, is modelled on the Temple of Vesta at Tivoli. Built of local basalt and sandstone from Ballycastle in 1785, the building was used as a library by the Bishop, who allowed the local Roman Catholic priest to say Mass here.

▶ *Continue west on the A 2.*

Beyond the Lion Gate, the sea and the strand become visible: where once the Bishop held horse races, the present generation indulges in surfing. The Bishop's Road across the Binevenagh Mountain was built as a short cut home from Limavady.

▶ *Bear left into the Bishop's Road.*

Gortmore Viewpoint★★

High up on the northeast slope of Binenvenagh Mountain, there is a superb **view** of Magilligan Strand across the mouth of Lough Foyle towards the Inishowen Peninsula.

▶ *Return downhill; turn left onto A 2.*

Magilligan Strand★★

The long stretch of golden sand dunes (6mi/10km) is equipped with sports facilities at Benone. The Point, where a Martello Tower (1812) was built during the Napoleonic Wars to guard the narrow approach to Lough Foyle, is now a Nature Reserve.

SPERRIN MOUNTAINS★

These lonely smooth-topped mountains, dividing the Londonderry lowlands from northeastern Ulster, rise to their highest point in Sawel Mountain (2 224ft/678m). Composed of schist and gneiss, they were once covered in magnificent forests, but their upper slopes are now grazed by sheep and clad in blanket bog and purple heather, and woodland is confined to the deep gorges worn by mountain streams. Over the moorland hover birds of prey; the rare hen harrier is sometimes seen, and the Sperrins are the only site in Ireland where cloudberry grows. The rocks contain minute deposits of gold, the extraction of which gives rise to periodic controversy about the future of these mountains, which have largely remained outside the mainstream of modern life.

- **Information:** Burn Road, Cookstown; ☎028 86766727. 7 Connell Street, Limavady; ☎028 7776 0307; www.limavady.gov.uk. Strule Arts Centre, Townhall Square, Omagh; ☎028 8224 7831. Alley Arts & Conference Centre; 1a Railway Street, Strabane; ☎028 7138 4444; www.strabanedc.com/leisure-and-tourism. www.sperrinstourism.com.
- ▶ **Orient Yourself:** The Sperrin Mountains are bounded to the west by the A 5 between Londonderry and Omagh, to the east by the A 29 between Cookstown and Coleraine, south by the A 505 between Cookstown and Omagh and north by the A 2 between Londonderry and Limavady.
- **Don't Miss: the** Ulster American Folk Park.
- **Also See:** DUNGANNON, LONDONDERRY, LOUGH NEAGH.

A Bit of History

In the 17C certain areas were granted to four of London's City livery companies – the Drapers, Skinners, Grocers and Fishmongers – who brought in settlers, mainly from Scotland, to inhabit their new towns and villages. In fact by the early 19C the region was overpopulated so assisted emigration was introduced and the land was re-allocated in holdings of 20–30 acres/8–12ha of neatly-hedged fields. Model farms were established to promote modern methods and roads and bridges, churches, schools and dispensaries were built.

Driving Tours

1 Uplands and Coast

▶ *From Londonderry take the A 2 eastwards; turn right.*

Eglinton

This elegant little village (1823–25) with its **Courthouse** was developed by the Grocers' Company around a tree-shaded green beside the Muff River which tumbles down through **Muff Glen**, a narrow tree-lined valley of pleasant walks.

Ballykelly

This community was established early in the 17C by the Fishmongers' Company. The model farm on the north side of the road consists of a two-storey block linked to two one-storey pavilions by curtain walls enclosing a farmyard. Opposite is the Presbyterian Church (1827). The Anglican Church (1795) was one of several built by the Earl Bishop of Derry (*see PORTRUSH*).

Limavady

The town takes its name from the Irish for Dogleap since the original settlement was farther upstream (2mi/3.2km) by the 13C O'Cahan castle in what is now the Roe Valley Country Park. It was re-founded as Newtown-Limavady in the 17C by Sir Thomas Phillips, Chief Agent of the City of London in Ulster. It is now a pleasant Georgian market town where the famous song, *Danny Boy* (*The Londonderry Air*), was noted down by Jane Ross (1810–79) who lived at 51 Main Street.

▸ *Take the B 68 south.*

Roe Valley Country Park★

(HM) ⊙*Park: open daily. Visitor Centre: open daily year-round 10am–6pm (5pm Oct–Mar).* ⊑. ☎ *028 772 2074. www. ehsni.gov.uk.*

The country park extends along a stretch *(3mi/4.8km)* of the wild thickly wooded valley, where the peaty red River Roe runs over rocks and through gorges on its way north to the sea. The **Countryside Centre** at the Dogleap Bridge provides information on the local flora and fauna, old industries and on the 17C Plantation. As well as great natural beauty and scenes of the O'Cahans' legendary exploits, the park preserves evidence of early industrial activity, particularly related to the linen industry: bleach greens, weirs and mill races, and 18C water-powered mills for sawing wood, scutching flax, weaving and beetling linen. An unusual feature is the stone-built **Power House** (1896), the site of early success in generating hydroelectric power *(open on request)*.

▸ *Take the B 192 south to Burnfoot.*

Bovevagh Church

In the churchyard of a ruined medieval church stands a **mortuary house** similar to the one at Banagher (◔*see below*); its ruined state reveals the cavity, which contained the body, and the hand hole in the east end through which the faithful could touch the relics.

▸ *Continue south; turn left onto the A 6 and make a detour east.*

Glenshane Pass★

The pass between Mullaghmore (1 818ft/555m – south) and Carntogher (1 516ft/462m – north) carries the main Belfast-Londonderry road through the Sperrin Mountains. The northern approach through dramatic mountain scenery overlooks Benady Glen on the River Roe; the southern approach provides a **panoramic view**★★ across Lough Neagh in the mid-Ulster plain to Slemish.

▸ *Continue east on the A 6. At the north end of the main street turn right into Bank Square.*

Address Book

◔*For coin ranges, see the Legend on the cover flap.*

WHERE TO STAY

⊖ **Ballyhenry House** – *172 Seacoast Road, 0.75mi north of Limavady. 3rm.* ☎*028 7772 2657. michaeljkane@hotmail. co.uk.* Attractive farmhouse B&B in Roe Valley. Ideal for outdoor activities (fishing, riding, golf, walking) around the farm estate.

⊖⊖**B&B Tullylagan Country House** – *40B Tullylagan Road, Sandholes, 4mi south of Cookstown.15rm.* ☎*028 8676 5100. www.tullylagan.co.uk.* Peaceful country house on the Tullylagan River. The interior has a Georgian feel and the period-style bedrooms all have an individual personality; popular new wine bar and restaurant.

WHERE TO EAT

⊖⊖**Lime Tree** – *60 Catherine Street, Limavady.* ☎*028 7776 4300. www.lime treerest.com.* Seasonal produce, modern Irish cuisine; daily fish specials, good wine list. Booking recommended.

SPORTS AND LEISURE

The **Ulster Way**, a long-distance footpath, passes through the eastern slopes of the Sperrins.

The Owenkillew and the Glenelly are both good trout streams. Several good angling streams flow north and west down the River Roe and the Foyle tributaries into the Foyle estuary or southeast into Lough Neagh.

TRACING ANCESTORS

Ulster-American Folk Park – *(◔see Western Valleys Driving Tour) Centre for Migration Studies: Mon–Fri 10.30am–4.45pm.*

Maghera

This little town at the foot of the Glenshane Pass has a picturesque ruin, **St Patrick Church** (c 10C), which boasts an outstanding west door (added c 12C), with inclined jambs, wonderful floral and animal decoration and a lintel carved with an elaborate Crucifixion scene. In the graveyard stands a rough pillar stone, carved with a ringed cross, which, according to tradition, is the grave of St Lurach, who founded an important monastery on this site in the 6C (*key from The Bridewell/Megherafelt Tourist Information Centre;* ☎ *028 79631510; www.magherafelt.gov.uk*).

▸ *Return west on the A 6.*

Dungiven

Before it was redeveloped by the Skinners' Company, Dungiven was the base of the fierce O'Cahan clan. Just outside the town is an imposing natural strongpoint above the River Roe, the site of a pre-Norman monastery and ruined Augustinian **priory**. The church remains are impressive, but the main attraction is the magnificent **tomb** of the O'Cahan chieftan Cooey-na-Gal, who died in 1385. It consist of an effigy beneath a traceried canopy, protected by heavily armed Scottish mercenaries ("gallowglasses") in kilts. Similar tombs dating from the 15C survive in western Scotland.

In the 17C Sir Edward Doddington, who constructed the walls of Londonderry, built himself a house in the cloister.*(HM)* 😊 *Check with Megherafelt TIC.* ☎ *028 79631510.*

North of the path is a **bullaun**, a hollowed stone originally used for grinding grain – it now collects rainwater which is deemed to cure warts. The rags tied to the overhanging tree are an ancient tradition, either left as a offering (once they would have been full garments, but in time dissolve to rags) or as a good luck symbol.

▸ *In Dungiven turn left into a minor road.*

Banagher Church

In the graveyard of the ruined church (c. 1100) stands a 12C **mortuary house**, built of dressed stone probably to house relics disturbed by the addition of a chancel to the church. The panel on the west gable depicts a figure with a hand raised in blessing and bearing a crozier. According to tradition it is the tomb of St Muiredach O'Heney and sand from his tomb brings good luck.

▸ *Return direct to the A 6, or take the B 74 west through Feeny and Claudy to rejoin the A 6 later.*

Ness Wood Country Park

From the car park walk through the picnic area into the wood to the waterfall. There is a woodland walk along both sides of the stream meeting at a bridge about 600yd/548m from the car park.

The spectacular 30-ft/9-m high waterfall was created, together with a series of gorges, potholes and rapids, by the River Burntollet eroding a channel through the metamorphic schist rock since the end of the last Ice Age.

2 Eastern Foothills

Cookstown

Once an important linen centre, Cookstown is now an important market centre for the area. Its most notable feature is the extraordinarily long and very broad main street which, under 10 different names, extends north from the River Ballinderry towards the silhouette of Slieve Gallion (1 732ft/528m). This is the result of one of the most ambitious attempts at urban planning ever imposed on the Irish landscape, devised c. 1750 by James and William Stewart, after the original Plantation settlement of Cookstown had been destroyed in the rebellion of 1641. The new street extended south to their own property at Killymoon Castle *(private)* which was redesigned by John Nash in 1803; its grounds are now a golf course.

▸ *From Cookstown take the A 29 south; bear left onto the B 520. Turn left on a blind corner into the car park; it is 10min there and back on foot to the fort.*

Beaghmore Stone Circles

Tullaghoge Fort

The tree-crowned earthworks of this hillfort are replete with memories of the ancient rulers of Ulster, having enclosed the residence of the O'Hagans: the chief justices of the old kingdom of Tyrone. It was here that the rulers of Tyrone were inaugurated, the last of them being Hugh O'Neill in 1593. Their stone throne was broken up by Lord Mountjoy in 1602. The **view** from the fort is extensive: southwest to the circular walled graveyard at Donaghrisk where the O'Hagans were buried; east towards Lough Neagh; north to Slieve Gallion with the River Ballinderry in the foreground and Killymoon Castle in the trees by the river.

▸ *Return to Cookstown; take the A 505 west for 2.5mi/4km.*

Drum Manor Forest Park

&⊙*Open 10am–dusk.* ⊗*£1 pedestrian, £3 per car.* ⚏*Jul–Aug.*
The old country house of Drum Manor has long been a ruin, but its walled gardens and open parkland now form part of Drum Manor Forest Park. One of the gardens has lent itself perfectly to conversion into a **butterfly garden**, while in the ruins of the manor house an attractive **flower garden** has been created.

▸ *Continue west on the A 505; turn right (signposted).*

Wellbrook Beetling Mill★

(NT) ⟜*Admission by guided tour only, Jul–Aug Sat–Thu 2pm–6pm. Apr–Jun*

& Sept Sat–Sun & Bank Hols 2pm–6pm. Sat–Mon around St Patrick's Day 2pm–6pm. Sat–Tue around Easter weekend 2pm–6pm. ⊗*£3.45.* ☎*028 8675 1735. www.nationaltrust.org.uk.*
Beetling is the last stage in the production of linen where the cloth is beaten to close up the weave and give it a smooth sheen. The first mill at Wellbrook came into operation in September 1767; the present mill, known as no 6, dates from about 1830 and worked until 1961.
The drying loft contains an excellent display on the production of linen and the history of the Irish linen industry, while the lower floor houses the seven **beetling machines** turned by an external wooden water-wheel. The amount of noise produced by two beetling engines operating for a few minutes explains why deafness was common among beetlers, who worked from early morning to nine at night.

▸ *Continue west on the A 505; at Dunnamore Bridge turn right across the river.*

Beaghmore Stone Circles★

Mid-Ulster is particularly rich in prehistoric stone circles. This site, used in Neolithic times, has seven from the Bronze Age, comprising quite small stones set on, rather than in, the ground. Six circles are arranged in pairs, with a cairn and a row of stones near the point of intersection. The area enclosed in the seventh circle is studded with close-set stones known as "Dragons' Teeth" – used to calculate the rising and setting of the sun and moon.

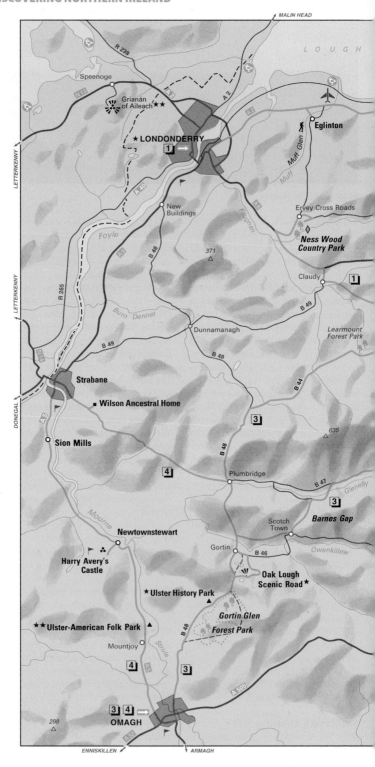

MALIN HEAD

LOUGH

R 238

Speenoge

Grianán of Aileach ★★

★ LONDONDERRY

1

Eglinton

Muff Glen

Muff

LETTERKENNY

New Buildings

Ervey Cross Roads

Ness Wood Country Park

Foyle

Faughan

371 △

Claudy

1

LETTERKENNY

R 265

Burn Dennet

B 48

Dunnamanagh

B 49

Learmount Forest Park

DONEGAL

Strabane

■ Wilson Ancestral Home

B 49

B 48

B 44

635 △

3

Sion Mills

4

B 48

Plumbridge

B 47

Glenelly

3

Barnes Gap

Mourne

Newtownstewart

Scotch Town

Owenkillew

Harry Avery's Castle

Gortin

B 46

Oak Lough Scenic Road ★

★ Ulster History Park

★★ Ulster-American Folk Park

Gortin Glen Forest Park

B 48

Strule

Mountjoy

4

3

A 505

3 4 →

OMAGH

298 △

A 32

ENNISKILLEN

ARMAGH

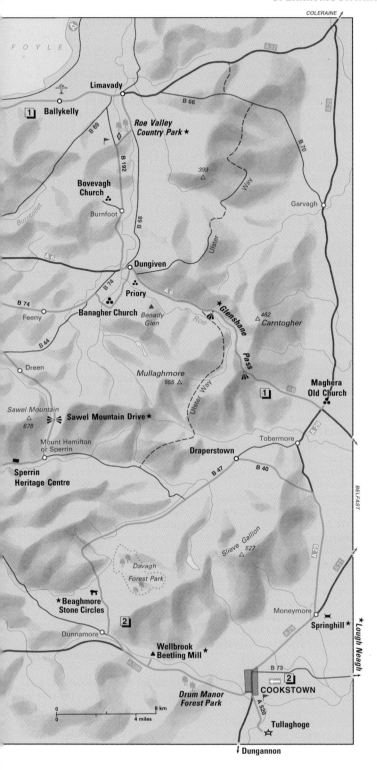

▶ *Continue north; turn right onto a minor road which joins the B 47.*

Draperstown

This pleasant little town, a classic settlement from the time of the Ulster Plantation in the early 17C, is now a busy market centre in the heart of Sperrin Mountain country.

▶ *From Draperstown take the B 40 east; turn right onto the A 29 to Moneymore.*

Springhill★

(NT) ☝ ♿ *Admission by guided tour only, Jul–Aug 1pm–6pm; late Mar–Jun &Sept Sat–Sun & Bank Hol Mon 1pm–6pm; Sat–Mon around St Patrick's Day 1pm–6pm; Sat–Tue around Easter weekend 1pm–6pm.* ☞£5.45 house and grounds and costume collection. £3.72 grounds and costume collection only. ☕ 🅿. ☎028 8674 8210. www.nationaltrust.org.uk.

This attractive country house was the family home of the Conynghams, who came to Ulster from Ayrshire early in the 17C. Built around a deep courtyard flanked by service buildings, it is a rare survivor of the kind of comfortable residence built by Plantation families at this time, despite the difficult and sometimes dangerous conditions. The property was altered and enlarged by subsequent generations of Conynghams, who usually followed military careers.

Family portraits hang throughout the house, which is furnished with **fine 18C and 19C furniture**. Note the splendid oak **staircase** with a yew handrail. The older rooms contrast with the more spacious interiors added later like the early-19C dining room graced by an Italian marble chimney-piece presented by the notorious Earl Bishop of Londonderry. The gun room collection includes flintlocks used during the Siege of Derry and a pair of pikes from the Battle of Vinegar Hill.

The courtyard buildings house an acclaimed **costume collection** of 2300 articles, from the 18C to the 1930s.

▶ *From Moneymore take the A 29 south to return to Cookstown.*

3 Central Heights

▶ *From Omagh take B48 north.*

Gortin Glen Forest Park

🕐*Open 10am–dusk.* ☞*£1 pedestrian; £3 car.* ☎*028 8164 8217.*

This coniferous woodland park is part of the larger Gortin Forest, a commercial plantation. The forest drive *(5mi/8km – one way only)* offers great vistas over the Sperrin Mountains. Information on trails and where to see Sika deer is supplied in the Nature Centre.

▶ *From the B 48 turn right.*

The **Oak Lough Scenic Road**★ loops round a cluster of lakes, much favoured by canoeists, and provides a fine **view** of Gortin on the Owenkillew River.

▶ *Turn left onto the B 46. In Gortin turn right onto the B 48; after crossing the river turn right onto a minor road; in Scotch Town turn left.*

The **Barnes Gap** carries the road through a narrow cleft in the hills between the valleys of the Owenkillew and Glenelly Rivers.

▶ *At the T-junction turn right; at the next T-junction turn left; cross the river at Clogherny Bridge; turn right; turn right onto the B 47.*

Sperrin Heritage Centre

🕐*Open Apr–Oct 11.30am (2pm Sun) to 5.30pm (6pm Sat–Sun)* ☞*£2.60.* ☎*028 816481423.*

The Centre has been sensitively designed to fit with three adjoining cottages. Videos, computers and exhibitions enable visitors to explore the local flora and fauna, history and culture.

▶ *Continue east on the B 47; in Sperrin/ Mount Hamilton turn left.*

The **Sawel Mountain Drive**★, a narrow unfenced road along the east face of Sawel Mountain (2 229ft/678m), the highest peak, passes through the wild and austere beauty of the open moorland; the **views**★★ are spectacular.

▶ *Continue east on the B47;*
in Sperrin/Mount Hamilton turn left.
Beyond Dreen turn left onto the
B 44 ; turn left onto the B 48 to
return to Omagh via Plumbridge.

4 Western Valleys

Omagh

The former county town of Co Tyrone
is normally a quiet market town, built
on a steep slope overlooking the point
where two rivers, the Camowen and the
Drumragh, join to form the Strule.
Sadly, in 1998, Omagh was the site of
the worst single atrocity of Northern Ireland's Troubles, when the "Real IRA", a
dissident republican grouping, exploded
a bomb in the town centre, killing 29 and
injuring over 200 people.

▶ *From Omagh take the A 5 north.*

Ulster-American Folk Park★★

&⏱*Open 17 Mar–Sept Mon–Sat 10.30am*
–6pm, Sun and Bank hols 11am–6.30pm.
Oct–17 Mar Mon–Fri 10.30am–5pm. Last
admission 1hr 30 min before closing (all
year).⊜*£4.50.* ▱*.*☎*028 8224 3292. www.*
folkpark.com.
Of all the establishments in Ireland celebrating the country's intimate links
with America, this extensive open-air
museum is perhaps the most evocative.
Opened in 1976 as part of the American bicentennial celebrations, it is laid
out around the ancestral cottage from
which **Thomas Mellon**, of the banking
dynasty, emigrated with his family at
the age of five in 1818. There is also a
Centre for Migration Studies, with a
library, extensive database, and facilities for research.
The Matthew T Mellon Information
Centre and the **Emigrants' Exhibition** give the historical context for
mass emigration, citing life stories of
particular individuals who settled in
the New World. Various other buildings, some replicas, others transferred
from elsewhere in Ulster or America,
are laid out in chronological order
starting with the typical 18C and 19C
Ulster buildings like a humble cabin
from the Sperrins, a complete "Ulster
Street" lined with shops, workplaces,

Ulster-American Folk Park

and Reilly's pub-cum-grocery. The cottage in which Thomas Mellon was born
in 1813 was built by his father with his
own hands; it was transported here in
1976 to form the nucleus of the park.
The **Ship and Dockside Gallery** marks
the transition to America, and features
the brig Union moored at the Belfast
quayside. The **American Street** with
its all-important General Store has a
replica of the 1870 First Mellon Bank
of Pittsburgh, shielding a series of log
cabins and a complete mid-18C stone
dwelling, brought from frontier territory
in Pennsylvania, where it was built by an
emigrant from Co Donegal.
In the workshops and cottages local
people in **period costume** demonstrate
the old crafts: cooking, spinning, weaving, the making of baskets, candles and
soap; blacksmithing and carpentry; turf
fires burn throughout the year.

Newtonstewart

The village is set near the confluence of
the River Mourne and the River Strule. On
a nearby hilltop stands **Harry Avery's
Castle**, two D-shaped towers from a 14C
O'Neill stronghold. There are fine views
of the surrounding countryside.

Sion Mills

This model village was established by
the three Herdman brothers, who in
1835 started a flax-spinning operation
in an old flour mill on the Mourne. The
buildings are an appealing mixture of
Gothic Revival terraced cottages in poly-

chrome brick, and black and white half-timbered edifices, of which the most striking is Sion House, and the Church of the Good Shepherd, a splendid Italianate Romanesque building (1909).

Strabane

This small town stands at the confluence of the Finn and the Mourne. In the 18C Strabane was famous for printing, celebrated behind the bowed Georgian shopfront at 49 Main Street, where **Gray's Printing Press** (NT. &.*⁀⁀ admission by guided tour ony; call for times ⁀£3; ☎028 8674 8210 , www.nationaltrust.org.uk) a 19C printing shop has been preserved with its original hand- and foot-operated presses.

Two of Gray's apprentices, John Dunlap (1747–1812), printed the American Declaration of Independence in his newspaper the *Pennsylvania Packet*, while James Wilson became editor of a Philadelphia newspaper after leaving for America in 1807.

The **Wilson Ancestral Home** (*⁀⁀ admission by guided tour only, Jul–Aug Tue–Sun 2pm–5pm; ☎028 7138 4444, www.strabanedc.com/leisure-and-tourism) is a whitewashed thatched cottage on the south side of town, home to James Wilson, the grandfather of **President Woodrow Wilson**. The house contains original furniture, including a cupboard bed by the kitchen fire and curtained beds in the main bedroom. The Wilson family still live in the modern farmhouse behind the cottage.

▷ *Continue on this road; in Plumbridge turn right onto the B 48 to return to Omagh.*

STRANGFORD LOUGH ⋆

This inland sea, 18m/29km long with its 80mi/142km coastline, has a tranquillity and beauty that is disturbed only when the tides rip through the narrow channel linking it to the Irish Sea. Strangford Lough was formed when the sea level rose at the end of the Ice Age, drowning the drumlins – the most characteristic features of its landscape – and converting them into countless whale-backed islands. The lough lends itself to sailing and boating, supports an exceptional wealth of bird-life, while its shores and islands are rich in historical remains.

- ▯ **Information:** 31 Regents Street, Newtownards; ☎028 9182 6846. The Stables, Catle Street, Portaferry; ☎028 4272 9882. www.ards-council.gov.uk/visitor-information.
- ▷ **Orient Yourself:** Strangford Lough lies 10mi/16km south east of Belfast at its closest point.
- ⊙ **Don't Miss:** Castle Ward.
- ▦ **Especially for Kids:** Exploris. Castle Ward. Delamont Country Park.
- ⟳ **Also See:** BANGOR, DOWNPATRICK, LISBURN, MOUNT STEWART.

A Bit of History

The old Irish name for the lough was Lough Cuan but the name bestowed by the Vikings – "violent fjord" – prevails, acknowledging the regular spectacle of 350 million tonnes of sea water racing through the strait between Portaferry and Strangford village as the tide changes.

Conditions in the lough itself vary between the exposed eastern shore on the Ards Peninsula and the sheltered western shore.

The whole of the Lough is a **Marine Nature Reserve**, the first in Northern Ireland managed by public bodies including the National Trust and the Royal Society for the Protection of Birds.

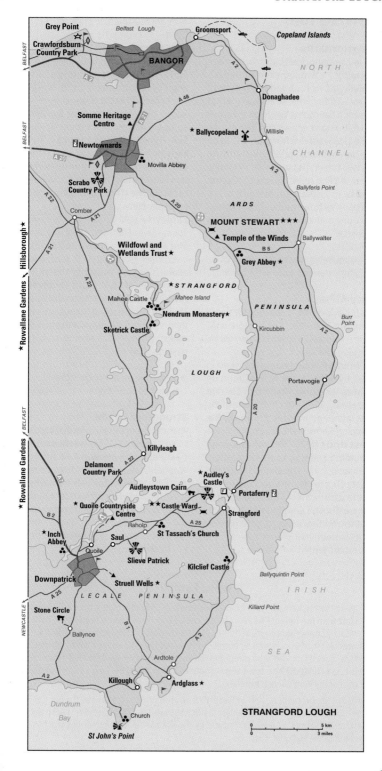

STRANGFORD LOUGH

0 — 5 km
0 — 3 miles

Driving Tour

Newtownards

An ancient priory predates the modern dormitory town annexed to Belfast, which was re-founded in Plantation times. Today, the spacious market square, a handsome Georgian town hall in Scrabo stone and a distinctive market cross (1635) survive from the 17C, as do the unremarkable priory ruins and the burial vault of the Londonderry family. There is a fine collection of of 13C **cross slabs**★ inscribed with foliage crosses. These come from nearby Movilla Abbey, once one of the most important abbeys in Ulster.

▷ *From Newtownards take the A 20 along the east shore of the lough.*

Grey Abbey★

(HM). 🕐*Open Apr–Sept Tue–Sat 9am–6pm, Sun 2pm–6pm. Oct–Mar Sat only, 10am–4pm. ☎028 90546552. www.ehsni. gov.uk/greyabbey.*

A Cistercian abbey was established in 1193 by Affreca, the wife of John de Courcy, for monks from Holm Cultram Abbey in Cumbria. Its church, one of the first in Ireland to exhibit traces of the dawning Gothic style, has a magnificent **west door** (1220–30) with elaborate moulding and dog-tooth decoration. Damaged in the Elizabethan wars, the abbey church was restored and served as the parish church. The small **visitor centre** displays descriptions of monastic life and the abbey; a herb garden stocks medicinal plants typical of a Cistercian garden.

▷ *Continue south on the A 20.*

Portaferry

A busy coastal town until the mid 19C, Portaferry is now a yachting and sea angling centre, famed for its sunsets. **Portaferry Castle** (🕐*open Apr–Jun & Sept Mon–Sat 10am–5pm, Sun 2pm–6pm; Jul–Aug Mon–Sat 10am–5.30pm, Sun 1pm–6pm)* was probably built early in the 16C by the Savage family. Its stables houses the tourist information centre while the keep is now home to "Art in The Loft', exhibitions by local craftspeople.

Exploris★ (Kids 🕐*open daily Apr–Aug 10am–6pm, 11am Sat, noon Sun; Sept–Mar 10am–5pm, 11am Sat, 1pm Sun; ☜£7, child £4; ☎028 4272 8062; www. exploris.org.uk)* presents the varied marine life of Strangford Lough and the Irish Sea. It has a touch tank where children enjoy getting "hands-on" with (non-stinging) stingrays, and open-sea tanks, which attract passing seals and basking sharks.

▷ *Take the car ferry across the strait to Strangford.*

Strangford Castle

At the heart of this picturesque harbour town stands a 15–16C **tower house** *(HM.* 🕐*Key at house opposite).* An internal wooden stair climbs the three storeys to a very narrow roof walk from where there is a fine **view** of the ferry running between the Narrows and Portaferry.

▷ *Make a detour (2.5mi/4km) south by the A 2 coast road.*

Ward Family

Late in the 16C Bernard Ward from Capesthorne in Cheshire bought the Castle Ward estate from the Earls of Kildare. In 1610 Nicholas Ward built a tower house, Old Castle Ward, by Strangford Lough. In the 18C the Ward estates extended from Castle Ward to the coast of Dundrum Bay; nothing remains of the 18C house built by Michael Ward, a good landlord, who promoted the linen trade, developed the lead mines on his estate, built the new town and harbour of Killough and became a Justice of the Court of the King's Bench in Ireland.

In 1812 the property passed to Robert Ward, who preferred to live at Bangor Castle. In 1827 the 3rd Viscount Bangor (a title bestowed in 1781) started restoring the estate. In 1950 the house was received by the state in lieu of death duties and presented to the National Trust.

Kilclief Castle

(HM)

♿🕐*Open Jul–Aug, Tue–Fri 10am–6pm. Sat–Sun 2pm–6pm. ☎028 9181 1491.*
This 15C gatehouse style **tower house**, with two defensive projections was built to guard the entrance to the Narrows.

▶ *From Strangford take the A 25 west.*

Castle Ward★★   Kids

(HM).

♿🕐*Grounds: open 10am–8pm (4pm Oct–Mar). House: ♿━ Admission by guided tour only, daily Jul–Aug 1pm– 6pm. Early Apr–Jun & Sept Sat–Sun & Bank Hol Mon 1pm–6pm. Sat–Mon around St Patrick's Day 1pm–6pm. Easter week daily 1pm–6pm. House, grounds and wildlife centre: ⊜£4.36, child £2.18; House only, £2.70. ☕. ☎028 4488 1204. www. nationaltrust.org.uk.*

This Great House surrounded by superb parkland overlooking Strangford Lough is an odd but endearing architectural compromise between the conflicting tastes of Bernard Ward, later the first Lord Bangor, and his wife Anne. The main facade is Palladian, the garden front is Gothick. The interiors exhibit a similar dichotomy.

The entrance to the **house** (1760–75) opens into the hall, exuberantly deco-rated with stuccowork. The rooms on the northeast side reflect the Gothick style favoured by Lady Bangor – the boudoir **fan vaulting** is modelled on Henry VII's Chapel in Westminster Abbey; window panels in the saloon are deemed to be 17C Flemish. By contrast, the **dining room** on the Classical side of the house has 18C panelling and Chippendale chairs (c 1760).

When the new house was built, the for-mal gardens were replaced by a natu-ralistic landscape of grass, trees and deer park around such features as the **Temple Water**, created in 1724, and the **ice house** on the east bank, close to where the former early 18C house stood. The Walled Garden, which originally provided the house with cut flowers and produce now contains pens for the **Wildfowl Collection**.

Children can dress up and play with period toys in the Victorian Past Times centre, visit the horses, pigs and hens in the farmyard and let off steam in the adventure playground.

The 17C **tower house**, known as Old Castle Ward on the lake shore, was the first dwelling built on the estate by a Ward; today it is surrounded by farm-yard buildings – the original 18C mill, once a tidal mill, was later adapted to be powered by the Temple Water. One

Gothick Boudoir, Castle Ward

A von Einsiedel/National Trust Photographic Library

building houses the **Strangford Lough Wildlife Centre**.

The estate's latest venture is **The Clear Sky Adventure Centre** including kayak, canoeing, coasteering, archery, rock-climbing, abseiling, orienteering, mountain biking and clay-pigeon shooting.

▶ *Either walk from the north entrance to the estate or drive by the minor road west of the estate.*

Audley's Castle★

The ruins of this 15C gatehouse-type **tower house** stand on a spit of land projecting into Strangford Lough. It was built by the Audley family, who sold it in 1646 to the Wards of Castle Ward. The hamlet of Audleystown was demolished in the 1850s and the inhabitants are thought to have emigrated to the USA.

Audleystown Cairn

Walk across the fields. The cairn, which is retained with drystone walling, is a dual court tomb with a forecourt at each end opening into galleries. Excavations in 1952 revealed 34 partly burned skeletons, Neolithic pottery and flint implements.

▶ *Continue west on the A 25.*

Quoile Countryside Centre★

&. ⏰*Open Apr–Aug daily 11am–5pm. Sept–Mar Sat–Sun 1pm–5pm. Castle island hide year-round daily 10am–4pm.* ☎*028 4461 5520. www.ehsni.gov.uk*

In 1957 a barrage was built at Hare Island excluding the sea from the Quoile estuary, turning the tidal flats into a freshwater lake with sluice gates. The Nature Reserve comprises 494 acres/200ha of woodland, grassland and reedbed habitats enjoyed by birds and otters.

From **Quoile Quay**, which was built in 1717 by Edward Southwell and served as a port for Downpatrick until 1940, the road reaches **Quoile Castle**, a late-16C tower house inhabited by the West family until the mid 18C.

The **visitor centre** provides descriptions of the local history, flora and fauna.

▶ *From Downpatrick take the A 7.*

Inch Abbey★

2mi/3.2km NW of Downpatrick via the A 7; after 1mi/1.6km turn left.

This abbey, built on an island in the marshes, is now accessible by road. The daughter house of the Cistercian abbey at Furness in Lancashire, ir was founded c 1180 by John de Courcy. Among the ruins are the remains of a 13C church and detached buildings presumed to be an infirmary *(southeast)*, a bakehouse and a guesthouse.

▶ *From Downpatrick take the A 22 north.*

Delamont Country Park [Kids]

⏰*Open: Park 9am–dusk. Railway: Jun–Aug and Bank Hols daily noon–6pm, rest of year Sat–Sun noon–dusk.* ☞*£2.50, child £1.50.* ☕. ☐*(charge).*☎*028 4482 8333. www.delamontcountrypark.com.*

The park contains a walled garden with formal beds and extends to the shore of Strangford Lough. A spacious bird hide is ideal for bird watching; the longest miniature railway in Ireland, boat trips a blue-flag beach and an adventure playground are more fun for children.

▶ *Continue north on the A 22.*

Killyleagh

The picturesque turreted **castle** redesigned in 1850 by Charles Lanyon, has two circular towers (13C and 17C). The original castle, built by de Courcy, was acquired by the O'Neills and destroyed by General Monk in 1648. Killyleagh was the birthplace of **Sir Hans Sloane**, whose collections formed the nucleus of the Natural History and British Museums in London.

▶ *Continue north on the A 22; bear right onto a minor road along the shore.*

Sketrick Castle

The approach to Sketrick Island is guarded by the ruins of a massive four-storey tower house which collapsed in a storm in 1896.

▶ *Continue north along the shore. Note that there is a very narrow road approach to the monastery.*

Drumlins in Strangford Lough

J Cornish/National Trust Photographic Library

Mahee Island
Nendrum Monastery★

(HM) ◷*Open Apr–Sept Tue–Sun 9am–6pm (2pm Sun); Oct–Mar, Sat 10am–4pm.* ☎*028 9181 1491.www.ehsni.gov.uk.*
This inspiring Early Christian site stands on an island in the lough and is now linked by causeways to a chain of islands. Nendrum was excavated and partly restored in the 1920s. A visitor centre tells the story of the three concentric enclosures (cashels) defined by drystone walls, and the monastery founded in the 5C by St Mochaoi (Mahee), sacked by Vikings and re-established in the 12C by the Anglo-Norman John de Courcy, who staffed it with Benedictine monks from Cumbria. In the 14C it was abandoned. The remains of the 10C monastic church stands in the central enclosure.

▶ *Continue north along the shore.*

Wildfowl and Wetlands Trust
(Castle Espie Centre)★

♿◷*Open Mar–Oct Mon–Fri 10.30am–5pm (5.30pm Jul–Aug), Sat–Sun 11am–5.30pm (5pm Mar–Jun); Nov–Feb daily 11am–4pm (4.30pm Sat–Sun).* ☕🅿. 🐦*£5.39.* ☎*028 9187 4146. www.wwt.org.uk.*
The protected area on the west shore of Strangford Lough includes freshwater lakes, flooded clay and limestone quarries. These are now home to endan-gered species bred in captivity and a broad range of wild species. In winter, thousands of wildfowl arrive here from the Arctic.

▶ *Continue north on the A 22; in Comber take the A 21; turn left up a steep minor road.*

Scrabo Country Park

(HM) ◷*Tower: open Apr–late-Sep, Sat–Thu 10.30am–6pm.* ☎*028 91811491. www.ehsni.gov.uk/scrabo.*
The upper end of Strangford Lough is dominated by **Scrabo Tower** on Scrabo Hill, the 135-ft/41m-tall centrepiece of this popular country park. Dolerite, a form of volcanic lava extruded at the same time as at the Giant's Causeway, has protected the underlying sandstone from erosion. Both rocks have been quarried in the past, the dark dolerite for Mount Stewart, the light sandstone for many Belfast buildings. Both were used in Scrabo Tower, which was built in 1857 to commemorate the 3rd Marquess of Londonderry (1778–1854), a compassionate man who showed great concern for his tenants during the Great Famine. There is a video and display about the park in the tower; on a clear day **views**★★ *(122 steps – viewing maps)* extend as far as the Scottish coast and the Isle of Man.

INDEX

INDEX

INDEX

INDEX

WHERE TO STAY

INDEX

WHERE TO EAT

COMPANION PUBLICATIONS

A map reference to the appropriate Michelin map is given for each chapter in the Selected Sights section of this guide

MICHELIN MAP 712 – IRELAND

● Scale 1 : 400 000 - 1cm = 4km - 1in : 6.30 miles   covers the Republic of Ireland and Northern Ireland, and the network of motorways and major roads. It provides information on shipping routes, distances in miles and kilometres, town plans of Dublin and Belfast, services, sporting and tourist attractions and an index of places; the key and text are printed in four languages.

MICHELIN TOURIST AND MOTORING ATLAS GREAT BRITAIN & IRELAND

● Scale 1 : 300 000 - 1cm = 3km - 1in : 4.75 miles (based on 1 : 400 000) covers the whole of the United Kingdom and the Republic of Ireland, the national networks of motorways and major roads. It provides information on route plan-

ning, shipping routes, distances in miles and kilometres, over 60 town plans, services and sporting and tourist attractions and an index of places; the key and text are printed in six languages.

MICHELIN MAP 713 – GREAT BRITAIN AND IRELAND

● Scale 1 : 1 000 000 - 1cm = 10km - 1inch : 15.8 miles   covers the whole of the United Kingdom and the Republic of Ireland, the national networks of motorways and major roads. It provides information on shipping routes, distances in miles and kilometres, a list of Unitary Authorities for Wales and Scotland; the key and text are printed in four languages.

INTERNET:

● Users can access personalised route plans, Michelin mapping on line, addresses of hotels and restaurants listed in The Red Guide and practical and tourist information through the internet: www.ViaMichelin.com

MAPS AND PLANS

LIST OF MAPS

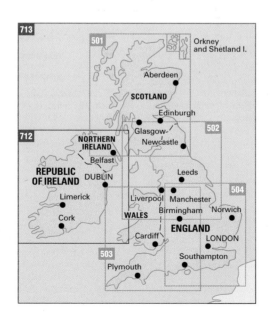

Special symbols

 M3   Motorway

A2   Primary route

Forest, Country Park,
National Park

Selected monuments and sights

    Tour - Departure point

   Ecclesiastical building

   Synagogue - Mosque

   Building

■   Statue, small building

   Calvary, wayside cross

◎   Fountain

   Rampart - Tower - Gate

   Château, castle, historic house

   Ruins

   Dam

   Factory, power plant

☆   Fort

   Cave

   Troglodyte dwelling

   Prehistoric site

   Viewing table

   Viewpoint

▲   Other place of interest

LEGEND

	Sight	Seaside resort	Winter sports resort	Spa
Highly recommended ★★★	☆☆☆	✳✳✳	‡‡‡
Recommended ★★	☆☆	✳✳	‡‡
Interesting ★	☆	✳	‡

Additional symbols

🛈	Tourist information
═══ ═══	Motorway or other primary route
❶ ❶	Junction: complete, limited
⊨═══ ═══	Pedestrian street
⊥═════⊥	Unsuitable for traffic, street subject to restrictions
⊓⊓⊓⊓ ----	Steps – Footpath
🚆 🚉	Train station – Auto-train station
🚌 SNCF	Coach (bus) station
•━━•━	Tram
⊙	Metro, underground
P℞	Park-and-Ride
♿	Access for the disabled
✉	Post office
☎	Telephone
⊠	Covered market
•⚔•	Barracks
△	Drawbridge
⊍	Quarry
✕	Mine
B F	Car ferry (river or lake)
🛥	Ferry service: cars and passengers
⛴	Foot passengers only
③	Access route number common to Michelin maps and town plans
Bert (R.)...	Main shopping street
AZ B	Map co-ordinates

Sports and recreation

🏇	Racecourse
⛸	Skating rink
🏊 🏊	Outdoor, indoor swimming pool
🎥	Multiplex Cinema
⛵	Marina, sailing centre
⛺	Trail refuge hut
□━■━■━□	Cable cars, gondolas
□++++++□	Funicular, rack railway
🚂	Tourist train
◇	Recreation area, park
🐬	Theme, amusement park
Ψ	Wildlife park, zoo
⊛	Gardens, park, arboretum
⊙	Bird sanctuary, aviary
🚶	Walking tour, footpath
🙂	Of special interest to children